AF705681

THE HISTORY AND THEORY
OF INTERNATIONAL LAW

Nineteenth-Century Perspectives on Private International Law

THE HISTORY AND THEORY OF INTERNATIONAL LAW

General Editors

NEHAL BHUTA

Professor of Public International Law, European University Institute

ANTHONY PAGDEN

Distinguished Professor of Political Science and History, University of California Los Angeles

BENJAMIN STRAUMANN

Alberico Gentili Senior Fellow, New York University School of Law

In the past few decades the understanding of the relationship between nations has undergone a radical transformation. The role of the traditional nation-state is diminishing, along with many of the traditional vocabularies which were once used to describe what has been called, ever since Jeremy Bentham coined the phrase in 1780, "international law." The older boundaries between states are growing ever more fluid, new conceptions and new languages have emerged which are slowly coming to replace the image of a world of sovereign independent nation states which has dominated the study of international relations since the early nineteenth century. This redefinition of the international arena demands a new understanding of classical and contemporary questions in international and legal theory. It is the editors' conviction that the best way to achieve this is by bridging the traditional divide between international legal theory, intellectual history, and legal and political history. The aim of the series, therefore, is to provide a forum for historical studies, from classical antiquity to the twenty-first century, that are theoretically-informed and for philosophical work that is historically conscious. It is the editors' hope that a new vision of the rapidly evolving international world, its past and its possible future, may emerge.

PREVIOUSLY PUBLISHED IN THIS SERIES

International Law and Religion
Historical and Contemporary Perspectives
Edited by Martti Koskenniemi, Mónica García-Salmones Rovira, and Paolo Amorosa

The Hidden History of International Law in the Americas
Empire and Legal Networks
Dr. Juan Pablo Scarfi

Nineteenth-Century Perspectives on Private International Law

ROXANA BANU

OXFORD
UNIVERSITY PRESS

OXFORD
UNIVERSITY PRESS

Great Clarendon Street, Oxford, OX2 6DP,
United Kingdom

Oxford University Press is a department of the University of Oxford.
It furthers the University's objective of excellence in research, scholarship,
and education by publishing worldwide. Oxford is a registered trade mark of
Oxford University Press in the UK and in certain other countries

© Roxana Banu 2018

The moral rights of the author have been asserted

First Edition published in 2018

All rights reserved. No part of this publication may be reproduced, stored in a retrieval system, or transmitted, in any form or by any means, without the prior permission in writing of Oxford University Press, or as expressly permitted by law, by licence or under terms agreed with the appropriate reprographics rights organization. Enquiries concerning reproduction outside the scope of the above should be sent to the Rights Department, Oxford University Press, at the address above

You must not circulate this work in any other form
and you must impose this same condition on any acquirer

Crown copyright material is reproduced under Class Licence
Number C01P0000148 with the permission of OPSI
and the Queen's Printer for Scotland

Published in the United States of America by Oxford University Press
198 Madison Avenue, New York, NY 10016, United States of America

British Library Cataloguing in Publication Data
Data available

Library of Congress Control Number: 2018942148

ISBN 978–0–19–881984–4

Links to third party websites are provided by Oxford in good faith and
for information only. Oxford disclaims any responsibility for the materials
contained in any third party website referenced in this work.

Series Editor's Preface

The deep contemporary challenges to the nation-state as the structuring frame for law—both national and international—and the emergence of complex forms of hybrid legal ordering beyond the state, have led to a systematic questioning of the presuppositions of legal order in a number of subfields of law. This questioning, in turn, has led to renewed interest in the historicity of the sub-field itself, a turn to the historiography of the field in order to reflect on its past and present potentialities in an epoch of global and transnational law. In the realms of constitutional law, international organizations law, and public international law, history and theory have become significant objects of scholarly time and attention, as means of puzzling through the transformations of the present.

Dr. Roxana Banu's very learned study represents a welcome addition to the breadth of these inquiries, by re-examining the historiography of private international law. Her fundamental concern is the aptness of contemporary private international law for the complex problems of inter-personal and inter-relational justice raised by concrete human lives under conditions of globalization. She challenges profoundly the received historiography and understanding of the field as liberal, individualist, and preoccupied with property relations, and also the alternative position that sees private international law as having capitulated to the logic of the nation-state long ago. This challenge is mounted through an impressive re-reading and contextualization of jurists—some renowned and many forgotten—in order to redraw and rearrange our perceptions of the lineages of the present, but also to argue for the many possibilities for global inter-relational justice immanent to the history of the field and perhaps recoverable in the present. In a time when our understandings of the divisions between public and private are being unsettled, Dr. Banu's book will be an important source of inspiration and provocation for rethinking the tools at our disposal to reconstruct relationships of justice across borders.

Nehal Bhuta
Florence and Edinburgh
May 2018

Acknowledgments

This book grew out of my doctoral dissertation at the University of Toronto, which benefitted from funds provided by the Law School of the University of Toronto, the Ontario Graduate Scholarship, the Strauss Fellowship in International Law, and the Alan Marks Medal.

I am indebted to Toni Fine at Fordham Law School who always believed in me, supported and encouraged me to pursue a doctoral program and an academic career. Without her relentless mentorship and kindness I might have never embarked on the journey of pursuing a doctoral degree.

For having guided, encouraged, and mentored me every step of the way in writing this book, I am forever indebted to my supervisor, Professor Karen Knop, at the University of Toronto. Her unparalleled knowledge, creativity, thoughtfulness, remarkable hard work, and elegance never cease to amaze me and continue to inspire me. It is impossible to thank her adequately for all the dedication and kindness she has offered me throughout these formative years. She has been and remains a role model for me in more ways than I could list here.

Catherine Valcke and Robert Wai have been a rock of support and inspiration. I am grateful for all the kind ways in which they challenged me to sharpen my arguments and my analysis. Diego Fernandez Arroyo has been most generous in offering invaluable thoughts and suggestions on this book and much needed encouragement in finalizing this project.

I have benefitted tremendously from the support and encouragement of David Dyzenhaus in the last stages of my doctoral program and in bringing this book to light. I am extremely grateful for the many ways in which he has guided my way as a starting academic.

Although my intellectual home and shelter for the past five years has been the University of Toronto and its remarkable doctoral program, two other institutions have also offered valuable intellectual and financial resources. The Institute for Global Law and Policy (IGLP) at Harvard Law School has been a comforting environment of like-minded people who have supported and encouraged my writing. I am particularly indebted to Horatia Muir Watt for the comments and suggestions she made on earlier chapters during the 2015 IGLP workshop.

NYU Law School welcomed me as a Visiting Doctoral Researcher from 2014 to 2016 and has offered a whole range of resources invaluable for this project, especially innumerable interlibrary loans. The SJD students in residence at NYU Law School in 2014–2016 and the 2014–2015 visiting doctoral researchers at NYU Law School were generous enough to read and offer many suggestions on various chapters of this book. Stef Feyen and Bartosz Marciniak in particular spent numerous hours supporting and challenging me in my thought process on various parts of this book. They have made a whole year of writing this book much more enjoyable and inspirational.

I am also grateful for suggestions from and conversations with Benedict Kingsbury and Liam Murphy during my visitorship at NYU Law School. Eyal Benvenisti has been most gracious in guiding and motivating me at crucial times. Chapter 4 in particular grew out of conversations with Eyal Benvenisti.

Hanoch Dagan has been a most thought-provoking partner of conversation and an invaluable source of support in the final stages of writing this book.

Due to the very generous invitation by Annelise Riles to the 2016 International Governance Seminar at Cornell Law School, I benefitted from valuable comments and suggestions on Chapter 6 from Stéphanie Francq, Jan Kleinheisterkamp, Chantal Thomas, Annelise Riles, and Ralf Michaels.

For their wonderful friendship and moral support I am grateful to my SJD colleagues and dear friends, including Danielle Bertollini, Lindsey Carson, Cecilia Fernandez, Ema Iancu, Simona Soare, Andrew Martin, and David Sandomierski. My friend and artist Simona Soare has been most generous in allowing me to display one of her amazing etchings on the cover of the book.

I am particularly grateful to Joanna Langille, my colleague, then and now, for enduring endless conversations on virtually every aspect of this book. Having her as a friend, a partner of conversation, and a huge supporter has made the entire experience of writing this book much more enjoyable.

Finishing this book would have never been possible without the love and help of my family, especially my relentlessly supportive mother. Since I had two wonderful children in the process of writing this book, I am particularly grateful to every caretaker, family member or friend who spent even an hour taking care of my children, allowing me the peace of mind to concentrate on the book.

Above all, I am grateful to my husband, Andrei Banu, who stood by me, helped and supported me at every trying moment during these years. His love and patience have kept and keep me going.

Table of Contents

1
Introduction

On a daily basis, courts all over the world hear cases involving an incredibly wide range of interpersonal relationships with a foreign element: international contracts or accidents, marriages, adoptions, divorces involving different nationals or individuals domiciled in different jurisdictions, and so on. Some of these relationships sound unfortunate but mundane, such as a minor car accident involving individuals domiciled in different states. In other cases, the high stakes are evident, such as when multinational corporations engaged in massive mining operations in developing countries cause serious environmental and health problems for the indigenous population. In today's extremely interconnected world, a staggering proportion of our interpersonal relationships escapes the purely national context and exhibits links to various national communities.

It is at this fragile border between the national and the transnational reach of interpersonal relationships that the stakes increase dramatically. As an interpersonal relationship floats somewhere in the transnational realm, it appears simultaneously to implicate the correlative expectations of the individuals within the relationship, their links to various other individuals and communities, the interests and regulatory needs of the states affected by the dispute, as well as broader notions of interpersonal and interstate international justice. This makes it difficult to understand how such various considerations should be weighed or reconciled when they lead to different results. It also makes it particularly difficult to integrate them into a coherent theoretical and methodological framework.

Take, for example, the couple that entered into a same-sex marriage in Canada and subsequently sought a divorce in Ontario in 2011.[1] At the time of entering into the marriage the couple appeared "local": two individuals wishing to enter into a marriage legally permissible in Canada. At the time of divorce the matter had to be revisited through the transnational lens of the couple's existence: the Ontario court's jurisdiction over their divorce was complicated by the fact that the spouses had established their domicile in Florida and the United Kingdom. The same-sex marriage

[1] Application for Divorce of V.M. and L.M. <http://s3.documentcloud.org/documents/283180/l-and-m-application-amended.pdf> accessed April 19, 2017 (hereafter "Divorce Application"). For an overview of the general legal context in which this case arose, as well as the legal changes made after it, see Martha Butler and Cynthia Kirkby, 'Same-Sex Marriage, Divorce and Families: Selected Recent Developments' (Library of Parliament Research Publications, 2013) <https://lop.parl.gc.ca/content/lop/ResearchPublications/2013-74-e.htm> accessed April 19, 2017.

Nineteenth-Century Perspectives on Private International Law. Roxana Banu. © Roxana Banu 2018. Published 2018 by Oxford University Press.

they entered into in Canada had been recognized in neither Florida nor the United Kingdom.

The Attorney General noted that:

> In order for a marriage to be legally valid under Canadian law, the parties to the marriage must satisfy both the requirements of the law of the place where the marriage is celebrated (the *lex loci celebrationis*) with regard to the formal requirements, and the requirements of the law of domicile of the couple with regard to their legal capacity to marry one another.[2] [. . .] In this case, neither party had the legal capacity to marry a person of the same sex under the laws of their respective domicile—Florida and the United Kingdom.[3]

As a result of this blend of international elements, "their marriage is not legally valid under Canadian law," even though it was entered into in Canada.[4] The rule was based on the assumption that only the law of the place of domicile would have the authority to determine an individual's right to marry and to divorce.[5] Therefore, allowing the parties to divorce according to Canadian law might offend the foreign states of domicile and their respective sovereignty. As an interstate matter, this consideration weighed heavily.

In contrast, none of this was immediately apparent or relevant to the spouses. To them, marriage and divorce appeared as "a central component of the freedom to live life with the mate of one's choice" and were "intensely personal decisions that engage a complex set of social, political, religious and financial considerations"; their relevance flowed "from the incalculable value placed on public recognition of the marital relationship."[6] From the parties' perspective the fact that their marriage was not recognized at their place of domicile and that they could not get a divorce outside Canada should weigh in favor of marriage recognition in Canada as an element of international justice and judicial recourse. The parties stressed that "they are prevented from severing the legal and psychological bonds of marriage in a way that other couples routinely take for granted."[7]

The couple asked the court to consider the equality of treatment between the spouses:

> Even if the United Kingdom was prepared to dissolve the union as a civil partnership, it is unfair to place all of the responsibility with her [the spouse domiciled there]. Either party should be able to initiate and participate in her own divorce proceedings.[8]

The spouses also asked the court to consider the implications that its decision would have for their relationship to various communities and family members. The couple stressed that they could not move to Canada, "a new country, alone and isolated, to engage in the already lonely and isolated process of obtaining a divorce."[9]

Furthermore, regardless of the spouses' individual affiliations to Canada, their marriage itself could be thought of as embedded in Canada, the country in which

[2] Statement of the Attorney General of Canada, 2.a., court file number FS-11-367893, para. 4 <http://s3.documentcloud.org/documents/283173/l-and-m-answer.pdf> accessed April 19, 2017.
[3] Ibid., 5. [4] Ibid. [5] Ibid.
[6] "Divorce Application" (n. 1) paras 14 and 15. [7] Ibid., para 16.
[8] Ibid., para 22. [9] Ibid., para 23.

the relationship was entered into and which changed the lives of the spouses in significant ways.[10] Obtaining a divorce in the country where they got married was a means to:

[A]fford them respect and dignity to legally end their marriage. Without this, they cannot move on from this chapter in their lives. The fact that they continue to be connected by the legal institution of marriage impinges their ability to pursue new relationships and to feel comfortable doing so.[11]

Juxtaposing the couple's statements in the application for divorce with the Attorney General's submission reveals two very different ways of describing the transnational context of an interpersonal relationship: one fundamentally premised on a division of sovereignty in the international realm and a sense of the interstate accommodation of sovereign control, the other focused on various complex elements of individual self-determination and relational considerations.

Private International Law (PrIL) operates in the realm of these different normative justifications and policy implications. The field is central to any private law relationship involving foreign elements. Its norms designate which state's court should adjudicate a cross-border legal relation (jurisdiction), which state's law (not necessarily that of the forum) should determine the rights and liabilities of individuals involved in the relationship (choice of law), and in which courts the resulting judgment can be recognized and enforced (recognition and enforcement of judgments).

Although crucial to the regulation of interpersonal cross-border relationships, PrIL is repeatedly criticized harshly for failing to "offer any systemic vision, or sense of meaning, to the changes affecting law and authority in a global environment" and for "leaving untended the private causes of crisis and injustice."[12] For Horatia Muir Watt, for example, the future direction of the field should be to adopt a "planetary perspective" that would "connect up with the politics of international law."[13] Jacco Bomhoff proposes that PrIL be thought of "as a constitution" to strengthen it "as a site for deliberation and contestation over the identity and boundaries of polities,"[14] while Alex Mills aims to re-envision PrIL as a set of rules for a kind of global federalism.[15]

These and other critical projects in PrIL converge less on the solution than on the problem of PrIL's "tunnel vision." The perception is that the autonomy of private individuals is unfettered in PrIL and that this is due to its individualism as a form

[10] Ibid., para 24. [11] Ibid.

[12] Horatia Muir Watt, 'Private International Law Beyond the Schism' (2011) 2 Transnatl Leg Theory 347, 350 (hereafter Muir Watt, "Beyond the Schism").

[13] Ibid., 347.

[14] Jacco Bomhoff, 'The Constitution of the Conflict of Laws' in Horatia Muir Watt and Diego Fernández Arroyo (eds.), *Private International Law and Global Governance* (OUP 2015) 262, 263 (hereafter Bomhoff, "Conflict of Laws").

[15] Alex Mills, *The Confluence of Public and Private International Law: Justice, Pluralism and Subsidiarity in the International Constitutional Ordering of Private Law* (CUP 2009) (hereafter Mills, *Justice, Pluralism and Subsidiarity*).

of *private* law.[16] Furthermore, the repeatedly referenced "neutral" and apolitical dimensions of PrIL are thought to keep PrIL unaware of the systemic, global implications on the world's current injustices and abuses brought or sustained by the operation of its norms.[17]

A. The Fault of History

In diagnosing the problems and portraying the solutions, the normative critical project intersects, directly or indirectly, with a particular, by now conventional, account of PrIL's historical development. Much of this "tunnel vision" is blamed on PrIL's nineteenth-century history for two reasons. First, since the main PrIL theories were developed in the nineteenth century, the common assumption is that they inevitably borrowed from the then dominant liberal ideology and incorporated the private/public, market/government, and individual/state dichotomies. The main target is German legal scholar Friedrich Karl von Savigny (1779–1861), who, we are repeatedly reminded, wrote at the height of liberalism.[18] Second, by the end of the nineteenth century PrIL disconnected from Public International Law (PublIL) and it is generally assumed that this division has enabled PrIL to remain oblivious to global public concerns.[19]

[16] Bomhoff, "Conflict of Laws" (n. 14) 262: "the appeal to constitutionalist ideas pursued in this chapter is one attempt to restoratively invoke some form of 'the public' in the face of increasing threats of private hegemony"; Muir Watt, "Beyond the Schism" (n. 12) 387:

> the liberal paradigm favors an approach to legal problems in terms of the "micro" or the individual—individual civil or political rights; private property; discrete contracts; non-mass torts. In addition, "private" law adopts a backward-looking perspective, providing the tools for solving inter-subjective conflicts *ex post*, on a case-by-case basis. Issues relating to collective goods often tend to be confiscated or occulted by private conflicts. Private international law has internalized these limitations and disconnected from the macro-perspective which focuses on the surrounding social and political context.

Horatia Muir Watt, 'Party Autonomy in International Contracts' in Horatia Muir Watt (ed.), *Private International Law and Public Law*, vol. 2 (Elgar Press 2015) 382.

[17] Muir Watt, "Beyond the Schism" (n. 12) 360, n. 62: "The supposed 'naturality' of the principles of private international law owes an initial debt to Von Savigny's great *Treatise of Roman Law System des heutigen Römischen Rechts, 1849,* whose famous chapter VIII is believed to be the fount of modern conflicts methodology."

[18] Many references could be included here. See, e.g. Henri Batiffol, 'Les intérêts du droit international privé' in Alexander Lüderitz and Jochen Schröder (eds.), *Internationales Privatrecht und Rechtsvergleichung im Ausgang des 20. Jahrhunderts. Bewahrung oder Wende?* (Alfred Metzner 1977) 11, 15.

[19] Joel R. Paul, 'The Isolation of Private International Law' (1988) 7 Wis Int L J 149. For Muir Watt the separation of the two fields led to "the construction of the closet." Muir Watt, "Beyond the Schism" (n. 12) 375–7:

> Indeed, gradually disconnected from the substance of public international law while espousing the limits it prescribed, private international law closed in on itself. Inhibited from interfering with interstate clashes of power, it continued to focus on private and domestic issues, developing for that purpose a specific methodology which consolidated its axiological neutrality and widened the breach between itself and international politics.

In contrast, in this book I argue that theories that connected PrIL with PublIL did not connect it "with the substance of public international law" and did not focus on "interstate clashes of power" in

These two common intuitions inform much of the discourse about reform in PrIL today. Nineteenth-century intellectual history is portrayed as the classical liberal legacy that PrIL must shed; courts and scholars often appeal to reversing the historical split of private from public international law; and much of the critical literature pleads for restoring the lost political and regulatory space by refocusing on state interests rather than individual rights and interests. Inevitably, PrIL is now divided between the "classicists" and the critical scholars, between individualistic theories focusing on individual autonomy and state-centered theories focusing on state interests and regulatory policies.

While PrIL's nineteenth-century intellectual history looms large in the critical normative project, there is little examination of that history up close.[20] This is not so surprising. If nineteenth-century PrIL, and Savigny as its main protagonist, are viewed as marked by individualistic liberalism, it seems easy, indeed advisable, to not dwell on the period. Similarly, if the intellectual "height" of the period is thought to have been the association between PrIL and PublIL, it seems that we could bring it back by simply reclaiming the association today, rather than examining it in its own time. Nineteenth-century PrIL then represents both the problem and the solution for contemporary projects to reform the field. It appears desirable to recapture the PrIL-PublIL association and to refocus the field on states and state sovereignty, but only if one could simultaneously discard the perceived overly liberal individual-centered, private law-focused theories, which also marked the field in the nineteenth century.

Throughout this book, I show that this analysis is wanting as a matter of historical method, because it involves a certain atemporal essentializing of concepts. This essentializing prevents a thorough engagement with the theories of nineteenth-century PrIL scholars, or of any period for that matter, on their own terms. Our contemporary skepticism about private autonomy—which is well founded for the society we inhabit today—makes it difficult to imagine that nineteenth-century scholars might have referenced private autonomy and might have focused on individuals rather than states in a different intellectual, as well as sociopolitical context. And if we now assume that joining PrIL with PublIL would increase the public and political dimensions of PrIL, we feel entitled to both condemn any nineteenth-century scholars for having fought against such program, and to praise those who

the way that we understand these terms today. Therefore, the schism between the two fields cannot be understood as a move away from politics or from a focus on global public goods, since these were not the themes of the nineteenth-century PrIL-PublIL association.

[20] Notable exceptions are Ralf Michaels, 'Story, Joseph' in J. Basedow et al. (eds.), *Encyclopedia of Private International Law* (Edward Elgar 2017); Ralf Michaels, 'Waechter, Carl Georg' in J. Basedow et al. (eds.), *European Encyclopedia of Private International Law* (Edward Elgar 2017). Another more recent study of PrIL's pre-classical history, to which I did not have access while writing this book, is Nicholas Hatzimihail, *Pre-classical Conflicts of Laws* (SJD Thesis, Harvard Law School 2002). Among the earlier historical studies on PrIL see Maurits Meijers, 'L'histoire des principes fondamentaux du droit international privé a partir du moyen age, spécialment dans l'Europe occidentale' (1934) 49 Recueil des Cours 547; Rodolfo de Nova, 'Historical and Comparative Introduction to the Conflict of Laws' (1966) 116 Recueil des Cours 437; Max Gutzwiller, 'Le développement historique du droit international privé' (1929) 29 Recueil des Cours 237.

pled for it. The meanings we attribute to an individual-centered or a state-centered theoretical perspective in PrIL today are projected onto nineteenth-century intellectual history and then carried forward, unaltered, over two centuries.

From the perspective of historical methodology, recasting PrIL's intellectual history through contemporary biases is problematic on its own. But this lack of contextual engagement with PrIL's intellectual history also contributes to discrediting PrIL in various ways. It tends to encourage the perception of PrIL as an impoverished legal discipline, built on superficial analytical ground.[21] It also makes it possible to argue that we are still and perpetually marching in the footsteps of Savigny, even as the footprint is highly contested and not at all easy to discern.[22] More important, the lack of engagement with PrIL's intellectual history allows us to overlook the vast jurisprudential ground that PrIL covered every time that it constructed and re-constructed itself. Because of the nature of the problems it is meant to solve, PrIL had to struggle with questions of authority, sovereignty, individual autonomy, the nature of a legal system, and many other questions that are at the forefront of jurisprudence. This is not to say that PrIL necessarily found the best answer to any of these questions, but it is to say that there have been and continue to be intense academic discussions on all of these topics.

B. The State, the Individual, and the Relationships

This book recasts a succession of such intense academic discussions between the mid-nineteenth to the mid-twentieth century, which focused on whether PrIL should take the individual or the state as the analytical point of departure in constructing the field. This general question of course dissolved into a myriad of other questions: Does PrIL deal with interpersonal or interstate relationships? Is PrIL interested in the rights and interests of states or the rights and interests of individuals? Does PrIL "answer" to individuals or to states? What space for contestation is allowed to each? How does taking the state or the individual as the reference point impact PrIL's techniques and methodology?

In recent times these questions have become increasingly relevant, especially to those interested in emphasizing PrIL's global regulatory dimensions and PrIL's social dimensions generally. But these questions are far from novel. They have marked PrIL as a legal field since its inception. Contemporary PrIL scholars

[21] Horatia Muir Watt, 'Future Directions?' in Horatia Muir Watt and Diego Fernández Arroyo (eds.), *Private International Law and Global Governance* (OUP 2015) 363 (questioning whether PrIL should still be considered as a separate legal field or whether we should instead start discussing about "the end of choice of law"). But see Horatia Muir Watt, 'Theorizing Private International Law' in Anne Orford, Florian Hoffmann, and Martin Clark (eds.), *The Oxford Handbook of the Theory of International Law* (OUP 2016) 862 (suggesting that one might revise and reframe PrIL's own methodological and theoretical arsenal).

[22] For a very interesting discussion and refutation of the thesis that PrIL is always walking in Savigny's footsteps see Klaus Schurig, 'Das Fundament trägt noch' in Heinz-Peter Mansel (ed.), *Internationales Privatrecht im 20. Jahrhundert, Der Einfluss von Gerhard Kegel und Alexander Lüderitz auf das Kollisionsrecht* (Mohr Siebeck 2014) 9, 17 (hereafter Schurig, "Das Fundament").

generally recognize this, but they tend to assume that the field operated with only two extreme positions, which I will call individualistic and state-centered, respectively.

PrIL theories that conceptualized PrIL by reference to private law and focused on the individual are believed to have adopted an individualistic, self-interested image of the individual in her transnational existence. This perspective allegedly entailed a sharp distinction between private and public law and between law and politics, and excluded any meaningful element of the social responsibility of individuals in their cross-border dealings.[23] By contrast, state-centered theories are generally associated with the desire to curb private power and to emphasize the public and political dimensions of transnational legal matters. This assumption often translates into a general aim to recover state-centered theories, especially if they could re-connect PrIL with PublIL.

This book recovers the "untapped" resources of PrIL's nineteenth-century intellectual history. It argues that insofar as current scholars have recourse to this history, they tend to idealize the nineteenth-century relationship of private to public international law, on the one hand, and to demonize any individual-centered perspective, on the other. The result is that we have lost sight of an important position of the nineteenth century, which I have termed "relational internationalist." I show that this perspective was meant to be a reaction to both the state-centered and the libertarian position, and as such would be extremely useful for contemporary debates on rethinking the regulatory function of PrIL in light of our increasingly interconnected world.

This book shows that in its current depictions, the nineteenth century is as much the "history of an illusion" for PrIL as it is for PublIL.[24] Far from injecting an awareness and concern for global public goods or restraining private power and abuse, the association of private with public international law during the nineteenth century injected much of the formalism and isolation of today's PrIL. For example, as shown in Chapters 2 and 3, when continental European scholars constructed PrIL as the field dealing with the universal distribution of sovereign authority in the nineteenth century, the PrIL-PublIL analogy discouraged any engagement with individuals'

[23] Schurig, "Das Fundament" (n. 22) 8 (discussing and refuting the thesis that Savigny's theory should be seen as apolitical and removed from public law considerations):

> One also needs to immediately refute the legend which emerged in the second half of the previous century under the influence of the so-called political school and which can still be seen today in the scholarship of several authors and which appears ineradicable. This thesis argues that the so conceived PrIL [in Savigny's theory] is apolitical, removed from the state and disconsiders material goals, especially those of political economy and social goals. [Translated by author. All materials cited in this book, originally published in a language other than English, are translated by the author, unless otherwise specified].

Bomhoff, "Conflict of Laws" (n. 14) 275: "But classical private international law is also importantly incomplete in this respect, for example in the way notions of responsibility are almost entirely absent from its dominant mode of discourse."

[24] I take this line of argument from David Kennedy, 'International Law and the Nineteenth Century: History of an Illusion' (1998) 17 Quinnipiac L Rev 99 (hereafter Kennedy, "History of an Illusion").

interests and pleas for justice, as well as any reflection on the consequences of the distribution of sovereignty on global justice and global public goods. When English scholars constructed PrIL as a site for the recognition of universal rights in the twentieth century, the PrIL-PublIL analogy led primarily to an exacerbation of contract and property rights, as well as individual liberty, ignoring any debates around social justice in the transnational realm.

Furthermore, the contemporary lament for the "lost" relationship between PrIL and PublIL is misplaced. In keeping with the idea that our contemporary impressions of nineteenth-century PrIL are "the history of an illusion," I suggest that the "classical" relationship between PrIL and PublIL is actually quite well entrenched in PrIL theory and methodology—so well entrenched, in fact, that whenever PrIL tries to move closer to PublIL, many of the tenets of the nineteenth-century association are revived.[25] As Kennedy said of nineteenth-century PublIL, it has never been as thoroughly rejected as the usual account suggests, but instead "survives in the most progressive of contemporary polemics for a new international law."[26]

Contrary to the other common attitude to the PrIL of the period, I further suggest that the demonization of all nineteenth-century individual-centered perspectives is too quick and too shallow. Many of the nineteenth-century authors who argued for an analogy between PrIL and domestic private law or for a focus on individuals' interests were not simultaneously pleading for a strict private/public, market/politics distinction. Rather, they were countering the formalism and injustices of the state-centered internationalist perspective, which emerged from the PrIL-PublIL association. Since the PrIL-PublIL analogy did not represent the enlightened quest for the public good it is portrayed to have been, nineteenth-century theories that dispelled the association should not be understood as a reaction against the pursuit of global public goals or global justice generally.

Rather, the historical analysis in this book aims to show that many nineteenth-century individual-centered perspectives can be viewed as motivated by insights focused on individuals' agency as well as responsibility in transnational interpersonal interactions. Central to these perspectives was the appeal to disaggregate state interests or appeals to sovereignty, in order to allow for the voice of various individuals and groups. Furthermore, they encouraged courts to ponder on the level of consideration, respect, dignity, and care that individuals owe each other in their cross-border private law relations. Similarly, they were particularly attuned to the way in which individuals pursue particular claims in particular courts as part of their quest for recognition and integration in various communities. Finally, they contended that courts have fiduciary duties toward the litigating parties directly,

[25] Roxana Banu, 'Assuming Regulatory Authority for Transnational Torts: An Interstate Affair? A Historical Perspective on the Canadian Private International Law Tort Rules' (2013) 31 Windsor YB Access Just 197 (arguing that the Canadian Supreme Court's attempt to "adapt Private International Law to modern realities" can, in fact, be best understood as recasting the nineteenth-century PrIL-PublIL association).

[26] Kennedy, "History of an Illusion" (n. 24) 102.

and are therefore bound to an equitable weighing of the interests of domestic and foreign parties alike.

The book reconstructs this lost "relational internationalist" perspective primarily from the writings of three scholars, each developing and refining their predecessors' relational insights: Joseph Story (1779–1845), Friedrich Karl von Savigny (1779–1861), and Josephus Jitta (1854–1925). It shows how each of them developed and refined the relational insights of their predecessors and, in turn, how traces of this perspective, culminating in Jitta's writings, were recast and refined in a different context by the American legal realist school in the 1930s and by several continental European scholars after the Second World War. In the case of Story and Savigny, while both are famous in PrIL and beyond, this book incorporates thus far overlooked writings and historical accounts, to suggest new interpretations of their PrIL theses. Jitta does not figure in the historical memory of PrIL and one of the goals of the book is to show the surprising relevance of his theories for PrIL and beyond.

The fact that this book aims to reconstruct a relational internationalist perspective is not meant to suggest that the three authors to whom I have ascribed a "relational internationalist" perspective fully acknowledged or deliberately set to create such a perspective. Both the label and the reconstruction of their theories as a "relational internationalist" perspective are my own. What can be discerned from their writing is that all three authors rejected both extreme individualism and state-centrism in PrIL. What emerges as an alternative to individualism and state-centrism following a thorough engagement with the theories of these authors, I argue, is an attempt to theorize various levels of relationships amongst individuals and with various communities in the transnational realm.

The distinctive feature of the "relational internationalist" perspective is the attempt to bring out an increasingly broad range of factors, as constructing the transnational context of a particular interpersonal relationship. This perspective avoids the libertarian image of the isolated individual, as well as the image of the individual inevitably subsumed under the notion of a state or a particular community. Instead, it outlines a view of relational, rather than individualistic vested rights in a transnational context. Furthermore, it departs from the consent-based or state sovereignty-based theories of legitimacy, drawing instead on a variety of sources to determine the level of interpersonal responsibility within a particular private law relationship and beyond. Lastly, it situates itself within the two extreme positions of universalism and relativism. It blends natural law and *jus gentium* insights with an appreciation for national particularities.

Overall, the "relational internationalist" perspective this book aims to recover constructs the individual as a social being, whose existence is embedded within a variety of relationships, including her relationships to the other party(ies) in the private law relationship, with the community(ies) in which the private law relationship is embedded, as well as with humanity generally. This relational insight made it less plausible for the authors referenced in this book to create a strict separation between the individual and larger social communities, between private and public, and between freedom and social responsibility.

C. History and Theory

1. The devil is in the details: refocusing PrIL historiography

Arguing that one can reconstruct a "relational internationalist" perspective from nineteenth-century PrIL theories might come as a surprise for scholars both within and outside the field. This is primarily due to the way in which intellectual history in PrIL has traditionally been written.

As already mentioned, reading contemporary concepts and debates into nineteenth-century PrIL scholarship prevented us from engaging with the nuances and unique motivations of nineteenth-century PrIL theories. Equally unhelpful in encouraging more detailed and contextual intellectual historical analysis in PrIL are the diluted historiographies that are prevalent in PrIL. Generally, PrIL intellectual history is either catalogued based on major schools of thought (i.e., the Dutch, German, French, Italian school of thought) or on broad normative currents, which are thought to have repeated cyclically in the development of PrIL as a field (nationalism, internationalism, unilateralism, multilateralism, etc.).

Friedrich Juenger's "Page of History" for example takes PrIL history from Antiquity, to the Middle Ages, to the American realist revolution; it breaks down PrIL theories geographically into the Italian, the French, the Dutch school and isolates as particular cases the "English deviation," the German authors, and various U.S. theories.[27] Juenger's account is not only considered "the most common English-language reference on the history of the conflict of laws."[28] It is also representative for a genre of historical account in PrIL which, while not focused on an analysis of original texts, makes broad claims about the impact of particular authors or schools of thought on the development of PrIL as a legal field. Characteristic of the type of historical account exemplified by Juenger is also the breaking down of PrIL theory and methodology into "epochs" of pre-classical, classical, and modern PrIL thought. Each period is then ascribed a certain geography and a certain broad unified "ethos."[29]

A related and equally common type of historical account describes PrIL as a cyclic sequence of big theoretical and methodological "moves," from universalism to particularism, multilateralism to unilaterialism, personality to territoriality, conflicts justice to material justice, and so on.[30] The goal is not to understand what motivates

[27] Friedrich Juenger, 'A Page of History' (1984) 35 Mercer L Rev 419.

[28] Nikitas Hatzimihail, 'Pages of History: Friedrich Juenger and the Historical Consciousness of Modern Private International Law' in Leonel Pereznieto Castro, Tullio Treves, and Francesco Seatzu (eds.), *Tradition and Innovation of Private International Law at the Beginning of the Third Millenium—Liber in Memoriam of Professor Friedrich K. Juenger* (Juris Publishing 2006) 81, 82 (hereafter Hatzimihail, "Pages of History").

[29] For a very good account and critique of Juenger's historical account in PrIL see Hatzimihail, "Pages of History" (n. 28).

[30] Symeon Symeonides, 'The American Choice-of-Law Revolution in the Courts: Today and Tomorrow' (2002) 298 Recueil des Cours 9, 357–417. Symeonides also relies on these broad theoretical and methodological moves in order to describe and explain trends and attempts at codifying choice of law around the world. Symeon Symeonides, *Codifying Choice of Law Around the World* (OUP 2014).

any one of these perspectives at any given time, but rather to characterize particular developments in PrIL in light of familiar and broad theoretical and methodological developments. One is led to believe that these theoretical and methodological "moves" have a certain coherence and meaning that can be discerned whenever, wherever, and regardless of who invokes them. The agency of the scholars who constantly shape and reframe these perspectives at any given moment is lost, as is the context, which defines the many iterations underlying any of these broad theoretical and methodological currents.

According to conventional PrIL historiography, nineteenth-century PrIL theory, which is central to this book, is generally described as the classical period of PrIL. Methodologically, this period is thought to have been characterized by clear, intransigent and uniform rules of PrIL, which did not take account of the substance of the laws "in conflict." Rigidity, naiveté and agnosticism toward politics and policy analysis are thought to describe nineteenth-century PrIL scholarship. From the perspective of broader sociological and epistemological changes, nineteenth-century PrIL receives a different characterization:

> On the one hand, classical conflict of laws is the culmination of certain developments in private law and international law: the creation of legal categories such as "family law" or "extracontractual obligations," the increased emphasis on the concepts of subjective right and legal relation, the notion of gapless legal systems—as well as the concept of sovereignty and the notion of ordering the international relations through a clear allocation of jurisdictional powers. On the other hand, classical conflict of laws stands for the eventual separation of "private international law" from both private law and international law, for the construction of an autonomous discipline with its own methodology, philosophy, instruments and . . . economics.[31]

This book departs from the conventional broad historiographies of PrIL generally, and of its nineteenth-century theories in particular. Instead, it portrays each broad theoretical and methodological direction in PrIL in the nineteenth century as a placeholder for much more detailed and consequential debates. For example, while Hatzimihail might be right that nineteenth-century PrIL theory is characterized by an increased focus on subjective rights, legal relations, state systems, and national sovereignty, choosing any one of these notions as analytical starting points in PrIL theory divided PrIL scholars and often created fundamentally different visions in constructing "an autonomous discipline." There is hardly a unified cluster of nineteenth-century notions giving rise to a unified classical nineteenth-century PrIL. Rather, nineteenth-century PrIL is characterized by intense, consequential and often extremely detailed debates about precisely which concepts underlying private law and PublIL should be borrowed and allowed to shape the theory and methodology of PrIL. The mere question whether those concepts should be borrowed from private law or from PublIL was no small quarrel among nineteenth-century PrIL scholars.

[31] Hatzimihail, "Pages of History" (n. 28) 94.

For the intellectual historical account presented in this book, the devil is in the details. Therefore, rather than presenting the nineteenth-century universalist current as a unified theory, this book portrays it as a placeholder for a series of debates about whether universalism[32] should be constructed by analogy to private law or PublIL, or whether it should be constructed around universal rights, equal sovereignty, transnational relationships, and so on. Similarly, rather than assuming that individual-centered notions characterized a particular unified individual-centered vision of PrIL,[33] this book shows that theories constructed by reference to individual autonomy, vested rights, or jural relations differed quite substantially from each other. Rather than leveling nuances, this book reveals and engages with the nuances of PrIL intellectual history, in order to distill overlooked or marginalized ways of constructing the theory and methodology of PrIL.

2. Texts and contexts

In order to expose marginalized or overlooked PrIL theories and methodologies this historical study further departs from the way in which we have traditionally separated the field between various large camps of nationalist/internationalists and positivists/non-positivists.

One example of such historical generalization can be seen in Arthur Nussbaum's contention that "nearly all of the leading continental writers of the period [from 1870 to 1930] espoused the Law-of-Nations conception"[34] which in his view represented "a virtually unified conception [...] despite some quibbling differences between the Savignyan and Mancinian schools of thought."[35] This unified front of legal scholarship is then simply defined by a "cosmopolitan feature" and a "focus on international in Private International Law."[36]

There are many ambiguities in this remark, including the reference to "leading" writers and the extremely large period of time to which such ideological uniformity is attributed. But it is the allegation of the ideological uniformity of internationalism in PrIL that is most problematic, and Nussbaum was hardly alone in making it.[37]

[32] Because in PrIL intellectual history internationalism and universalism were used interchangeably to describe a school of thought, which pled for an analysis of PrIL matters in light of interests and concerns transcending national boundaries, the two terms are also used interchangeably in this book.

[33] Erik Jayme argued that a "human rights paradigm" existed in PrIL in the nineteenth century, returned in PrIL theory in the last quarter of the twentieth century, and is now re-articulated in the increasing focus on party autonomy in PrIL. Erik Jayme, 'Völkerrecht und internationales Privatrecht—eine entwicklungsgeschichtliche Betrachtung' in Stefan Leibe and Matthias Ruffert (eds.), *Völkerrecht und IPR* (Jenaer Wissenschaftliche Verlagsgesellschaft 2006) 23. By contrast, this book aims to show that the individual-centered theoretical paradigm of the nineteenth century differed from that of the twentieth and the twenty-first centuries. Furthermore, it argues that even in the nineteenth century there existed different variations of the individual-centered perspective, some focusing on an atomistic, others on a more relational image of the transnational agent.

[34] Arthur Nussbaum, 'Rise and Decline of the Law-of-Nations Doctrine in the Conflict of Laws' (1942) 42 Columbia L Rev 189, 198 (hereafter Nussbaum, "Rise and Decline").

[35] Ibid., 194. [36] Ibid., 195, 198.

[37] Frank Kahn is notorious in discussing the divide between internationalism and nationalism in PrIL. Franz Kahn, 'Gesetzeskollisionen, Ein Beitrag zur Lehre des Internationalen Privatrechts' (1890) 30 Jherings Jahrbücher für die Dogmatik des Bürgerlichen Rechts 1 and (1898) 39 Jherings Jahrbücher

The fact that internationalism was constructed differently depending on whether these internationalists took the state or the individual as the point of reference—a central thesis of this book—is simply lost either in the alleged "unity" of internationalism or subsumed under the "quibbling differences."

Internationalism was portrayed as being grounded in the association between PrIL and PublIL and having as its point of departure "the community, based on international law, of the nations (independent states) having intercourse with one another."[38] Internationalism was defined by its state-centered variation and we inevitably lost sight of any individual-centered internationalist perspectives. By contrast, this book, especially in its first chapter, aims to break this unity of universalism by showing the philosophical questions that divided universalists between those taking the individual and those taking the state as their point of reference. At the same time, just as universalism is presented in this book as a school of thought with many iterations, state-centered and individual-centered perspectives are not presented as unified subdivisions of universalism. In particular, the book aims to highlight the philosophical arguments within individual-centered theories which sought to construct a more individualistic or more relational image of the transnational agent.

In order to be attuned to such "philosophical" quarrels within the internationalist school and with their critics this book views nineteenth-century academic debates as one among other gateways to understand the meaning the respective authors meant to ascribe to their texts. In his project, while trying to recover a certain kind of internationalism in PrIL, Alex Mills distinguishes between an "intrinsic" and an "extrinsic" perspective from which to tell the story of universalism in PrIL.[39] He describes the extrinsic perspective he adopts as one which "looks at the role played by broader ideas of international law and international order" in the development of PrIL.[40] In this context he describes the role of certain legal and political currents first in the development of PrIL as a branch of international law, and then in its development as an extension of national private law.[41] This perspective helps him characterize the fall of universalism as a historical contingency. It can always be re-challenged at the same time as legal positivism, the relationship between private and public law, and the description of international law as the law of sovereign states, are also challenged.[42] In contrast, Mills describes an intrinsic historical perspective as one that sees developments of PrIL as particular to this field of law, without linking them to broader developments in our view of law and legal order.[43]

It is generally with reference to an extrinsic perspective that PrIL is thought to have aligned itself with liberalism or natural law thought, positivism, or any other theoretical perspective dominant at particular times. The idea that PrIL academic

für die Dogmatik des Bürgerlichen Rechts 1 and (1899) 40 Jherings Jahrbücher für die Dogmatik des Bürgerlichen Rechts 1. For a discussion of the impact of Kahn's analysis on the development of PrIL see Chapter 3. Otto Kahn Freund, *The Growth of Internationalism in English Private International Law* (Magnus Press 1960); Henri Batiffol, 'Les tendences doctrinales actuelles en droit international privé' (1948) 72 Recueil des Cours 1, 9–33.

[38] Nussbaum, "Rise and Decline" (n. 34) 195.
[39] Mills, *Justice, Pluralism and Subsidiarity* (n. 15). [40] Ibid. [41] Ibid., Chapter 2.
[42] Ibid., 68. [43] Ibid., 27.

debates might reference ideas and perspectives particular to its development at different times is challenged as an overly intrinsic perspective.

This book captures the extrinsic and intrinsic background as simply referencing different contexts, which one can use as gateways to understand the meaning the original authors wished to attribute to a particular text.[44] Each one or both can appear more or less plausible in deciphering the meaning of such text. To the extent the distinction is made simply to show that there are a variety of contexts to which one can refer, this is an important observation.[45] But it seems misleading to suggest that an extrinsic perspective is better or more helpful for intellectual history in general and PrIL intellectual history in particular.[46]

For example, Phocion Franceskakis, whose PrIL theory is outlined in Chapter 4, challenged a Marxist interpretation of the statutory school of thought in PrIL on the basis that the statutory theory developed and survived as a product of PrIL theorists, without much connection to the general socioeconomic background.[47] Furthermore, from the historical account in this book it should become apparent that labeling Savigny as a natural law scholar,[48] or a Kantian,[49] misrepresents the context of the historical school of thought, which Savigny grounded and which was a reaction to both Kantian philosophy and natural law. Similarly, the characterization

[44] The intrinsic/extrinsic distinction usually carries a different meaning in intellectual history. The former is associated with a purely textual analysis of different writings, while the latter is associated with a contextual analysis of texts. The context, however, can capture both the socioeconomic and political situation at the time of the writing of the text, as well as the academic debates within a legal field. For an argument that one should not derive the meaning of a text exclusively from a textual analysis or the sociopolitical context of the time it was written see Quentin Skinner, 'Meaning and Understanding in the History of Ideas' (1969) 8 Hist Theory 3 (hereafter Skinner, "Meaning and Understanding"). For an argument that there are multiple contexts which can and should be employed in the reading and interpretation of texts see also Dominick LaCapra, 'Rethinking Intellectual History and Reading Texts' (1980) 19 Hist Theory 245, 254 (hereafter LaCapra, "Rethinking Intellectual History"): "An appeal to *the* context is deceptive: one never has—at least in the case of complex texts—*the* context."

[45] Annabel Brett, 'What is Intellectual History Now?' in D. Cannadiene (ed.), *What is History Now?* (Palgrave Macmillan 2002) 116 (hereafter Brett, *What is History Now?*): "context can be multidimensional: a specific political situation, a social or cultural milieu, an institutional context like a courtroom."

[46] Skinner, "Meaning and Understanding" (n. 44).

[47] Phocion Franceskakis, 'De coflictu legum, Melanges offerts a R.D. Kollewijn et J. Offerhaus a l'occasion de leur soixante-dixieme anniversaire', reviewing M. Blagojeviç, 'Théorie des statuts à la lumière générale de l'évolution de la société' in Phocion Francescakis, *La pensée des autres en droit international privé: comptes rendus bibliographiques (1946–1984) réunis en hommage à leur auteur* (Université Aristote de Thessalonique, Faculté de droit 1985) 211. See also Skinner, "Meaning and Understanding" (n. 44) 42–3:

> It is my essential contention, however, that none of this panic or equivocation is at all well-judged, since the methodology of contextual reading, in both its Marxist and Namierite versions (they are oddly similar) can itself be shown to rest on a fundamental mistake about the nature of the relations between action and circumstance. Despite the possibility, therefore, that a study of social context may *help* in the understanding of a text, which I have conceded, the fundamental assumption of the contextual methodology, that the ideas of a given text should be understood *in terms of* its social context, can be shown to be mistaken, and to serve in consequence not as the guide to understanding, but as the source of further very prevalent confusions in the history of ideas.

[48] Mills, *Justice, Pluralism and Subsidiarity* (n. 15) 68.

[49] Sagi Peari, 'Savigny's Theory of Choice-of-Law as a Principle of "Voluntary Submission"' (2014) 64 UTLJ 106.

of the Dutch school, or of Story as positivist would ignore or misrepresent Story's numerous references to natural duty, morality, general principles of justice, and so on.[50]

It is therefore equally misleading to suggest, as Nussbaum and others did, that an idea—such as internationalism—may have retained a unitary morphology during an entire century, and that the various authors discussed in this book must be understood in light of the dominant view of law and justice at any particular moment.[51] Instead, this book subscribes to Skinner's remark that "there *is* no history of the idea to be written, but only a history necessarily focused on the various agents who used the idea, and on their varying situations and intentions in using it."[52]

On this premise, I make certain arguments about the intellectual history of PrIL. First, internationalism cannot be understood as a unitary theory, especially when looked at throughout an entire century. There are indeed many nuances and perspectives which differentiate internationalists, and which are significant on their own. This book underscores one such significant difference and argues that internationalism, especially in the nineteenth-century, was conceptualized differently depending on whether its proponents took the individual or the state as the point of departure in their theories. It also highlights the difference between individual-centered and state-centered internationalist perspectives of the second half of the nineteenth-century and those of the twentieth century. The individual-centered internationalist perspectives of each period can only be understood in light of the state-centered internationalist theories of their time, since they are typically thought of as a reaction or an alternative to them.

Second, not all nineteenth-century individual-centered internationalist theories endorsed an individualistic ideology. That is, not all individual-centered international theories of a century referencing autonomy and liberty should be understood, especially when this understanding is informed by our contemporary biases, as premised on an atomistic image of the individual or a libertarian perspective.

Third, any one PrIL author's statements or theories can be understood in light of a variety of contextual elements, two of which are the main focus of this book. When available and especially in Savigny's case, each author's PrIL theory is read in connection with his writings on law and justice more broadly. Blaine Baker's reading of Story's PrIL theory in light of his general writings and court decisions, especially in constitutional law, seems therefore, persuasive.[53] Similarly, it is helpful, indeed

[50] Mills, *Justice, Pluralism and Subsidiarity* (n. 15) 68.

[51] Skinner, "Meaning and Understanding" (n. 44) 46:

> Even if we could decode what a given statement must mean from a study of its social context, it follows that this would still leave us without any grasp of its intended illocutionary force, and so eventually without any real understanding of the given statement after all. The point is, in short, that an unavoidable lacuna remains: even if the study of the social context of texts could serve to *explain* them, this would not amount to the same as providing the means to *understand* them.

[52] Ibid., 38.

[53] Blaine Baker, 'Interstate Choice of Law and Early-American Constitutional Nationalism. An Essay on Joseph Story and the Comity of Errors: A Case Study in Conflict of Laws' (1993) 35 McGill LJ 454.

necessary to read Savigny's PrIL theory in light of his general theory about law and in light of the various schools of thought to which he subscribed or explicitly rejected. At the same time, this book focuses primarily on the general academic context in which these authors were writing, their conversations with one another, their descriptions and misdescriptions of each other's theories and the general academic directions that they meant to dispel or to react against.

PrIL as a field, and especially that of the nineteenth century, is characterized by intense discussions among scholars, who were reacting to one another's writings. It is almost impossible to understand the direction of reform an author intended to introduce in PrIL without paying attention to the way in which he described his intellectual opponents' or allies' theories. Chapter 2, for example, shows that Antoine Pillet (1857–1926) understood Savigny's theory as overly vague and unstable and thought his own theory, referencing sovereignty and PublIL, in contrast, managed to provide a truly universal and intransigent theory. It would be hard to understand what the PrIL-PublIL association meant for PrIL at the end of the nineteenth century without understanding how this association was used as an alternative to other theories of the time, including Savigny's.

3. Dialogues as entry points

In an attempt to capture the questions with which PrIL scholars struggled as they were developing the field, the intense debates that occurred between PrIL scholars, either directly, or through their various reviews of one another's works, are of paramount importance for this book.[54] Chapter 3 outlines three articles written in 1899 and 1900, featuring an academic conversation between Josephus Jitta and Ludwig von Bar (1836–1913), in which the authors debated and contested each other's internationalist theoretical positions focused on the individual or the state. This exchange provides not only a good basis for understanding the positions of the two authors, but also an insight into the way in which the field was struggling to find itself alongside PublIL at the end of the nineteenth century.

Chapter 4 describes the way in which Henri Batiffol (1905–1989) in France, Gerhard Kegel (1912–2006) in Germany, and R. H. Graveson (1911–1991) in England were, intentionally or not, aligning their theories in combining the description of PrIL as a coordinator of legal systems with remnants of the vested rights doctrine. This explains not only the way in which Batiffol's and Kegel's theories increased the technical nature of the field but also how this combined with an increased focus on an atomistic overly liberal image of the individual after the Second World War.

[54] LaCapra, "Rethinking Intellectual History" (n. 44) 263:

> In this sense, the history of critical response, including the book review, is an important chapter in the history of social impact, especially with reference to the constitution and development of disciplines. One can often learn more about the operative structure of a discipline from its book reviews and from their differential distribution in different sorts of journals than one can from its more formal institutional organization.

Chapter 5 introduces the 1957–1958 letters between two prominent American legal realists, David Cavers (1902–1988) and Brainerd Currie (1912–1965), as they shed new light on the motivations behind Currie's focus on state interests in PrIL. This correspondence also provides an entry point into the intense, often overlooked debates within the American realist school over the proper balancing of individual and state interests in PrIL in the twentieth century.

Whereas Chapters 3, 4, and 5 focus on dialogues between scholars who were contemporaries, the last three chapters reveal the analytical contours of the nineteenth-century relational internationalist perspective by placing it in dialogue with modern scholars. Chapter 6 relates Horatia Muir Watt's account of current debates on the individuals' rights to the recognition of their interpersonal relationships in the EU to the way in which recognition featured in the nineteenth-century "relational internationalist" perspectives centered on rights and reasonable expectations. Chapter 7 relates Lea Brilmayer's account of political legitimacy in PrIL to perspectives on legitimate authority under the state-centered and the "relational internationalist" perspectives of the nineteenth century. Chapter 8 compares and contrasts ways of underscoring the cosmopolitan dimensions of PrIL and the relationship between private interests and broader theories of justice within the twentieth century German interest jurisprudence, as opposed to the nineteenth-century "relational internationalist" perspective.

4. International themes within an international dialogue

This book aims to highlight the way in which PrIL scholars were struggling with extremely important theoretical themes of international interest by engaging in an international conversation, if not collaboration. The fact that it references the writings of authors from six different jurisdictions is a reflection of the international nature of the process of thinking and rethinking PrIL's theoretical foundations.

While the way in which Savigny influenced the development of PrIL in Germany, or Story the development of PrIL in the U.S. are certainly important studies on their own, this book focuses primarily on the way in which these ideas migrated across jurisdictions, thereby creating an international dialogue over the proper theoretical fundaments of PrIL. This cross-reference between authors in different jurisdictions is explicitly included in the writings of the authors referenced in this project. Savigny acknowledges having read and been influenced by Joseph Story's writings. Josephus Jitta, Antoine Pillet, and others explicitly construct their theories by reference to or distinction from Savigny. Therefore, these references themselves form part of the context through which to understand the writings of these scholars.

The dialogue of course is international also due to the international nature of the themes being discussed. As these authors were trying to identify the contours of rights claims in the transnational context (Chapter 6), the basis of legitimate authority for interhuman transnational legal matters, and the contours and limits of individual autonomy (Chapter 7), or else the proper blend of national particularities and universal justice principles, and cosmopolitan dimensions of PrIL generally (Chapter 8), they inevitably found themselves in an international dialogue on international themes. This book traces both the international nature of that dialogue as well as the international nature of the issues debated.[55] It highlights the way in which in PrIL "ideas *travel*, who transports them, what baggage they carry on their journeys and how they become domesticated and naturalized upon arrival."[56] At the same time, it reveals the way in which PrIL debates about the national, the international, the transnational, or the global "need to be placed into contexts construed almost entirely as temporal and linguistic not physical or spatial."[57]

While the historical study in this book focuses on the migration of ideas and theories in PrIL throughout Europe and the U.S. between the mid-nineteenth to the mid-twentieth century, it also insists on underscoring the particularities of each iteration of what appear as similar ideas. For example, the notion of autonomy relied upon by early nineteenth-century German scholars constructing a notion of vested rights is different from the notion of autonomy relied upon by Savigny, which in turn is different from the notion of autonomy relied upon by twentieth-century English writers constructing their own variation of the vested rights doctrine. Yet these different iterations of autonomy or vested rights used by different authors in different countries did not "emerge in ignorance of each other, but rather in dialogues mediated by local conditions of the reception, circulation and hybridization of arguments."[58]

Furthermore, while this study focuses on the internationalization of ideas, it insists that this internationalization should not be generalized to an entire doctrine or school of thought. A central thesis in this book is that once we understand that the universalist doctrine contained state-centered and individual-centered variations, it also becomes clear that at particular times, one or several of these variations "internationalized," while others did not. Chapter 2 shows that the state-centered variation dominated the period discussed in this book. Chapter 4 shows that even when individual-centered perspectives gained in importance, primarily after the Second World War, it was individualistic theories focused on an isolated image of the transnational agent that took center stage, particularly in English reconstructions of universalism. The relational underpinnings of various PrIL theories were never underscored as much as individualistic and especially state-centered universalist variations. The historical account in this book confirms Samuel Moyn's contention that "it is impossible to isolate the globalization of one concept from the *nonglobalization of another*."[59]

55 For a very helpful exposition of a study of international intellectual history, including a description of its methodology see David Armitage, *Foundations of Modern International Thought* (CUP 2013).

56 Ibid., 22.

57 Ibid., 22 and 32: "Historicizing conceptions of space—of the national, the international, the transnational and the global—may in fact be one implied agenda for intellectual history after the international turn."

58 Ibid., 30.

59 Samuel Moyn, 'The Nonglobalization of Ideas' in Samuel Moyn and Andrew Sartori (eds.), *Global Intellectual History* (Columbia University Press 2013) 193. Interestingly, Moyn concludes that "the

5. Time, people, places

This book's historical account of individual- and state-centered internationalist perspectives is in many ways prompted by current debates within PrIL. What prompts a return to nineteenth-century PrIL scholarship is the fact that we nowadays identify individualistic and state-centered theories as the only ones available in PrIL's intellectual history and that we trace the construction of both these extremes to the nineteenth century. My goal is to show that we have lost sight of a possible individual-centered internationalist perspective that constructed the individual not as an atomistic, but rather as a relational being and that did not create a strict separation between the individual and the state, and between liberty and social responsibility.

It is also in the nineteenth century that the conceptualization of PrIL as a conflict of sovereignties was first articulated.[60] It is with the help of this conceptualization that the association between PrIL and PublIL was created. Furthermore, it was in the nineteenth century when the major theories underlying contemporary PrIL scholarship were formulated.

This is not at all to say that the individual/state duality was not discussed or did not influence earlier theories and perspectives, which in turn impacted the nineteenth-century authors included in this book. Rather, it is primarily in the nineteenth century that the early articulations of individual autonomy, state sovereignty, comity, etc. triggered the emergence of broader theories on the nature and methodology of PrIL and it was primarily those nineteenth-century treatises which have marked the development of PrIL in its current variations.

The series of the main nineteenth-century studies on PrIL began with Joseph Story's 1840 *Commentaries on the Conflict of Laws* and that work also marks the beginning of this book's intellectual historical account. Savigny, the second protagonist of the relational internationalist perspective, had read and admitted to having been influenced by Story's Commentaries in the writing of the eighth volume of his System in 1848.[61] I argue that what united those two PrIL scholars was the attempt to construct a relational image of the individual who is both in need of autonomy and self-determination and socially responsible, as she is embedded in a large web of relationships. This conceptualization was picked up and refined in 1880 by the Dutch scholar Josephus Jitta, the third protagonist of the relational internationalist perspective presented in this book.

At the end of the nineteenth century Jitta recast the relational internationalist perspective as an attempt to counter the dominant state-centered theories of his

victory of self-determination politics resulted in the greatest dissemination of sovereignty as a concept and a practice in world history and it created the very situation the human rights movement later set itself the task of qualifying or overcoming." Moyn 193–4. See also Moyn, 201: "If there is to be a global concept history, it must put comparison and competition of potentially global concepts at its heart."

60 André Bonnichon, 'La notion de conflit de souverainetes dans la science des conflits de lois' (1949) 39 Rev crit dr int privé 615 and (1950) 40 Rev crit dr int privé 11.

61 Gerhard Kegel, 'Story and Savigny' (1989) 37 Am J Comp L 39 (for a general discussion of the commonalities between Story's and Savigny's PrIL theories).

time, which associated PrIL with PublIL. From among these state-centered theories, this book focuses on those of the French scholar Antoine Pillet (1857–1926) and the German scholar Ernst Zitelmann (1852–1923), arguably some of the strongest state-centered internationalist theories of the late nineteenth century in PrIL. Gutzwiller viewed Zitelmann's doctrine as the only one truly developed out of PublIL and founded on the international community of states.[62] Similarly, Pillet's theory was praised as one of the most original internationalist theory.[63]

There is of course a wealth of scholars apart from those here singled out as protagonists of the state-centered and the relational internationalist perspectives. The writings of some of them are discussed in the first four chapters, as I trace the rise and fall of the state-centered and relational internationalist perspectives. But many authors are inevitably left out. This study therefore should not be read as a purported complete historiography of the field spanning over a century and several jurisdictions.[64]

6. The dialogue between past and present

In his 2007 Hague course Spyridon Vrellis invited us not to lose sight of the fact that the subject of law in general and of PrIL in particular "is the human being, a moral being; 'a subject worthy of esteem and respect."[65] But Vrellis clarifies that taking the individual as the point of departure does not need to translate into an individualistic normative theory:

> From this point of view, law, all law in its entirety, expression of politics or one of the expressions of politics, both in its origin and in its finality, is at the same time *private*, because it only exists for the human being and because of her, and *public*, because the interest of the human being finds its perfection in the general interest, in the general good, and the individual only becomes virtuous, that is highly moral, as part of a human society. This is why the tendencies manifested in the field, among others, of PrIL, which interests us in particular, which insist either on the interests of states (for example, Currie), or on the interests of individuals in isolation, are only partial. Those tendencies are correct, but only partially correct. The entire truth is found in their synthesis.[66]

[62] Max Gutzwiller, 'Zitlemann's völkerrechtliche Theorie des Internationalprivatrechts' (1923) 16 ARWP 468, 473–4.

[63] A.V. Dicey, *A Digest of the Law of England with Reference to the Conflict of Laws* (Stevens and Sons 1908) 13, n. 1 (citing Pillet's theory as a very good exposition of how to conceptualize the relationship between PrIL and PublIL, while maintaining the concept of vested rights).

[64] Because this study focuses on the theories, which have marked and defined the contours of PrIL primarily in the nineteenth century, it references primarily Western European and American theories. The way in which these theories have influenced PrIL in a variety of other jurisdiction beyond Europe and the United States would, of course, be worthy of a thorough examination, but is beyond the scope of this book. In Chapter 4 I briefly discuss, by reference to Duco Kollewijn's scholarship, the Eurocentic and imperial dimensions of nineteenth-century PrIL and the way in which the individual-centered/state-centered duality mapped onto the recognition/misrecognition of colonized territories as legal systems.

[65] Spyridon Vrellis, 'Conflit ou coordination de valeurs en droit international privé a la recherché de la justice' (2007) 328 Recueil des Cours 189, 196.

[66] Ibid., 198–9.

Andreas Bucher also observed in his general Hague course that "the interest of the person and individual liberty are surrounded by the general interest of the society and of the state. Conflict of laws rules should be equally inspired by this orientation."[67] The "social dimension of PrIL" then rests on this constant rebalancing of the relationships between individuals and between the individual and the broader social community.[68]

In the same vein, Ralf Michaels showed that PrIL constantly struggles with such questions as:

> Is choice of law about conflicts between states and their desires to regulate? (as the governmental-interest analysis dictates it?) Or is it about conflicts between private rights acquires in one state and public regulation in another (as in vested-rights theory)? Or is it not about conflicts at all, but merely about the technical designation of the applicable law?[69]

Much as Bucher and Vrellis, Michales concludes that a recalibration, rather than radicalization of the individual-centered and state-centered positions was a normative direction PrIL failed to construct.[70] This historical study aims to show that this recalibration can be reconstructed from relational internationalist perspectives of nineteenth-century PrIL theories.

This does not mean that simply bringing these nineteenth-century writings into our intellectual and sociopolitical context of today would immediately solve PrIL's problems as the current critics see them. More important, it does not mean that relationality as it was seen and conceptualized by these nineteenth-century authors maps onto current strands of relationality in jurisprudence, private law, or feminist writings. As I conclude this book I contemplate how the relational internationalist perspective might relate to, but also what might need to be traded off in light of contemporary insights. [71]

I am, in other words, much in agreement with Annabel Brett's view that "intellectual history does not merely unravel the structure of what we have inherited but can also unearth what we have lost: ways of speaking and ways of seeing the world, once current, now exotic and (perhaps) full of possibility"[72] and that "in trying to unravel the mental worlds of the past, we give ourselves the opportunity to re-weave

[67] Andreas Bucher, 'La dimension sociale du droit international privé: cours general' (2009) 330 Recueil des Cours 1, 99.

[68] Ibid.

[69] Ralf Michaels, 'Economics of Law as Choice of Law' (2008) 71 L & ContempProbs 73, 78.

[70] Ibid., 69: "[t]his is a combination that traditional doctrine [of conflict of laws] has not yet addressed accurately."

[71] A more thorough analysis of how the nineteenth-century relational internationalist perspective could reform today's PrIL and what might need to be traded off in light of newer strands of thought on relationality is the subject of an ongoing research project. For a connection between the relational internationalist perspective presented in this book and relational feminism see Roxana Banu, 'A Relational Feminist Approach to Private International Law' (unpublished paper, awarded the 2016 ASIL PILIG Prize in Private International Law, on file with author). For an analysis of how relational feminism could reform PrIL theory and methodology see Roxana Banu, 'A Relational Feminist Approach to Conflict of Laws' (2017) 24 Mich J Gender & Law 1.

[72] Brett, *What is History Now?* (n. 45) 127.

our own."[73] The relational internationalist perspective might give us a frame of reference for the ways in which PrIL could recover the image of the individual whose autonomy is embedded and constructed through a variety of relationships and affiliations and whose liberty and social responsibility are constantly interwoven in the transnational realm.

[73] Ibid., 128.

2

Individual- and State-Centered Perspectives in Nineteenth-Century Private International Law

A. Introduction

Erik Jayme opened his book on the intellectual history of PrIL focused on the work of Pasquale Mancini and Anton Ehrenzweig with the proposition that "the embeddedness of history in the present is nowhere more obvious than in Private International Law. The methods and instruments currently used were developed and tested much earlier, primarily in the 19th century."[1]

Franz Kahn summarized the fervor and significance of nineteenth-century academic debates in PrIL in his famous statement "[t]he battle of opinions in Private International Law starts already from the title page."[2] This dispute was not over terminology. It was one over identity, self-expression, and recognition of a legal branch, struggling to find its place within the legal system. The hybrid nature of PrIL, at the crossroad between private and public law, and between national and international law was and still is indicative of the "fighting contradictions typical of private international law."[3] In recent times these contradictions have taken center stage, as PrIL underwent major changes, including the intense national codifications of PrIL, as well as the remarkable efforts to harmonize PrIL within the EU and globally under the Hague Conventions.[4]

But as Jayme remarked, those newer developments, as well as the deficiencies and contradictions that they reveal within PrIL as a field, are often disconnected from PrIL's own intellectual and methodological past.[5] For example, Jayme suggested that one must reflect on the distinction EU PrIL makes between disputes involving

[1] Erik Jayme, *Internationales Privatrecht: Ideengeschichte von Mancini und Ehrenzweig zum Europäischen Kollisionsrecht* (C.F. Müller 2009) 1 (hereafter Jayme, *Ideengeschichte*).

[2] Franz Kahn, *Über Inhalt, Natur und Methode des internationalen Privatrechts* (G. Fischer 1899) 5.

[3] Pavel Kalenský, *Trends of Private International Law* (Czechoslovak Academy of Sciences 1971) 158. See also Arthur Nussbaum, *Principles of Private International Law* (OUP 1943) 3 (stating that the definition of PrIL as the part of private law dealing with foreign relations is accurate at least "in that it embodies the actual indefiniteness in past and contemporaneous literature").

[4] For a review of the major PrIL codifications, see Symeon Symeonides, *Codifying Choice of Law Around the World* (OUP 2014).

[5] Jayme, *Ideengeschichte* (n. 1) 1.

Nineteenth-Century Perspectives on Private International Law. Roxana Banu. © Roxana Banu 2018.
Published 2018 by Oxford University Press.

EU nationals and those involving "third state nationals."[6] This level of injustice, he argues, was precisely what past PrIL theories had tried to avoid: "[c]lassical PrIL was built upon the principle of equality [between nationals and foreigners]."[7] In particular, Jayme argues that we lost the particular humanistic perspective of "classical" PrIL, which he found in nineteenth-century PrIL generally and in Mancini's theory in particular.[8]

In his writings on the intellectual history of PrIL, Jayme tried to shift our understanding of the historical development of PrIL theory and methodology. He suggests that although it is common to consider the transition from the statutory school to Savigny's theory of the localization of legal relations as the "Copernican revolution," the true Copernican revolution should be seen in the transition from a state-centered to an individual-centered paradigm in PrIL, which Jayme believes had started with Mancini.[9] Jayme attempts, much as I do in this book, to recover a humanistic paradigm in PrIL, which he believes had been lost or gravely misunderstood.[10] His historical recovery focuses on three interrelated arguments.

First, Jayme argues that the principle of nationality, which Mancini and other members of the Institute of International Law had considered the anchor of both private and public international law, should be understood as a freedom-enhancing analytical notion, which incorporated a human rights paradigm into PrIL.[11] In Jayme's view, the concept of nationality was relied upon by several nineteenth-century PrIL scholars, most prominently Mancini, to simultaneously incorporate PrIL into PublIL and to "privatize Public International Law."[12] By grounding an international obligation to recognize rights of foreigners, Jayme believes the concept of nationality incorporated a human rights paradigm in both private and public international law.[13]

Second, once Jayme characterizes Mancini's humanistic premises grounded on nationality as a human rights paradigm, he attempts to create a genealogy of this paradigm from the nineteenth century onwards. Allegedly, Mancini's thought, after having been initially gravely misunderstood and discredited,[14] reappears in PrIL under the influence of human rights codifications, especially in Europe, then in the

6 Ibid. 7 Ibid. 8 Ibid.

9 Erik Jayme, *Internationales Privatrecht und Völkerrecht* (C.F. Müller 2003) 102–3 (hereafter Jayme, *IPR und Völkerrecht).*

10 Ibid., 109:

> Private International Law is repeatedly criticized for allegedly overshadowing material justice considerations through its soulless method of choosing among laws. In my view one should recognize that Private International Law has a human rights dimension. This incorporates a particular kind of material justice into Private International Law, which better explains not only the public policy exception, but certain ground aspects of the choice of law question. In the end it is about the consideration due to the individual, in Mancini's sense, with respect to values, the direct relevance of which has become clearer and clearer after the Second World War.

11 Ibid., 12: "Public and Private International Law were united under the concept of the nation. This concept is the common root of both areas of law."

12 Ibid. 13 Ibid., 32–3, 67. 14 Ibid., 70.

recognition of cultural and religious rights, and ultimately in the increasing relevance given to party autonomy in PrIL.[15]

Third, Jayme clearly marks a distinction between nineteenth-century scholars who argued for an obligation to apply foreign law and recognize the rights of foreign citizens and those who suggested that this was merely a voluntary concession made by states.[16] Jayme seems to suggest that the human rights paradigm can only be fully realized if private and public international law are united and if an obligation to recognize rights of foreigners is incorporated in PrIL via PublIL.[17]

The intellectual historical account presented in this book differs from Jayme's in various important respects, although it too aims to recover an individual-centered paradigm in PrIL theory and methodology. Jayme is certainly right that we tend to underestimate and fail to underscore the particular humanistic tenets of various nineteenth-century PrIL theories and even that we might have lost them altogether. This book aims to restore precisely the humanistic perspective of various nineteenth-century scholars. Yet it rejects the assumption that humanism in PrIL is a unitary and linear concept and even that it has always been and must be grounded in PublIL.

First, the intellectual historical account in this book focuses on the complexity and the variations within individual-centered theories. Even within the "classical" period, as Jayme calls it, assuming this refers to the nineteenth century generally, the humanistic perspective was hardly uniform and highly contested. The nineteenth century represented a time of intense academic discussion for and against individual-centered perspectives, as well as a time when much of the misunderstanding of the individual-centered perspective was solidified and carried through to the twentieth century and possibly to contemporary PrIL.

But the nineteenth century was also a time when the various ways in which PrIL might take the individual as the focus point were considered, even among those who generally subscribed to a humanistic paradigm. In other words, this book not only underscores the existence of a humanistic perspective within several nineteenth-century PrIL theories as such, but also reveals the complex range of its conceptualization among various theorists.

As this chapter shows, the humanistic perspective that Mancini took via the principle of nationality is different from the humanistic perspective that Savigny took via private law, and in turn Savigny's humanistic perspective is different from that of several earlier German scholars focusing on individual liberty and vested rights. Furthermore, this chapter, in its discussion of Mancini's theory, suggests some skepticism in anchoring humanism in Mancini's concept of nationality. It suggests that the freedom-enhancing function of nationality that Jayme pleads for should be analyzed with caution, rather than fully embraced. Furthermore, it remains unclear how much the principle of nationality departed from a state-centered perspective and even more unclear and uncertain that it would have necessarily created a human

[15] Ibid., 97, 98, 99, 107, 109, 155.

[16] Ibid., 27 (Jayme argues that Savigny opted for mere voluntary concession, while Mancini pled for an international obligation to apply foreign law).

[17] Ibid., 43, 63, 70.

rights paradigm. To understand how the principle of nationality navigated somewhere in between the concept of sovereignty and an individual-centered premise, one might recall the remarks of Mailher de Chassat:

> The laws of each nation might well define, within their respective limits, the capacity of its subjects . . . But outside of the nation's territory, questions of capacity are no longer individual-centered questions or questions of statute, but questions of nationality. And nationalities, even in the instances of individual exercises of civil rights on a foreign territory, reflect above all and immediately relationships between two nations, the laws of which may collide.[18]

Unlike Jayme's account, this book therefore does not take the theories of nationality of the nineteenth century, including Mancini's, as the "Copernican" shift to an individual-centered theory in PrIL.

Furthermore, this book also does not search for individual-centered theories in PrIL primarily in theories connecting PrIL with PublIL. Instead, it suggests that much of this paradigm can be found in various private law theories in PrIL. Similarly, it introduces a distinction between the universalist *justifications* scholars underscored for recognizing foreign rights and laws and the *aims and functions* they committed PrIL to. While Jayme suggests that an individual-centered, human rights paradigm was forged primarily by those who introduced an obligation from PublIL into PrIL to apply foreign laws and recognize foreign rights, this chapter shows that the individual-centered paradigm was in no way diminished by references to comity, rather than international duty, in Story's and Savigny's writings.

Lastly, this book rejects the linear genealogy that one might be tempted to forge between nineteenth-century individual-centered theories, twentieth-century human rights treaties, and ultimately the contemporary increased relevance given to the notion of party autonomy. A central thesis of this book is that each individual-centered theoretical instantiation might and often does incorporate a different image of the individual in her transnational existence. For example, while Jayme sees a linear genealogy between nineteenth-century PrIL individual-centered theories, twentieth-century human rights arguments in PrIL, and twenty-first-century appeals to party autonomy in PrIL, Horatia Muir Watt associates these different moments in the history of PrIL with different images of the transnational agent. In her account, nineteenth-century PrIL theories and twenty-first-century appeals to private autonomy share an individualistic, libertarian image of the individual,[19] which differs from the more socially constructed and socially responsible image of the individual in human rights norms and arguments.[20] The historical account in

[18] Mailher de Chassat, *Traité de Statuts (Lois Personelles, Lois Réelles), d'après le Droit Ancienes et le Droit Moderne, ou du Droit International Privé, Consideré comme Conséquence ou Reproduction, dans le Sens Individuel, du Droit International Public* (A. Durand 1845) 332 (hereafter De Chassat, *Traité de Statuts*).

[19] For the way in which Muir Watt associates recent pleas for an increased role of party autonomy in PrIL with nineteenth-century liberal theories in PrIL, see Horatia Muir Watt, 'Party Autonomy in International Contracts' in Horatia Muir Watt (ed.), *Private International Law and Public Law*, vol. 2 (Elgar Press 2015).

[20] For Muir Watt's account of the way in which human rights norms can and have reformed the field of PrIL, see Horatia Muir Watt, 'Future Directions?' in Horatia Muir Watt and Diego Fernández Arroyo (eds.) *Private International Law and Global Governance* (OUP 2015).

this book reaches different conclusions about the image of the individual at particular historical moments in PrIL's development than those that can be discerned from Horatia Muir Watt's writing. However, Muir Watt's account provides a very useful counternarrative to the idea that an individual-centered perspective in PrIL has a unitary meaning and that it should always be associated with an idealized notion of human rights.

The juxtaposition of different ways of understanding individual-centered theories in PrIL in Jayme's and Muir Watt's work should lead us to conclude that different individual-centered theories focus on different constructions of the transnational agent and that the particularities of such constructions can only be discerned from a detailed contextual analysis of any individual-centered theory. Through such contextual analysis, this book shows that the image of the individual constructed in Mancini's theory is different from that constructed in Friedrich Karl von Savigny's theory, and in turn different from the image of the individual underlying twentieth-century human rights theories in PrIL (Chapter 4), as well as contemporary theories of party autonomy in PrIL.

This book tries to discern precisely the different ways in which the transnational agent is conceptualized within a variety of individual-centered theories in PrIL. Within this range of conceptualizations I am interested in a particular variation of the humanistic perspective, which I will call relational-internationalist and will try to recover from the writings of Joseph Story, Friedrich Karl von Savigny, and Josephus Jitta. I show that in many ways each of these scholars built upon the insights of their respective predecessor to construct a theory, which was profoundly individual-centered, yet not individualistic. All scholars, I argue, try to integrate the individual within a private law relationship and then embed the individual and the private law relationship in various social spheres, and ultimately within humanity.

While Josephus Jitta espoused the latest and possibly most elaborate such relational internationalist perspective, this book does not aim to present his theory in isolation. Rather, this chapter starts by broadly underscoring the thinking of the first two "giants of the 19th century,"[21] Joseph Story and Friedrich Karl von Savigny, since Jitta's thinking is very much influenced by Savigny and in turn Savigny was influenced by Story's writings. The full scope of relational internationalist thinking can only be fully appreciated by tracing this academic triad.

While Story's and Savigny's writings have had a profound influence on the development of PrIL, they have not remained unchallenged. The rise and fall of the humanistic underpinnings of Story's thinking in the development of PrIL in the United States will become apparent in Chapter 5. This chapter shows the way in which the individual-centered perspective underlying Story's and Savigny's writings was challenged in Europe under the rise of the association between PrIL and PublIL. Within this school of thought, Mancini's nationality principle kept the humanistic premises but Mancini both diminished and enlarged the scope of freedom and

[21] I take this metaphor from Kurt H. Nadelmann, 'Bicentennial Observations on the Second Edition of Joseph Story's Commentaries on the Conflict of Laws' (1980) 28 Am J Comp L 67 (hereafter Nadelmann, "Bicentennial Observations").

self-determination envisioned by Story and Savigny. In contrast, the predominantly state-centered theories within the school of thought associating PrIL with PublIL eliminated almost entirely and occasionally quite explicitly denounced humanistic premises in PrIL.

As the nineteenth century comes to an end, Josephus Jitta will make a remarkable attempt to recover the humanistic underpinnings of Savigny's theory and to counter what he perceived as the excessively state-centered development of PrIL in complete disregard for individuals' interests and appeals to justice. To the extent Josephus Jitta even registers in the memory of PrIL's intellectual history, he is known as the founder of the political school of thought in PrIL in Europe, which is generally associated with an anti-individualistic position, a focus on legislative and social policies, as well as with the unilateral method in PrIL.[22] The fact that Jitta was simultaneously the most vigorous individual-centered theorist of the nineteenth century shows precisely the way in which an individual-centered perspective in PrIL can be integrated within a social justice framework and the unilateral method.[23]

Jitta was also called both a disciple[24] and a critic of Savigny.[25] Both labels are to a certain extent accurate. Jitta very openly and explicitly adopts Savigny's individual-centered premises and encourages PrIL as a field to reconsider them at the end of the nineteenth century. But he simultaneously reconstructs Savigny's individual-centered premises to further emphasize the social, relational image of the individual that he wished to integrate within PrIL theory and methodology. Therefore, while the nineteenth-century relational internationalist perspective might be said to culminate in the writings of Josephus Jitta, many of its premises can be traced to Savigny and Story.

[22] Thomas Decker, 'Das kollisionsrechtliche Werk Ernst Zitelmanns (1852–1923)' (PhD dissertation in law, Osnabrück University 2004) 109.

[23] According to the unilateral method each state would determine the extraterritorial reach of its own substantive norms. By contrast, according to the multilateral method, the reach of norms is determined irrespective of the country they pertain to. For one of the most notorious accounts of the unilateral method, see Pierre Gothot, 'Le renouveau de la tendance unilatéraliste en droit international privé' (1971) 60 Rev crit dr int privé 1, 209 and 417.

[24] Josephus Jitta, *The Renovation of International Law on the Basis of a Juridical Community of Mankind* (Martinus Nijhoff 1919) 90 (hereafter Jitta, *The Renovation*): "I have been called, by a benevolent critic—he was too benevolent, I should think—*the best* disciple of Savigny." In this passage Jitta alludes to the fact that while he embraced Savigny's focus on the jural relation, he did not subscribe to Savigny's focus on the community of nations and instead focused on the community of people. I argue below that Savigny also focused on the community of people and that it was a common misreading of Savigny to suggest that he focused on the community of states. See also Jitta, *The Renovation* 1:

> In one of my works published some years ago, on the *Method of Private International Law*, I have respectfully but decidedly rejected the basis, assigned by Savigny to private international law. According to the opinion of this illustrious predecessor, private international law should be based on the community of *the nations*, united by regular intercourse. My conviction, however, is that the community of nations may exist, but that it is not the basis of private international law. The real basis of the said law is the juridical community of *mankind*.... It was also said that there was no essential difference between my view and that of the illustrious scientist. The last objection has induced me to make new investigations.

[25] G.J. Steenhoff, 'Daniël Josephus Jitta (1854–1925)' in *The Moulding of International Law: Ten Dutch Proponents* (T.M.C. Asser Instituut 1995) 237, 240–1 (hereafter Steenhoff, "Daniël Josephus Jitta").

B. The First Two Giants of the Nineteenth Century

1. Joseph Story

In his inaugural lecture at Harvard, Joseph Story introduced what would become one of the most influential writings in PrIL. He announced:

> I shall adventure far more than has been usual with publicists into those general principles of jurisprudence which affect the contracts, govern titles, and limit the remedies of the subjects of independent powers who acquire rights or contract obligations or succeed to property or are in any measure subjected to the municipal law in a foreign country. This will include a variety of delicate and interesting topics belonging to the operation of foreign jurisprudence or, as it is sometimes called, the *lex fori et lex loci*.[26]

Story wrote his Commentaries on the Conflict of Laws in 1834, at a time when despite a growing body of case law on interstate conflicts matters, there was virtually no in depth analysis of the field of conflict of laws.[27] Livermore, a Louisiana lawyer, had written a treatise defending the European theory of statutes as a response to a case in which such defense was unsuccessful.[28] Livermore's book did not have much of an impact on the development of PrIL and Story did not adopt the European school of statutes per se.[29] But Livermore had donated his library to Harvard Law School and Story was able to incorporate much of the existing European literature, although he criticized it for its "theoretical distinctions, which serve little other purpose than to

[26] Nadelmann, "Bicentennial Observations" (n. 21) 77, n. 69.

[27] Joseph Story, *Commentaries on the Conflict of Laws: Foreign and Domestic, in Regard to Contracts, Rights, and Remedies, and Especially in Regard to Marriages, Divorces, Wills, Successions, and Judgments* (1st edn., Hilliard Gray 1834) 9 (hereafter Story, *Commentaries on the Conflict of Laws*):

> The subject has never been systematically treated by writers on the common law of England; and indeed, seems to be of very modern growth in that kingdom; and can hardly, as yet, be deemed to be there cultivated, as a science, built up and defined with entire accuracy and precision of principles. More has been done to give it form and symmetry within the last fifty years, than in all preceding time. But much yet remains to be done to make it what it ought to be, in a country of such a vast extent in its commerce, and such universal reach in its intercourse and polity.

[28] Rodolfo de Nova, 'The First American Book on Conflict of Laws' (1964) 8 Am J Leg Hist 136, 137 (hereafter De Nova, "The First American Book on Conflict of Laws"). See also Story, *Commentaries on the Conflict of Laws* (n. 27) 10, n. 2 (praising Livermore's dissertation "as very able and clear" and for "enumerating the principal continental writers, who have discussed this subject at large").

[29] De Nova "The First American Book on Conflict of Laws" (n. 28) 136, n. 1. For Story's discussion of the statutory school, see Story, *Commentaries on the Conflict of Laws* (n. 27) 11–18 and 17:

> It is not my design to engage in the controversy, as to what constitutes the true distinction between personal and real statutes, or to examine the merits of the various systems propounded by foreign jurists. It would carry me too far from the immediate purpose of these commentaries, even if I felt myself possessed (which I certainly do not) of that critical skill and learning, which such an examination would require, in order to treat the subject with suitable dignity.

See also Gerhard Kegel, 'Story and Savigny' (1989) 37 Am J Comp L 39, 51.

provoke idle discussions, and with metaphysical subtleties, which perplex, if they do not confound, the inquirer."[30]

One of the most impressive aspects of Story's treatise was precisely the way in which he navigated between, and paid equal due regard to an extensive body of European literature as well as roughly 500 American conflicts cases.[31] Yet indeed, as Ralf Michaels remarked, despite its comparative nature, the treatise "remains explicitly Anglo-American in its focus" rather than "a general theory or an assumed universal law of conflicts."[32]

Despite its focus on case law, Story had postulated Ulricus Huber's three maxims[33] as the theoretical anchor for the field:

> 1) every nation possesses an exclusive sovereignty and jurisdiction within its own territory;[34] 2) no state or nation can, by its laws, directly affect, or bind property out of its own territory, or persons or residents therein, whether they are natural born subjects or others;[35] 3) whatever force and obligations the laws of one country have in another depends solely upon the laws and municipal regulations of the latter, that is to say, upon its own proper jurisprudence and polity and upon its own express or tacit consent.[36]

On the premise of these axioms Story had further postulated that states did not have a duty to apply foreign law:

> The true foundation, on which the administration of [private] international law must rest, is, that the rules, which are to govern, are those, which arise from mutual interest and utility, from a sense of inconvenience, which would result from a contrary doctrine, and from a sort of moral necessity to do justice, in order that justice may be done to us in return.[37]

Story is clear that even moral duty should only be seen as one "of imperfect obligation, like that of beneficence, humanity, and charity. Every nation must be the final judge for itself, not only of the nature and extent of the duty, but of the occasions, on which its exercise may be justly demanded."[38] He concludes that "there is, then, not only no impropriety in the use of the phrase 'comity of nations,' but it is the most

[30] Story, *Commentaries on the Conflict of Laws* (n. 27), 10 (acknowledging that "the civilians on continental Europe have examined the whole subject in all its bearings with a much more comprehensive philosophy, if not with a more enlightened spirit").

[31] According to Kurt Nadelmann's count. See Nadelmann, "Bicentennial Observations" (n. 21) 67.

[32] See Ralf Michaels, 'Story, Joseph' in J. Basedow et al. (eds.), *Encyclopedia of Private International Law* (Elgar 2017). See Story, *Commentaries on the Conflict of Laws* (n. 27) 17–18: "My object is rather to present the leading principles upon some of the more important topics, and to use the works of the civilians, to illustrate, confirm, and expand the doctrines of the common law, so far at least, as the latter assumed a settled form."

[33] Ulrich Huber, 'De conflict legum Diversarum in Diversis Imperiis' in *Praelectionum Iuris civilis tomi tres* (2nd edn., Title 3, Part 2, Book 1, Expensis Iosephi et Ioannis Roland fratrum 1788). For a translation and discussion, see Ernest G. Lorenzen, 'Huber's de Conflictu Legum' (1919) 13 Ill L Rev 375.

[34] Story, *Commentaries on the Conflict of Laws* (n. 27) 19. [35] Ibid., 21.

[36] Ibid., 24. [37] Ibid., 34.

[38] Ibid., 33, 34: "And, here again, every nation must judge for itself, what is its true duty in the administration of justice. It is not to be taken for granted, that the rule of the foreign nation is right, and that its own is wrong" and 35: "But of the nature, and extent, and utility of the recognition of foreign laws, respecting the state and conditions of persons, every nation must judge for itself, and certainly is not bound to recognize them, when they would be prejudicial to its own interests."

appropriate phrase to express the true foundation and extent of the obligation of the laws of one nation within the territories of another."[39]

Indeed it would be primarily the theory of comity with which Story would be associated, and the contours of his PrIL philosophy would be examined around his exposition of the comity theory. On the one hand, Alan Watson blamed Story for distorting the universalist implications of Huber's concept of comity and for turning it into a discretionary and primarily nationalistic notion.[40] The comity metaphor also led to the interpretation of Story's theory as primarily state-centered and even as an early exposition of Brainerd Currie's state interest analysis.[41] On the other hand, Joel R. Paul praised Story as a proponent of the association between PrIL and PublIL and for incorporating primarily a public law dimension into PrIL through his reference to the notion of comity.[42]

Indeed Story not only presented himself as a "publicist" venturing in the domain of the private, but he repeatedly referred to PrIL as a branch of public law:

> The jurisprudence, then, arising from the conflict of the laws of different nations, in their actual application to modern commerce and intercourse, is a most interesting and important branch of public law. [...] This branch of public law may be fitly denominated private international law, since it is chiefly seen and felt in its application to the common business of private persons, and rarely rises to the dignity of national negotiations, or national controversies.[43]

In his introduction to the second edition of his Commentaries, Story also invites "the genius and learning and labors of more gifted minds" to "mould and polish and expand" his writings "into an enduring system of public law."[44] Story also occasionally references the notion of "law of nations" as an anchor for PrIL, although in his theory the term seems to stand for a general sense of global justice, or customary practice and legal principles.[45]

But it would be a mistake to think that Story's references to sovereignty, comity, and the law of nations translate primarily into a state-centered theory. Blaine Baker argued forcefully that one should read Story's *Commentaries on the Conflict of Laws* in line with his *Commentaries on the Constitution of the United States* and

[39] Ibid., 37.

[40] Alan Watson, *Joseph Story and the Comity of Errors: A Case Study in Conflict of Laws* (University of Georgia Press 1992).

[41] See Donald Earl Childress III, 'Comity as Conflict: Resituating International Comity as Conflict of Laws' (2010) 44 UC Davis L Rev 11. See also Ernest G. Lorenzen, 'Story's Commentaries on the Conflict of Laws—One Hundred Years After' (1934) 48 Harv L Rev 15, 35.

[42] Joel R. Paul, 'The Isolation of Private International Law' (1988) 7 Wis Int'l LJ 149.

[43] Story, *Commentaries on the Conflict of Laws* (n. 27) 9.

[44] Joseph Story, *Commentaries on the Conflict of Laws, Foreign and Domestic in Regard to Contracts, Rights, and Remedies, and Especially in Regard to Marriages, Divorces, Successions, and Judgments* (3rd edn., Charles C. Little and James Brown 1846), ix (hereafter Story, *Commentaries 3rd Edition).*

[45] Story, *Commentaries on the Conflict of Laws* (n. 27) 4 and 5:

> New rules, resting on the basis of general convenience, and an enlarged sense of national duty, have been, from time to time, promulgated by jurists, and supported by courts of justice, by a course of juridical reasoning, which has commanded almost universal confidence, respect, and obedience, without the aid, either of municipal statutes, or royal ordinances, or international treaties.

with his general views on the scope of state sovereignty. Through this association, *Commentaries on the Conflict of Laws* become "a heuristic, constitutional essay on the correlative scope of private and public sovereignty."[46] And through this lens one becomes attuned to the fact that Story makes a distinction between the justification for the mere possibility of applying foreign law—which he grounds in comity—and the regulatory scope of PrIL—which he grounds in weighing and securing peoples' rights and reasonable expectations in the transnational realm:

> Indeed, in the present times, without some general rules of right and obligation, recognized by civilized nations to govern their intercourse with each other, the most serious mischiefs and most injurious conflicts would arise. Commerce is now absolutely universal among all countries, the inhabitants of all have such a free intercourse with each other; contracts, marriages, nuptial settlements, wills, and successions, are so common among all persons, whose domicils are in different countries, having different and even opposite laws on the same subjects; that without some common principles adopted by all nations in this regard there would be an utter confusion of all rights and remedies; and intolerable grievances would grow up to weaken all the domestic relations, as well as to destroy the sanctity of contracts and the security of property.[47]

In Story's *Commentaries* PrIL matters are described as issues of "mixed rights"[48] and the goal is to analyze and secure the various rights and reasonable expectations of individuals as they cross national boundaries, while being mindful of the social context in which they are exercised. Overall, the aim was to eliminate "the grossest inequalities which will arise in the administration of justice between the subjects of the different countries."[49]

At the same time, as Baker notes, Story's "conception of national sovereignty prevented him from admitting directly the universality of private rights."[50] Therefore, a state's obligation to enforce rights and reasonable expectations in PrIL cases had to be explained in a different way. First, in accordance with his views of constitutional law, Story relied on a theory of limited state sovereignty, which meant that in a national context the state has a direct obligation toward its constituents to respect and secure their rights and reasonable expectations.[51] Secondly, as a corollary to this internal obligation, the state acts as the agent of its nationals in an international realm to ensure that other states extend such recognition to the rights of its nationals. Emerging from their internal/constitutional obligations, states had the external/PrIL obligation to negotiate rules of PrIL, which would ensure the widest possible recognition of "naturally vesting rights."[52]

[46] Blaine Baker, 'Interstate Choice of Law and Early-American Constitutional Nationalism. An Essay on Joseph Story and the Comity of Errors: A Case Study in Conflict of Laws' (1993) 35 McGill L J 454, 488 (hereafter Baker, "Interstate Choice of Law"): "As Story said repeatedly, his choice-of-law rules were designated to regulate the domestic behavior of states and nations, and thereby secure the mixed private rights of citizens operating in national or international markets."

[47] Story, *Commentaries on the Conflict of Laws* (n. 27) 5. [48] Ibid., 3. [49] Ibid., 6.

[50] Baker, "Interstate Choice of Law" (n. 46) 496. [51] Ibid., 494.

[52] Ibid: "With regard to other nations, the United States could also claim sovereign status. Unlike its citizens, the United States enjoyed no inherent sovereignty vis-à-vis other nations, but only those powers conveyed to it by its citizenry in an express social contract."

Comity was thus used in a loose sense, both as the recognition of this unrestrained sovereignty of states in relationship to each other, and as an indicator of a "rational" basis of coordination of PrIL among states to fulfill their internal obligations toward their nationals. Comity in Story's doctrine is thus the point of connection between individual-centered and universalist state-centered principles. As a state-centered concept, comity confirms that in PrIL states have no direct duties toward each other. However, as a loose concept signifying a sort of implied reciprocity,[53] comity can serve as a "function of the security of mixed private rights."[54] This implied consent of states to coordinate their rules to ensure the stability of private rights in an international context would translate in what Baker referred to as an "imaginary confederation" among states on PrIL matters.[55] According to Baker's reading of Story's Commentaries on the Conflict of Laws, "nation-states participated in Story's imaginary convention as agents of their citizens, authorized to compromise national independence in specific instances of interstate conflict to secure extraterritorial protection for the private rights of their citizens."[56] For Story, coordination of PrIL rules with a view to secure private rights ultimately symbolizes "an enlarged sense of national duty."[57]

But just as it would be wrong to assume that Story adopted a state-centered theory from his references to comity, it would be equally wrong to assume that Story meant to subscribe to an individualistic theory because of his many references to private rights. First, as showed in Chapter 6, Story does not set particular boundaries between individual interests and expectations and larger public values, and fluctuates indiscriminately between the two. Second, Story incorporates a broad notion of public policy to secure general principles of morality and justice, as well as political goals:

> No nation can be justly required to yield up its fundamental policy and institutions in favour of those of another nation. Much less can any nation be required to sacrifice its own interests in favour of another; or to enforce doctrines, which, in a moral, or political view, are incompatible with its own safety or happiness, or conscientious regard to justice and duty. In the endless diversities of human jurisprudence many laws must exist in one country, which are the result of local or accidental circumstances, and are wholly unfit to be engrafted upon the institutions and habits of another. Many laws, adapted to heathen nations, would be totally repugnant to the feelings, as well as to the justice, of those, which embrace Christianity. A heathen nation might justify polygamy, or incest, contracts of moral turpitude, or exercises of despotic cruelty over persons, which would be repugnant to the first principles of Christian duty. The laws of one nation may be founded upon a narrow selfishness, exclusively adapted to promote the personal or propriety interests of its own subjects, to the injury or even ruin of

[53] Story, *Commentaries on the Conflict of Laws* (n. 27) 37: "in the silence of any positive rule, affirming, or denying, or restraining the operation of foreign laws, courts of justice presume the tacit adoption of them by their own government, unless they are repugnant to its policy, or prejudicial to its interests."

[54] Baker, "Interstate Choice of Law" (n. 46) 505.

[55] Ibid., 495: "Much like the signatories of the United States' Constitution, nations acceded to a circumscription of their juristic sovereignty in conflicts matters to provide institutional safeguards for the private rights of their citizens."

[56] Ibid., 496.

[57] Story, *Commentaries on the Conflict of Laws* (n. 27) 5.

> those of the subjects of all other countries. A nation may refuse all reciprocity of commerce, rights, and remedies to others. It may assume a superiority of powers and prerogatives for the very purpose of crushing those of its neighbors, who are less fortunate or less powerful. In these, and in many other cases which may easily be put, without any extravagance of supposition, there would be extreme difficulty in saying, that other nations were bound to enforce laws, institutions, or customs, so subversive of their own morals, justice, interest, or polity.[58]

This extended account of public policy shows two distinctions, which Story makes in his account of PrIL. On the one hand, comity is not equated with particularism. In Story's own words, "mutual utility presupposes that the interest of all nations is consulted, and not that of one only."[59] Comity does not mean an absolute preference for national interest, but rather a principled analysis and weighing of all interests involved. On the other hand, the goal of securing rights and expectations is not set in contrast to public and political goals, but rather in contrast to "despotic power."[60]

It is this last point, which becomes even clearer through an addition that Story made in the second edition of the *Commentaries*. In the introductory remarks to the first edition, Story had searched for "any distinct system of principles applicable to international cases of mixed rights in the antiquity."[61] He argued that we do not have a clear understanding of how questions of mixed rights were disposed of in antiquity and that since "the Law of Nations, strictly so called, was in a great measure unknown to antiquity, and is the slow growth of modern times, under the combined influence of Christianity and Commerce,"[62] one must acknowledge that "the invasions of the Barbarians of the North, the establishment of the feudal system in the middle ages, and the military spirit and enterprise cherished by the Crusades, struck down all regular commerce, and surrendered all private rights and contracts to mere despotic power."[63]

But in the second edition Story adds a five-page translation from Savigny's History of the Roman Law in the Middle Ages.[64] He referred to Savigny as "a most learned and eminent jurist," considered the passage in which Savigny described the origins of personal laws as "exceedingly interesting and curious" and felt compelled to cite it at large.[65] In that passage Savigny shows that the Goths, Burgundians, Franks, and Lombards allowed the conquered people to maintain their laws and customs. Savigny argues that it is "from this state of society that arose that condition of civil rights, denominated Personal Rights or Personal Laws, in opposition to Territorial Laws."[66] Savigny refutes the "customary" explanation of the recognition of these personal laws by reference to "the love of freedom" and argues instead that the recognition of personal laws by the conquerors can be best explained as a result of increased interpersonal contact between individuals belonging to the different races:

58 Ibid., 26. 59 Ibid., 36.

60 Ibid., 4: "the invasions of the Barbarians of the North, the establishment of the feudal system in the middle ages, and the military spirit and enterprise cherished by the Crusades, struck down all regular commerce, and surrendered all private rights and contracts to mere despotic power."

61 Ibid., 3. 62 Ibid., 4. 63 Ibid.

64 Story, *Commentaries 3rd Edition* (n. 44) 4, n. 3, citing Friedrich Karl von Savigny, *The History of the Roman Law During the Middle Ages* (E. Cathcart tr., Adam Black 1829).

65 Ibid. 66 Ibid.

> Further, the want of such an institution as the Personal Laws, could never have been felt, in a country without trade, and where few foreigners resided. In these circumstances, its introduction was impossible. If only a single Goth lived in the Burgundian empire, none of his countrymen could be found to administer Gothic law, and the Burgundians themselves were entirely ignorant of it. [. . .] The truth is that the want of such an institution, and the possibility of introducing it, could occur only after the nations were blended together in considerable masses. The internal condition of each kingdom could then produce what could never have been brought by mere benevolence toward individual foreigners.[67]

Much of this resonated with Story. In his view this significant interpersonal intercourse and trade defined the society of his time. And it was precisely the despotic disregard of peoples' rights and reasonable expectations, which PrIL had to avoid, much like the system of personal laws seemed to have contemplated. In other words, the goal of recognition of rights and reasonable expectations was meant to avoid the arbitrary disregard of human agency and reasonable expectations by different public powers. As argued in Chapter 5, Story places the reasonable expectations of individuals within a social context and shifts indiscriminately from the rights and expectations of individuals to the broader social and public context. His references to rights and reasonable expectations are meant to signal the need for "moderation" in the exercise of public power, which might be inclined to entirely disregard the voice and the interests of individuals in their transnational relations.

2. Friedrich Karl von Savigny

Joseph Story's treatise had a profound influence on the development of PrIL in the nineteenth century and beyond, both in the United States and abroad.[68] Story also sent a copy of his *Commentaries* to Friedrich Karl von Savigny, whose own treatise on PrIL was published fifteen years later, in 1849.

Despite the time gap between Story's first edition of the *Commentaries* and Savigny's eighth volume of the *System*, the discipline still appeared to Savigny "in a state of growth, incomplete and unfinished."[69] He found a striking opposition between an almost universal interest and debate on the nature of PrIL and the lack of consensus on any "universally admitted principles."[70]

Yet precisely because academic debates in PrIL had intensified since Story's writing, Savigny had more intellectual material to draw from in his own account of PrIL. Story's book was already published and two German scholars, Karl Georg von Wächter (1797–1880) and Wilhelm Schäffner (1815–1897) had already published valuable expositions of PrIL.[71] Savigny does indeed cite all three accounts

67 Ibid., 4–5, n. 3.

68 See Nadelmann, "Bicentennial Observations" (n. 21).

69 Friedrich Karl von Savigny, *Private International Law and the Retrospective Operation of Statutes: A Treatise on the Conflict of Laws and the Limits of their Operation in Respect of Place and Time* (William Guthrie tr., T&T Clark 1880) 1 (hereafter Savigny, *Private International Law*).

70 Ibid.

71 Karl Georg von Wächter, 'Über die Collision der Privatrechtsgesetze verschiedener Staaten' (1841) 241 AcP 230 and (1842) 251 AcP 1, 161 and 361; Wilhelm Schäffner, *Entwicklung des internationalen Privatrechts* (J.D. Sauerländer 1841). See also Gerhard Kegel, 'Story and Savigny' (1989) 37 Am J Comp L 39, 40 (hereafter Kegel, "Story and Savigny") (noting the influence of the theories of Schäffner and

extensively and praises Story, in his letter of recognition for receiving Story's book,[72] as well as in his preface to the eighth volume.[73]

Yet in historical accounts of PrIL's development Story is often juxtaposed to Savigny. Gerhard Kegel described Story as a publicist and Savigny as a privatist, Story as focused on the community of states and Savigny on the community of laws.[74] From the preceding account of Story's cross-reference between comity and private rights it would have become apparent that the classification of Story as a state-centered publicist is overly simplistic. But even through the lens of Savigny's writings, the parallels to Story become quite obvious.[75] Kegel observes that "Story's influence on Savigny went beyond the universal international connection and is stronger than the influence of other jurists. Gutzwiller even presumes that Savigny took his partiality for Hert and Boullenois from Story."[76]

Wächter on Savigny). Ralf Michaels also noted the influence of Wächter's writing on Savigny. See Ralf Michaels, 'Wächter, Carl Georg' in J. Basedow et al. (eds.), *Encyclopedia of Private International Law* (Elgar 2017). For a discussion of Wächter's essay, see Kurt Nadelmann, 'Wächter's Essay on the Collision of Private Laws of Different States' (1964) 13 Am J Comp L 414.

[72] See Wm.W. Story, ed., *Life and Letters of Joseph Story*, vol. 2 (John Chapman 1851) 378.

[73] See Savigny, *Private International Law* (n. 69) 43: "A remarkable picture of this imperfect but hopeful state of things is presented in the excellent work of Story, which is also extremely useful, as a rich collection of materials, for every inquirer."

[74] See Kegel, "Story and Savigny" (n. 71) 58–9 arguing that it is first with Savigny that PrIL has been truly "privatized." Ralf Michaels also adopted this reading. See Ralf Michaels 'Public and Private International Law: German Views on Global Issues' (2008) 4 J P Int'l L 121 at 127:

> Story had defined private international law as a subdiscipline of international law, and connections to public international law and/or federalism were always important in his work. This understanding of comity as concerning relations between governments established private international law as a discipline of conflicts between different governments, and thereby lent itself nicely to 20th century conceptions of conflict of laws as conflicts of governmental interests, at heart very much a public law conception of conflict of laws. Savigny, by contrast, came not from international law but from private law.

But see Ralf Michaels, 'Story, Joseph' in J. Basedow et al. (eds.) *Encyclopedia of Private International Law* (Elgar 2017) referencing Blaine Baker's reading of Savigny, which underscores Story's focus on private rights and private law.

[75] Despite the juxtaposition between Story and Savigny, Kegel also remarks that "although civil and common law remained at the time (and further on) separate in the field of private international law, the strong links between them are striking." See Kegel, "Story and Savigny" (n. 71) 48.

[76] Ibid., 49. Boullenois had already described conflict of laws issues as "mixed questions," a term that Story used repeatedly throughout his commentaries. By virtue of this term, Boullenois explained the variety of issues which are involved simultaneously in conflict of laws matters: state-centered and individual-centered aspects, written and customary law, as well as natural law, personal, and territorial elements and so on. Underscoring the variety of elements involved in conflict of laws and the attempt to reconcile and make sense of them was, in line with my reading of Story and Savigny throughout the book, a theoretical and methodological direction which united Story and Savigny. It seems natural then that they would both be drawn to this perspective in Boullenois's writing. See Louis Boullenois, *Traité de la personalité, et de la réalité des lois, coutumes, ou statuts, par forme d'observations* (Guillaume Desprez 1762). Story included a quote from Boullenois on the front cover of his Commentaries. Story, *Commentaries on the Conflict of Laws* (n. 27), front cover citing Louis Boullenois, *Traité de la personalité, et de la réalité des lois, coutumes, ou statuts, par forme d'observations* (Guillaume Desprez 1762), preface: "There will always be a constant contrariety of laws between nations; maybe it will always exist on many aspects. This makes it necessary to devise rules and principles, which allow us to decide questions, which arise from this contrariety of laws."

Savigny references Story's emphasis on the "strict right of sovereignty" and recognizes that this "might certainly, among other things, go so far as to require all judges of the land to decide cases that come before them solely according to the national law, regardless of the perhaps different rules of some foreign law with whose territory the case in question may have come in contact."[77] And certainly, "in the first place, we must admit, that if the domestic laws give directions for the treatment of cases of conflict, they must be applied absolutely by the judges of our state."[78] There was in other words indeed no positive obligation of states to apply foreign law. Yet in practice states commonly apply foreign law and "this has resulted from that reciprocity in dealing with cases which is so desirable, and the consequent equality in judging between natives and foreigners, which, on the whole, is dictated by the common interest of nations and of individuals."[79]

At first sight Savigny's account might appear as a departure from Story's theory of comity. Yet the grounds he offers for tempering the initial postulates of sovereignty and comity are the same as in Story's theory.[80] The gradual recognition of equality between natives and foreigners,[81] Christian morality,[82] and "the real advantages which result from it to all concerned"[83] were precisely the same grounds that Story had referenced to push his quasi-federation of states to the adoption of common rules and practices. Therefore what could at first sight be perceived as a departure from Story's comity seems at second glance much of a restatement of Story's notion of comity. Savigny writes:

> This equalization, as contrasted with the strict law above mentioned, may be designated as friendly concession among foreign states; that is, an admission of statutes originally foreign among the sources from which native courts have to seek for their decision as to many cases (legal relations). Only this deference must not be regarded as the result of mere generosity or arbitrary will, which would imply that it was also uncertain and temporary. We must rather recognize in it a proper and progressive development of law, keeping pace with the treatment of cases of conflict between the particular laws of the same state.[84]

Like Savigny, Story had also associated comity with a progressive development of law and certainly did not think that the application of foreign law as based on comity would be arbitrary and temporary and not even uncertain.

For Savigny this translates into a community of law, which "lies in reality at the foundation of the universal customary law"[85] and:

> Neither can it make any difference that there is a dispute as to the substance and the limits of that customary law. The general assumption that it exists, and the general attempt to determine its contents, are decisive in favor of our assertion. We cannot, however, be surprised to find wavering and conflicting opinions in a branch of jurisprudence, which, like that now before us, is presented to us in a state of growth.[86]

[77] Savigny, *Private International Law* (n. 69) 69. [78] Ibid. [79] Ibid.
[80] Jayme, *IPR und Völkerrecht* (n. 9) 10 (arguing that Story and Savigny joined in their adoption of comity as the anchor for PrIL, while Mancini pled for an obligation to apply foreign law).
[81] Savigny, *Private International Law* (n. 69) 69. [82] Ibid., 70. [83] Ibid.
[84] Ibid., 70–1. [85] Ibid., 72. [86] Ibid., 72.

Kegel saw in Savigny's conceptualization of the community of laws both a distinction to later theories grounded in PublIL and as a departure from Story's comity doctrine. As to the former he argues:

> Thus, Savigny did not derive private international law from international law (something Zitelmann will later do unsuccessfully). [. . .] The "*völkerrechtliche Gemeinschaft*" was not a community of international law, but a legal community of peoples. For Savigny, it was, so far as private international law was concerned, the counterpart to the national legal community in which the interstate conflict of laws unfold.[87]

As to the distinction between Savigny's community of people and the later invoked community of states by the PublIL school of thought, Kegel is right. The next chapter shows how Savigny was for a long time misunderstood as a precursor of a state-centered theory, precisely because of his reference to the "völkerrechtliche Gemeinschaft." But Kegel also believed Savigny's principles leading to "a common system of rules"[88] "serve Savigny to form carefully a transition from a *comitas* doctrine, retained by Story, to a developing law, in principle universally applied, that is of advantage to the states and the individuals (in the sense of a true advantage to all parties concerned)":[89]

> With his "*völkerrechtliche Gemeinschaft,*" Savigny left the public law context (from which the *comitas* doctrine was derived; Story subsequently viewed private international law as "a system of public law") and moved into the field of private law (where the interstate conflict of laws had been situated to start with.) The "*völkerrechtliche Gemeinschaft*" thus had the double task of privatizing private international law and of driving it toward universal uniformity (so that it will be judged according to the same law everywhere).[90]

This distinction might be too quick. On the one hand, it underestimates Story's goal to move states to coordinate their rules of PrIL, while overestimating Savigny's universalist theory. Blaine Baker's analysis identifies comity precisely as a term, which is mindful of state sovereignty, while pushing states toward an imaginary confederation and a quasi-transnational common law practice. Furthermore, the last chapter of this book shows that Savigny's plea for uniformity was much more restrained and nuanced than it is commonly assumed. On the universalist premises therefore, Story and Savigny were not that far from each other.

On the other hand, Kegel equates a move away from a state-centered perspective with a move away from public law. Yet the individual/state and private/public distinctions should be kept separate in the analysis of PrIL's intellectual history. It is true that Savigny did not conceptualize PrIL matters as questions of division of sovereignty as many PrIL scholars would later do. And it is also true that Savigny referred to a general community of law and of people, rather than a community of states. But this does not mean Savigny took what would now be thought of as public law completely out of the purview of PrIL.

[87] Kegel, "Story and Savigny" (n. 71) 59.
[88] Savigny, *Private International Law* (n. 69) 72.
[89] Kegel, "Story and Savigny" (n. 71) 58.
[90] Ibid., 59.

The way in which public law rules and principles are integrated precisely within an individual-centered perspective through a relational image of the individual will be showed throughout the various chapters. Here I merely want to introduce a few themes, which are developed in further chapters and which offer an initial glimpse into the way in which an individual-centered starting point does not translate into individualism in Savigny's PrIL theory.

On the one hand Savigny made famous a methodological transition from analyzing the nature of laws (as personal, real, or mixed) to analyzing the nature of legal relations.[91] This was indeed a trademark of all relational internationalist theories. It was also not a novel metaphor originating with Savigny's theory. Story had already referenced the nature of legal relations and frequently referred to inter-personal relationships as the unit of analysis in PrIL.[92] Furthermore, Savigny's two German predecessors, Karl Georg von Wächter and Wilhelm Schäffner had already introduced the notion.[93] But Savigny made it analytically sharper and drew various new methodological conclusions from it. Yet shifting from an analysis of the nature of laws to an analysis of the nature of legal relations does not represent a turn to individualism. When distinguishing his theory from the previous statutory school, Savigny argued that it should not make a difference whether one starts from the legal relation and asks which law it is submitted to, or whether one starts from the law and asks whether it covers this particular legal relation.[94] Searching for the "nature of a legal relations" was an analytical exercise which incorporated the extra-legal social expectations of individuals in relationship to each other, as well as the rules and principles, which regulate such relationship.[95] As Chapters 3 and 6 show, searching for the nature of a legal relation was a rather fluid and complex analytical step that was not anchored in an underlying concept of unrestrained individual freedom.

On the other hand, Savigny references a concept of "voluntary submission," arguing that the seat of a legal relation would, among others, be located by reference to individuals' free submission under particular laws. Recently, this metaphor was understood as a proxy for a theory of free choice of law.[96] Yet, as showed in Chapter 6, Savigny himself distinguishes this principle from the theory of free choice of law.[97]

[91] For Savigny's analysis of the statutory school, see Savigny, *Private International Law* (n. 69) 47–8 and 141–2. For his discussion of the legal relation, see Savigny, *Private International Law* (n. 69) 57, 70, 133. See also Kegel, "Story and Savigny" (n. 71) 57–8 with further references on writings about Savigny's focus on the legal relations at n. 129.

[92] For more on this, see Chapter 6.

[93] For this notion in the earlier German writing, see Kegel, "Story and Savigny" (n. 71) 55–6.

[94] See Andreas Bucher, *Grundfragen der Anknüpfungsgrechtigkeit im internationalen Privatrecht (aus kontinentaleuropäischer Sicht)* 22 Schriftenreihe des Instituts für Internationales Recht und internationale Beziehungen (Helbing & Lichtenhahn 1975) 40 (arguing that Savigny's focusing on both the legal relation and the law was underappreciated).

[95] See Pierre Gothot, 'Le renouveau de la tendance unilatéraliste en droit international privé' (1971) 60 Rev crit dr int privé 1, 10, n. 1: "the legal relations (*Rechtsverhältnisse*) derive from institutions (*Institutionen*), notions which, for Savigny, are at the same time social and juridical and in which the *Volksgeist* is manifested."

[96] Sagi Peari, 'Savigny's theory of choice-of-law as a principle of "voluntary submission"' (2014) 64 UTLJ 106.

[97] Duco Kollewijn, an author I introduce in Chapter 4, pointed out that Savigny did not consider individuals' choice of law as a connecting factor in determining the seat of a legal relations, while in

Mancini praised Savigny precisely for making this distinction and avoiding any individualistic theoretical and methodological premises. Rather, Chapters 6 and 7 argue that Savigny's concept of voluntary submission is an expression of what Okko Behrends called empirical elements of freedom, namely the actual ability of individuals to travel, purchase things abroad, enter into contracts in other jurisdictions and so on.[98] The call is for the application of the law to be generally linked to the actual actions and expectations of individuals in the myriad of inter-personal transnational relations. But Savigny argues not only that "this link must not be regarded as unlimited," but also that its value will be considered differently among a wide variety of inter-personal relations.[99]

Therefore, neither Savigny's shift to the analysis of the legal relations, nor his reference to voluntary submission represent a shift to individualism and unrestrained individual liberty. Instead, Savigny takes the equality between nationals and foreigners as an anchor for PrIL, just as Story had argued previously. This postulated equality, as well as the social image of the individual he constructs make him focus on a legal relation, rather than an isolated individual,[100] and allowed him to argue for the possibility of an increasingly universal treatment of PrIL matters.[101] As described in Chapter 6, this was different from previous attempts of vested rights theorists to anchor PrIL and its universality in individual freedom and autonomy.

Furthermore, the fact that Savigny does not take either Kantian rationalism or an intransigent concept of individual liberty as the reference point of law is further reflected in his general theory of law and state. Chapter 7 in particular discusses the way in which Savigny's theory of the Volksgeist, his anti-Kantian philosophy, and the historical school of thought he grounded, enabled him to construct a relational, socially constructed image of the individual. Indeed within his PrIL volume, Savigny refers his readers to his general theoretical expositions on the concept of law

Kollewijn's time, choice of law was viewed as such a connecting factor. Kollewijn thought that even though Savigny had included a concept of voluntary submission, the fact that he did not incorporate an individual choice of law as a connecting factor allowed him to calibrate the level of freedom allowed for different categories of private law, rather than anchoring PrIL as a field to a concept of freedom. Furthermore, this distinction allowed him to distinguish and calibrate "objective" elements that define the "international" nature of a private law relationship from "subjective" intentions and appreciations by the parties. See Roeland Duco Kollewijn, 'Quelques considerations a propos de la doctrine de Savigny' (1968) 15 Nethl Int'l L Rev 237.

98 Okko Behrends, 'Geschichte, Politik und Jurisprudenz in Savignys System des heutigen römischen Rechts' in Okko Behrends, Wulf Eckart Voss, and Malte Diesselhorst (eds.), *Römisches Recht in der Europäischen Tradition: Symposion aus Anlass des 75. Geburtstages von Franz Wieacker* (R. Gremer 1985) 257.

99 See Savigny, *Private International Law* (n. 69) 134–6.

100 Ibid., 143.

101 Ibid., 69:

> For it is the necessary consequence of this equality, in its full development, not only that in each particular state the foreigner is not postponed to the native (in which equality in the treatment of persons exists), but also that, in cases of conflict of laws, the same legal relations (cases) have to expect the same decision, whether the judgment be pronounced in this state or in that.

See Chapter 8 for a detailed discussion of this aspect. For a general account of Savigny's principle of equality and its relationship to PrIL's cosmopolitan premises, see Egon Lorenz, *Zur Struktur des internationalen Privatrechts. Ein Beitrag zur Reformdiskussion* (Dunkler & Humblot 1977).

and state, the various categories of law and the concept of legal relation found in other volumes within his System.[102] Much of this parallel between his PrIL writings and his general theory of law and state is made in subsequent chapters, especially Chapter 7. Suffice it here to note that Savigny outlines the entire method of PrIL as a search for the embeddedness of individuals and legal relation in a larger "whole":

> In order to discover the connection by which a person is attached to a particular positive law by subjection to it, we must remember that the positive law itself has its seat in the people as a great natural whole, or in an ethnical subdivision of this whole. It is only another expression of the same truth, when we say that law has its seat in the state, or in a particular organic part of the state, because, as it is only in the state that the will of individuals is developed into a common will, it is there only that the nation has a realized existence. In pursuance of this general plan, we have then to determine more minutely how this whole is constituted, and how this unity is defined, within which the rules of law, as constituent parts of the positive law, have their seat. Thus we shall know through which tie individuals are held together in the common possession of the same positive law.[103]

C. Conflicts of Laws as Conflicts of Sovereignty

Both Story's and Savigny's theory represented a departure from the previous European statutory school, which divided statutes into personal, real, or mixed (depending on whether they were dealing primarily with people or with territory), in order to determine their extraterritorial reach. It was both a departure from the formalist nature of the classification of laws and an attempt to center PrIL on the interpersonal relationships in both their extra-legal social and legal dimensions.

Yet a focus on laws would make a comeback in the nineteenth century after Savigny, as a way of conceptualizing conflict of laws matters as conflicts of public powers. André Bonnichon traced the beginnings of this new conceptualization to the French author Mailher de Chassat and his 1845 treaty on statutes.[104] Bonnichon argued that the conceptualization of PrIL matters as conflicts of sovereignty should be understood as a corollary to the concomitant theories of public law, which increasingly emphasized the formal origins of law as an attribute of sovereignty, as well as to the PublIL theories of the time, postulating fundamental rights of states.[105]

Initially, at least in Pasquale Mancini's theory, this new conceptualization of PrIL by analogy to PublIL translated into a way of reflecting on the obligations of states toward individuals, especially toward foreigners. This maintained the cosmopolitan ethos of Story's and Savigny's theories, while also changing its contours and its premises. Yet as the nineteenth century was coming to an end, the conceptualization of PrIL as conflicts of sovereignty translated more and more into a focus away from the

[102] See Savigny, *Private International Law* (n. 69) 77, n. (a). [103] Ibid., 57.

[104] See André Bonnichon, 'La Notion de conflit de souverainetés dans la science des conflits de lois' (1950) 39 Rev crit dr int privé(hereafter Bonnichon, "La Notion") 11, 12–13 citing Mailher de Chassat, *Traité de statuts (lois personelles, lois réelles), d'après le droit ancienes et le droit modern, ou du Droit International Privé* (A. Durand 1845).

[105] Ibid.

humanistic premises of Story, Savigny, and Mancini, and toward theorizing interpersonal relations as particular kinds of interstate relations. The idea emerged, and the French civil code at the time adopted it as well, that every individual right would need to be claimed by his/her state.[106] Bonnichon thought this transition implied a shift, already started by Mancini, from underscoring the agency of individuals in the transnational realm to portraying the individual as subsumed under nationality or citizenship: "the political allegiance to a prince or a nation would initially not be confused with the civil condition of the individual, the one was nationality, the other domicile. But now the political and the civil are one."[107] Bonnichon thought it was telling that Mailher de Chassat had already emphatically declared "my birth gives me the quality of a French man I am thereby."[108] Progressively, from Mailher de Chassat to Mancini and his Italian disciples, the notion of personal sovereignty of the state would join the previous Dutch theory of territorial sovereignty in order to complete the imagery of conflict of laws as conflict of sovereignty.[109] It was at this junction point that Bonnichon remarked ironically:

> Now all the conditions are united for the modern idea to emerge that conflict of laws is a conflict of sovereignty; now we consider in the law its formal source, the imperative of a sovereign; we admit that this imperative is addressed above all towards people and that it can follow them everywhere; we imagine a wrap-around of a clear idea and by this idea we can connect Private International Law with Public International Law. The science of Private International Law can finally come out of the limbo in which it was stuck for so long.[110]

The limbo that the PrIL-PublIL association was meant to counter was precisely that allegedly caused primarily by Story and Savigny. On the one hand, Story was famous for having explicitly argued that there is no obligation to apply foreign law or to apply the same law as other national courts did. That was in fundamental contradiction to the PublIL school, which worked tirelessly to ground an obligation to adopt uniform rules of PrIL derived from PublIL. Virtually all scholars pleading for the PrIL-PublIL association fundamentally rejected the comity doctrine. On the other hand, Savigny pled for situating a legal relation according to its nature. To universalists focusing on the PrIL-PublIL relationship, this seemed a much too fluid analytical notion, which could not possibly lead to universal rules of PrIL. It allowed for too much interpretation and too many nuances, and was not anchored in an overarching principle of theoretical justification that could be accepted by all states.[111]

Instead, those who structured the PrIL-PublIL association thought "realizing finally that conflict of laws is a conflict of sovereignty means to finally build [PrIL] solidly."[112] To build solidly was to operate with high abstractions and very general principles around which universal consensus could be reached. The last few

[106] Ibid., 15 citing Joseph Beale, whose scholarship is discussed in Chapter 5 and Eugen Ehrlich, 'Les tendances actuelles du droit international privé' (1908) 4 Rev dr int privé 902, 916.

[107] Bonnichon, "La Notion" (n.104) 11, 15. [108] Ibid., 14. [109] Ibid., 14 and 16.

[110] Ibid., 16.

[111] See below for a discussion of how both Mancini and Pillet refuted the fluidity of Savigny's theory. For a more detailed discussion of Pillet's critique, see Chapter 7.

[112] Bonnichon, "La Notion" (n. 107), 14.

decades of the nineteenth century displayed a tremendous variety of scholarly efforts to theorize the PrIL-PublIL association and thereby to build PrIL "solidly" and uniformly.[113] To show this trajectory of the PrIL-PublIL association this section starts by broadly outlining the philosophy of Pasquale Mancini, the "third giant" of the nineteenth century, alongside Story and Savigny. It underscores both the particular humanistic premises of his theory and distinguishes them from those underlying Story's and Savigny's thinking. The second section considers the way in which Mancini's initial humanism dissipated as the PrIL-PublIL association became increasingly state-centered in the theories of the French scholar Antoine Pillet and the German scholar Ernst Zitelmann.

1. Pasquale Mancini

In his account of the contours of Mancini's nationality principle in PrIL, Kurt Nadelmann rightfully ranked Mancini "with the other two giants of the nineteenth century conflicts theory—Joseph Story and Friedrich Carl von Savigny," and noted his fame as both a statesman and jurist.[114] In his inaugural lecture as professor of international law, Mancini had already postulated the principle of nationality as the pillar of PublIL.[115] From a political standpoint the principle of nationality was meant to support the movement of national unity in Italy, and when Mancini became the draftsman of the committee on legislation in the Italian Parliament during the Risorgimento, he urged that the principle of nationality become the pillar of conflicts rules in the new civil code.[116] The law of nationality would thereby govern status and capacity, family relations, and successions.[117] Mancini became the president of the Institute of International Law in 1873 and at the Institute's second session in 1874 Mancini prepared a report on PrIL, which was later published in the first edition of the Journal du Droit International Privé et de la Jurisprudence Comparée, founded by Mancini with Chretien Clunet and Charles Demangeat.[118]

The report became the manifesto of the universalist theory for uniformity of PrIL. But as an expression of Mancini's philosophy of PrIL, it went much beyond its general plea for uniformity. Mancini starts his report with the same ode to the past that Story and Savigny had incorporated in their own writings on PrIL. The time when Romans had allowed the conquered races to live by their laws and customs is presented with the same nostalgia that marked Savigny's and Story's own accounts.[119]

[113] Ibid.

[114] See Nadelmann, 'Bicentennial Observations' (n. 21). For a detailed account of Mancini's thought, see Jayme, *Ideengeschichte* (n. 1).

[115] P.S. Mancini, *Della nazionalitá come fondamento del diritto delle genti* (Istituto Suor Orsola Benincasa 1988); P.S. Mancini, *Diriti Internazionale, Prelezioni* 1 (Giuseppe Marghieri 1873).

[116] Nadelmann, "Bicentennial Observations" (n. 21), 420.

[117] Ibid.

[118] P.S. Mancini, 'De l'utilité de rendre obligatoires pour tous les Etats, sous la forme d'un ou de plusieurs traités internationaux, un certain nombre de régles generales du droit international privé pour assurer la decision uniforme des conflits entre les différentes legislations civiles et criminelles' (1874) 1 Journal du droit international privé et de la jurisprudence comparée 221 and 286 (hereafter Mancini, "Decision uniforme des conflicts").

[119] Ibid., 221–2.

And it was precisely this ability of individuals to maintain their national laws while within the purview of another state that Mancini wanted to recover for PublIL and PrIL alike. Yet pushing for this direction required the conceptualization of a strong theoretical foundation, which would motivate all countries to accept it as the basis for PrIL. Furthermore, it required refuting the notion of domicile as a primary connecting factor for PrIL matters, which was incorporated in both Story's and Savigny's theories.

The first step for Mancini was to refute the theory of comity, in order to construct a true obligation to apply foreign law generally, and the law of nationality in particular.[120] Mancini accepts the independence of states as "no more or less inviolable than individual freedom"[121] and charges scholars like Story with having "confused the absolute legislative power of a state with the legitimacy of its exercise."[122]

It would be illegitimate to apply the law of the forum in all circumstances because this could violate individual liberty and rights:

> Laws and codes, fallible works and relative expression of the truth, as it is conceived by the legislature of a state, do not create the rights and liberties of man, but have the duty to recognize them their just domain, even for foreigners. If they do not, they violate the laws of justice and at the same time the law of nations, because each state has an interest in ensuring the legitimate rights and liberties of its members and to have them respected by other nations.[123]

Recognizing rights and liberties was an actual obligation grounded concomitantly in international justice and PublIL. Thus, comity could be completely refuted and Mancini cites the overwhelming consensus of members of the Institute of International Law[124] and many other PrIL scholars[125] in having entirely rejected the comity doctrine. To ensure the universal recognition of rights and liberty, what was needed was "the most complete equality in the extent to which each political sovereign determines the limits of the accomplishment of its duties in terms of recognizing the rights of individuals and foreign nations."[126] PrIL rules would need to be "equal and identical."[127]

But to move away from comity and ground an obligation to apply foreign law inevitably introduced a duality. This obligation was at once an obligation of justice owed to individuals directly and an obligation under the law of nations owed to the countries to which individuals belonged. To reconcile this duality, Mancini postulated that the individual could make claims of recognition from other states via the PublIL notion of nationality:

> Just as in the relationships of mere private law within a state, the principle of liberty protects the legitimate and inviolable autonomy of individuals and places a limit to the political and legislative power of government, in the same way the principle of nationality places a limit between foreigners and other nations or states. The reason rests in individual and reciprocal autonomy, legitimate and inviolable autonomy. And, as the law of nationality, which belongs to the entire nation, is not different in substance from the right to liberty belonging to individuals, it follows that the individual can demand of nations and states in the name of foreign

[120] Ibid., 228. [121] Ibid. [122] Ibid., 229. [123] Ibid., 231.
[124] Ibid., 230. [125] Ibid., 231. [126] Ibid., 232. [127] Ibid.

nationality the same respect for his patrimony of private law, that he can demand in its own state from his co-nationals. [128]

This state/individual ambivalence was also present in Mancini's description of rights and liberty generally and in the way in which Mancini subscribed some of these rights to the law of nationality.

First, focusing on rights, liberty, and personal laws generally, showed much resemblance to the personal statutes under the statutory school. Mancini recognized as the great merit of this theory the fact that it was "an a priori theory, conceived broadly and capable of encompassing the entire area of conflicts of laws and statutes."[129] Mancini too was in search of a highly general theory and a universal principle to ground his theory in order for it to be acceptable to all states. But he criticized the statutory school for having failed to "justify rationally the existence of laws which by their own and intense nature, maintain their authority over people even while abroad."[130] The highly general theory of personal statutes had to be sustained by a highly general theory of law, of the state, and of individual liberty. Mancini meant to provide precisely such a theory. This theory starts from Mancini's remark that:

The juridical order consists in the accommodation between private and individual liberty and the exercise of social power, that is in the relationship between the laws of a state and individual prerogatives, between political order and the civil order of domestic and private relations. The activity of social power stops where it meets the inoffensive and therefore legitimate liberty of individuals.[131]

This inoffensive and legitimate liberty extends above national borders and must be recognized by all states:

Once these premises are established, if from the consideration of individual liberty of each individual within a civil society, we move a step further to the examination of the collective constitution of nations, and the relationships between them, it is easy to recognize that individual liberty is so to speak the root of the nationality of a people. In effect, if we multiply the exercise of such inoffensive liberty by the mass of individual liberty of all citizens of a nation, what result are certain constant and spontaneous qualities, traditions, requirements, tendencies and customs. This is what represents the special juridical character by which we can distinguish a people from another [...] Alongside this free activity of individuals we have the activity of the public power, to which are entrusted the administration and guarantee of the public order and social progress within its entire political territory. Private laws respond to individual liberty; laws that guarantee the public order and the organization of public power belong to the sovereignty of the state. We can therefore affirm, without fear of error: just as individual liberty cannot suffer unjust limitations through the recognition of rights to other individuals living in society under the same social power, this liberty does not cease to exercise itself when it goes beyond the sphere of such society and manifests itself within the sphere of other peoples and nations. In effect, such rights of private law belong to people as people and not as members of a political society.[132]

In other words "civil private law is personal and national, and, as such, must accompany the person beyond its nation; public law, by contrast, is territorial."[133] In the

[128] Ibid., 293. [129] Ibid., 290. [130] Ibid. [131] Ibid., 292. [132] Ibid.
[133] Ibid., 297.

relationship between an individual and a foreign state, the individual's private rights and liberty are inoffensive and apolitical and therefore easily recognizable, indeed recognizable *as* human rights:

> We have substituted to these traditional formulas [of personal and real statutes] two other formulas which are easily comprehensible: *private and domestic law, public and political law*. If we make this terminological shift, we can easily understand why the laws of the first category can and must maintain all their force and rule the conditions of the person and of the family even beyond the territory; we understand why the sovereign power of a state has the duty to recognize them to all foreigners of all nations who find themselves within its territory; why, by contrast the laws of the second category rigorously rule within the limits of each state.[134]

Yet within the relationship between the individual and her own nation, private law was not entirely "inoffensive." Rather, it was broken down into a "necessary" part comprising of personal status, family, and wills[135] and a "voluntary" part comprising "goods, contracts, obligations generally and things of that nature."[136] The voluntary part is "inoffensive" to both the state of nationality and the foreign state and individuals can choose whichever law they please.[137] As to the "necessary" part of private law Mancini says:

> In effect, it does not depend on the will of individuals to alter or modify this necessary part. Nobody can renounce its state or family relations that are attributed to him by the law of his nationality. An individual's status and family represent an ensemble of attributes and qualities, which are not attributes of all human beings, but of each individual belonging to a particular nation. Attributing to a person Italian, French or German nationality is, in effect, suddenly awakening the idea of all personal rights relative to the organization of the family, which belong to all individuals as part of each nationality. A person can change his nationality by accepting that of another country, but it cannot maintain it, while repudiating its conditions, since these conditions are like the mirror that reflects nationality itself.[138]

It is in this image of the private individual as "inoffensive" in relationship to foreign states, but permanently linked to his state of nationality at least in certain legal components of his "private" status that one can best discern the similarities and differences between Mancini on the one hand and Story and Savigny on the other.

On the one hand, it is true that the theories of all three authors had a profound humanistic dimension and were motivated largely by the fear of despotic power exercising arbitrary power and judgment over individuals in their transnational existence. Erik Jayme showed the strong humanistic premises of Mancini's theory and argued that the notion of nationality has the potential to bring human rights considerations, as well as sociological considerations, under the purview of PrIL.[139]

[134] Ibid., 297–8. [135] Ibid., 294. [136] Ibid., 295.

[137] Ibid., 295: "the state [of nationality] has no interest to prevent the exercise [of inoffensive liberty]."

[138] Ibid., 294.

[139] See Jayme, *Ideengeschichte* (n. 1). For his emphasis on cultural affiliations, see Erik Jayme, 'Die kulturelle Dimension des Rechts—ihre Beudeutung für das internationale Privatrecht und die Rechtsvergleichung' (2003) 67 RabelsZ 211. For his discussion of the recognition of human rights within the PrIL-PublIL association, see Erik Jayme, 'Völkerrecht und internationales Privatrecht—eine entwicklungsgeschichtliche Betrachtung' in S. Leibe and M. Ruffert (eds.), *Völkerrecht und IPR* (Jenaer Wissenschaftliche Verlagsgesellschaft 2006). See also Erik Jayme 'Menschenrechte und Theorie

Furthermore, the theories of all three authors were premised on a strong recognition of equality between nationals and foreigners. It is also true that none of the three authors subscribed to a libertarian theory of private law. Mancini's strict duality between private and public law might surprise. But this is due primarily to the idealized assumptions about the theoretical premises of the PrIL-PublIL association. As Chapter 7 shows, by reference to Pillet's theory, the private/public distinction was in many ways much more present in the theories of those who associated PrIL with PublIL than in the theory of those who associated PrIL with private law. State-centered internationalists, including Mancini, relied heavily on the private/public distinction as a way of defining a strict, predictable, and uniform division between territorial and extraterritorial application of laws and ultimately as a way of ensuring a number of uniform rules of PrIL acceptable to all states and based on highly abstract philosophical assumptions.

Yet it would not be accurate to assume that Mancini encouraged a despotic and individualistic notion of autonomy, or that he did not allow for public law to trump private values. Rather, both in his theory and in the Italian code, Mancini included a fairly large "corrective" provision stipulating that states would not need to recognize any judgments or private dispositions and conventions that would constitute a derogation from or violation of public order, good morals or the prohibitive laws of public law within a state.[140] Furthermore, while he did not subscribe to Savigny's theory of the nature of a legal relation, which he considered too flexible and incapable of generating intransigently uniform rules of PrIL,[141] he praised Savigny for having already refuted an individualistic notion of autonomy:

> [Savigny] victoriously refuted a different principle proposed especially by professor Hans of Göttingen, who elevated the autonomy of individual will to the level of the power of law, and who placed it even above the level of law of particular countries. This considers individual will almost as regulatory authority for transnational relations. This system, by interpreting in contra sense the ancient well-known juridical rule: *provisio hominis vincit provisionem legis (Arg. G. fin. C. de pact. Convent.),* pretends that, in all cases of conflict, we should apply to all jural relations the law, which we could prove to have been chosen by the parties, and to which individuals were willing to submit their actions.[142]

Yet despite these similarities there are important nuances that differentiate the humanistic premises underlying Mancini's theory from Story's and Savigny's theories. In his placement of the individual between his state of nationality and the foreign state, Mancini both narrowed individual liberty and ignored an important element of social responsibility.

des internationalen Privatrechts' in Erik Jayme (ed.), *Internationales Privatrecht und Völkerrecht* (C.F. Müller 2003). Jayme, together with Heinz-Peter Mansel also organized a symposium and edited a volume on the concepts of nation and state within PrIL theory and history. See Erik Jayme and Heinz-Peter Mansel (eds.), *Nation und Staat im internationalen Privatrecht. Zum kollisionsrechtlichen Staatsangehörigkeitsprinzip in verfassungsrechtlicher und internationalprivatrechtlicher Sicht* (C.F. Müller 1988) (hereafter Jayme and Mansel, *Nation und Staat*).

140 Mancini, "Decision uniforme des conflicts" (n. 118) 303.

141 Ibid., 287.

142 Ibid., 288.

Mancini narrowed what relational internationalists believed was a fundamental ability of individuals to immerse themselves in the social life of various communities and submit to their laws.[143] At least within the "mandatory" part of private law Mancini subsumed the individual under the nation. Bonnichon marked the transition from Story's and Savigny's emphasis on domicile to Mancini's emphasis on nationality in these words:

The political allegiance to a prince or a nation would initially not be confused with the civil condition of the individual, the one was nationality, the other domicile. But now the political and the civil are one.[144]

Certain important nuances might emerge from the fact that Mancini does not subsume the individual under the state, but rather under the nation. Erik Jayme has argued that PrIL needs to maintain the notion of nationality in addition to the notion of the state, because nationality can emphasize the "cultural belonging" of individuals, going beyond the formal relationship between individuals and the state.[145] Placing the individual within the nation bears much resemblance to Savigny's placing of the individual within the Volk. Yet while Savigny emphasized the intimate relationship between the individual and the Volk, he was also keen to avoid subsuming the individual under the Volk. And indeed Savigny,[146] as all relational internationalists, for that matter, separated the civil from the political condition of the individual and thereby introduced a distinction that Karen Knop conveyed forcefully, between private and public citizenship.[147] The individual is thereby allowed to integrate herself in a community other than her own nation and to have the laws of the foreign community applied to her. This is the case both for what Mancini described as the mandatory and the voluntary part of private law, so that personal and family status, as well as contracts and property matters can be regulated by another state than that of nationality.

In other words, relational internationalists understood the identity of individuals as formed by links to a variety of communities. While Mancini might have linked one's "cultural belonging" to a particular nation, relational internationalists had a more fluid understanding of culture and identity[148] and were more likely to accept individuals' reference to the norms and values of a variety of communities for different aspects of their transnational life.[149]

[143] See Ferdinando Treggiari, 'Nationales Recht und Recht der Nationalität—Mancini' in Jayme and Mansel, *Nation und Staat* (n. 139) 145, 163.

[144] Bonnichon, "La Notion" (n. 104) 15.

[145] See Jayme, *Nation und Staat* (n. 139) 316.

[146] For a detailed account of the transition in Savigny's writing from the individual as the citizen of the *Volk*, to the cosmopolitan individual as part of humanity, see Hans-Cristof Kraus, 'Begriff und Verständnis des "Bürgers" bei Savigny' (1993) 110 Zeitschrift der Savigny Stiftung für Rechtsgeschichte. Romanistische Abteilung 552.

[147] Karen Knop, 'Citizenship Private and Public' (2008) 71 L & Contemp Probs 309.

[148] For a contemporary argument that one's culture is constructed through concomitant affiliations to multiple communities and that it is fluid and fluctuating, see Samuel Scheffler, 'Immigration and the Significance of Culture' (2007) 35 Phil & Public Affairs 92.

[149] This is especially the case with Jitta who argued that virtually all links (nationality, domicile, territory etc.) matter and that they might be cumulated, or alternatively referenced in different cases and circumstances. See, e.g., Jitta, *The Renovation* (n. 24) 106. For an argument that individuals routinely

But relational internationalists also held individuals socially responsible to the communities in which they immerse themselves "in proportion to the penetration" of these individuals within various communities.[150] Mancini portrayed the individual as "inoffensive" in relationship to the foreign state, but relational internationalists made no such assumption.

Furthermore, Mancini tried to dissociate himself from Savigny's analytical method of localizing the legal relation according to its nature because he rightly foresaw that the legal relation could be embedded in a variety of communities, which inevitably leads to simultaneous pleas from several states to regulate the relationship.[151] However, Josephus Jitta would later welcome this intuition. He emphasized the complex dimensions of private law's social embeddedness in the transnational realm and pled in some cases for the application of a blend of the laws of various states in order to take full account of the transnational nature of the dispute.

Overall, while Mancini maintained the humanistic underpinnings of Story's and Savigny's theories, his political commitment to ensure the national unity of Italy did not allow him to account for the full scope of individual liberty and social responsibility in relationship to foreign states. While he rightly underscored the intimate relationship between an individual and her state of nationality, little further reflection

appeal to the norms and values of multiple communities, inspired by cultural anthropology, see Annelise Riles, 'Cultural Conflicts' (2008) 71 L & Contemp Probs 273.

150 See Jitta, *The Renovation* (n. 24) 103:

> Nationality, as the basis of private international law, is not necessarily dependent on the same conditions as nationality in the domain of public international law, but the admission of two kinds of nationality, a private, and a public one, would accentuate the discrepancy between nationality, considered as a feeling, and nationality as a juridical qualification, so that in a State there is generally only one conception of nationality, depending on fixed juridical marks.

And at 106:

> It is a general guiding thought that a man ought to be subjected to the civil law, in force in a local sphere of social life, *in proportion to his penetration into such a sphere.* According to this thought an absolutely reasonable rule could easily be found, if the divergences between the various laws, with regard to persons, were only founded on the differences of the local social life. Every man would then, as a rule, be subjected to the law of the local sphere of social life in which he has settled, unconditionally and durably, *cum animo perpetuitatis.* The reference to this domiciliary law would by no means be a mechanical and supernational rule for the solution of conflicts between laws, but only a guiding thought, allowing the other points of contact the influence they deserve.

151 See Mancini, "Decision uniforme des conflicts" (n. 118) 287. See also Eugène Gaudemet, 'La thèorie des conflits des lois dans l'ouvre d'Antoine Pillet et de la doctrine de Savigny' in *Mélanges Antoine Pillet* (Rec Sirey 1929) 89, 91:

> Savigny announces by contrast an entirely analytical method, foreign to *a priori* principles, applying to each legal relation a rule determined by reasons particular to this relationship. And this is in effect the line of reasoning he will follow, refuting deliberately the old categories of real and personal statutes, eliminating the theory of territoriality, to mold its doctrine to the infinite variety of most complex problems which juridical life had to offer to legal science. Due to this characteristic, Savigny rests in such stark contrast to the Italian school, founded two years after the publishing of his book, through Mancini's famous discourse in 1851. Just as the principle of territoriality of law, the antithetical Italian rule of personality, is an *a priori* general rule: Savigny's method refutes it as such.

has been given to the wider range of affiliations of individuals in their transnational existence.

2. Antoine Pillet and Ernst Zitelmann

In his universalist manifesto for PrIL, Mancini repeatedly referenced the cohort of internationalists that was part of the movement to connect PrIL with PublIL.[152] Indeed his PrIL account was part of a larger intellectual movement to unite the two fields and provide a philosophical justification for this connection. While for Mancini the philosophical justification for the unity between the two legal fields was premised on liberty and national unity, the association between the two fields was progressively premised on a reconceptualization of PrIL matters as conflicts of sovereignty. At least incidentally, Mancini had contributed to this reconceptualization by introducing personal sovereignty as the flipside of territorial sovereignty, which had already been heavily referenced in the Dutch school and in Story's theory.[153]

Progressively, the conceptualization of PrIL matters as conflicts of sovereignty became such a powerful imagery that in 1899 the French scholar Etienne Bartin wrote: "[t]his assertion is nowadays not contested by anyone."[154] Henri Batiffol described this imagery in the following words:

> In a world divided into independent states, all relationships, even between individuals, which cross the borders of a particular state, involve the relationship between states: the international society is one made up of states; if an individual enters into a relationship, even a purely commercial one, with another individual pertaining to another state, this relationship is considered to belong to public international law because no relationship can be established between individuals belonging to different states but within the framework of inter-state relationships, in other words within the framework of public international law.[155]

Conceptualizing PrIL matters as conflicts of sovereignty inevitably required several analytical steps. On the one hand, it required a certain extrapolation from interpersonal relationships to interstate relationships. This in turn generated a progressive attempt to exclude the individual from within the purview of PrIL matters. One had to argue that when a court is asked to recognize the application of foreign law and rights granted by such law, the request does not come from "a person, a simple individual," but rather "a foreign sovereign," and failure to apply this law would

[152] Mancini, "Decision uniforme des conflicts" (n. 118) 230: "Without referencing additional authorities, all the members of the commission named by the Institute already had occasion to offer similar views on this question [of refuting the notion of comity and pleading for a universal obligation to apply foreign law]. (Bluntschli, Heffter, Beach Lawrence, Massé, Westlake)."

[153] Bonnichon, "La Notion" (n. 104) 14, 16.

[154] Etienne Bartin, *Études de droit international privé* (A. Chevalier-Marescq 1899) 146 (hereafter Bartin, *Études*). Bonnichon notes ironically: "the universality of this reconceptualization was so powerful that even those who do not directly subscribe to this view (such as Arminjon) simply deny it in passing." See Bonnichon, "La Notion" (n. 104) 615.

[155] Henri Batiffol, 'Principes de Droit International Privé' (1959) 97 Recueil des Cours 431, 437–8.

result in "an infringement of the public law of the foreign sovereign."[156] This transition from thinking about the rights of individuals to the rights of states was facilitated by the concomitant efforts to develop a theory of fundamental rights of states within PublIL.[157] Reconceptualizing PrIL matters as conflicts of sovereignty meant focusing on the rights of states in relationship to each other and showing that "PrIL is not concerned with private interests but with questions of state sovereignty."[158] In other words, "even if a PrIL matter might be occasioned by a private interest, this interest has been considered so important that it has been elevated to the level of a public interest."[159] Private matters become state matters and questions of mixed rights as Story had called them[160] become questions of mixed sovereignties.[161]

It is precisely its focus on state sovereignty that might suggest to contemporary scholars that the PrIL-PublIL association focused on regulatory goals and global public goods. But this idealized assumption is far from the meaning attributed to sovereignty around which the PublIL-PrIL association was constructed in the nineteenth century. Rather, the notion of sovereignty, which rested at the foundation of the PrIL-PublIL analogy was almost deliberately assigned a formalistic meaning as part of a perceived need to introduce easy and clear concepts into PrIL in order to achieve coherence and uniformity in PrIL.[162] Focusing on the intransigent element of the imperative character and source of law meant avoiding the flexibility of the notions of justice, comity, nature of legal relation etc.[163] Furthermore, the notion of sovereignty employed in PrIL was often explicitly apolitical. Bartin had been explicit that one must "dissociate political sovereignty in Public International Law from legislative sovereignty in civil law."[164]

One of the first scholars to provide a theory grounded in the association between PrIL and PublIL that illustrates the formalistic underpinnings of the notions of sovereignty was the German scholar Ernst Zitelmann. In 1897 Zitelmann portrayed his state-centered internationalist theory as entirely novel.[165] While the PrIL-PublIL association had been postulated by Mancini, virtually all members of the Institute, and many other PrIL and PublIL scholars, no one, in Zitelmann's view, had provided an entire theory grounded in this association and nobody had been able to "prove" that this association had a solid philosophical foundation.[166] For Zitelmann this philosophical

[156] Mailher de Chassat, *Traité de statuts (lois personelles, lois réelles), d'après le droit ancienes et le droit modern, ou du Droit International Privé* (A. Durand 1845) 214. Referenced favorably in Antoine Pillet, *Principes de droit international privé* (Allier Frères 1903) 61, n. 1 (hereafter Pillet, *Principes*).

[157] See Bonnichon, "La Notion" (n. 104) 13. See also Gilbert Gidel, 'Droits et devoirs des nations, théorie classique des droit fondamentaux des États' (1925) 10 Recueil des Cours 537, 559.

[158] Antoine Pillet, 'Droit international privé consideré dans ses rapports avec le droit international public' in *Annales de l'enseignement superior de Grenoble* (F. Allier Père & Fils 1892) 309, 336 (hereafter Pillet, "Rapports").

[159] Ibid., 345.

[160] Story, *Commentaries on the Conflict of Laws* (n. 27) 3.

[161] Pillet, "Rapports" (n. 158).

[162] Bonnichon, "La Notion" (n. 104) 13.

[163] Ibid., 14–15.

[164] Bartin, *Études* (n. 154) 224–5. Bonnichon found this impossible to understand precisely because those authors argued that the bases of PrIL are set within public law. See Bonnichon, "La Notion" (n. 104) 30.

[165] Ernst Zitelmann, *Internationales Privatrecht*, vol. 1 (Dunkler & Humblot 1897) 27–8 (hereafter Zitelmann, *Internationales Privatrecht*).

[166] Ibid., 24.

foundation started from an emphasis of the "true danger," which exists if every judge makes a case by case determination "based on the nature of things," without any guidance in the positive law.[167] For this reason, Zitelmann thought the only way to develop uniform rules of PrIL would be to commit PrIL to an overarching principle, which all states agree on and are committed to. Such principle can only be found in PublIL,[168] and it was the responsibility of scholars to develop unified principles of PrIL from general and universal concepts of PublIL.[169]

Interestingly, state-centered internationalists, such as Zitelmann and Pillet relied on PublIL to establish PrIL as positive law, despite the fact that PublIL's positivity was itself contested. That is because these scholars attempted to establish PrIL as positive *international* law and PublIL appeared as the only hope for such achievement. At the end of the nineteenth century, as the next chapter shows, this argument will be turned on its head. Precisely by emphasizing PublIL's contested pedigree as "positive law" it was later argued that PrIL can only be positive law if it is national law.

Zitelmann nevertheless attempted to anchor PrIL to PublIL through two general postulates. First, in PrIL as in PublIL one had to center the analysis on states rather than individuals by acknowledging that objective law precedes subjective rights and that individual freedom becomes legal freedom only because it is granted by the state through the legal order.[170] Story and Savigny had distinguished between a pre-political notion of liberty as an attribute of humanity and the liberty within private law categories, which had a profound political dimension.[171] For relational internationalists, liberty would be a highly complex and nuanced concept, but under the PrIL-PublIL association the nuances had to be downplayed in order to operate with highly abstract and intransigent concepts. If individual liberty were granted by the state, the shift from the individual to the state would be relatively easy to make.

But Zitelmann still openly acknowledged that PublIL deals with interstate relationships in a more direct way than PrIL seemed to. Therefore, there could not be a direct relationship between the subjective private rights of individuals, which PrIL seemed to reference, and PublIL.[172] To demonstrate such relationship one had to determine a relationship between private rights and the state, and then a relationship among states with respect to private rights.[173]

Such determinations culminated in the conclusion that:

> private rights can be created with a well-founded claim to international recognition by that state only which possesses the general governmental control, recognized by the principles of international law, over the subject with respect to which the subjective private law confers authority and that state alone can revoke such private rights again.[174]

In effect PrIL would be concerned with conflicts of legislative jurisdiction of states in the international realm.[175] Such rules of division of jurisdiction in the international realm could only be deduced from general principles of PublIL, recognized by and binding on all states.

[167] Ibid., 6. [168] Ibid., 17. [169] Ibid., 20. [170] Ibid., 60.
[171] See Chapter 7. [172] Zitelmann, *Internationales Privatrecht* (n. 166) 41.
[173] Ibid. [174] Ibid., 68. [175] Ibid., 25 and 40.

The only two such principles that could prove useful in PrIL as well, were territorial and personal sovereignty.[176] All questions of PrIL could be solved by determining for each category of cases whether "proper jurisdiction" existed based on broad appreciations of a state's territorial or personal sovereignty.[177] Zitelmann admitted that PublIL does not directly offer rules delimiting the legislative authority of states according to these principles.[178] However, to establish a relationship between PublIL and PrIL, allegedly one did not need to prove that PublIL offers norms of PrIL. One only had to prove that the norms of PrIL must be based on principles of PublIL, and this can only be the case if PrIL relations have the same scope as those of PublIL. To extract PrIL norms from PublIL principles was the "responsibility of the legal scientific community."[179]

Since no norms of PublIL could directly determine which of the two types of sovereignty takes precedence in a particular case or category of cases,[180] this distribution of authority had to be deduced primarily from state practice. For example, Zitelmann talked about "a consensus amongst states that the state, which has territorial sovereignty must give way to the one with personal sovereignty."[181] To Zitelmann, personal authority was subsidiary to territorial (in a clash between citizenship as the personal link and domicile as the territorial link) only to the extent that the state of domicile must exercise authority over the domiciled individual to fulfill its public order functions.[182]

This intransigent a priori choice between territorial and personal sovereignty in a large category of cases became inevitable once the PrIL-PublIL association was forged. PrIL would now learn from PublIL that "each state is obliged not to attribute to itself a legal authority, which is not recognized by public international law"[183] and that "a state's authority is always exclusive."[184] Once PrIL was grounded in PublIL and was described as a clash of sovereignty, it seemed obvious that the decision, which law to apply in a particular case, must always be the same.[185] Any deviation from the uniform division of authority would imply a breach of sovereignty and a breach of PublIL. Of course, such uniformity was not possible if states had an interest in widening their legal authority in relationship to other states. Even though this was possible in other fields, Zitelmann believed that in PrIL states had less of an interest to increase the area of legal authority in private law matters than to achieve uniform solutions: "[T]his community of interests makes a legal community not only possible but also necessary."[186]

Once it was shown that the legal relations governed by PrIL were the same in nature as those governed by PublIL, the connection between the two branches became uncontestable. However, having its roots in PublIL, PrIL now borrows from PublIL's possible uncertainty, lack of development and incoherence. Thus, on the one hand, Zitelmann acknowledged that these unified principles of PrIL derived from PublIL could only have subsidiary effect until they are incorporated into national law.[187] Until then, national rules of PrIL trump those unified principles, even

[176] Ibid., 66 and 83. [177] Ibid. [178] Ibid., 97. [179] Ibid., 20.
[180] Ibid., 97. [181] Ibid., 107. [182] Ibid., 99. [183] Ibid., 70.
[184] Ibid., 73. [185] Ibid. [186] Ibid., 80. [187] Ibid., 74.

though states are under a moral obligation to act in conformity with PublIL.[188] Zitelmann openly acknowledged that:

> Once one understands the dependence of private international law on public international law, the attainable can be easily distinguished from the unattainable. If public international law does not provide for clear principles of division of legal authority among states, no uniform principles of private international law can be found. If uniformity in private international law is missing it is entirely attributable to the state of play of public international law.[189]

Furthermore, the pool of states among which such absolute uniformity of PrIL would be achievable would also need to be discerned by reference to PublIL. This is because a prerequisite of harmonization was that states considered themselves as equals in the international community.[190] Zitelmann thought that PrIL could only include this as a postulate, while PublIL would need to determine the conditions and extent of such equality among states.[191]

Overall Zitelmann had provided the platform for the reconceptualization needed in order to associate PrIL with PublIL. But the French scholar Antoine Pillet thought it was entirely wrong to suggest that this was indeed a "reconceptualization." If PrIL relationships were ever described in any other way than as interstate relationships, it was due to a misunderstanding of the "true nature of PrIL" and a rather superficial examination of the relationship between PrIL and PublIL.[192]

In 1892 the French scholar Antoine Pillet started what he perceived as a fundamental investigation in the nature of the PrIL-PublIL association and was keen to portray the perplexing state of academic debates trying to establish this association.[193] On the one hand the question had been "dealt with a hundred times, a commonplace because we can say that there is no author who does not consider himself obliged to dedicate it a few lines."[194] On the other hand, after a thorough examination of the variety of European authors who had touched upon the association between the two fields, Pillet concluded that "the majority of them considered it as an object of curiosity, rather than an aspect the full understanding of which is essential for the mere intelligibility of the field [of PrIL] and for the establishment of a proper method of its study."[195] He thought what had confused scholars most in their attempts to associate PrIL with PublIL was the apparent difference in the subjects of the two fields: PrIL dealing with interindividual relationships and PublIL dealing with interstate relationships. Yet for Pillet this distinction "emerges from a superficial and erroneous analysis and the truth is, on the contrary, that both private international law, as well as public international law deal with relationships between states."[196]

According to Pillet, any question or conflict of authority or state law in an international context was a form of conflict of sovereignty[197] because any law is based

[188] Ibid. [189] Ibid., 78. [190] Ibid., 16. [191] Ibid., 6.
[192] Pillet, "Rapports" (n. 158) 325, 329. [193] Ibid., 312. [194] Ibid.
[195] Ibid., 320. [196] Ibid., 329. [197] Ibid., 339.

solely on the legislative sovereignty of the state.[198] The question PrIL must answer is which sovereign to grant the authority to govern the particular legal matter.[199] "The conflict is between two sovereigns and it involves one of their essential attributes, namely their legislative functions; such conflict of sovereignties automatically falls under the scope of Public International Law."[200] No private interests are involved because the limit of the authority of law is nothing more than a limit of the "public power of a state" in relationship to another.[201]

The more challenging task for Pillet was to describe this public power and the various ways in which the public powers of states could collide. He thought it was astonishing that this question had not been thoroughly examined in PrIL before.[202] It was precisely because this clash of state interests/public powers had not been noticed and properly examined that the organic relationship between PrIL and PublIL had been overseen.

To explain the nature of states' interests involved in both PrIL and PublIL, Pillet employed a functionalist theory of the state.[203] All states must perform the same functions for their individuals.[204] These state functions could and often do collide in the international realm. PrIL was but one example of such a clash.[205]

Employing a functionalist theory of the state was not just one more way of describing state sovereignty, but rather a necessary answer to what Pillet thought was the main question of the PublIL school: on which basis to establish the relationship between the two fields.[206] He disagreed with Johann Kaspar Bluntschli that the association could be made on the basis of human nature mandating equality, because "we are not dealing with individuals, but with states."[207] For the same reason, Mancini's theory was unacceptable as well, even though Pillet praised the clarity of Mancini in establishing a firm relationship between PrIL and PublIL.[208] But Mancini had failed to realize, according to Pillet, that:

> among states individual rights only have the force derived from the authority of the state, under the control of which they are exercised and that individual liberty, which within a state, can only manifest itself through a permission granted by the law, should not have a higher force vis-à-vis foreign states.[209]

As showed in Chapter 7, despite this theoretical controversy, Pillet adopted Mancini's private/public and individual/social duality as a way of determining the extraterritorial scope of laws. Yet the theoretical controversy itself was important for Pillet, because these distinctions would not be made via individual liberty, human

198 Ibid., 333; Antoine Pillet, *Recherches sur les droits fondamentaux des états dans l'ordre des rapports internationaux et sur la solution des conflits qu'ils font naitre* (A. Pedone 1899) 63 (hereafter Pillet, *Droits fondamentaux*).

199 Pillet, "Rapports" (n. 158) 333. 200 Ibid. 201 Ibid., 335.

202 Pillet, *Droits fondamentaux* (n. 198) 69.

203 Antoine Pillet, 'Le droit international public, ses elements constitutifs, son domaine, son objet' (1894) 1 RGDIP 1, 4.

204 Ibid.

205 Ibid., 34 (Pillet conceived of PrIL as an instance of conflict between one state's territorial sovereignty and another state's right to international commerce).

206 Ibid., 4. 207 Ibid. 208 Pillet, "Rapports" (n. 158) 318. 209 Ibid.

nature, nationality or even individual expectations generally. Rather, the distinctions were introduced through an analysis of the law as public power and taking the law as an initial point of departure was necessary since the relationship between PrIL and PublIL was based on the assumption that both fields deal with interstate relationships.

Pillet had argued that individuals are connected to "three societies": the national, the international, and humanity.[210] Each society has to have its own law and the three societies correspond to three types of law: national, international, and the law of humanity.[211] PrIL corresponded neither to national law, nor to the law of humanity. Those who associated PrIL with national law, including with national private law, were certainly wrong according to Pillet.[212] But to the extent Mancini would have meant to reference a notion of human rights or pre-political rights and liberty as the anchor point for PrIL, he was wrong too. He had failed on the "philosophical method."[213]

As showed throughout the book, for relational internationalists, liberty was a complex notion having both a political and a pre-political dimension and one that manifested itself differently depending on the PrIL relationship involved. The individual was simultaneously embedded in all three societies Pillet referenced and the intensity of one's affiliations which each one would need to be determined based on the circumstances, the type of PrIL relationship involved, elements of justice, social reality, and so on. For Pillet, this image was too fluid. One needed to commit to clear and intransigent distinctions. PrIL was not about individuals or liberty, but about states. And it operated neither in the realm of the national, nor in that of mankind, but rather in the realm of the international. The international was made up of states and comprised of two kinds of laws: those which do not require consent because consent is implicit in the fact that states have to perform certain functions together, and those which required consent because the state functions are not necessary, but desirable.[214] PrIL allegedly belonged to the first category.[215] Through these sets of analogies it would now be clear that the individual is not a subject of international law, neither private nor public. The individual is an international subject only under exceptional circumstances or because of an express delegation that he is performing a state function.[216] It was therefore clear that no association between the two fields could be established via the individual or a general concept of human nature.

But it was equally wrong to establish the relationship between the fields on a postulate of equality among states. Pillet took stock of the constant enlargement of the international community and was critical of it. He noted that at some point we had replaced the idea of a Christian community with that of a European community and that we had started to find even that too restrictive. To Pillet, this was entirely wrong because "as much as we can speak of the natural equality among individuals there is no corresponding exact equality among nations. In fact the degree of a state's

[210] Pillet, *Droits fondamentaux* (n. 198) 3. [211] Ibid., 7.
[212] This is what Pillet thinks of Jitta for example. See Pillet, "Rapports" (n. 158) 317.
[213] Ibid., 318. [214] Pillet, *Droits fondamentaux* (n. 198) 7–8.
[215] Ibid., 8 and 28–30. [216] Ibid., 32.

civilization is the measure of its right."[217] Pillet adopted James Lorimer's classification to argue that no full rights can be recognized to semicivilized states by fully civilized states.[218]

Consequently anchoring the PrIL-PublIL association in the concept of state functions, rather than human or state equality, was necessary and quite innovative.[219] Pillet proposed that a judge ruling in a PrIL matter apply the law of the state whose function/interest is most significant.[220] Both PublIL and PrIL allegedly aimed to apply the law of "least sacrifice,"[221] namely that which causes the least amount of intrusion of state sovereignty understood as public power/ public function.[222]

Pillet was careful to distinguish his "interest methodology" from the German *Interessenjurisprudenz*, and implicitly from variations of the modern American interest analysis methodology proposed much later.[223] In Pillet's theory, the state interests that are at stake and collide with one another both in PublIL and in PrIL should be found based on a general classification.[224] Included in the classification should be only those interests that are indispensable to a state in performing its functions. It cannot be left to the discretion of the judge to determine and weigh the interests on a case by case basis.[225] This is too uncertain and can lead to arbitrary decisions and abuses. Furthermore, such classification is possible because only a handful of predetermined interests that are essential for the performance of state functions can be reasonably claimed by states under PublIL principles. Pillet therefore purported to achieve such classification of state interests and their conflicts both for PublIL[226] and for PrIL.[227] The determination of the applicable law in PrIL matters is a direct result of these predetermined solutions to conflicts of state functions.[228] Pillet criticized Zitelmann for having produced an abstract division between personal and territorial sovereignty and between territorial and extraterritorial application of law. He argued that in order to choose between sovereignties one must use another concept at a higher level of abstraction. For Pillet, the social scope of the law would serve as such a concept meant to determine whether a law applies territorially or extraterritorially. Chapter 7 shows how Pillet used a highly formalistic and abstract notion of "the social scope of the law" precisely as a way to ensure absolute uniformity and systematicity for PrIL. Bonnichon described Pillet's focus on the social scope of the law in these terms:

217 Ibid., 24.

218 Ibid., 27. Since Pillet established the relationships between PrIL and PublIL by reference to interstate relationships he incorporated Lorimer's distinctions with respect to states, rather than Lorimer's discussion about "the private citizen of the world." For an illuminating account of Lorimer's account of the private citizen, see Karen Knop, 'Lorimer's Private Citizens of the World' (2016) 27 Eur J Int L 447.

219 For an account of the way in which Pillet's theory was situated within the internationalist school of the time, see Maurice Bernard, 'Review of Antoine Pillet, Principes de Droit International Privé' (1904) 31 Journal de Droit international privé et de la jurisprudence comparée 769, 770–1.

220 Pillet, *Droits fundamentaux* (n. 198) 41. 221 Ibid., 42. 222 Ibid.

223 Ibid., 68–9. See also Marti Koskenniemi, *The Gentle Civilizer of Nations: The Rise and Fall of International Law (1870–1960)* (CUP 2004), 282.

224 Pillet, *Droits fondamentaux* (n. 198) 68–9. 225 Ibid. 226 Ibid.

227 Ibid. See also Pillet, *Principes* (n. 156). 228 Pillet, *Droits fondamentaux* (n. 198) .

Since this is a conflict of equal sovereignty, to choose between them you need a notion external to the notion of sovereignty. In essence this notion is social justice, or the nature of the legal relations. But in order to make sure that the test can easily be associated with sovereignty, we talk about the social scope of the law. In so doing, we do not even realize that we have narrowed the analysis.[229]

Yet the analysis had to be narrowed because much like Zitelmann, Pillet thought "uniform rules of conduct among states are the unifying element of public and private international law."[230] Both are concerned with clashes of state sovereignty, which can only be solved in a uniform manner. Furthermore, if the distribution of sovereignty were deduced from PublIL, any deviation from such distribution would constitute a violation of PublIL. The distinctive line of arguments in state-centered universalist doctrines ends up conceptualizing uniformity as a right of states. It all proceeds from the realization that PrIL cannot be uniform unless states have an obligation to pursue such uniformity. However, states can only have an obligation toward each other.[231]

Either private international law is not truly law and has no mandatory character for states or it does have a mandatory character but then it becomes a part of public international law and according to Rolin, becomes a doctrine which settles relationships between states and establishes the limits of their respective legislative competence with respect to rights and private interests.[232]

Once this link is created, individuals cannot claim or choose that a certain law be applied, let alone claim uniformity, because states and not individuals are the subjects of PrIL.[233] Furthermore, the individual allegedly does not dispose of what is at stake in PrIL, namely state sovereignty. Both Pillet and even more so Zitelmann commence their studies with an overview of the hardship created to individuals absent uniformity in PrIL. Uniformity is certainly meant at least *also for* individuals. If it ends up being described as a right of states, this is for two reasons. First and most important, only states are at least formally "equal" with rights and obligations toward each other in an international community.[234] Second, for Pillet, in the context of a conflict of laws, any law, including private law, is a form of public authority. It is an attribute of the public power of a state, regulating for the entire community.[235] According to Pillet, in the analysis of courts in PrIL "the litigating parties disappear for a while."[236] Allegedly it is "entirely wrong to assume that the individual has a right to the application of a certain law, because the limits of the authority of law are not fixed by consideration to private interests, but result from the limits of the public powers which enacted them."[237]

229 Bonnichon, "La Notion" (n. 104) 22.

230 Pillet, "Rapports" (n. 158) 327.

231 Pillet, *Droits fondamentaux* (n. 198) 20: "states are the only ones able to deal from equal to equal within a foreign community."

232 Pillet, *Principes* (n. 156) 56.

233 Pillet, *Droit fondamentaux* (n. 198).

234 Ibid., 20, 36.

235 Ibid., 83.

236 Pillet, "Rapports" (n. 158) 335: "The litigating parties disappear for a while: instead there are two sovereigns in attendance and their respective rights and obligations can only be determined by Public International Law."

237 Ibid.

Zitelmann's and Pillet's theories were variations on the same theme: the reconceptualization of PrIL as conflicts of sovereignty and the implicit association of PrIL with PublIL. By the end of the nineteenth century this theme had become nearly universal. According to Bonnichon writing in 1950:

The vast majority of authors view in this notion of conflict of sovereignty the best way to frame the issue and the central principle that will offer the solution. The idea can incorporate around it the most diverse tendencies: and this explains in part its success. You can use the idea of sovereignty to link Private International Law to Public International Law as Pillet did. But if you want to turn Private International Law into national law the idea of sovereignty can serve that purpose too.[238] Bartin uses the idea of sovereignty in another way saying that it is up to each state to define for itself the restrictions it accepts to its own sovereignty.[239] This is also a sovereign prerogative. And if you want to group the entire field around the idea of sovereignty you can do that with Mancini: the personal link, which unites the individual to the national. This would be personal sovereignty. The many exceptions to bring to the application of the national law would be founded on the idea of a public order imposed in the name of the general interest of the state, which stands for territorial sovereignty.[240]

D. Josephus Jitta

The conceptualization of PrIL matters as conflicts of sovereignty was indeed predominant within PrIL academic circles of the late nineteenth century. The Dutch PrIL scholar Josephus Jitta would react precisely to this dominant way of conceptualizing PrIL.[241] He purported to show at the end of the nineteenth century that the PrIL-PublIL association leads to highly questionable methodological conclusions for PrIL.[242] An outcast of his time, placing himself both outside the dominant law of nations theory and the particularistic school of thought,[243] Jitta's scholarship remained outside the canons of PrIL theory.[244]

Although his writings are little known today, Jitta's scholarship was very well received in common law jurisdictions.[245] Yet the value of his scholarship was put

238 J.P. Niboyet, *Traite de droit international privé français*, vol. 1 (Rec. Sirey 1938) 61 (for the proposition that PrIL can only be national because the formal source of its rules can only be national).

239 Bartin, *Études* (n. 154) 14–16. See also Étienne Adolphe Bartin, *Principes de droit international privé selon la loi et la jurisprudence françaises*, vol. 1 (Domat-Montchrestien 1930) 113.

240 Bonnichon, "La Notion" (n. 104) 18–19.

241 For a biography of Josephus Jitta, see Steenhoff, "Daniël Josephus Jitta" (n. 25).

242 Josephus Jitta, *La methode du droit international privé* (Belifante Fréres 1890) (hereafter Jitta, *La Methode*).

243 See Steenhoff, "Daniël Josephus Jitta" (n. 25) 256 showing how Jitta incorporated both the unilateral and the multilateral, the national, and the supranational perspective: "Jitta, when faced in 1890 with the two trends distinguished by Kosters (the nationalist and the internationalist one), made no choice. [. . .] Jitta acknowledged a right to exist for both branches."

244 See for example Comp. J. Offerhaus, 'L'Université d'Amsterdam et le Droit international privé' in *Ius et Lex—Festgabe zum 70. Geburtstag Max Gutzwiller* (Helbing & Lichtenhahn 1959) 283–302: "However brilliantly conceived and written, Jitta's publications have failed to influence legal practice significantly. His views did not properly link up with the current legal thinking of his time in which the concepts of nationality and sovereignty were the dominant elements."

245 In the United States, Ernest Lorenzen thought his "remarkable" works "will remain landmarks in the science of private international law." See Ernest G. Lorenzen, 'The Renovation of International Law

on hold. His extreme departure from the Austinian theory of state sovereignty as applied to PrIL,[246] his plea for a modern *jus gentium*, his analysis of the scope of a legal relation, his countering of mechanical rules and solutions, and his focus on the ultimate substantive result of the dispute[247] made Thomas Baty (1869–1954) think that "Professor Jitta's exposition of a novel and eminently natural principle is well worthy of attentive consideration, even if the time is not ripe for the immediate adoption by our Courts of his doctrine."[248]

For state-centered internationalists, situating PrIL above national private laws and safe from the particularistic tendencies of national legislators and courts was the ultimate triumph. However, for Josephus Jitta, thought to be "one of the most original thinkers" in PrIL,[249] it was particularly worrying that if PrIL must establish harmonious relationships between laws, "our science becomes a species of supreme law, a law of laws, placed to such extent above the individuals, that it can disregard them."[250] Jitta argued that the conceptualization of PrIL as conflicts of sovereignty and its association with PublIL made the field openly disinterested in the way in which the distribution of sovereignty affects individuals; that PrIL had become increasingly formalistic, lacking any sense of regulatory perspective, and that the field had become obsessed with uniformity at all cost.

Jitta acknowledged that the "contradiction of adjectives" in the term "private international law" is not easy to explain.[251] However, to the extent the term "international" has led authors to conclude that PrIL is similar to PublIL in that it deals with "conflicts of states, or relationships between states and individuals, or conflicts of laws," it must be the "limits of our modern terminology" that have led scholars to such erroneous conclusions.[252] He explained "there is nothing per se in the name 'international' that leads PrIL to PublIL."[253] Instead, he thought our conceptualization of PrIL matters as conflicts of laws can be explained historically and traced back to the statutory theory, in that "the interpreters of our science, who did not have a clear idea of PrIL's goal, but who were perfectly aware of the obstacle created by territorial sovereignty, placed all their attention on the obstacle, and ignored the more distant goal."[254]

by D. Josephus Jitta' (1920) 29 Yale LJ 700, 700 (hereafter Lorenzen, "The Renovation"). In England, Baty thought Jitta's works take "one out of the electrically-lighted salons of conventional theory, heated and illuminated regardless of expense, and a little stuffy, into the dim, fresh dawn of open air." Thomas Baty, 'A Modern Jus Gentium' (1909) 20 Jurid Rev 109 (hereafter Baty, "A Modern Jus Gentium").

[246] See Jitta, *The Renovation* (n. 24) 7: "According to the reasonable principles of international social life, sovereignty, the paramount power in the juridical community of the human species, belongs to mankind, the personification of the human species, and, strictly speaking, exclusively to mankind."

[247] See Steenhoff, "Daniël Josephus Jitta" (n. 25) 238: Jitta was against the idea that one should apply the law of the forum in all cases because "this is false; this is not a proper criterion. You might as well say: take the oldest law, that is the wisest; or take the youngest, for it has benefitted from the others" and 241: "Jitta rejected all neutral choice of law rules. [. . .] A reasonable solution should be sought not by means of abstract rules and general principles, but by means of comparison of law in each separate case."

[248] Baty, "A Modern Jus Gentium" (n. 245) 120.

[249] See Lorenzen, "The Renovation" (n. 245).

[250] Jitta, *La methode* (n. 242) 5.

[251] Ibid., 4.

[252] Ibid., 34–5.

[253] Ibid., 36.

[254] Ibid., 41.

Jitta thought it was a mistake to think that PrIL resembles PublIL more than it resembles private law.[255] Associating PrIL with PublIL would inject the illusion that PrIL deals with some abstract notion of sovereignty, rather than real life problems of people. Also he thought that the mere term "conflict of laws" encouraged overly mechanical solutions and turned PrIL into a "conflicts guillotine." PrIL's obsession with uniformity was also attributed to the conceptualization of PrIL as conflicts of sovereignty: if the field was viewed as settling conflicts between sovereignty and between states, then a uniform "settlement" of such conflicts appeared an ideal outcome. In contrast, analogizing PrIL to private law would make all these assumptions appear ridiculous.

For Jitta, in line with the scope of private law, the purpose of PrIL is not to determine some law as applicable, but rather to analyze the social purpose of a legal relation[256] and to determine what rules of law would be most suitable for the attainment of its social purpose in the international society.[257] According to him "Private International Law is not the science relating to the conflict of laws or lawgivers, but the science of the jural relations between people in a community larger than a State."[258]

Because in Jitta's view PrIL should regulate the international existence of mankind, it could not be limited to choosing between laws, completely disregarding the actual result of the application of such law:[259]

> It is an erroneous idea that private international law has attained its objective when it has chosen from among the laws that touch upon a legal relation ... It is this idea which has converted our science into a conflicts guillotine and has produced these badly chosen questions that the legislator can only resolve by a "sic jubeo" (so ordered).[260]

The association between private law and PrIL made the proposition that PIL performs a structural function of merely choosing between different national laws seem even more ridiculous: "[w]ho, we ask, ever dreamt to see in private law the science which has as its aim the settlement of possible conflicts between different articles of a civil code and deciding which one is applicable in each case?"[261]

In Jitta's view, linking PrIL to private law would allow the field to escape many misconceptions. First of all, it would bring back a profoundly humanistic perspective. PrIL could no longer fail to examine the results the operation of its rules has on

[255] See, e.g., Jitta, *The Renovation* (n. 24) 119: "In searching such a solution, we must bear in mind that private international law is not the science relating to the conflict of laws or lawgivers, but the science of the jural relations between men in a community larger than a State."

[256] Ibid., 90. [257] Jitta, *La methode* (n. 242) 217. [258] Ibid., 119.

[259] See C.C.A. Voskuil, 'A Survey of Dutch Scholarly Practice Concerning Private International Law from 1938 till Present' (1970) 17 Nethl Int'l L Rev 11, 12: "in the universal legal community of man—the pattern of legal relations between individuals, as looked upon by Jitta—the rights and interests of the individual should not be judged by common national or domestic rules and principles, but by standards which might be regarded as *reasonable* from an international or rather universalist point of view."

[260] Jitta, *La methode* (n. 242) 44; Friedrich K. Juenger, 'The Lex Mercatoria and Private International Law' (2000) 60 La L Rev 1134, 1139.

[261] Jitta, *La methode* (n. 242) 43. To use Friendlich Juenger's classification, Jitta is therefore not a "conflictualist," but an "internationalist." See Friedrich K. Juenger, 'The Lex Mercatoria and Private International Law' (2000) 60 La L Rev 1134.

the lives of people. Second, it would eliminate the overly technical focus on settling conflicts and encourage PrIL to focus directly on its regulatory function. To Jitta, private law had a strong and complex regulatory function, and PrIL qua private law would need to recover precisely the strongly normative direction of a substantive area of law like private law, rather than the highly abstract nature of PublIL. Third, understanding and transplanting the regulatory dimensions of private law into PrIL methodology would temper the abstract universalist tendencies of the time. If one understood the various regulatory dimensions of private law norms and concepts one had to develop any degree of universalism from a thorough comparative analysis, rather than any abstract pursuit of uniform general rules.

This was in many ways a revolutionary shift in the PrIL of the late nineteenth century. Jitta was indeed perceived as overly revolutionary, completely changing the landscape of PrIL in ways that were almost incomprehensible for the scholars of the time.[262] Jitta himself was convinced that future generations would be in a much better position to understand his message and his vision.[263] At the same time, Jitta thought the building blocks of his philosophy were already found within the history of the field.

In particular, Jitta pled for a return to the analysis of a legal relation proposed by Savigny. He thought focusing the analysis on legal relations, rather than statutes, was "the dawn of the modern development" of PrIL and had to be recovered and rethought.[264] Jitta would try to forge precisely that recovery and reconstruction of many of Savigny's precepts and to underscore their significant implications.

First, focusing on legal relations meant a revival of the humanistic spirit. "Not the will of a sovereign, but the requirement of a reasonable social intercourse of people, is the decisive element."[265] The applicable law in PrIL cannot possibly be determined in accordance with the sovereign's perception of the reach of its law in defiance of the consequences of its application for the private international relations between individuals. Jitta argued that "[t]he community of nations may exist, but that is not the basis of private international law. The real basis of the said law is the juridical community of mankind. A system of reasonable principles for the international intercourse of people can only be built on such a community."[266]

Jitta blamed Savigny for having been unclear about the contours and implications of his humanistic perspective: "Savigny stopped one step away from the truth, by

[262] See Steenhoff, "Daniël Josephus Jitta" (n. 25) 244: "The method presented by Jitta was received very critically. The idea of a 'legal community of the human race' was generally rejected by all reviewers, whereas the method itself was considered to be too little factual to entrust legal practice to it."

[263] Ibid 237:

> Jitta himself was convinced that he was ahead of his time, and that future generations would be more appreciative of his views. He was in fact a visionary who lived more in the future than in the present, regarding it as his duty to awaken the consciousness of his contemporaries and to prepare them for a concept of private international law based on the "legal community of mankind," a concept he himself never gave up, notwithstanding the terrible First World War and its aftermath.

[264] Jitta, *The Renovation* (n. 24) 90. [265] Ibid., 125. [266] Ibid., 1.

conceptualizing the need for universalism in PIL by reference to the community of states, as opposed to a juridical community of mankind."[267]

Second, recovering a humanistic foundation in PrIL by focusing on interhuman relationships also meant that one could fundamentally challenge the notion of sovereignty, which was used to link PrIL to PublIL. To Jitta, the limitations of state sovereignty in PrIL are not explained in relationship to other states, but rather in relationship to the international community of mankind: "The sovereignty of the State is a derived, a relative and a limited one. It is derived from the sovereignty of mankind, and, as such, it is only a relative one."[268] Therefore, "the state must abstain from measures constituting a violation of the reasonable order of the international social life and it has to act when the said order is requiring an action."[269] Jitta started from the premise of the existence of a "juridical community of mankind."[270] He thereby concluded that the sovereignty of the state is derived, relative, and limited.[271] There are limits on state sovereignty, in the state-citizen, state-foreigner, and state-state relationships.[272] His theory focuses almost exclusively on a thorough understanding of the limits of state sovereignty in the first two relationships, rather than those in the state-state relationship. This is because in Jitta's theory "the duties of the State towards individuals exist, even when the individuals are not its 'subjects'." The State has direct duties toward the individuals, only because they are people, members of the human species, and not because they are subjects of another State; therefore the said duties are independent of reciprocity and do not admit retortion."[273] This was a departure both from the comity and the state-centered theories:

Even in the relations between the State and its own subjects, also in the domain of the pure municipal law, the existence of juridical limits of the sovereignty of the State is scarcely admitted, and, as to the relations between the State and aliens, positive law does not go any farther than the admission of the so called *comitas juris gentium*, a latin, not easily translatable expression, originally implying only a kindliness *between States*, so that reciprocity was a condition and retortions were absolutely lawful. We shall see however, in many parts of the

[267] Jitta, *La Methode* (n. 242) 55. [268] Jitta, *The Renovation* (n. 24) 9.

[269] Ibid., 10.

[270] Ibid., 3. How inclusive the juridical community of mankind would have been is not entirely clear. As I show in Chapter 3, Jitta disavowed the civilized/non-civilized distinction and pled for equality between men and women. Yet in a biography of Jitta, G.J.W. Steenhoff argued Jitta most likely had in mind precisely the European environment of the "mobile" individual with multiple affiliations and that the European community would represent a regional counterpart to his universal community of mankind. See G.J.W. Steenhoff, 'Daniël Josephus Jitta' in *The Moulding of International Law: Ten Dutch Proponents* (T.M.C. Asser Institute 1995) 238, 267–8. In that way, certain parallels between Jitta's theory and contemporary debates around the notion of EU citizenship might be made. On the concept of EU citizenship, see, e.g., Percy B. Lehning, 'European Citizenship: Towards a European Identity' (2001) 20 L & Philosophy 239; Dimitry Kochenov, 'European Citizenship and the Difficult Relationship Between Status and Rights' (2009) 15 Colum J Eur L 169. For the recognition of rights and relationships as a corollary to the mobility of individuals within the EU, see Muir Watt, 'European Federalism and the New Unilateralism' (2008) 82 Tulane L Rev 1983; See also Loïc Azoulai, 'The European Individual as Part of Collective Entities' in Loïc Azoulai, Ségolène Barbou des Places and Etienne Pataut (eds.), *Constructing the Person in EU Law: Rights, Roles, Identities* (Hart 2016) 203.

[271] Jitta, *The Renovation* (n. 24) 8. [272] Ibid., 9–11.

[273] Ibid., 10: Jitta admits that "I am fully aware of the fact that positive law is not in accordance with the principles."

system, that the *kindliness towards nations* is gradually evolving in the direction of the *conscience of a duty towards people*. The interest of the State is a moving-spring in this evolution, but not its basis.[274]

Following his analysis of state sovereignty, Jitta argues that the focus on conflict of laws, as opposed to the nature of legal relations, is caused by a misperception of the social nature of interhuman relationships. Allegedly,

[W]ithin the sphere of national private law, the role of the statute is not disputed. It is not the source, but the product of "law" and law itself is the normal rule of social life, the ensemble of precepts, which allow the individual to enter into relations with other members of the human species, by limiting his liberty against those of others, and the liberty of others against his own.[275]

Why then, he asked:

[O]nce we enter the larger scheme of private international law, everything changes and the statute takes the place of honor, placing law and life at the back-end? Is it that within humanity social life is manifested differently than within a nation? Within humanity, are relationships between individuals established through public authorities or directly, from individual to individual?[276]

This analysis made Jitta conclude that the applicable law is determined based not on the will of the sovereign state, but on the social scope of the legal relation as "a link between two persons or juridical subjects, a link formed and maintained by the social public power, the link being at one end a duty, and at the other end a claim corresponding to the duty."[277]

The practical application of the way in which Jitta reconstructed the notion of sovereignty is best exemplified in his explanation of the citizenship versus domicile debate in PrIL. Jitta thought that the absolute imposition of the law of citizenship for individuals who have established their domicile abroad disregards the limits of state sovereignty in relationship to its own citizens. He was appalled by the fact that "many lawgivers, moved by religious or social-philosophical considerations, have such a high idea of their own absolute and unlimited sovereignty, that they regard themselves entitled to impress the rules of their own laws on their own subjects as an indelible mark."[278] He thought it would be wrong to associate the scenario in which "individuals have established their home abroad, cum animo perpetuitatis" to the idea of "the evasion of law," "sometimes qualified as a fraud."[279] Because the state is the organizing framework of a particular people, but also the local representative of mankind, the free choice of individuals to move to a new state and thereby submit to a different law is not felt by a state as an affront to its authority. Because Jitta sees the juridical community of mankind as the basis of states' sovereignty, a state encourages rather than restricts individuals' tendency to enter into another local sphere of social life:

[274] Ibid. [275] Jitta, *La Methode* (n. 242) 43. [276] Ibid.
[277] Jitta, *The Renovation* (n. 24) 89. [278] Ibid., 106. [279] Ibid.

All individuals have the right to participate in the universal social life by submitting themselves to the laws of different social groups, which constitute humanity, and they will be regulated by them to the degree of the penetration of their activity within the social life of these groups.[280]

On the one hand, unlike in Mancini's theory, the individual is not subsumed under any particular social community, but rather linked to and thereby regulated by various social communities in proportion to the respective social links, including domicile, residence, citizenship, place of contracting etc. Every element of an interpersonal relationship is therefore perceived as a social link, which in turn generates various regulatory needs. Yet the individual was not subsumed under a larger and more vague notion of humanity either. Jitta did not feel the need to separate nationality from other social links or to separate the national from the international, and from mankind. Rather, individuals' existence implicated all these affiliations and all these levels of social embeddedness simultaneously, but to different degrees depending on circumstances and the relationships involved. He perceived the individual as an inherently social being and it is her relational nature which makes her simultaneously embedded in smaller communities of families, friends, nations etc., as well as in a larger notion of humanity.[281] Jitta, as well as Story and Savigny, were both highly skeptical of pushing for universal fraternity given the example of the French revolution, or of inhibiting the individual from engaging in cross-border relationships.

Focusing on legal relations then meant focusing back on the people whose life in the transnational realm is in dire need of a regulatory framework. It meant transferring the focus from an abstract notion of states and state sovereignty to real people. But this did not mean shifting the focus to isolated individuals or to an abstract notion of human reason or individual liberty. Rather, Jitta thought that PrIL needs to focus on interpersonal relationships and their social scope. To Jitta, every PrIL determination represented a projection of a particular social goal for particular relationships between people in the transnational realm.

At the same time, Jitta directly acknowledged that judges in different states might have different understandings of the "social nature" of each legal relation in the transnational realm, because they are inevitably influenced by their national legal and socioeconomic background.[282] Since every judicial determination is influenced by and becomes a symbol of each state's historical, political, social, and judicial individuality, PrIL decisions could vary widely.[283] Yet this did not mean national judiciaries and legislatures would offer arbitrary solutions for PrIL matters. Jitta thought that national judiciaries would neither set their national legal system as a

280 Josephus Jitta, *La substance des obligations dans le droit international privé*, vol. 2 (Belifantes Fréres 1906) 505.

281 For a more detailed analysis of this aspect of Jitta's theory see Chapters 6–8. For a brief exposition, see Steenhoff, "Daniël Josephus Jitta" (n. 25) 242.

282 This problem is reflected in today's analysis of "characterization" which is the process by which a legal matter is "characterized" as pertaining to a particular category of private law (i.e., contract, tort, property) and thereby assigned a particular choice of law rule for that category.

283 Jitta, *La Methode* (n. 242) 75.

procrustean bed for transnational private law relationships,[284] nor could they entirely avoid being influenced by their own legal system.[285] They had to analyze the social scope of legal relations of various degrees of internationality and therefore had to consult and weigh the policies and legal appreciations of these relationships in all states concerned.[286] It is true that individual judges pertaining to different states might reach different decisions on the applicable rules of law, in spite of the fact that they share the same goal and duty toward the international community of mankind.[287] But Jitta perceived this divergence as a direct result of different appreciations of the social nature of particular transnational interpersonal relationships, which could not be overridden by a blind uniform designation of a particular law as applicable, regardless of the social implications.

It is this "absence of universal certainty" with respect to the social scope of a legal relation,[288] which obliges states to cooperate and achieve legal certainty in PrIL.[289] "Each State is bound to collaborate with the other States, and to take by mutual agreement the measures required for the maintenance of the reasonable order of international social life." [290] This duty was portrayed as an expression of a juridical limitation of the State's sovereignty in relationship to individuals.

For Jitta, the universality of PrIL did not rest in the absolute uniformity of PrIL rules at all cost. The universality of PrIL was the expression of a common regulatory goal shared by all states and courts. Because the purpose of PrIL is to apply the law most appropriate for the nature of the legal relation, meaning that law which allows it to develop in the universal community according to its social scope, "every state, even when it is acting in isolation, is bound to recognize, as a source of a duty correlative to a right, every jural relation established in conformity with the requirements of the reasonable order of international social life."[291] The stability of these jural relations and their universal recognition is the symbol of states' direct duty toward individuals and the international society as a whole.

Juxtaposing the eminently regulatory nature of PrIL with the universal nature of the judicial task in PrIL is an important way in which Jitta incorporated universalist elements while at the same time challenging the abstract focus on uniformity within the PrIL-PublIL association. Another important way of looking for this balance was to rethink Savigny's principle of localizing interpersonal relationships. On the one hand, Jitta added to the social lens brought into PrIL by focusing the analysis on interpersonal relationships, a social theory of localizing transnational interpersonal relationships. He argued that localization represents the analysis of "the link that may exist, in a social sense, between the fact and a local sphere of social life."[292]

[284] Josephus Jitta, 'Le Droit commun international comme source du droit international privé' (1908) 4 Revue de droit international privé et de droit pénal international 553, 569–570.

[285] Ibid., 568.

[286] Jitta thought the primary method of analysis in PrIL should be comparative law. For a detailed account of the use of comparative law, see Josephus Jitta, 'Le Droit commun international comme source du droit international privé' (1908) 4 Revue de droit international privé et de droit pénal international 553 and (1909) 5 Revue de droit international privé et de droit pénal international 485.

[287] Jitta, *La Methode* (n. 242) 177–9 and 455.

[288] Ibid., 456.

[289] Ibid., 456, 457.

[290] Jitta, *The Renovation* (n. 24) 11.

[291] Ibid., 91.

[292] Ibid., 97.

Localization "is a matter which requires a thorough analysis of its [the inter-personal relationship's] social aim."[293] A transnational interpersonal relationship can only be definitively localized in one jurisdiction "if it has a predominant social element and if that element caused the legal relation to penetrate in a local sphere of social life."[294]

On the other hand, Jitta opposed the idea that all legal relations can be localized in one jurisdiction.[295] If localization was defined as searching for the social link between an interpersonal relationship and a particular sphere of social life, and if this analysis was guided by an understanding of the social scope of that relationship, it seemed natural that one relationship could have a social impact in a variety of jurisdictions. This was precisely the insight that made Mancini avoid the entire analysis of the nature of jural relations, in order to ensure intransigently uniform rules of PrIL. But to Jitta this was simply an insight that could not be brushed aside, but rather should form the center stage of the method of localizing PrIL matters.

Allegedly, "it is perfectly reasonable to submit a jural relation to the civil law of the local sphere of social life, to which it belongs in accordance with its peculiar nature, provided that the relation belongs to such a local sphere."[296] If a legal relation is not predominantly localized[297] in a national social sphere, one cannot arbitrarily choose an applicable state law simply to give authority to some sovereign. "The jural relation is submitted to the international-common rules of law if these are to be found, and when they are not, to the reasonable principles of the international social life,[298] as a subsidiary source of positive law."[299]

Jitta admitted that this injects quite a high degree of uncertainty in the law and therefore pled for the development of treaties on uniform rules of private law or on matters of PrIL, but with a focus on the substantive result to be achieved by the adoption of particular choice of law rules.[300] When such uniform provisions are absent and when PrIL legal relations do not penetrate in a local sphere of social life,[301]

[293] Ibid., 99.

[294] Josephus Jitta, *La substance des obligations dans le droit international privé*, vol. 2 (Belifantes Fréres 1907) 498.

[295] Jitta's methodology focused on individual legal relations, rather than on the nature of whole private law categories. He therefore viewed choice of law rules developed for entire private law categories as mere presumptions, "a guiding thought." See Jitta, *The Renovation* (n. 24) 106.

[296] Ibid., 91.

[297] Ibid., 97. (For Jitta, localization represented the analysis of "the link that may exist, in a social sense, between the fact and a local sphere of social life.") As to contracts, for example, Jitta explained that the localization of a contract "is a matter which requires a thorough analysis of its social aim ... This restriction is the main difference between the principle of localization and the classical rules for the solution of the conflicts between the national laws, relating to contracts." Jitta, *The Renovation* (n. 24) 99.

[298] In Jitta's theory the judge uses her "judicial consciousness" to find those principles. Josephus Jitta, *La substance des obligations dans le droit international privé*, vol. 2 (Belifantes Fréres 1907) 501–3. Jitta recognized that the judge is connected to the national legal consciousness, which guides her in determining the social scope of a legal relation and the appropriate rules to be applied. Jitta, *La Methode* (n. 242) 75.

[299] Jitta, *The Renovation*, (n. 24) 91.

[300] Josephus Jitta, 'The Development of Private International Law Through Conventions' (1920) 29 Yale L J 497, 500.

[301] Jitta clarified that a PrIL legal matter can only be localized if it has a predominant element and if that element caused the legal relation to penetrate in a local sphere of social life. Josephus Jitta, *La substance des obligations dans le droit international privé*, vol. 2 (Belifantes Fréres 1907) 498.

but rather belong to the international social life, to ask the judge to apply a particular law based on predetermined assumptions about the reach of laws in broad private law categories, in defiance of the ultimate result, would be to "put a judge's judicial consciousness to sleep."[302]

E. Conclusions

PrIL has always been in search of its place within the legal system, as well as of its particular regulatory function. During the nineteenth century, this search was part of larger attempts to connect PrIL either to PublIL or to private law and to focus the theoretical and methodological analysis either on the individual or on the state. To date, the swing of the pendulum between individual-centered and state-centered premises in PrIL has not been thoroughly analyzed in the field, whereas this chapter has shown that it was at the core of PrIL academic debates during the nineteenth century. As nineteenth-century PrIL scholars considered the extent to which PrIL should take the individual or the state as the analytical point of departure, they reveal the contours and implications of an individual-centered or state-centered perspective in PrIL. Many of our current perceptions of the PrIL-PublIL association, or of individual-centered theoretical premises within PrIL can be revisited through a thorough engagement with the nineteenth-century academic debates.

What emerges from revisiting this nineteenth-century academic context within PrIL, I have argued, is that in the theories of the main figures of the nineteenth century, in particular Joseph Story and Friedrich Karl von Savigny, the individual-centered theoretical direction introduced neither an individualistic notion of individual liberty and autonomy, nor an abstract notion of free choice of law. Rather, the individual-centered premises referenced both a concern for human agency and self-determination opposing potentially "despotic" state power, and a social, relational context for individual agency and self-determination in relationship to other people and social communities. Much of PrIL analysis is centered on the interpersonal relationship as an analytical unit evoking both extra-legal social expectations and national regulatory policies. In turn, this interpersonal relationship is linked to particular national communities, as well as to a general notion of humanity and enlarged community of laws. Because of its more complex image of the individual's transnational existence, the methodology proposed in both Story's and Savigny's accounts is highly analytical and sequential, engaged in a constant back and forth between liberty and social responsibility, between the extra-legal social and the legal domain, and between the spirit of the *Volk* and national sovereignty, on the one hand, and the international legal community and humanity, on the other.

It was in large part the complex, analytical background of the individual-centered analysis that prompted state-centered internationalists to switch their focus to the state. In the second half of the nineteenth century the search was for abstract,

[302] Ibid., 503.

unchangeable, and uniform philosophical premises from which uniform PrIL rules were to be constructed. State sovereignty and public authority were among the terms on which PrIL as a field could allegedly "build solidly." The meaning attributed to these notions however remained unclear. And while PrIL would be linked to PublIL, *jurisdictional* sovereignty in PrIL would still be separated from *political* sovereignty in PublIL. This meant that sovereignty in PrIL could be used as a much more abstract notion that appeared not only to overlook, but to explicitly avoid a thorough engagement with policy considerations and political goals. In the PublIL school of thought, the *international* would be set as the priority, and the *public* would be allowed only to the extent that it did not disturb the international. While the association with PublIL did not manage to retain the public dimensions, it did manage to exclude the private, especially in Pillet's and Zitelmann's theories. In those theories, sovereignty and public power are set in opposition to the individuals involved expressing their own expectations for the application of one law or another, or broader appeals to justice. Once PrIL becomes a form of interstate division of sovereignty, it seemed only logical that the individual had no role to play.

At the end of the nineteenth century the Dutch scholar Josephus Jitta aimed to restore the field back to its humanistic foundations. In his view the conceptualization of PrIL as a conflict of sovereignty made the field increasingly formalistic and openly disinterested in the needs and wants of individuals in their transnational existence. But in refocusing the analysis from states to individuals, Jitta did not introduce an atomistic image of the individual, nor did he disconnect private law and PrIL from politics and state regulatory goals. Rather, he reconciled the two by referencing a social, relational image of the individual. He pled for a return to Savigny's focus on the legal relation between individuals, which he used as an anchor to situate the individual within ever wider spheres of relationships: in relationship to the other party(ies) of the private law dispute; in relationship to other individuals and communities, and finally embedded, through their relationships, within one or more communities and within a broader notion of humanity. To achieve that, Jitta departed from what he perceived as a somewhat essentialized localization in Savigny's theory. Instead, he created a theory of the social localization of private law relationships and differentiated between various degrees of internationality of private law relationships. Furthermore, he built upon Savigny's analytical method of searching for the nature of private law relationships by shifting back and forth from extra-legal social considerations to political and policy considerations revealed through a comparative analysis.

3

Individual- and State-Centered Perspectives in Nineteenth-Century Europe

A. Introduction

In an article included in a volume dedicated to Paul Lagarde, the French PrIL scholar Pierre Gothot made some reflections on what he calls "the saga of conflict of laws," namely "the chapter which can be found at the beginning of virtually any treaties or textbook of private international law and which 'narrates' the history of conflict of laws."[1] Gothot noted the irony of the fact that while most—primarily European—PrIL scholars feel compelled to include an account of PrIL's intellectual history in their respective books, few if any engage with the original texts and the meanings their authors meant to attribute to them.[2] Instead, what emerges, according to Gothot, is a sort of diluted, vulgar version of original PrIL theories and methods, to the point where the "narrated" history can depart entirely from the original texts.[3]

Gothot criticizes classical historical accounts for painting PrIL's intellectual history in too broad brush-strokes,[4] for their lack of critical spirit,[5] and for naively portraying a "progressive emergence" of PrIL theories, which does not allow for the refutation of any one of them.[6] Gothot sees in classical accounts a history openly disinterested in an engagement with disruptive debates and critiques among PrIL theorists, as well as disinterested in rediscovering and reconstructing the meaning of original texts.

By contrast, this book aims to highlight precisely the internal debates, critiques, and misunderstandings that generated particular theoretical and methodological directions in PrIL. It also does not focus on a "saga" of theories and methodologies in PrIL over time, but rather on a particular issue, namely the implications of taking the state or the individual as an analytical point of departure in PrIL.

The next three chapters consider the trajectory of the individual-centered and the state-centered perspectives in the intellectual history of PrIL until roughly the

[1] Pierre Gothot, 'Simples Réflexions à Propos de la Saga du Conflit des Lois' in *Le Droit International Privé: Esprit et Méthodes. Melanges en l'honneur de Paul Lagarde* 342 (Daloz 2005) (hereafter Gothot, "Simples Réflexions").

[2] Ibid., 344. [3] Ibid., 344, 346. [4] Ibid., 346.

[5] Ibid: "history conserves, still today, a prestige which does not directly depend on the rigor of the critique and the quality of the erudition."

[6] Ibid., 347.

Nineteenth-Century Perspectives on Private International Law. Roxana Banu. © Roxana Banu 2018. Published 2018 by Oxford University Press.

middle of the twentieth century. Specifically, they create a transnational genealogy of these perspectives as they rose and fell while being transplanted, re-interpreted, and incorporated in various countries. They show that individual-centered perspectives were often ignored, misunderstood, or unduly associated with an individualistic, overly liberal ideology. In order to recover and partly reconstruct the individual-centered perspective that I term "relational internationalist" it is therefore necessary to explain how and why individual-centered arguments were misunderstood or ignored.

The first of these three chapters focuses on the main academic debates in nineteenth-century Europe. These debates centered on PrIL's relationship to private law and PublIL, as well as on the extent to which individual or state interests should be the focus of PrIL theory and methodology.

This chapter begins with an account of the way in which Savigny's scholarship has been interpreted and incorporated in German PrIL theory and beyond. In particular, it shows that initially Savigny's theory was stripped of its individual-centered underpinnings and occasionally even interpreted as entirely state-centered. This interpretation is significant, given the wide-ranging influence of Savigny's scholarship in a large number of countries.

Second, by looking at an academic debate between Josephus Jitta and the German nineteenth-century PrIL scholar Ludwig von Bar (1836–1913), this chapter shows that nineteenth-century internationalists[7] failed to fully engage with or even acknowledge the "relational internationalist" perspective. In other words, the very academic debates among internationalists contributed to the overshadowing of the distinction between individual-centered and state-centered internationalist perspectives. By misunderstanding, misstating, or completely ignoring each other's arguments, internationalists made the distinction less sharp and less relevant for scholars outside the internationalist school.

This, among other factors, made it possible for Franz Kahn to split PrIL theory at the end of the nineteenth century between internationalists and particularists without there being a sense that any distinctions were lost within the internationalist school of thought. The third section of this chapter explains how creating the divide between nationalists and internationalists solidified the lack of engagement of the discipline with a particular relational variation of the internationalist perspective. Furthermore, this chapter reveals how the nationalist school of thought made a name for itself by associating PrIL with domestic private law,

[7] Throughout this book "internationalism" and "universalism" are used interchangeably, as they were used in the majority of nineteenth- and twentieth-century PrIL scholarship. Pierre Gothot however made a distinction between "internationalist universalism" and "universalism," although it is not entirely clear what motivated this distinction. On the one hand, the former could presumably describe the universalist school which focused on the interstate framework of co-operation generated by the PrIL-PublIL association, while the latter could describe alternative (including, presumably relational internationalist) universalist perspectives. On the other hand, it is likely that Gothot classified "multilateral" PrIL rules under the term "universal internationalist" while classifying the combination between multilateral and unilateral rules, which was prevalent at the time of his writing, as "contemporary universalism." Pierre Gothot, 'Le renouveau de la tendance unilatéraliste en droit international privé' (1971) 60 Rev crit dr int privé 417, 430.

failing to acknowledge the private-law focused internationalist arguments of the previous generation. Late nineteenth-century scholars offered a new meaning for the PrIL-private law association, which remained engrained in the consciousness of PrIL.

Last, this chapter looks at the way in which the individual-centered versus state-centered distinction crystalized in the beginning of the twentieth century in England, and whether this was a reflection or even a transplant of the continental debates. In particular, it highlights the way in which English nineteenth-century PrIL scholars reasoned on the conflicts that may arise between considerations of private justice and state sovereignty.

Overall, then, this chapter tries to map how the European academic discourse in the second half of the nineteenth century reflected on the way in which PrIL should incorporate and respond to state—or individual—interests and rights.

B. Savigny's Legacy

Savigny's PrIL theory is considered one of the most important, if not the most important, PrIL theory of the nineteenth century, having influenced an impressive number of scholars, national courts, and codifications.[8] It might therefore be assumed that, at least since the English translation of his eighth volume, the individual-centered aspects of his PrIL theory have been part of that virtually worldwide influence. Yet, as noted in the first chapter, PrIL theory appeared predominantly state-centered, particularly in continental Europe in the nineteenth century.[9]

This section explains how the predominantly state-centered underpinnings of PrIL theory can not only be reconciled with, but partly explained by the way in which Savigny's PrIL theory was received and interpreted in the nineteenth century. In particular, it aims to show that as opposed to the individual-centered underpinnings of his theory, it was mostly his reference to an ever-growing community of law and his formal maxim of the "seat of a legal relation" that were influential in the shaping of nineteenth-century PrIL theory and methodology. State-centered theories have referenced and heavily relied on the notion of the community of law/states in ways that can hardly be reconciled with Savigny's own theory.[10] Similarly, the concept of the seat of a legal relation was brought to a much higher level of abstractness, which in contrast to Savigny's own theory, disconnects this principle

[8] For a detailed account of the influence of his theory on the development of PrIL in Germany, the United States, England, France, and Belgium, see Max Charles Gutzwiller, *Der Einfluss Savignys auf die Entwicklung des Internationalprivatrechts* (Gschwend, Tschopp 1923) (hereafter Gutzwiller, *Der Einfluss Savignys*).

[9] See André Bonnichon, 'La Notion de conflit de souverainetés dans la science des conflits de lois' (1949) 38 Rev crit dr int privé 615: "it is a common statement among the modern scholars of PrIL that the conflict of laws boils down to a conflict of sovereignties."

[10] See Gutzwiller, *Der Einfluss Savignys* (n. 8) 42–4 (arguing that "while this notion [of the community of states] has exercised a significant influence on PrIL theory and methodology, Savigny himself drew virtually no conclusions from this notion for his own theory").

from both the individual interests and rights at stake in PrIL relationships and the principles underlying the laws which regulate them.[11]

Pierre Gothot is therefore right to note in his "reflections" on the saga of conflict of laws, that we should distinguish between Savigny and "Savignism."[12] As he notes:

> Savigny's extraordinary prestige made it possible for his disciples, very different from one another, to have not retained much else from Savigny's theory than his principle of the community of laws and the analytical method.[13]

Gothot argues that the saga of conflict of laws' intellectual history generally portrays the "vulgar" version of Savigny's theory—Savignism—rather than the meaning Savigny meant to attribute to his theory.[14] Thus, notes Gothot, "the thinking of Savigny, by far the most prestigious author of the theory of conflict of laws, remains so little known in its totality and entailment."[15]

This section confirms Gothot's intuition that it is precisely the individual-centered starting point that was lost from Savigny's theory.[16] Overall, however, this book argues that Savigny's theory can be subject to two different kinds of biases: on the one hand, ignoring the individual centered-premises of his theory and on the other hand associating his individual-centered premises with a libertarian ideology. By contrast, Gothot seems to believe that ignoring its individual-centered premise made it possible for scholars to idealize Savigny's theory, rather than subject it to a thorough critique (presumably for being overly individualistic).

1. The international community of states

Although Savigny constructed an individual-centered theory to determine the applicable law in a transnational legal matter, he did not argue directly that the application of a particular foreign law is mandated by a direct obligation of states toward individuals. Whereas Savigny argued that the application of a particular law must reflect the litigating parties' submission under that law,[17] Pillet noted that Savigny offered no explanation for why states must recognize such submission.[18]

[11] See Andreas Bucher, *Grundfragen der Anknüpfungsgrechtigkeit im internationalen Privatrecht (aus kontinentaleuropäischer Sicht)* 22 Schriftenreihe des Instituts für Internationales Recht und internationale Beziehungen (Helbing & Lichtenhahn 1975) 10–14 (hereafter Bucher, *Grundfragen der Anknüpfungsgrechtigkeit*) (arguing that Savigny's principle of the seat of the legal relation was unduly interpreted as overly abstract and individualistic. Bucher argues that Savigny's notion of the "seat of a legal relation" focused on individual interests and rights, as well as the policies and principles of the various national laws relating to specific PrIL relationships). See also Gutzwiller, *Der Einfluss Savignys* (n. 8) 44–5 (arguing that post-Savigny, his notion of the seat of the legal relation, is used without recourse to any normative considerations).

[12] Gothot, "Simples Réflexions" (n. 1) 348ff. [13] Ibid., 350. [14] Ibid., 354.

[15] Ibid., 354. [16] Ibid., 352.

[17] For my interpretation of Savigny's concept of "voluntary submission," see Chapter 6.

[18] Antoine Pillet, 'Droit international privé consideré dans ses rapports avec le droit international public' (F. Allier Père & Fils 1892) 309, 336, and 367–8. (Pillet agreed with the principle of "the unity of successions" meaning that the entire estate had to be distributed according to the personal law of the decedent, irrespective of the type of property. However, he thought that it would be impossible to oblige states to respect this principle by reference to the individual's personal autonomy. This would change, however, if it could be showed that "the unity of successions is a natural consequence of the nature of

Rather, Savigny suggested that the mutual recognition and application of different national laws is grounded in the constantly evolving community of law.[19] Yet, while he invokes the community of law/nations in order to construct a universalist theory that moves states to recognize one another's laws, he does not derive any choice of law rules from it.[20] Gutzwiller noted that "Savigny's reference to the community of states and his concept of the seat of the legal relation run parallel to each other and are not brought into connection by any legal construction."[21] Savigny did not seem "to derive any of the many possible conclusions from his reference to a community of states. In particular, he does not derive his own theory from it."[22]

Despite the fact that Savigny did not construct a state-centered theory from his concept of the "ever evolving community of law among states," Gutzwiller was able to observe in 1923 that "Savigny's Public International Law starting point has been universally recognized."[23] PrIL theories everywhere started referencing in one form or another Savigny's maxim of the "ever evolving community of states."[24] However, rather than being used, as in Savigny's theory, as a convenient slogan to push states toward universalism, it later became the basis for PrIL theory and methodology. Most universalist theories developed after Savigny were not only primarily state-centered, but portrayed their theories as a continuation of Savigny's doctrine by referencing his "community of states."[25] Yet the

laws of this sort and that a certain state cannot refuse the recognition of this unity without implicitly rejecting the authority of the foreign law and offending the sovereign which enacted the law and its interests of seeing it enforced.") For the way in which Pillet tried to reach similar results to Savigny, while justifying them by reference to state sovereignty, see André Bonnichon, 'La notion de conflit de souverainetes dans la science des conflits de lois' (1950) 40 Rev crit dr int privé 11, 22:

> By the nature of things, we are left with what we have called the functional or essential principle. We search for a just and useful solution; we examine the nature of the legal relation in dispute. But in order to remain faithful to the line of reasoning we have adopted, we disguise such motives under the cover borrowed from the term sovereignty. This way, for example, the social scope of a law will reveal whether the attribute of permanence of this law will make way to that of generality. This can be examined from the angle of justice or the nature of a legal relation. But we add: this way [by referencing sovereignty] the necessary sacrifice will be demanded from the sovereignty, which will incur the least detriment. In reality this is reverting to a criterion of justice or social utility, but at the same time attributing the term of reference, not without sacrifice, to the concept, allegedly fundamental, of conflict of sovereignty.

[19] Friedrich Karl von Savigny, *Private International Law and the Retrospective Operation of Statutes: A Treatise on the Conflict of Laws and the Limits of their Operation in Respect of Place and Time* (William Guthrie tr., T&T Clark 1880) 44 ("community of legal convictions"), 45 ("community of different nations"), 59 ("community of laws"), 71 ("community of law among independent states"), 76 ("community of law obtaining between different states") (hereafter Savigny, *Private International Law*).

[20] Gutzwiller, *Der Einfluss Savignys* (n. 8) 44. This also mirrors Blaine Baker's observation that while Story uses comity to push states to cooperation, he does not derive a state-centered PrIL theory from it. See Blaine Baker, 'Interstate Choice of Law and Early-American Constitutional Nationalism. An Essay on Joseph Story and the Comity of Errors: A Case Study in Conflict of Laws' (1993) 35 McGill L J 454. For a discussion of Baker's interpretation of Story, see Chapters 2 and 6.

[21] Gutzwiller, *Der Einfluss Savignys* (n. 8) 44.

[22] Ibid., 38, n. 23 (Gutzwiller also includes references to previous works by other PublIL and PrIL scholars mentioning the community of states. Yet he argues that this reference and the relationship between PrIL and PublIL remain quite vague until the post-Savigny literature).

[23] Ibid., 44. [24] Ibid., 45. [25] Ibid.

community of states finds a very different place in these theories, both conceptually and analytically.[26]

At the end of the nineteenth century the community of states is even more explicitly linked to and included in a theory of PrIL elaborated on the basis of PublIL, primarily by Zitelmann and Pillet.[27] These authors constructed their theories as a reaction both to previous universalist theories relying on Savigny and to emerging nationalist skeptics. As to the former, they charged universalists with being overly vague about the way in which PrIL connects to PublIL.[28] They saw themselves as the first ones truly carrying Savigny's universalist credo to fruition by establishing a theory entirely relying on the PrIL-PublIL association.[29] In arguing this way, it appeared as though this association was implicit or inevitable for the internationalist theory of PrIL. What they saw themselves doing was simply explaining in a more substantiated way why it was correct to invoke the association and how it could translate into a PrIL methodology. Success in this endeavor was also meant to counter the nationalists who were arguing that a universalist theory in PrIL via the PrIL-PublIL association was not conceptually tenable.[30]

Whether acknowledged or not by universalist writers themselves, these developments created a shift in perspective from Savigny's writings.[31] Savigny's choice of law methodology was modeled according to what he perceived to be the rights and interests of the "community of individuals," which could be discerned through an analysis of individual legal relations.[32] The "community of laws among states" appeared as a convenient construct that enabled the universal recognition and enforcement of individual reasonable expectations and interests.

With Pillet and Zitelmann the relationship between the community of states and community of mankind within PrIL theory is reversed. The interests and rights of the states within a community become the basis for choice of law rules. The community of individuals is merely the beneficiary or victim of a formal and uniform distribution of authority, which is otherwise based on the rights and interests of states.

[26] See Gutzwiller's description of how the French scholars Frantz Despagnet and Jules Valery refer to Savigny's community of states as well as his maxim of the seat of a legal relation, but use those concepts in very different ways and draw different conclusions from Savigny's. Gutzwiller, *Der Einfluss Savignys* (n. 8) 140.

[27] Ibid., 45.

[28] For a description of Pillet's and Zittelmann's theories, see Chapter 2.

[29] See Gutzwiller, *Der Einfluss Savignys* (n. 8) 45.

[30] See Franz Kahn, 'Gesetzeskollisionen, Ein Beitrag zur Lehre des Internationalen Privatrechts' (1890) 30 Jherings Jahrbücher für die Dogmatik des Bürgerlichen Rechts 1; Franz Kahn, 'Abhandlungen aus dem internationalen Privatrecht' (1898) 39 Jherings Jahrbücher für die Dogmatik des Bürgerlichen Rechts 1 (hereafter Franz Kahn, "Abhandlungen 1898") and (1899) 40 Jherings Jahrbücher für die Dogmatik des Bürgerlichen Rechts 1 (hereafter Franz Kahn, "Abhandlungen 1899").

[31] André Bonnichon, 'La notion de conflit de souverainetes dans la science des conflits de lois' (1950) 40 Rev crit dr int privé 11, 11–13 (describing the transition from Savigny's theory to the theory of conflict of sovereignties).

[32] Gutzwiller, *Der Einfluss Savignys* (n. 8) 42.

2. The seat of the legal relation

Legal scholarship not only relied on Savigny's concept of the ever-increasing community of states in ways that depart from Savigny's own theory. They also overwhelmingly incorporated his maxim of the "seat of the legal relation," while disconnecting it from Savigny's normative justifications, both by stripping it of its individual-centered tenets and by raising its level of abstraction.[33] Gutzwiller noted that "the concept has become so widely used,[34] that one would be inclined to see a worldwide spread of the Savignyan doctrine, while at a closer look the concept has lost almost any relationship to Savigny's own theory."[35]

First, the maxim of the "seat of the legal relation" was disconnected from its individual-centered justification and occasionally directly linked to a view of PrIL as the division of sovereign authority among states.[36] In his account of Savigny's influence on the development of PrIL Gutzwiller noted that "for the most part only the convenient and graphic term of the 'seat' remained from Savigny's theory. Nobody concerned himself anymore with the individual-centered analysis which led Savigny to his concept."[37]

In Savigny's theory, the "seat of the legal relation" was not an entirely abstract, normatively empty concept, but rather centered on the way in which he viewed the relationship between the individual, the legal relation, and law.[38] Savigny was clear that laws are a necessary pre-requisite for the existence of individual rights and that the state and state law are an absolute necessity for the legal expression of

[33] For a general account of Savigny's use of the term, see Paul Heinrich Neuhaus, 'Savigny und die Rechtsfindung aus der Natur der Sache' (1949) 15 RabelsZ 364.

[34] Gutzwiller, *Der Einfluss Savignys* (n. 8) 84: "The Savignian principle of the seat of the legal relation has become a common good of the jurisprudence. The concept of the 'seat' has been so widespread that it appears as though it would have something to do with the technical concept of the law or with an old inventory of the common science. The idea that each legal relation has a seat and that only the law of the seat must be applied has become a common sense principle for which there is no need of a justification for the jurisprudence."

[35] Ibid., 84–9. Andreas Bucher reaches the same conclusion arguing that the concept has reached such a high level of abstraction that it has lost virtually any normative grounding (either individual-centered or policy-centered). Bucher, *Grundfragen der Anknüpfungsgrechtigkeit* (n. 11). See also Theodor Niemeyer, *Vorschläge und Materialien zur Kodifikation des internationalen Privatrechts* (Duncker & Humblot 1895) 59: "the Savignian theory [of the seat] has been adopted by the scholars and courts of most civilized states and in particular in Germany (here primarily through the influence of von Bar's writing) and it has reached such influence that its principles have become the customary law." Some PrIL scholars writing after Savigny have replaced Savigny's term of the "nature of the legal relation" with the concept of the "nature of things," drawing different conclusions and different methodologies than Savigny. See Ludwig von Bar, *The Theory and Practice of Private International Law* (George Robertson Gillespie tr., W. Green & Sons 1892). For Gutzwiller's account of von Bar's theory, see Gutzwiller, *Der Einfluss Savignys* (n. 8) 62ff & 85. For a discussion of the distinction between Savigny's term of the nature of a legal relation and von Bar's term of the nature of things, see Eugène Gaudemet, 'La théorie des conflits de lois dans l'ouvre d'Antoine Pillet et la doctrine de Savigny' in *Mélanges Antoine Pillet* (Sirey 1929) 89, 101, n. 1: "We must also observe that Savigny's formulation, *nature of a legal relation,* is more precise than that of von Bar, *nature of things*, with which Pillet seems to confuse it (*Principes,* p. 281), and is not that different from Pillet's. There is without a doubt a strong similarity between the *nature of a legal relation* and *the social scope of the law* which regulates it."

[36] See Gutzwiller, *Der Einfluss Savignys* (n. 8) 45. This mirrors a distinction made in Chapter 6 between state-centered and individual-centered perspectives pertaining to the concept of vested rights.

[37] Ibid., 40. [38] Ibid., 43.

the people.[39] However, while acknowledging and reinforcing the state and state law, he did not conceptualize PrIL as the delimitation of sovereign authority between states.[40] Rather, his conceptual points of departure are the individual and the "community of individuals," rather than a community of states.[41] Savigny framed the PrIL question in dual terms: one could start from a legal norm and ask what its sphere of application is, or start from the legal relation and ask what norm it is governed by.[42] He believed the two questions should lead to the same answer because both ways of framing the question capture the same link between the individual, the legal relation, and the state.[43]

In other words, regardless of how the question is framed, both the analysis of a PrIL matter and the ultimate answer to the dispute must consider the way in which individuals have decided to structure their legal relations, the way in which they relate to each other and to various communities, as well as their aims and expectations.[44] Gutzwiller summarizes Savigny's individual-centered premises thus:

> Only through this detour to the individual and only because Savigny localizes the legal community of individuals in the actual territory to which they submit, rather than the state that grants them citizenship,[45] does he come to ask which territorial law must be applied to each legal relation. The seat of the legal relation is therefore a concept that connects individuals with the legal relations they enter into and, in turn, connects the latter to a geographical space and its laws. The mere confluence with the traditional question of choosing between different national laws is not the obvious point of departure for the Private International Law problem for Savigny, but rather the result of a much larger construction that starts off with the individual.[46]

Second, in subsequent scholarship inspired by Savigny, his concept of the seat of the legal relation not only lost its individual-centered premises, but was also brought to a much higher level of abstractness than Savigny had provided for.[47] The process of finding the "seat" would either be portrayed as quasi-scientific and therefore objective, or simply commonsensical and therefore not requiring much justification.[48] Gutzwiller noted that in Savigny's theory, the process of localizing a legal relation according to its nature instructs the judiciary or legislator to:

[39] Savigny, *Private International Law* (n. 19) 57.

[40] Gutzwiller, *Der Einfluss Savignys* (n. 8) 41.

[41] Ibid., 42.

[42] Ibid., 41; Savigny, *Private International Law* (n. 19) 47.

[43] Bucher, *Grundfragen der Anknüpfungsgrechtigkeit* (n. 11) 40 (arguing that Savigny's double starting point had been underappreciated and might have caused us to interpret Savigny's theory as overly individualistic).

[44] See Chapter 6.

[45] Savigny refers consistently to the concept of the people ("das Volk"), which would suggest that nationality would be an important concept of his theory. For an explanation of how and why Savigny adopted domicile as the most relevant connecting factor for private law and PrIL, see Hans-Christof Kraus, 'Begriff und Verständnis des "Bürgers" bei Savigny' (1993) 110 Zeitschrift der Savigny Stiftung für Rechtsgeschichte Römische Abteilung 552.

[46] Gutzwiller, *Der Einfluss Savignys* (n. 8) 42.

[47] See Bucher, *Grundfragen der Anknüpfungsgrechtigkeit* (n. 11); Gutzwiller, *Der Einfluss Savignys* (n. 8) 40, 85, 140. For an account of German jurisprudence relying on the concept in a variety of ways, see Gutzwiller, *Der Einfluss Savignys* (n. 8) 84, n. 13.

[48] Gutzwiller, *Der Einfluss Savignys* (n. 8) 84, 85.

> [C]onsider the legal (maybe even factual) elements of the legal relation, the subjective rights, etc. and to draw conclusions from these elements which can be useful for the Private International Law question. From this point of view, the "nature of things" is simply a helpful element in the process of interpretation. Yet a quick look at the jurisprudence shows that it has not used the concept in this harmless way, but that it has turned this into a heuristic principle, which can easily lead to very different conclusions. Now the concept should be used with much more care.[49]

For Savigny the seat of the legal relation was to be justified and determined by an analysis of the way in which the legal relation was constructed, its defining elements, the legal rules which apply to it, and so on.[50] Later, it was transformed into a maxim that surreptitiously leads to a variety of conclusions while necessitating almost no analysis and no justification.[51]

C. The Debate Among Universalists

At the end of the nineteenth century Josephus Jitta took stock of the state-centered direction in which PrIL theory was developing. He too argued that Savigny's ambiguous use of the term "community of laws among states" had made him "stop one step away from the truth" and had overshadowed and made less apparent the individual-centered tenets of his theory.[52] In his first book on PrIL[53] and an article published in the *Archiv für Öffentliches Recht* in 1899,[54] Jitta argued that PrIL scholars failed to realize the different directions in which PrIL could develop, depending on whether the individual or the state becomes the conceptual point of departure.[55]

Ludwig von Bar, one of the most prominent PrIL scholars in Germany at the time, reviewed the "new principles and methods" in late nineteenth-century PrIL, including Jitta's work, in order to determine whether they were truly bringing fundamental critiques of the prevailing theories (including his own).[56] This led to an interesting academic exchange between Jitta and von Bar in three articles published in the *Archiv für Öffentliches Recht* in 1899 and 1900. This exchange offers a valuable glimpse into the way in which the individual-centered/state-centered distinction was perceived at the time within the universalist school. It represents a rare occasion in which the distinction itself is brought to the surface for discussion and critique.

In 1899, Jitta published an article in the *Archiv für Öffentliches Recht* on the "nature of PrIL," in which he tried to contest the leading view that PrIL should

[49] Ibid., 85. [50] Bucher, *Grundfragen der Anknüpfungsgrechtigkeit* (n. 11) 9–17.

[51] Gutzwiller, *Der Einfluss Savignys* (n. 8) 88.

[52] Daniel Josephus Jitta, *La Méthode du droit international privé* (Belinfante 1890) 111 (hereafter Jitta, *La Methode*).

[53] For a discussion of Jitta's theory, as espoused in his first book on PrIL, see Chapter 2.

[54] Josephus Jitta, 'Das Wesen des internationalen Privatrechts' (1899) 14 AOR 301 (hereafter Jitta, "Das Wesen").

[55] Ibid.

[56] Ludwig von Bar, 'Neue Prinzipien und Methoden des internationalen Privatrechts' (1899) 14 AOR 1 (hereafter von Bar, "Neue Prinzipien").

produce rules that choose between different national laws.[57] He argued that this view's insistence on describing PrIL rules as fundamentally different from private law norms had made scholars oblivious to the fact that PrIL norms nevertheless regulate interpersonal relationships, rather than relationships between states qua relationships between their laws.[58] Jitta invited us to think of PrIL as a sort of private law itself, just as focused on the regulation of interpersonal relations as private law. The only one, albeit highly relevant, factor that distinguishes the two fields is that while PrIL is supposed to respond to and incorporate the legitimate interests and expectations of a wider society, domestic private law will consider primarily the national society's interests.[59]

In light of this analogy with private law and the underlying emphasis on PrIL's regulatory function for individuals, it should become clear, in Jitta's view, that devising rules of legislative jurisdiction (choice of law rules) is only one of many possible methods that PrIL could employ to respond to the legitimate interests of a wider society, and as such, it must always be subordinate to the actual goal of regulating a society wider than the national one.[60] In other words, PrIL's goal is the regulation of a society of individuals beyond the national borders, and choosing between the laws of different states is simply one of many possible means to achieve this goal. Jitta believed that only the state-centered framing of PrIL matters made it appear as though choosing between different national laws is itself the goal.[61] Jitta pled "not for norms of choice between laws but for norms of application (Anwendungsnorm) for a wide law of interactions (Verkehrsrecht)."[62]

Furthermore, Jitta argued that shifting from a state-centered to an individual-centered perspective on PrIL meant that states, individually as well as collectively, had direct obligations toward the international society as a whole. One would no longer justify a decision to apply a certain law in terms of comity or reciprocity, but rather directly as an obligation toward individuals.[63] It is important to note that Jitta generally does not refer to the obligation of states or courts toward the litigating parties alone, but rather to the international society as a whole.[64] Because he believed that private law relationships and norms are always embedded in a larger social context, implicating not only the litigating parties, for Jitta the social scope of each legal relation referenced the international society. In his theory, not only the litigants, but international society as a whole, had a legal claim, an interest, in a legal dispute being decided in a certain way.[65] This implicitly acknowledged that adopting certain approaches to solving private law and PrIL matters had systemic implications for the whole society (national in the case of private law and international for the international society).[66] In this sense, "Private international law must analyze each legal claim of international society in itself, and if one agrees that private law must be social, then PrIL must be *doubly social*."[67]

[57] Jitta, "Das Wesen" (n. 54) 304. [58] Ibid., 307. [59] Ibid., 309.
[60] Ibid., 309. [61] Ibid., 310. [62] Ibid., 326. [63] Ibid., 314.
[64] Ibid., 307, 309, 321. [65] Ibid.
[66] See Chapter 2; Josephus Jitta, 'Alte und neue Methoden des internationalen Privatrechts' (1900) 15 AOR 564 at 568 (hereafter Jitta, "Alte und neue Methoden").
[67] Jitta, "Das Wesen" (n. 54) 321.

Last, while most internationalists embraced the PrIL-PublIL association as progressive, Jitta believed that breaking the relationship would be liberating for PrIL. Freeing PrIL from PublIL meant that PrIL would detach itself from the many ambiguities and concerns at the heart of PublIL.[68] Connecting PrIL to private law, in Jitta's view, would make PrIL more analytical than structural, and more directly focused on individuals' rights and interests in the international context.

As such, Jitta's critique of PrIL's common path up to that point appeared quite crushing of previous PrIL scholars, as well as of several of his contemporaries. Ludwig von Bar was one of the authors that Jitta's critique is quite directly addressed to. Jitta described von Bar's methodology in the following way:

> For each legal institution Von Bar creates a patterning of the different laws and legal systems with which it might be connected, for example the lex domicilii or originis personarum, the lex rei sitae, fori, actus or contractus etc.; then he makes a choice between those identified laws, based on different rationales, sometimes reason, sometimes custom, sometimes by reference to other authors or rules set up by international congresses. This choice represents the law that each judge of the world, given the alleged universal binding force of international private law must apply, as long as there are no diverging norms in the laws of its country.[69]

To Jitta this was the classical definition of creating "laws about laws," while completely failing to engage with the regulatory needs and legal claims of international society.[70] Von Bar responds to Jitta's critique in an article in the same volume of the *Archiv für Öffentliches Recht*. While defending the leading academic current of the time, of which he was clearly part, von Bar struggles to understand Jitta's claims. First, he found it astonishing that Jitta had "changed" Savigny's postulate of the international community of states to that of mankind.[71] Von Bar seemingly perceived this as a significant departure from tradition that could not be so easily made.[72]

Second, von Bar was critical of the fact that Jitta contented himself with creating an approach, a theory, without devising a catalogue of norms that courts would apply to different PrIL cases.[73] He was concerned that shifting the conceptual point of departure—from states to individuals—not only might change something in the substance and the results of PrIL decisions, but also seemed to change the contours of the methodology by injecting more complexity.[74] In some sense it seemed as though the individual-centered perspective (even if one agreed that it was indeed a separate internationalist perspective) would be even more difficult to embrace if it made the field more complex.

Third, von Bar found it preposterous that Jitta was actually challenging the usefulness of the PrIL-PublIL association, and even challenged the activity of the Institute

[68] Ibid., 320. [69] Jitta, "Alte und neue Methoden" (n. 66) 574. [70] Ibid.

[71] Von Bar, "Neue Prinzipien" (n. 56) 2.

[72] Jitta himself understood this as a departure from Savigny because he too thought Savigny had referenced a community of nations, rather than a community of law. See Josephus Jitta, *The Renovation of International Law on the Basis of a Juridical Community of Mankind* (Martinus Nijhoff 1919) 1. (Jitta references directly von Bar's criticism: "I was asked how I dared to disagree with such an authority as Savigny; this is a question not deserving any answer.")

[73] Von Bar, "Neue Prinzipien" (n. 56) 3, 8. [74] Ibid.

for International Law, blaming it for uncritically connecting PrIL with PublIL.[75] For von Bar, it was hard to see how any level of internationalism could emerge outside of the Institute and outside of PublIL. Jitta was making the more complex argument that internationalism is not useful in itself, but only if it allows PrIL to regulate the international society in a coherent and substantive way. Von Bar found it hard to understand how anybody could challenge internationalism especially on any other ground than the usual positivist critique.[76]

Von Bar was not only puzzled by the methodological changes that Jitta suggested would follow from taking the individual-centered perspective seriously. He also struggled to understand how the individual-centered perspective could be understood as different from a state-centered perspective. He believed his own principle of looking for "the influence that should be attributed to a territorial law over a legal relation with a foreign element" is just as individual-centered as any other.[77] In broad terms, even when one "speaks of the jurisdiction of a norm, one still thinks of people."[78] Similarly "all PrIL scholars reference vested rights"[79] so it must be that under a state-centered perspective an individual-centered perspective is always subsumed. This also made it hard for von Bar to understand how the legal claims of the international society that Jitta referenced repeatedly would not find their materialization in the national laws from which one had to choose.[80] It appeared, as though for von Bar a state was merely the aggregation of individuals; the international, the aggregation of different states; and the transnational, the aggregation of national laws, so that every state-centered approach would imply an individual-centered one. After all, even the formalism that Jitta criticized "leads to legal certainty which is for the benefit of the individuals."[81]

Lastly, von Bar found it puzzling that Jitta resisted what he described as overly formalistic and naïve internationalist tendencies in the scholarship of the time while pleading for the recognition of a worldwide community of mankind. Von Bar was concerned that focusing on individuals everywhere would expand internationalism beyond the "civilized (Kulturstaten) states."[82] In some sense this showed that Jitta

[75] Ibid., 6, 9, 15. In his first book Jitta also analyzed the activity of the Institute of International Law with respect to Private International Law. See Jitta, *La Methode* (n. 52) 398 (arguing that "from the beginning and without any hesitation [the Institute] connected PrIL with PublIL, by considering it not as a series of inter-individual relationships, but as a series of conflicts that arise among the civil and penal norms and which are meant to be settled through international treaties." The Institute "does not take any account of the duties of individual states towards the international society of individuals" and it is obsessed "with general rules.") Von Bar was worried that splitting the Institute in two parts would cast a shadow on the institute itself. See von Bar, "Neue Prinzipien" (n. 56) 15–16.

[76] In the last section of the paper von Bar responds to the positivist critique to internationalism made by Franz Kahn. See von Bar, "Neue Prinzipien" (n. 56) 39.

[77] Ibid., 8. [78] Ibid.

[79] Ibid., 4, 5. Chapter 6 shows how, although many PrIL scholars of the time refer to vested rights, they create different theories of vested rights depending on their theoretical standpoint.

[80] Ibid., 7.

[81] Ibid., 9, 10. (Von Bar thought that pursuing uniformity of PrIL rules meant that "one proposes individual states to give up on parts of their national legislation (sovereignty) which is not essential, in order to achieve general legal certainty and the effectiveness of their own laws across the purely physical legal sphere.")

[82] Ibid., 14: "The international conceptualization of the law of marriage within the European cultured states cannot be placed in connection with that of the Negro people (Negervolke), which does

was perhaps even more naively internationalist than those he was attacking, so it seemed hard to understand what Jitta was reacting to.

In the subsequent volume of the *Archiv für öffentliches Recht,* Jitta responded to von Bar's "more stingy than decisive" critique.[83] He purported to show that von Bar failed to understand the distinction between making the international community of mankind, rather than the international community of states, the point of departure in PrIL, because von Bar, like many of his contemporary PrIL scholars, was not aware of a contradiction within their own theories.[84]

Jitta argued that in the theories of most PrIL scholars of the time, including von Bar, even if the goal of PrIL might be individual-centered, the underlying principle and method were state-centered.[85] For Jitta there was a disconnect between arguing that PrIL aims to "provide for and protect the coherent and peaceful engagement in inter-human relationship between individuals" and then providing a method that aims to "choose between different national laws according to the nature of things"[86] or on a division of sovereignty.

Jitta thought the fact that PrIL scholars maintained this duality in their writing meant either that authors did not genuinely believe in the individual-centered goal of PrIL and simply used it as rhetoric, or that they failed to understand that the goal would lead to certain conclusions incompatible with their state-centered methodologies.[87] In response to von Bar, Jitta aimed to show how the latter is most likely the case and particularly damaging for the development of PrIL.

Jitta argued that if PrIL scholars agreed with him that "PrIL is the private law of mankind and that its goal is to satisfy the legal demands of this society and ensure a dignified relationship between all individuals,"[88] then one needed to develop a method that was "the road taken in full awareness of the goals and nature of the particular legal field and which is meant to find the means to achieve these goals."[89]

Jitta did not consider von Bar's appeal to the "nature of things" as a method capable of ensuring a regulatory goal for PrIL, but rather as helpful advice in the interpretation process, thus reverting to Savigny's view.[90] Jitta argued, as Gutzwiller later would as well, that "the nature of things" was being used as a transcendental notion or as an appeal to rationality that prevented an actual analysis of the legal demands of the litigating parties and of the international society.[91] This in turn was made possible because PrIL did not perceive itself as having any actual substantive dimension, but simply a role of coordinating legal systems in a structural way. But if PrIL was focused on the individuals, it would be impossible to deny it a substantive dimension. Instead, Jitta argued that the structural obsession of PrIL is the result of the state-centered imagery of "choosing between laws."[92]

not yet know the concept of a marriage, at least not in the conventional and practical way in which one deals with PrIL matters."

[83] Jitta, "Alte und Neue Methoden" (n. 66) 564. [84] Ibid. [85] Ibid., 566–8.
[86] Ibid., 568. [87] Ibid., 571. [88] Ibid., 567.
[89] Ibid., 566 (arguing that "only scholars who at least agree about the goals can argue about method").
[90] Ibid., 566. [91] Ibid. [92] Ibid., 572–4.

The concern was less to inquire into the demands of regulating international society properly and more to devise a way of choosing between laws because the latter is arguably what would interest states in relationship to each other.[93] In other words the coordination that may be required from a state-centered perspective may be different from the one required by individuals for their international existence. In the process of merely "choosing" it was easy to imagine that the goal is to reconcile the field of application of those laws and the sovereignty of the states, rather than to fulfill some regulatory aim for the society.[94]

Conceptualizing PrIL as the area of "laws about laws"[95] also created the impression, in Jitta's view, that the only way to regulate an international society, if that was even a uniform understanding of PrIL's goal, is through the application of one national law or the other. This in turn obscured the fact that national laws do not always take into consideration and do not reflect the international dimensions of individuals' legal existence. To Jitta, von Bar's argument that the individual could simply be subsumed under the state and the national under the international was just confirmation that PrIL scholarship fails to account for the divergence between the individual-centered and the state-centered internationalist perspective.[96] Similarly, if Jitta was not ready to move beyond a method to secure a catalogue of rules that would apply intransigently, as von Bar required, it was because he was skeptical about the extent to which general choice of law rules (just as national substantive rules) would be able to fully capture the complexities of transnational legal matters, or rather would manage to prevent an actual engagement with the international society's legal requirements.[97] Furthermore, Jitta argued that the civilized/uncivilized distinction that von Bar was eager to maintain made little sense from an individual-centered perspective.[98]

Last, Jitta addressed what seemed to be an underlying consideration in von Bar's skepticism about the individual-centered internationalist perspective, namely the fear of discretion, complexity, and lack of positivity that an individual-centered perspective might generate.[99] Jitta was aware that the PrIL rules that would result from a determination of the "ideal rules demanded by the international society" could only serve as "a norm of reason," rather than a positive norm:[100]

> When the legislator has issued its command, the international society and the judges are slaves of the laws, even to the detriment of reason. If the legislator is silent, the judge must, with unrestrained freedom, determine how the state should have reasonably regulated. In such circumstances positive norms are modeled after the reasonable requirements of the international society. However, this is the case both for national, as well as international private law,

so it should not be given additional relevance in the transnational context.[101]

Overall, in the context of this academic exchange between Jitta and von Bar, Jitta indirectly offered three possible ways of understanding the relationship between

[93] Ibid., 573. [94] Ibid., 572, 574. [95] Ibid., 574. [96] Ibid., 568, 572, 573.
[97] Ibid., 574. [98] Ibid., 569; Jitta, "Das Wesen" (n. 54) 315.
[99] Jitta, "Alte und neue Methoden" (n. 66) 576, 577. [100] Ibid., 576. [101] Ibid.

individual-centered and state-centered arguments at the end of the nineteenth century. It is particularly interesting to take account of them, since they might be helpful in imagining the relationship between the two perspectives today.

One possibility is that authors do not actually agree on whether PrIL's concern should be the sound intercourse of people, or the preservation of state sovereignty within interstate relationships. If this is the case, then the divergence of methodology is a clear consequence of the different ways in which the goals are conceptualized.[102]

Another possibility is that scholars do indeed envision an individual-centered goal, but do not realize the tension between this goal and the state-centered methodologies they are offering. Of course, in the same vein it is possible that the international community of individuals was simply not a conceptual possibility at the time. When Batiffol noted that for internationalists all "inter-human relationships take place as inter-state relationships," he seemed to suggest not that scholars do not wish to make the difference between the two, but that they do not have the ability, conceptually and analytically, to separate the two.[103] It is worth thinking whether this imagery is available today.

Last, Jitta believed that the quest for positivism might explain the state-centered approach and the relationship between PrIL and PublIL. On the one hand, the positivist movement might explain the need to construct PrIL relationships as conflicts of national laws.[104] It is easy to understand why grounding PrIL analysis in existing national laws, rather than Jitta's sociological analysis of the legal claims of the international society, would appeal to positivists. However, he believed that we must account for the fact that the tension between positivism and the reasonable requirements of social life is just as present in PrIL as in national private law, so it should not look more surprising in the transnational context and certainly should not move one more toward positivism in PrIL than it would in domestic private law.[105]

On the other hand, Jitta did not think that constructing the relationship between PrIL and PublIL should be a necessary step for a positivist, because he doubted that PublIL itself fulfilled the criteria of positivism any more than PrIL did.[106] The fact that authors like Franz Kahn constructed their nationalist theory on the argument that the relationship between PrIL and PublIL does not provide PrIL with a solid positivist foundation seems to have confirmed Jitta's intuition.[107] However, within the universalist theory, Zitelmann and Pillet both believed that constructing a relationship between PrIL and PublIL would give a firm legal grounding to the obligation of states to implement one law or another. They criticized Savigny precisely for the fact that his theory, by not linking PrIL with PublIL, failed to explain why states would be obliged to apply foreign law and a particular law in each case.[108]

[102] Ibid., 566.
[103] Henri Batiffol, 'Principes de Droit International Privé' (1959) 97 Recueil des Cours 431, 437–8.
[104] Jitta, "Alte und neue Methoden" (n. 66) 576–7.
[105] Ibid.
[106] Jitta, "Das Wesen" (n. 54) 320.
[107] See the next section for a discussion of Franz Kahn's main insights.
[108] See Chapter 7.

D. Universalism Versus Particularism

At the end of the nineteenth century the three developments alluded to in the previous two sections—the alleged continuity in the internationalist school with reference to Savigny, the impact of positivism on PrIL, and the lack of proper engagement with one another's arguments within the internationalist school—crystalized in what would be "a new era" for PrIL.[109] This new era was generated by Franz Kahn's splitting PrIL scholarship between nationalists and internationalists.[110]

In general terms Franz Kahn's distinction between nationalists and internationalists solidified the cover of ideological differences within the universalist school and in particular the individual-centered versus state-centered distinction. Franz Kahn perceived the internationalist school as a unified conception. The vast differences in methodology, theoretical precepts and legal conclusions, generated by those theories, were likely viewed as minutia that could be subsumed under the larger umbrella of universalism. All the authors described in the first chapter were included in the internationalist school without the sense that any important distinctions were thereby overlooked.[111] Whatever disagreements existed within the international school were viewed as a sign of incoherence, rather than important normative distinctions.[112]

This leveling of ideological differences is not only the consequence of failing to properly engage with the theories of the various internationalist writers, but is also caused by the way in which Franz Kahn seems to define internationalism. Interestingly for example, Jitta is included in both the internationalist and the particularist school of thought: his plea for the co-operation of states for the good of the international society makes him an internationalist,[113] whereas the part of his writing focusing on the "individual method," namely on the individual state, places him in the nationalist school.[114] This completely overlooks the way in which Jitta argued that the state acting individually through its legislature or judiciary (the individual method) and states acting together all have the same goal of coherently

[109] Gutzwiller, *Der Einfluss Savignys* (n. 8) 74. [110] Ibid.; Franz Kahn, various (n. 30).

[111] Franz Kahn, "Abhandlungen 1899" (n. 30) 20, n 1 and 2.

[112] Ibid., 25:

> If only those theoreticians were in agreement we could at least view that, if not as an existing, at least an evolving international conviction. We would see the mountain from the sun of the emerging international law, whereas we [the particularists] would still be covered in the darkness of confusion. Yet that is not so. Our internationalist theoreticians are in the middle of the darkness. They keep fighting about the content of their international law; they are only in agreement that despite all doubt, international law exists and must exist.

See also Arthur Nussbaum, 'Rise and Decline of the Law-of-Nations Doctrine in the Conflict of Laws' (1942) 42 Colum L Rev 189, 194–5 (describing the universalist doctrine as "a virtually unified conception [. . .] despite some quibbling differences between the Savignian and Mancinian schools of thought").

[113] Franz Kahn, "Abhandlungen 1899" (n. 30) 20, n. 2 and accompanying text.

[114] Ibid.

regulating an international society of individuals.[115] The fact that an individual-centered perspective can create an internationalist perspective in itself seems to not be acknowledged. Rather, the split between nationalists and internationalists is made according to the level of constraint imposed on states by other states in devising their PrIL rules and methods.

It is the association of internationalism with the level of interstate obligation of coordination that made it possible for Franz Kahn to lay out the entire internationalist theory under the rubric of "the relationship between PrIL and PublIL"[116] and to often contrast it with a theory that connects PrIL with private law.[117] Allegedly, "PublIL is the law whose subjects are only states. Only the specialized PrIL theorists managed to inject some confusion into an otherwise universally recognized principle of PublIL."[118] He charged PrIL scholars for either not recognizing that PrIL deals with individuals and their interests, while PublIL deals with states, or for creating the impression that although PrIL deals with individual interests, it is still a branch of PublIL or of a larger area of international law.[119] Clearly he does not acknowledge the scholarship of Jitta and Savigny as trying to devise a universalist theory that is precisely based on the relationship between PrIL and private law and focused on individuals.

Franz Kahn is happy to make the observation (which he perceives quite novel) that if one acknowledges that PrIL deals with individuals one would connect PrIL with private law, rather than PublIL.[120] But the individual-centered internationalist authors had made this claim all along. However, Franz Kahn attributes a different meaning to the observation.

On the one hand Kahn thought that if PrIL is connected with private law, it must be domestic private law and it then becomes clear that states are acting in the realm of the national again. No constraint on their activity in the realm of PrIL can be imposed on them by other states. And, again, only constraints from other states appear relevant. The way in which states would be constrained by their duties to individuals directly, citizens and foreigners, is simply out of sight.[121] It is in this way that the

[115] See Chapter 2 for a discussion of Jitta's general universalist premises. See also Jitta, 'Alte und neue Methoden' (n. 66) 577.

[116] Franz Kahn, "Abhandlungen 1899" (n. 30) 18ff. [117] Ibid., 23.

[118] Ibid., 29. At n. 2 Franz Kahn cites PrIL authors who, while separating international law into private and public, depending on whether they deal with states or individuals, still refer to PrIL as a law dealing with interstate relationships regarding their laws.

[119] Ibid., 29. [120] Ibid., 30.

[121] The obligation of "international justice" is equally refuted. See Frank Kahn, "Abhandlungen 1899" (n. 30) 32 and 34 (arguing that scholars who try to connect PrIL with PublIL would need to "prove more, namely that PublIL really does impose the recognition and enforcement of individual rights," whereas if PrIL was a form of national private law, there would be no obligations at all that the state would need to take into consideration). Frank Kahn cites favorably Thomas Erskine Holland, *The Elements of Jurisprudence* (Clarendon Press 1880) 345: "It follows from the independence of each State within its own borders that it might without contravening any principles of international law regulate every set of circumstances which calls for decision exclusively by its own law." See also Franz Kahn, "Abhandlungen 1899" (n. 30) 39 (alleging that the "credo of the nationalist school" is the acknowledgment that "the legislator is completely free when assessing the influence of international elements, its discretion is in no way limited by PublIL," while admitting that in extraordinary circumstances, the exclusive application of the forum's law could be seen as an "abuse under PublIL").

PrIL-private law association gets a new meaning and becomes the emblem of a more particularistic view of PrIL that can make the field as oblivious to its global systemic implications as the state-centered internationalist perspective did.

On the other hand, Kahn is careful to remind us that the fact that PrIL does not generate substantive norms is "an undisputable fact that cannot be underscored enough."[122] While the association between PrIL and private law is useful in "nationalizing" PrIL, it is not useful if it could lead to the impression that PrIL has a direct regulatory function. Here again the "new" PrIL-private law association is different from the one, which grounded the relational internationalist perspective, in particular for Jitta.

Similarly, for Franz Kahn, thinking of PrIL as public law would not be useful either because it might resonate with internationalists who were trying to think of PrIL as a sort of international law of federalism.[123] PrIL therefore is "neither public, nor private," but nevertheless domestic.[124] Allegedly, only this way of thinking about PrIL would support the view that states have no obligations whatsoever in their assessment of PrIL matters, with the exception of extreme cases, which could be classified as "abuses under international law,"[125] or "certain concessions that states might make towards the international community."[126]

Kahn's analysis had an almost entirely underappreciated impact on the development of PrIL. His distinction between particularism and internationalism was uncritically adopted as a way of telling the history of nineteenth-century PrIL.[127] Kahn's leveling of nuances within the internationalist school of thought continued in subsequent accounts of internationalism versus nationalism in PrIL.[128] At the same time, the meaning he attributed to the PrIL—private law association—survived and managed to define and limit the way in which we perceive of the association today. Contemporary PrIL scholars often suggest that PrIL's private law dimensions make the field less focused on its systemic global implications and attempt instead to recreate the PrIL-PublIL association, as the only viable internationalist route.[129] The individual-centered internationalist perspective is not conceived as an option and in fact it is unclear whether it is even historically acknowledged as part of PrIL theory.

Aside from creating a powerful imagery of the ideological division within PrIL and of the (new) relationship between PrIL and private law, Kahn also solidified a distinction between internationalism and positivism. Theodor Niemeyer in Germany

[122] Ibid., 52. [123] Ibid., 40. [124] Ibid., 53.

[125] Ibid., 40 and 42 ("the international community has a claim against abuses").

[126] Ibid., 41.

[127] Henri Batiffol, 'Principes de droit international privé' (1959) 97 Recueil des Cours 431; Arthur Nussbaum, 'Rise and Decline of the Law-of-Nations Doctrine in the Conflict of Laws' (1942) 42 Colum L Rev 189; Juan Antonio Carillo Salcedo, 'Le Renouveau du Particularisme en Droit International Privé' (1978) 160 Recueil des Cours 181.

[128] See Gutzwiller, *Der Einfluss Savignys* (n. 8) 74.

[129] See Joel R. Paul, 'The Isolation of Private International Law' (1988) 7 Wis Int L J 149; Horatia Muir Watt, 'Private International Law Beyond the Schism' (2011) 2 Transnatl Leg Theory 347; Jacco Bomhoff, 'The Constitution of the Conflict of Laws' in Horatia Muir Watt and Diego P. Fernández Arroyo (eds.), *Private International Law and Global Governance* (OUP 2015) (arguing that recreating the PrIL-PublIL association would be an alternative to the constitutionalist framework he develops).

for example was building upon Kahn's ideas when he pled for a clear "method in the sense of a positivist theory of PrIL and a clear distinction between lex lata and lex ferenda."[130] Internationalism is now contrasted with positivism[131] and as such allowed to enter the PrIL analysis only as a gap-filler. Internationalist arguments are occasionally brought to bear to temper overly nationalist tendencies or "abuses" as Franz Kahn called them. Similarly, when there is no clear guidance in positive law, scholars occasionally rely on "the spirit of the law, the legal science, legal interpretation, legal relation, or the nature of things" as fundamentally "diluted Savignyan concepts" without any kind of unified normative understanding of PrIL's regulatory goals.[132] Rather, they reconstruct those terms to create a variety of theories that can be understood as the early expressions of vested rights[133] and interest-analysis theories,[134] none of which was envisioned by or easily subsumed under Savigny's theory.[135]

Because Kahn began the dilution of internationalism as a whole and because what was now contrasted with internationalism would be constructed by reference to private law, the PrIL-private law association becomes an emblem of the nationalist movement. It became hard to appreciate that another association with private law, in both a substantive and internationalist direction ever existed. Furthermore, a relationship between nationalism, private law, and positivism was created in a way

[130] Gutzwiller, *Der Einfluss Savignys* (n. 8) 74; Theodor Niemeyer, *Zur Methodik des internationalen Privatrechts* (Duncker & Humblot 1894) 5, 9, 26, 34, 38.

[131] See Franz Kahn, "Abhandlungen 1899" (n. 30) 23, 24, 27, 28. This contrast is particularly pervasive in Anglo-American writing. See for example the Lord Chief Justice of England (Russel) in the speech on international law before the American Legal Congress of Saratoga Springs cited in Franz Kahn, "Abhandlungen 1899" (n. 30) 24–5, n. 1:

> Whereas in the latter (the continental school of thought) what I shall call the ethical and metaphysical treatment is followed, in the former (the Anglo-American), while not ignoring the important part which ethics play in the consideration of what international law ought to be, its writers for the most part carefully distinguish between what is, in fact, international law from their views of what the law ought to be. Their treatment is mainly historical. By most continental writers ... theory and fact, law and so-called rules of nature and of right, are mixed up in a way at once confusing and misleading.

[132] Gutzwiller, *Der Einfluss Savignys* (n. 8) 77.

[133] See for example Carl Crome, *System des deutschen bürgerlichen Rechts* (J. C. B. Mohr 1900) 218: "One must assume that the facts and inter-human relationships must be analyzed according to the moment when they arise (originate) and when they are created with legal consequences by a particular territorial law; this legal consequence must be subsequently recognized and considered everywhere else." See also Friedrich Endemann, *Lehrbuch des bürgerlichen Rechts. Einführung in das Stadium des Bürgerlichen Gesetzbuchs*, vol. 1 (9th edn., C. Heymann 1903) 81: "the starting point is the fact that each legal system is limited territorially by the sphere of its sovereignty. The private law elements must be distributed among the territorial legal spheres."

[134] See for example Konrad Cosack, *Lehrbuch des deutschen bürgerlichen Rechts* (1st edn, Gustav Fischer 1910) 41: "the general principle underlying German PrIL is that a PrIL legal matter must be determined in German courts by the law of the state which has the highest interest to determine the matter according to its discretion" and 47: "If Germany has such an interest it is mandated to apply its law and reject the application of a foreign law. If Germany does not have such an interest, it must apply the foreign laws which are potentially applicable together, as long as they do not give rise to a fundamental contradiction." See Gutzwiller, *Der Einfluss Savignys* (n. 8) 78, n. 75 (calling this early version of interest-analysis the most "astonishing amateurishness").

[135] The distinction between relational internationalist theories on the one hand and individualistic vested rights and interest-analysis theories on the other hand will become apparent in Chapters 6 and 7.

that does not allow for the kind of elaborate reasoning and sociological observation regarding the regulatory needs of the international society that Jitta was advocating and believed would derive precisely from associating PrIL with private law.

E. Sovereignty and Vested Rights in Late Nineteenth-Century English PrIL Scholarship

The relationship between positivism and internationalism in both its state-centered and individual-centered counterparts becomes particularly relevant in late nineteenth-century English PrIL scholarship. In England positivism was an argument to resist the internationalist movement in PrIL on the continent. Albert Venn Dicey famously distinguished between the Continental "theoretical" method and the British "positive method."[136] In the PrIL context, this characterization of the English positive method was meant to counter the assumption that "fundamental principles of private international law can be ascertained by study and reflection and that the soundness of the rules maintained, say in England, as to the extra-territorial recognition of rights, can be tested by their conformity to, or deviation from, such general principles."[137] In other words, there neither is a "common law" nor is it possible to assume that if it did exist it was "tacitly adopted by all civilized nations" and even less so that they might have an obligation to adopt it.[138] To say that PrIL was part of some universal law was wrong. If the precepts of positivism are to be taken seriously, one had to think of PrIL as national law.

Then again, the positivist/non-positivist distinction does not entirely overlap the nationalist/internationalist distinction, as Franz Kahn occasionally suggested.[139] This is most evident in late nineteenth-century English PrIL scholarship in two ways. First, PrIL scholars, including most prominently Dicey, argued that the application of foreign law is not a matter of "caprice or option," but rather flows directly from a sense of "justice" and "inconvenience," "logical and practical necessity."[140] Second, the fact that no state is directly constrained by any other to apply a particular law does not mean that there is no convergence. Rather, there is a natural convergence,[141] "a community of the aim," which flows from the universal goal to "secure the extra-territorial effect of rights."[142] In other words, states were not in

[136] A.V. Dicey, *A Digest of the Law of England with Reference to the Conflict of Laws* (Stevens & Sons 1908)(hereafter Dicey, *Digest of the Law of England*) 16.

[137] Ibid. [138] Ibid.

[139] Franz Kahn, "Abhandlungen 1899" (n. 30) (Kahn believed that positivism leads to nationalism, which might then be tempered by some level of comparative analysis).

[140] Dicey, *Digest of the Law of England* (n. 136) 10–11. See also John Westlake, 'Relations Between Public and Private International Law' in Lassa Oppenheim (ed.), *The Collected Papers of John Westlake on Public International Law* (CUP 1914) 305 (hereafter Westlake, *Collected Papers*): "It is not a vague comity, but the force of reason, which binds us to recognize foreign laws and the rights which they originate."

[141] Dicey, *Digest of the Law of England* (n. 136) 11: "The selection of one or more of these laws is not a matter of caprice, but depends upon more or less definite reasons which are likely to influence all courts and legislators."

[142] Ibid., 12.

any way constrained to apply foreign law by other states, but they were constrained directly by the principles of justice associated with the concept of vested rights and these constraints might actually move them toward uniformity of decisions.

In this way, positivism was used in late nineteenth-century English scholarship as a means both to free the consciousness of the national judge/legislator and maintain the sovereignty of states in relationship to each other,[143] and to inject "vested rights" as a universal and presumably stable and constant concept to guide PrIL theory and practice. Thus "the application of foreign law does not arise from the desire of the sovereign of England, or of any other sovereign, to show courtesy to other states. It flows from the impossibility of otherwise determining whole classes of cases without gross inconvenience and injustice to litigants, whether natives or foreigners."[144]

But while positivism might have been a factor that indirectly facilitated an individual-centered reasoning for *the possibility of applying* foreign law in general,[145] it had the opposite effect when determining the *factors* to be included in choice of law rules, which is most evident in John Westlake's theory. Both Westlake and Dicey argued that states have obligations directly toward individuals to apply the law of the state under which their rights vested. However, when determining where those rights vested, Westlake was clear that one could not rely on "abstract justice and moral claims."[146] Rather, one had to rely on some body of "positive law" that could establish the limits of the authority of states in enacting laws and creating rights.[147] It is at the point of *substantiating* "vested rights"[148] that PrIL reconnects to PublIL.[149] Westlake's reconstruction is worth quoting at length:

Without the help of Public International Law the problem of Private International Law cannot be solved. For if we admit that such questions [of vested rights] are not to be left to the unstable equity of tribunals, which at the command or with the support of their governments may read the law of nature by the light of prejudice and interest, then must the idea of their solution contain two things: the selection on common principles of some positive law by which the rights of parties are to be determined in their inception, and the universal recognition of rights which have once sprung from the appropriate law. [. . .] The limits of the respective national authorities that enact laws, and any validity conceded in one country

[143] Ibid., 10: "If the assertion that the recognition or enforcement of foreign law depends upon comity means only that the law of no country can have effect as law beyond the territory of the sovereign by whom it was imposed, unless by permission of the state where it is allowed to operate, the statement expresses, though obscurely, a real and important fact."

[144] Ibid., 11.

[145] See for example Westlake, *Collected Papers* (n. 140) 306: "Perhaps, if we discussed this subject to a merchant, we should find that the universal validity of a right which has once accrued was his leading idea of it, as, in spite of manifold lapses in its application, it certainly has been the leading idea of courts of justice." For a history of the development of English conflict of laws, see Alexander N. Sack, 'Conflicts of Laws in the History of the English Law' in A. Reppy (ed.), *Law, a Century of Progress, 1835–1935: Contributions in Celebration of the 100th Anniversary of the Founding of the School of Law of New York University* (New York University Press 1937) 342 (hereafter Sack, "Conflicts of Laws").

[146] Westlake, *Collected Papers* (n. 140) 296–7.

[147] Ibid., 297.

[148] Chapter 6 elaborates on how a theory of vested rights that relies on the PublIL-PrIL association differs from the nineteenth-century relational internationalist theory recovered in this book.

[149] Westlake, *Collected Papers* (n. 140) 297. See also Dicey, *Digest of the Law of England* (n. 136) 13, n. 1 (citing Pillet's theory as a very good exposition of how to conceptualize the relationship between PrIL and PublIL, while maintaining the concept of vested rights).

to the rights, which have arisen by the law of another, must depend on the express or tacit agreement of nations.[150]

British PrIL theory of the nineteenth century was constructed as a middle ground: the universal validity of a right should be taken as the "leading idea of the merchant," whereas the "public law of nations" would help us "ascertain who in each case has the authority to originate a right by giving a command."[151] The determination of where a right vested is made by considering which state has the authority to vest it "in its inception," which in turn mirrors the analytical framework which Pillet and Zitelmann attempted to include in PrIL through the PrIL-PublIL association.[152]

In late nineteenth-century English PrIL, there is, in other words, a blend between a non-territorial "general equity" and an individual-centered justification for the application of foreign law, on the one hand, and the territorial view of law's legitimacy and a reliance on state sovereignty in determining formal criteria for when rights vested, on the other hand.[153] As the next two chapters show, in the twentieth century each of the two elements generated different PrIL theories derived from the notion of vested rights. In the United States, Joseph Beale relied primarily on the concept of territoriality and state sovereignty to identify formal elements that connect rights to particular jurisdictions and ensure their universal recognition once "vested" in a territory. In England the concept of "justice" became the signpost for a PrIL theory focused on a liberal recognition of rights and individual liberty.

F. Conclusions

Despite Jitta's efforts to recover the individual-centered premises underlying Savigny's theory while emphasizing a fundamental social component, PrIL in the nineteenth century was moving in between the Continental theory of PrIL as conflicts of sovereignty and the English model of focusing on vested rights and often creating a mix of the two perspectives. Jitta thought that emphasizing the social, relational

[150] Westlake, *Collected Papers* (n. 140) 297. [151] Ibid., 306.

[152] Ibid., 307–8. (While the ascertainment of the limits of legislative authority on which the concept of vested rights rests connects PrIL with PublIL "through the idea of sovereignty," there are cases that Westlake believed are either "beside" or "even opposed to a theory" connecting PrIL with PublIL.) Westlake admitted for example: "I do not know that I could justify the law of the domicile, as the rule of testaments and successions, to one who did not admit the conception of a continuation of the person of the defunct." While it seemed difficult to show that states had agreed among themselves, even tacitly, that the law of domicile should regulate all testaments and successions, Westlake argued that:

> ... the history of European law contains nothing more beautiful than the evolution of the idea of the person from that of the family and the mysterious perpetuity which clings to the former as a memory of its source. [...] That it is clear that the rule must be taken from that spot to which the deceased had his most intimate and permanent attachment, where is the seat of that family from whose broken continuance the idea of his own representation is derived.

[153] See Sack, "Conflicts of Laws" (n. 145) 398. (Arguing that this blend of arguments can be explained historically by the "special features of the law and of the administration of justice which left their imprint upon the course of development of the English law on conflicts of laws in the 19th century, and even upon the English law on the subject as it stands today.")

component of transnational interpersonal relations would integrate the individual into ever-wider social spheres and thereby achieve a perpetual cross-reference between the interests of various individuals and social groups. Associating PrIL with private law was meant to create a more normative, regulatory and socially focused alternative to what he perceived to be an overly formalistic state-centered perspective, which explicitly eliminates any scope for individual agency and contestation.

By the end of the nineteenth century Jitta was not alone in attacking the PublIL school. Yet the attack coming from scholars like Franz Kahn was focused on the naiveté of internationalism, rather than its dogmatism. This meant that the attack could be directed at every scholar presuming any degree of universalism for PrIL, not just those who framed universalism in state-centered terms. PrIL was then split between universalism and particularism, without there being a sense that the universalist thesis was constructed in fundamentally different terms by those whose point of departure was the individual and those whose point of departure was the state. Whereas for Jitta focusing on private law and on the individual were cast in juxtaposition to formalism, as well as both individualistic and statist perspectives, for Franz Kahn focusing on the individual and private law meant focusing on the national, rather than the international.

Much of the critique of universalism that Franz Kahn started resonated with Dicey. From a positivist perspective there was no doubt that states had no obligation to apply each other's laws. But there was an obligation grounded in a larger sense of justice and fairness to individuals to recognize their vested rights. In turn the notion of vested rights would split in two directions. One option, favored by Westlake, was to reference vested rights to answer the question why a court would ever apply foreign law and then to reference PublIL to find out which state had the authority to vest which rights in which cases. Another option was to maintain a certain vagueness about the pool of considerations employed to find out under which law a right vested. This meant that vested rights could also be drawn from more general notions of liberty, autonomy, and justice. One can find this way of conceptualizing vested rights in Dicey's theory. As outlined in the next chapter, this conceptualization was recast in twentieth-century English PrIL theories, which referenced broad notions of justice and individual liberty.

4

Tracing the Relational Internationalist Perspective in Europe After the Second World War

A. Introduction

Franz Kahn's late nineteenth-century writing on PrIL split the scholarship into two broad camps of nationalists and internationalists, thereby writing off many of the nuances in each camp, while his nationalist premises started a new way of thinking. Both nationalism and internationalism would keep reoccurring in many variations during the twentieth century. And within this recasting of an old debate the individual-centered/state-centered duality reappears as well in a different context and with different arguments.

Nineteenth century state-centered arguments were derived from a vague and formal notion of state sovereignty pushing states toward uniformity of PrIL rules and principles. Jitta's revival of individual-centered arguments was meant to counter the formalism of the sovereignty thesis as well as the structural internationalism of the PrIL-PublIL association. By contrast, early twentieth-century state-centered arguments recast state sovereignty precisely as a reaction to internationalism and as a symbol of unfettered discretion in setting up PrIL norms and regulations in each state. In the twentieth century, individual-centered arguments are offered to push for systematicity, predictability, and universal recognition of vested rights. All these arguments are meant to bring PrIL back to internationalism or at least to a philosophy of moderation where internationalism is tempered by nationalism, individualism by state-centered arguments, private law by public law etc. They are part of a renewed interest in the philosophy of PrIL and a search for the higher principles of the field.

Toward the middle of the twentieth century, European scholars like Henri Batiffol and Gerhard Kegel would derive PrIL philosophy from PrIL methodology. For those scholars the methodological arsenal of PrIL is explained by and justified through a theory of "coordination of legal systems" or "conflicts justice." This represents both a revival of a theoretical interest in PrIL and a restatement of old methods and techniques.

English PrIL scholars also take part in this quest to rewrite a theory of PrIL. Whereas in the nineteenth century Dicey had contrasted the English practical

Nineteenth-Century Perspectives on Private International Law. Roxana Banu. © Roxana Banu 2018.
Published 2018 by Oxford University Press.

method with continental theoretical idealism, twentieth-century English PrIL scholars take center stage in the theoretical debates on the higher principles of PrIL. Perhaps most surprisingly, English twentieth-century PrIL scholars are also the ones to revive the PrIL-PublIL association of the nineteenth-century debates centered primarily on the continent. However, whereas nineteenth-century continental European scholars had argued that PrIL can learn from PublIL by incorporating the prevailing notions of state sovereignty, peaceful coexistence of states, and fundamental rights of states, mid twentieth-century English writers argued that it is PublIL that can learn from PrIL by recognizing the individual as a subject of law and ensuring the recognition of vested rights.

Despite these strong individual-centered arguments in twentieth-century English PrIL scholarship, as late as 1970 F.A. Mann will try to revert the field to the nineteenth-century rapprochement between PrIL and PublIL on the basis of international jurisdiction. Yet he too joins fellow English scholars in arguing that it is PublIL that can now learn from the theory of international jurisdiction developed in PrIL. Allegedly, the expertise of uniformly dividing jurisdiction among states was, by the time of Mann's writing, firmly anchored in PrIL and from there it can be incorporated into PublIL more generally.

The "new" European philosophy of PrIL in the twentieth century is a combination of a broad—and often quite vague—concept of coordination of legal systems and the thesis of transnational recognition of vested rights; both of these concepts are now thought of as the philosophical gifts that PrIL can offer PublIL, bringing these fields back together via a different route.

This chapter outlines the way in which state-centered and individual-centered arguments reappear in the European theories of the twentieth century. It starts by briefly describing the state-centered nationalist arguments that dominated PrIL in the first few decades of the twentieth century. Those arguments reject an overall philosophy of PrIL—especially grounded in internationalism—and instead proclaim an unfettered discretion of states in designing their own rules and principles of PrIL. The third part of this chapter shows that the individual-centered internationalist perspective of the post-Second World War period was decisively liberal and that it was structured around the combination of the vested rights theory and Henri Batiffol's "system coordination" theory. In this combination, private law is often explicitly or implicitly separated from public law and the role of PrIL is described as the universal liberal recognition of vested rights and individual autonomy. Nationalism is no longer placed in tension with the needs of humanity or the international society of mankind as Jitta saw it, but with a particular understanding of the needs of international commerce focused on order and predictability. This chapter shows how these themes circulated among some of the main PrIL European authors of the time, including Henri Batiffol, Gerhard Kegel, W.A. Wortley, R.H. Graveson, and F.A. Mann.

Inevitably, as the role of the state was shifting from facilitator to regulator, the "tendence privatiste" eventually came under attack as well. Interestingly, the arguments used to push for national political sentiment, as well as global public concerns, are often those of the nineteenth century relational internationalists. The last section of the chapter shows how the Dutch scholar Duco Kollewijn carried on Jitta's tradition, as well as Jitta's reconstruction of Savigny's theory. Similarly, one of the strongest proponents of a public dimension of PrIL, Phocion Franceskakis, will re-emphasize Jitta's critique of "the conflicts guillotine"[1] and his focus on truly international relationships.

Yet while the arguments and the directions of reform might resonate with those of the nineteenth century relational internationalist perspective, the justification is different. Because the individual-centered perspective of the twentieth century was decisively liberal, primarily focused on methodology, and overly internationalist, tempering those tendencies meant focusing away from the individual toward the state, toward national politics, and toward PublIL.

However, even then it was unclear how national politics and even PublIL would reform PrIL. When Phocion Franceskakis reviewed Jessurun D'Oliveira's work on "The Pollution of the Rhine and Private International Law,"[2] he was somewhat surprised by the analysis.[3] Like Franceskakis, D'Oliveira argued that PrIL was overly liberal and overly technical, as opposed to being focused on the substantive result, especially with respect to international environmental matters.[4] But when it came to integrating a substantive environmental policy, it appeared to D'Oliveira that the "classical" PrIL rule calling for the application of the law of the place of tort was the best, the only caveat being that the plaintiff should be given the choice of whichever law demands greater compensation, as between the law of the place of the tortious act and the law of the place of damage.[5] It appeared that the common good and the international public concern were best captured within PrIL, as opposed to PublIL, and in the claims of individual plaintiffs toward tortfeasors, as opposed to an interstate framework.[6]

B. The Various Facets of Nationalism

When Franz Kahn wrote his "manifesto" against the internationalist movement at the end of the nineteenth century, Kahn's own normative commitments were not entirely clear. While attacking the naiveté of internationalism, he also portrayed himself as a moderate nationalist and argued that the goal of uniformity and a concern

[1] Phocion Franceskakis, 'De conflictu legum, Mélanges offerts à R.D. Kollewijn et J. Offerhaus à l'occasion de leur soixante-dixième anniversaire' review of 'Les règles de droit international privé materiel' by M. von Overbeck (1963) 53 Rev crit dr int privé 866, 872 (hereafter Franceskakis, "De conflictu legum"): "the author teaches us immediately that the utility of the concept (of material rules) was advocated in the Dutch doctrine by the great theoretician of our field who was Jitta and that this opinion was further developed by Kosters, Hijmans and for interpersonal law by M. Kollewijn".

[2] Jessurun D'Oliveira, 'La Pollution du Rhin et le droit international privé' in R. Hueting (ed.), *Rhine Pollution: Legal, Economic and Technical Aspects* (Tjeenk Willink 1978) 81–127 (hereafter D'Oliveira, "La Pollution du Rhin").

[3] Phocion Franceskakis, review of D'Oliveira (n. 2) (1979) 59 Rev crit dr int privé 266 (hereafter Franceskakis, "Review D'Oliveira").

[4] D'Oliveira, "La Pollution du Rhin" (n. 2) 103–4.

[5] Ibid., 97, 100.

[6] Franceskakis, "De conflictu legum" (n. 1) 268.

for comparative law should still have some role in PrIL.[7] Kahn in Germany and Etienne Bartin in France,[8] the main protagonists of what became known as the nationalist movement, were, in effect, not always arguing that internationalism is not desirable, but rather that it was unrealistic. Their main goal was to show that contrary to the internationalists' theories, PublIL did not actually offer universal norms of PrIL and that there was no universal nature of a legal relation.[9] Furthermore, the discovery of the characterization and incidental question problematique, as well as of renvoi, was in effect a "scientific" methodological critique, rather than a decisive normative critique of internationalism.[10] It is not surprising then that Duco Kollewijn thought Kahn's and Bartin's attacks on internationalism were still coming from a "supranational" angle.[11]

However, when the French scholar J.P. Niboyet wrote the first volume of his PrIL treatise in 1938, it was clear that, for him, nationalism came with a normative agenda.[12] He wrote that "law does not have a universalist aim, like the new messianic internationalism presupposes, but rather aims to satisfy the needs of each country through legislation, which is adapted to it as much as possible."[13] In other words, "each state, before having any obligations without reciprocity towards humanity, has obligations to itself and the interests it must cater to."[14] The theory of his contemporary Georges Scelle—that a state has a double function vis-à-vis its society and vis-à-vis international society—seemed unacceptable to him.[15]

Instead, for Niboyet, not only should the state not hesitate, it should embrace the application of its law for transnational relations. The application of foreign laws would cause too much heterogeneity, which in turn would "endanger the ethical principles of a particular nation."[16]

These reflections were particularly important for France in the context of the large wave of immigrants at the time, and Niboyet did not hesitate to reinforce France's interest to "assimilate" the foreign population.[17] Franceskakis thought it was France's particular demographic situation that made Niboyet plead for the

[7] See Chapter 3.

[8] Etienne Adolphe Bartin, *Principes de droit international privé: selon la loi et la jurisprudence françaises*, 3 vols. (Domat-Montchrestien 1930–1935).

[9] Phocion Franceskakis, 'Permanence de l'ouvre de Niboyet' in Henri Batiffol (ed.), *La pensée des autres en droit international privé: comptes rendus bibliographiques (1946–1984) réunis en hommage à leur auteur* (Université Aristote de Thessalonique, Faculté de droit 1985) 451 (hereafter Franceskakis, *La pensée des autres*).

[10] See, e.g., Etienne Bartin, 'La doctrine des qualifications et ses rapports avec le caractere national du conflit des lois' (1930) 31 Recueil des Cours 561.

[11] Roeland Duco Kollewijn, 'Quelques considerations a propos de la doctrine de Savigny' (1968) 15 Neth Int L Rev 237, 241 (hereafter Kollewijn, "Quelques considerations").

[12] J.P. Niboyet, *Traité de droit international privé français*, vol. 1 (Sirey 1938) (hereafter Niboyet, *Traité, vol. 1*).

[13] J.P. Niboyet, *Traité de droit international privé français*, vol. 3 (Sirey 1944) para 918 (hereafter Niboyet, *Traité*, vol. 3); J.P. Niboyet, *Cours de droit international privé: à l'usage des étudiants de licence et de doctorat* (Sirey 1946) para 374.

[14] Niboyet, *Traité*, vol. 3 (n. 13) para 907.

[15] Franceskakis, *La pensée des autres* (n. 9) 448–9.

[16] Ibid., 451; Franceskakis, *Traité*, vol. 3 (n. 13) para 881.

[17] Franceskakis, *La pensée des autres* (n. 9) 453.

principle of territoriality of law, rather than the previous PublIL theory, or the vested rights theory, which were also developed on the basis of law's territoriality.[18]

Niboyet was therefore careful to point out that political interest will serve as a correcting factor for any result of the application of the territoriality principles.[19] As Franceskakis showed, nothing prevented France from serving its political interest by applying the law of nationality for French citizens abroad and the principle of domicile for foreigners domiciled in France.[20] All of this seemed natural if states are understood to have a direct interest in how a transnational private law relationship is regulated and if private law is understood as being as much the expression of "the national genius" as any other law.[21]

C. The Post-War Critique of Nationalism

In 1952 the Greek PrIL scholar living in France, Phocion Franceskakis, wrote a review of French international law scholar Henri Batiffol's second edition of his treatise on PrIL.[22] Franceskakis took this review as an opportunity to outline the changes in the theory of PrIL from the beginning of the century until the end of the Second World War. He thought that "the current tendencies are the antithesis of those in 1939,"[23] and that "one day this will appear as a sudden impulse of internationalism, reversing the direction of the previous evolution."[24] Franceskakis described the nationalist movement before the Second World War thus:

> In France, especially, legal thought would exhibit impatience with all legal imperatives not emanating from the national legal order. We would proclaim voluntarily that France, as all other sovereign states, will recruit its citizens in whichever way it considers necessary, without any regard to double nationality or statelessness. We would applaud legislative restrictions of foreigners' rights. We would adopt in conflict of laws the famous statement of the councilor Denis: "I love French law more than foreign law."[25]

In contrast, Franceskakis thought the period after the Second World War was showing a decisive liberal tendency.[26] Access to "French justice" would be widely, Franceskakis feared "too widely," opened to foreigners; public policy would be applied with more restraint to foreign acquired rights than national ones; and French law would no longer apply to every relationship involving at least one French national.[27]

[18] Ibid. [19] Ibid. [20] Ibid.

[21] Ibid., 460: "By emphasizing the necessity of maximum homogeneity in the various legal orders, Niboyet not only reminds us that private law is a powerful way of manifestation of the national genius, but also deduces from this, for the first time, consequences for our field regarding the involvement of the state in the private life."

[22] Phocion Franceskakis, 'Perspectives du Droit international privé actuel a propos de la deuxième édition du Traité de M. Henri Batiffol' review of Henri Batiffol, *Traité élémentaire de droit international privé*, 2nd edn. (1955) 7 RIDC 349 (hereafter Franceskakis, "Perspectives").

[23] Ibid., 359. [24] Ibid., 358. [25] Ibid., 351. [26] Ibid., 359.

[27] Ibid., 358–9.

Franceskakis believed that three elements contributed to this shift in policy direction, at least in France. First, the wave of immigrants decreased substantially and the ones who immigrated were by then substantially integrated in French society; second, after an initial socialist tendency, the involvement of the state in the international economy was substantially weakened; and third, the increasing interdependence of states made the nationalist ideology generally less appealing to the jurists and politicians of the time.[28]

But Franceskakis also believed that jurisprudential trends in PrIL were generally strongly influenced by scholars in the field. In particular, he believed that French jurisprudence and the PrIL scholarship of the French scholar Henri Batiffol were influencing one another.[29]

Indeed it was Henri Batiffol who tried to reawaken an interest in the philosophical aspects of PrIL.[30] The period after the Second World War was a time to take stock of past theories and insights in the field. In particular, for Batiffol in France, as for Gerhard Kegel in Germany, the philosophical exercise was mostly one of synthesis and reframing of well-established theories. The philosophical movement was also one of distilling higher principles and goals of PrIL from the established methodology of the field. The next section outlines how both the French scholar, Henri Batiffol, and the German scholar, Gerhard Kegel, synthesized and reframed the philosophy of PrIL. It also shows the role that individual-centered and state-centered arguments played in this exercise.

D. Continental European Philosophical Debates in PrIL After the Second World War

1. Henri Batiffol

In 1948, the year of his election to the Institute of International Law, Henri Batiffol was charged by the Hague Academy of International Law with the task of giving a lecture on the current tendencies in PrIL.[31] In this first—out of four—course at the Hague Academy one can already distill Batiffol's view of the field, as well as the

[28] Ibid., 359–60.

[29] Ibid., 360. Franceskakis was also generally skeptical of attempts to explain PrIL theories exclusively by reference to the social context. For example, he thought that the Marxist interpretation of the statutory school of thought left out the possibility that the theory was actually produced by PrIL scholars somewhat removed from the social context. See Franceskakis, *De conflictu legum, Melanges offerts a R.D. Kollewijn et J. Offerhaus a l'occasion de leur soixante-dixieme anniversaire,* review of M. Blagojeviç, 'Théorie des statuts à la lumière générale de l'évolution de la société' in Franceskakis, *La pensée des autres* (n. 9) 211.

[30] Horatia Muir Watt, 'Batiffol, Henri' in Jürgen Basedow et al. (eds.), *Encyclopedia of Private International Law*, vol. 1 (Edward Elgar 2017) 64, 68: "Henri Batiffol was perhaps the last of the civil lawyers to attempt to entertain any serious interdisciplinary project [between conflict of laws and philosophy]" (hereafter Muir Watt, "Henri Batiffol").

[31] Henri Batiffol, 'Les tendances doctrinales actuelles en droit international privé' (1948) 72 Recueil des Cours 1 (hereafter Batiffol, 'Tendences Actuelles').

roots of his theory of coordination of legal systems, which he argued for in the 1967 Hague Course.[32]

Batiffol starts his course on the tendencies in PrIL in 1948 by announcing that he is not offering an account of PrIL's intellectual history, which can not only be "fastidious" but which also requires "attention to nuances, often subtle, which separate the theory of one scholar from that of the other."[33] Instead, Batiffol aims to provide an overview and discussion of academic debates around three main themes: the conflict between universalism and particularism; the discussion whether PrIL encompasses only conflict of laws rules for private law matters or also questions of nationality, the condition of foreigners, criminal, and administrative law etc.; and debates centered on the development of an inductive or deductive method.[34] Batiffol's aim is therefore not to distill nuances or trace a particular line of thought he finds most useful for PrIL, but instead to group PrIL scholars into camps of particularists or universalists, those embracing the inductive versus deductive method etc. and then to appreciate the value of each broad theoretical position.

Once these opposing categories are constructed, it appears natural for Batiffol that one must plead for a synthesis: between individual and public interests,[35] international, and national order.[36] It is in these initial thoughts on the theoretical dichotomies of the field that one can already trace Batiffol's philosophy of moderation, described by Horatia Muir Watt as "enlightened liberalism."[37]

Despite this general plea for synthesis and combination of broad philosophical positions, Batiffol does not hesitate to take stronger positions on some of the main theoretical debates of his time. He pleads for limiting the field of PrIL to matters of private law, rather than expanding it to questions of nationality, the legal condition of strangers, criminal, or administrative law.[38] He shows significant skepticism toward a more analytical, empirical method, especially toward the realist attempt to hold PrIL rules and decisions to the standard of achieving "better social results."[39] Batiffol is weary of broadening the field of PrIL to the status of "an encyclopedia"[40] as well as diluting the deductive method to the point of transforming PrIL into a system of ad hoc decisions.[41]

Keeping a coherent structure and order in PrIL as a field seems extremely important to Batiffol, such that method might come before theory in a double sense. First, Batiffol constructs an often sharp distinction between the role of the "theoretician" to speculate about various directions in the field and the role of the judge in creating a workable set of rules and principles for PrIL.[42] Whatever doubts theoreticians might have toward multilateral over unilateral rules or toward the appeal to a universal nature of private law relationships, the fact that judges continue to base their decisions on these assumptions is an indirect reflection of their wisdom,

[32] Henri Batiffol, 'Réflexions sur la coordination des systèmes nationaux' (1967) 120 Recueil des Cours 165 (hereafter Batiffol, "Réflexions sur la coordination").

[33] Batiffol, "Tendences Actuelles" (n. 31) 6. [34] Ibid., 7–8. [35] Ibid., 25.

[36] Ibid., 33. [37] Muir Watt, "Henri Batiffol" (n. 30) 66.

[38] Batiffol, "Tendences Actuelles" (n. 31) 41, 50–1. [39] Ibid., 54–64.

[40] Ibid., 39. [41] Ibid., 54. [42] Ibid., 48.

if only meant to construct a coherent system of PrIL rules.[43] Second, Batiffol often conflates theoretical distinctions within methodological debates. For example, he analogizes the United States' realist school of thought's reluctance to mechanical rules to the arguments in favor of party autonomy in choosing the applicable law.[44] The nuances of the realist philosophy, especially Cavers's theory, which Batiffol references repeatedly, are lost under the assumption that both realist scholars and party autonomy proponents plead for "better social results" and display a skepticism to rules, which in turn Batiffol associates with the analytical method opposing the deductive method.[45]

Virtually all of the initial thoughts Batiffol includes in his account of the tendencies of PrIL in 1948—philosophy of moderation, strong deference to court decisions, and deducing theory from method—crystalize in his own way of describing PrIL as a field ensuring the coordination of legal systems.

The thesis of coordination of legal systems reflects Batiffol's moderate position within the particularist/universalist spectrum. In keeping with the main insights of the nationalist movement at the beginning of the century, Batiffol agreed that an important principle of PrIL is to preserve the national interest. Yet he insisted that in private law, the state's interest is mediated through the interests of individuals.[46] Furthermore, while national private law is the expression of the national interest and conditions of life, for Batiffol there is undoubtedly an international order as well, which caters to a larger social context. Yet, because national society is historically antecedent to the international one and because the national spirit and culture are more developed than the international, the national takes precedence over the international.[47] Therefore, rather than subscribing to either the particularist or the universalist theories, Batiffol felt more drawn to the German so-called "third school of thought" of his time, which he interpreted as being focused on the comparison of different legal systems.[48]

As a result, for Batiffol, PrIL focuses on distinct national legal systems, rather than the international as such. This realization conjures up for Batiffol the imagery of PrIL as a "coordinator of legal systems"[49] and makes PrIL the "system of systems."[50]

Batiffol also positions the systems coordination theory somewhat vaguely in between the state-centered/individual-centered positions. While Batiffol opposed the state-centered internationalist theories of the nineteenth century,[51] it is not entirely clear what differentiates his theory, other than replacing the emphasis on

[43] Ibid., 50–1. [44] Ibid., 50. [45] Ibid., 58–9.

[46] Franceskakis, "Perspectives" (n. 22) 354.

[47] Henri Batiffol, *Aspects philosophiques du droit international privé* (Dalloz 1956) 229 (hereafter Batiffol, *Aspects philosophiques*).

[48] Henri Batiffol, 'Principes de droit international privé' (1959) 97 Recueil des Cours 431, 442–3 (hereafter Batiffol, "Principes"). See also Henri Batiffol, 'Pluralisme des méthodes en droit international privé' (1973) 139 Recueil des Cours 79, 80–1 (hereafter Batiffol, "Pluralisme").

[49] Batiffol, *Aspects philosophiques* (n. 47) 16. See also Batiffol, "Réflexions sur la coordination" (n. 32).

[50] Phocion Franceskakis, 'Philosophie du droit international privé a propos du livre de M. Batiffol' review of Henri Batiffol, *Aspects philosophiques du Droit international Privé* in Franceskakis, *La pensée des autres* (n. 9) 173 (hereafter Franceskakis, "Philosophie").

[51] Batiffol, "Principes" (n. 48) 437–8.

states with an emphasis on legal systems. It is certainly not the internationalism of the nineteenth-century state-centered theories that he rejected, since his theory was also decisively internationalist. Rather, Batiffol seemed to believe the term "co-ordination" entails more and tells a richer story of the regulatory aims of PrIL than the nineteenth-century focus on "division" of state sovereignty.[52] Nonetheless, Franceskakis believed Batiffol had not drawn as much from the term as might have been possible. While coordination shifted the perspective from a one-shot division of sovereignty to a "process of regulation," Franceskakis believed Batiffol did not go so far as to plead for any substantive regulatory dimension of PrIL for an international society.[53]

The metaphor of the coordination of legal systems represents also a moderate position in between the analytical method and the preservation of a systematic nature of PrIL.[54] Batiffol's earlier work which focused on the philosophical aspects of PrIL shows a duality in his thinking. Batiffol exhibited skepticism about any extreme theoretical position: PrIL is neither exclusively international nor exclusively national, there should be no extreme division between individual and community interests,[55] and there should be a multiplicity of methods, including Savigny's search for the nature of the legal relation, the sociological perspective, and the method focused on the social scope of rules and relationships.[56] Yet Batiffol was also very drawn to the systematic character of law.[57]

Substituting the legal system for the state as the point of reference therefore alludes to more than might be immediately apparent. Franceskakis thought it was a reference to Hans Kelsen's imagery of the ascendant organization of norms.[58] This, in turn, makes it possible for Batiffol to speak of PrIL as the system of systems and the law of laws, precisely the terms against which Jitta had positioned his entire theory. For Batiffol there must be a systematic way of assigning legal matters to legal systems, which in his theory translates into an assignment based on a quantitative accumulation of connecting factors even though various mechanisms remain in place to test the results of the localization in view of the values and interests of the forum.[59]

Lastly, insisting on the "systematic" nature of law in general and of PrIL in particular made Batiffol extremely favorable to the variety of techniques of PrIL, including renvoi, characterization, incidental question etc.[60] Batiffol explained those techniques not only as instruments to pursue or guide the analytical process to

[52] Franceskakis, "Perspectives" (n. 22) 133. [53] Ibid.

[54] Henri Batiffol, 'Droit et nature de choses dans la philosophie française du droit' in *Choix d'articles. Rassemblés par ses amis* (Librairie generale de droit et de la jurisprudence 1976) 387, 388 (relating the analytical dimension of Savigny's search for the nature of a legal relation to his theory of coordination of legal systems).

[55] Batiffol, *Aspects philosophiques* (n. 47) 225, 264. [56] Ibid., 227, 229.

[57] Franceskakis, "Philosophie" (n. 50) 172. [58] Ibid., 173.

[59] Franceskakis, "Perspectives" (n. 22) 135.

[60] Henri Batiffol, " Principes" (n. 48) 467ff (for the proposition that as the diversity of substantive rules led to the creation of norms for their coordination, so does the diversity of conflict of laws rules lead to renvoi, as the tool to determine the field of application of those different conflict of laws rules. For Batiffol the coordination of legal systems was operating on two levels).

certain results, but as fundamental elements preserving the systematic nature of PrIL as a coordinator of legal systems.[61]

Batiffol's last three Hague courses therefore represent an effort to both explain and justify PrIL's techniques as tools to achieve the coordination of legal systems. Batiffol attempts both to synthesize PrIL's methodology through the metaphor of coordination of legal system as well as to validate his theoretical postulate by showing that French PrIL jurisprudence at least indirectly, namely through PrIL techniques, aims to achieve the coordination of legal systems. Batiffol therefore re-creates a philosophy of PrIL from PrIL methodology and jurisprudence. In his 1959 Hague course Batiffol argued that through various techniques such as characterization, PrIL aims to coordinate the *rules of private law* belonging to different legal systems, while through renvoi PrIL aims to coordinate *PrIL rules* belonging to different legal systems.[62] In Batiffol's view not only are PrIL techniques best understood as coordinating rules pertaining to different legal systems; judges also at least subconsciously employ PrIL techniques in this way and perceive PrIL's regulatory function as coordinating legal systems.[63]

Much of Batiffol's scholarship aims to defend the understanding of PrIL as a coordinator of legal systems and to show its continued relevance, despite major socioeconomic changes.[64] In his 1969 Hague Course, Batiffol defends PrIL's methodology and the thesis of PrIL as coordinator of legal systems despite two main critiques: that PrIL methodology is ill suited to respond to the "publicisation of private law"[65] and that it fails to account for the international, systemic implication of PrIL matters.[66] Six years later Batiffol suggests that the critiques overestimate both the role of the state in private law matters[67] and the particularity of transnational over national private law matters[68] and that PrIL methodology can adapt to any socio-economic changes. The breadth and vagueness of the thesis of PrIL as a coordinator of legal systems therefore helps to restore the prestige of PrIL methodology:

> This method of settling issues which arise from private relations of an international character, or those which require considering several legal systems within a single country, has enjoyed considerable prestige because it allows for subtle, ingenious analyses based on more or less general principles; it thus provides an excellent exercise for the mind, and promotes well-ordered international relations.[69]

As late as 1985, Batiffol's 1967 Hague Course was translated in English and reprinted in *The Seton Hall Review* as an enduring defense of "the conflict of laws method" in light of "contemporary challenges."[70] Batiffol argues that, viewed through the metaphor of coordination of legal systems, the PrIL method makes it possible to avoid

[61] Franceskakis, "Perspectives" (n. 22) 135–6.

[62] Henri Batiffol, " Principes" (n. 48) 467ff.

[63] See Batiffol, "Principes" (n. 48) (describing various court decisions that Batiffol interprets as attempting precisely to coordinate legal systems through the PrIL methodology).

[64] Batiffol, "Réflexions sur la coordination" (n. 32) 169. [65] Ibid. [66] Ibid.

[67] Batiffol, "Pluralisme" (n. 48) 139. [68] Ibid., 132.

[69] Henri Batiffol, 'Reflections on the Co-ordination of National Systems' (1985) 15 Seton Hall L Rev 793 (hereafter Batiffol, "Reflections").

[70] Ibid.

"mutual ignorance between two legal systems" and instead to achieve "an overall superstructure,"[71] "an objective, happy medium between complication and over-simplification"[72] and to provide "synthesis and continuity."[73]

A long-time collaborator of Henri Batiffol and very attentive reviewer of his work, Phocion Franceskakis, argued that the term "system" had progressively acquired "an existential meaning" for Batiffol.[74] Although it initially appeared that "coordination" was meant to be a fluid term signaling a plurality of methods and perspectives in the determination of a PrIL matter, it progressively collapsed into favoring the "technical" and "conflictual" underpinnings of PrIL norms.[75] It also eventually collapsed into the old doctrine of "division of states' sphere of action" in the international realm.[76]

According to Franceskakis's reading, three ideas combine to revive an old doctrine. First, states are again the agents, the subjects of PrIL;[77] the international realm is perceived as an accumulation of national states, rather than a sphere of social life with its own particularities and regulatory needs;[78] and the focus is on international order, rather than on substantive principles of social life.[79]

By 1967 when Franceskakis reviewed the fourth edition of Batiffol's treatise on PrIL, it appeared to Franceskakis that Batiffol's theory focused on the "mission of distributive justice, to give each law involved its role" had become universal.[80] Although he does not cite Jitta, whom he calls elsewhere "the great theoretician of PrIL,"[81] Franceskakis criticized Batiffol in the same way Jitta criticized the state-centered internationalists and Savigny.

He argued that the obsession with "conflict of laws" makes scholars oblivious to the results of this "division of sovereignty."[82] He further argued that the appeal to focus on individual laws and individual states makes us oblivious to the operations of truly international economic and social conditions, such as the economic conditions of the world market[83] or matters of international environmental law.[84] He argued, as Jitta did, that the process of localization and the "conflictual approach" is only one among many possible methods (a notable one for Franceskakis, as for Jitta, were substantive international rules) to search for "just and efficacious rules for international inter-human relations."[85]

Franceskakis argued that by its fourth edition, Batiffol's writing in PrIL "ceased to be merely a treatise, but rather the expression of positive law" in France.[86] The liberal and internationalist tendencies at the end of the Second World War found

[71] Ibid., 797. [72] Ibid., 798. [73] Ibid., 811.

[74] Franceskakis, "Philosophie" (n. 50) 173. [75] Ibid., 173. [76] Ibid., 178.

[77] Ibid., 178. [78] Ibid.

[79] Ibid., 177–8 (Franceskakis thought it was "a symptomatic change of terms" when Batiffol shifts from "the international society" to "the objective of international order").

[80] Phocion Franceskakis, Book Review of Henri Batiffol, *Droit international privé*, 4th ed., in Franceskakis, *La pensée des autres* (n. 9) 236 (attributing this framing of PrIL's role to Savigny).

[81] Franceskakis, "De conflictu legum" (n. 1).

[82] Phocion Franceskakis, Book Review of Henri Batiffol, *Droit international privé*, 4th edn., in Franceskakis, *La pensée des autres* (n. 9) 237.

[83] Ibid., 237. [84] Franceskakis, "Review D'Oliveira" (n. 2) 387.

[85] Franceskakis, *La pensée des autres* (n. 9) 237. [86] Ibid., 240.

inspiration in, and occasionally went beyond Batiffol's thesis of coordination of legal systems.[87] In turn, the increasingly liberal and internationalist directions of the jurisprudence influenced and found a grounding in Batiffol's own writing so that "there is in this work [Batiffol's] a progressive equilibrium between his ideas and their consecration by the courts."[88]

2. Gerhard Kegel

The liberal and the technical aspects defining PrIL theory as found in Batiffol's theory were prevalent not only in France. The idea of coordination of legal systems seemed to be the common way of describing the goals of PrIL after the Second World War.[89] PrIL scholars were now merely debating the consequences, the conditions, or the tempering of such blind coordination. Hans Lewald for example asked how one should understand the goals of coordination of legal systems when this leads to a result that is unacceptable to both legal systems involved.[90] As Franceskakis described it,

> The classical case involves German spouses married without contract and subsequently acquiring Swedish citizenship. According to German marital law there is a separation of goods—according to Swedish marital law there is a communion of goods between the spouses, which dissolves at the end of marriage. For the German law of succession the surviving spouse inherits even when there are children—he does not according to Swedish law. According to German PrIL matrimonial matters are determined by German law and inheritance matters by Swedish law. So the spouse doesn't recover anything, either according to marital law or according to succession law.[91]

The preoccupation of the time was therefore to understand what to make of the clashes between "rules dividing legislative competence in space" and "a larger sense of justice."[92] One option was, as Franceskakis pointed out repeatedly, to eliminate the tension and realize that PrIL matters can be determined based on a variety of factors, including choice of law, but also direct appeal to "substantive" principles.[93] In other words, one option was to give up on Batiffol's insistence on the absolute systematic nature of PrIL understood as the coordination of legal systems. But another option, taken up by Gerhard Kegel in Germany, was to make use of a variety of technicalities to justify a preferred result, even if Kegel did not explain it as such.[94]

[87] Ibid. (Franceskakis argued that by the time the second edition of Batiffol's treatise was published, French jurisprudence was even more liberal and more internationalist than Batiffol's theory, at 139).

[88] Ibid., 240.

[89] Ibid., 1 (citing the post Second World War Greek author Pierre G. Vallindas, defining PrIL rules as "the ensemble of rules of law meant to regulate the parallel coexistence of multiple legal orders and organs functioning within each of these legal systems").

[90] Hans Lewald, *Règles générales des conflits de lois; contributions à la technique du droit international privé* (Helbing & Lichtenhahn 1941).

[91] Phocion Franceskakis, review of Gerhard Kegel, 'Begriffs- und Interessenjurisprudenz im internationalen Privatrecht' (1954) 43 Rev crit dr int privé 238, 238–9 (hereafter Franceskakis, "Review Kegel").

[92] Ibid., 239. [93] See n. 1.

[94] Franceskakis, "Review Kegel" (n. 91) 241. For a more detailed account of Kegel's theory, as well as subsequent interest jurisprudence writings in Germany, see Chapter 8.

Overall, a scholarly effort of the time, reflected in Gerhard Kegel's writings on "conflicts justice" and cited repeatedly by Batiffol[95] was to outline how the coordination of legal systems achieved its own kind of justice and how this justice could be reconciled with more substantive versions precisely through PrIL's methodological repertoire. In effect, one would resort to renvoi, characterization, incidental questions, or even arguments relating to the "systemic nature of legal norms" within each legal system,[96] in order to maintain the systematic character of PrIL's coordination function while avoiding absurd results.[97]

In Germany, Kegel came to argue for the pursuit of "conflicts justice" that operates with its own logic and arguments, independent of the substantive result, and having no substantive agenda of its own.[98] Within this conflicts justice, private law is distinguished from public law, individual interests in private law are distinguished from any public goals of the state, and the assignment of legal matters to different jurisdictions can be made based on broad appreciations of individual "interests."[99]

When Kegel wrote a critique of the American realist writings in PrIL, which was translated and republished in the American Journal of Comparative Law,[100] he noted that a striking difference between his conflicts justice theory and the American realist theories is that in the latter "public law arguments are invoked in the context of private law and the results are thereby distorted."[101] Kegel is explicit about his distaste for referencing any public law in the area of PrIL when stating that "[i]t also burdens international discussion whenever rules of public law appear in private law contexts, e.g. when tort and social security are put on the same level for conflicts purposes."[102]

Furthermore, preserving the systematic nature of PrIL was as vital to Kegel as it was for Batiffol. Comparing his conflicts justice theory to the American approach favoring the "better law" Kegel remarks:

> Preference of the better law is exactly the opposite of PIL: the conflicts "process" is disrupted before the end on account of conflicts decision-weakness and replaced by comparative law and legal policy. Such a process is insecure, because it lacks binding value criteria, and it is awkward because it awards grades.[103]

For Kegel, as for Batiffol, the methodological arsenal of PrIL is supposed to provide precisely such order and structure to PrIL. According to Kegel's account of conflicts

[95] See, e.g., Batiffol, "Reflexions sur la coordination" (n. 32) 176, 178, 181, 183, 185.

[96] Franceskakis, "Review Kegel" (n. 91) 242. [97] Ibid., 240. [98] Ibid., 241–2.

[99] See Chapter 8 for a discussion of Kegel's theory.

[100] Gerhard Kegel, 'Paternal Home and Dream Home: Traditional Conflict of Laws and the American Reformers' (1979) 27 Am J Comp L 615. The editors' note reads:

> This article is a translation (by your Editor-in-Chief) of a contribution to the *Festschrift für Günter Beitzke* 551–73 (1979). We have deviated from our customary editorial policy of not republishing writings that have already appeared in print elsewhere, because of its singularly forceful (but rather inaccessible) continuation to a debate stirred by the preceding paper from Professor Audit. Since most American commentators have joined in the bandwagon of the radical reform movement or at best remained on the sidelines, it seems we have fallen to outsiders to espouse at long last the role of devil's advocate.

[101] Ibid., 618. [102] Ibid., 632. [103] Ibid., 632.

justice one starts from a "blind" assignment of PrIL to a particular jurisdiction and then adjusts through techniques.[104] "The American reformers, on the other hand, put the cart before the horse if they seek to proceed from analysis of substantive rules to the allocation of their special scope of application."[105]

For example, according to Kegel, the idea that one should appreciate whether a state has an interest in its law being applied is wrong, not only because it brings public law considerations into private law, but also because it conflates substantive law and substantive justice with conflicts law and conflicts justice. Instead, any review of whether the state does not wish to have its law applied should be made after an initial blind assignment of the case to a particular jurisdiction and then re-evaluated with the use of PrIL techniques, in this case "renvoi." Kegel's distinction between the focus on substantive law of the American methodology based on state interests and his approach based on conflicts justice and relying on renvoi is worth citing at large:

> The best example is *renvoi*. It gets "squeezed" in the dream home [the American realist school of thought] in being understood as part of the analysis of substantive rules. So in the case of the guest passenger, the prohibition against wives going surety and charitable immunity.
>
> What is then being misunderstood is that *renvoi* turns on an absolutely fundamental question. Namely on whether the decision should be absolutely the same as in the foreign state whose law is being invoked. [. . .] But it is always conflicts interests (spatially correct solution) that decide, not those of substantive law (substantive correct solution) [. . .] It is the same with characterization . . . in any case characterization involves the interpretation of specific conflicts rules. Because questions of characterization deal with the limits of specific conflicts rules vis-à-vis each other: they appear on the frontiers of those rules.[106]

Interestingly, when Batiffol reviewed Kegel's writing, he found it strikingly similar to his own and he believed any differences that might arise would be mostly on the margins of either theory, rather than being fundamental and consequential.[107] The last chapter outlines how this preoccupation for the systematic and universal nature of PrIL norms and principles is different from the universalism underlying the relational internationalist theory.

Here I am simply interested in revealing that the idea of coordination of legal systems, itself resembling to a large extent the nineteenth-century state-centered internationalist imagery of division of sovereignty, led to a heightened interest in systematicity and technicality and traveled freely between various European jurisdictions at the time. Critics of the "conflicts guillotine" after the Second World War, such as Franceskakis, were quick to refute the illusion of the neutrality of the coordination function and to point to the abstract and artificial methodological play within PrIL. But Franceskakis was also quick to attribute the overly technical and neutral character of PrIL norms to the Savignian legacy.[108] Yet this can be misleading.[109]

[104] Ibid., 625. [105] Ibid., 628. [106] Ibid., 627. [107] See Chapter 8.

[108] See numerous references throughout Franceskakis' review collection. See, e.g., Franceskakis, *La pensée des autres* (n. 9) 236.

[109] See, e.g., Klaus Schurig, 'Das Fundament trägt noch' in Heinz-Peter Mansel (ed.), *Internationales Privatrecht im 20. Jahrhundert: Der Einfluss von Gerhard Kegel und Alexander Lüderitz auf das Kollisionsrecht* (Mohr Siebeck 2014) 17 (explaining how for every new development in PrIL, Savigny's

First, the techniques of PrIL (renvoi, incidental question, characterization) were "discovered" after Savigny by Savigny's critics, and it is not clear how they would feature, if at all, in Savigny's theory. They were meant to question the possibility of universal rules of localization of legal relations. When those techniques were taken up as essential to preserve the systematic nature of PrIL by Batiffol or Kegel, they were part of a renewed interest in the systematic structure of PrIL as such, rather than a revival of Savigny.[110]

Second, implying that the increased technical or methodological interest of PrIL scholars in the twentieth century was necessarily part of moving Savigny's theory forward is also misleading. As the previous chapter has shown, Jitta also tried to move Savigny's theory forward while at the same time disavowing the overly technical nature of the field. Furthermore, as Karen Knop, Annelise Riles, and Ralf Michaels showed persuasively, PrIL's technicalities can also be embraced as means of structuring and guiding the argumentative and interpretive process, rather than as essential elements of PrIL as a system.[111]

E. English PrIL Theory After the Second World War

The fact that continental European scholars such as Batiffol and Kegel were trying to rethink the philosophical foundations of PrIL after the Second World War was not entirely surprising. Continental European scholars had always been preoccupied with PrIL theory and methodology and Batiffol and Kegel were only following in the long line of continental European theoreticians of PrIL. Furthermore, both authors were primarily concerned with validating and reclaiming PrIL's traditional methodology despite what appeared to be "the crisis" of PrIL in light of socioeconomic changes after the Second World War.[112]

What at first sight may appear more surprising is that the philosophical current after the Second World War was picked up and intensified in England. While at the end of the nineteenth century Dicey made a sharp distinction between English pragmatism and the somewhat naïve continental European philosophy, after the Second World War English PrIL scholars found themselves at the forefront of philosophical debates in PrIL. However, rather than simply subscribing to Batiffol's enlightened

system is mentioned, "as if there had been no development of PrIL in the last 150 years." For example, the question is posed "what Savigny would have thought of Rome I-VO." "The picture of 'the closest relationship' becomes almost a fetish. That this is only a short form for the appropriate constellation of PrIL interests falls under the table. What remains is nothing more than an empty slogan").

[110] Franceskakis describes this interest: "One must remember that the end of the previous [nineteenth] century marked for PrIL a complete renewal of its rational structure. The famous controversies over qualification and renvoi, we remember, provided this occasion. Subsequently, an intense theoretical debate was developed by scholars to outline and systematize the methods of reasoning and interpretation particular to conflict of laws." Franceskakis, *La pensée des autres* (n. 9) 181.

[111] Karen Knop, Ralf Michaels, and Annelise Riles, 'From Multiculturalism to Technique, Feminism, Culture, and the Conflict of Laws Style' (2012) 64 Stan L Rev 589.

[112] Gerhard Kegel titles his Hague Academy Course 'The Crisis of Conflict of Laws'. See Gerhard Kegel, 'The Crisis of Conflict of Laws' (1964) 112 Recueil des Cours 91.

liberalism or the focus on methodology, English writers claimed and described a particular English philosophy of PrIL, which distinguished itself from continental theories of the time.

First, while continental European scholars were trying to distill whether and how public law and politics could enter the PrIL analysis or how to position classical PrIL methodology in light of American theories centered on state interests, for the most part English PrIL scholars were unapologetic about focusing PrIL on private justice and individual rights, and displayed a clear skepticism of public policy analysis.

Second, while continental European scholars were still trying to understand what PrIL can learn from PublIL or how and whether the two fields can connect in a more substantive way, English scholars were clear that it was PublIL that had much to learn from PrIL. B.A. Wortley would argue that PrIL can "teach" PublIL how to incorporate the individual as a subject of law and how to achieve the universal recognition of individual rights and liberty. This was after all a repurposing and validation of the English vested rights theory of late nineteenth century, which English PrIL scholars engaged in with great pride. Furthermore, even when F.A. Mann reclaimed the association between PrIL and PublIL based on the notion of international jurisdiction, he argued that the expertise of distributing legislative jurisdiction among states flows from PrIL to PublIL. While both PrIL and PublIL speak the language of international jurisdiction, PrIL had developed the expertise and methodology of how to design universally acceptable grounds for dividing such jurisdiction among states.

What united PrIL philosophy in continental Europe and in England after the Second World War was the attempt to reclaim a certain prestige and enduring wisdom for PrIL. While continental European scholars praised the adaptability of PrIL methodology to virtually any socioeconomic changes, English scholars praised PrIL's focus on the "rights of man" and its expertise in devising uniform bases of distributing jurisdiction among states.

The following section outlines the efforts of three English scholars to reclaim the philosophical bases of PrIL as a field, either as a form of "judicial justice" in R.H. Graveson's account, or as a jurisprudence of the concept and rights of man in W.A. Wortley's account, as an expertise in distributing international jurisdiction in F.A. Mann's account.

1. R.H. Graveson—Judicial justice and vested rights

In her recent account of the significance of Henri Batiffol's scholarship in PrIL Horatia Muir Watt already noted that Batiffol's scholarship left a profound influence on the jurisprudence of PrIL in France as well as on many French scholars who had worked with Henri Batiffol or had been his supervisees.[113] Furthermore Muir Watt noted that Batiffol's distinctive approach to PrIL was influenced by his keen interest

[113] Muir Watt, "Batiffol" (n. 30) 65.

in philosophy. This prompted him to search for the philosophy of PrIL, or at least to attempt an interdisciplinary exercise in philosophy and PrIL.[114]

What may be less well known is that Batiffol's attempt to reclaim PrIL's prestige by outlining a philosophy of PrIL theory influenced not only French PrIL jurisprudence and scholarship. In a 1962 article the British PrIL scholar R.H. Graveson[115] inquired whether Batiffol's theory and philosophy of PrIL had found any resonance in England.[116] Graveson was particularly interested in "attributing a philosophy to English Private International Law"[117] or even to Private International Law in the common law world generally.[118]

Overall, Graveson thought that PrIL in England was developing very much along the lines espoused by Batiffol. As far as Batiffol's theory can be understood to plead for:

> an analysis of foreign law and a deepening of national legal concepts in order to enable foreign concepts to be brought within national categories […] [s]o far as English law is concerned, however, Professor Batiffol has an audience of the converted, for our judges have long used wider and more flexible concepts in private international law than municipal law.[119]

English PrIL scholars and courts were in effect already "practicing" PrIL in light of an underlying philosophy, though they might not recognize it as explicitly as continental European scholars and courts had done.[120] But while they were certainly "practicing" PrIL along the philosophical dimensions described by Batiffol, English courts in particular could not openly commit to a philosophy of PrIL, because they would thereby "transgress the limits of legal respectability."[121] And for those who

[114] Ibid., 67.

[115] R.H. Graveson was the dean of the Faculty of Laws, University of London between 1951–1954 and 1972–1974 and the dean of the Faculty of Laws, King's College London between 1951–1970. He retired as a Professor Emeritus of Private International Law in 1978. Among his publications are R.H. Graveson, *Conflict of Laws,* 7th edn.(Sweet & Maxwell 1974); R.H. Graveson, 'Comparative Aspects of the General Principles of Private International Law' (1963) 109 Recueil des Cours 1; R.H. Graveson, 'The Comparative Evolution of Principles of the Conflict of Laws in England and the United States' (1960) 99 Recueil des Cours 21.

[116] R.H. Graveson, 'Aspects philosophiques du droit international privé anglais' (1962) 51 Rev crit dr int privé 397 (hereafter Graveson, 'Aspects philosophiques').

[117] R.H. Graveson, 'Philosophical Aspects of the English Conflict of Laws' in R.H. Graveson, *Comparative Conflict of Laws. Selected Essays*, vol. 1 (North Holland 1977) 14, 14 (hereafter Graveson, "Philosophical Aspects").

[118] Ibid., 20. Elsewhere he confesses that he "sought to explain the development of the system in the common law in terms of a new theory of justice." See R.H. Graveson, 'The Special Character of English Private International Law' in R.H. Graveson, *Comparative Conflict of Laws. Selected Essays,* vol. 1 (North Holland 1977) 1, 7. See also Graveson, "Philosophical Aspects" (n. 117) 46:

> This common tradition of the common law, expressed in a common language and for the most part in a common way of political thought, has become part of the law of England in the sense of Pound's "taught tradition" in a way which naturally gives a wider outlook to problems of conflict of laws than would be possible in a different situation.

However, he also described in detail many of the differences between the English and the American conflict of laws theories of the time. See R.H. Graveson, 'The Comparative Evolution of Principles of the Conflict of Laws in England and the U.S.A.' in R.H. Graveson, *Comparative Conflict of Laws. Selected Essays*, vol. 1 (North Holland 1977) 225.

[119] Graveson, "Philosophical Aspects" (n. 117) 19. [120] Ibid., 14. [121] Ibid.

might have thought that English PrIL scholarship was simply opposed to theory ever since Dicey's distinction between "the theoretical and the positive methods"[122] Graveson reminds them that in Dicey's remarks one can see "not simply the positivist persuasion in favor of the vested rights theory which he adopts, but the non-positivist reasons which led him to do so. One can find not only effectiveness and convenience but justice, too, in those reasons."[123]

Therefore, although Graveson admits that "the doctrine of the vested right has now become old-fashioned" he aims to restore its philosophical foundation in a larger "principle of justice."[124] Thus, the vested rights theory can be stripped of its formalism and repurposed as a symbol of universal justice. Graveson's account of "the only modern English exponent of the doctrine of the vested rights" in Graveson's time, C.M. Schmitthoff, is particularly telling:[125]

> Dr. Schmitthoff's view of the vested rights theory is more developed than the sources from which he drew it. It is based on a sense of internationalism with affinity to natural law concepts, on the idea that there exist human rights, which should be recognized and protected by the courts of all civilized countries, subject to the exigencies of municipal public policy. Schmitthoff, indeed, finds in the same conception of justice the origins of the doctrine of vested rights, the Universal Declaration of Human Rights and the Convention on Human Rights. In his writings, therefore, one can find a link between the extreme narrowness of territorialism and the undue generality of internationalism and it would, it is submitted, be fair to say that that link is found in the idea of justice and fundamental human needs.[126]

By reclaiming English theories of vested rights as human rights and by drawing attention to a large wave of English internationalists such as Norman Bentwich and B.A. Wortley, Graveson attempts to place English PrIL at the forefront of a new internationalist philosophy of PrIL, much in line with Batiffol's work on a philosophy of PrIL. Even English pragmatism, once associated with particularism and positivism is now described as a larger sense of justice, because while J.H.C. Morris noted that "common sense is a quality with which even the least learned English judge is liberally endowed"[127] Graveson quickly notes that "common sense in adjudication would appear to be a way to the achievement of justice."[128] It was therefore possible to restate Batiffol's philosophy of PrIL as a coordinator of legal systems in terms that would resonate in England.

First, Graveson thought it was telling that in England already in 1878 Frederic Harrison had described the role of PrIL as providing for the coordination and coexistence of legal systems, in line with the thesis later developed by Batiffol.[129] Second, Graveson believed many of the propositions about individual liberty found in Batiffol's theory were found and given even more significance in English PrIL

[122] Ibid., 21. [123] Ibid., 21. [124] Ibid., 22.

[125] Ibid., citing C.M. Schmitthoff, *The English Conflict of Laws* (3rd edn., Stevens 1954).

[126] Graveson, "Philosophical Aspects" (n. 117) 23.

[127] J.H.C. Morris, *Cases in Private international law*, 2nd edn.(Clarendon 1951) 18.

[128] Graveson, "Philosophical Aspects" (n. 117) 24–5.

[129] Graveson, "Aspects philosophiques" (n. 116) 399 referring to Frederic Harrison and A.H.F. Lefroy, *On Jurisprudence and the Conflict of Laws* (Clarendon 1919) 135. Although Harrison's book was published in 1919 the lectures comprised in the book were given in 1878 and 1879.

theory and jurisprudence.[130] Third, and more important, he argued that the English legal system had in fact materialized, perhaps more than any other legal system, the goal of the "positive coexistence of different legal systems."[131] By positive coexistence Graveson means the liberal recognition of vested rights and individual liberty. In other words, the thesis of vested rights qua theory of justice and that of the coordination of legal systems combined to foster and encourage individual liberty. PrIL as a coordinator of legal systems could now incorporate an updated notion of vested rights qua human rights.[132]

Graveson described the result of this combination as "the principle of justice" underlying English PrIL theory and practice.[133] He argued that there were five elements that made up "the principle of justice," namely:

> individual liberty; maintenance of validity of acts; equality between English and foreign rules of PrIL and between the people they apply to; the sentiment of responsibility towards the international society, which leads to a movement towards the uniformisation of the law; and limiting the use of public policy as much as possible in order to allow for the normal functioning of rules of conflict of laws.[134]

Regarding individual liberty, Graveson argued that this principle is found as a justification for adopting the principle of domicile over nationality,[135] in the decisions refusing the recognition of slave laws,[136] in the absolute liberty and autonomy of individuals in the area of contract law,[137] and in the absence of any principle of "fraude à la loi" in English PrIL.[138]

[130] Graveson, "Aspects philosophiques" (n. 116) 407–8. [131] Ibid., 414.
[132] Graveson, "Philosophical Aspects" (n. 117):

> At the end of the nineteenth century there was still an element of novelty in the recognition of foreign acquired rights and the determination of their nature by the law under which they were acquired. Dicey's remark that "The recognition of rights acquired under foreign laws is a leading principles of modern civilization" might well be read in conjunction with the explanation (Dicey, *Conflict of Laws*, 1st edn., 29) that the term "civilised country" for the purpose of these General Principles included France and the U.S.A., but not Turkey and China.

[133] Graveson, "Aspects philosophiques" (n. 116) 407. [134] Ibid. [135] Ibid., 409.
[136] Ibid., 407.
[137] Ibid., 408 (On this point Graveson is in absolute accord with Batiffol).
[138] Ibid., 408. He argued that the justification for not including such a principle rests in the attachment of English law to individual liberty but also in the fact that:

> For the English jurist, given the general rules of PrIL and international law, there are certain limits to the legislative jurisdiction of a state. If a state edicts laws respecting such limits, it cannot complain that individuals go beyond the territory of those jurisdictions (therefore evading its jurisdiction) in order to enter into acts, which are valid according to the *lex loci actus*. The application of English PrIL rules which recognize the validity of such acts do not have to depend on the fact that the parties preferred to make those acts beyond the limits of the jurisdiction of English law. The two factors which for English PrIL, may influence the rules of conflict of laws, are the act and the intention, not the act and the motive. We are in according with Aristotle on this point. The rules of PrIL allow us to evade internal law and the judges respect the limitations that these laws impose on them, as they are interpreted in the context of the philosophy of English PrIL.

See also R.H. Graveson, 'The Doctrine of Evasion of the Law in England and America' (1937) 19 Journal of Comp Legislation and Int'l L 21.

As to the maintenance of the validity of acts, Graveson considered it "the positive politics" of PrIL.[139] It stands "for the tendency of the English judge to say yes rather than no" when it comes to the liberal recognition of foreign rights and institutions.[140] This, he argued, is meant both to allow for the maintenance of transactions and to satisfy the reasonable expectations of individuals.[141]

As to the restrained use of public policy, Graveson considered it to be "a fundamental principle of English jurisprudence."[142] He argued that it is an undeniable principle of English PrIL to show "repugnance" to the use of public policy, and instead to limit it as much as possible in order to allow for the "normal" functioning of conflict of laws rules.[143] He argued that this is not just "a play of words or etiquette," but rather represents the judges' conviction that one must "remain faithful to the rule of law, meaning the normal functioning of PrIL rules."[144] Furthermore,

> Public policy presents a further example of a special character of English private international law, which derives from the distrust of the courts for Parliament and politics manifested since the seventeenth century. Public policy has always been constructed narrowly and treated as a negative rather than a positive principle.[145]

Overall, Graveson believed that the "politics favorable to individual liberty" and "the internationalist approach" combine to ensure "the positive coexistence of different legal systems" which he believed Batiffol had tried to pursue in his theory.[146] The principle of justice underlying the English PrIL theory described by Graveson is certainly liberal and undoubtedly focused on the individual and individual liberty. The relational insight underlying the relational internationalist perspective seems much diluted in the English scholarship focused on liberty and vested rights. For example, Graveson responds to critiques of the English theory of the proper law of contract favoring the free will of the parties thus:

[139] Graveson, "Aspects philosophiques" (n. 116) 409.

[140] Ibid., (showing how this made it possible to recognize polygamous marriages and legitimation by subsequent marriage, even if those legal institutions did not exist in domestic law).

[141] Ibid., 410.

[142] Ibid., 413. For a much more detailed account of the English approach to public policy reasoning in PrIL, including a comparison with the American approach, see R.H. Graveson, 'The Limits of Private International Law: Public Policy' (1963) 109 Recueil des Cours 38.

[143] Graveson, "Aspects philosophiques" (n. 116) 413. However, Otto Kahn Freund argued that English PrIL indirectly relied on public policy considerations, for example by ensuring the application of *lex fori* through increased reliance on party autonomy or characterizing legal issues as procedural or by treating norms found in statutes differently than norms laid down in judicial decisions: "I shall submit that public policy has been a formative factor in the conflict of laws in cases which are not normally referred to as public policy cases at all." O. Kahn Freund, 'Reflections on Public Policy in the English Conflict of Laws' (1953) 39 Transactions of the Grotius Society 39, 49. Graveson rejected this way of analyzing public policy cases and instead pled for gaging the frequency of the application of the public policy exception only based on the cases in which the exception is explicitly cited and relied upon by courts. O. Kahn Freund, 'Reflections on Public Policy in the English Conflict of Laws' (1953) 39 Transactions of the Grotius Society 39, 70.

[144] Graveson, "Aspects philosophiques" (n. 116) 413.

[145] R.H. Graveson, 'The Special Character of English Private International Law' in R.H. Graveson, *Comparative Conflict of Laws. Selected Essays*, vol. 1 (North Holland 1977) 1, 9.

[146] Graveson, "Aspects philosophiques" (n. 116) 414.

Most English writers do not share Professor Batiffol's concern about the role of free will in law. [. . .] English writers find it slightly exaggerated to regard the property law problem as a manifestation of the classic one of conflict of law and liberty. Such a formulation is really too extreme a statement of the position in the English conflict of laws, where the question is regarded as one of the utmost freedom of the exercise of the individual will within the limits allowed by law. What these are in any particular country is largely a question of its political views. But whether those limits are fixed by concepts of individualism or socialism or other views seems immaterial to the proposition of allowing the utmost liberty of the exercise of the free will within the limits so defined.[147]

At first sight Graveson seems to suggest that PrIL can simply frame its norms and principles around the notion of liberty while recognizing that each legal system understands and curbs liberty in different ways. PrIL can commit to a goal of liberty, while being somewhat agnostic to its contours. But of course PrIL norms are meant precisely to choose a particular legal system and therefore to choose a particular standard of liberty over another. This becomes most clear precisely in the case which Graveson considered "the triumph of justice"[148] and which he discusses in his article titled "Judicial Justice as a Contemporary Basis of the English Conflict of Laws."[149]

In *The National Bank of Greece and Athens v. Metliss* Mr. Metliss claimed the recovery of interest on bond, which had been issued by the National Mortgage Bank of Greece in 1927.[150] In 1941, following the German and Italian invasion of Greece, payment of interest ceased and in 1953 The National Bank of Greece, the guarantor was amalgamated with the Bank of Athens forming a new corporation, called The National Bank of Greece and Athens. In Graveson's assessment, "Viscount Simmonds, delivering the first judgment, went straight to the root of the problem when he spoke in terms of justice."[151] Although the controversial question in conflict of laws terms was whether the issue should be characterized as status, contract, or succession—with different laws potentially applicable to each of these questions—Simmons based his reasoning "on a principle of rational justice"[152] and concluded that "clearly the obligations in English law (the proper law of the contract) could not be affected by the Greek law which purported to vary its terms."[153]

In 1956 Greece passed a law clarifying that the National Bank of Greece and Athens would not take over any rights and liabilities of the bank it replaced. Action was brought by Mr. Adams and others before the Queen's Bench, which also ruled that Greek law could not modify a contractual liability which was vested in the plaintiffs according to English law, the "proper law" of the contract.[154]

On appeal however, the decision was unanimously reversed, according to Graveson "on grounds which leave one with an uneasy sense of being unwillingly convinced."[155] In the judgment of the court:

[147] Graveson, "Philosophical Aspects" (n. 117) 37.

[148] R.H. Graveson, 'Judicial Justice as a Contemporary Basis of the English Conflict of Laws' in R.H. Graveson, *Comparative Conflict of Laws*, vol. 1 (North Holland 1977) 51, 65 (hereafter Graveson, "Judicial Justice").

[149] Ibid., 51.

[150] *The National Bank of Greece and Athens v. Metliss* [1958] A.C. 509.

[151] Graveson, "Judicial Justice" (n. 148) 56.

[152] Ibid., 53.

[153] Ibid., 57.

[154] Ibid., 59.

[155] Ibid., 59.

It seems to us that those who seek recourse to Greek law must take it as they find it. If they assert that Greek law can endow, they must recognize that Greek law can disendow. If they aver Greek law can create, they must accept that Greek law can change.[156]

The court noted that the law simply withdrew a benefit to the bondholder but that does not mean that the decree:

[W]as either confiscatory or discriminatory in its scope or was in the nature of a penal or revenue law or that English public policy could demand that it be not recognized. All bondholders alike could be affected by the change in the law.[157]

For the court of appeal what was significant was that the law did not discriminate among national and foreign bondholders. Certainly the court did not agree that Greek law could not alter rights previously granted. Allowing the law to operate also seemed to comply with a notion of justice, albeit not the kind of justice Graveson had in mind. For Graveson the goal of PrIL was to achieve a just result "beyond the frontiers of strict legalism" and in PrIL "this is particularly important because it shares a common frontier with public international law."[158] Graveson describes the distinction between the legalism of state sovereignty and of PublIL and the principle of justice in PrIL thus:

No one can doubt the legislative power in public international law of the Greek Government, the Russian Government or any other government to make whatever changes it wishes in the existence and constitution of a corporation which it creates. From a purely legalistic standpoint the position of any government legislating to affect private obligations is unimpeachable. But beyond the legalism of strict international law there are standards of international morality which come into conflict from time to time with the purely legal standard. [. . .] The English courts as representing the interests of a long-established and internationally-minded commercial community have always sought to strengthen the concepts of good faith and the fulfillment of obligations freely entered into. They have sought where possible to give remedies to creditors.[159]

Whereas Graveson initially suggested that PrIL only commits to a standard of individual liberty within the bounds of different national laws, in his assessment of judicial justice in the English PrIL cases of the time, it becomes clear that the English standard of liberty is not likely to defer to the laws of other states. Thus, Graveson could only declare the "triumph of justice" in the case he reviewed once the House of Lords reversed the decision of the Court of Appeal and re-emphasized the high standard of individual liberty underlying the goal of universal recognition of vested rights.

2. B.A. Wortley—The concept and the rights of man

R.H. Graveson's characterization of the cases involving the National Bank of Greece and Athens as a tribute of justice implicitly represented a characterization of the English approach to conflict of laws theory and methodology after the

[156] Ibid., 60. [157] Ibid., 62. [158] Ibid., 62. [159] Ibid., 62–3.

Second World War. The many cases of nationalization and expropriation especially after the Second World War brought English PrIL theory and methodology to the forefront. These cases raised precisely the central aims of English PrIL theory at the time: ensuring the protection of vested rights, especially property rights, across borders; connecting private and public international law by conflating the notion of vested private rights with human rights; and the recognition of the individual as a subject of international law precisely through the alignment of private and public international law via vested rights theories.

All these issues were especially prevalent in the scholarship of Ben Atkinson Wortley who in his 1954 Hague Course confessed that:

> It was when preparing my lectures on Expropriation in private international law for this Academy in 1939 that I began to see more vividly than ever how often modern problems necessitate a wide approach. The outbreak of war and the consequent expropriations, captures and confiscations, convinced me that in the future, for most of us it would not be good enough to label ourselves "public international lawyers" or "private international lawyers", or to keep our minds running in mutually exclusive and separate channels.[160]

In Wortley's view pleas made by individuals or corporations to recover property or the value thereof from governments showed how private and public international law "interact with each other, and, occasionally, the rules of one will correct and supplement the other, much as in English and Roman law, equity corrected the traditional law."[161] The issue of expropriation was the perfect case study to reclaim the unity of international law (public and private) in its ancient form as *jus gentium*[162] precisely through the universal recognition of private rights as "the rights of man" against the "new national sovereign ... acclaimed 'all powerful'."[163]

Wortley decried that:

> In this international law [Bentham's], operating between territorial sovereigns, the individual was rarely if ever treated as a subject of international law but, essentially, as a subject of his own sovereign law-giver, and his personal international relations were regarded as a matter primarily for the rules of private international law contained in the civil code with which he was connected.[164]

Instead of this positivist understanding of international law, Wortley claimed a return to a universal customary law: "A sphere in which the Law, both international and municipal, recognizes individual rights independently of the direct or specific approval of the State."[165] Wortley "look[s] ahead"[166] by remarking that:

> [T]reaties and customs may soon make it clear that ordinary individuals have certain fundamental human rights protectable and even enforceable in international law. These rights, we suggest, are there even before they are fully enforceable. When all rights attaching to individual human beings, alone or in groups, are enforceable, there will be little reason for distinguishing between public and private international law [...].[167]

160 B.A. Wortley, 'The Interaction of Private and Public International Law Today' (1954) 85 Recueil des Cours 239, 245.

161 Ibid., 246. 162 Ibid., 248. 163 Ibid., 249. 164 Ibid., 251.

165 Ibid., 252, 253. 166 Ibid., 254. 167 Ibid.

A truly international law would combine, in Wortley's assessment, the focus on the individual and individual rights from PrIL with the access to international tribunals and international organizations of PublIL:

When international co-operation results in the recognition and protection of fundamental human rights there will arise again a body of *international* law concerned with individuals and the group life of individuals, and cognizable in national and international courts; though for the present, until the establishment of international courts of human rights, any denial of fundamental rights by a misapplication of the rules of conflict of laws by a national court can only be put right (if at all) by diplomatic claims for denial of justice, or, in the case of an injury to an international organization, by demanding reparation, by representatives of that organization.[168]

At first sight Wortley's remarks seem to resonate with those of many contemporary critics pleading for PrIL norms and principles to account for human rights violations across borders, such as those of mining corporations.[169] Yet the parallel between Wortley's remarks and contemporary critiques is complicated by the way in which Wortley describes the "concept" and the "rights" of man.

On the one hand, in his book on "Jurisprudence" Wortley praises the Kantian approach in international law because:

[I]t has supported the need for a rule of law against anarchy; it has stressed man's duty to his fellows and the need for distributive justice (including fair taxation), and the value of the human being as a person with a will of his own. In private international law, it has favored the autonomy of the will, including the notion of the proper law of the contract. In public international law it favoured the notion of the self-determination of peoples.[170]

Nevertheless, he admits "Vinogradoff may have been right when he criticized the individualistic approach of Kant."[171]

Wortley argues that in law generally and PrIL in particular, the "crux of the matter" is "must the public law of States always prevail over private rights? Must the power or the will of the ruler always prevail over the restraints of reason?"[172] Fear of despotism in other words translates into a fear of subsuming the individual under the state and merging the private with the public. Yet Wortley is also cautious of embracing an individualistic philosophy so that "despotism and servitude can be prevented, at any rate in this country, if we keep firmly to the high common law ideal of that person of good character, 'the reasonable man'."[173] Wortley therefore acknowledges that the goal of universal recognition of vested rights is strongly related to the "concept of man" underlying a particular legal system:

Even the most liberal statements of human rights, such as the Rome Convention on Human Rights, contain as we saw certain safety valves in the shape of conceptions of public policy

[168] Ibid., 257.

[169] For a claim that human rights might be a strong source of reform for PrIL, see Horatia Muir Watt, 'Future Directions?' in Horatia Muir Watt and Diego P. Fernández Arroyo (eds.), *Private International Law and Global Governance* (OUP 2015) 343.

[170] B.A. Wortley, *Jurisprudence* (Oceana 1967) 405.

[171] Ibid.

[172] Ibid., 259–60.

[173] Ibid., 260.

and public order imposed in the general interest. If we bear in mind that all rights are subject to possible limitations, and that not all enunciations of rights are liberal, we can usefully analyze the nature of rights and duties among the right-bearers and the duty-subjects of a legal order. Such analysis will, however, tell us little about the values guaranteed in that order: for these we have to look primarily at the notion of man held in any particular legal order and protected by its rules.[174]

It is no wonder then that Wortley titles his speech in front of the Grotius Society in 1947 "The Concept of Man in English Private International Law."[175] In his account, English laws "long stood as bulwarks of the essential personal liberties of the reasonable man of the developed common law; a man loyal to the Crown and conscientious and responsible in his behavior to his fellows."[176] Furthermore:

No complex theories of state, no jurisprudential doctrines of the nature of the *homo juridicus* are needed to explain or justify the essential rights of the common man in our courts: they are an integral part of our civilization, and they are safeguarded by our judges.[177]

Therefore:

the ideal standard of conduct of the reasonable man of the common law is based upon a firm belief that man's fundamental rights and duties which Holland calls his antecedent rights *in rem,* arise from the simple fact of his manhood, or, if you like, from his human nature: in that sense his rights and duties in Society are natural rights."[178]

It is through this universal notion of man that the concept of justice and its underpinnings of individual liberty underlying English PrIL that the field should be associated, in Wortley's view, with human rights.[179] In 1947 Wortley wrote:

The revival of interest in the rights of man is symptomatic of our deepest anxieties, so much so that even public international lawyers are becoming increasingly reconciled to the emergence of the human person as a subject of public international law, having rights and duties of his own, whilst private international lawyers who have always been accustomed to deal with human rights on an international plane, welcome the rapprochement between the two branches of international law.[180]

Wortley describes many of the PrIL rules and principles precisely as a way of preserving "the high concept of man" and recognizing his "natural rights."[181] By focusing on domicile versus nationality for example, PrIL ensures that freedom of choice for matters relating to personal status can empower individuals to evade an oppressive regime or circumstances and take hold of her life.[182] Furthermore:

[174] Ibid., 292.

[175] B.A. Wortley, 'The Concept of Man in English Private International Law' (1947) 33 Transactions of the Grotius Society 147 (hereafter Wortley, "The Concept of Man").

[176] Ibid. [177] Ibid. [178] Ibid. [179] Ibid. [180] Ibid., 148.

[181] Ibid., 149.

[182] Ibid., 154, 155: "First, English judges do in fact try to do right to all manner of people coming before them, by minimizing the effects of any unfree status which a foreign domicile may appear to engender."

Failure to retain or to acquire a nationality will not prevent our courts from giving a man a civil status; and in these days when it is not uncommon for men to be deprived of their nationality for political reasons, the English attitude robs de-nationalization of some of its terrors. Statelessness does not mean rightlesness in English law.[183]

Furthermore, by describing slavery laws and any laws providing for an "unfree status" and "limitations on freedom" as "penal," Wortley argues that English PrIL "placed liberty before property."[184] The focus on liberty has also led to "reopening a foreign judgment for the fraud of a party to a suit [...] particularly in view of some of the experiences of litigants in totalitarian countries"[185] and to "enforce[ing] a high standard of conduct upon contractors, trustees and others."[186] Moreover, Wortley argues that the focus on liberty and natural rights led to a wide application of the standard of care and damage underlying English tort law based on the following justification:

We fear, however, that to accept this view [of applying the law of the place of tort] might result in accepting too low a standard of human values for, to suggest that damages for a tort "should be measured according to the law of the place from which it has derived its origin," might, if some foreign laws were followed, result in an unduly restrictive view of common right and liberty, and fail to do justice as between man and man as required by our law. We see no reason why a person subject to our jurisdiction, should not be compelled to do justice according to our standards. This is especially so in actions of negligence when the claim is for damages resulting from a failure to observe the standard of conduct English law expects of a reasonable man.[187]

Progressively Wortley's thesis of recognition of universal rights derived from a universal concept of man makes it possible for him to describe indiscriminately virtually all private rights falling under the purview of PrIL cases as human rights. Not only does PrIL commit to human rights by "refus[ing] to recognize penalizing disabilities" and by "favor[ing] complete liberty of choice of spouse"[188] but also by committing to party autonomy in contract law.[189]

The way in which the notion of natural rights flows freely from one private law category to another is clear when Wortley argues that just as:

English courts allow a very wide freedom to the parties and tend to recognize the existence of the legal obligation of marriage whenever possible ... [s]o with contract: English courts will recognize contracts wherever possible in order to do justice between the parties and, what is more, they will follow the reasonable intentions of the parties.[190]

[183] Ibid., 152.

[184] Ibid., 155. See also 156, 157:

It would be attended with peculiarly serious consequences in the present state of Europe; since then the property of foreigners, who are daily resorting for refuge to this country, from confiscations at home, would not be protected against the designs of artful man who could gain possession of it by any means.

[185] Ibid., 163. [186] Ibid., 166. [187] Ibid., 161.

[188] B.A. Wortley, 'The General Principles of Private International Law from the English Standpoint' (1947) 71 Recueil des Cours 1, 34 (hereafter Wortley, "General Principles—English Standpoint").

[189] Ibid., 44. [190] Ibid., 44.

The idea that no man can be without domicile leads to the idea that no contract can be without a proper law and the liberty of individuals to choose a domicile spills into party autonomy in contract law.[191] Freedom of marriage is also equated to freedom of contract.[192] And just as general rules of PrIL operate to preserve liberty, the public policy exception is limited and/or invoked "in the interests of personal liberty."[193]

The way in which Wortley's concept of natural rights and liberty travel freely between various private law categories and the way in which the concept and the rights of man he describes shift from more relational, socially responsible, to more individualistic variations is best seen in his work on the question of expropriation.

In 1958 Wortley describes issues related to the protection of property as "the most controversial of all topics in private international law."[194] And although Wortley admits that different states "have differing conceptions of property, and there are as many gradations between the completely individualist and the completely collectivized State" Wortley believes property can be properly understood as a human right because:

> [I]n every civilized country in the world, the law provides machinery to protect the right of property and this includes the U.S.S.R ... For this reason one would have liked to have seen some reference to the right to property in Lauterpacht's impressive book entitled *An International Bill of the Rights of Man* (1945, New York), and we should have preferred something more than an oblique reference in article 15, in the British White paper on *An International Bill of Human Rights* (H.M.S.O.Jan: 1947).[195]

And while in 1958 he quite realistically refers to property as "power" and problems of power "are at the root of most international problems,"[196] just a year later, in his lecture delivered at the Tulane University Law School, Wortley describes property as a pre-political, natural right:

> What is the theoretical basis of the claim to protect property? The historical answer is, we would suggest, that the claim is based on the customs and usages of reasonable men ... Customs with regard to the use, abuse and appropriation of property exist from early times, and certainly precede the state with its modern power to legislate and its closely delimited boundaries.[197]

Claims to recover expropriated property or the value thereof brought in a state other than the expropriating one are therefore described as claims to recognize vested rights qua human rights:

> The prima facie right to recover possession of a thing seized is based upon the elementary notion of corrective justice, i.e., that the man whose thing is seized, without explanation, is entitled to recover it, or its equivalent. Restitution is based upon restoring a disturbed *status quo ante* and the prima facie right to restitution of possession is recognized in most legal systems as a matter of justice and fair dealing between man and man. Contractual, inherited

[191] Ibid., 45. [192] Ibid., 44. [193] Ibid., 51.

[194] B.A. Wortley, 'The General Principles of Private International Law' (1958) 94 Recueil des Cours 85, 192 (hereafter Wortley, "General Principles").

[195] Wortley, "General Principles—English Standpoint" (n. 188) 71. [196] Ibid.

[197] B A Wortley, 'The Protection of Property Situated Abroad' (1961) 35 Tul L Rev 739, 740 (hereafter Wortley, "Protection of Property").

and other claims to objects of property and to the repayment of debts, have existed and been recognized by legal customs, long before the arrival of the modern state with its elaborate court and police machinery.[198]

Since property rights are portrayed as pre-political universal human rights, obligations to restitution are also understood as "moral obligations," "natural obligations," or "natural rights in the creditor."[199] Wortley is unapologetic in his answer to a critic asking "how a legal right can exist unless protected by law."[200] Wortley replies:

The position is very simple: claims to the possession of things, to the repayment of debts and to the fulfillment of obligations or promises incurred, are prima facie protected in all civilized customary and codified systems alike which have any regard for justice. Claims to justice are protected, not *created,* by these systems ... [E]xperience shows that the fact that one legal system will not give a remedy to a man in respect of a claim to justice does not mean that will *necessarily* fail to obtain a legal remedy for that claim in another legal system, or by procedures of international law.[201]

The ambivalence between a more individualistic and a more relational perspective on the concept and rights of man is also reflected in the way in which Wortley fluctuates in his description of the injustice created by expropriation. In a paper read before the Grotius Society in 1947 he acknowledges that property is "power."[202] He argues:

The reason for expropriating and the method thereof must not be contrary to that conception of justice, which is an integral part of international law. There is a conception of justice in international law, historically European, but universal in character, which is based on the nature of man himself, and which would guarantee every man his rights of life and liberty and at least as much property as is necessary to support life. The present-day proposed statements of human rights, like all other statements, merely confirm a right inherent in man's nature, and in the nature of civilized society, the aim and purpose of which society is to promote life and not to destroy it. Grave infringements of elementary rights are international injuries of "torts," calling for diplomatic or other redress. Such international "wrongs" are not to be presumed; they must be proved. States are societies to protect life and hence *prima facie* entitled to have their authority respected.[203]

In the debates at the Grotius Society on Wortley's paper, G.C. Cheshire challenges Wortley precisely on his conception of justice and his definition of property:

He [Wortley] says that an expropriation must not be contrary to that conception of justice, which is an integral part of international law. "Justice" is a word that bears different meanings in different countries, and its vagueness and ambiguity arouse the instinctive suspicions of the lawyer. Professor Wortley attempts to give a more concrete shape to the conception and to bring it a little nearer to earth by explaining that its object is to guarantee to every man his rights of life and liberty and at least as much property as is necessary to support life. It is the last limb of this definition that I find a little puzzling and disturbing. Is international law

[198] Ibid. [199] Ibid. [200] Ibid. [201] Ibid.

[202] B.A. Wortley, 'Expropriation in International Law' (1947) 33 Transactions of the Grotius Society 25, 27.

[203] Ibid., 28.

satisfied as long as the victim of expropriation can eke out an existence? This certainly seems to be a case where the poor have the advantage of the rich, for apparently it is not objectionable to natural justice that a rich man should be deprived of the greater part of his wealth.[204]

And just as Cheshire expressed the hope that this inconsistency will "clear up,"[205] Wortley does not rely on the same definition of property or the wrongfulness of expropriation in subsequent writings. In an article published in the American Journal of Comparative Law in 1956 he argues that "states are interested in the economic well-being of their subjects, and a loss of foreign property usually makes the owner less able to discharge his obligations at home."[206] Therefore:

Unless a state is bound to do so by treaty, it will not usually recognize an expropriation of its subjects as valid in public international law if it considers that due restitution, or at least full compensation, has not been secured. This approach to expropriation in public international law finds its parallel in the field of private international law when an owner considers that expropriation is unjust if it deprives him of his ownership so as to leave him unable to satisfy obligations that he has assumed under various municipal laws either to his own creditors, to his family or, in the case of an ecclesiastic, to his superiors under Canon Law; such a feeling will prompt the dispossessed owner to sue in whatever home or foreign court he is advised that he can obtain restitution or damages.[207]

By 1959 when he delivers a lecture at Tulane University Law School, Wortley describes expropriations as international wrongs and violations of natural law, since property rights are inherent in human nature.[208] While in 1947 he wrote that such wrongs cannot be presumed and that the reason and method of expropriation might make some difference, he now argues that the wrongfulness can simply be presumed from the taking of property without consent.[209] The seizure is thus characterized as "internationally illegal" and entitles states to take recourse against the expropriating state:

A state protects its nationals' property which is in danger of confiscation by a proposed legislative program not only from motives of self-interest, in that it is better able to tax a wealthy subject, but also from the fact that every state has an interest to maintain the rule of law in international affairs, and to discourage any arbitrary and therefore internationally illegal seizures of property.[210]

His work on expropriation represents the culmination of various moves combining to create the universal recognition of rights: first, alleging a more or less universal, or at least "Western" concept of man and placing the individual at the center of both public and private international law; second, blurring the border between the more relational and more individualistic traits of the "high standard of man" incorporated in both private and public international law; third, describing virtually all private rights as pre-political universal human rights, and finally committing

[204] Ibid., 37. [205] Ibid., 38.
[206] B.A. Wortley, 'Observations on the Public and Private International Law Relating to Expropriation' (1956) 5 Am J Comp L 577, 579.
[207] Ibid., 579–80. [208] Wortley, "Protection of Property" (n. 197) 740. [209] Ibid.
[210] Ibid., 744.

international law, private and public, to the recognition of vested private rights qua human rights.

All these moves make it possible for Wortley to finally suggest that claims for restitution following nationalizations and expropriations should not allow for any justifications by the expropriating state and certainly should not allow for mere allegations of national interest. The alignment of private with public international law ultimately meant that stricter tort law claims could be enforced and recognized worldwide, at least in the spirit of "natural justice," against the nationalizing or expropriating state:

> It should be stressed then that the claim for restitution need not be made on the basis of any alleged "fault" or negligence. Such allegations usually (like those of discrimination already alluded to) impair international claims by raising a barrier of national pride—of face. It is better to make international claims on the lines of conversion or detinue in tort at common law, *i.e.*, solely on the basis that the property of the claimant has been detained or dealt with without the consent of the owner, without going into the innocence or otherwise of the detention. The owner had the property until it was taken and that entitles him prima facie to protection in international law.[211]

By reframing "vested private rights" as human rights Wortley argues not only for the connection of private and public international law, but also for a much stricter and often acontextual plea for the universal recognition of rights across borders. And as Wortley is keen to suggest, in this new realignment between private and public international law, it is private international law that is supposed to teach PublIL how to properly recognize private rights qua human rights.

The move from PrIL to PublIL culminating in the plea for the "protection of vested rights in international law" especially in the context of nationalizations and expropriations following the First and Second World War was very well underscored and critiqued in 1936 by G. Kaeckenbeeck, president of the Arbitral Tribunal for Upper Silesia.[212]

Kaeckenbeeck made two arguments, which are particularly relevant in the context of this chapter. First, he suggested that the notion of vested rights, which English scholars attempted to bring into PublIL is different from that of Savigny's.[213] On the one hand, Savigny rejected the notion of vested rights as an anchor for conflict of laws in space and argued that it should be used only in the context of conflict of laws in time.[214] On the other hand, he made a distinction between mere expectations and vested rights. As Kaeckenbeeck notes with respect to Savigny's theory:

> By *vested right*, however, is not as a rule here meant every legal relation of a determinate person. Abstract faculties or qualities of all men or of whole classes of men, as well as expectations founded on the law, are not vested rights, and are normally destroyed by a new law.[215]

[211] Ibid., 764.

[212] G. Kaeckenbeeck, 'The Protection of Vested Rights in International Law' (1936) 17 Brit YB Int'l L 1 (hereafter Kaeckenbeeck, "Vested Rights in International Law").

[213] For a description of Savigny's notion of vested rights and a comparison of different perspectives of vested rights in the intellectual history of PrIL, see Chapter 6.

[214] Kaeckenbeeck, "Vested Rights in International Law" (n. 212) 2.

[215] Ibid., 3.

Furthermore, by arguing that the whole question of vested rights "should be withdrawn from the province of absolute right and transferred to that of legislative policy, which is its true place" Savigny meant to avoid precisely the kind of acontextual argument that vested rights always trump legislative reform.[216]

By contrast, Kaeckenbeeck argued that English theories of vested rights anchored both private and public international law to a notion of vested rights which is broader (incorporating virtually "all legal positions that would be enforceable by the law under which they were created"[217]) and also more rigid as it is meant as a counterbalance to the principle of territoriality and the general view of late nineteenth-century English PrIL scholars that there is no obligation per se to apply foreign law:

> The object of this notion is not indeed to select rights especially entitled to preservation, but to give validity outside the territorial limits to all rights duly created. In this way it is the necessary postulate of any system of private international law based on territoriality and which in principle refuses to apply foreign law. As any system of law necessarily provides for the creation of rights and for the protection of the rights thus created, so also for internationally vested rights and, if this is to have any sense, for their international recognition and enforcement.[218]

Second, Kaeckenbeeck argued that precisely because the notion of vested rights incorporated from PrIL into PublIL takes a stricter approach than that favored by Savigny, there is a conflation between the suppression of vested rights and the question of compensation.[219] By contrast, Kaeckenbeeck argues, also in line with the Savignian notion of vested rights:

> ... the question when the legislature should overrule vested rights or capitulate before them is always and exclusively a question of policy, of public interest, which the state alone is competent to decide. And we must not forget that almost every social change, almost all so-called progress, plays havoc with some vested rights.[220]

The issue of protection of vested rights and the question of compensation—which need to be kept separated in Kaeckenbeeck's view[221]—take a more communitarian and more contextual form:

> If a state grants an indemnity to the holder of a suppressed vested right, I submit that it does not pay it as compensation for a tort, in order to redeem an illegal act [as Wortley suggested], but simply as an equitable alleviation, from funds of the community, of the economic sacrifice demanded on behalf of the community ... [I]t is in my opinion essential to keep clearly

[216] Ibid., 4.

[217] Ibid., 6 (also noting that this broader notion of vested rights as an anchor of international law broadly understood is a corollary to the concept of territoriality).

[218] Ibid., 6. [219] Ibid., 15. [220] Ibid., 15.

[221] Ibid:

> Another question, then, is whether the sacrifice imposed on the holders of the rights overruled is so considerable and exceptional as justice to require alleviation in the form of an indemnity. Many see one single issue in these two questions and speak in one breath of a duty not to suppress vested rights without compensation. Expediency from the point of view of public interest, and the equitableness of granting an indemnity are in my opinion two absolutely distinct questions, the solution of which depends on different facts and considerations.

in mind that the ground of compensation here is not reparation of a wrong but alleviation of an exceptional hardship, and that the aforementioned standard exists only as a requirement or, so to say, as a reservation of elementary justice ... Only, and this is worth insisting on, the application of this standard must always take into account all the elements of the case, for the very reason that it is a standard of justice and fairness. It can never be stereotyped, nor can it be subjected to hard and fast rules.[222]

3. F.A. Mann—Uniting PrIL and PublIL through the concept of international jurisdiction

A prevalent way of looking at the issue of expropriation in between the wars and after the Second World War was to consider it, vaguely, as a case of injustice, as Graveson did, or as a suppression of vested private rights, as Wortley did. In both cases connections were made in both directions between PrIL and PublIL. To view it as an injustice Graveson raised individual liberty under private law to the status of a universal natural right recognized internationally. To view it as a violation of human rights, Wortley described property as a human right and expropriation as an international tort which PublIL and PrIL alike must provide redress for, without the possibility of any justification.

But another way to look at the question of expropriation was to suggest that laws purporting to expropriate simply cannot be recognized abroad by virtue of their penal or confiscatory nature. Such an account, provided most vividly by F.A. Mann, also operates with various connections flowing in between PrIL and PublIL.[223]

[C]onflict rules are a product of municipal law, which has to stand the test of the international doctrine of jurisdiction. In other words, it is the function of jurisdiction to define the international scope, which the municipal legislator is entitled to give to his enactments. The conflict rule implements and gives effect to the requirements of public international law.[224]

It is PublIL that renders such laws unenforceable for being "based upon the *jus imperii*."[225] Even if the confiscatory legislation provides for compensation, the law allegedly cannot apply extraterritorially because:

[It] is still a manifestation of sovereignty, which no State may carry out so as to change title to property in another State. If this were not so the decree of a State would have greater legal effect in another state than the dispatch of a battalion of soldiers. It is, therefore, not the payment of compensation, but the character of the measure that is decisive, for no State has jurisdiction so as to bind property outside its borders.[226]

[222] Ibid., 16–17.

[223] For a useful account of F.A. Mann's scholarship and its placement in between private and public international law, see Lawrence Collins, 'F.A. Mann (1907–1991)' in Jack Beatson and Reinhard Zimmermann (eds.), *Jurists Uprooted: German Speaking Emigré Lawyers in Twentieth-century Britain* (OUP 2004) 381.

[224] F.A. Mann, 'The Doctrine of Jurisdiction in International Law' (1964) 111 Recueil des Cours 1, 19 (hereafter Mann, "Jurisdiction in International Law").

[225] F.A. Mann et al., 'Prerogative Rights of Foreign States and the Conflict of Laws' (1954) 40 Transactions of the Grotius Society 25, 29 (hereafter Mann, "Prerogative Rights").

[226] Mann, "Jurisdiction in International Law" (n. 224) 62.

For Mann, PrIL connects with PublIL precisely through the concept of international jurisdiction, a thesis the novelty of which he is unclear. On the one hand, he acknowledges Zitelmann, von Bar, "and numerous other scholars" to have "put this view forward toward the end of the 19th century"[227] and even recognizes the identity between this thesis and Pillet's framing of PrIL's function as "the fair distribution of sovereignty."[228]

At the same time he notes "that those interested in municipal law, including the conflict of laws, almost invariably ignore it [the issue of international jurisdiction], is perhaps less surprising if their deeply regrettable, yet general, *insouciance*, about public international law, is remembered."[229] He notes Beale however, as "a notable exception."[230] This characterization is even more surprising, since Mann locates the expertise on international jurisdiction firmly within PrIL:

> [T]he suggestion that the origin of the international doctrine of jurisdiction lies in the conflict of laws would not have caused surprise in the earlier days. Its correctness is even today unlikely to be questioned, for a fruitful and effective history of public international law starts some four centuries later than the history of the conflict of laws.[231]

And although the history of the doctrine of international jurisdiction takes Mann almost to a history of the entirety of PrIL, he seems to argue that it is now PublIL that commits PrIL to a theory of international jurisdiction based on territoriality—possibly initially borrowed from PrIL.[232] And while PublIL may have borrowed and internalized territoriality as a basis of international jurisdiction from PrIL, to update this principle PublIL can once again look to PrIL.[233] Mann argues that just as Savigny had modernized PrIL methodology by shifting from the analysis of statutes to the localization of a legal relation:

> Perhaps public international lawyers should now discard the question whether the nature of territorial jurisdiction allows certain facts to be made subject to a State's legislation. Rather should they ask whether the legally relevant facts are such that they "*belong*" to this or that jurisdiction.[234]

Once the expertise of distributing legislative jurisdiction among states—a framing of PrIL's goals, which Mann seems to attribute equally to Savigny and Zitelmann—is incorporated in PublIL, the two fields of law can once again reunite.

> The conclusion, then, is that a State has (legislative) jurisdiction, if its contact with a given set of facts is so close, so substantial, so direct, so weighty, that legislation in respect of them

[227] Ibid., 17. [228] Ibid., 18. [229] Ibid., 23. [230] Ibid., 23, n. 3.
[231] Ibid., 24. [232] Ibid., 24–44.
[233] Ibid., 54:

> It is due to the close historical connection between the two subjects that private international law reflects the effects and requirements of the doctrine of legislative jurisdiction more faithfully than any other branch of the law. Private international law proves, in particular, the familiar reluctance to transgress those limits of jurisdiction which public international law recognizes, as well as the development from a strictly territorial to a more flexible doctrine of closeness of connection.

[234] Ibid., 44–5.

is in harmony with international law and its various aspects (including the practice of States, the principles of non-interference and reciprocity and the demands of inter-dependence). A merely political, economic, commercial or social interest does not in itself constitute a sufficient connection.[235]

At first sight, reuniting PrIL and PublIL through the concept of international jurisdiction might appear to reconnect PrIL with the politics of PublIL, as Horatia Muir Watt notoriously pled for.[236] Mann himself for example argued that "no rule of international jurisdiction requires or, indeed, permits any distinction in the scope of public and private law legislation."[237] Yet, he also argued that it was wrong to suggest, as various German authors at the time did, that there should be special conflict of laws rules ensuring that the laws of various states whose interests are affected, may apply.[238] Instead, Mann suggested that one should stick to general rules of conflict of laws based on the principle of international jurisdiction:

[E]xcept in a very specific and limited type of case, there is, or should be, no room in the conflict of laws, for attributing a distinct role to public law: if foreign law is applicable it should, in principle, be applied as it is, without regard to legal classifications of provisions or rules.[239]

Furthermore, it is unclear to what extent the substantive part of public international law is incorporated into PrIL. Mann argues that acts of a foreign state, whether legislative or executive, can be scrutinized by the forum either in light of the public policy exception which should include norms of public international law or based on a violation of public international law directly:

Even if the validity of the foreign act of State under public international law may not be investigated under the law of the foreign State, it is open to the forum to do so to the extent to which it allows public international law to be applied by its courts.[240]

Yet he does not reflect much on how conflict of laws norms can be devised precisely in order to incorporate substantive norms of PublIL into PrIL. Instead, based on the principle of international jurisdiction, in Mann's framework conflict of laws norms still attempt a rather neutral distribution of sovereign authority, much as nineteenth-century state-centered internationalists had argued. For example, according to Mann, the principle of international jurisdiction mandates the strict application of the law of the place where the tort occurred, rather than the application of the wrongdoer's nationality or domicile.[241] Furthermore, it rejects the application of antitrust law based on effects felt within the state:

It is submitted that "effect", whether intended or merely foreseeable or unexpected, does not constitute a sufficiently close connection with the importing country so as to permit the

[235] Ibid., 49.

[236] Horatia Muir Watt, 'Private International Law Beyond the Schism' (2011) 2 Transnatl Leg Theory 347.

[237] Mann, "Jurisdiction in International Law" (n. 224) 72.

[238] See F.A. Mann, 'Conflict of Laws and Public Law' (1971) 132 Recueil des Cours 107, 157 (hereafter Mann, "Public Law").

[239] Ibid., 116. [240] Ibid., 154.

[241] Mann, "Jurisdiction in International Law" (n. 224) 58.

assumption of legislative jurisdiction by the latter; from the point of view of public international law the *Alcoa* decision cannot, therefore, be justified, and if the rules of customary construction imposed by international law had been observed it is also unlikely to be supported by a proper interpretation of the Sherman Act itself.[242]

Overall, F.A. Mann's account represented a counter narrative to the individual-centered position of his fellow English scholars after the Second World War. It was also a return to the state-centered internationalism that dominated continental European PrIL scholarship at the end of the nineteenth century. In turn, the individual-centered position he provided a counter narrative to, resembled early nineteenth-century European vested rights theories based on natural law and individual liberty.[243] In the second half of the twentieth century one could find in English PrIL scholarship both the individualistic and the state-centered extremes of PrIL theory and methodology, although one could argue that the former was certainly more prominent. Overall in Europe the liberal internationalism of vested rights and international jurisdiction theories combined quite easily with the technical, methodological focus of the system coordination and conflicts justice theories.

F. Critique of the "Tendence Privatiste"

1. Phocion Franceskakis

The liberal and technical directions in the development of PrIL, though widely accepted, also had their critics. The French scholar of Greek origin, Phocion Franceskakis, was an avid critic of both tendencies, which he considered typical of PrIL's development after the Second World War.[244] For Franceskakis PrIL had become almost obsessed with its methodology and its respective tools.[245] He disavowed the rigidity and often incomprehensibility of the field[246] and also the particular liberalization and facilitation of cross-border relationships that had come to accompany internationalism, as opposed to a substantive regulatory framework for such relationships.[247] At the same time, he was avidly searching for traces in

[242] Ibid., 104. [243] For an account of those theories, see Chapter 6.

[244] See, e.g., Franceskakis, *La pensée des autres* (n. 9) 48:

> I do not believe that the object of our discipline should be limited to international commerce in the sense used by Lerebours-Pigeonniere. Apart from the phenomenon of international exchange—undeniable factor of progress—our field has also focused on different phenomena. We are talking about the problem of human migration, of their transfer (or the transfer of their activity) voluntarily from one legal order of private law to another. The private law legal order of a state is focused increasingly on the social. [...] Consequently, the state is more and more directly interested in the activity of private individuals.

[245] Ibid., 198: "the complication as well as the excessive proliferation of so called mechanisms." See also at 235: "the increased role in PrIL of the method of conflict of laws."

[246] Ibid., 198: "the necessity for PrIL to internalize an ambition to become intelligible to the average jurist."

[247] Ibid., 134: "for internationalists [...] the immediately discernable goal is their [the legal relations'] increased frequency and liberty."

the scholarship of the post-war period trying to reconnect PrIL with PublIL. For example, in Franceskakis's more than eighty reviews of PrIL writings between 1946 and 1984, one can trace the frustration in his relentless search for any indication that PrIL scholars might be trying to reconnect PrIL with PublIL.[248]

Much like PrIL scholars trying to emphasize the global regulatory function of PrIL today, Franceskakis thought connecting PrIL with PublIL would come with a particular normative agenda. It would emphasize the public, political implications of each PrIL legal matter; it would challenge the individualistic premises of the dominant current of his time and it would question PrIL's obsession with mere distribution of authority regardless of the substantive result.[249] But that vision was nowhere to be found.

In the relational internationalist perspective, that vision came with an argument for focusing from the individual upwards, to his relationships, his community, his state, and humanity. That was because the state-centered perspective at the time was formalistic and ignored the needs and interests of individuals. In the twentieth century the individual-centered internationalist perspectives were quite explicitly liberal, so it seemed implausible to argue that an individual-centered internationalist perspective could exist that would encourage, rather than diminish, social responsibility. Furthermore, because Savigny was associated with both blind distribution of authority and liberal ideology and because Jitta's development of Savigny's theory was mostly unacknowledged or misunderstood, there was no relational internationalist perspective to fall back on. Now, the only way to push for a socially just system of PrIL was, for Franceskakis, as for many contemporary global governance scholars, to put one's hope in PublIL and focus on states and politics. This of course ignores the fact that historically the PrIL-PublIL association generally offered little space for politics and a substantive agenda for social justice.

In his attempt to push for the public, the political, and social justice, Franceskakis repeated the three main arguments that Jitta had made at the end of the nineteenth century. First, he argued that PrIL had become overly obsessed with its methodology, its systematic structure, and technicalities.[250] Franceskakis believed this distracted PrIL from its direct regulatory function, the substantive goals of the international society.[251] Like Jitta, Franceskakis argued that PrIL should stop focusing on distributing legislative authority based on conflict of laws norms and instead focus on

[248] Ibid., 320–4, 345, 356, 358, 387–9, 408.

[249] Ibid., 319 and 309: "under current conditions the distinction between private and public law becomes less and less consistent and PrIL was never easily placed within this distinction." But see 312: "makes one wonder whether, when the collaboration of states is exercised solely in the sense of simple tolerance of rules elaborated outside its purview, 'the judicial creativity' of merchants would not operate in favor of weakening the influence of states on international economic life." See also 323 (suggesting that the relationship between the two fields would lead to an increased focus on international public policy).

[250] Ibid., 198: "The complication and proliferation of so-called mechanisms [makes it less likely] for PrIL to internalize the need to make itself intelligible to the average jurist."

[251] Franceskakis, *La pensée des autres* (n. 9) 48.

direct substantive rules for the international society, a proposition that would later be made by Arthur von Mehren[252] and Friedrich Juenger.[253]

Franceskakis rehearsed Jitta's main insight that the conflict of laws norm is only a method and furthermore only one amongst many methods to achieve a just regulation of international interhuman relationships:[254]

> The procedure of direct rules implies, as we will see, a direct engagement with the purpose of international legal relations. The generalization of this approach would lead to the perfection of the international society, which is in question. In this case, law would impose or validate human actions only by direct reference to the structure and finality of such society.[255]

Focusing on substantive goals for an international society meant, second, that Franceskakis believed the international social context has its own particularities, which lead to different regulatory needs. He therefore shared Jitta's skepticism that you could always situate a legal relation in one jurisdiction or even that you could serve international regulatory needs by extrapolating from the national ones:

> My main argument [against the idea of conflicts justice as developed by M. Kegel] is that the conflict of laws method, by calling for the regulation of the international matter through the accumulation of national laws and by making us believe that the regulation of the international matter is a question of equilibrium between the states implicated, of their national affairs, ignores the specificity of international inter-human relationships, which cannot be accounted for merely by the application of purely national laws.[256]

It is not surprising then that Franceskakis thought of renvoi merely as a technique, rather than a principle enshrined in the very nature of PrIL as a legal system.[257]

Last, it seemed obvious and advisable to Franceskakis that each state and each legislator would need to judge for themselves which PrIL rules are appropriate in each case.[258] It is not always clear whether Franceskakis thought each state would be free to apply its law or serve its political interests whenever it had jurisdiction over a PrIL matter,[259] or whether he believed, like Jitta, that even when the judge and the legislators act unilaterally in PrIL, they still need to have in view humanity as a whole.[260] But in his review of Jacques Maury in 1982, Franceskakis seems to have largely adopted Jitta's general insights:

[252] See Arthur Taylor von Mehren, 'Special Substantive Rules for Multistate Problems: Their Role and Significance in Contemporary Choice of Law Methodology' (1974) 88 Harv L Rev 347.

[253] Friedrich K. Juenger, *Choice of law and multistate justice* (M. Nijhoff 1993).

[254] Franceskakis, *La pensée des autres* (n. 9) 407.

[255] Ibid., 168.

[256] Ibid., 237 (Yet Franceskakis was certainly not a deregulator and he criticized repeatedly the idea that PrIL is too much focused on international commerce as well as the fact that international contracts would be allowed to "flow in a no man's land," at 48).

[257] Ibid., 238 and 217: "in my opinion the progress of our discipline does not rest in complicating matters but rather making them accessible to the practice and why not, to the people."

[258] Ibid., 77.

[259] Ibid., 238 (mentioning that unlike Batiffol, he always believed the application of foreign law is exceptional: "M. Batiffol places, at least in principle, foreign law on a footing of equality with the internal law of the forum. We have, on our part, always considered the inferior position of foreign law in relationship to the law of the forum, based on the idea that the application of foreign law is merely an exceptional case to the normal application of the lex fori.").

[260] Ibid., 77.

Private International Law, national as it is according to its sources [...] should not be abandoned to the goodwill of states, no less than certain sectors of PublIL. For the legal matters pertaining to it, the solution demanded from PrIL should be, for all courts and arbitrators, the result of an examination of the kind that Maury advocated for an international judge. As to the possibility of a "non conflictual" solution by formulating material rules, we are not too far from Maury in thinking that they are incumbent on an international law, understood according to its ancient term, as the jus gentium privatum.[261]

2. Duco Kollewijn

During his lifetime, Jitta was more or less an outcast in PrIL. In the Netherlands Jitta's PrIL theory was quite overtly undermined and marginalized, including by his colleague T.M.C. Asser.[262] But many Dutch international law scholars, knowingly or not, recast many of his insights. A prominent example is Roeland Duco Kollewijn. In PrIL circles Kollewijn made a name for himself primarily with respect to what he called "intergentiel" private law, otherwise known as "inter-personal," "colonial law," or "inter-religious law."[263] After writing his dissertation on the concept of "ordre public" in private international law at Leyden University, Kollewijn took the exam that qualified him for the judiciary in the then Netherlands Indies.[264]

As his biographer noted:

he came to live in a plural society, where plurality of law was prevailing within the boundaries of a single territory: the law for the several Indonesian people, for Europeans, for Chinese and others. In addition, a system of law in the colony, which even for Europeans was different in many points from that in force in the metropolis. Rich fields indeed for the study of the conflict of laws, ripe for harvesting.[265]

Kollewijn thought "contacts between different civilisations are a fascinating field of study"[266] and he "emphatically rejected the view, that in colonies adhering to plurality of law, priority should be accorded to one (and then of course the metropolitan) system."[267] He believed PrIL should come to terms with "conflicts of Western and Non-Western law" and give proper respect to both:

When we are brought face to face with legal relations unknown to our own law, we may well find that we have no rules of conflict appropriate to these unknown institutions. But we ought not therefore to refuse to recognize, or even in appropriate circumstances to give effect to, an institution or status unknown in our Western countries; rather, we should work out

[261] Ibid., 409.

[262] For the way in which Jitta was perceived relative to other Dutch scholars of his time, especially T.M.C. Asser see G.J.W. Steenhoff, 'Daniel Josephus Jitta—1854–1925' in *The Moulding of International Law: Ten Dutch Proponents* (T.M.C. Asser Instituut 1995) 231.

[263] Franceskakis, *La pensée des autres* (n. 9) 210.

[264] J.H.A. Logemann, 'Biography of Roeland Duco Kollewijn' (1962) 9 Nethl Int'l L Rev 17, 18 (hereafter Logemann, "Duco Kollewijn").

[265] Ibid.

[266] R.D. Kollewijn, 'Conflicts of Western and Non-Western Law' (1951) 4 Internat'l L Quarterly 307, 324 (hereafter Kollewijn, "Western and Non-Western Law").

[267] Logemann, "Duco Kollewijn" (n. 264) 20.

new rules applicable to the interplay of these strange institutions with our own. International private law is not merely a static group of fixed rules confined to the legal institutions of a definite number of Christian or Western States, but a dynamic entity, which is constantly growing with the progressive integration of what is after all (and more obviously as time proceeds) a single world.[268]

He therefore focused on uncovering the principles, theories, and norms that can be borrowed and adapted from PrIL to deal with clashes between fundamentally different laws, values, and cultures. What is most interesting for the purpose of this chapter is that in so doing Kollewijn recast many of Jitta's insights, including, without referring to him, Jitta's reconstruction of Savigny's theory. Furthermore, it is often precisely the relational insight underlying Savigny's and Jitta's theories that Kollewijn seems to rely on.

a) Colonial law

Kollewijn was most critical of "the earliest attitude of Westerners [. . .] which is not yet wholly extinct, to regard the rules of social intercourse observed in non-Western communities as not being in any true sense law: according to this view, they may be usages or customs or they may have been imposed by force but they cannot be recognized as law. This conception has been nourished by purely material interests and defended by bombastic theories."[269]
Instead, he believed that "before such law can be acknowledged it must be studied and understood; and down to the present day the failure to appreciate non-Western law at its true value is commonly based on ignorance."[270]

Kollewijn thought it repugnant that German, French, and British colonial theory for a long time maintained the superiority of the law of the colonizing state and often denied the status of law to the rules in the colonies.[271] What is more, he found it unacceptable that one would feel comfortable in "passing a sweeping judgment on the indigenous law as a whole without going into the examination of separate rules."[272] There was in other words "a generalization of ignorance."[273]

Interestingly, Kollewijn believed this blatant disregard for different cultures and values was solidified when PrIL started to be perceived as a law of sovereigns and focused primarily on distribution of sovereignty. For example, he noted a legal matter decided in 1932 by the Court of Justice of Algier, which involved an Italian woman who married a Tunisian Jew in Tunis. Her husband repudiated her by ghett under Tunisian Jewish law, but the woman refused to accept and filed for divorce. Kollewijn had this to say:

[268] Kollewijn, "Western and Non-Western Law" (n. 266) 325. [269] Ibid., 308.
[270] Ibid.
[271] Ibid., 313 (citing the minister for the French overseas territories, writing in 1948, 37 Rev crit dr int privé 545: "In the case of a conflict between the normal French legal system and a local legal system, it is the former that must necessarily win. That is to say, French law is the norm; indigenous law is abnormal, temporary, transient, jurisprudence d'exception, and limited in its scope").
[272] Ibid., 312. [273] Ibid., 310.

This conflict was not between the French law of the Civil Code and the Tunisian Jewish law, but between the Italian law of the wife and the law of the French protectorate, regarding a marriage celebrated in Tunisia in Tunisian fashion, between parties living in Tunis, the husband being a Tunisian Jew. Had this been an ordinary case of international private law, either the lex loci celebrationis or the law of the matrimonial domicile [...] would have applied. In either case the result would have been the same, namely, the application of Tunisian law. But the Algerian court held that the rules of private international law presupposed a certain equality between the laws which may be applied and this equality is lacking in a conflict between European and Tunisian Jewish law. The court says that Tunisia is a protectorate and that the raison d'etre of the political position is a certain limitation of the sovereignty of the protected State and not only in matters of public law but also in matters of private law in order to secure the predominance of the European law, in this case the Italian law of the wife, over the Tunisian law of Oriental origin.[274]

Kollewijn fundamentally disagreed with this line of reasoning and praised the Dutch system of equality of all laws since:

no one can ever call one legal system in itself, higher or lower, better or worse, than another, there is no standard by which to measure it. The question whether a legal system is good or not can only be considered in connection with a group of persons to be governed by it.[275]

Kollewijn therefore believed the only way to judge a matter of conflict of western and non-western law is like any other matter of PrIL, namely to inquire into the social connection between a particular relationship between individuals and a particular community and a set of norms that regulate it. He thought the idea of localization of a legal relation had precisely this in view, a cosmopolitan understanding that no law is as such superior to another, but that a law could plausibly regulate particular people and particular relationships that fall under its purview.[276] Therefore, he thought it outrageous that French law for example would not recognize a polygamous relationship in which one spouse was French:

The quintessence of this position is not merely that the marriage contracted in France was governed by French law, but that it continued to be governed by French law even after the couple had made their matrimonial domicile in Annam, and consequently that a French marriage could never be converted into an Asiatic marriage permitting polygamy, no matter how long a married couple may remain in Annam.[277]

[274] Ibid., 313. [275] Ibid., 314.

[276] This is very well reflected in his analysis of Savigny's method. See Kollewijn, "Quelques considerations" (n. 11).

[277] Kollewijn, "Western and Non-Western Law" (n. 248) 317. As to the position that the *lex fori* should judge the nature of marriage according to its own law, Kollewijn stated, at 320:

> It would probably be agreed, first and foremost, that when the term "marriage" occurs in a British statute territorially intended for the homeland only, it must be understood in the English sense. But I venture to suggest that if English municipal law is applied in international relations in accordance with English doctrines of the Conflict of Laws, this does not necessarily mean that the word should have in its international relation exactly the same sense as it had in its internal or municipal aspect; some modifications become necessary when the Act is applied to a situation which is not in contemplation of Parliament when it was passed.

Overall, Kollewijn believed conflict of laws rules could achieve precisely the kind of cosmopolitan respect for different communities, cultures, and values that was needed when confronted with conflicts of Western and non-Western law. But that meant PrIL itself had to sustain, rather than undermine, that goal. And PrIL itself had its problems. For example, like Jitta, Kollewijn was critical of the lack of empiricism and pragmatism of PrIL. He noted that interpersonal law had been developed in the Dutch East Indies primarily by case law: "The study of law here plays a careful and modest role. In recent years—conscious of the harm that a priori theories have inflicted on private international law—it has been more concerned to determine, summarize and explain than to be creative."[278]

Therefore, "the choice of law rules of private international law ought not to be indiscriminately applied in interregional cases. The court should be aware that choice of law rules might have been formed or created in the narrow-minded spirit of a chauvinistic legal consciousness that did not wish to take proper account of the requirements of international coexistence."[279]

Interestingly, Kollewijn's ideal view of PrIL traced four of Jitta's main insights. First, he thought a certain degree of freedom must be allowed to the judge in order to appreciate all the facets of the international relationships subject to the dispute:

> Facts themselves possess a force that to an extent determine the court's decision (the fait accompli), but only to a certain extent, for statute and justice each impose their own demands which the court must obey. Judges must in this also take heed of developments in society. If rules of law are absent, judges must follow their own personal convictions of what justice is and ought to be.[280]

Often his view of the role of the judge is as controversial as Jitta's:

> No judge can avoid that he perceives life in his own individual manner and that his judgment of the law and fact bears the stamp of his own personality. And that is good, for being called upon to participate in the development of the law of his country he must give so as he is; he should have the courage to follow the principles that he personally holds true.[281]

Second, like Jitta, he thought every principle, such as the one of nationality, should serve merely as a guiding thought rather than as an a priori tool to assign vast numbers of relationships indiscriminately to particular jurisdictions.[282] Third, Kollewijn adopts the same relational perspective as Jitta. For example, he criticized the famous French Ferrari decision in which French courts determined that the French national who married an Italian in Italy could obtain a divorce in France, although their entire married life occurred in Italy and the spouse still lived there. He argued that:

> the French court took account only of the French party while in fact it was concerned with a legal relation that existed in relation to two or more persons. [. . .] The court thereby disregarded the fact that it could not intervene in the legal relation of the French party without also affecting the rights of the other party.[283]

278 G.J.W. Steenhoff, 'Roeland Duco Kollewijn—1892–1972' in *The Moulding of International Law* (n. 244) 382.

279 Ibid., 384. 280 Ibid., 396. 281 Ibid., 379. 282 Ibid., 385.

283 Ibid., 386:

Furthermore, again like Jitta, he repeatedly criticized the unilateral application of the law of domicile of the husband because this disregards the interests and community affiliations of the wife.[284] He argued repeatedly for the repeal of the provision held in the Dutch East Indies' Civil Code whereby the recognition by the European parent of a child born of a native woman removed all civil law relations between the mother and the child.[285]

Last, Kollewijn subscribed to Jitta's duality between the "unilateral" and the "multilateral" method and Jitta's proposition that even when the court applies the unilateral method, it must still have in view humanity and the international dimensions of the legal relation.[286] Kollewijn also adopted the constant duality between particularism and universalism that underlined both Jitta's and Savigny's theories.[287]

He argued that "even States are parts of a greater whole and that therefore decisions in cases involving international relationships must also be responsible to the international community."[288] Furthermore, he blamed the academic community for the extreme focus on sovereignty and nationalism at the beginning of the century. As Steenhoff noted, Kollewijn thought:

> The fact that it was a nationalistic period in history was an explanation for that phenomenon but certainly not a justification for it. Private International Law was strongly under the influence of academic commentators who should have protected it from sub-division under national law but who instead were those same people who, far more than the courts and the legislature, made the fatal connection between application of national law and sovereignty.[289]

> For private international law is still international in the sense that it concerns international relationships and international relationships cannot be properly judged unless one calls to mind before judgment and incorporates therein the reception and consequences that the judgment will have abroad. Legislators, courts and commentators who neglect this, on the ground that private international law should after all be national, fail to recognize the task that is laid on the national body in the process of the formation of international law.

284 Ibid., 392. 285 Ibid., 384. 286 Ibid., 386.

287 Ibid., 387:

> I notice that even the greatest of the great, probably as a result of these combined theories, namely, that private international law is conflicts law and that private international law is national law, are led to conclusions that are less than correct. They draw the conclusion that, as it is the national legislator that defines the scope of operation of its own law and only that body has the right to do so, it is unacceptable, as Pillet says, that a sovereign should take notice of the view of another in order to discover how far the prerogatives of its own sovereignty extend, and in particular how far its law extends in order to apply its own laws. But is this nothing more than shutting one's eyes to legal conceptions from abroad even though one is faced with an international relationship? When one is of the view that, simply by querying the sphere of operation of the national law, it can be ascertained whether it must be applied or not to a relationship to which also foreign law has a claim to be applied, is this not in fact the application of a national solution to an international issue?

288 Logemann, "Duco Kollewijn" (n. 264) 18.

289 Steenhoff, "Roeland Duco Kollewijn" (n. 260) 390.

b) Recasting Jitta's reconstruction of Savigny's theory

In 1968 Kollewijn wrote his last major article "Several Considerations About Savigny's Theory."[290] When reading the article, one has the impression that the author tried to show the way in which his entire life-long engagement with questions of PrIL and interregional law relates to, but also departs from, Savigny's theory. Kollewijn also thought it was generally necessary to understand how, in his view, Savigny's theory is particularly useful for the social realities of his time, but also to what extent Savigny's theory must be refined in light of those social realities. Most strikingly, although Kollewijn cites Jitta only once throughout the article, he recasts almost entirely Jitta's revision of Savigny's theory.

Like Jitta, Kollewijn thought that the "grand and durable merit of Savigny" was to focus the PrIL analysis on the legal relation.[291] He also thought that Savigny, contrary to the common understanding, had thought of the "nature of a legal relation" as a fluid concept, which encourages rather than distracts from a thorough analysis.[292] He agreed with Kahn's[293] and Bartin's[294] critique that a legal relation could not have a universal nature, but that instead each court and legislator would perceive the legal relation from their national perspective. Kollewijn thought "the issue of qualification had been enormously exaggerated."[295] He thought, like Jitta, that "while it is self-evident that a judge is situated in her own state's point of view and it is just as evident that the judge will apply her own PrIL,"[296] that does not mean she applies her own substantive law.[297] Rather, the conflict of laws norms must be interpreted and "it is only in contact with the figures of foreign laws that the national conflict of laws can be comprehensible."[298]

Kollewijn adopted entirely Jitta's distinction between the unilateral and the multilateral method. With no universal consensus on the nature of the legal relation, each court and legislator decides on the nature of an international legal relation.[299] Yet even when courts and legislators apply the unilateral method, they still understand that they are in effect determining the nature of an international, rather than national, relationship, and that the views, values, and principles of foreign communities would need to be factored in.[300]

[290] Kollewijn, "Quelques considerations" (n. 11).

[291] Ibid., 258. See also 238: "from the beginning he [Savigny] opposes the person as such [. . .] to legal relations in which individuals might find themselves." For his discussion of the controversy over whether the analysis is centered on the legal or the factual relationship, see 248–9.

[292] Ibid., 251:

> Savigny does not adopt a purely rational justification [for the nature of the legal relation], as he brings to bear as many rationales as possible and justifies them in relationship to one another. It is the interpretation of the nature of a legal relation and the weighing of the elements that display the talent of the jurist who finds an acceptable, even though not always easy to explain, solution to the PrIL matter.

[293] Ibid., 241. [294] Ibid. [295] Ibid., 241. [296] Ibid., 241.

[297] Ibid., 242. [298] Ibid., 242. [299] Ibid., 242.

[300] Logemann, "Duco Kollewijn" (n. 264) 18.

Furthermore, Kollewijn adopted Jitta's insight that it would not always be possible to "localize" legal relations in only one community. Kollewijn writes:

> We have become more modest: we do not believe there is one veritable nature of a legal relation, one veritable law for all legal relations. But we have not lost sight of the demands of the world community [. . .] While Savigny so to speak tries from above to achieve the unity of conflict of laws solution through a universal nature of all legal relations, we believe that this unity is achieved from below, through our acknowledgment of the relative value of our judgment. [301]

In this account Kollewijn outlines one of the main characteristics of the relational internationalist perspective as it culminated with Jitta. The way in which one could be "mindful of the demands of the world community" while acknowledging the "relative value of our judgment" represents precisely the restrained universalist connotations of this perspective outlined in Chapter 8.

G. Conclusions

Franz Kahn's awakening of the national sentiment in PrIL at the end of the nineteenth century influenced the development of the field into the first few decades of the twentieth century. Within that movement, the relational internationalist perspective was lost because of both its internationalist, and its individual-centered premises.

Yet the post Second World War period will bring internationalist perspectives into law generally and PrIL in particular. The internationalism of the post -war period seems connected to an awakened interest in methodology and systematicity under the label of systems coordination, and a refocusing on individual vested rights and liberty. The combination translates into a uniform recognition of individual rights and liberty across legal systems, into Graveson's positive coordination of legal systems. In other words, internationalism is linked to the atomistic image of the individual and of individual liberty and to states' alleged duty to recognize and foster this liberty as much as possible, as well as to suppress the application of public policy. Inevitably, the possibility of combining individual liberty and public policy under the image of relational rights and freedom is hard to find.

Normatively, though not conceptually, the arguments that rested at the core of Jitta's reconstruction of the relational internationalist perspective are often recast by critics of extreme internationalism and individualism. Yet, because of the individualistic tendencies of the international individual-centered perspectives of the time, arguments in favor of public law and social justice are often state-centered. Much as in contemporary debates, Franceskakis thought realigning PrIL with PublIL and focusing on state regulatory objectives might be a way to reach those goals. But like in contemporary debates, it was unclear even for Franceskakis how the PrIL-PublIL relationship would be structured and what impact it would have on PrIL as a field.

[301] Kollewijn, "Quelques considerations" (n. 11) 255–6.

Similarly, as for Brainard Currie in the United States, once Franceskakis started focusing on state regulatory interests, he inevitably argued for "the inferiority of foreign law, based on the idea that the application of foreign law would only constitute an exception of the formal application of the law of the forum."[302] In other words, if the public, social element was to be identified with the state and state regulatory policies, it was hard to understand precisely what the international dimension of PrIL could be, if any.

[302] Franceskakis, *La pensée des autres* (n. 9) 238.

5

Individual-Centered and State-Centered Internationalist Perspectives in American Private International Law Theory

A. Introduction

The previous chapters described the role that the individual-centered/state-centered analytical distinction played in the development of PrIL in Europe in the nineteenth century and after the Second World War. They showed that the Story-Savigny-Jitta trio could be viewed as a progression of individual-centered internationalist arguments, which were meant to provide a counternarrative both to the purely structural state-centered perspective, and to the overly individualistic perspectives of the nineteenth century. As it culminated in Jitta's account, the relational internationalist perspective was meant to inject a more substantive and more pragmatic engagement with the transnational existence of individuals embedded in a progressively wider social context (the private law relationship—the state(s)—humanity).

Yet as the nineteenth century came to an end, this perspective had disappeared from sight. The end of the century saw both the much more robust articulation of the state-centered internationalist perspective in Pillet's and Zitelmann's account and the emergence of the nationalist private law perspective of Franz Kahn and his disciples. Furthermore, after the Second World War, variations of the vested rights theory combined with the thesis of coordination of legal systems, which increased the focus on individual liberty and the technical dimensions of PrIL.

This chapter follows the state-centered/individual-centered duality within American PrIL theory and methodology from the 1920s onwards. The classical account of that history does not track the individual-centered/state-centered analytical duality, which is the focus of this book. However, read from this perspective, classical historical accounts give the impression that American PrIL theory and methodology developed from Joseph Beale's (1861–1943) rights-based perspective to Brainerd Currie's (1912–1965) state-centered perspective, which was then followed by several attempts to temper the state-centered perspective through a revival of rights-based discourse, most notably by

Nineteenth-Century Perspectives on Private International Law. Roxana Banu. © Roxana Banu 2018.
Published 2018 by Oxford University Press.

Lea Brilmayer and Perry Dane.[1] In contrast, this chapter tries to inject several different perspectives and nuances into this historical account.

This chapter argues that we tend to mischaracterize Beale's account as individual-centered—or at least fail to articulate the contours of the vested rights ideology in light of the European state-centered internationalist arguments that Beale rehearsed in his own theory. The first part of this chapter presents a different reading of Beale's vested rights theory, as an extension to, rather than a break from the state-centered internationalist theories of Pillet and Zitelmann.

Furthermore, this chapter argues that the classical historical account is unhelpful because it fails to unpack the variety of individual-centered arguments, which feature both within the American realist school of thought in PrIL and in the arguments of its critics. After briefly describing the first wave of the realist theory in the writings of Walter Wheeler Cook and Ernest G. Lorenzen and then Brainerd Currie's much more developed state-interest theory, this chapter outlines a rich and underexplored debate among the realist scholars, and their critics, about the implications of choosing the individual or the state as the analytical point of departure in PrIL theory and methodology. It underscores three different ways in which individual-centered arguments were used to try to temper Currie's state-centered premises. In reviewing critiques against Currie's state-centered perspective, the analysis in this chapter distinguishes between arguments focused on fairness, those based on equity and equality, and those based on a sociological notion of disaggregated state interests. When properly engaged with, each of those arguments offers an additional layer explaining the function of individual-based arguments within PrIL theory and methodology. While it is less clear what role these arguments played in the development of American PrIL theory,[2] they provide a valuable perspective on the role that they could play in rethinking PrIL's regulatory function today.

B. Beale's Vested Rights Theory

Beale's vested rights theory represented the first more thoroughly articulated theory of conflict of laws in the United States since Story's writings, as well as the theoretical foundation of the First Restatement.[3] Beale's later critics, who started the realist "revolution" in the 1930s, portrayed him as a formalist, overly concerned with dogmatism and positing unexplained axioms.[4] By contrast, for the

[1] For an account of the development of American PrIL, see Symeon Symeonides, *American Private International Law* (Wolters Kluwer 2008); Symeon Symeonides, 'The American Choice-of-Law Revolution in the Courts: Today and Tomorrow' (2002) 298 Recueil des Cours 1.

[2] For an account of how the current approach of American courts on conflict of laws matters is both influenced by but also departs from previous theories, see Lea Brilmayer, 'The Problem of Provenance: The Proper Place of Ethical Reasoning in the Selection of Applicable Law' in Donald Earl Childress (ed.), *The Role of Ethics in International Law* (CUP 2012) (hereafter Brilmayer, "The Problem of Provenance").

[3] See, e.g., Ernest Lorenzen and Raymond Heilman, 'The Restatement of the Conflict of Laws' (1935) 83 U Pa L Rev 555.

[4] See, e.g., Walter Wheeler Cook, 'The Logical and Legal Bases of the Conflict of Laws' (1924) 33 Yale LJ 457 (hereafter Cook, "Logical and Legal Bases"); Walter Wheeler Cook, 'The Jurisdiction

counter-revolutionaries[5] the Bealean theory would serve as a point of reference in tempering what they perceived to be the chaotic and overly state-centered premises underlying the realist school.[6] At first glance, PrIL theory in the United States seems to have developed from the individual-centered theory of Beale to the state-centered theory of Currie and then to a less successful attempt to temper the state-centered development with certain rights-based arguments (partly inspired by Beale's theory). Thus portrayed, Beale's theory is thought to provide—possibly stripped of its formalist foundation—a germ of the individual-centered ideology.

This chapter provides a different historical narrative and a different reading of Beale's theory. It argues that while Beale's theory references "vested rights," it should not be thought of as primarily individual-centered. When placed in relationship to the European state-centered theories described in the first chapter—which Beale cited and relied upon—Beale's vested rights theory could be interpreted as an extension of the state-centered theory describing PrIL as a division of sovereignty among states. Furthermore, this chapter shows that the realist school, while a *shift* from Beale's theory, is not entirely dissimilar from the relational internationalist perspective. It recovers the rich spectrum of individual-centered—yet not individualistic—arguments that realists introduced into the debate about the proper theory and methodology of PrIL.[7]

In order to construct this alternative narrative, this chapter starts by providing an analysis of Beale's theory and links it to the arguments of the state-centered theories described in the first chapter. Providing this link illuminates how Beale's theory is almost indistinguishable from Zitelmann's, and shows that the term "vested right" has brought no significant individual-centered elements, at least not in the sense of the relational internationalist theories described in the first chapter.

The next chapter provides a richer discussion of Beale's vested rights theory, by comparing it to other authors' rights-based theories, especially those of Story and Savigny. It shows that the term "vested rights," which can be found throughout PrIL theories of the nineteenth century hides a wide range of ideological differences and should certainly not be perceived as a uniform individual-centered perspective. By contrast, this chapter focuses less on Beale's account of rights, and more on the way in which Beale connects his theory to that of the state-centered internationalist

of Sovereign States and the Conflict of Laws' (1931) 31 Colum L Rev 368 (hereafter Cook, "The Jurisdiction"); Ernest Lorenzen, 'Territoriality, Public Policy and the Conflict of Laws' (1924) 33 Yale LJ 736 (hereafter Lorenzen, "Territoriality"); David Cavers, 'Review of Walter Wheeler Cook, The Logical and Legal Bases of the Conflict of Laws' (hereafter Cavers, "Review of Cook") and 'A Critique of the Choice-of-Law Problem' in David Cavers, *Selected Essays 1933–1983* (Duke Univ Press 1985).

5 The term is taken from Albert Ehrenzweig, 'A Counter-Revolution in Conflicts Law? From Beale to Cavers' (1966) 80 Harv L Rev 377.

6 See, e.g., Perry Dane, 'Vested Rights, "Vestedness," and Choice of Law' (1987) 96 Yale LJ 1191 (hereafter Dane, "Vested Rights"); Terry S. Kogan, 'Toward a Jurisprudence of Choice of Law: The Priority of Fairness over Comity' (1987) 62 NYUL Rev 651 (hereafter Kogan, "Fairness Over Comity"); Lea Brilmayer, 'Rights, Fairness, and Choice of Law' (1988) 98 Yale LJ 1277 (hereafter Brilmayer, "Rights").

7 For an account of how the legal realist perspectives in PrIL can be understood as compatible with a rights-based perspective see Michael Green, 'Legal Realism, Lex Fori, and the Choice-of-Law Revolution' (1995) 104 Yale LJ 968 (hereafter Green, "Legal Realism").

authors in continental Europe.[8] To underscore that connection this chapter first offers a broad description of Beale's account of law and rights and then shows how this account leads Beale to connect PrIL with PublIL through the concept of legislative jurisdiction.

1. Law and rights

In order to understand the particularity of Beale's PrIL theory one must first understand the meaning that he attributes to law and legal rights and then appreciate the way in which those concepts become interrelated and linked to legislative jurisdiction and PublIL. For Beale, law emanates from and becomes almost synonymous with the state. "Law is at once the source and the expression of sovereignty. Law creates the state and the state creates law by a common and mutual impulse; the two are born at an instant, are inseparable through life, and must die together."[9] Law is the command, indeed the "function" of a sovereign,[10] which means that any degree of individual autonomy (even with respect to choice of law in contracts) is impermissible. "To allow the parties to choose the rule [that governs a transnational legal matter] is to grant them legislative functions."[11]

Law for Beale has its internal logic and coherence "absolutely distinct from any rule of conduct based on a moral ground no matter how strong."[12] This leads him to argue that "courts are sworn to enforce the law, not to make it."[13] In fact a "really learned judge" internalizes law "as a part of himself." "Such a man solving a legal problem presented to him does not say, such and such a solution seems reasonable or reaches a practical result, he says it is the law."[14] It is no wonder then that Beale finds Jitta "striking" in arguing that one should be less obsessed with choosing between laws because "positive law (loi) is not the source, but the product of legal principles (droit)."[15] Beale overall offers an idyllic, if not a naïve view of the law when arguing that "truth in law, like beauty in architecture, is simple, clear, restful."[16] Continuity and predictability become fundamental attributes of law.

At the same time, law and a legal system are to Beale "a succession of right upon right,"[17] which leads him to argue that "if law be regarded as a right-producing principle, then every act must in accordance with the law change or not change existing

[8] Because he offers a more detailed analysis of the continental authors he found inspiration from in his "first essay," which later provided the basis for his conflict of laws treaties, I focus my reading primarily on the earlier, 1916 work. See Henry Joseph Beale, *A Treatise on the Conflict of Laws or Private International Law*, vol. 1, part 1 (Harvard University Press 1916) (hereafter Beale, *A Treatise on the Conflict of Laws*).

[9] Ibid., 115. [10] Ibid., 6.

[11] Ibid., 80. Note that the possibility of choosing the applicable law is disavowed even in those areas generally viewed as underlying private autonomy, such as certain aspects of contract law. In his review of Dicey, Beale agreed with Dicey's account of vested rights, but objected to the possibility of the parties' actual choice of law in contract law matters. See J.H. Beale, 'Dicey's Conflict of Laws' (1896) 10 Harv L Rev 168.

[12] Beale, *A Treatise on the Conflict of Laws* (n. 8) 153.

[13] Ibid., 135: "and though it is strenuously contended that they do in fact make the law, it must be admitted at least that they make it before they enforce it."

[14] Ibid., 136. [15] Ibid., 65. [16] Ibid., 85. [17] Ibid., 185.

rights."[18] Beale cites Dicey and Westlake and relies on Westlake's description of the way in which rights are created. Allegedly, "law's method of creating a right is to provide that upon the happening of a certain event a right shall accrue. Law annexes to the event a certain consequence, namely, the creation of a legal right. The creation of a right is therefore conditioned upon the happening of an event."[19] Depending on the particular classification of rights—and Beale admits that "legal rights might be analyzed in almost as many ways as there are analysts"[20]—different "events" will determine where and when different rights were "created."[21]

2. Legislative jurisdiction and the move to PublIL

Through a series of analytical steps, Beale goes on to connect law and rights to the issue of legislative jurisdiction and PrIL to PublIL. First, given that law is viewed as a sequence of rights and is almost synonymous with the state, Beale argues that the state itself has "an interest in the continued existence of rights."[22] Second, if law and rights:

> cannot exist without the will or at least the acquiescence of a political sovereign [. . .] there is no law, then, without a sovereign; and the fundamental inquiry in any study of the application of law must be, what sovereign created the law [and implicitly the right] in question.[23]

"As law-giving is a function of sovereignty, this amounts to fixing the limits of jurisdiction"[24] and in his view, as in Zitelmann's and Pillet's, the "whole great subject of jurisdiction is purely international"[25] pertaining to the "right of nations."[26] Beale describes the relationship between PrIL and PublIL in the following way:

> The legal bounds of a nation's power are fixed by the accepted law of nations. If they are so fixed, no nation claiming to belong to the family of civilized states can by any means extend or alter the legal exercise of its own powers to the prejudice of other states. While therefore the question of legal jurisdiction is a question to be determined by the law treated as a whole, it cannot properly be settled either by legislation or by decision, but must be left for settlement to the body of doctrine which the particular state in question has accepted in accepting the general principles of international law.[27]

It thus becomes clear that "sovereign power could be subjected to no restraining force except that of another political association *more powerful than itself*."[28] Beale is unclear whether power or law is what constrains states' legislative jurisdiction amongst each other and seems to settle for a mix: "It will be noticed that personal jurisdiction is based only on law, while territorial jurisdiction is based upon power and upon law. The latter is the stronger, and personal jurisdiction must always yield to it."[29] Since "the object of international law is to avoid conflict between sovereigns," international law creates a presupposition in favor of territoriality.[30]

[18] Ibid., 154. [19] Ibid., 106–7. [20] Ibid., 115. [21] Ibid., 169, 183, 185.
[22] Ibid., 166. [23] Ibid., 115. [24] Ibid., 6. [25] Ibid., 8. [26] Ibid., 53.
[27] Ibid., 146. [28] Ibid., 117. [29] Ibid., 120. [30] Ibid., 120.

The entire framework of division of legislative jurisdiction under PublIL continues to support PrIL because "the desire of a sovereign to find himself included in the number of civilized nations is so great as to constrain his acceptance of the principles of international law, and among them, the rules governing international jurisdiction."[31]

What is more, the concept of vested rights itself becomes the mark of civilization symbolizing and uniting *civilized* states:

> If the national law is a civilized law this [recognizing vested rights] will of course be done; and if it is not, the principles of a supposed private international law would not constrain its actions. The binding force for the dictates of justice is not created, and cannot be created, by extra-national constraint. No civilized law, national or international, could be oblivious to the just requirements of recognizing the legally accomplished fact. All civilized countries have the common ideal of justice.[32]

In other words, recognizing vested rights is what unites and defines civilized states. While no body of external law can impose the recognition of vested rights, one could easily infer from Beale's observation that states aspire to be included in the family of civilized states under international law, and that the concept of vested rights operates as a standard of civilization and inclusion.

Many of the quotes extracted from Beale's writing will have reminded the reader of Zitelmann and Pillet. Indeed Beale cites Zitelmann, Pillet, and Bustamante extensively. He considers Pillet's theory "a remarkable original theory,"[33] "ingenious, interesting and specious."[34] He is only concerned that it might be too "uncertain in its application" and that to make it operable one would need to add—as Beale does in his own theory—that "true continuity in law, namely that which is necessary to prevent the failure or forfeiture of acquired rights—demands territoriality, in order that this continuity may be enforced."[35] Indeed, as the next chapter outlines, Beale's theory is distinguishable from Pillet's only in concretizing the concept of continuity through the concept of vested rights.

Beale also considers Zitelmann "the most advanced author of the internationalist school"[36] and reproduces a five-page detailed description of Zitelmann's theory by Eugen Ehrlich.[37] When reading Ehrlich's description of Zitelmann's theory one might mistake it for Beale's. The following passage cited by Beale from Ehrlich's description of Zitelmann's theory is particularly telling:

> That Zitelmann sees in a state the source of the objective law is a very natural thing in a modern internationalist. For him, as for all of them, conflicts between laws of different states are the only ones with which private international law occupies itself. But Zitelmann draws from this idea the most extreme conclusions. He sees in the state the source of every subjective right. When a person has a right, he always gets it in the last analysis by reason of a concession of the state or of a recognition of this right by the state.[38] [. . .] These principles constitute an integral part of the law of nations, and therefore individuals cannot evoke them any more

[31] Ibid., 117. [32] Ibid., 112. [33] Ibid., 80. [34] Ibid., 85.
[35] Ibid., 85. [36] Ibid., 91. [37] Ibid., 91–5. [38] Ibid., 93.

than any other rule of the law of nations; for the law of nations confers rights only on states and imposes obligations only on states.[39]

Beale continues this state-centered line of thought himself when arguing that "within the boundaries of states there are roving tribes who form no part of the nation within whose territory they exist and have no standing among the sovereign states of international law. Such are tribes of Indians in the United States and Canada."[40] Clearly their views are excluded from the ambit of PrIL by now fully connected to the state-centered ideology of PublIL.

Lastly, Beale points to Bustamante's theory as "one of the most interesting theories based on the doctrine of vested rights."[41] Again, the passage he quotes from Bustamante could stand as a description of Beale's own theory:

The simultaneous existence of sovereignties, makes it necessary to fix limits in space for their respective legislative jurisdiction. There can exist on the face of the earth no legal relations without some law, jurisprudence, custom, precedent or principle applicable to it. Since humanity is divided into nations and they are fundamentally equal in the exercise of legislative power, there must exist some principle, precedent, custom, jurisprudence of law, of universal and absolute application to all things and persons. To assert the coexistence of nations is to assert the coexistence of law, and to suppose coexistent laws is to suppose them limited in application. That the power of the world may not be wasted in strife, science must assign to each its sphere of action; and it is fighting with reality to deny the name international to a law which proposes to keep the peace between the laws of different states.[42]

C. The Realist School—Cook and Lorenzen

Beale's theory came under serious attack by the American realist school of thought in PrIL starting in the 1930s. Its first protagonists were Walter Wheeler Cook[43] and Ernest Lorenzen.[44] The move from what was perceived to be undue formalism to a more pragmatic approach of conflict of laws was made by attacking Beale's understanding of law and rights, and his deductive methodology, as well as what was perceived to be a focus on sovereignty and territoriality inherited from Story.[45] The fact that the relationship between these two sets of critiques has not been fully appreciated led later twentieth-century authors to argue that the realist movement inevitably brought more parochialism and an overly state-centered perspective into conflict of laws.[46] In particular, because the principle of territoriality had informed some internationalist theories of conflicts (including Beale's), Cook's and Lorenzen's

[39] Ibid., 91. [40] Ibid., 118. [41] Ibid., 109. [42] Ibid., 110.

[43] For a description of Cook's "realist" initiatives in Conflict of Laws and in law generally, see David Cavers, "Review of Cook" (n. 4) 41. See Cook "Logical and Legal Bases" and "The Jurisdiction" (n. 4).

[44] See Lorenzen "Territoriality" (n. 4).

[45] Brainerd Currie referred to the "hypnotic power of the ideas of territoriality and vested rights [...] We need not pause to inquire *why* courts behave in such strange ways. The history of conflict-of-laws theory makes that plain enough." See Brainerd Currie, 'Married Women's Contracts: A Study in Conflict-of-Laws Method' (1958) 25 U Chicago L Rev 227, 245, 246.

[46] See Brilmayer, "Rights" (n. 6) and Dane, "Vested Rights" (n. 6) .

attack on territoriality was implicitly perceived as an absolute attack on internationalism.[47] Similarly, what became known as Cook's local law theory was interpreted as an endorsement of the forum's policy over other states' policies.[48]

In contrast, this chapter suggests that a careful reading of Cook's article attacking the principle of territoriality and sovereignty underlying his reading of Story mirrored Jitta's attack of the state-centered internationalist theories and opened up the space for pragmatic and just results for individuals within and beyond the legal relation in dispute. Similarly, by uncovering Lorenzen's very positive review of Jitta's work, it suggests that at least certain elements of the American realist school of thought could be seen or reconceptualized as a continuation of the relational internationalist perspective in Jitta's theory.

1. The critique of Beale's theory

Cook's critique of Beale's theory emanated from the broader realist view that any claims about law and legal rights cannot be more than claims and predictions of judicial behavior:

> "Right", "duty" and other names for legal relations are therefore not names of objects or entities which have an existence apart from the behavior of the officials in question, but merely terms by means of which we describe to each other what prophecies we make as to the probable occurrence of a certain sequence of events—the behavior of the officials.[49]

Rights, in other words, cannot be considered some "inherent or immutable principle limiting the jurisdiction of a state" because under the realist framework "a right is entirely non-normative until brought to life by the judge's own ethical views."[50] That means that nothing other than "purely pragmatic" considerations "as to what, all things considered, it is desirable to do"[51] can inform the decision of the judge in a PrIL dispute. It is not that any pre-existing vested rights constrain the decision of the judge, but rather that "social desirability" informs whatever content the judge ultimately gives to rights or entitlements in the dispute.[52] This line of reasoning becomes most clear in Cook's insistence that there is a constant confusion in PrIL writing, between the creation and the enforcement of rights. In his view we must be speaking figuratively when saying "that the plaintiff owns *something* and we give *it* to him."[53] "The figurative language may or may not be a convenient way of stating a result; it cannot be the reason for the result."[54] Aiming at "better social results" is the reason for "predicting" that a right will be given effect in the forum.[55]

[47] Ibid.

[48] See Dane, "Vested Rights" (n. 6); Brilmayer, "Rights" (n. 6). For a different understanding of Cook's local law theory, see Green, "Legal Realism" (n. 7).

[49] Cook, "Logical and Legal Bases" (n. 4) 476.

[50] Green, "Legal Realism" (n. 7) 983.

[51] Cook, "Logical and Legal Bases" (n. 4) 464.

[52] Ibid., 466. See also Green, "Legal Realism" (n. 7) 981: "Because he accepted that the law amounts to what the courts decide, he concluded that the application of the laws has no intrinsically legal limitations of the sort that the vested rights theorists hoped to discover."

[53] Cook, "Logical and Legal Bases" (n. 4) 481.

[54] Ibid., 481.

[55] Ibid., 481, 483.

This ambiguity goes together with what Cook perceived as another "ambiguity in the word 'law' involved in the question as usually asked: Shall Q apply Xs 'law,' or Y's 'law,' or Z's 'law?' "[56] Since it is a judge's decision in the realist framework, which should be understood as law (rather than a pre-existing principle or right) it appears aberrational to say that a forum's judge applies foreign law. A judge belonging to the forum inevitably applies (creates[57]) the forum's law. Whatever comes from another state (a law, a judgment, a right) is fact[58] and will inform the decision of the forum's court (or not) in its own (forum) decision. It is this line of reasoning that informs Cook's statement that "the forum *enforces* not a foreign right but a right *created* by *its own law*."[59]

Perry Dane interpreted Cook's insistence that a forum enforces a domestic right, rather than a foreign one, as a sign of parochialism.[60] Yet Michael Green argued that this statement is explained by the realist ideology of the concept of law and the role of the judge.[61] Indeed, as Green observed:

> Cook thought that all use of foreign law is grounded in the policies of a forum, but that does not mean that he thought it must be grounded in the policies behind domestic legislation and precedent. Rather, he believed that all law, foreign and domestic, has its source in the policies of the adjudicator, which will often, but not always, be equivalent to the policies behind domestic legislation and precedent.[62]

Cook's rather obscure way of describing the role of "rights" in conflict of laws adjudication[63] not only qualified him as parochial, but also made it possible for his later critics to argue that Cook does not take into consideration any legitimate expectations or considerations of fairness regarding what law the parties might have expected to govern their relations.[64] Yet this is in no way implicit in his views of rights. By arguing that there are no rights (foreign or domestic for that matter[65]) which a priori constrain the judgment of courts, Cook meant to suggest that there are no entitlements that are closed off or barred from assessment, balancing or re-evaluation

[56] Ibid., 468.

[57] According to Cook, a judge "must legislate, whether he will or no." See Walter Wheeler Cook, 'The Scientific Method and the Law' (1927) 13 ABA J 303, 308. See also, Cook, "Logical and Legal Bases" (n. 4) 487 for his discussion of precedent: "In doing this, the rule or principle as it existed has not been applied; it has been extended to take in the new situation."

[58] Cook, "Logical and Legal Bases" (n. 4) 470.

[59] Ibid., 469 (emphasis added) and 477: "As we are prophesying what Massachussets officials are going to do, the meaning we have given to 'right' compels us to say that a Massachussets right exists, identical in scope with the Maine right, and that the Massachussets court is going to 'enforce' this Massachussets right."

[60] Dane, "Vested Rights" (n. 6). [61] Green, "Legal Realism" (n. 7). [62] Ibid., 983.

[63] See Elliot E. Cheatam, 'Review of The Logical and Legal Bases of the Conflict of Laws' (1944) 93 U Pa L Rev 112, 113: "The local law theory here given is only one possible analytical explanation of how it happens that in deciding a case the court of one state may employ the law of another state. The theory is free from the particular rigidity of the vested rights doctrine. Yet it would substitute for the territoriality of the place of occurrence a conceptually necessary territoriality of the state of the forum."

[64] See Brilmayer, "Rights" (n. 6); Dane, "Vested Rights" (n. 6).

[65] Cook, "Logical and Legal Bases" (n. 4) 486: "But I may be asked, if the answer to conflict of laws cases cannot be deduced from certain pre-existing principles relating to 'jurisdiction,' how are they to be decided? The only answer that can be given, by the same methods actually used in deciding cases involving purely domestic torts, contracts, property, etc."

in light of the circumstances of the case.[66] But that does not mean that individuals' expectations regarding the applicable law are irrelevant or should not enter the choice of law analysis.[67]

2. Critique against sovereignty, territoriality, and Story

Once Cook established that rights are not transcendental "entities" that constrain PrIL decisions,[68] he went on to dispel what he viewed as yet another "fiction," namely territoriality and the alleged limitations that international law places on legislative "jurisdiction."[69] Ernest Lorenzen joined in the same endeavor.[70] Cook emphasized that:

> Law is not a material phenomenon, which spreads out like a light wave until it reaches the territorial boundary and then stops. Whatever be the legal limitations upon the power of a state or country to affect the legal relations of persons anywhere in the world, they must be found in positive law of some kind—be the same international law or constitutional law, and do not inhere in the constitution of the legal universe.[71]

Both Cook and Lorenzen argue that the Anglo-American world had been induced to derive PrIL from a fictitious concept of the territoriality of law and sovereignty due to Story's treatise.[72] The first chapter showed, in line with Blaine Baker's interpretation, that while Story focused on sovereignty, comity, and territoriality in the first few pages of the treatise, these considerations did not seem to inform his analysis of the field as much as one would assume. Cook recognizes this as well and finds it somewhat puzzling that Story has an initial theoretical treatment of sovereignty and comity at the beginning of the treatise, while later into the treatise he seems to adopt views similar to his own.[73] Yet regardless of whether or not sovereignty, territoriality,

[66] Ibid., 480:

> The decision thus appears not as an inevitable outcome from fixed premises (that the forum is enforcing an *obligation* created by foreign law, and *must* inevitably take it or leave it, just as it is), but for what it is, and for what Mr. Justice Holmes undoubtedly knew it was—a practical result based upon the reasons of policy established in prior cases.

[67] The following passage from Cook's assessment of *Milliken v. Pratt*, cited in Green, "Legal Realism" (n. 7) 986 is particularly telling:

> The wife did no acts in Maine; all her acts were done in Massachussets. If one rather than the other state has "jurisdiction," it would seem to be Massachussets, not Maine ... It is pertinent to inquire 1) Why should the offerees expect her to be bound by the "law" of their own state rather than by that in force where she is living and acting? 2) Why should her own state be expected to recognize that she can escape the limitations of its law merely by sending a communication ("offer") to the partners in another state? The partners must know that if they ever have to sue her, it will in all probability be in the state where she lives. Why ought the offerees, the partners, expect the courts there to apply their law rather than hers to her acts done in her own state?"

See Walter Wheeler Cook, *Selected Essays on the Conflict of Laws, Reprinted from the Harvard Law Review* (Harvard Law Review Association 1940) 435–6.

[68] Cook, "Logical and Legal Bases" (n. 4) 476. [69] Cook, "The Jurisdiction" (n. 4).

[70] Lorenzen, "Territoriality" (n. 4). [71] Cook, "Logical and Legal Bases" (n. 4) 484.

[72] Cook, "The Jurisdiction" (n. 4) 368.

[73] Cook, "Logical and Legal Bases" (n. 4) 483, n. 70.

and comity really did motivate Story's treatment of the field, Cook's and Lorenzen's critique of these concepts is telling of what these authors viewed themselves as reacting against.

Both Cook and Lorenzen agreed with Story's postulate that "every nation possesses an exclusive sovereignty and jurisdiction within its own territory," but "only if properly interpreted," namely in the sense that there is nothing that a priori constrains the policy judgment of the court.[74] On the face of it, one might interpret this statement as an invitation to parochialism. Yet this would not be an appropriate assessment.

Cook's critique of territoriality is not an absolute critique of internationalism. Rather, he is reacting against the formalism of the a priori deductions that were made from the concept of territoriality.[75] In particular, he argues, as did Jitta,[76] that the distinction between territorial and personal jurisdiction is unsound and is not based on any practical policy consideration.[77] More important for present purposes, his critique of sovereignty and territoriality, like Jitta's, is grounded in an attempt to focus more pragmatically on the regulatory needs of the individuals implicated in or affected by the relationship in dispute, as well as on broader policy considerations. The following passage is particularly telling:

> If we look at the rules for the solution of problems in the conflict of laws as intended to regulate human conduct so as to bring about desirable and convenient results, we shall doubtless all agree that since a piece of lawn is as such "immovable," and only the officials of the state in which it is physically situated can—consistently with the existing territorial organization of modern political society—rightfully deal with its physical possession, it will be convenient for other states to apply to deeds of land the rules which the state of physical situs would apply to them. It is therefore useful to group together the cases involving rights relating to such "immovable" objects and deal with them as a unit. However, we must not from this grouping on practical grounds draw conclusions, which will not stand analysis. For example, it would seem to be no infringement of the existing territorial organization of modern society, if a sovereign state, say England, should decide not to follow the land of the situs in dealing with the validity and effects of deeds to foreign land.[78]

Like Cook, Lorenzen also insists throughout his article that "each sovereign state can determine the rules of the conflict of laws in accordance with its own notions of what is just and proper,"[79] but he is quick to acknowledge that "under modern conditions such an administration of justice often demands that a state shall take into consideration the rules of other states. Whether it will do so in a particular situation or not will depend upon the conclusion it reaches as to what is right and proper."[80] This, in

[74] Cook, "The Jurisdiction" (n. 4) 370. See also Lorenzen, "Territoriality" (n. 4).

[75] Cook, "The Jurisdiction" (n. 4) 370–3.

[76] See Chapter 1.

[77] Cook, "The Jurisdiction" (n. 4) 380–5, esp. 380:

> Whenever jurisdiction is exercised, i.e., whenever a state "creates rights," these rights affect persons even though they relate to "things," and that therefore the postulates in question contain inherently contradictory assertions, and so can never furnish a satisfactory basis for a sound doctrine in the field of the conflict of laws.

[78] Ibid., 382.

[79] Lorenzen, "Territoriality" (n. 4) 748.

[80] Ibid.

other words, is not to encourage parochialism, but is simply a realistic acknowledgement, which Story and Jitta stated as well, that:

> as justice can be administered only in accordance with the sense of what is right existing in the community in which the court sits, the feelings of the local community cannot be disregarded altogether. The general problem is therefore always the same: What are the demands of justice in the particular situation; what is the controlling policy?[81]

This reading of Lorenzen is also confirmed by the very positive review he makes of Jitta's "The Renovation of International Law" in a 1920 article published in the Yale Law Journal.[82] Lorenzen believed "The Renovation of International Law" to be "a most remarkable book"[83] that "will help us all to lay aside our own prejudices and to become more earnestly desirous of participating in any movement that will bring mankind nearer to this goal."[84] The following passage is particularly telling of the way in which Lorenzen read Jitta's internationalist theory:

> To persons accustomed to the Austinian theory of sovereignty, the views expressed by Professor Jitta may be those of a visionary; yet no assumption could be further from the truth. There is probably no living writer who is more fully cognizant of the realities of life than is Professor Jitta, or who understands better the actual requirements of international intercourse. His mind rebels, however, against the mechanical application of rules of law. Law to him is not a collection of abstract rules, but a vital force arising directly from the social conditions under which men live. So far as the intercourse among men has become cosmopolitan, and it is becoming more and more so every day, it is necessary, therefore, that a cosmopolitan law, a *jus gentium* as it were, be created.[85]

This reception of Jitta's work not only by Lorenzen, but also by Roscoe Pound[86] and David Cavers[87] should make one realize that at least in its inception the American realist school was fully compatible with both an individual-centered—yet not individualistic—perspective, and an internationalist vision in PrIL.

D. Brainerd Currie

Although Cook's theory was perceived as "a dramatic triumph over the 'territorial' and 'vested rights' theories," it was triumphant mostly in analytical terms.[88] The first restatement reflected entirely Beale's views and theories, rather than Cook's. Furthermore, Cook "did not offer a substitute order. His approach would lead to

[81] Ibid., 748.

[82] Ernest Lorenzen, 'Review of The Renovation of International Law by Josephus Jitta' (1920) 29 Yale LJ 700. Regardless of whether Jitta might have inspired Lorenzen's own work, it is worth noting that the review was published before any of the main realist theories had been developed.

[83] Ibid., 700. [84] Ibid., 702. [85] Ibid., 701.

[86] Roscoe Pound, 'Uniformity of Commercial Law on the American Continent' (1909) 8 Michigan L Rev 91.

[87] David Cavers, 'A Critique of the Choice-of-Law Problem' (1933) 47 Harv L Rev 173, 193, n. 35 (calling Jitta "a vigorous critic of mechanical rules for choice of law") (hereafter Cavers, "A Critique").

[88] See Cavers, "Review of Cook" (n. 4) esp. 41–2.

a far narrower role for precedent and to a wider role for social and economic considerations,"[89] but offered little guidance as to how PrIL might or should develop further in this direction. It was Brainerd Currie who, being a disciple of Cook and embracing his jurisprudence,[90] sought to provide a concrete and workable theory of conflict of laws.

Currie's main claim was that conflict of laws rules had to consider the purposes or policies underlying the particular laws potentially applicable in the dispute,[91] as well as their intended range of application.[92] He identified a "presumption" that for the most part states would have an interest in having their policies implemented when they benefited their domiciliaries.[93]

Because of the particular "configuration of parties to the dispute relative to the configuration of state interests represented by various rules of decision invoked by those parties"[94]—only one state (false conflict)[95] or several states (real conflict) would have an interest in having their laws applied.[96] In the latter case:

> The sensible and clearly constitutional thing for any court to do, confronted with a true conflict of interests, is to apply its own law. In this way it can be sure at least that it is consistently advancing the policy of its own state. It should apply its own law ... simply because a court should never apply any other law except when there is a good reason for doing so.[97]

While Currie's theory went a step forward in the more concrete elaboration of the realists' principles, the critical reception of Currie's theory has been aptly described by Perry Dane:

> Much of Currie's work has been severely criticized. His analysis of state interests, for example, is often arbitrary, dogmatic, narrow, and vaguely unrealistic. Indeed, Currie's domiciliary-centered scheme of choice of law is in many ways as rigid and unconvincing as the territorial catch-phrases of Beale and Dicey. Moreover, a number of commentators have suggested that Currie's analysis of true conflicts slighted both the importance of values such as comity, reciprocity, and uniformity, and the fact that courts often balance competing policies and interests and might be expected to manage the task as well in their efforts at choice of law.[98]

The development of Currie's theory is traditionally understood as a moment when American choice of law moved in both a parochial and a state-centered direction.[99] The claim is that Currie's theory implied a reaction against both an

[89] Ibid., 42: "Professor Cook has defended his work against the charge that his criticism is 'merely destructive' by replying that 'the removal of the weeds [in the intellectual garden] is ... as constructive in effect as the planting and cultivation of the useful vegetables.' This is true, but it assumes that we have vegetables to plant and planters to plant them."

[90] See Dane, "Vested Rights" (n. 6) 1201. See also Brainerd Currie, *Selected Essays on the Conflict of Laws* (Duke University Press 1963) (hereafter Currie, *Selected Essays*) 6: "Walter Wheeler Cook discredited the vested-rights theory as thoroughly as the intellect of one man can ever discredit the intellectual product of another".

[91] Currie, *Selected Essays* (n. 90) 117–18, 143–6.

[92] Ibid., 144–5.

[93] Ibid., 85, 143–6, 719. But cf. id. at 186 (recognizing the possibility of "rational altruism").

[94] Dane, "Vested Rights" (n. 6) 1202.

[95] Currie, *Selected Essays* (n. 90) 107, 163, 189, 726.

[96] Ibid., 119.

[97] Ibid., 119.

[98] Dane, "Vested Rights" (n. 6) 1203.

[99] Ibid. Brilmayer, "Rights" (n. 4).

individual-centered, and an internationalist perspective in choice of law. As Cavers noted, Currie's theory was bound to be interpreted as such.[100] The next section describes three types of individual-centered arguments made by various scholars in an attempt to temper the state-centered premises of Currie's theory, which in fact mirror those made by the relational internationalists presented in the first chapter.

The remaining of this section, however, offers some insights from the correspondence between David Cavers and Brainerd Currie in order to suggest two points: first, regardless of how his theory was later interpreted, Currie did not mean to inject a complete shift from an individual-centered to an extreme state-centered perspective and second, his preference for the application of forum law, as well as his general state-centered arguments were linked to his broader aim to provide a workable theory that would diminish judicial discretion. This reading of Currie's theory in light of his exchange with Cavers shows that the development of Currie's "state interest" theory should not be seen as a particular moment in the history of PrIL in which individual-centered internationalist perspectives were analytically refuted.

In order to provide some context for the academic debates between Brainerd Currie and David Cavers, it is necessary to first understand how David Cavers's theory, itself grounded in the realist school, differed from Currie's.

1. David Cavers

David Cavers was a legal realist writing after Cook and Lorenzen. While embracing the pragmatic approach of his predecessors, his "Critique of the Choice of Law Problem"[101] "assailed state-selecting rules for the fact that, given their disregard of the content of the laws whose application they dictated, they could not assure justice in the individual case."[102] Cavers thus continued Jitta's critique that PrIL had become obsessed with choosing between states and drafting rules of jurisdiction, rather than rules that achieve a proper regulatory goal:

> Again, so long as the court was in search of a "foreign-created right," it would seek an appropriate jurisdiction, not an appropriate substantive rule, for metaphorical consistency demands that the creation or non-creation of rights be attributed only to states and not to their legal rules. [. . .] With the reaction against the restrictions of theory, there has come a recognition that considerations of justice and social expediency should be, and in many cases have been, the dominant determinants of problems in this field. Yet these considerations are still harnessed to the old task of devising (or justifying) rules for selecting the appropriate jurisdiction whose law should govern a given case.[103]

[100] David F. Cavers, *The Choice-of-Law Process* (University of Michigan Press 1966) 72: "I predict that, for years to come, he (Currie) will be held by many to insist that the law of the forum must always be applied in a case in which the court can find any reasonable basis to apply the forum's law" (hereafter Cavers, *The Choice-of-Law Process*).

[101] Cavers, "A Critique" (n. 87).

[102] David Cavers, 'Contemporary Conflicts Law in American Perspective' (1970) 131 Recueil des Cours 85, 152 (hereafter Cavers, "Contemporary Conflicts"). But see David Cavers, *The Choice of Law Process* (n. 100) 76: "I am not the champion of justice in the individual case that I have been made to seem. I never have been."

[103] Cavers, "A Critique" (n. 87), 178.

Cavers pled for an alternative appreciation of conflict of laws cases that comes remarkably close to that of Jitta. He argued that any conflict of laws determination "requires an equally complete depiction of the facts, but to determine what their effect upon the choice of the competing laws should be, would necessitate their careful appraisal with this end in view."[104] In order to ensure a proper regulation of cross-border legal matters, one would need to focus on the acts of the individuals and provide a thorough analysis of their relevance in relationship to the policies of the potentially applicable law. A substantive analysis of the rules is necessary because:

> It is difficult to see how the facts so selected could be properly appraised except in relation to the provisions of the laws whose application is at issue. The court is not idly choosing a law; it is determining a controversy. How can it choose wisely without considering how that choice will affect the controversy?[105]

In his "Critique," Cavers adopts the following hypothetical to illustrate his proposed methodology:

> A salesman induces a married lady, not yet 21, in state A to order several feet of belles lettres. Her order is received and accepted by the publishers at their office in state B, and they express the books to her residence in state A. After reading through two inches and paying for six, the customer repents of her bargain. The publishers sue in state A. The lady pleads want of capacity to contract.[106]

Cavers argued that a proper determination of the dispute implies a thorough analysis of the facts and their relevance in relationship to the substantive provisions of the respective laws. Furthermore, he argued that the weight or assessment of the facts will differ depending on which country has the policy enforcing such contracts.[107] A factual analysis of the case might proceed as follows:

> The fact that the publisher's agent went to the defendant's home would be material. Had she first "clipped the coupon" that fact might be accorded some weight. It might also be material that his sale was part of a sales campaign waged in that state and not an isolated transaction. Certainly such a case presents quite a distinct picture from one where the bargain is struck by mail, either solely as a consequence of correspondence or as a result of preliminary negotiations in the seller's state. The fact that the transaction comprises a sale of books might lead to it being viewed in a different light than if its subject were, on the one hand, shares of stock whose edges alone were gilt, or, on the other hand, some article, a vacuum cleaner perhaps, which barely lay beyond the concept of the "necessary."[108]

Furthermore, he argues, again like Jitta, that "in the course of this evaluation, the court's opinion as to the desirability of limitations upon the contractual capacity of

[104] Ibid., 188. [105] Ibid., 189. [106] Ibid., 180.

[107] Ibid., 190: "Of what real importance is it now that state A's law should have been applied had its provisions been exactly the reverse of what they are? The fact that now the application of state A's law will defeat the contract confers a radically different aspect upon the problem. The degree to which sustaining this bargain would impair the protection which state A insists is due its infant matrons must be measured against the degree to which its avoidance will frustrate the reasonable expectations of business men from without the state."

[108] Ibid., 189.

infants and married women will inevitably enter. Any effort to exclude it would operate only to distort the intellectual processes of adjudication."[109]

Whereas this earlier essay was meant to open up the space for pragmatic interest balancing and case by case determination, Cavers' later work focused on devising principles of preference, which were meant to provide some predictability and consistency to the choice of law process, while still being committed to the substantive evaluation of choice of law problems.

While both Cavers and Currie were writing in roughly the same school of thought,[110] Cavers believed two aspects distinguished their choice of law writings. First, while Cavers was keen to broaden the space for interest analysis (state and individual) and then construct presumptive rules in the form of principles of preference, Currie believed that the ordinary process of construction and interpretation would ultimately resolve choice of law problems.[111] Second, and more important for present purposes, Cavers felt that Currie's:

> terminology may create difficulties in the application of those processes [of construction and interpretation] by tending to exaggerate the interest of a state in the application of its own law and to undervalue the importance of factors that are not reflected in the doctrine and policies of the respective laws between which a choice is to be made.[112]

These included both multistate policies[113] and individual-centered considerations.[114] It was these two points of disagreement on which Cavers pressed Currie in an exchange of letters between 1957 and 1958.

This correspondence sheds new light on Currie's interest analysis theory. It shows that both the state-centered and the parochial connotations of his theory were motivated mostly by pragmatic, rather than fundamental normative and ideological, rationales.

2. Cavers–Currie correspondence

The correspondence between Cavers and Currie was motivated by Currie's articles on two conflict of laws cases, *Miliken v. Pratt*[115] concerning the choice of law governing a married woman's capacity to contract, and *Grant v. McAuliffe*[116] involving survival of actions. Because Currie believed that each state has an interest in

[109] Ibid., 190.

[110] Dane argues that Currie was not really a realist. See Dane, "Vested Rights" (n. 4). Both Cavers and Currie however were Cook's disciples. As will become apparent from their exchange of letters discussed below, the main difference between Currie and Cavers ideologically was their attitude to judicial discretion.

[111] Cavers, "Contemporary Conflicts" (n. 102) 74.

[112] Ibid.

[113] For a broader discussion of the multistate policies see Arthur Taylor Von Mehren and Donald Theodore Trautman, *The Law of Multistate Problems; Cases and Materials on Conflict of Laws* (Little, Brown, 1965) esp. 237ff; Cavers, "Contemporary Conflicts" (n. 102) 99.

[114] Cavers, "Contemporary Conflicts" (n. 102) 99.

[115] *Miliken v. Pratt*, 125 Mass. 374 (1878). See Brainerd Currie, 'Married Women's Contracts: A Study in Conflict-of-Laws Method' (1958) 25 U Chicago L Rev 227.

[116] *Grant v. McAuliffe*, 41 Cal.2d 859 (1953).

applying its policy favorable to its respective domiciliaries, he argued that when the creditors and debtors come from different states neither of the two states "should yield the policy embodied in its own law to that of the other state."[117] Massachussets law granting immunity to married women could not apply to women domiciled outside the state, just as the California law allowing for the survival of the tort action following the death of the tortfeasor could not apply if the plaintiff was domiciled outside the state.

Cavers challenged Currie on this line of reasoning and on Currie's implicit "unreadiness to admit that the individual parties may have interests, distinct from the states' interest, that should be taken into account in a conflicts case."[118] He argued that while:

> residence is almost certain to be a significant, though not necessarily controlling contact in a married woman's capacity case, while dropping a letter in a box probably won't be, there are other elements in the conduct of the parties that might be important in a decision whether to deny or grant the protection each party claims: planning a transaction to by-pass a known law, for example.[119]

Cavers charged Currie for refusing "to consider the claims of human beings to justice unless he can fit them into his conception of state interests."[120] In line with his own conflict of laws theory, Cavers argued that there is no reason to assume—absent a very detailed analysis of the state policies[121]—that states do not have an interest in applying their policies for the benefit of non-domiciliaries.[122] Similarly, one could conclude that the application of the protective policy to the benefit of the domiciliary is unwarranted, for example, when the domiciliary had an upper hand in relationship to the non-domiciliary.[123] Cavers argued that judges should be able to make such "justice determinations" without being overly constrained by the "procrustean bed" of the "state interest analysis."[124]

Currie replied to these charges by trying to clarify his intentions behind the adoption of the state interest methodology. He conceded that he "has had a feeling of inadequacy" about the fact that a focus on state interests might ignore important

[117] David Cavers, 'A Correspondence with Brainerd Currie, 1957–1958' (1982) 34 Mercer L Rev 471, 475.

[118] Ibid., 477. [119] Ibid. [120] Ibid., 485.

[121] Ibid., 484 (Cavers charged Currie for being overly concerned with a "demonstration of exercise in methodology" by forcing a finding of an interest of the state to protect its domiciliaries) and 486 (Cavers thought that rather than forcing a finding of a state interest, it would be more important to engage in a more thorough "identification of state interest").

[122] Ibid., 480. As to Currie's view that Massachusetts must have meant to protect only its domiciliary women, Cavers stated:

> it may be that the legislators' objectives were more inclusive. They started with the view that wives are likely to be unduly influenced by husbands who, being in financial straits, seek their guaranties. They didn't like this type of transaction and wanted to discourage it. If a Maine wife were to go up to Boston with her husband and be talked into giving surety for him on a note to a Boston wholesaler, I'm not at all sure that the legislators would expect her to have to pay. Maybe she would on a note drawn in Maine but we here in Massachusetts have our own standards. At any rate it's a view that ought not to be brushed aside.

[123] Ibid., 476. [124] Ibid., 476, 479.

individual interest but that he was "far from sure how the problem should be handled."[125] The way in which he clarified his normative position is worth quoting at large:

> Of course I shall not admit that I am unwilling to consider the claims of human beings to justice unless I can fit them into the conception of state interests. I am just a little less sure what constitutes justice in a conflict of laws case, and I am very much concerned about a method that will be found operational by the courts. I have, to repeat, found it useful to compare the results reached by traditional methods with those, which would be reached if the selfish interests of the states involved were alone consulted. No doubt the "justice" of the result would in many cases be improved if we assumed a benevolent and far-reaching purpose instead of a selfish one; but I am certain that this is not so in all cases. [. . .] Similarly, I have never felt that either missionary zeal or altruism should justify American courts in awarding damages to German citizens against German employers who discharged them under the odious Nuremburg decrees.[126]

Throughout the letters Currie explained that he was concerned with "a method of general utility"[127] which springs from his pressing "concern about judicial discretion."[128] This general stance explained his view on what Cavers had called the "differentiating facts" of the cases, which should inspire one to a more flexible approach with an eye to the interests and claims to justice of the parties. Currie explained:

> Over the years, however, this conception [of the differentiating facts] has come to have two meanings for me. The first has embraced such circumstances as whether the transaction was part of a sales campaign and the others [. . .] These have gradually lost significance for me, largely because I have never been able to make them very meaningful, much less to conceive of standards for their evaluation. The other meaning has been the one strongly though implicitly suggested by the reverse-hypothesis discussion, where, without reference to who clipped the first coupon, the significant change is that the posture is such that the state policies, or interests, are presented in an entirely different light. Thus the significant differentiating facts have come, for me, to be identical with those, which relate to the incidence of state policy.[129]

In other words, as Green argued in his interpretation of Currie's theory, "it is not that traditional rights-based jurisprudence has been rejected in favor of other forms of reasoning."[130] Rather, Currie's theory was based on a twofold evaluation of the

[125] Ibid., 481.

[126] Ibid., 488, citing *Holzer v. Deutsche Reichsbahn-Gesellschaft*, 277 N.Y. 474, 14 N.E.2n 798 (1938).

[127] Ibid., 487.

[128] Ibid., 490 and 491:

> I have never been entirely comfortable with the idea that conflicts problems should be resolved through the exercise of a freedom which the court does not enjoy in a domestic case, however; and I have reached the conclusion that as far as I am concerned I have to get along without that idea. [. . .] I have tried to dissociate myself from the course of judicial discretion. [. . .] I am afraid that somehow I have to dissociate myself from the Cavers thesis, which is rather widely identified with the course of judicial discretion, since otherwise my position is so nearly identical with yours that it will be assumed to be the same and will arouse the old fears. It has already been so interpreted by a few.

[129] Ibid., 490.

[130] Green, "Legal Realism" (n. 7) 994.

general context in which conflict of laws matters arise. First, the large variety of factual circumstances, if evaluated with an eye to achieving justice and taking account of the parties' various claims to justice, might make the conflict of laws method inoperable. Second, the balancing act that would be required when embracing the variety of "significant facts" might lead to unrestrained judicial discretion. The move from individual interests to state interests was therefore not normatively inevitable, but rather pragmatically necessary. Similarly, the forum bias was not an absolute policy preference for particularism over internationalism, but also part of the methodological arsenal of restraining judicial discretion.

Within this different image of Currie's theory lies an insight into the extent to which the respective view of the role of the judge may shape the direction of development of PrIL, including on the individual-centered/state-centered spectrum. For realists prior to Currie, especially for Cook and Cavers, the judge's "ethical principles stand above and assess" the policies underlying the forum's law. "Thus, paradoxically in claiming that all adjudication is the expression of the judge's ethical principles, the local law theory explains how a judge can *avoid* applying local law."[131]

In other words, allowing for some level of judicial discretion meant that "the gap between state policy and court policy allows for a critical space in which state policy may be weighed—and perhaps rejected—in cases of true conflicts."[132] If one disavows judicial discretion, as well as the elaboration of statutory and international rules, as Currie did, the policy space inevitably narrows, not only on the individual-centered/state-centered, but also on the particularist/internationalist spectrum.

E. Individual-Centered Arguments Against Currie

Regardless of what policy direction Currie meant to provide for PrIL, his theory was justifiably understood as being overly state-centered. Three perspectives were offered to temper this direction. Each of them provides a useful element that illustrates the way in which PrIL's regulatory function might be shaped by individual-centered perspectives.

1. Fairness over comity

The recurring critique against Currie's theory is very well captured in the title of an article by Terry Kogan: "fairness over comity."[133] The underlying concern of this critique was that while Currie provided a methodology aimed at discerning and restricting when states should exercise comity and therefore compromise on their own policy for the benefit of another state, the reasonable expectations of individuals were largely left out. Currie's critics argued that legitimacy should not be considered in relationship to states. "Fairness concerns focus on the litigants' affiliating

[131] Ibid., 984. [132] Ibid. [133] Kogan, "Fairness Over Comity" (n. 6).

contacts, contacts that in political theory justify a person's obligation to a governmental entity."[134]

Lea Brilmayer explains that the "fairness" perspective, while borrowing the rights-based approach from Beale's theory, is different from it in several respects. Most important, the rights implicated in jurisprudential considerations of fairness "are primarily negative rights rather than positive rights; not swords, but shields. By and large they are rights to be left alone. Their source is also different from the sources that Beale relied upon. They are founded on principles of political fairness that specify preconditions for the exercise of legitimate state coercion."[135]

Stated in these terms, the fairness perspective makes the application of a particular law dependent on the political relationship between the state, whose law ends up being applied, and the parties. Several different perspectives were offered in order to discern the circumstances that would make coercion by law legitimate in a transnational setting.[136] For example, Kogan argued that in order for a particular state's law to apply, there must be a correlation between one party having taken the benefits of a state's law in a manner related to a dispute, with the other party having contributed to the state in some way related to the dispute.[137] Lea Brilmayer argued that a state could only legitimately impose a burden or duty on its own domiciliaries.[138] This was the reverse of Currie's view that a state would apply its law only to the benefit of its domiciliaries, regardless of whom it might implicitly burden.

Despite these different nuances these theories share a premise of individual autonomy and liberty rights. On the one hand, because the rights Lea Brilmayer was concerned with are "mostly negative rights instead of positive rights and they are vertical rights that the individual possesses against the state directly, rather than horizontal rights against the other party to the litigation,"[139] they are less concerned, if at all, with the substance of the rules in conflict and the consequences of choosing one over the other.[140] Indeed, the approach disavows consequentialism entirely.[141]

134 Ibid., 656.

135 Brilmayer, "Rights" (n. 6) 1280. See also at 1279: "Rights analysis only establishes what Robert Nozick has called 'side constraints,' namely principles or limits, based on fairness, on what the state may do."

136 For a discussion of the federal context of the United States, see Kogan, "Fairness Over Comity" (n. 6) with further references at n. 3; Elliot E. Cheatham and Willis L.M. Reese, 'Choice of the Applicable Law' (1952) 52 Colum L Rev 959, 970–2 (calling "protection of justified expectations" one of nine relevant policies in choice of law); Harold Korn, 'The Choice-of-Law Revolution: A Critique' (1983) 83 Colum L Rev 772; Amos Shapira, 'Protection of Private Interests in the Choice of Law Process: The Principle of Rational Connection Between Parties and Laws' (1970) 24 Sw L J 574.

137 Kogan, "Fairness Over Comity" (n. 6) 706: "1. In order for a litigant to be subjected to the burden of a state's law, it must be shown that the litigant previously took advantage of the benefits of that law in a manner related to the dispute. 2. In order for a litigant to invoke the benefit of a state's law, that litigant must demonstrate that she previously made a contribution to the state, in some way related to the dispute, that justifies her enjoying of that benefit."

138 See Brilmayer, "Rights" (n. 6).

139 Brilmayer, "Rights" (n. 6) 1295 and n. 59 and 60.

140 See also Kogan, "Fairness Over Comity" (n. 6) 679: "Fairness contacts are unrelated to state interests or regulatory policies."

141 Brilmayer, "Rights" (n. 6) 1292: "There is an alternative conception of rights that does not require prior identification of the applicable substantive law."

By determining legitimate authority without considering the substance of the laws in conflict, Lea Brilmayer's approach presupposes that individuals never operate in the transnational sphere in full awareness of the substance of the rules in conflict, sometimes constructing their legal relation in such a way as to avoid the imposition of a particular law while taking full advantage of "negative rights."

Chapter 7 provides an analysis of the different ways in which legitimate authority has been conceptualized in PrIL theories and distinguishes what could be called "individualistic legitimacy" notions underlying theories of "fairness" from Cavers's and Jitta's alternative "social legitimacy" theories, premised on a view of relational autonomy and rights. While Brilmayer's "strongly held moral intuition that human beings are not just means to an end, but must be treated as ends in themselves"[142] is clearly valuable, an individualistic notion of autonomy ends up allowing some people to treat others as means under the protection of the law.[143] Therefore, a territorial individualistic assumption that only the state of domicile can impose duties on its defendants runs counter to the myriad of elements informing a transnational legal relation and the expectations of the individuals. Focusing on the actions of the individuals should not only lead to a view attempting to minimize state intrusion or coercion, but rather to make individuals responsible for their actions in the transnational field.

On the other hand, because the rights identified by Brilmayer represent merely "side-constraints" to the process of determining the applicable law, they do not provide a solution or a prescription for what law should be chosen, they merely reveal which one "cannot" be chosen.[144]

Perry Dane argues the stronger thesis that one needs to apply the norms to which the litigants were expected to conform at the time of the events being adjudicated.[145] As Green noted "Dane does not flesh out what choice-of-law principles follow from his theory. He does argue, however, that because adjudication must recognize and enforce forum-independent rights, any choice-of-law principle should be nonrelativist, that is, any forum applying the same principle to the same set of facts should come to the same choice of law."[146]

Here Dane might appear to come close to the classical understanding of Savigny's theory as arguing that an analysis of the nature of a legal relation focused on the law which individuals would have assumed guides their relationship will generally lead to only one possible answer to the choice of law question. But in adopting this view, Dane leaves out Jitta's critique to Savigny's theory, as well as some of the American realists' insight. First, as Jitta argued, the nature of a legal relation is itself a fluid concept, which will inevitably depend on the views of the judge deciding the matter. Second, the parties might have and often do have, or at least assert, different expectations regarding the applicable law. This means, as Cavers made clear, that what is ultimately involved is an assessment of whether or not each of the party deserves the

[142] Ibid., 1291. [143] See Chapter 7.

[144] Green, "Legal Realism" (n. 7) 971: "such negative rights do not determine but merely constrain choice of law."

[145] Dane, "Vested Rights" (n. 6) 1218–23. [146] Green, "Legal Realism" (n. 7) 972.

application of the law he/she is claiming. At this stage of the assessment the judge should be constrained by ethical considerations, such as avoiding prejudice and even a *lex-fori* bias, and should focus more on the actions and communications of the parties. But a wide variety of factors might play a role, including the intentions of the parties, the expectations that they generated in one another and in the communities affected by their actions, the power relations between the parties etc. This means that, contrary to Dane's intuition, the process of discerning the norms to which the parties were supposed to conform is much more fluid and inevitably influenced by the views of the adjudicating forum. Indeed, Brilmayer admits that "it may turn out that in numerous instances there are several different states whose law might apply without violating the parties' rights. In such cases, policy analysis could properly come into play."[147]

It is in this context that one should appreciate Green's intuition that:

> with ease of movement, the ethical certainty of what law the litigants had a duty to obey has, in many cases, disappeared. Without this certainty, the rights that norm-based jurisprudence claims the courts must recognize and enforce also disappear. This leaves the courts with literally nothing to do in such cases unless they are willing to experiment with innovative reasons for applying law.[148]

2. Equity

One might be convinced by Green's assessment that "it is not that traditional rights-based jurisprudence has been rejected in favor of other forms of reasoning, but that traditional rights-based jurisprudence has become irrelevant and other forms of reasoning are all that is left to fill the gap."[149] But the fact that the complex patterns of interhuman transnational relations make *traditional* rights-based jurisprudence, and some would now argue, even governmental interest analysis[150] unhelpful, does not mean that one should immediately either go back to "good old fashioned choice of law rules,"[151] or abandon any arguments focusing on individuals' and communities' rights and interests.[152] Arguing that there is no a priori rule that determines individuals' rights and expectations in broad categories of cases doesn't mean that one should abandon any individual-based perspectives as Currie could be understood to have implied.

Cavers argued that neither an obsessive procrustean bed in the form of state interest analysis, nor the illusion of "conflicts justice" should distract one from thinking about what a just, equitable solution to the legal matter might look like. While in the correspondence with Currie he showed that state interest analysis

[147] Brilmayer, "Rights" (n. 6) 1279.

[148] Green, "Legal Realism" (n. 7) 994.

[149] Ibid.

[150] John Hart Ely, 'Choice of Law and the State's Interest in Protecting its Own' (1981) 23 Wm & Mary L Rev 173 (hereafter Ely, "Choice of Law").

[151] Ibid.

[152] As became apparent from his correspondence with David Cavers, Currie implied that the complexity of such analysis is too great.

might make it less likely for a state to apply its policy altruistically,[153] elsewhere he argued that a proper understanding of reasonable expectations of individuals would reveal that it is entirely justified for a state's policy to apply in order to hold responsible its domiciliaries for conduct abroad.[154]

In an article entitled "Cipolla and Conflicts Justice" Cavers reflects on different "true conflicts" scenarios in the area of tort law. In particular, he argues that in cases in which the parties are domiciled in different countries, "it does not follow that, because the domiciliary contacts conflict, their significance is equal. Rather, the court has to evaluate the position of the two parties with reference to the two states' conflicting rules since the forum must prefer one state's rule to that of the other."[155] Thus, in a case involving a plaintiff "who lives in the accident state with the lower standards and the defendant who comes from the other state with the higher standards" he asks:

> ... whether it would be unjust to the out-of-state defendant to hold him to the higher standards of liability or financial protection existing in his own state, thereby benefiting the plaintiff who, of course, would have been restricted by his own state's rule to a lower recovery if the tortfeasor had been a fellow-citizen.[156]

He shows that even from a state-centered perspective, one might argue for the interest of the defendant's domicile state to "hold to the full measure of damages or the standard of care which that state's law provides for."[157] He then goes on to argue that a proper understanding of the expectations of individuals shows that it is entirely equitable for a state's law offering higher compensation to regulate a domiciliary abroad for the benefit of non-domiciliaries. Indeed, anything else would amount to invidious comparisons.[158] As Cavers put it: "a defendant may complain of the harshness of his own state's rules when he is subjected to them in a case involving extraterritorial conduct or consequences. However, he can seldom complain that he was thereby been denied conflicts justice."[159]

Applying either the law of the tort or the law of the tortfeasor's domicile might be considered fair from a conflicts justice perspective.[160] But whether or not one should apply a law to hold domiciliaries accountable for conduct abroad will depend on an

[153] See Ely, "Choice of Law" (n. 150) (showing that Currie's proposition that a state would only protect its own domiciliaries has actually become the credo of the state interest analysis methodology.) See also David Cavers, 'Cipolla and Conflicts Justice' (1970) 9 Duq L Rev 360, 363 (hereafter Cavers, "Cipolla and Conflicts Justice"): "The idea that a state has an interest in protecting the claims of its citizens to the benefits of their own law when they are itinerant plaintiffs but not to the protection of their own law when they are stay-at-home defendants has begun to manifest itself among courts venturing upon governmental interest analyses".

[154] Cavers, "Cipolla and Conflicts Justice" (n. 153). [155] Ibid., 362.

[156] Ibid., 368. [157] Ibid., 369.

[158] For a similar perspective, see Arthur von Mehren, 'Recent Trends in Choice-of-Law Methodology' (1974) 60 Cornell L Rev 927; Arthur von Mehren, 'Choice of Law and the Problem of Justice' (1977) 41 Law & Contemp Probs 27.

[159] Cavers, "Cipolla and Conflicts Justice" (n. 159) 372.

[160] Note that Kogan, "Fairness Over Comity" (n. 6) would have argued that regardless of whether it is fair to apply the law against the defendant, it is not fair for the plaintiff to invoke it, because in order for the law to apply, each one of the parties (not just the defendant) must have a relationship to the law invoked.

assessment of equity between domiciliaries and non-domiciliaries and a view of social justice for transnational matters. All this means going back to Jitta's insight that one needs to understand what social function one attributes to a transnational legal relation (such as transnational torts of multinational corporations) and apply the law that allows it to perform such function.

3. Disaggregating state interests

So far, this chapter has shown that the American realist school placed the focus on surfacing and analyzing the policies underlying the respective laws in conflict. Occasionally, and especially because of the conventional understanding of Currie's theory, this perspective made analysts oblivious to the consideration of individual interests. Yet this chapter focused on Cavers's writing precisely because he attempted to show that the determination of the application of the policies of the laws should not be disjoined from, but rather informed by, the actions, beliefs, expectations, prior relationships between the parties and so on.

But while Cavers, in contrast to Brilmayer and Dane, suggested that a focus on individuals and their interests and expectations goes hand in hand with a focus on the substance and the policies of the laws, he was less clear about why that should be the case and how this relationship might be conceptualized.

A 1959 article by Robert Kramer seems to offer some valuable insight into this question.[161] Kramer aimed to connect Currie's theory focusing on state interests with the sociological jurisprudence of Thomas Cowan and Roscoe Pound in order to suggest that a conflict of laws analysis should disaggregate state interests.[162] He started from the premise that the realist school had rightfully brought attention to the substantive values underlying the laws in conflict. Like many critics of Currie, Kramer too argued that the theory might have adopted an overly state-centered approach. Yet in his view, this realization should not distract one from the substantive analysis of the policies underlying the laws. Rather, he argued that the policy in question needs to be analyzed by first "identifying and separating from each other the various interests—individual, group, social" and the way in which the respective law is trying to reconcile "conflicts among or between the identified interests."[163]

[161] Robert Kramer, 'Interests and Policy Clashes in Conflict of Laws' (1959) 13 Rutgers L Rev 523 (hereafter Kramer, "Clashes in Conflict of Laws"). Interestingly, Kramer himself is not clear about the novelty of his thesis of disaggregating state interests. While he suggests that focusing on state interests is misleading and obscures the individual, group and social interests underlying it, at 531, he also states that other authors had argued for a "frank recognition that the social, economic, political reasons behind the policy or law of a state must and should be ascertained," at 533–4. But in this evaluation he fails to appreciate the extent to which underscoring these interests amounts to simply suggesting that there might be policies underlying state interests beyond those initially recognized by Currie, as opposed to proposing an inquiry into how individuals, groups, and communities would be impacted by one decision or another.

[162] Ibid., 532: "If that policy is, as I believe, the outgrowth of clashes of individual, group, and social interests, if it is a legislative, judicial or administrative attempt to compromise, adjust, or prevent these clashes of interests, then the better we can identify these interests, their real nature, their conflicts, the better we can grasp the legitimate reasons and governmental interests behind the policy in question."

[163] Ibid., 526.

He presents the challenge of such an analysis in a purely domestic context in the following way:[164]

A just, decent, and orderly adjustment of these clashes of interests demands that each interest—individual, group, social—be adequately represented and have a chance to present its case before a decision is made. Yet courts have rarely, if ever, devised adequate methods for handling such multi-party clashes, and legislative and administrative hearings frequently are so dominated and overwhelmed by the clamors of powerful groups that social or individual interests may be overlooked or neglected. Markets may cease to function in a representative manner if dominated by powerful groups, and groups may callously disregard individual and social rights and interests.[165]

When moved to the transnational setting the challenge is even greater:

Here we have clashes of interests between individuals, groups, and communities located, not all in one sovereign state, but in two or more states. In a sense we move from the three-dimensional universe of individual, group and social interests, into a multidimensional universe. We have not simply conflicts of interests—individual, group, and social—among themselves and with each other; we have a clash between the policy of one state—how it adjusts the clashing interests—and the policy of another state—the different solution that state has for a similar clash of like interests. And, of course, more than two states may be involved; we may have policy conflicts here of several states.[166]

This disaggregation of interests means that whenever a court decides on the validity of guarantees offered by married women when one of the laws in conflict does not allow for such guarantees, for example, it must consider "the individual, group and social interests involved."[167] Kramer's analysis of the interests that might underlie such a decision is worth quoting at large:

Perhaps A cared not at all about married women but, responding to the wishes of a special group of creditors—professional sureties—enacted this statute to prevent the all-too-frequent substitution of a wife for a professional surety as a guarantor for a husband's credit. Thus A's policy is one to regulate creditors here, not debtors. Or perhaps state A felt its courts were too often thrust into family affairs when wives were sureties for husbands, that such transactions were too productive of perjury and fraudulent transactions, so that the courts of A should not be forced to try such actions. Or such suretyship transactions may be too prone to lead to husbands and wives having title to property really owned by them either held by others on secret or oral trusts for them or placed in the names of their children. Similar conjectures may be made about the reasons and interests behind the policy of B. Perhaps the policy of B was really meant to aid married women, to encourage them to take a more active part in business affairs, to add to their financial knowledge about their husbands' businesses in cases of early widowhood, to enable them to enter the business of suretyship. Or perhaps

[164] Note that in addition to revealing the complex web of interests that need to be evaluated in any judicial decision (and especially in transnational ones) Kramer also underscores that a difficult question is also "who in our society—legislature, administrative agency, court, executive official—is to decide the conflicts, to make compromises and adjustments, to assign priorities, to determine the values of the competing interests and which shall prevail to what extent. The problems of valuation alone present perplexing questions—the interdependency of ends and means, the relative importance of both reason and feeling or intuition, the need for acute semantic analysis." Ibid., 526.

[165] Ibid., 527. [166] Ibid., 527. [167] Ibid., 530.

B felt that a contrary policy encouraged fraud and perjury in its courts, led to husbands placing all property in the names of their wives. Or perhaps the policy was an attempt to aid and foster small family businesses, which could not otherwise obtain needed credits.[168]

For Kramer a disaggregation of state interests implies a much wider policy space and policy consideration. It was this particular broadening of the interests that Currie meant to avoid for various pragmatic reasons.[169] However, by showing how wide ranging the considerations and interests are, Kramer revealed how much is at stake for the individuals, groups, and communities who are affected by the application of these policies.

The exposure of individual, group, and social interests behind legislative policies means that ultimately the application of one law over the other, or of a combination of the laws,[170] implies a projection in the transnational space of a particular kind of rebalancing of these relevant interests. This is likely what we should understand by Jitta's claim that PrIL is ultimately concerned with applying the law that allows a legal relation to fulfill its social purpose in the transnational space. This means that whenever a determination of the applicable law is made, one is in essence engaged in determining the social scope of this relationship in the transnational space and this entails a certain preference for certain individual, group, and social interests over others.[171] Kramer explains that:

> If we recognize and appreciate fully the fact that we are often dealing with policies here which, under the mask or guise of a broad public social interest, actually reflect and represent comparatively narrow selfish group interests, we may, as judges, be strongly inclined to reject a local policy, benefiting a small, powerful group at public expense, in favor of another state's policy which curbs this group interest for the benefit of the interest of a far larger group or of the public as a whole.[172]

F. Conclusions

The conventional account of American PrIL theory as developing from a rights-based, to a state-interest based perspective and then back to rights-based arguments as a means of tempering the state-centered perspective is not particularly

[168] Ibid., 540.

[169] Kramer agrees with Currie that policy balancing is not a task meant for the judges.

[170] Note that Jitta envisioned the possibility of applying a substantive norm that results from the combination of the different national laws relevant to the dispute. Arthur von Mehren argues for the same possibility. See Arthur von Mehren, 'Special Substantive Rules for Multistate Problems: Their Role and Significance in Contemporary Choice of Law Methodology' (1974) 88 Harv L Rev 347.

[171] Much of this complex analysis revealed by Kramer's disaggregation of interests is well captured and illustrated by Joseph Singer in two articles published in 1989 and 1990. See Joseph Singer, 'Real Conflicts' (1989) 69 BU L Rev 3, 35; Joseph Singer, 'A Pragmatic Guide to Conflicts' (1990) 70 BU L Rev 731.

[172] Kramer, "Clashes in Conflict of Laws" (n. 161) 547. In the end it is telling that in a recent article Lea Brilmayer seems more inclined to accept this broadening of the substantive analysis as a natural development of PrIL from an individual-centered perspective. Brilmayer, "The Problem of Provenance" (n. 2).

illuminating. This chapter showed that even when detached from its formalist underpinnings Beale's theory is not properly understood as individual-centered; rather, it represents a continuation of the state-centered internationalist theories described in the first chapter. Similarly, in line with Green's assessment, this chapter revealed that the realist school of thought is not only compatible with relational internationalist perspectives, but in many ways conducive to such an approach. By offering a different reading of Currie's theory, found in his correspondence with David Cavers, it suggested that the state-centered and parochial elements that Currie's theory injected into American PrIL theories were based on pragmatic, rather than absolute normative considerations.

Shedding new light on the American realist school of PrIL made it possible to capture the variety of individual-centered internationalist arguments that realist scholars offered to counter Currie's state-centered premises. From outside the realist school, Currie was criticized for ignoring "fairness" concerns, understood as rights limiting the coercive power of states in a transnational setting. Yet from within the realist school the individual-centered arguments were much richer and more nuanced. Cavers argued that courts should discern the legitimacy of applying a particular law by evaluating the acts of the individuals in relationship to the state and the policy underlying its laws. Kramer argued that state interests must be disaggregated in order to capture the variety of individual, group, and social interests, which are balanced and captured under a legal policy. He argued that choice of law rules must inevitably capture and appreciate the right balance of those interests given the transnational context of PrIL matters.

Overall, much as Beale's theory could be seen as a continuation of Pillet's and Zitelmann's state-centered internationalist theories, there are many overlooked arguments underlying the realist theories that represent a continuation of the relational-centered internationalist perspective, especially Jitta's.

To deepen our appreciation of the difference that the state-centered/individual-centered distinction makes for the development of PrIL, the next three chapters pick up respectively on three themes already apparent in the historical analysis developed in this and the previous chapters: rights and reasonable expectations (Chapter 6), legitimacy and autonomy (Chapter 7), and the cosmopolitan dimensions of PrIL (Chapter 8). Describing the different ways in which these issues were analyzed from an individual-centered and a state-centered perspective will reveal in greater detail the impact for the development of PrIL theory and methodology of choosing the state or the individual, in relational terms, as the analytical point of departure.

6

Recognition, Rights, and Reasonable Expectations

A. Introduction

Following an overview of the ideological and analytical contours of the state-centered and individual-centered perspectives in Chapter 2, Chapters 3 to 5 traced the rise and fall of these perspectives in Europe and the United States. The next three chapters distill from this historical material the implications of adopting any one of these perspectives for the understanding of rights and reasonable expectations (current chapter), legitimacy and autonomy (Chapter 7), and the cosmopolitan dimensions of PrIL (Chapter 8).

The goal of these chapters is to reveal the ways in which the conceptualization of some of PrIL's analytical categories depended on whether particular PrIL scholars took the state or the individual as the point of reference and on what image of the individual in her international existence they referenced. In particular, the aim of these chapters is to explore individual-centered perspectives that have been marginalized to date and that offer alternatives to overly liberal or libertarian individualistic theories, as well as to exclusively state-centered theories of PrIL. These marginalized perspectives focus on the recognition, as well as the responsibilization of individuals in the transnational context; relational, rather than individualistic notions of autonomy; and substantive, socially informed, rather than libertarian conceptualizations of legitimate authority.

When PrIL theory and methodology are constructed in state-centered terms, they exclude an important space for private versus private contestation, as Robert Wai calls it,[1] where parties' arguments for justice, fairness, rights, and reasonable expectations can be made. As shown in Chapters 2 and 3, the state-centered internationalist perspective, which developed at the end of the nineteenth century, imagines individuals as bystanders to an interstate affair based on a neutral division of sovereign authority. Similarly, as alluded to in Chapter 5, the American state interest theory may often be interpreted to suggest that individual interests and appeals to justice are comfortably reflected and subsumed under state interests.

[1] Robert Wai, 'Private v. Private: Transnational Private Law and Contestation in Global Economic Governance' in Horatia Muir Watt and Diego P. Fernández Arroyo (eds.), *Private International Law and Global Governance* (OUP 2015).

Nineteenth-Century Perspectives on Private International Law. Roxana Banu. © Roxana Banu 2018. Published 2018 by Oxford University Press.

Furthermore, as Joseph Singer points out, while the state interest theory allows utilitarian or regulatory policies designed to maximize the general welfare to enter into the analysis, it ignores rights-based or moral principles designed to promote social justice by defining moral obligations within social relationships.[2] Indeed Singer argues that "the decision to ignore moral policies" that provide for different ways of understanding individuals' responsibilities and moral conduct in relationship to each other in a transnational context "is crucial to modern conflicts theories."[3]

At the same time, while this book recovers these "rights-based or moral principles designed to promote social justice,"[4] it does not inevitably focus on the neutral, libertarian position. As shown in the next chapter, in reacting against the utilitarian model, Lea Brilmayer developed an individual-centered theory based on individual liberty and political neutrality. This theory might reveal an image of individuals as isolated and exclusively autonomous agents who should be "protected" from what is uncritically understood as intrusive state authority.[5]

In contrast, the goal of this book is to recover a different position by resurfacing the image of a relational individual whose existence in the international realm is determined by overlapping relationships with various individuals and communities. Focusing on these relationships inevitably means focusing on the rights, duties, legal, and moral responsibilities individuals have in relationship to each other. It means focusing on the way in which they impact and alter each other's opportunities, rights, autonomy, etc. This chapter argues that several rights perspectives found in the theories of Joseph Story, Friedrich Karl von Savigny, and Josephus Jitta, offer an initial step in developing this alternative relational internationalist perspective in PrIL. This picture will be further completed in the next two chapters with a discussion of legitimate authority and PrIL's cosmopolitan dimensions.

B. Breaking the Alleged Unity of the Vested Rights Theories to Make Space for Recognition

In the recent collection *Private International Law as Global Governance*, which she edited with Diego Fernández Arroyo, Horatia Muir Watt considered possible "future directions" for the development of PrIL.[6] Muir Watt suggests that PrIL and PublIL might currently undergo significant transformations through the incorporation of recognition as a proxy for emphasizing individual identity and dignity, as well as creating a decent international society.[7] "In a nutshell, the idea is that

[2] Joseph Singer, 'Real Conflicts' (1989) 69 BU L Rev 3, 35. [3] Ibid. [4] Ibid.

[5] Lea Brilmayer, 'Rights, Fairness, and Choice of Law' (1989) 98 Yale L J 1277.

[6] Horatia Muir Watt, 'Future Directions?' in Horatia Muir Watt and Diego P. Fernández Arroyo (eds.), *Private International Law and Global Governance* (OUP 2015) 343 (hereafter Muir Watt, "Future Directions?").

[7] Ibid., 366. As regards PublIL Muir Watt cites Emmanuelle Jouannet for the proposition that "recognition could be the most promising candidate for a re-foundation of the discipline, as geared to the establishment of a fair and decent international society," citing Emanuelle Tourme-Jouannet, *Qu'est-ce qu'une société international juste? Le droit international entre développement et reconnaissance?*

personal relationships created elsewhere, under a foreign law (and according to a potentially different understanding of their meaning and content), should be given a place (within the society and under the law of the forum) as such, respecting their specific, initial characteristics."[8]

Muir Watt notes that in the case of PrIL "the potential implications of recognition may well be less immediately perceptible than in the discipline's public international counterpart. Indeed, the vocabulary of recognition has always been central to the conflict of laws—encompassing vested rights, judgments, public acts, personal status, and now under the influence of European Union law, mutual recognition."[9] However, she argues that the vocabulary of recognition within PrIL, at least as it is commonly understood, is fundamentally different from the one she is trying to recover by reference to feminist writings and human rights norms, among others.

With this cautionary remark, Muir Watt introduces certain ambivalences that she sees as underlying PrIL as a field. First, PrIL's methodological tools and techniques might signal a propensity for recognition, but in PrIL recognition may be part of an acontextual and dogmatic ideology. By focusing on recognition, Muir Watt has in mind neither a return to Mancini's recognition of personal status according to the law of citizenship,[10] nor a blind reference to vested rights.[11] Second, recognition may be confused with an overly liberal, possibly individualistic concept. Transported to the wide variety of private law relationships with which PrIL deals, it could simultaneously achieve the recognition of identity and dignity, on the one hand, and of individualistic property and contract claims, on the other. In other words, Muir Watt does not have in mind a revival of individual liberty underlying English justice theories in PrIL, which were described in the previous chapter and which would lead indiscriminately to self-determination and identity as well as strong property and contract claims. In Muir Watt's view recognition should be limited to "personhood and family relationships."[12]

(Pédone 2012). See also Emanuelle Tourme-Jouannet, 'The International Law of Recognition' (2013) 24 EJIL 667.

[8] Muir Watt, "Future Directions?" (n. 6) 367. [9] Ibid., 368.

[10] Ibid., 378: "a different epistemological frame is proposed by human rights law in this context, substituting a concrete, individualized approach for the more abstract concern for continuity and permanence of status whatever the circumstances."

[11] Ibid., 367, n. 100 (expressed disagreement with Prof. Ralf Michaels' thesis of associating the mutual recognition principle underlying EU law with the PrIL vested rights theory: "the thesis according to which 'mutual recognition' under European Union has anything to do with 'vested rights' is not really convincing; or at least, no more so than any attempt to correlate mutual recognition and the recognition debate considered above") citing Ralf Michaels, 'EU Law as Private International Law—Re-Conceptualizing the Country-of-Origin Principle as Vested-Rights Theory' (2006) 2 J Priv Int'l L 195.

[12] Muir Watt, "Future Directions?" (n. 6) 367, n. 102:

> The scope of recognition cannot be defined dogmatically, in the way in which traditional methodological tools determine their purview, for the epistemological reasons that will be explained later. Recognition responds, rather, to a need stemming from the denial of identity, which will tend to circumscribe its use to personhood and family relationships [. . .] A tort or criminal case may ALSO involve issues of recognition, if only through procedural issues of standing, for example.

Given these ambivalences, Muir Watt finds it unsurprising that "for the moment, recognition in PrIL is perceived largely as a competing, and opposing, methodological approach to individual trans-border relationships, for which traditional tools have had to make room, owing to the direct vertical and horizontal effects of hard-core human rights instruments."[13] Indeed it seems that in the EU context, for example, a "human rights-based perspective" is necessary in order to achieve the "cross-border continuity of a parent-child relationship on the dignitarian ground of the right to a normal family life"[14] or the recognition of a family name across borders as the corollary of the necessary "coherence of individual status of mobile citizens within the internal market."[15] The paradigm of recognition that Muir Watt seeks to introduce into PrIL focuses on "social reality,"[16] rather than dogmatic and abstract notions of law and rights; on fluid notions of reasonable expectations, rather than methodological play;[17] on "open-textured and deliberative normative modes, sensitive to life experiences with which it interacts, rather than 'formal rationality of the law',"[18] and on "a method of care, respect for alterity, protection of dignity and identity, which are to a large extent excluded by the abstraction of private international law methodology."[19]

Interestingly, although not directly focusing on the concept of recognition, Loïc Azoulai has argued that European Union law also attempts to recognize and validate individuals' social—"real links"—to particular European Union communities. Azoulai argues that in the European Union context:

> EU law's intervention means special protection for individuals who have developed multiple affiliations within the Union, whether they are nationality bonds, family or professional ties. The core of the EU law regime consists in imposing on Member States the obligation to grant a legal status corresponding to the concrete life of these European individuals who are anchored in different points of the European territory. That this regime collides with a state territoriality concern recognized by the Court as a public policy concern is not surprising [. . .] This pre-empts, in practice, Member States to recognize the status of multi-anchored individuals within their legal order and to organize their integration into the host society.[20]

Azoulai further argues that an acknowledgment of Europeans' "multi-anchored" existence translates into an attempt to create a coherent framework, which recognizes different levels of social integration in different European communities simultaneously, based on their existing integration in the social life of these communities:

> Integration into society instead of political community means integration into a group of people whose members are bound by various kinds of connecting factors based on residence,

[13] Ibid., 369. [14] Ibid.

[15] Ibid: "If concerns for individual and collective dignity and identity, associated in other disciplinary fields with the recognition paradigm, have made a recent entrance into private international law, it has been through the transnational effects of fundamental rights."

[16] Ibid., 372. [17] Ibid., 373. [18] Ibid., 375. [19] Ibid., 378.

[20] Loïc Azoulai, 'The European Individual as Part of Collective Entities (Market, Family, Society)' in Loïc Azoulai, Ségolène Barbou des Places, and Etienne Pataut (eds.), *Constructing the Person in EU Law: Rights, Roles, Identity* (Hart 2016) 203, 216 (hereafter Azoulai, "Collective Entities").

employment, family ties, education and so on, and not exclusively or primarily by the nationality bond.[21]

This shift from the image of an individual linked to a political community through citizenship to a relational individual embedded in various social systems and communities furthers and increases the level of recognition granted to this social embeddedness:

Unlike bounded political communities, societies and discrete social groups are deemed to be capable of mutual recognition. The institutional and personal parties to these groups, be they hospitals and patients, universities and students, tax authorities and taxpayers or social security and insured persons, may develop direct relations even though they do not belong to the same nation, or if they do, do not operate within the same national borders.[22]

The recognition granted through EU law is not only stronger—because more directly premised on a pre-existing integration in social life—but also more nuanced because it responds to multiple concurrent social affiliations. While Horatia Muir Watt considers it a significant advance that human rights norms in the *Wagner*[23] case facilitated the recognition "as such" of a pre-existing relationship—an adoption—from Peru to the Netherlands, EU law tries to make sense and coordinate individuals' embeddedness in multiple relationships and multiple communities. Azoulai describes this distinction in the following way:

In that decision [*Wagner*] the European Court of Human Rights forced the Luxembourg authorities to recognize an adoption judgment passed in Peru as legally valid. It referred to the "social reality" of the situation created under Peruvian law. But, in *Wagner*, social reality essentially means family ties as attested to by foreign law. By contrast, in the Court of Justice's case-law on surnames, the family perspective is only one aspect of the situation. What really matters is that the individual concerned is "closely connected" to different societies and to different aspects of social life: the family, the profession, the social protection or the education system. In these cases, the Court's concern is not so much the preservation of a family group but to secure a smooth mode of circulation of individuals between these distinct social spheres and institutions.[24]

The parallel between the level and degree of recognition that Muir Watt argues should be granted in PrIL and the level and degree of integration that Azoulai believes is achieved through EU law is instructive both in revealing different gradations of recognition needed for a relational individual and for revealing the limitations of achieving such recognition in the transnational realm absent the level of economic and social integration present within the European Union.

But Muir Watt is clear that even the more limited framework of recognition of a single relationship from one jurisdiction to the other is somehow at odds with the methodology of PrIL.[25] Given this tension between the formalistic dogmatic image

[21] Ibid., 212. [22] Ibid., 213. [23] ECtHR June 28, 2017 req. no. 76240/01.

[24] Azoulai, "Collective Entities" (n. 20) 214.

[25] Pierre Mayer has argued that the question of recognition is in fact very easily placed "under the domain of conflict of laws" and that "the method of recognition is simply one of the solutions to the conflicts of systems." See Piere Mayer, 'Les methods de la reconnaissance en droit international

of PrIL presented by Muir Watt and the framework of recognition focused on individual dignity, identity, and interpersonal care, Muir Watt posits two alternative positions as "future directions" for PrIL. One position would welcome the overcoming of PrIL's dogmatism by the contextual and fluid human rights methodology, as well as insights from feminist writings, sociology, philosophy, and so on, even to the point when PrIL might no longer constitute an independent legal discipline.[26] Alternatively, the enterprise might be to connect the framework of recognition to PrIL's own underlying philosophy:

> The scope of recognition cannot be defined dogmatically, in the way in which traditional methodological tools determine their purview. This is because recognition responds, rather, to needs stemming from the denial of identities in real life. However, these are salient in the field which, in the vocabulary of the conflict of laws, belong to "personal status," and involve the impact of cross-border mobility on personhood and family relationships. Does this mean that, in this field, the tools and methods of this discipline are disqualified? The question, now, is the extent to which recognition could be seen to represent the excavation of an alternative axiological project which has always been contained implicitly within the conflict of laws.[27]

This chapter attempts precisely such an "excavation of an alternative axiological project" underlying the relational internationalist perspective which, I argue, connects in many respects to the paradigm of recognition described by Muir Watt. In engaging in this excavation, this chapter reveals precisely the ambivalence in PrIL, ranging from the utter misrecognition of individuals' pleas for identity, justice, and dignity to an overly liberal individualistic recognition. The liberal individualistic paradigm can be found in early nineteenth-century theories of vested rights, which described the application of foreign law as an attribute of personal autonomy and liberty. On the other side of the spectrum, regardless of whether Horatia Muir Watt is right that PrIL and PublIL could now reconnect via the recognition paradigm,[28] I suggest that historically the misrecognition of individuals and their pleas for justice was in fact a corollary to the state-centered internationalist position under the PrIL-PublIL association.

In contrast, I argue that a much more nuanced and contextual framework of recognition can be "excavated" from the premises of the relational internationalist

privé' in Pierre Mayer and Marie-Noëlle Jobard-Bachellier (eds.), *Droit international privé, esprit et methods: mélanges en l'honneur de Paul Lagarde* (Dalloz, 2005) 547, 548.

[26] Horatia Muir Watt portrays this as "a methodological enquiry: the end of choice of law?" See Muir Watt, "Future Directions?" (n. 6) 363.

[27] Ibid., 378.

[28] Muir Watt argues that the incorporation of a method of recognition in PrIL via human rights highlights two different aspects. Ibid., 382.

> The first is drawing attention to similarities between the two sets of methods, and the values they carry with them. Thus, absorption of the conflict of laws relating to personal status by human rights, has not only had a radical effect on the existing legal tools, but has also served to highlight the convergence between the axiological project of recognition and the pre-modern statutist ideal. The second is suggesting that schism between public and private international law may be in the (incremental) process of being bridged. In this latter perspective, it is remarkable that recognition is now associated with a re-foundation of international law on both sides of the looking glass.

perspective, especially as it culminated in Jitta's theory. First, the relational internationalist perspective emphasized precisely the spectrum from liberty and self-determination to social responsibility, based on the differentiation of the various types of private law relationships in the transnational realm. Implicitly, the recognition of individual reasonable expectations and appeals to justice and of larger sociopolitical considerations are involved to different degrees, depending on the kind of relationship at issue. Second, the relational internationalist perspective engages in an analysis of the nature of the relationship by incorporating both extra-legal social expectations of the individuals involved and the relevant legal policies. Furthermore, as shown below, Story refers to a notion of "naturally vesting rights" precisely to emphasize the recognition of expectations and relationships that have manifested themselves in the lives of individuals, rather than being formally granted through law. As it culminated in Jitta's account, this perspective focused explicitly on achieving the coherence of individuals' existence in the transnational realm, emphasized a needed loosening of PrIL's methodology, and pled for a purposeful and contextual analysis of international social life. Furthermore, Jitta emphasized the complexity of individual identity by underscoring the myriad of affiliations and relationships in which the individual is embedded as she navigates the transnational realm. As such, Jitta's theory may be read as pleading for an even stronger and more layered framework of recognition akin to that described by Azoulai as underlying EU law.

Throughout her account, Horatia Muir Watt repeatedly cites vested rights theories in PrIL as the element—at least conceptually—most closely related to recognition, although she seeks to dissociate the methodological and policy justifications that separate the two notions.[29] Indeed it is through the lens of rights theories that one can appreciate the level of recognition granted to individuals and their relationships. This chapter therefore takes rights theories as the terrain on which to distinguish between perspectives highly focused on individual liberty, state-centered perspectives that eliminate the voice of individuals, and relational internationalist perspectives that construct a relational, social image of the individual.

To appreciate the diverse ways in which the identity and regulatory needs of individuals are portrayed in PrIL, one must first break the perceived unity of vested rights theories. In 1908 Albert Dicey argued that PrIL is almost universally unified through the concept of vested rights.[30] He claimed there was a natural convergence,[31]

[29] Muir Watt, "Future Directions?" (n. 6) 367, n. 100 and 368:

> Indeed the vocabulary of recognition has always been central to the conflict of laws—encompassing vested rights, judgments, public acts, personal status, and, now under the influence of European Union law, "mutual recognition"; moreover, traditional concern for the understanding of the "foreign" has always existed, at least in the discourse of the discipline, so that under cover of a common signifier, there is a tendency to assume substantive similarity between the conventional goals of private international law as "management of pluralism" with more recent, collectively identitarian or individually dignitarian, forms of recognition.

[30] Albert Venn Dicey, *A Digest of the Law of England with Reference to the Conflict of Laws* (Stevens 1908) (hereafter Dicey, *A Digest of the Law of England*).

[31] Ibid., 11: "The selection of one or more of these laws is not a matter of caprice, but depends upon more or less definite reasons which are likely to influence all Courts and legislators."

"a community of the aim" that flows from the universal goal to "secure the extra-territorial effect of rights."[32] Westlake in England,[33] Ernst Zitelmann in Germany,[34] Vareilles-Sommières in France,[35] and Joseph Beale in the United States[36] all made the same claim in the last few decades of the nineteenth and the first few decades of the twentieth century.[37]

At first sight, this overwhelming consensus between PrIL scholars in different countries suggests a uniform rights-based understanding of the regulatory goals of PrIL all through the first few decades of the twentieth century. But of course not only does this tell us little about the consequences of adopting a rights-based perspective in PrIL. It also tells us little about how these and other scholars in PrIL conceptualized rights in a transnational context. Behind this façade of doctrinal uniformity hide different underlying assumptions about the contours of rights, which have a strong impact on the regulatory function of PrIL.[38] In particular, our perspective on the content and function of rights tends to change depending on whether we take the individual or the state as the analytical point of reference in PrIL theory and methodology and whether we portray an atomistic or a relational image of the individual in her international existence. We inject different assumptions, biases, and analytics into our view of rights depending on whether we think of PrIL as a space for promoting individual liberty, determining conflicts of sovereignty among states, or for contesting and constructing the requirements for the reasonable social intercourse of individuals in the transnational sphere.[39]

This chapter reveals these different contours of rights by focusing on three main yet different perspectives. The first section pursues the common intuition that rights theories are overly individualistic and premised on unrestrained individual autonomy. It outlines several theories within the intellectual history of PrIL that seem to fit this model. The following section describes the formalistic state-centered internationalist perspective of Pillet, Zitelmann, and Beale. From this perspective,

[32] Ibid., 12.

[33] John Westlake, 'Relations Between Public and Private International Law' in Lassa Oppenheim (ed.), *The Collected Papers of John Westlake on Public International Law* (CUP 1914) 285, 305.

[34] Ernst Zitelmann, *Internationales Privatrecht* (Duncker & Humblot 1897) (hereafter Zitelmann, *Internationales Privatrecht*).

[35] Gabriel Vareilles-Sommières, *La synthèse du droit international privé* (Pichon 1897). For a synthesis, see Marquis de Vareilles-Sommières, 'La synthese du droit international privé' (1900) 27 Journal de droit international privé et de la jurisprudence comparée 5 and (1900) 27 Journal de droit international privé et de la jurisprudence comparée 158.

[36] Joseph Henry Beale, *A Treatise on the Conflict of Laws: Or, Private International Law*, vol. 1, part 1 (Harvard University Press 1916) (hereafter Beale, *A Treatise on the Conflict of Laws*). Beale relied heavily on the European authors referencing the vested rights doctrine, including Pillet, Zitelmann, Westlake, and Vareilles-Sommieres. He described Vareilles-Sommieres's theory, for example, as "a singular original, well-reasoned and careful work, which will repay careful study. He holds the theory of vested rights, and his work is therefore one of special interest to an American scholar."

[37] For an overview and critique of the different vested rights theories, see Pierre Arminjon, 'La notion de droit acquis en droit international privé' (1933) 44 Recueil des Cours 1.

[38] For an account of the different vested rights theories in PrIL and their relationship to the "country of origin" principle underlying EU law, see Ralf Michaels, 'EU Law as Private International Law? Re-Conceptualizing the Country-of-Origin Principle as Vested-Rights Theory' (2006) 2 J Priv Int'l L 195 (hereafter Michaels, "EU Law as Private International Law").

[39] For a general description of these various theoretical perspectives in PrIL, see Chapter 2.

individuals' pleas for justice and recognition are almost entirely excluded from the determination of the applicable law. While rights perspectives are targeted as overly liberal or libertarian, it is important to acknowledge that "vested rights" perspectives in PrIL can also stand for state-centered, rather than individual-centered theories. These perspectives make it possible to exclude individuals entirely, to argue that their reasonable expectations are "fictitious concepts,"[40] and that their role is that of bystanders to the interstate affair of distributing rights and authority amongst each other.

Although the first section of the chapter reveals highly liberal theories of rights that treat the application of a particular law as an attribute of individual autonomy and liberty, we should not be too quick to classify all rights theories under this category, or at least not discard all such theories simply because they appear to focus on autonomy. The third section argues that Savigny's theory has been wrongly associated with the extreme individualistic perspective. Savigny in fact reacted against the overly individualistic perspective and his theory resembles in many respects Story's method of analyzing legal relations. To provide further support for this reading of Savigny, this chapter outlines how the German socialist Josephus Lassalles used the conceptualization of the relationship between rights, autonomy, and the people (Volk) that Savigny relied on, in order to counter the individualistic theory of vested rights and to provide an impetus for social justice in PrIL. Furthermore, it shows how Jitta elaborated both on Savigny's concept of the legal relation and on his view of autonomy and voluntary submission.

C. Individualistic Vested Rights Theories

One might assume that "vested rights" theories originated with Albert Dicey and Joseph Beale. However, this perspective can be traced to at least the early nineteenth century, in the scholarship of Friedrich Wilhelm Tittmann, Karl Friedrich Eichhorn, and Georg Friedrich Puchta. This earlier scholarship could serve as a proxy for the intuitive case that vested rights theories foster an overly individualistic perspective. These authors offer the clearest justifications for a theory of vested rights grounded in an individualistic philosophy and correlated with a certain theory of individual freedom and autonomy. These particular vested rights theories were indeed among the earliest articulations of this perspective in PrIL, even though both Wächter and Savigny would later entirely refute them.

It is in these theories that one finds a clear "tension between the individual and the state,"[41] and an overemphasis on individual freedom and autonomy. Under this

[40] For the way in which this argument features in the state-centered internationalist theory of the Supreme Court of Canada in *Tolofson v. Jensen*, see Roxana Banu, 'Assuming Regulatory Authority for Transnational Torts: An Interstate Affair? A Historical Perspective on the Canadian Private International Law Tort Rules' (2013) 31 Windsor YB Access Just 197.

[41] Horst Müller, *Der Grundsatz des wohlerworbenen Rechts im internationalen Privatrecht* (De Gruyter 1935) 185 (hereafter Müller, *Der Grundsatz*).

ideology the individual is self-sufficient, independent, and autonomous and must be protected from state intrusion. Similarly, the role of the state is merely to respect, recognize, and foster individual freedom. Transposed to the PrIL context, individual freedom translates into a freedom to choose the law or deviate from the applicable law, rights and freedom are natural pre-legal expressions of individuality, and the application of the *lex fori* is viewed as a "falsification of individual will."[42]

1. Friedrich Tittmann

In his 1822 dissertation, the German scholar Friedrich Tittmann focused on a question he perceived as overlooked in the theory of PrIL, namely why a court would apply foreign law to begin with.[43] Viewed from this angle he believed the fundamental question PrIL must answer is the extent to which laws that vest private rights must apply extraterritorially. The fact that vested rights must in fact be recognized is posited as an axiom deduced from individual autonomy.[44] The task was merely to connect rights and individual autonomy to the choice of law problem. This makes him argue that "a vested right is not recognized because a foreign law which vested it is recognized, but rather, the law is recognized as a 'fact' proving that a right vested."[45] An individual right is the object of recognition, while the law is just the medium through which the right finds recognition in another state.[46]

More important, law is not the source of rights. Rights are understood by Tittmann, given his natural law ideology, as pre-legal. "A right is created when the fact required by natural law, in particular a form-free contract exists. The positive law simply concretizes the content of this right further."[47] This means that the existence of a right is determined not by "submission under a law, but is a direct consequence of autonomy. Foreign law is applied therefore simply because this is what the parties want."[48] Whether a right is vested therefore "does not depend on a particular legal order, but on natural law and autonomy."[49]

This inevitably creates "a tension between the individual and the state," where the relationship rests in the individual's right, based on a social contract, to claim from the state "protection of its personhood and its legal features."[50] The stakes of PrIL are described accordingly: "if a court applies forum law over the law desired by the

[42] Ibid.

[43] Friedrich Wilhelm Tittmann, *De competentia legum externarum et domesticarum in defiendis potissimum iuribus coniugum* (Gebauer 1822). Tittmann's dissertation was written in Latin. The discussion of his writing therefore relies on Müller's review of Tittmann's theory. See Müller, *Der Grundsatz* (n. 41) 180–7.

[44] Müller, *Der Grundsatz* (n. 41) 181.

[45] Ibid., 183.

[46] For a brief description of Tittmann's vested rights theory, see Michaels, "EU Law as Private International Law" (n. 38) 220.

[47] Müller, *Der Grundsatz* (n. 41) 184.

[48] Ibid., 184. The distinction between deriving the application of a law from voluntary submission to that law and deriving it directly from individual autonomy matters because it reflects the way in which individual rights and entitlements are considered pre-legal (Tittmann) or derived from law (see the discussion of Savigny below).

[49] Ibid., 185.

[50] Ibid., 185.

individuals, it offends not foreign law and the foreign state, but the individual and her rights vested in accordance with party autonomy. It would falsify her will."[51]

In his 1935 review of Tittmann's vested rights doctrine, Müller notes that Tittmann's theory was acknowledged, but had no followers.[52] However, he argued that:

> one should not downplay its historical relevance. Tittmann was still the first writer who purposely and because of its underlying premises inevitably introduced the concept that vested rights must be recognized in PrIL. Thereby he certainly exposed the issue fully. The critique of Wächter then illuminated the problems. Ever since, the idea keeps reoccurring in PrIL.[53]

2. Friedrich Eichhorn

Tittmann's views were later picked up by the well known Germanist Friedrich Eichhorn (1781–1854).[54] In 1935 Müller noted that Eichhorn's fame "might be the reason why Tittmann's dissertation was not completely forgotten."[55] Eichhorn, like Tittmann, argued that party autonomy determines the law under which particular rights vest and that this autonomy can only be limited through the absolute laws of the domicile (not the forum).[56] For torts for example, he argued that the law of the place where the tortious act occurred should apply "because the tortfeasor [through his tortious act] submitted to this law."[57] Because the application of a law must be the consequence of individual freedom, presumably the tortfeasor has a vested right in the application of this law.

Overall Eichhorn believed that the law of domicile should govern, most likely because this is the law to which individuals presumably submit.[58] Yet for Eichhorn even derogations from the law of domicile can be made freely by the parties. Any application of the law ultimately rests on party autonomy, of which individuals dispose freely, subject to restrictions in the law of domicile.[59] In this spirit Eichhorn argued that while the law of the place where immovable property is located should govern rights related to property, the principle "autonomy breaks state law"[60] should make it possible for individuals to "subscribe to rights with a different content" subject to the absolute laws of the *lex rei sitae*.[61] Müller noted that this line of reasoning makes it possible to "determine applicable, by virtue of party autonomy, another law than the one generally considered applicable."[62]

[51] Ibid. [52] Ibid., 186. [53] Ibid., 187.

[54] Karl Friedrich Eichhorn, *Einleitung in das deutsche Privatrecht: Mit Einschluss des Lehenrechts* (Vandenhoeck & Ruprecht 1836) §34, 37, 97–9, 108–11 (hereafter Eichhorn, *Mit Einschluss des Lehenrechts*).

[55] Müller, *Der Grundsatz* (n. 41) 187.

[56] Eichhorn, *Mit Einschluss des Lehenrechts* (n. 54) §36 and 104–8; Müller, *Der Grundsatz* (n. 41) 188.

[57] Müller, *Der Grundsatz* (n. 41) 188.

[58] As I will show in the next chapter, it is at this point that an individualistic vested rights theory connects with Lea Brilmayer's negative rights theory. See Müller, *Der Grundsatz* (n. 41) 190 (discussing that Eichhorn imagined the main role of the state as protecting the individual and her freedom).

[59] Eichhorn, *Mit Einschluss des Lehenrechts* (n. 54) 108, §37. [60] Ibid., 88, §27.

[61] Ibid., 104, §36.1.

[62] Müller, *Der Grundsatz* (n. 41) 188, 189; Eichhorn, *Mit Einschluss des Lehenrechts* (n. 54) 104, §36.1.

In Eichhorn's theory, as in Tittmann's, the state is merely meant to protect and mostly leave individuals alone to pursue their autonomy.[63] But by abandoning the natural law tradition, himself being part of the historical school, Eichhorn had great difficulty in explaining how states' alleged obligation to respect vested rights and autonomy should be explained theoretically.[64]

3. Georg Friedrich Puchta

In an attempt precisely to provide the philosophical ground for the concept of recognition of vested rights, the German scholar Georg Friedrich Puchta (1798–1846) later equated recognition of vested rights with the recognition of the person.[65] Allegedly, the application of foreign law must be considered exceptional only:

> if it is not based on the principle that a state, by recognizing an individual as a legal subject, must also recognize her vested rights (unless the state does not recognize such rights at all in its legal system); in other words, that a state cannot date the existence of a person from the time when the individual and her rights come in contact with the legal institutions from which he seeks protection.[66]

For Puchta the individual has an inherent freedom and her legal relations are simply the consequences of such inherent freedom. This "will power and freedom" is given to individuals naturally, qua individuals, not by law.[67] Freedom is the fundament of law and all legal relations emanate from it. In other words, legal relations are the expression of freedom and the application of a law must ultimately have its source in individual freedom.[68]

D. The State-Centered Internationalist Perspective

The individualistic connotations of the foregoing vested rights theories indicate why PrIL is commonly criticized for being overly liberal and failing to curb private power in the transnational realm. Yet it is important to recognize that PrIL moves quite easily between the overly liberal mode and the state-centered mode and can be equally criticized for completely failing to focus on what Jitta called "the reasonable social life in the transnational space."[69] The state-centered variation is now simply less acknowledged in social justice debates.

Although the term "vested rights" suggests an individual-centered analysis focused on individuals' entitlements to a particular outcome or the application of a particular law, the following section shows that many rights-based perspectives in

[63] Müller, *Der Grundsatz* (n. 41) 190. [64] Ibid., 191.

[65] Georg Friedrich Puchta, *Pandekten* (10th edn., Johann Ambrosius Barth 1866) 172–5, §113.

[66] Ibid., 173. [67] Ibid.

[68] Georg Friedrich Puchta, *Vorlesungen über das heutige römische Recht* (5th edn., Bernhard Tauchnitz 1862) 55–7, §22.

[69] For an account of Jitta's general theory, see Chapter 2.

PrIL actually leave no space for individuals to contest or voice any of their assumptions with respect to the applicable law.

In order to understand how such apparently recognition-focused concepts such as vested rights, manage to completely obscure and exclude individuals' interests and reasonable expectations, we must acknowledge the "state-centered ethic"[70] under which the main vested rights theories were created. The next section outlines five main elements that characterize such state-centered vested rights theories, such as those developed primarily by Beale, Zitelmann, and Pillet in the late nineteenth and early twentieth century. It shows that these elements make it possible to exclude the reasonable expectations of the individuals from the determination of the applicable law.

1. Rights of states

As discussed above, Horatia Muir Watt observes that many of PrIL's methodological tools and concepts fail to account for individuals' claims for recognition and justice. The "traditional tools" appear not to incorporate human rights perspectives and to fail to appreciate the interests of the individuals claiming recognition of their legal relations. Muir Watt attributed this lack of engagement with the complexity of individuals' existence in the transnational realm to the field's seemingly dogmatic and technical nature. However, the lack of engagement is due in part to the state-centered ideology under which many "vested rights" theories in PrIL developed. According to this ideology, the question is not what rights and duties individuals have to one another or what rights and duties states have toward individuals. Rather, the question is what rights states have in their relationship to one another. In Pillet's words, "the principle of respect of vested rights presents itself as an obligation of states in relationship to each other."[71]

The underlying question becomes, for example, whether the state of citizenship (or domicile) should recognize the authority of the state where the individual acted, to regulate her conduct.[72] In other words, does territorial sovereignty trump personal sovereignty or the other way around?[73]

As to why these categories apply, state-centered internationalist authors would argue that they are PublIL categories, and since PublIL and PrIL both have the function of settling conflicts of sovereignty, PrIL must inevitably import the categories from PublIL.[74] If there is a connection between sovereignty, territory (or

[70] For the proposition that PrIL should move past the state-centered ethics borrowed from PublIL, see H. Patrick Glenn, 'The Ethic of International Law' in Donald Earl Childress (ed.), *The Role of Ethics in International Law* (CUP 2012).

[71] A. Pillet, *Principes de droit international prive* (Pedone 1903) 503 (hereafter Pillet, *Principes*).

[72] Zitelmann, Pillet, and Beale all structure their theories in this way. See Chapter 2.

[73] Zitelmann, *Internationales Privatrecht* (n. 34) 107: "a consensus amongst states that the state, which has territorial sovereignty must give way to the one with personal sovereignty." See also Beale, *A Treatise on the Conflict of Laws* (n. 36) 120: "It will be noticed that personal jurisdiction is based only on law, while territorial jurisdiction is based upon power and upon law. The latter is the stronger, and personal jurisdiction must always yield to it."

[74] Antoine Pillet, *Recherches sur les droits fondamentaux des États dans l'ordre des rapports internationaux et sur la solution des conflits qu'ils font naître* (Pedone 1899) 26 (Pillet argues that these categories should

citizenship), and jurisdiction under PublIL, PrIL will incorporate it as well, along with all assumptions and limitations that it carries.[75]

Either way, from the state-centered internationalist perspective the relevant rights are the rights of states (determined a priori and neutrally) to regulate large sets of transnational legal matters. Rather than asking, as Cavers did, whether a balance of various interests entitles individuals to the application of the law they claim, the question becomes whether a state is entitled to regulate a particular legal matter in accordance with PublIL principles.[76]

As Zitelmann put it, the assumption is that:

> private rights can be created with a well-founded claim to international recognition by that state only which possesses the general governmental control, recognized by the principles of international law, over the subject with respect to which the subjective private law confers authority, and that state alone can revoke such private rights again.[77]

PrIL is thereby in search for the state with the right to "vest" rights in accordance with PublIL principles.

Similarly, for Beale, as Ralf Michaels showed, the vested rights methodology was also cast within an interstate framework through the principle of territoriality:

> For Beale . . . vested rights and territoriality went hand in hand: rights could be acquired only under the law of the sovereign on whose territory the relevant act took place, and other sovereigns had to enforce the rights created by the sovereign.[78]

Furthermore, Pillet clarifies that the right of the state to vest private rights is "the patrimony of all nations."[79] At its strongest, it would appear that an individual state cannot derogate from the "right" to regulate a legal matter because such right was determined by reference to the entire "community of states."[80]

be imported from PublIL, but also that a further principle is needed to help choose between them) (hereafter Pillet, *Droits Fondamentaux*). For a contemporary recasting of the personal/territorial sovereignty as a corollary to the PrIL-PublIL association, see Alex Mills, *The confluence of Public and Private International Law: Justice, Pluralism and Subsidiarity in the International Constitutional Ordering of Private Law* (CUP 2009).

75 See the Helsinki Summer Seminar 2015 discussing how "in PublIL the concepts of sovereignty, territory, and jurisdiction are often seen as inextricably linked," online: <http://blogs.helsinki.fi/helsinkisummerseminar/about/previous-helsinki-summer-seminar-topics/2015-2/>accessed February 13, 2018. See also Zitelmann, *Internationales Privatrecht* (n. 34) 78:

> Once one understands the dependence of Private International Law on Public International Law, the attainable can be easily distinguished from the unattainable. If Public International Law does not provide for clear principles of division of legal authority among states, no uniform principles of Private International Law can be found. If uniformity in Private International Law is missing it is entirely attributable to the state of play of Public International Law.

76 On Cavers's theory and its relationship to the European relational internationalist theories, see Chapter 5.

77 Zitelmann, *Internationales Privatrecht* (n. 34) 68.

78 Michaels, "EU Law as Private International Law" (n. 38) 216.

79 Antoine Pillet, 'Essai d'un système general de solution des conflicts de lois' (1894) 21 Journal de droit international privé et de la jurisprudence comparée 417, 423 (hereafter Pillet, "Essai").

80 Ibid.

2. Empty rights?

For the state-centered conceptualization what matters is not so much an analysis of the substantive interest underlying a particular right or the context in which this interest was given legal recognition. Rather, there is a presumption that states have an interest in the *permanence* of rights or denial of rights (whatever their content and context).[81] This becomes merely a replay of the personality/territoriality and territoriality/extraterritoriality distinctions.[82] Pillet for example tried to devise a theory that would determine a priori the cases in which states had the right to the extraterritorial application of their laws, which they could claim vis-à-vis other states.[83] To make an a priori division possible, he argued we must operate with a highly reified concept of law[84] that serves no particular interests of individual states or of the parties. Rather, the law that legitimately applied would be determined by abstracting from a very broad and general social interest for various private law categories.[85]

Alternatively, Beale opted for territoriality over personality, arguing the "true continuity of law—that which is necessary to prevent the failure or forfeiture of acquired rights—demands territoriality in order that this continuity may be enforced."[86] In other words, for Beale territoriality determined legislative jurisdiction under principles of PublIL by recognizing the interest of the territorial state in the continuance of the rights it created.[87] Such rights are recognized as an expression of the principle, which Pillet embraced as well,[88] that "the state itself is interested in the continued existence of all static rights which it does not choose to terminate [...]."[89] Beale thought for example that "rights of property, also, are of interest to the state."[90] Not recognizing a property right is therefore tantamount to an infringement of a state interest and of its sovereignty (in creating the right). Conversely, recognizing a property right means recognizing the sovereignty of the state, not the value of the interest

[81] See for example Beale, *A Treatise on the Conflict of Laws* (n. 36) 166: the characteristics of rights are "the quality of permanence, the relation of third parties to it, and the interest of the state in its existence."

[82] Ibid., 81–5, citing Pillet:

> We shall declare to be territorial all laws the object of which could not be attained if in each country they did not apply as well to foreigners as to citizens; extraterritorial, all laws the object of which requires that they should follow everywhere the person who comes under the force of their provisions [...] Laws for individual protection should be extraterritorial while laws of which only the entire community can require the protection must be territorial.

[83] See Pillet, "Essai" (n. 79) 724.

[84] Ibid., 422: "One must use law in its most general sense, which eliminates any contingent and accidental factors that would make it impossible to deliver a truly general theory of PrIL, but would instead lead to a relative and limited reality" and 423: "I look at the law anew, the law as sovereign order over its subjects, without any specifications as to its content or object."

[85] Ibid. (Pillet is allegedly interested in the social scope of law, at 715. However, for him the notion of law and implicitly its social scope must be "common to all," at 724. Therefore "the only nature of law that interests us is the law as seen from the point of view that is most abstract, independent of its form, independent of the people to whom it applies, even independent of the modalities that the "caprice" of the legislator gives it," at 724.)

[86] Beale, *A Treatise on the Conflict of Laws* (n. 36) 85.

[87] Ibid., 120–1 (arguing that the objective of international law is to avoid conflict between sovereigns which is why it creates a presumption in favor of territoriality).

[88] Pillet, *Principes* (n. 71) 515.

[89] Beale, *A Treatise on the Conflict of Laws* (n. 36) 166.

[90] Ibid.

underlying a property right. A state has the right to the permanence of the rights it created, regardless of what other states or affected individuals and communities might think of its merits (subject to the public policy exception).

This abstraction away from any substantive consideration allegedly achieves "a perfect agreement, far from raising a conflict."[91] It is only in this sense that "vested rights" become a "pillar of PrIL"[92] for state-centered internationalist authors.

3. Ethics, morality, and law

The abstraction from any substantive considerations is also made possible by a clear delimitation between ethics, morality, and law. To ensure neutrality in the distribution of authority among (equal) states, PrIL must be in the business of recognizing legal rights. A state can only have a duty to enforce a right created by another state if it is easily recognizable in a positivistic sense.

This means first that rights created under non-state norms are excluded.[93] Muir Watt, for example, notes that debates in Europe now focus on "whether a purely 'factual relationship' (such as a common law marriage or a de facto partnership), should be subjected to the same methodology [of recognition under human rights norms of the ECHR]"[94] because it is unclear "whether the object of recognition in such circumstances is the factual situation, the law under which it grew up, or the relationship as thus formed."[95] Under the state-centered internationalist perspective only rights "created" by positive law can be recognized.

It also means, second, that rights are not recognized "on a balance of equities."[96] If a particular right is recognized, it is because the authority of a state to "vest" such a right is recognized. A shift to "open-textured and deliberative normative modes sensitive to the life experiences with which it interacts," such as Muir Watt pleads for,[97] appears incompatible with the state-centered internationalist framework because individuals' transnational life experience cannot be integrated into a framework focused on a neutral and uniform distribution of state authority. PrIL is perceived as a "grand law of respect" where respect is granted to an empty notion of sovereign authority, rather than life experience.[98]

[91] Pillet, *Principes* (n. 71) 515.

[92] Ibid.

[93] Beale, *A Treatise on the Conflict of Laws* (n. 36): "law is at once the source and the expression of sovereignty. Law creates the state and the state creates law by a common and mutual impulse; the two are born at an instant, are inseparable through life, and must die together," at 115. On Zitelmann's account of the state being the source of any objective law and rights, see Beale, *A Treatise on the Conflict of Laws* (n. 36) 93.

[94] Muir Watt, "Future Directions?" (n. 6) 372, n. 137: "it is difficult to see why not, to the extent that it is effective. If effective, it must be recognized under art. 8 of the ECHR."

[95] Ibid., 372, n. 138 citing S. Bollée, 'L'extension du domaine de la method de la reconnaisance unilatérale' 2007, 96 Rev crit dr int privé 307.

[96] Beale, *A Treatise on the Conflict of Laws* (n. 36) 136: "the learned lawyer solving a legal problem presented to him does not say, such and such a solution seems reasonable or reaches a practical result, he says it is the law" and 154: "If law be regarded as a command, then every act done must either be permitted or forbidden. If law be regarded as a right-producing principle, then every act must in accordance with the law change or not change existing rights."

[97] Muir Watt, "Future Directions?" (n. 6) 375.

[98] Pillet, *Principes* (n. 71) 515.

For the same reason, no flexibility or proportionality is allowed in the PrIL realm under the state-centered internationalist framework. Because recognizing and enforcing legal rights represents the recognition of state authority and sovereignty, any "tweaking" or balancing of rights implicitly means a misrecognition or an infringement of the state sovereignty granted authority to "vest" it. The adage "PrIL recognizes already vested rights, it does not create new ones" had become a credo of PrIL precisely to ensure that no derogation from the authority of a state to "vest" a right would be permissible.[99]

4. National versus transnational context; recognition versus misrecognition

Consequently, any analysis of the relevance of the transnational context under which rights are constructed, exercised, misused and so on is precluded. Rights are necessarily "national" because nation states recognize one another and therefore also what each of them, in isolation, has created. As Beale put it, "law (and legal rights) is at once the source and the expression of sovereignty. Law creates the state and the state creates law by a common and mutual impulse; the two are born at an instant, are inseparable through life, and must die together."[100] Under the state-centered internationalist framework, rights are created in the territorial state and then recognized as such, their content unaltered, in another state.[101] Nothing is either lost or added as a result of the transnational context in which the rights are exercised.

The way in which the national element features in the transnational context, in fact, sets the stage for the recognition or misrecognition of individual rights and expectations. State-centered internationalists seemed to envision mainly what Jitta called "relatively international cases," meaning cases in which most elements of the legal relation are connected to one jurisdiction, a case that Jitta believed was extremely rare.[102]

The reversed and much more complicated scenario in which a relationship is simultaneously connected to multiple jurisdictions is hard to classify as a case of recognition of a vested right, or rather it becomes a case of misrecognition by default. Pillet explains that when a case is connected to more jurisdictions from its inception (e.g., citizenship of the adoptive parent different from the place of adoption), the question raised is that of the applicable law, rather than the recognition of rights.

[99] Dicey, *A Digest of the Law of England* (n. 30) 9: "the object of a legal decision or judgment is to enforce existing rights, or give compensation for the breach thereof, and it is not the object of a legal decision or judgment to create new rights, except in so far as such creation may be necessary for the enforcement or protection of rights already in existence."

[100] Beale, *A Treatise on the Conflict of Laws* (n. 36) 115.

[101] See David Kennedy, 'Law and the Political Economy of the World' (2013) 26 Leiden J Int'l L 7, 13 (for a very useful account of the tension between the "free movement" of rights compared to the territorial limitation of politics).

[102] Daniel Josephus Jitta, *La Méthode du droit international privé* (Belinfante 1890) 200–16 distinguishing between national (connected exclusively to the forum), relatively international (connected exclusively to another jurisdiction), and absolutely international relationships (connected to multiple jurisdictions) (hereafter Jitta, *La Méthode*).

Since the applicable law, in Pillet's theory, is determined based on a broad framework of division of sovereignty, it is unpredictable—and in a sense secondary—whether this leads to the recognition or misrecognition of a particular right or relationship. As Michaels explained:

> The important difference from Dicey (and Beale) is that Pillet created a full system of designating the applicable law *in addition* to his theory of vested rights. In fact, Pillet considered a right duly acquired only under the law applicable according to general private international law.[103]

Pillet therefore explains that when a relationship is connected to multiple jurisdictions, the legal relation was:

> [F]rom inception international. Here there is a conflict. For the right created in such relationship to be recognized, the conflict must have been determined according to the rules of Private International Law, in other words that the competent law was applied. We easily perceive the great difficulty, which this causes. The rules of Private International Law might differ between the two states. The law determined competent by one state is not the same as the one determined competent by the forum, which will determine that the legal relation should have been judged by another law. To which body of law should the forum court look in determining this question? Here we have an issue of an international character, which is implicitly part of the international patrimony. Each state has, as to the solution of conflict of laws, equal rights and we cannot impose on one judge the solution of another. The issue must be resolved by the law of the forum. It follows that a right considered acquired in one legal system will be denied in another. As bad as these consequences might seem, they result evidently from the independence of states in determining their obligations towards other states.[104]

The result can be summarized as follows: Once a state is thought to have authority under principles of PublIL, then its authority and the rights that it created would have been recognized by other states because Pillet assumes that no actual "conflict of laws" arises in such a case. But when a legal matter is connected to more jurisdictions, then a conflict of laws exists. And here, Pillet acknowledged that even though conflict of laws are determined according to PublIL, different states might define their conflict rules differently depending on how they understand/incorporate PublIL.[105] In such a case, the misrecognition of a legal relation is inevitable. Since Pillet was always clear that no individual interests/rights/legitimate expectations can enter the analysis of conflict of laws understood as conflict of sovereignties, there is no alternative framework of contestation to enable the recognition of legal relations.

5. Civilized/non-civilized states

Under the state-centered internationalist framework the recognition of vested rights (unaltered) is considered a sign of respect for state sovereignty and ultimately as a mark of civilization.[106] Beale posited that "no civilized law, national or international,

[103] Michaels, "EU Law as Private International Law" (n. 38) 217.
[104] Pillet, *Principes* (n. 71) 536. [105] Ibid., 81–3.
[106] Beale, *A Treatise on the Conflict of Laws* (n. 36) 112.

could be oblivious to the just requirements of recognizing the legally accomplished fact. All civilized countries have the common ideal of justice [understood as the recognition of vested rights]."[107] He noted that "if the national law is a civilized law this [recognizing vested rights] will of course be done; and if it is not, the principles of a supposed PrIL would not constrain its actions. The binding force of the dictates of justice is not created, and cannot be created, by extra-territorial constraint."[108] However, "the desire of a sovereign to find himself included in the number of civilized nations is so great as to constrain his acceptance of the principles of international law, and among them, the rules governing international jurisdiction."[109]

The analogy between PrIL and PublIL under which the state-centered internationalist theory of rights is created thus constrains states to recognize vested rights as the mark of civilization. But "civilized" states are by no means constrained in failing to recognize the rights of individuals belonging to "less civilized states." A condition of the framework of recognition of rights as an interstate affair is that states perceive each other as equals.[110] Pillet argued that "a state's degree of civilization is the measure of its rights" as much in the PrIL context, as in the PublIL one.[111]

It is by virtue of this state-centered framework of analysis that the recognition of rights and legal relations translates into an uneasy conflict of sovereignty, rather than a contextual analysis of the life experience and expectations of individuals in their transnational relations.

E. The Relational Internationalist Theories

The gist of the individualistic theories is usually attributed to or at least associated with Savigny. The previous chapter showed that until the end of the nineteenth century many state-centered internationalist theories were developed based on what was perceived to be Savigny's key theoretical element, namely the international community of states. Yet after the first few decades of the twentieth century, his theory was described and criticized as liberal, Kantian, and overly individualistic.[112] While

[107] Ibid. [108] Ibid., 110. [109] Ibid., 117.

[110] Zitelmann, *Internationales Privatrecht* (n. 34) 6. Zitelmann would later comment on the "imperfections of public international law" in Ernst Zitelmann, *Die Unvollkommenheit des Völkerrechts* (Duncker & Humblot 1919). See also Martti Koskenniemi, *The Gentle Civilizer of Nations: The Rise and Fall of International Law 1870–1960* (CUP 2004) 230.

[111] Antoine Pillet, 'Le droit international public, ses éléments constitutifs, son domaine, son objet' (1894) 1 RGDIP 1, 24, 27; Pillet, *Droit fundamentaux* (n. 74) 6: "il n'existe égalitè de droit entre les États civilizes et les États non civilises ou moin civilisés" (there is no legal equality between civilized and non-civilized or less civilized states).

[112] See, e.g., Christian Joerges, *Zum Funktionswandel des Kollisionsrechts: Die Governmental Interest Analysis und die Krise des Internationalen Privatrechts* (Mohr Siebeck 1971) 4–16; Müller, *Der Grundsatz* (n. 41) (Although Müller does not attribute the vested rights doctrine to Savigny, at 175, he argues that the vested rights doctrine represents simply a "reconstruction" of the individualistic, liberal ideology found in Savigny's theory, at 177); Jessurun D'Oliveira, 'La pollution du Rhin et le droit international privé' in R. Hueting, *Rhine pollution: legal, economic and technical aspects* (Tjeenk Willink 1978) 91; Sagi Peari, 'Savigny's theory of choice-of-law as a principle of "voluntary submission"' (2014) 64 UTLJ 106 (for a Kantian reading of Savigny's PrIL theory).

the previous chapters showed that Savigny did not construct a state-centered internationalist theory from his concept of the international community of states, this chapter outlines the ways in which Savigny avoided an overly individualistic perspective at the same time.

This section focuses on how Savigny countered the overly individualistic notion of vested rights and distinguished his theory of "voluntary submission" from the concept of autonomy used by the individualistic authors discussed above. It then shows how the German socialist Ferdinand Lassalle (1825–1864) in fact used Savigny's main relational insights precisely to counter the individualistic underpinning of the vested rights theory and to plead for social justice as a guiding principle of PrIL. Lastly, it describes the way in which Jitta further developed and clarified Savigny's theory in order to counter any extreme individualistic connotations of the vested rights theories, while at the same time keeping his individual-centered premises.

Because Savigny's individual-centered theory can be better understood by comparison to that of his predecessor, Joseph Story,[113] this section introduces three elements of Story's theory that are particularly relevant. First, the way in which Story refers interchangeably to rights and reasonable expectations mirrors the way in which Savigny shifts from the concept of absolute rights to claims and expectations. Second, the way in which Story moves back and forth between individual rights and broader social interests and his argument that the recognition of a right is itself a policy choice can both be found in Savigny's discussion of ethical consideration with respect to vested rights. Third, the way in which Story connects rights/reasonable expectations with life experience, in addition to law, mirrors Behrends' description of Savigny's theory as "sociological-empirical."[114]

1. Joseph Story

As argued in the first chapter, while Story relied on the concept of sovereignty, he did not imagine PrIL as a body of rules neutrally distributing legislative sovereignty. Story described PrIL relations as instances of "mixed rights." For him PrIL rules were meant to prevent the "confusion of rights" and of "the personal and conjugal relations," and overall to prevent the "pernicious consequences" for individuals that could result from the diversity of laws.[115] His theory is based on the observation, framed most explicitly in his discussion of marriages, that "infinite mischief and confusion must necessarily arise to the subjects of all nations with respect to legitimacy, succession, and other rights, if the respective laws of different countries were

[113] Gerhard Kegel, 'Story and Savigny' (1989) 37 Am J Comp Law 39 (for a general account of the relationship between the theories of the two scholars).

[114] Okko Behrends, 'Geschichte, Politik und Jurisprudenz in Savignys System des heutigen roemischen Rechts' in Okko Behrends, Wulf Eckart Voss, and Malte Diesselhorst (eds.), *Römisches Recht in der Europäischen Tradition: Symposion aus Anlass des 75. Geburtstages von Franz Wieacker* (R. Gremer 1985) (hereafter Behrends, "Geschichte").

[115] Joseph Story, *Commentaries on the Conflict of Laws: Foreign and Domestic, in Regard to Contracts, Rights, and Remedies, and Especially in Regard to Marriages, Divorces, Wills, Successions, and Judgments* (1st edn. Hilliard, Gray & Co. 1834) 113 (hereafter Story, *Commentaries on the Conflict of Laws*).

not to be observed, as to marriages contracted by the subjects of those countries abroad."[116]

Thus, applying foreign law is acknowledged as necessary to achieve a coherent existence for individuals across borders, as Jitta would later describe it. Comity is consequently used as a catchphrase and a useful symbol to illustrate, for example, as to the validity of marriages, "that all nations have consented, or are presumed to consent, for the common benefit and advantages that such marriages shall be good or not, according to the laws of the country where they are celebrated."[117] This is necessary, not in order to prevent an infringement of state sovereignty, but rather because "by observing this rule, few, if any, inconveniences can arise. By disregarding it, infinite mischief must ensue."[118] In other words, it is necessary for purely pragmatic considerations, which are deduced from empirical observation of individuals' existence in the transnational space.

These pragmatic considerations are often described by Story in terms of infringement and confusion of rights. Story talks about the "sanctity of contracts" and property. But the conceptualization of rights in Story's theory is different both from that of the individualistic and of the state-centered internationalist authors.

Unlike the individualistic authors, Story is clear that individuals do not have a right to the application of a particular law as an extension of individual autonomy. In the area of contract law, he argues:

> The ground of this doctrine, as commonly stated, is, that every person, contracting in a place, is understood to submit himself to the law of the place, and silently to assent to its action upon his contract. [. . .] It would be more correct to say, that the law of the place of the contract acts upon it, independently of any volition of the parties, in virtue of the general sovereignty possessed by every nation to regulate all persons, property, and transactions within its own territory.[119]

In other words, the law of the place where the contract was made may legitimately apply to such contracts, independent of the will or choice of the parties. And if this law is applied by other states, it is neither because they recognize a right generated by the individual will/choice/autonomy of the individuals, nor due to an interstate respect for sovereignty, but rather because:

> Nothing can be more just than this principle. For when a merchant of France, Holland, or England, enters into a contract in his own country, he must be presumed to be conusant of the laws of the place, where he is, and to expect, that his contract is to be judged and carried into effect according to those laws; and the merchant with whom he deals, if a foreigner, must be supposed to submit himself to the same laws, unless he has taken care to stipulate for a performance in some other country, or has in some other way excepted his particular contract from the laws of the country, where he is.[120]

This is described as a reasonable expectation, not an absolute right. Should the parties not have reasonably known or inferred that this law would apply the analysis

[116] Ibid., 112. [117] Ibid. [118] Ibid. [119] Ibid., 217–18.
[120] Ibid., 232.

might change. But the analysis might also easily change if some other interest is at stake. Story for example referred to a case, decided by the Supreme Court of Louisiana, in which "a transfer of a part of a ship was made in Virginia, the ship, at the time of the sale, being locally at New Orleans; and, before any delivery, she was attached by the creditors of the vendor."[121] Story tellingly describes this as "a conflict between the creditor and the purchaser."[122] The Supreme Court of Louisiana, while acknowledging the consensus among "civilized countries" that the law of the domicile of the property owner should apply to this kind of contract, reasoned that the application of such law can cause "serious inconvenience to the citizens of this country." The reasoning is worth quoting at large:

> This distinction appears to us founded on the soundest reasons. The municipal laws of a country have no force beyond its territorial limits; and when another government permits these to be carried into effect within her jurisdiction, she does so upon a principle of comity. In doing so, care must be taken, that no injury is inflicted on her own citizens; otherwise justice would be sacrificed to courtesy. Nor can the foreigner or stranger complain of this. If he sends his property within a jurisdiction, different from that, where he resides, he impliedly submits it to the rules and regulations in force in the country, where he places it. [...] We proceed to examine, whether, giving effect to the law of Virginia, on the contract now set up, would be working an injury to this state, or its citizens. In doing this, we must look to the general doctrine, and the effect it would have on our ordinary transactions, as well as its operation in this particular case. This valuable provision [delivery necessary for property transfer], by which all our citizens are bound in their dealings, protects them from the frauds, to which they would be daily subjects, were they liable to be affected by the previous contracts, not followed by the giving of possession. The exemption contended for here, would deprive them of that protection, wherever their rights, as purchasers, came in contact with strangers; a protection, which, it may be remarked, it is of the utmost importance, owing to our peculiar position, that we should carefully maintain. This city is becoming a vast storehouse for merchandise sent from abroad, owned by non-residents, and deposited here for sale; and our most important commercial transactions are in relation to property so situated. If the purchasers of it should be affected by all the previous contracts made at the owners' domicile, although unaccompanied by delivery, it is easy to see, to what impositions such a doctrine would lead; to what inconvenience it would expose us; and how severely it would check and embarrass our dealings.[123]

Story believed that:

> no one can seriously doubt, that it is competent for any state to adopt such a rule in its own legislation, since it has perfect jurisdiction over all property, personal as well as real. Nor can such a rule, made for the benefit of innocent purchasers and creditors, be deemed justly open to the reproach of being founded in a narrow or selfish policy.[124]

On the other hand, it is not easy to say:

> to what extent [a court] may be pressed in subversion to the general rule [that the law of domicile of the owner applies] since every country has so many minute regulations in regard to the transfers of personal property incorporated into its municipal code, each of

[121] Ibid., 319. [122] Ibid. [123] Ibid., 320–2. [124] Ibid., 324.

which may be properly deemed beneficial to its own government, or to the interests of its citizens.[125]

This particular case affords the best understanding of the way in which Story identifies the reasonable expectations of individuals as an important interest—albeit not the only relevant interest—to be considered in the PrIL analysis. The individual's expectation, here those of the owner and the purchaser, may conflict with a state policy in the creditor's home jurisdiction. There is no doubt in Story's theory that such policy should be identified and factored into the analysis. At the same time, the expectation of the individuals cannot be taken lightly and one should acknowledge that a contrary policy could always be found in some law of the forum that will invalidate any possible individual entitlement. Story, as Savigny, therefore invited moderation in the balancing between reasonable expectations and broader social interests. In this line of reasoning, Story appears to be anticipating both the rise of the state interest theory and its subsequent critique by scholars like Cavers.

Hence, for Story any question of enforcing a reasonable expectation in light of contravening policies is itself a policy choice. For example, Story argued that it is very possible that:

The principle that moveables follow the person [. . .] had not its origin in any distinction as to real or personal laws, or in any fictitious annexation of them to the person of the owner, or their incapacity to have a fixed situs: but in an enlarged policy growing out of their transitory nature and the general convenience of nations. If the law rei sitae were generally to prevail in regard to movables, it would be utterly impossible for the owner, in many cases, to know, in what manner to dispose of them during his life, or to distribute them at his death; not only from the uncertainty of their situation in the transit to and from different places, but from the impracticability of knowing with minute accuracy the law of transfers inter vivos, or of testamentary dispositions and successions in the different countries, in which they might happen to be.[126]

Similarly:

The English doctrine in relation to Scotch marriages by parties domiciled in England, and going to Scotland to marry, though a plain violation of the English marriage act, has been upheld unquestionably upon a like policy. It is the least of two evils, in a political, a civil, and a moral sense. We have already seen that the positive code of France has promulgated an opposite doctrine, with unrelenting severity.[127]

Story also stated:

[I]t is admitted, that the doctrine is repugnant to the general principles of law relating to contracts; for a fraudulent evasion of the laws of the country, where the parties have their domicile, would not be protected. But the exception in favor of marriages is maintained upon principles of public policy, with a view to prevent the disastrous consequences to the issue of such a marriage, which would result from the loose state, in which persons so situated would live.[128]

[125] Ibid., 324. [126] Ibid., 311. [127] Ibid., 117. [128] Ibid., 116.

Story's vested rights have little in common, then, with the individualistic perspective outlined above. But Story's vested rights theory is also far from the state-centered internationalist theory. As Blaine Baker noted, unlike state-centered internationalists, "Story was not constrained by analytically-rigorous, regional descriptions of positive legal rights."[129] Instead, he:

> used vested rights in a non-positivistic, unofficial, almost commonsensical way to describe popular appreciations of natural entitlement and promissory expectations. His vested rights had more to do with the realistic presumptions of parties to a transaction, and with the policies perceived to underlie fields of private law about which he wrote, than with analytically-rigorous rights created by sovereigns, foreign or domestic.[130]

Because Story did not describe PrIL as a conflict of rights, nor sovereignties, he could afford to be quite eclectic about the "sources" from which he derived the rights qua reasonable expectations. Unlike the state-centered internationalist authors, those rights/reasonable expectations did not need to have a positive source in the laws of one particular country and certainly not in the country a priori assigned legislative jurisdiction. The current European debate about whether factual relationships could be recognized as much as legal relations might find fruitful arguments in Story's theory. According to Blaine Baker, because Story thought of rights in the transnational context as substantiated by commonsensical expectations and the values he perceived to underlie categories of private law, "Story was much less interested than Dicey or Beale in the decrees of a national sovereign technically necessary to vest positive rights."[131]

Story's notion of rights, then, is much more fluid, more pragmatic, and empirically grounded in the experience of individuals in their transnational existence. For example, Story:

> justified his rule that contracts for interests in land were governed by the law of the place where the land was situated on the basis that parties to American real estate transactions had long relied upon the interplay of local requirements of writing and county-by-county systems of title registration, and that they distinguished investments in land from moveable or intangible property dealings on the basis of land's stationary character.[132]

Similarly, the application of the law of the place where a bill of landing was drawn was promoted based on the "confidence, which the commercial world have hitherto reposed in the universal validity of the title acquired under a bill of landing."[133] The application of the law of the place where the property is situated was also based on the observation that "in the ordinary course of trade with foreign countries, no one thinks of transferring personal property according to the forms of his own domicile;

[129] Blaine Baker, 'Interstate Choice of Law and Early-American Constitutional Nationalism. An Essay On *Joseph Story and the Comity of Errors: A Case Study in Conflict of Laws*' (1993) 35 McGill LJ 454, 504 (hereafter Baker, "An Essay").

[130] Ibid., 503. [131] Ibid., 504.

[132] Ibid., 504; Story, *Commentaries on the Conflict of Laws* (n. 115) 358.

[133] Story, *Commentaries on the Conflict of Laws* (n. 115) 327.

but it is transferrable according to the forms prescribed by the law of the place where the sale takes place."[134]

2. Friedrich Karl von Savigny

Contrary to the usual reading of Joseph Story's theory as state-centered or even an early expression of the state interest analysis methodology,[135] this chapter adopted Blaine Baker's alternative reading of Story's theory as individual-centered and rights-based. At the same time it outlined Story's emphasis on individuals' reasonable expectations, as a way of departing from overly individualistic theories focusing on absolute rights and liberty.

Unlike the general reading of Story, Savigny's theory is currently perceived as an overly liberal and individualistic account of PrIL. In contrast, in what follows I underscore the way in which Savigny criticized both the overly individualistic account of vested rights and individual autonomy and show that Savigny's account of PrIL mirrors in many respects that of Story.

In contrast to the individualistic authors, Savigny explicitly rejected the vested rights theory as a way of finding solutions to choice of law problems and adopted Wächter's critique that the vested rights theory is premised on an illogical assumption and a vicious circle: to know whether a right has vested, you must determine under which law it vested.[136] This critique should not be perceived as a mere technicality. Rejecting the vested rights theory based on this reasoning implicitly brings to light a certain view about the relationship between rights and state authority and about individual autonomy and social life. Only by understanding Savigny's views on these matters is it possible to understand how Savigny managed to avoid an overly individualistic premise in his PrIL theory.

a) Rejection of the vested rights doctrine

Savigny's thoughts about "equitable considerations" with respect to rights are espoused in the often-ignored last five pages of his eighth volume. These reflections have most likely been ignored because they appear in the sections of the book dealing with "conflicts of laws in time," as opposed to "conflicts of laws in space." In Savigny's view, vested rights are only relevant to questions of retroactivity (conflicts between earlier and later laws of the same state) and not helpful for conflicts of different national laws. Accordingly, his discussion of vested rights is integrated into the topic of conflict of laws in time. Yet these pages are useful in understanding why

134 Ibid., 18; Baker, "An Essay" (n. 129) 505.

135 Donald Earl Childress III, 'Comity as Conflict: Resituating International Comity as Conflict of Laws' (2010) 44 UC Davis L Rev 11.

136 Friedrich Karl von Savigny, *Private International Law. A Treatise on the Conflict of Laws: And the Limits of Their Operation in Respect of Place and Time, vol. 8* (William Guthrie tr., 2nd edn., T. & T. Clark 1880) 147 (hereafter Savigny, *Private International Law*).

Savigny did not adopt the vested rights theory into PrIL and how he managed to avoid the overly individualistic theory of his predecessors.

Savigny begins his analysis of "equitable considerations" with regard to vested rights (in the purely national context) by noting the prevailing assumption that "every violation of an acquired right, without the assent of the person interested, is simply impossible from the standpoint of moral rights, and this impossibility is regarded as a supreme and absolute principle."[137] Savigny argued that this "assumption cannot be admitted" for two reasons:

> In the first place [this assumption cannot be admitted] because it is incompatible with the general nature and origin of law. Law has its root in the common consciousness of the nation. This is, on the one hand, entirely different from the easily and quickly changing, the accidental and momentary consciousness of the individual man; but, on the other hand, it is subject to the law of progressive development, and cannot therefore be conceived as fixed and immovable.[138]

The "contemplation of the nation in whose sense of rights the law itself has its roots"[139] is contrasted with the idea that law has its roots in individual will, which Eichhorn often described as a legal source.[140] Savigny relied on the integration of individual autonomy within the "Volk" (People) in order to explain how laws abolishing slavery cannot be thought of as infringing upon a vested right, but simply as laws reflecting the way in which "this status [slavery] is regarded as totally impossible, and utterly contrary to all sense of right."[141]

The idea that law has its origin in the people is used precisely to explain that laws restricting individual will are not per se illegitimate. Therefore, Savigny rejects the common view of "those who assert the absolute inviolability of acquired rights by new laws, merely protest[ing] against the compulsion involved in such violations, and allow the fairness and justice of the change as soon as the assent of the party interested is given to the abolition or modification of his acquired right."[142] If the individual is part of the people and the will and values of the people are the source of law, it cannot be that the legitimacy of a law restricting vested rights depends on the consent of the individual.

To support the legitimacy of laws restricting vested rights, Savigny adds "a second argument" relating to "the individual man as the possessor of acquired rights."[143]

[137] Ibid., 428. [138] Ibid., 428. [139] Ibid., 430.

[140] See Section C, part 2 in this chapter, for the discussion of Eichhorn.

[141] Savigny, *Private International Law* (n. 136) 429, n c. The note he adds to this passage is also telling:

> Many writers have sought to obscure or to weaken this contrast by comparing the status connected with those severe punishments of modern times which consist of deprivation of freedom, with the mild and often friendly condition of the slaves of antiquity. But the true relations of things are thus unaltered. In order to keep the contrast before our eyes in all its clearness, two things must be remembered: First, the origin of slavery by birth; secondly, the legal position of the slave in the same line with domestic animals, as a kind of merchandise (Ulpian, XIX.1.). Modern slavery in the East, as well as the totally different slavery of America, are not here taken into account.

[142] Ibid., 430. [143] Ibid.

Savigny believes one must "examine the character of those who are the possessors of acquired rights. Such a right appears as an extension of the power of an individual man, and is always of a more or less accidental nature."[144] Furthermore, "the individual man has a limited and transient existence."[145]

In other words the individual cannot be the only focus in an analysis of rights. Rather, he is portrayed as part of the people, his existence is "limited and transient," and his power is "arbitrary" while the law must regulate for the continual existence of "the people." This is why Savigny, like Story, ends up describing individual entitlements as "claims and expectations"[146] which must be carefully balanced against the principles and values of the people. Therefore, Savigny concludes in an almost forgotten passage that "the whole question [of balancing individual rights against broader social interests] should rather be withdrawn from the province of absolute right, and transferred to that of legislative policy, which is its true place, and where many ruinous errors may be avoided by caution, prudence, and moderation."[147]

b) Voluntary submission

Unlike in Tittmann's account, rights in Savigny's account are not pre-legal entitlements of individuals, but rather entirely dependent on and linked to a people and a state. Ralf Michaels rightly points out that Savigny has been misunderstood as a proponent of non-state law and *lex mercatoria*.[148] On the contrary, Savigny is explicit that state law predates individual rights, and as has been seen in the passages quoted above, that individual rights are granted by and integrated within the law emanating from the "people" crystallized in a state.[149]

Yet Savigny constructs a principle of voluntary submission as a guide to the determination of the applicable law. Other scholars, in particular Puchta and Eichhorn, also referred to the concept of voluntary submission and they seemed to base this principle on unrestrained individual autonomy, describing it as a reflection of the respect for personhood and the ability of individuals to give themselves a law.[150] It is this description of the principle of voluntary submission that makes it possible for these authors to then describe the application of a law as a vested right, which must be respected and recognized by the state. Applying forum law is therefore portrayed as an infringement of autonomy, of personhood, and of vested rights.

144 Ibid. 145 Ibid. 146 Ibid., 431. 147 Ibid.

148 Ralf Michaels, 'Globalizing Savigny? The State in Savigny's Private International Law and the Challenge of Europeanization and Globalization' in Adrienne Windhoff-Héritier, Michael Stolleis, and Fritz Wilhelm Scharpf (eds.), *European and International Regulation After the Nation State: Different Scopes and Multiple Levels* (Nomos 2004).

149 See Friedrich Karl von Savigny, *System des heutigen Römischen Rechts*, vol. 1 (Bei Deit & Comp 1840) (hereafter Savigny, *System 1*). See also Chapter 2.

150 See Section C in this chapter for discussion of individualistic theories.

But Savigny reacts precisely against Eichhorn and Puchta and their understanding of autonomy, alleging that their theories might exacerbate both the content and the consequences of autonomy in PrIL:

> Although great unanimity prevails as to the influence which voluntary submission to a particular local law actually exercises, I must yet object to a mode of expression, which has lately come into use. Modern writers are accustomed to designate this very general effect of the free will as autonomy [citing Eichhorn and Mittermaier among others]—a technical expression which has been applied, from an early time, as indicating a very peculiar relation in the development of the German law; namely, the competence of the nobility and of many corporations independently to regulate their own relations by a kind of internal legislation [citing Eichhorn and Puchta]. In this sense the expression is indispensable; and its usefulness in the proper meaning is impaired by its superfluous application to the entirely dissimilar relations of the subject with which we are here engaged, which gains nothing by it in clearness and distinctness. If this phrase be justified by asserting that the parties subject themselves to a law (already subsisting) and in that sense assign a law to themselves, the same is true in a still higher degree of the free choice of domicile; and yet no one thinks of describing that as the result of autonomy. Accordingly it seems advisable, in regard to voluntary subjection to any local law, the choice of domicile, and the countless other voluntary actions from which legal consequences flow, to avoid the word autonomy.[151]

Although Savigny remarks that the notion of voluntary submission was at the time of his writing almost universally employed,[152] he cautions against the all too free association of voluntary submission with a notion of autonomy that suggests individuals are placed above the law. He was very critical of authors who managed to confuse "acts which originate legal relations" with "law sources"[153] and argued that only the "loose use of the concept of autonomy has made it possible to place entering into a contract and the law validating such a contract on the same level as legal sources."[154]

In making this distinction between his concept of voluntary submission and the notion of autonomy, Savigny seems primarily concerned with explaining that his term references individuals' submission to an existing national law, rather than the ability of creating one's own law. Apart from this clarification, much of his writing focuses on explaining the various facets of individuals' liberty underlying the notion of voluntary submission. To understand the complexity of the notion of voluntary submission it is important to capture Savigny's distinction between dispositive laws—which give a wide scope to individual autonomy—and imperative laws (discussed under heading (i) below) and then to understand the apparently eclectic, yet sequenced analysis of the nature of legal relations (discussed at (ii)).

i) Dispositive and imperative laws

Savigny places at the forefront of his treatise on conflict of laws the postulate of "an international common law of nations having intercourse with one another" and argues that "this view has in the course of time always obtained wider recognition, under the influence of a common Christian morality, and of the real advantages which results

[151] Savigny, *Private International Law* (n. 136) 136. [152] Ibid., 134.
[153] Ibid., 136. [154] Savigny, *System 1* (n. 149) 12.

from it to all concerned."[155] Savigny conceives of the "international community of law" as "the foundation and highest aim of our whole doctrine."[156] Laws that fall under this broader umbrella of "international common law" can be applied freely among states, without regard to territorial delimitations. However, notes Savigny:

> [T]his principle must be limited with respect to many kinds of laws, whose peculiar nature does not admit of so free an application of the community of law obtaining between different states. Where there are such statutes, the judge will have to apply the domestic law more exclusively than that principle allows, and must, on the one hand, leave the foreign law unapplied, even where that principle would justify its application.[157]

Savigny assumes that one could break law generally and private law in particular, into two classes. One class comprises "dispositive, permissive or suppletory laws" which:

> [A]llow free scope to individual will, and only step into its place where it has omitted to exercise its power, in order to give the necessary certainty and precision to the legal relation.[158]

Such laws can be applied freely among states, regardless of territorial limits. Because Savigny assumes that such laws cater primarily to the interests of the individuals within the private law relationships, he deduces the applicable law from various circumstances, which reflect primarily parties' reasonable expectations as to where their relationships are centered and therefore as to which law the parties submitted themselves.

A second class of laws is that of "absolute, or imperative laws." Those are:

> [I]ntended to rule with inflexible necessity, without allowing any play to individual will. This necessity may have its origin in the peculiar nature of the particular positive law; or in political or economical considerations; or may flow directly from moral considerations.[159]

These laws are out of the purview of the "international community of laws" and therefore the forum must apply its own imperative laws.[160] Savigny understood that this latter category of laws can be quite broad. Therefore, when comparing his PrIL theory to that of scholars who pled for the application of the law of the forum in all circumstances he notes "it will become apparent that the practical difference between this theory and the view which I maintain is, in fact, not so great as it at first appears."[161]

Savigny argues that "whether any law is to be reckoned among the exceptional cases depends principally on the purpose of the legislator."[162] Virtually all of the laws which were heavily discussed by American realist scholars under the term of "state interests" are also discussed by Savigny, including restrictions on suretyship for women,[163] restrictions on donations among spouses,[164] age-related restrictions on capacity,[165] and even rules of succession which aim to protect a certain class of individuals, such as the peasantry.[166]

[155] Savigny, *Private International Law* (n. 136) 70. [156] Ibid., 138.
[157] Ibid., 76. [158] Ibid., 77 n. 1. [159] Ibid.
[160] Savigny also believed that the logical consequence of this postulate is that the forum cannot apply the imperative laws of another state. Understanding Savigny's rationale for these postulates shows why it would be wrong to trace a "public law taboo" to Savigny. Savigny did not think there was a taboo in applying public law, but rather that states were simply unwilling to apply each others' imperative laws and therefore cannot create a community with respect to such laws.
[161] Savigny, *Private International Law* (n. 136) 146. [162] Ibid., 78, 145.
[163] Ibid., 158. [164] Ibid., 297. [165] Ibid., 152. [166] Ibid., 279.

Much like the American realist scholars, Savigny also relies on a method of statutory interpretation to determine the scope of such laws and the interest of the state in their application.[167] And like American realist scholars, Savigny did recognize the need to reference, in some instances, wider, public regulatory goals in PrIL. Furthermore, Savigny did not argue that the public policy exception would only cover a highly exceptional category of laws that are fundamental to the values of a particular state. His exceptional category of mandatory rules is much larger than that which is currently described as the public policy exception. In this respect, Savigny is much closer to American realist scholars than other classical continental PrIL scholars. What distinguishes Savigny from the American realist school is rather Savigny's general methodology, taken from classical Roman law writing, of distinguishing between rules and exceptions. Savigny describes this methodology of classical Roman law in this way:

> [Rules of Roman law] certainly seem at first glance to place, as is commonly done by the moderns, rule and exception alongside of one another; whereas in fact it only lays down tentatively and apparently general propositions, and then, by adding limitations, leads the reader to find by abstraction the true rule, which it does not directly enunciate;—all quite in accordance with the method of the old jurists.[168]

The rule/exception dichotomy penetrates Savigny's entire thinking, including in PrIL. He postulates general PrIL rules for a large category of private law relations, while arguing that individual circumstances might necessitate exceptions;[169] he separates, analytically, binding and indiscriminating rules from principles of equity[170] and distinguishes between legal institutes and legal relations.[171] Within this analytical framework private law rules, which consider primarily the interest of the parties, are distinguished from mandatory rules, which focus on the interests of a larger community including its economic and social well being, as well as its moral framework.[172] Unlike American realist scholars, Savigny does not collapse the entirety of

[167] Ibid., 78, 296, 297, 324, 152, 279. [168] Ibid., 199 n (a).

[169] Ibid., 224. See also 199 (describing the circumstances which make it necessary to apply, as an exception, the law of the place where the contract was made, rather than the law of the place of fulfillment); 281 ("The Roman law has certainly appointed a special forum for the *fideicommissa* where the greater part of the inheritance is situated; but of course this arbitrary and exceptional direction, in regard to a solitary legal institution, cannot create a rule for the local law of succession in general") 351 (for guardianship he argues that "the necessity of the individual case may justify a complete deviation from the principle, especially if, according to the family relations, no influence on the future condition of the ward is to be ascribed to the last domicile of the father").

[170] Ibid., 211–12: "if the obligation is for delivery of a certain individual moveable of a *certa species* there is this alleviation for the debtor, that he can free himself by delivery at the place where the thing happens to be at the time, and therefore he is not bound to bring it at his own cost and risk to the place where the action is raised . . . If we take this exceptional rule, as it has here been stated, as a mere equitable favour to the debtor, it is clear that it has nothing at all to do with the place of fulfillment and a jurisdiction founded on that; for there, on the contrary, are binding and restrictive to the debtor."

[171] Ibid., 274: "the foundation of the Roman law of succession is the *succession per universitatem*, which must be assumed in every succession, and beside which all other legal relations take up a secondary position. This, however, is merely the legal form into which the substance of succession, as above explained, is brought."

[172] Ibid., 223, 251, 253, 255, 279.

law under the latter category, but like the American realist scholars it recognizes the possibility that much of the law could fall under this "exceptional" category.

The 1928 debates on choice of law in contracts within the Conflict of Laws Committee of the International Law Association illustrate precisely the distinction between Savigny's category of mandatory laws and the exception of public policy as it is generally understood in PrIL.[173]

In a paper read before the Grotius Society in 1934 Stephen de Százy[174] argued that "the question of the choice of law by the parties to a contract [. . .] may, without exaggeration, be called the most intricate question of Private International Law."[175] He argued that the dominant theory at the time of his writing argued for the freedom of the parties to choose the law applicable to their contracts such that "not only the legal effects but also everything relating to essential or intrinsic validity of the contract" falls under the scope of parties' choice of law.[176] He suggests that this move is unsupported by some of the main writings in PrIL, including Savigny[177] and Story.[178] First, Szászy argues that one should appreciate a distinction made in Story's writing—and as I have shown, in Savigny's as well—between references to the applicable law based on inferences of parties' reasonable expectations and the plea for the autonomy of individuals to choose the applicable law.[179] Szászy argues that whereas the former is merely a consideration that enters the analysis of the "proper law" of the contract, the latter assumes that parties have the freedom to decide which law applies to their transactions in any circumstances, and regardless of the nature of the laws selected.[180] Second, Szászy argues that a very narrow understanding of the public policy exception has left many so called "compulsory non-ordre public rules" under the purview of parties' choice of law.[181] Whereas there is widespread agreement that public policy may trump any choice of law by the parties, Szászy argued that at the time of his writing, compulsory contract rules which did not fall under the public policy exception[182] fell under the scope of parties' choice of law, such that "the laws which are compulsory in municipal law lose their compulsory nature in international law."[183]

173 Report of the Conflict of Laws Committee of the International Law Association (1928) 35 Int'l L Ass'n Rep Conf 135.

174 Judge of the Royal Court of Justice of Budapest, attached to the Royal Hungarian Ministry of Justice, Lecturer at the University of Budapest.

175 Stephen de Szászy, 'Choice of Law by the Parties to a Contract with Principal Reference to the English and American Law' (1934) 20 Transactions of the Grotius Society 156 (hereafter Szászy, "Choice of Law by the Parties").

176 Ibid., 158.

177 Ibid., 159 citing Savigny, *Private International Law* (n. 136) 223, 224, 251.

178 Ibid., 162, 163. 179 Ibid., 163. 180 Ibid., 168.

181 Ibid., 158. For a discussion of the distinction between public policy and mandatory laws outside the purview of public policy, see the Report of the Conflict of Laws Committee of the International Law Association (1928) 35 Int'l L Ass'n Rep Conf 135, 141–4.

182 As examples, he cites "rules making the contract invalid by reason of error, of fraud, or of the illegality of the object of the contract, or by reason of provisions invalidating clauses of non-responsibility in certain cases, etc." See Szászy, "Choice of Law by the Parties" (n. 175) 157–8.

183 Ibid., 172.

Szászy therefore suggested that one should reconsider the distinction—made by Savigny[184]—between facultative or supplementary rules and compulsory rules, and to determine that in contract law, as well as in many other areas of private law "the liberty of parties is absolute all over the province of facultative or supplementary rules of law and that only compulsory rules of law are exempt from the autonomy of the parties."[185]

ii) Sequenced analysis of the nature of legal relations (formal principles; practical considerations in the transnational social realm; relational justice)

Within Savigny's distinction between suppletory and mandatory laws, the principle of voluntary submission applies only to the former category. Yet even within this category the principle of voluntary submission is understood to have "a more objective [. . .] character."[186]

In Savigny's own words, "voluntary subjection to a local law is manifested in various kinds and degrees."[187] This will depend on the different kinds of legal relations individuals enter into and the various interests and expectations that underlie such relations. Therefore, the application of a particular law is not a "vested right" from which there is no derogation. Rather, as Gutzwiller noted, the applicable law is determined based on the way in which Savigny determined the nature of a particular legal relation by underscoring a very broad and very eclectic set of factors and interests.[188] After all, Pillet confessed that the "true reason" why he could not accept Savigny's theory was because it offered an eclectic pool of elements from which to deduce the nature of the legal relation. The theory was abstract, not stable, and not precise enough.[189]

Savigny argued that because the individual extends himself into a wide network of relationships with various individuals, he inevitably "comes under the authority of the most various laws"[190] and one needs to look for a decisive factor which will connect a legal relation to a territory.[191] Much like Jitta, Savigny takes the freedom of individuals to enter into legal relations across borders for granted. Savigny's notion of voluntary submission is linked to people's presumed freedom to establish their domicile in different places, to travel to a different country to purchase property

184 Savigny, *Private International Law* (n. 136) 77 n a) and translator's note 1, citing Friedrich Karl von Savigny, System des heutigen römischen Rechts, vol. 1 (Veit & Comp 1840) 57:

> Absolute or imperative (absolute, gebietende) laws are those, which "are intended to rule with inflexible necessity, without allowing any play to individual will. This necessity may have its origin in the peculiar nature of the particular positive law; or in political or economical consideration; or may flow directly from moral considerations." Dispositive, permissive, or suppletory (vermittelnde) laws are those which "allow free scope to the individual will, and only step into its place where it has omitted to exercise its power, in order to give the necessary certainty and precision to the legal relation. The latter class of laws may therefore be regarded as interpreting the imperfectly expressed will."

185 Szászy, "Choice of Law by the Parties" (n. 175) 177.

186 Savigny, *Private International Law* (n. 136) 196.

187 Ibid., 134.

188 Max Charles Gutzwiller, *Der Einfluss Savignys auf die Entwicklung des Internationalprivatrechts* (Gschwend, Tschopp 1923) 85.

189 Pillet, "Essai" (n. 79) 422–3.

190 Savigny, *Private International Law* (n. 136) 133.

191 Ibid.

there, and to engage in potentially tortious activity in different jurisdictions. To the extent the law does not prevent them from doing so, people are free to travel, to buy foreign property, to enter into marriages with other nationals and so on. In doing so they do not also legislate for themselves, but they inevitably bring their relationships under the purview of a variety of laws. This "empirical human will" as Behrends called it,[192] extends for Savigny into a quasi-empirical analysis of legal relations[193] which enables him to localize them in a particular community. Thereby one "deduces" from what Behrends called "empirical elements of freedom"[194] "the subordination of the individual to a particular local law, and consequently the relation of the person to a particular territory."[195]

Savigny therefore pleads for a very thorough investigation of the wide variety of legal relations because "only by the complete solution of this problem will it be possible to make a safe and exhaustive application to actual life of any principles that shall be established."[196] Savigny rejected any overarching principle that attempts to "reduce under a common absolute rule as to their seat" all legal relations because "the various legal relations are of such diverse nature."[197] He therefore not only rejected the proposition that the law of domicile should apply to all legal relations,[198] but also the principle that "every legal relation should be judged according to the local law of that territory within which it has come into existence."[199] According to Savigny:

> This principle is not only arbitrary, because the place of origin in itself, and irrespective of the circumstances in which the legal relation may have been brought into existence, cannot determine the local law to be applied; but it has only the appearance of a substantive principle, while it is in reality of a merely formal nature. For the place where each legal relation comes into existence, in the legal sense, can only be known by more minute examination of its specific nature; and in this a predominant and capital regard paid to the place of origin will only obstruct us.[200]

Savigny therefore provided a detailed, and as Gutzwiller points out, very eclectic analysis determining the "nature of the legal relation."[201] When he discussed the law applicable to transfers of property, he engaged in a comparative analysis of different laws that determine alienation based on delivery of the thing or based on the contract.[202] When he discussed prescription he noted that "possession is a relation of facts."[203] As to obligations he referred to "well-founded expectations"[204]

[192] Behrends, "Geschichte" (n. 114) 285.

[193] Unlike Behrends, Rückert argued that "it is a misunderstanding of Savigny when one interprets references to 'life' and so on as sociological-empirical requirements." Joachim Rückert, *Idealismus, Jurisprudenz und Politik bei Friedrich Carl von Savigny* (R. Gremer 1984) 347.

[194] See Behrends, "Geschichte" (n. 114) 285.

[195] Savigny, *Private International Law* (n. 136) 132.

[196] Ibid., 133.

[197] Ibid., 141.

[198] Ibid., 143: "The law that governs the person as such is not necessarily the law that governs the particular legal relation in which that person may be concerned, and through which he may come under the authority of the most different laws."

[199] Ibid., 147.

[200] Ibid., 147.

[201] Gutzwiller (n. 188).

[202] Savigny, *Private International Law* (n. 136) 184.

[203] Ibid., 186.

[204] Ibid., 196.

as well as the role of "visible facts" in determining the fulfillment of the obligation, distinguishing between those "accidental, transitory, foreign to the substance of the obligation and to its further development and efficacy."[205] For different kinds of obligations he examined the "relation in which the nature and length of the residence stand to the substance of the obligation."[206] And even once Savigny determined an applicable law for obligations, he was careful to point out that:

> Although the seat of the obligation, and, at the same time, the local law that governs it, may upon the whole be determined with certainty by the rules here laid down, yet it must not be asserted that all possible questions of law occasioned by an obligation must be determined only by this local law. A more thorough investigation of such questions of law, in their whole connection, is required to settle this point.[207]

For many of the legal relations he analyzed, Savigny discussed the way in which individuals act within the legal relations and the variety of expectations they raise in each other.[208] Furthermore, Savigny classified the area of tort law as "quasi-penal"[209]and "coercive, strictly positive,"[210] and involving such a wide variety of interests[211] that it should be regulated by the *lex fori*.

To understand the way in which Savigny avoided anchoring the principle of voluntary submission to a formalistic notion of autonomy, one must understand the sequenced reasoning through which Savigny determined the applicable law based on an analysis of a legal relation. Savigny's analysis starts with a rather abstract description of private law relationships from which one can deduce which law the parties submitted themselves to. This analysis is sometimes informed by a comparative analysis of various laws based on statutory interpretation. Following this abstract description, Savigny offers various assumptions about the implications of applying one law or another for the life of individuals in the transnational realm. Finally, Savigny provides various considerations of interpersonal justice to support the application of particular laws and particular interpretations of legal relations. More will be said regarding the last two elements of Savigny's analysis in the next chapter in the context of discussing various conceptions of legitimate authority in PrIL theory. Suffice it here to note a few examples to illustrate the way in which this sequenced analysis

[205] Ibid., 198. [206] Ibid., 207. [207] Ibid., 224.

[208] Ibid., ("the important fact, that the larger number of legal relations concern not a single person, but several," at 143; "The circumstances, therefore, under which an obligation arises may often excite in others a definite and well-founded expectation, and in such a case this expectation is not to be disappointed," at 196; "If that debtor capriciously changes his domicile, or if he dies, his previous forum domicilii has, as such, entirely ceased. But in the quality here established, as the special forum of the obligation, it still continues: it follows the emigrant in his new domicile; it binds the heir in case of death, although he should have a different domicile. The reason of this peculiar rule is, that the debtor, by undertaking the obligation here, creates an expectation that he will also submit to its consequences at the same place," at 205; "This doctrine is not only correct in principle, but it is also recommended by a certain equity, since every capricious exercise of free will by one party to the detriment of the opponent, is excluded by the clear settlement of the period of prescription that results from it," at 250; "Precisely in order to exclude this unjustifiable one-sided power of the husband over the rights of the wife, was the existence of a tacit contract presumed by the defenders of the first opinion," at 294).

[209] Ibid., 255. [210] Ibid., 253. [211] Ibid., 253–5.

of the nature of legal relations—rather than any abstract postulate of autonomy—feeds into the concept of voluntary submission.

For example, when discussing the law applicable to succession, Savigny starts by arguing that the nature of successions:

> [C]onsists in the passing of an estate, at the death of its owner, to other persons. This implies an artificial extension of a man's power, and therefore his will, beyond the limits of his life, which continuing will may either be an expressed intention (in the testament), or a tacit one (in intestate succession) . . . This second kind of continuing will stands in connection with the continuation of the individuality of man by relationship. This relation is entirely and immediately connected with the person of the deceased.[212]

Savigny argues that framing the analysis in terms of searching for the nature of a legal relation avoids the formalism of deducing the applicable law from technical differences in the law. Rather, by anchoring the application of a law to a certain view of the nature of a legal relation, one acknowledges that determining a particular law applicable is precisely a reflection of a particular understanding of the nature of a legal relation. He describes the position of those deriving the applicable law from technical differences in the laws thus:

> In the countries, which treat succession (according to the Roman principle) as universal succession, the domicile, he says, is decisive for the whole estate. In those countries, on the other hand, which do not recognize the theory of universal succession (such as England and America), the succession to immoveables must be judges by the *lex rei sitae*.[213]

In response to these scholars he argues:

> This view originates in the mistaken notion that the adoption or rejection of universal succession is something absolute and independent, from which a further inference can be drawn to the seat of the right of succession, and the local law that governs it. But in fact the two are identical, and universal succession is only the legal form and the technical expression for that view of rights of succession, which places their seat universally at the domicile, without distinguishing between the different portions of the estate.[214]

Once the determination of the applicable law is anchored in a particular view of the nature of a legal relation, Savigny openly admits that this nature is contested:

> From the standpoint of the countries and the writers that deal with succession with reference to the estate as a whole, the *lex domicilii* is decisive, even for immoveables: from any other standpoint it is not. In this sense, the distinction is not disputed in any quarter.[215]

Precisely given different ways of appreciating the nature of a legal relation, in a second step Savigny adds some practical considerations that speak in favor of adopting a particular view of the nature of successions in the transnational context over another:

[212] Ibid., 272 and 272 n (a). [213] Ibid., 278. [214] Ibid., 278.
[215] Ibid., 278.

The correctness of this view is further confirmed by the following considerations. If we did not regard the domicile of the deceased as fixing the local law, there would be no other place with which we could connect the right of succession, except the place where the property is left, the inheritance or succession, is situated; so that then the *lex rei sitae* must determine. Where, then, is this place? The estate as a whole is an ideal object of perfectly indefinite contents possibly consisting of property and other rights in particular things, of obligations and debts, which last constituents at least have a quite invisible existence. This estate, therefore, is everywhere and nowhere, so that a *locus rei sitae* cannot be discovered for it all. It would be a very arbitrary expedient to adopt the place where the greater part is situated, both because this notion is fluctuating and uncertain, and because the lesser part has just as much claim to be considered as the greater. But if we give this up, it only remains to fix the place of succession wherever any single thing belonging to the estate is to be found. This, however, would lead, where the estate is extensive and widely scattered, to the assumption of many independent successions, subject possibly to quite different laws; and which after all would include only one portion of the succession (real rights), leaving the other part (obligations) altogether untouched. It is plain that this course would be entirely arbitrary and without principle, nay, would end in an empty show without any truth.[216]

Savigny then includes arguments about the statutory interpretation of the Prussian law of succession at the time,[217] as well as inferences about the reasonable expectations involved in transnational succession matters. As to the latter, he writes:

In intestate succession, however, the following consideration also comes into view: It rests chiefly on the presumptive, and therefore, tacit, intention of the deceased; not that such an intention can be asserted as a certain fact for this particular person with regard to his individual relations, but that every positive law establishes a general presumption in accordance with what appears to be the nature of the family relations. It is quite natural that such a presumption should take different shapes in different legislations. On the other hand, in would be quite unnatural, in a single given case of succession, to suppose that the deceased has had a different intention for the different parts of his estate, and thus to assume that he wishes one person to be heir to his house, and another to his landed estate or his money, if he has not expressly declared himself on the subject (by testament).[218]

A final stage in the sequenced analysis of the nature of a legal relation, from which Savigny deduces the applicable law, is a review of various principles of interpersonal justice. Savigny frequently refers to individuals' "expectations, based on circumstances."[219] These are not only expectations shared by the parties as to the applicable law, which ground the legitimacy of a state imposing its respective law. There are also expectations that individuals induce in each other and which must be calibrated

[216] Ibid., 273.

[217] Ibid., 288:

The legislator certainly cannot have intended to establish a principle that would involve the parties, especially the creditor, in quite useless embarrassment. This very practical argument appears to me far more important than the one urged by our opponents, viz., that, at the time when the Landrecht was compiled, the opposite doctrine was predominant in practice, and that an adherence to this practice in the Landrecht must be assumed where a deviation from it is not distinctly expressed.

[218] Ibid., 277. [219] Ibid., 202, 204.

through PrIL norms. For example, Savigny argues that statute of limitations rules should fall under the law of the contract, rather than the law of procedure since:

> This doctrine is not only correct in principle, but it is also recommended by a certain equity, since every capricious exercise of free will by one party to the detriment of the opponent, is excluded by the clear settlement of the period of prescription that results from it. Thus the plaintiff cannot select for his action just that one of several concurring jurisdictions under which there is the longest term of prescription. In the like manner, the defendant cannot, by changing his domicile to a place where there is a shorter term of prescription, obtain an advantage to himself, seeing that both the local law and the special forum of the obligation are immutably fixed for the debt contracted by him at the former domicile.[220]

Similarly, he argues that the law of the domicile of the husband at the time of marriage governs any claims to the matrimonial property based on the following rationale:

> If, at a place where the law establishes as the rule universal communion of goods of the most extensive description, a marriage is contracted by a rich man with a poor woman, the estate becomes common by the completion of marriage. If the man afterwards changes the domicile to a place where the dotal regime prevails, the wife must, according to the second opinion, lose in a moment, and against her will, the share of the estate to which she had already acquired right . . . The second opinion must indeed be adopted, if a law as to conjugal property of a strictly positive exclusive nature should exist at the new domicile. This would be presumed if a law were there enacted prohibiting any marriage whatever to be contracted, or if constituted elsewhere, to be continued, otherwise than under the dotal regime, or otherwise than with the communion of goods.[221]

3. Ferdinand Lasalle

I have argued above, in line with Behrend's general reading of Savigny's System that Savigny's concept of the legal relation, as well as of freedom, have an "empirical sociological"[222] dimension, such that legal relations are not constructed a priori, but following an analysis of transnational social life. Certainly Savigny's empiricism is limited to certain inferences about individuals' reasonable expectations on the application of particular laws in particular circumstances, rather than anchored in any view of the socioeconomic conditions of transnational life.

In 1880 the German socialist Lassalle picked up precisely on the interplay between individual rights, autonomy, and a people as a society. Unlike Savigny, Lassalle relied on this analytical framework to push for a particular, socialist political agenda. In Müller's view Lassalle meant to "capture, indeed undermine the principle which prevents any socialist (not all political) reform, namely the principle of vested rights."[223] Lassalle wrote two volumes titled "the principle of vested rights" in which he started from the premise that "rights, which are acquired through individual acts, cannot be altered by subsequent

[220] Ibid., 250. [221] Ibid., 296–7. [222] Behrends, "Geschichte" (n. 114) 284, 287.
[223] Müller, *Der Grundsatz* (n. 41) 195.

legislation"[224] and described private law as "the realization of individual freedom."[225] Lassalle argued that "the individual is free in the society. Whenever laws attach consequences to free acts of the individual, these consequences arise because the individual wished them. The individual has the choice to undertake a particular action or not."[226] This description appears to rehearse Savigny's view that the individual actions are not sources of law, but they simply constitute acts to which laws attach certain consequences.

Lassalle clarified that "the individual can acquire rights for himself or others, through individual or consensual actions, only insofar as laws allow him this."[227] He adopts Hegel's and Savigny's postulate that the ultimate legal source is the "consciousness of the people."[228] This led him to argue that enforcing a vested right to the detriment of a contrary legislative policy means breaking the relationship between the individual and the consciousness of the people.[229] If a legal right is granted through law and law emanates from the people, it would be impossible for an individual to claim a vested right—and thereby claim his relationship with the community—and at the same time refuse his relationship to the community by failing to recognize the new, contrary policy.[230]

Lassalle relied on the description of the relationship between the individual and the people that Savigny referenced as well, in order to argue that individual freedom and law might be perceived as competing only on the surface, while following a deeper analysis one would need to conclude that each one contains and relies on the other.[231] Lassalle developed these thoughts for the relationship of laws both in time (retroactivity) and in space.[232] This led him to argue that when the judge would need to apply the new law in the domestic context, he should apply *lex fori* in the transnational context. In circumstances in which he would need to apply the old law in the domestic context, he should apply the law of the domicile for issues of legal capacity; for issues of formal validity, the law of the place where the act ocurred; and for legal validity, the law that was determined by the parties, implicitly, if not explicitly.[233]

Lassalle offered virtually no explanation about why these particular laws would have to regulate those different categories of legal issues, and therefore his theory was mostly disregarded in the development of PrIL.[234] But Lassalle was less interested in enquiring under which law a right should vest in each category of cases. His interest was rather to explain why it cannot be viewed as an affront to autonomy or individual freedom to depart from vested rights. If vested rights are an expression of autonomy (or individual will expressed in a particular act which

[224] Sibylle Hofer, *Freiheit Ohne Grenzen? Privatrechtstheoretische Diskussionen im 19. Jahrhundert* (Mohr Siebeck 2001) 102.

[225] Ferdinand Lassalle, *Das System der erworbenen Rechte, Eine Versöhnung des positiven Rechts und der Rechtsphilosophie*, vol. 1 (Brochhaus 1880) 164, 170, 224, 300 (hereafter Lassalle, *Erworbene Rechte*).

[226] Müller, *Der Grundsatz* (n. 41) 195. [227] Lassalle, *Erworbene Rechte* (n. 225) 164.

[228] Müller, *Der Grundsatz* (n. 41) 197; Lassalle, *Erworbene Rechte* (n. 225) 302.

[229] Ibid. [230] Ibid.

[231] Müller, *Der Grundsatz* (n. 41) 197; Lassalle, *Erworbene Rechte* (n. 225) 360.

[232] Lassalle, *Erworbene Rechte* (n. 225) 303–5. [233] Müller (n. 41) 198. [234] Ibid.

leads to the acquisition of a right), a relational view of autonomy was needed in order to explain that departing from vested rights is not an infringement of but rather an expression of the social context of autonomy. In other words Lassalle's "true goal" and "the highest principle" was "the unity between individual freedom [individuelle Willensfreiheit] and community freedom [Willensgemeinschaft]."[235]

Lassalle thought an emphasis on, and reconstruction of, Hegel's and Savigny's ideas about the relationship between the individual and the people, would serve as fruitful intellectual ground to justify and push for socialist reform, both in the national and the transnational realm. He thought that by emphasizing the relational nature of autonomy one would be able to move from the protection of "individual freedom" to that of "the freedom of humanity."[236] Therefore, the goal of the state should not be to protect individual freedom and property,[237] but rather through the unity of the individual with the people, the state must "place the individual in a position to achieve such goals and such a level of development that they could not reach as isolated individuals; to enable them to achieve a level of education, power and freedom which they could not achieve as isolated individuals."[238]

Freedom and autonomy in a social context translate for Lassalle into the "progressive overcoming of powerlessness, that is of misery, ignorance and poverty of the working class."[239] Certainly Lassalle's political project, including the elimination of land and capital property[240] cannot be found in Savigny's theory. What is particularly interesting, however, is Lassalle's proposition that the integration of the individual will into the consciousness of the people, as well as Savigny's dual individual/community reference point throughout his System[241] can be used as a theoretical construct to further the social justice agenda, both nationally and internationally.[242] It is precisely Lassalle's linking of the political project with a theoretical model aimed at reconstructing autonomy in relational terms that made Müller suggest that "Lassalles' thought might be recast sometime in the future" in order to pursue social justice in PrIL.[243]

4. Josephus Jitta

Thus far this chapter has shown that Savigny's theory should not be understood in overly individualistic terms. The fact that Savigny took the individual and the legal relation as an analytical point of departure did not mean that he abandoned the

[235] Adolph Wagner, *Briefe von Ferdinand Lassalle an Carl Rodbertus* (Puttkammer & Muehlbrecht 1878) at 30 (hereafter Lassalle, *Letters*).

[236] Lassalle, *Erworbene Rechte* (n 225) 167.

[237] Ferdinand Lassalle, "Arbeiterprogramm" in Eduard Bernstein (ed.), *Ferdinand Lassalle's Reden und Schriften*, vol. 2 (Vorwärts 1891) 45.

[238] Ibid. [239] Ibid., 45–6. [240] Lassalle, *Letters* (n. 235) 46.

[241] For this duality and how it features in Savigny's System generally, see Behrends, "Geschichte" (n. 114) 277.

[242] Lassalle conceived of his work on the vested rights doctrine as "the reconciliation of vested rights with philosophy" (see the title of the book at n. 225).

[243] Müller, *Der Grundsatz* (n. 41) 198.

dual individual/community analysis that Behrends believed characterized all eight volumes of Savigny's System. Recognizing the fact that Savigny was reacting against the overly individualistic use of the concept of autonomy and that he incorporated Story's empirical dimensions provides much support for Okko Behrends' reading of Savigny's theory as "empirical-sociological."[244] However, Savigny's theory was not interpreted as such in the development of PrIL.[245]

Both the empirical and the sociological elements become much clearer in Jitta's writings and in particular in the way in which Jitta develops two elements of Savigny's theory that Jitta develops further. First, Jitta adopted Savigny's focus on the legal relation, which he believed was the "dawn of the modern evolution of PrIL."[246] Like Savigny, Jitta thought that centering the analysis in PrIL on the nature of a legal relation would counter the state-centered focus that PrIL had inherited from theories of sovereignty, as well as the overly formalistic focus it had inherited from the statutory school. And like Savigny, Jitta was keen to distinguish the analysis of the nature of a legal relation from vested rights theories.

Yet while Jitta kept Savigny's focus on the nature of a legal relation, the following section shows how Jitta fundamentally changed the contours of the analysis. The second section shows the way in which Jitta further clarified the distinction to which Savigny alluded between the freedom of individuals to immerse themselves in the social life of a particular local community and the application of a particular law. While Jitta, like Savigny, takes for granted a certain freedom of movement in the transnational realm and portrays it as natural, a part of human nature, he argues that the application of a particular law is derived from the "requirements of reasonable international social life" and deduced by reference to a much wider pool of interests of affected individuals and communities.[247] For example, Jitta argued that "he, who has acquired, in normal intercourse and in good faith, a right to a movable good, according to the law in force in the place where the good is de facto lying, must be considered as being entitled to the said right everywhere."[248] But "exceptions to this rule may be admitted when a social interest, stronger than the interest of the maintenance of a regular intercourse in good faith, is concerned with the matter."[249]

[244] Behrends, "Geschichte" (n. 114) 284.

[245] Savigny was generally perceived as formalistic and dogmatic. For many references to this reading of Savigny and a countering of this reading, see Behrends, "Geschichte" (n. 114) 279: "it always leads to serious mistakes, when one ignores the fact that the systematic expositions of legal terms is not meant to be classificatory, but rather follows from an empirical approach and is determined by the observed phenomena."

[246] Jitta, *La Méthode* (n. 102) 90.

[247] See D. Josephus Jitta, *The Renovation of International Law on the Basis of a Legal Community of Mankind, Systematically Developed* (M. Nijhoff 1919) (hereafter Jitta, *The Renovation*): "Social life necessitates a reasonable order, and this necessity is the basis of reasonable principles of international social life," at 3; "The only conclusion I deduce from the foregoing considerations is that reasonable principles are not to be found by philosophical abstraction, but by observation of life's phenomena," at 3.

[248] Ibid., 127. [249] Ibid., 127–8.

a) *Rethinking the analysis of the nature of a legal relation*

Jitta celebrated Savigny's "golden rule" that "for each legal relation we ought to seek the legal domain to which it belongs according to its peculiar nature and the civil law to which it is subjected in consequence."[250] He embraced the rule because it focused the analysis in PrIL on individuals, their relationships and their international existence, and because Jitta thought it could be used as a platform for a much more nuanced analysis of the applicable law.[251]

However, Jitta was careful to distinguish Savigny's golden rule from two other doctrines of the time that also focused on individuals. He noted that unlike Savigny's principle:

> The doctrine based on the respect of regularly acquired rights supposes that it is possible to determine, before applying the fundamental rule, when a right derived from a legal relation is a regularly acquired right. Mutatis mutandis, we find the same basis for the theory of the personal autonomy as a theory granting to the persons the faculty of freely choosing the law to which a legal relation between them is to be subjected.[252]

In other words, he saw Savigny and himself as relying on the notion of the legal relation and focusing on the individual differently than the individualistic authors focusing on vested rights and individual autonomy. But Jitta also departed from Savigny's analysis of the localization of legal relations in various respects.[253]

b) *Shifting the standpoint of analysis*

As a corollary to Savigny's distinction between suppletory and mandatory laws, Savigny analyzed the nature of a legal relation—at least with respect to suppletory laws—from the standpoint of hypothetical parties to a private law relationship. This is not to say that he thought private law is removed from a particular localized social context and that the nature of a legal relation can be deduced from natural law or *lex mercatoria*.[254] But since he envisioned suppletory laws of any national private law as catering to the interests and expectations of hypothetical individuals within particular sets of private law relationships, in Savigny's theory the localization of these relationships can also be made by considering the expectations and interests of such individuals.

[250] Ibid., 90.

[251] Ibid., 89: "The legal relation is a link between two persons or legal subjects, a link formed and maintained by the social public power, the link being at one end a duty, and at the other end a claim corresponding to the duty."

[252] Ibid., 90.

[253] Jitta, *La Methode* (n. 102) 26, §18 (discussing how his understanding of "the nature of the legal relation" methodology differs from Savigny's).

[254] Savigny, *Private International Law* (n. 136) 231 remarking ironically: "Differing entirely from these views, other writers have maintained that the contract concluded by correspondence must be judged by the law of nature; in regard to which it is only lamented that they have not also given us the system of natural law which they wish to be applied."

Jitta, in contrast, began from the premise that every legal relation has "a social scope."[255] Every legal relation is embedded in a social reality, and it is "society [that] attaches a duty connected with a claim" to particular "legal facts," which are "modifications of the state of things in social life [for example a prejudicial act or tort unjustly performed by an accountable subject]."[256] In his analysis of obligations he argues, for example, that "obligations are recognized and enforced because the reasonable order of the society demands it," not because of any particular right of the promisee.[257] Therefore, choice of law rules in contract law do not aim at recognizing any vested rights, but rather "consider obligations from the point of view of the demands of the legal community of mankind"[258] and establish "harmony between law and life."[259] While private law sets correlative rights and obligations among particular individuals within the relationship, the substance of these correlative rights and obligations depends on "the physical, intellectual, moral and economic conditions" of a particular nation:[260]

The law appropriate for the nature of a legal relation is that which allows it to develop in the universal community and to fulfill its social aim. Within national private law, it is the national legal community, which indicates the nature of the legal relation and the respective positive rules. To formulate them, the state would only need to take into consideration the physical, intellectual, moral and economic conditions of its own nation. In private international law, it is the universal legal community, such as it is, that must form the basis of analysis. Within this community, legal relations present themselves in much more complicated facets and the individuality of people is modified by their relationships with diverse legal groups within humanity. To formulate the law which is appropriate for the nature of legal relations in the universal society, the state has to take into consideration not only the physical, intellectual, moral and economic conditions of this enlarged and more varied community, but also the legal conditions which derive from the diversity of states. The legal rule which, under these conditions, allows the legal relation to fulfill its social goal within humanity, such as this state conceives of its goal, is the rule which it must apply.[261]

Jitta showed that shifting the standpoint of the analysis of a private law relationship from the individuals within a private law relationship to a broader social context brought many analytical and methodological consequences for PrIL.

First, Jitta thought the analysis of a private law relationship cannot be made in the abstract. On the one hand, this meant, contrary to what Savigny assumed, that one could not describe the nature of a legal relation from the standpoint of a hypothetical community of states:

There is no universal nature of a legal relation. The only way to "truly" focus on the nature of a legal relation is to start from the individual point of view [the point of view of an individual judge, court, country etc.] [. . .] It is only through the application of the individual method of our science that we can give a more precise meaning and a positive value to the expression

[255] Jitta, *The Renovation* (n. 247) 136; Jitta, *La Methode* (n. 102) 217.
[256] Jitta, *The Renovation* (n. 247) 97.
[257] D. Josephus Jitta, *La substance des obligations dans le droit international privé*, vol. 1 (Belinfante Frères 1906) 3 (hereafter Jitta, *Obligations* vol. 1).
[258] Ibid., 5. [259] Ibid., 20. [260] Ibid., 217–18. [261] Ibid., 217–18.

"the nature of a legal relation", expression of which everyone now makes use, but which does not prevent authors from disagreeing completely, even about the methodology of achieving a consensus.[262]

On the other hand, Jitta recognized the difficulty for the individual court and/or legislator in reconciling its responsibility to its own national society and toward this enlarged international social community:

By analyzing the matter from the point of view of a concrete state, by the nature of a legal relation, we understand its social scope in the universal legal community of people, such as this presents itself to the forum within its judicial function.[263]

Jitta thought it was inevitable and in some sense desirable that each national court/legislator would have to express a particular view about the nature of a legal relation in the transnational context. It was also inevitable that a national court/legislator's view of the nature of a legal relation would be influenced, even subconsciously, by its own national law and its own cultural, social, and political national environment.

Individual works, obtained through our method of reasoning, bear the print of the national legal consciousness, they are based on the particular way of appreciating the social scope of the legal relations. There would thus be neither unity of private law, nor harmony in the application of various private laws. These are undoubtedly the shortcomings of the individual method. Only the universal method may combat these shortcomings.[264]

Jitta thought that the only way to temper this subjectivism is to commit national decision makers in PrIL to a thorough comparative analysis, as well as a good grasp of the socioeconomic and political circumstances of the international society.

The nature of legal relations, examined from the individual point of view, does not allow for abstractions, derived from the philosophical law, but must take the society such as it is. An individual state cannot flatter itself to transform the legal conditions of a universal society, but must take them such as they are.[265]

The practical value of this inquiry can only be achieved if the legislator knows the legal elements of international life and the study of foreign legislations that a state finds in the universal legal society is indispensable for a good legislation of private international law.[266]

Second, and as a corollary to his focus on the social scope of private law relationships, Jitta argued, against Savigny, that one could not focus the analysis on broad categories of private law relationships because the social aim differs between the various relationships within a private law class. [267] Jitta not only broke down the category of obligations in many subcategories based on different social aims, but he also cautioned against taking any particular category of obligations as the benchmark.

[262] Ibid., 215–16. [263] Ibid., 217–18. [264] Ibid., 220. [265] Ibid., 218.
[266] Ibid., 218.
[267] See, e.g., D. Josephus Jitta, *La substance des obligations dans le droit international privé*, 2 vols. (Belinfante Frères 1906 and1907). See also Jitta, *La Methode* (n. 102) (criticizing Savigny for having been too general about the nature of the legal relation and for having focused on very broad categories of legal relations). See also Jitta, *The Renovation* (n. 247) 137 (The classification of obligations for example is "based on the social aim of a contract." Jitta also referred to "contracts based on the social value of goods," at 137, or contracts "based on the social value of change," at 139).

For example, although he distinguished contracts of employment as an important subclass of obligations, he argued that:

> The contract of employment is so much influenced by the economic position of the parties, by their profession, by the more or less temporary nature of their relations, by the nature of the work, and the results the parties aim to achieve, that it is of little use to develop principles for employment contracts generally.[268]

Similarly, for contracts of transportation of goods he argues that:

> Contracts of transport present all kinds of particularities, depending on the modes of transportation, the physical elements of the space in which the merchandise is transported, and depending on the particular kind of merchandise that is transported.[269]

Whereas Savigny had insisted that one can establish general principles for broad categories of relationships and then make exceptions from these general principles based on the circumstances of particular relationships, Jitta was keen to reverse the rule vs. exception dichotomy.

c) Different kinds of freedom

Once Jitta established that a legal relation has a social scope, he was quick to emphasize that the localization of any private law relation also had a profoundly social dimension. According to Jitta's methodology one must determine the "preponderant social element of a legal relation" as well as whether this element caused the legal relation to "penetrate within a particular local sphere of social life."[270] To "localize" a legal relation, what is needed is an "analysis of the link that may exist, *in a social sense*, between the fact and a local sphere of social life."[271] As a corollary to their different aims, different legal relations, even within a single private law category, may be linked to different social communities. This framing of the question of localization in PrIL also made it possible for Jitta to explain why the parties do not have an absolute right to the application of a particular law.

Much more will be said about Jitta's method of social localization in the next chapter, in order to reveal the way in which this method created a social, rather than individualistic principle of legitimate authority in the transnational realm. This section is meant to underscore that Jitta's method of localizing legal relations is based on a clear distinction between different ways of thinking about autonomy in the transnational realm.

Savigny's PrIL methodology had already anticipated a distinction between acts creating legal relations and legal sources, between the freedom of choosing a domicile and having the law of the domicile applied, and so on. Yet in Savigny's framework the distinction was not always very sharp, since voluntary submission was

[268] Jitta, *Obligations* vol. 1 (n. 257) 179. [269] Ibid., 182.

[270] D. Josephus Jitta, *La substance des obligations dans le droit international privé*, vol. 2 (Belinfante Frères 1907) 498 (hereafter Jitta, *Obligations* vol. 2).

[271] Jitta, *The Renovation* (n. 247) 97.

partly derived from presumptions about individuals' expectations of the applicable law and partly from a comparative analysis of law as well as general principles of interpersonal morality. Furthermore, since Savigny thought it was possible to distinguish, at least analytically, between suppletory and mandatory laws in the area of private law, the principle of voluntary submission was more or less premised on individuals' reasonable expectations depending on the type of laws potentially applicable.

Jitta, by contrast, envisioned a much more muddled regulatory space in private law, where it was hard if not impossible to separate norms between those granting and those limiting choice and autonomy. Therefore, Jitta posits that the localization of private law relationships must be made from the point of view of a larger social community and based on comparative law and sociological empirical analysis. There was thus a firm distinction to be made between the freedom of individuals to immerse themselves in the life of a local sphere of social life and the freedom to choose the applicable law. Jitta described the former kind of freedom in these words:

> I believe the individual is free to choose the local circle of social life in which to fulfill his social obligations.[272]
>
> All people have the right to take part in the universal life, by submitting themselves to the laws of different social groups, which form part of humanity.[273]

Jitta thought that emphasizing this type of freedom distinguishes his theory sharply from state-centered internationalist theories, especially Zitelmann's. He notes that:

> Zitelmann thought it was possible to derive from Public International Law a principle according to which only the *personal status [law]*—the law of citizenship and subsidiarily the law of domicile, can impose obligations to individuals, particularly legal obligations. For myself, I have replaced Zitelmann's public international law with the legal community of mankind and I cannot find Zitelmann's postulates in it.[274]

Chapter 2 already illustrated how Mancini, by adopting the principle of nationality, both narrowed and expanded individual liberty by, on the one hand failing to recognize the ability of individuals to disconnect from their national community, and on the other hand failing to appreciate the interests of other states in regulating individuals acting or establishing themselves in their community. Jitta thought the same could be said of Zitelmann and Jitta's stance toward Zitelmann's theory is unequivocal: "Zitelmann is not my man."[275]

While Jitta is keen to emphasize individuals' freedom to immerse themselves in the social life of different communities he does not equate this to a freedom to choose a law. Instead, from this initial postulate of a universal freedom of movement and establishment Jitta derived the applicable law, not as a free choice of individuals, but as an expression of social responsibility toward the communities in which individuals choose to act or establish themselves.[276] The application of a particular law

[272] Jitta, *Obligations* vol. 2 (n. 270) 458. [273] Ibid., 505. [274] Ibid., 458.
[275] Ibid., 459. [276] Ibid., 505.

is the consequence of an exercise of freedom, not a right derived from that exercise. Therefore, Jitta remarks:

> [Individuals] will be regulated by different national laws in proportion to their penetration within the social life of these groups.[277]
>
> I submit the individual to the national or international circle of social life where his initiative [of immersing himself in this social life] is exercised, and, subsidiarily, to the law of the local community where his activity is embedded and in this case, in the measure of its penetration.[278]

Thus, the application of a particular law is not a consequence of autonomy, understood as the freedom to choose a law. It is the consequence of the penetration of individuals in the social life of a community. "Individuals are autonomous only to the extent they are granted such autonomy by the laws that regulate their legal relations."[279] "Both local public policy and the public policy of the universal society will be applied with full force; instead of incorporating exceptions to the principle of autonomy, they will limit it, which is their true nature."[280] For example, after arguing that a contract for transportation of goods is preponderantly immersed in the social life of the place of shipment when both the contractor and the agent are professionally established in that community Jitta adds:

> We might arrive to the same result by referring to the common intention of the parties. It would not be unreasonable to assume, under these circumstances, that the parties had expected the law of the place of shipment to apply, but in basing the authority of the law of shipment on the penetration of the preponderant element of the contract within the local social life, we have a reasonable basis to apply this law also to the extent that it limits the autonomy of the parties, for example with respect to exemption clauses, and to the extent it imposes on an individual exercising a profession certain professional duties, based on the public interest.[281]

F. Conclusions

When Joseph Beale wrote his PrIL treatise based on the vested rights doctrine, he noted that "while [the theory of vested rights] has become the accepted theory in countries governed by the common law, it has been given scant attention on the European continent."[282] This impression is correct, given that despite the recurring references to "vested rights," the state-centered theories of Pillet and Zitelmann refer to rights only as a corollary to their discussion of state sovereignty and interstate duties.[283] Similarly Beale, along with Dicey and Westlake, also end up connecting the apparently individual-centered concept of "vested rights" to the universal interstate framework of distributing state authority to vest private rights.

[277] Ibid. [278] Ibid., 459.

[279] Ibid., 459, 505. See also Jitta, *Obligations* vol. 1 (n. 257) 254, 265.

[280] Jitta, *Obligations* vol. 2 (n. 270) 515. [281] Jitta, *Obligations* vol. 1 (n. 257) 254.

[282] Beale, *A Treatise on the Conflict of Laws* (n. 36) 108.

[283] Michaels, "EU Law as Private International Law?" (n. 38) 24.

This chapter showed that the state-centered way of framing "vested rights" in fact excludes any avenue of contestation by the individuals and communities affected by this distribution of sovereign rights to vest private rights. At the same time, it argued that resurfacing the individual-centered dimensions of rights theories in PrIL does not automatically mean pleading for unrestrained individual autonomy and choice of law. Rather, the aim of this chapter was to show that the history of PrIL yields various ways of reconciling the recognition of individuals' expectations and appeals to justice with their social responsibilization. Rather than establishing a tension between individuals and states, and between private rights and larger public concerns, Josephus Jitta created a relationship between the ability of individuals to immerse themselves in the social life of various communities and their responsibilities for the "social disturbances" they create for various social groups.

In turn, Jitta's emphasis on the social dimensions of rights and reasonable expectations represented a reconstruction of Savigny's emphasis on the legal relation and his concept of localization. A comparison with Story's fluid analysis of individuals' expectations in a social context revealed that Savigny too had paved the way for this reconstruction by adopting a relational image of the individual, as well as a more eclectic analysis of legal relations than is usually acknowledged.

7
Legitimacy and Autonomy

A. Introduction

Writing on American PrIL scholarship in 1989, Lea Brilmayer criticized the American realist school of thought for failing to provide a proper theory of legitimate authority, which would guarantee that individuals "cannot be treated as a means to an end."[1] She argued persuasively that the application of a particular law must be justified in relationship to the relevant individuals, rather than to the forum state or foreign states. In Brilmayer's view, this observation inevitably leads to the conclusion that the only elements that "define the situation, in which state coercion is proper" are "standards of political legitimacy" that underlie the relationship between a particular individual and a political community.[2] She argued that "negative rights," "rights to be left alone" should determine the legitimacy of the imposition of a state's law and that this is "the best" that an individual-centered "rights-based theory might have to offer."[3] Brilmayer's writings underscored many important limitations of the state interest analysis in PrIL and reopened a critique of this theory on both jurisprudential and methodological grounds.

This chapter shows how the relational internationalist authors envisioned different dimensions of legitimacy from those underscored by Brilmayer's account, by focusing on an interhuman relationship, as opposed to an isolated individual, and on private law, as opposed to constitutional or public law generally. In part, this particular relational, private law-centered perspective on legitimacy embraces Singer's appeal to "shift our focus from viewing individuals as abstract citizens whose relationships to each other are governed by rights enforced by the state to viewing them as active participants in shaping their relations in daily life."[4] Viewed in this light, the legitimacy question in PrIL begins with the particular relationship that is subject to dispute. The legitimacy of imposing one law over another is justified on different grounds, including by reference to the particular actions of the parties, the expectations they induced in each other, the advantages and disadvantages that define their

[1] Lea Brilmayer, 'Rights, Fairness, and Choice of Law' (1988) 98 Yale LJ 1277 (hereafter Brilmayer, "Rights").
[2] Ibid., 1294. [3] Ibid., 1279.
[4] Joseph William Singer, 'The Player and the Cards: Nihilism and Legal Theory' (1984) 94 Yale LJ 1, 65 (hereafter Singer, "Nihilism and Legal Theory").

Nineteenth-Century Perspectives on Private International Law. Roxana Banu. © Roxana Banu 2018. Published 2018 by Oxford University Press.

correlative duties, the values underlying private law relationships, and the embeddedness of a legal relation within one or several communities.

This chapter presents the particularities of this theory, uncovered in different segments of Savigny's and Jitta's writings, by contrasting it to both the formalist state-centered internationalist perspective and Brilmayer's account of negative rights. It focuses in large part on aspects of Savigny's general theory on law, the individual, and the legal relation. Much of this background analysis of his theory is generally ignored in studies of PrIL. And while it might be true, as Rückert suggested of Savigny's System generally, that many elements of his general theory were not always fruitfully employed by him in his analysis of the different areas of law,[5] uncovering these elements offers a new perspective on how Savigny's PrIL theory could be interpreted or reconstructed for today's reality.

Yet the account of Savigny offered here by reference, among others, to Joachim Rückert's[6] and Okko Behrends'[7] studies on Savigny's scholarship might surprise. Joachim Rückert described Savigny's theory as "objective idealist," leading Savigny to construct a series of distinctions and then to unite these different elements into a larger whole and within broader principles.[8] It is through this lens that Rückert explains how Savigny distinguishes between individual freedom and the social context, private and public, law and morality, and then reunites these elements within larger concepts such as the "Volk," Christianity, equal moral worth of individuals, and so on.[9] Rückert then argues that the distinctions Savigny makes are constantly fluctuating, are unstable, and can always be reconsidered.[10] It is precisely this flux between separating private from public, the individual from the social, and then constantly attempting to reunite them under a larger whole which is, I argue, a useful lens through which to understand Savigny's PrIL theory, as well as the way in which he avoids both state-centered, as well as individualistic premises. Furthermore, it is important to note that this reading of Savigny's theory as unstable, operating with constantly fluctuating analytical elements, maps onto the nineteenth-century state-centered internationalists' reading of Savigny. While it is quite common for PrIL scholars to now think of Savigny as unequivocally libertarian or Kantian, nineteenth-century internationalists and many contemporary

[5] Joachim Rückert, *Idealismus, Jurisprudenz und Politik bei Friedrich Carl von Savigny* (R. Gremer 1984) 347–8, 360 (hereafter Rückert, *Idealismus*).

[6] Ibid.

[7] Okko Behrends, 'Geschichte, Politik und Jurisprudenz in Savignys System des heutigen römischen Rechts" in Okko Behrends, Wulf Eckart Voss, and Malte Diesselhorst (eds.), *Römisches Recht in der europäischen Tradition: Symposion aus Anlass des 75. Geburtstages von Franz Wieacker* (R. Gremer 1985) 291 (hereafter Behrends, "Geschichte").

[8] Rückert, *Idealismus* (n. 5) 232–7 and 374 (noting the elasticity and "anchoring in the higher," as well as the constant back and forth between concepts).

[9] Ibid., 364–73 (on freedom and law and morality), 358–60 (on the private/public distinction), 312–28 (on the state and the "Volk").

[10] Ibid., 359 (arguing that the private/public distinction is flexible, unstable and fluctuating). See also Joachim Rückert, 'Friedrich Carl von Savigny, the Legal Method, and the Modernity of Law' (2006) 11 Juridica International 56, 67 (arguing that the private/public distinction was never very clear or stable and therefore "was too open for the enlightened project of modernity").

legal historians underscore precisely the way in which Savigny navigates in between and ultimately connects many of the elements within classical liberal dichotomies.

Emphasizing Savigny's idealist philosophy might expose his theory to the same critique offered by nineteenth-century state-centered internationalists who viewed Savigny's theory as imprecise and unstable. To a modern reader Savigny's theory might even seem contradictory. Joachim Rückert argued that one should not confuse the variability of substantive results with variability of method, since Savigny's theory is remarkably consistent within the objective idealist philosophy.[11] The goal of this chapter is not to prove or disprove that Savigny's theory is indeed clear or consistent, but rather to underscore that the understanding and critique of Savigny's theory as unstable and fluctuating in between divergent concepts (individual/state; liberty/social responsibility; private/public) is different and exposes an entirely different reading of Savigny than the typical critique of his theory as Kantian or libertarian. This chapter aims to recover precisely the way in which Savigny moves back and forth in between the classical liberal dichotomies and attempts to construct a cross-reference between the individual and the social, the private and the public, liberty and social responsibility.

To outline the contrast between state-centered and relational internationalist perspective on legitimacy, the chapter starts by outlining the state-centered internationalist perspective with reference to an essay by Antoine Pillet in which he sought to provide a justification for PrIL's universal legitimacy. It shows how Pillet overtly pled for ignoring individual-centered perspectives, including any reliance on private law relationships, in favor of value-neutrality, a high level of abstractness, and a strict separation of law and equity as the inevitable requirements for establishing the universal legitimacy of PrIL "amongst independent states."[12] The third section of this chapter outlines Brilmayer's proposal for a theory of legitimacy that takes the individual as the frame of reference. While Brilmayer rightfully suggests that the imposition of state authority must be justified in relationship to the relevant individuals, rather than states, she adopts a series of dichotomies and distinctions that result in a focus on the political relationship between an isolated individual and a state.

In contrast, the relational internationalist perspective starts from the premise that the individual is inherently social, and constantly embedded in a wide range of relationships, which she shapes and is shaped by. This relational image of the individual and of freedom make relational internationalist authors center their analysis in PrIL on private law relationships, rather than the relationship of an isolated individual to the state. At the same time, relational internationalists manage to ground, each to a different degree, a connection between politics and private law relations, between private and public law, and between freedom and social responsibility. Ultimately these analytical moves enabled by the relational analysis of the individual and liberty would make it possible to frame the legitimacy question in Cavers' terms of whether

[11] Rückert, *Idealismus* (n. 5) 375.

[12] Antoine Pillet, 'Essai d'un système general de solution des conflicts de lois' (1984) 21 Journal de droit international privé et de la jurisprudence comparée 417 and 21 Journal de droit international privé et de la jurisprudence comparée 711, 418, n. 1 (hereafter Pillet, "Essai").

or not the individual should be granted the protection of the law she claims in light of the variety of "differentiating factors," which form the background for parties' entitlements to each other, as well as the complex elements of the parties' interactions with each other.[13] This perspective, which could be called "social legitimacy" (by distinction to the negative rights-political legitimacy outlined by Brilmayer) manages to link the individual to the other party(ies) of the relationship, as well as to the communities their relationships are embedded in.[14]

B. Legitimate Authority—An Interstate Framework of Justification

While much of Pillet's general philosophy of PrIL has already been outlined in the first chapter of the book, this chapter focuses in particular on Pillet's proposition that PrIL must develop a theory and methodology according to which the application of a particular law is justified in an interstate relationship.[15] Pillet saw himself as putting forth "first order principles" or "first order truths"[16] that could ground PrIL's legitimacy universally within a framework of "independent states."[17] This way of framing his theory and the goal of PrIL pushes him in two directions, one state-centered and the other internationalist, which often produces a real tension.

The state-centered element made Pillet believe that the entire analysis of PrIL must be focused on the law. This makes him argue that the principle "least admissible" in PrIL is the one granting any scope to "the will" or "the intentions" of the parties.[18] It is significant that the only theory he identifies, and refutes, as being grounded in the will or the intentions of the parties is the theory "allowing individuals to choose the law which governs them [which] is to allow them to place themselves above the law, and to infringe the law and destroy its effect."[19] This is contrary to Pillet's own "idea of law," which is to "command or protect, depending on the case, in brief to impose itself upon the will of individuals because of a social interest."[20] According to Pillet all laws—including private laws—impose "sacrifices which the state representing the society asks of individuals, in the interest of the community."[21] "It is inadmissible, impossible to conceive that once we established them [the individual sacrifices made in the name of the society] we allow individuals to derogate from them."[22]

It is important to note that Pillet did not associate Savigny with the theory of "free choice." Rather, his understanding of Savigny's theory, as well as the passages in which he tries to distinguish his theory from that of Savigny, are particularly illuminating for what he sees the state-centered perspective as reacting against. Pillet criticized Savigny primarily for the flexibility of his theory, for not being abstract and universal enough, and not grounded in any single underlying principle.[23]

[13] For an initial account of this perspective in Cavers's theory, see Chapter 5.

[14] For such an account, see Rawi Abdelal and John Ruggie, 'Principles of Embedded Liberalism: Social Legitimacy and Global Capitalism' in David Moss and John Cistermino (eds.), *New Perspectives on Regulation* (Tobin Project 2009) 151.

[15] See Pillet, "Essaie" (n. 12). [16] Ibid., at 417. [17] Ibid., at 418, n. 1.

[18] Pillet, "Essai" (n. 12) 717 and n. 2. [19] Ibid., 718. [20] Ibid., 717.

[21] Ibid., 718. [22] Ibid. [23] Ibid., 419, 422–3, and n. 1.

In reference to Savigny's methodology, Pillet noted "attempting to search for conflict of laws solutions in the nature of things is a just idea, but too imprecise to serve as the principle for a doctrine."[24] Pillet therefore identified the very flexible and eclectic analysis of "the nature of … " methodology, not his focus on the jural relation, as the trademark of Savigny's theory. Interestingly, while Savigny's reviewer Gutzwiller charged many PrIL scholars with misunderstanding Savigny's methodology of centering a legal relation based on its nature as being abstract and dogmatic,[25] Pillet fully understood its non-dogmatic character and refuted it precisely for its flexibility.

In this light, Pillet believed that he had managed to incorporate two elements of Savigny's methodology, while avoiding its inherent flexibility. He thought that he was finally able to provide a solid analytical background for Savigny's postulate of the juridical community of nations by focusing on universal principles of interstate relationships, and that he had adopted Savigny's "nature of … " methodology, while changing its object and its looseness.

Therefore, Pillet argued that "the only nature of things that one must consider is the nature of the law (la loi) itself."[26] To search for the nature of law means to maintain the state-centered focus[27] because Pillet insisted repeatedly that law is "an instrument of authority" of a particular sovereign over its subjects.[28] At the same time, Pillet believed that PrIL must legitimize itself by a universal theory and methodology. Therefore, the search for the "nature" of law was to be made in a very particular way, in order to incorporate both a state-centered and a universalist perspective.

Allegedly, the need for universal legitimacy implies that:

> it is of sound method to think of the notion of law in its highest generality, by eliminating all contingent and accidental elements, where observation can only lead to a relative and limited truth, and which are therefore incapable of offering a truly general theory for the solution of conflict of laws.[29]

In other words, one must think of the "nature of law" at its most abstract, as the order of "a sovereign over its subjects, with no specificity to its content or object."[30] When Pillet contrasted his theory with Savigny's, he argued that his own "nature of … " methodology is able to ensure precise results because law is imagined:

> [I]n its most abstract sense, independent of its form, the persons to whom it applies and even independent of the modalities that the caprice of the legislator might give it. I only see in the law the instrument used by the legislator to exercise its authority over the people, and thus

[24] Ibid. [25] See Chapter 3. [26] See Pillet, "Essaie" (n. 12) 727.

[27] Ibid., 419, 422–3, and n. 1:

> This fault [of not focusing of the highest level of generality and abstractness] is precisely the reason why it is impossible for us to accept the system proposed by Savigny. Attempting to search for a conflict of laws solution in the nature of things is a just idea, but too imprecise, in order to serve as the principle for a doctrine. Furthermore, we notice that in Savigny's analysis to determine the seat of different legal relations, Savigny himself extracts from the most diverse areas his reasons for the decision of the seat, from the intention of the parties, to the location of an object, or this or other circumstance to which he ascribes arbitrarily a preponderant influence.

[28] Ibid., 423. [29] Ibid., 422. [30] Ibid., 423.

we have reached a notion of the law that is common to all societies, all states, a truly international notion of law.[31]

In order to ensure universal legitimacy for PrIL, Pillet believed it necessary to refer to the "indispensable character," the universal "nature, essence of law."[32] The only two such universally indispensable elements of an abstract notion of law understood as "an instrument of authority" are for Pillet "continuity and generality."[33] The former allegedly implies extraterritoriality, and the latter, territoriality.[34]

One must therefore search for a general principle that determines under which circumstances one or the other element must be sacrificed in order to reach uniform application of laws among states.[35] This determination cannot depend on "the will or the fantasy of the one determining the resolution of the conflict" or on "comity among states."[36] Rather, the principle is extracted, again, from the universal goal of law, as Pillet saw it:

the law is always the means employed by the legislator to achieve a well determined social goal. This is the same everywhere. Whether it regards public or private law, civil or criminal law, one of the fundamental laws of the state or a law of procedure, it is still true that the law is simply an instrument established in order to achieve a social goal.[37]

This realization however does not inject much nuance because "all laws everywhere have the same social goals."[38] Pillet prided himself that through this "analogy" or universality of social goals, he was able to "achieve the community of law amongst nations, as Savigny postulated it."[39]

The simplicity of the "social purpose" analysis, which is meant to be abstract and universal, becomes obvious when Pillet concludes that there are only two such legal purposes in the law: to protect individual interests and community, or social interests.[40] Laws protecting individual interests must be extraterritorial, while those protecting social interests must be territorial.[41] In Pillet's theory, an a priori, allegedly commonsensical analysis, as opposed to a thorough comparative or normative analysis would elucidate which category of laws serves to protect individual or community interests.[42]

At this culmination of his theory, Pillet felt the need to situate one last time his own theory within the rest of PrIL scholarship. In a quite telling passage, Pillet argued that:

[31] Ibid., 724. [32] Ibid., 423. [33] Ibid., 423.

[34] Ibid., 426. Unlike the statutists, Pillet argues that all laws, according to the essence of public power exercised over the subjects, are both territorial and extraterritorial, at 427. But PrIL is an "imperfect science," at 434; a "science of sacrifice" at 712, which makes it impossible for both characters to be maintained. Therefore, states must "sacrifice a certain element of laws' effectiveness in order to maintain ... international recognition which only such sacrifice can guarantee," at 712.

[35] Ibid., 712.

[36] Ibid., 713. At note 1, Pillet associated the comity doctrine with the nationalist perspective.

[37] Ibid., 725. [38] Ibid., 713. [39] Ibid., 728 and n. 1. [40] Ibid., 739.

[41] Ibid.

[42] Ibid., 740 (Pillet argued that such an analysis is possible, even if he acknowledged that the distinction is quite loose).

> if in our studies we have used a method so close to Savigny's [the nature of … method], in the result, we have reached conclusions very similar to the Italian school instead. Like Mancini and his disciples we have separated two classes of laws, those that serve individual interests, and those that serve social interests.[43]

In other words, Pillet quite accurately did not attribute the strict individual/social analytical duality to Savigny, but rather to the Italian school, and it was very likely the PublIL association of the Italian school that made him feel flattered at the thought of the possible analogies, since he also saw himself as part of the PublIL school of thought.[44] Even in this context, however, he was careful to point out that while he adopted the individual/community analytical duality, he did not accept any of the individual-centered connotations of the Italian school.

First, "if I [Pillet] accord the laws concerning individual interests an international effect, it is not because of an otherwise justifiable respect for the right of human personality […] It is from the law itself, the nature and its scope that we extract, necessarily its extraterritoriality."[45] Secondly, "Mancini takes as a point of departure nationality understood as a purely natural fact and pretends to derive from this purely philosophical notion practical consequences for PrIL, which is inadmissible. We take as a point of departure the state as it is in fact, its sovereignty, its duties … ."[46] Lastly, "my laws of social guarantee do not coincide with the laws of public policy of the Italian school, they go beyond them."[47]

Here Pillet came full circle. While he grounded his repetitive dismissal of any individual-centered premises and his state-centered ideology on the social purposes of law, his quest for universal and abstract premises made him construct a formalist duality between the individual and her social environment. This search pushed Pillet to overtly dismiss any quest for equity.[48] By separating laws into those fostering the interests of the individuals and those fostering the interests of a social group, he dismissed an important overlap and cross-referencing between the two, which makes him less attuned to the distributive background informing private law rules. Rather than fostering and enabling a social analysis and implications of PrIL rules as he initially suggested, Pillet managed to obscure it. Furthermore, while his theory at first sight aims at avoiding the understanding of the individual as an atomistic unit dissociated from the social context, his theory ends up creating precisely a separation of the individual from the social context. Lastly, by explicitly denying any voice to the litigating parties to express, contest, and balance each other's expectations, Pillet's state-centered theory also depletes the potential of the adversarial system and excludes any virtue in a pragmatic and policy oriented judgment of the judiciary.

The particular state-centered and the universal dimensions of Pillet's theory converge in the proposition that PrIL legitimizes itself relative to states as understood collectively, precisely through its alleged neutrality, abstractness, and policy-free substratum. This way of justifying the legitimacy of PrIL rules makes it possible to obscure any form of interpersonal justice that is not incorporated in the abstract

[43] Ibid., 745. [44] Ibid., 745. [45] Ibid., 745. [46] Ibid., 746.
[47] Ibid., 746. [48] Ibid., 714.

notion of the law identified by Pillet. Through Pillet's imagery that "the litigating parties disappear for a while"[49] it is possible both to exclude their voice and to avoid any responsibilization of individuals in their transnational legal relations.

C. Brilmayer's "Negative Rights" Theory as a Reaction to the Interest Analysis Methodology

Pillet himself described his theory as a rather formalist and very abstract state-centered internationalist perspective. The formalist aspects were a result of the particular way in which Pillet framed both the internationalist and the state-centered dimensions. In a different combination, a state-centered theory could look fundamentally different. Indeed, in the American realist school, and in particular in Brainerd Currie's theory, the state-centered dimension may present similarities to,[50] but also depart fundamentally from Pillet's. Like Pillet, Currie also centered the analysis on what he described as the social function of law, whether private or public.[51] Similar to Pillet, he argued that any method of determining the applicable law should be centered on an analysis of the social scope of law. Some of Currie's critics could arguably conclude that his analysis of the social scope is not much more sophisticated than Pillet's. The few nuances that Currie added to the analysis result primarily from his focus on the social scope of individual legal provisions, rather than whole categories of private law, and from the fact that Currie openly disavowed any a priori quest for uniformity. I have argued in the previous chapter, primarily through unearthing his correspondence with David Cavers, that Currie's apparent dismissal of universalist and individual-centered considerations was based mostly on pragmatic, rather than normative, considerations. I have conceded, however, as did Cavers, that Currie's theory was bound to be and was interpreted as primarily state-centered. It was this interpretation of his theory that generated much of the criticism discussed in the previous chapter.

In the context of this chapter, one critique made by Lea Brilmayer in 1989 is of particular importance. In *Rights, Fairness and Choice of Law* Brilmayer charges state-centered theories, in particular Currie's theory, for framing the question of legitimate authority as an interstate matter.[52] She argues that the legitimacy of imposing a particular law should be referable to the state-individual relationship.[53] She further argues that PrIL theory had, up to that point, been oblivious to "what the best possible rights-based theory might have to offer," namely, a framework of

[49] Antoine Pillet, 'Droit international privé consideré dans ses rapports avec le droit international public' Annales de l'enseignement superior de Grenoble (F. Allier Pere and Fils 1892) 335.

[50] Ralf Michaels, 'Economics of Law as Choice of Law' (2008) 71 Law and Contemporary Problems 73, 84, n. 64.

[51] For an initial outline of Currie's theory, see Chapter 5.

[52] See Brilmayer, "Rights" (n. 1).

[53] Even though she charges primarily Currie's theory because of its utilitarian foundation (as opposed to individual-rights based), she also rightly identifies Beale's theory as partly state-centered, as I have described it in the previous chapter. See Brilmayer, "Rights" (n. 1) 1292.

"negative rights" or "side constraints" of state authority vis-à-vis individuals.[54] Thus, Brilmayer distinguishes this "model of political rights in the inter-state setting" both from Beale's and from the realists or what she calls the "policy theorists."[55]

To Brilmayer, the vested rights theory discussed at greater length in the previous chapter dealt with "positive rights because the state has an affirmative obligation to act so as to help people realize their value,"[56] while her theory deals with rights "to be left alone" by the state, "not swords, but shields" "founded on principles of political fairness that specify the preconditions for the exercise of legitimate state coercion."[57] The distinction between her theory and Currie's or Cook's appears even stronger once Brilmayer argues that those theorists had completely lost sight of individuals and their "pre-existing rights,"[58] and focused exclusively on overall social utility.[59] Brilmayer is careful to add that Currie's utilitarian model is not only problematic for its focus on social values and not individuals' rights—although that was certainly an important aspect that Brilmayer was reacting against—but also because of its perceived particularistic, rather than universalist, focus. "Under a universalistic consequentialist theory, a state might adopt that substantive policy which it thinks is best for the world at large. This is not, however, what the modern choice of law theorists had in mind."[60]

Brilmayer criticized the state-centered theories on several grounds, four of which bring to light important considerations illuminating both her own theory and that of the individual-centered internationalist authors described in the next section. First, Brilmayer criticizes utilitarian theory for focusing on "the general social good, rather than the claims of the instant parties to fair treatment."[61] Second, she criticizes what "is fairly standard in interest analysis opinions and literature to allude to the needs of local nonparties whose economic interests will be affected by the decision."[62] Third, she argues that interest analysis "demonstrates a lack of concern with what the parties might deserve as a result of their past action."[63] Lastly, she decries interest analysis's indifference to "actuarial balance"[64] or "corrective justice,"[65] since in her view "choice of law seems an unpromising area of law in which to effect wealth redistribution."[66] In light of these considerations, she believes the interest

[54] Ibid., 1279. [55] Ibid., 1280. [56] Ibid., 1280, n. 11. [57] Ibid., 1280.
[58] Ibid., 1284. [59] Ibid., 1283–5. [60] Ibid., 1288. [61] Ibid., 1287.
[62] Ibid., 1289. [63] Ibid., 1289.

[64] Ibid., 1311. See also 1311–12: "to implement the notion of actuarial fairness, one might want to follow a general principle of mutuality. Mutuality would require that the substantive rule not be applied to an individual's detriment unless the individual would be eligible to receive the benefits if the tables were turned."

[65] Ibid., 1310.

[66] Ibid., 1311:

> In the interstate arena, a state's authority is at its most tenuous. However, if choice of law rules are to have redistributive consequences, at least they are better directed against insiders than outsiders. This is the effect of the domiciliary principles, because the state is granted the right to coerce its own people or business entities by imposing burdens upon them. Ideally, a choice of law rule would be actuarially balanced; however, a state's choice to redistribute wealth away from its own people is not automatically illegitimate. Such a law is unnecessarily generous, but so long as the burdens are self-imposed, the state may legitimately choose to

analysis perspective allows the state to treat the individual "merely as a means to an end."[67]

In contrast, an individual-centered theory, in Brilmayer's view, should be centered on "the political relationship between the state and the individual,"[68] namely, "on one's right to resist the imposition of a personal burden for the common good."[69] Based on this political relationship between the individual and the state, it appears wrong that "the claims of one of the parties are being sacrificed to further the general good of a community of which he or she may not even be a part."[70] Because the rights that Brilmayer is referencing are "negative rights instead of positive rights, and they are vertical rights that the individual possesses against the state directly, rather than horizontal rights against the other party to the litigation," the concern is with "political legitimacy" or "political rights,"[71] which underscore the fact that "persons have the right to be left alone" by the state.[72]

Brilmayer therefore concludes that "in a political rights analysis domiciliary connecting factors are of front-line importance, not secondary to territorial connecting factors. More important, under the political rights model, domiciliary factors function solely as a justification for the imposition of burdens; it is the party who is burdened who must have a local domicile."[73]

D. The Relational Internationalist Perspective

Lea Brilmayer's reaction to the state-centered analysis in PrIL is highly suggestive because her framing of the critique brings to light a series of assumptions at work in her own rights theory of legitimacy. Brilmayer pleads for PrIL theory and methodology to focus on individuals. She further assumes that PrIL must offer a framework of justification of the applicable law, and that this justification is owed to individuals. She argues rightfully that "the claims of the instant parties to fair treatment" matter.[74] Yet for Brilmayer this translates into equating "fair treatment" with "negative rights," and embracing a strong "philosophical distinction between deontological and consequentialist reasoning."[75]

Brilmayer's assumptions and distinctions lead her to frame her theory as one of political legitimacy, as a negative rights approach set within a relationship between the individual and the state. First, while she refers to the instant parties she does

> do so. The decision-maker imposing such a rule should be certain, however, that the costs are considered and found to be acceptable [...] Such a choice of law regime is not ideal. Adoption of such a regime should be a carefully considered choice, even if only local persons are disadvantaged.

[67] Ibid., 1291. [68] Ibid., 1292. [69] Ibid., 1292.

[70] Ibid., 1293. See also 1294: "one must show that the individual is properly subject to the state's authority before he or she can be called upon to contribute to the state's social good."

[71] Ibid., 1295. See also 1296: "one's choice of law rights, are, like personal jurisdiction rights, held against the state directly. They are not rights against the other party to the lawsuit (although, of course, they will affect one's legal claims)."

[72] Ibid., 1296. [73] Ibid., 1299. [74] Ibid., 1287. [75] Ibid., 1285.

not focus on their private law relationship but rather develops her own theory by reference to an isolated individual who has a right to be left alone by the state. The individual is separated from the collectivity and from the other party to the legal relation and exists in tension with state authority. Second, and consequently, she finds it plausible to distinguish between negative and positive rights, or to imply that a theory of legitimate authority can reference only negative rights. The state's "affirmative obligation to act so as to help people realize their value" is contrasted to, and separated from, the state's duty to "leave individuals alone." This, finally, creates a tension between corrective and distributive justice. Allegedly, the ideal choice of law rules would be "actuarially balanced" and centered on corrective justice.[76] "Actuarial balance is desirable, because choice of law seems an unpromising area of law in which to effect wealth redistribution. In the interstate arena, a state's authority is at its most tenuous."[77]

Brilmayer's theory of legitimacy is centered on the state-individual relationship in more ways than meets the eye. The relationship is important not only in the sense that the relevant inquiry is the legitimacy of imposing state authority (through its law) on individuals. The legitimacy theory is cast as a state-individual relationship also by suggesting that individuals' entitlements, benefits, burdens, and expectations can be thought of only by reference to a political relationship between the individual and the state. The following passage is particularly suggestive of how Brilmayer seeks to capture any benefits and entitlements within the state-individual relationship alone:

> In the usual domestic context, an individual would expect to experience both the benefits and the costs of a rule over the long run. Substantive rules, in other words, are actuarially fair, because an individual is eligible, in theory, to gain as much by application of the rule as he or she would lose if the tables were turned. To make a class of individuals ineligible to receive the benefits under a rule, while allowing the rule's burdens to be imposed upon them, results in an actuarial imbalance because over the long run the rule cannot be expected to work out evenly. The point is not merely a comparison of how insiders and outsiders are treated, although these are also problems of a distributional type. Rather, the problem is that of a single individual and his or her overall expectation of benefits and burdens.[78]

In Brilmayer's theory, then, the legitimacy of applying a certain law to an individual depends on the political relationship she has with a particular state. In contrast, the relational internationalist perspective highlighted in this section differs from Brilmayer's account of legitimacy in important ways.

First, the relational internationalist authors suggest that any kind of "connecting factor" or principle one might search for in order to determine the legitimacy of applying a particular law must focus on a legal relation rather than an isolated individual. The individual is viewed as inherently social and private law relationships are understood as important segments of people's social existence.[79]

[76] Ibid., 1277. [77] Ibid., 1311. [78] Ibid., 1309–10.
[79] Behrends, "Geschichte" (n. 7).

Second, because of the fundamentally relational account of the individual and individual freedom, the categories and dichotomies of negative/positive rights, corrective/distributive justice, and private/public are muddled and lose their a priori validity, although each scholar considers their importance to various degrees. PrIL is analyzed by analogy to and through the prism of private law (rather than PublIL or constitutional law) because the analysis is focused on the legal relations that individuals purposefully develop with each other. As opposed to being perceived or analyzed in a vacuum of isolated freedom or liberty, these relationships are placed in a political and social context.

To flesh out the perspective on legitimate authority which results from taking the legal relation—as opposed to an isolated individual or the state—as the analytical point of departure the next section outlines the general theoretical premises of the relational internationalist theorists generally. Just as Pillet and Brilmayer's perspectives on legitimate authority can be best understood once the background theoretical premises and dichotomies are revealed, so too the relational internationalist perspective can be best explained once we understand the way in which these authors described the social nature of the individual and of freedom; the extent to which they anchored private law relationships within a political context; how they conceptualize the relationship between private and public law and the way and extent to which they cross-reference freedom and social responsibility.

Once these theoretical premises are revealed, the final section of this chapter shows how Jitta and Savigny reasoned on the legitimacy of imposing a particular law in cases in which particular national laws impose limitations on contractual capacity for particular classes of individuals. Since these were also the paradigmatic cases discussed by American realist scholars, the section compares the reasoning of the relational internationalist scholars and that of the American realist scholars to underscore their shared pragmatism, as well as the distinction between a relational perspective and a state-centered perspective on legitimacy.

1. The social nature of the individual and of freedom

In the opening essay to the *Historical Legal Science Review*, which he founded together with Karl Friedrich Eichhorn, Savigny wrote that according to the historical school he embraced:

> There is no complete (vollkommen) individual and isolated human existence: rather, what can be perceived as atomistic, is, viewed from another angle, part of a larger whole. Therefore, every individual is at the same time part of a family, a people, a state: each historical period of a people is the continuation and development of all previous historical periods; any other analytical perspective is therefore one-sided, and when it is followed, it is false and pernicious.[80]

[80] Friedrich Karl von Savigny, 'Über den Zweck dieser Zeitschrift' (1815) 1 Zeitschrift für geschichtliche Rechtswissenschaft 1, 3 (Savigny contrasted the historical perspective with the historical perspective under which he included both rationalism and natural law theories) (hereafter Savigny, "Über den Zweck").

A theory that imagines a tension and "a complete separation between the individual and the state," does not therefore seem right to Savigny.[81] For Savigny, "the seeds of the state are in the families and the immediate constituents of the state are the families, not the individuals."[82] The social nature of individuals is reflected and embraced within the state and beyond. Savigny rejected the rational, individualistic notion of the law, the individual, and the state in a telling paragraph:

> Many start from the term of wrong to understand what right might be. Wrong appears to them the disturbance of freedom through another one's freedom, and this disturbance is believed to prevent individual developments and therefore must be eliminated. The elimination of this evil is believed to be achieved through law. The same is achieved, according to some, through a sensible convention, according to which each sacrifices a portion of her freedom to ensure the freedom of others ... The State appears to them as a mechanism of self-defense, which under conditions of a more equitable way of life, could disappear, instead of, as I believe, become even more glorious and powerful.[83]

Through an illuminating interpretation of Savigny's correspondence with friends and colleagues on various philosophical themes—particularly on human nature—Heinrich Jakobs argued that one could trace the roots of the historical school of law to Savigny's rejection of idealistic philosophy, especially his rejection of Kant's image of the rational agent.[84] In a 1799 letter between Savigny and F.C. Creuzer on Kantian philosophy—helpfully analyzed by Jakobs at length—Savigny considers most problematic Kant's description of human nature as a tension between "two opposing hostile elements" namely rationality on the one hand, and feeling and impulse on the other.[85] Savigny decries philosophy's attempt to construct people, through various abstractions, as "the most glorious snowmen"[86] devoid of any social experience, feelings, historical position etc.

Instead, Savigny finds a more suitable anchor point for "practical philosophy" in poetry.[87] Poetry, according to Savigny, shares philosophy's goal to emphasize and distinguish good and bad, moral and immoral character and action. Yet unlike philosophy, with its dogmatism and abstractions, poetry brings "the truth in us to life."[88] Savigny's alternative to philosophy—the historical school of law—was to borrow from poetry its focus on the particular, on details, and on life experience but it would

[81] Ibid., 5.

[82] See Friedrich Karl von Savigny, *System des heutigen Römischen Rechts*, vol. 1 (Bei Deit & Comp. 1840) 344 (hereafter Savigny, *System 1*). For an illuminating account of the role of the family in the structure of the Roman society and in private law, see Okko Behrends, 'Das Sozialrecht. Sein Wert und seine Funktion in historischer Perspektive' in Okko Behrends and Eva Schumann (eds.), *Gesetzgebung, Menschenbild und Sozialmodell im Familien- und Sozialrecht*, Neue Abhandlungen der Akademie der Wissenschaft zu Gottingen, Bd 3 (De Gruyter 2008) (hereafter Behrends, "Das Sozialrecht").

[83] Savigny, *System 1* (n. 82) 332–3. See also Rückert, *Idealismus* (n. 5) 365 (Rückert sees in this passage a glimpse of Savigny's general theory of the state, people and truth, none of which are linked to a theory of individual will. He believes these passages, among others, outline Savigny's absolute "rejection of Kant's theory"). For an account of Savigny's "positive anthropology" see Behrends, "Geschichte" (n. 7) 268.

[84] Horst Heinrich Jakobs, 'Der Ursprung der historischen Rechtswissenschaft in der Abwendung Savignys von der idealistischen Philosophie' (1989) 57 Tijdschrift voor Rechtsgeschiedeniss 241.

[85] Ibid., 253. [86] Ibid., 262. [87] Ibid., 263. [88] Ibid., 264.

borrow from philosophy its focus on "understanding" and distilling higher principles.[89] Those higher principles however were to be distilled after a detailed analysis of the individual case and positive law as opposed to natural law; of individual legal relations rather than abstract social life, and of individual states, histories, and cultural practices rather than humanity as a whole.[90] For Savigny it was possible to simultaneously think of the individual as a particular subject placed in a particular historical context, entering into particular relationships with other individuals and to draw general higher principles about his legal rights and obligations. But these rights and obligations were anchored in a particular national and historical context, rather than in "reason" and the abstractions of idealistic philosophy.

Once the individual was anchored in a particular social national and historical context it seemed plausible to argue that "he who mistakenly believes he is exercising free will (Willkuer), where only a higher communal freedom is possible, renounces his most noble claims."[91] For the social individual, freedom is experienced not by dissociation from the relationships with others but through these relationships.[92] Rückert believed Savigny was thus offering "a different way of talking about freedom" which differs strongly from the Kantian.[93] Rückert showed that Savigny's separation between law and morality does not derive from the universalization "of a subjective rational-autonomous premise" and from the "postulate of freedom according to general laws."[94] Rather, both law and morality are anchored not in individual freedom but in the "Christian way of life."[95] Law serves morality by "recognizing the equal moral worth and freedom of individuals"[96] where the "moral determination of human nature" rests in "the Christian way of life."[97]

It was therefore wrong to assume an isolated, atomistic image of the individual. But it was equally wrong to image the individual as subsumed under the state. Savigny repeatedly warned of "despotism," the loss of "spiritual freedom" through domination and suppression.[98] Therefore, one had to avoid imagining the state as a "brotherhood," "a fraternity" or the individual as an inseparable member of a larger whole,[99] not because Savigny wanted to disallow solidarity with others, but

[89] Ibid., 266. [90] Ibid., 264–6. [91] Savigny, "Über den Zweck" (n. 80) 4.

[92] See Rückert, *Idealismus* (n. 5) 368. [93] Ibid., 368–9. [94] Ibid., 365.

[95] Ibid., 365–6. [96] Savigny, *System 1* (n. 82) 55.

[97] Ibid., 53, 54. For a discussion of the way in which Savigny's religious outlook was not bound to the Christian period, see Behrends, "Geschichte" (n. 7) 263–4. For an account of the image of the individual's social responsibility under the Christian way of life in Roman law and under the historical school of thought, see Behrends, "Das Sozialrecht" (n. 82) 34–5.

[98] Savigny, *System 1* (n. 82), *Vorrede*, XI.

[99] Behrends, "Das Sozialrecht" (n. 82) 21 citing Otto Bähr, *Der Rechtsstaat: eine publizistische Skizze* (Scientia, 1961, reprint of 1861) 19:

> I consider it an incomplete account to find the contrast to private law in state law. In relationship to private law, that is the law, which concerns the individual as such, there is a larger legal field in which the person is an organic member of a larger whole, so that rights and obligations arise therefrom. We can call this higher term under which the individual is organically classified, and from which he acquires a legal existence, cooperatives. The most important such cooperative is the state.

Behrends considered Bähr's attributing to Savigny a clear separation between public and private law because he did not articulate an account of states as cooperatives "utterly unfounded," at 20. He also

because this would allow for and indeed foster arbitrary power of the ruler over the people.[100] It was therefore not the social responsibilization of the individual that had to be avoided, but the imposition of "the individual view and arbitrary will" of the ruler over the people, in the name of "the social body."[101]

Savigny, as well as Story and Jitta for that matter, shared with Brilmayer the fear that the state might treat the individual merely as a means to an end. Certainly Pillet's proposition that the "litigating parties disappear for a while" while states determine the proper distribution of authority amongst themselves was unacceptable. But this did not mean that the individual in isolation would become the central figure of law in general and PrIL in particular.

The proposition that the law of domicile of one individual should apply to govern all PrIL matters was therefore equally unacceptable.[102] Savigny indeed thought, like Brilmayer, that domicile "connects a person with a particular territory."[103] But unlike Brilmayer, he was keen to observe that "legal relations concern not a single person, but several."[104] "In such cases, this principle leaves us quite helpless, since we cannot find out from it which of the persons affected by the legal relation shall fix by his domicile the local law to be applied."[105] Savigny repeatedly rejected localizing a relationship by reference to only one of the parties in the relationship, in part because this would create all sorts of interpersonal inequities but also because choosing one individual over another as the benchmark for localization would inevitably be arbitrary and unprincipled.

For example, once Savigny derives the applicable law for legal claims to immoveable property from voluntary submission and the nature of the relevant legal rules, he adds the following consideration:

> This preference is also supported by another reason. Several persons may be concerned in the same right to a particular thing, of whom each may have a different domicile. If then, the law of the domicile is to regulate as to real things, it would remain doubtful in such a case which domicile should determine.[106]

In reaction to theories pleading for the application of the law of the person for claims to real estate, Savigny writes:

> But what person is thereby meant? Without doubt, the person interested in the legal relation to this thing. But this is a very ambiguous notion; and thereby the whole doctrine, even if it were admitted, becomes extremely indeterminate and uncertain. By the party interested we

explains that this would have been "under the circumstances of the modern state, encouraged by the French revolution, a fatal general claim," at 21).

[100] For a great discussion of the way in which Savigny's theory is compatible with the social state by preserving both duties of solidarity as well as individual self-responsibility, see Behrends, "Das Sozialstaat" (n. 82) 19–27 and 20–1 (explaining how Bähr hastily dismissed Savigny's private law/public law duality and thereby imagined the state as "a social body" which would in turn "enable despotic power").

[101] Savigny, *System 1* (n. 82) 57.

[102] Friedrich Karl von Savigny, *Private International Law and the Retrospective Operation of Statutes: A Treatise on the Conflict of Laws and the Limits of their Operation in Respect of Place and Time* (William Guthrie tr., T&T Clark 1880) 143, n. g. (hereafter Savigny, *Private International Law*).

[103] Ibid., 143. [104] Ibid. [105] Ibid. [106] Ibid., 178.

may understand the owner; but then it remains doubtful whether, in a transference of property, the old or the new owner is meant; so, too in a dispute as to property, which of the two competing parties, each of whom claims for himself the property. But we may also entirely give up thinking of the owner, and take the possessor as the party interested, by which, certainly, the matter is made simpler and easier. Besides property, various other real rights come under consideration; and each of these, when it exists or is even asserted, leads back to a new person interested in the thing.[107]

Unlike both Currie and Brilmayer, Savigny was not concerned with a theory of political legitimacy and none of what he says could be used to settle the controversy between Currie and Brilmayer. The application of the law of domicile of one party was unfair not because it would either unduly benefit or unduly burden him/her. It was unfair because it didn't simultaneously take account of all the other parties to the legal relation. It would simply arbitrarily choose one individual over another as the benchmark for answering the question of legitimate authority.

Shifting the analysis of legitimate authority from one individual to a relationship would not simplify, but often complicate the matters further because "legal relations are of such diverse nature, that they can hardly be reduced under a common absolute rule as to their seat."[108] But searching for "the essence and requirements of each legal relation" appeared more rewarding for Savigny precisely because he perceived it as less abstract and arbitrary than the a priori choice of one individual as the subject of analysis.[109]

2. Politics and private law relations

Emphasizing the social nature of individuals and of freedom makes it possible to connect private law relations with politics. This is most obvious in Jitta's theory, but as Okko Behrends has shown, it is also true of Savigny's theory.

Savigny's PrIL theory is usually described as apolitical and, in fact, as a deliberate effort to depoliticize the field.[110] If we equate politics with distributive justice, we could comfortably conclude that Savigny did not have in view a transnational scheme of distributive justice. And of course his localization of legal relations could often be criticized, as it was by Jitta, for failing to engage with or underscore the contentious policy elements of the "nature of legal relations."[111] Nevertheless, Behrends argued that it is a misreading of Savigny to suggest that he meant to discourage political engagement, or that his analysis of legal relations was meant to encourage a dogmatic perspective, rather than a more pragmatic perspective grounded in real life.[112]

[107] Ibid., 179–80. [108] Ibid., 141. [109] Ibid., 145.

[110] See, for example, Horatia Muir Watt, 'Private International Law Beyond the Schism' (2011) 2 Transnat'l L Theory 347.

[111] For an account of the different ways in which Jitta conceptualizes the legal relation as an analytical element, as opposed to Savigny, see Chapter 6.

[112] See for example, Behrends, "Geschichte" (n. 7) 279: "It always leads to great mistakes, when one loses sight of the fact that Savigny's legal terms exposition is not formalistic, classificatory, which is made prior to any real experience, but rather empirically grounded and based on the observation of real life phenomena." For a very interesting account of how Savigny tried to influence nineteenth-century agrarian reform in Germany through legal reform and through resurfacing Roman law concepts, see

Indeed Savigny criticized repeatedly Kant's formalism[113] and pleaded on various occasions for the revival of the political engagement of the Roman Republic, including in the area of private law.[114] Once we understand, as explained above, that the historical school of law was a reaction to the abstract, universal point of view of idealistic philosophy, we realize that the politics of a particular historical period and location mattered to Savigny. So too did political engagement of the people. For example, he decried what he perceived to be the citizenry's indifference to the legal institution of property, as well as its perception as "merely technical" by the jurists of his time. He argued that these attitudes are "a sign of a public state of affairs, which lacks the political spirit of legal development; when this spirit is present these relationships [of property] appear as everything but irrelevant."[115] Furthermore, the notion of the "Volk" as the source of the "people's spirit" was used to counter contractual theories of the state as well as despotic regimes.[116]

Savigny in fact recognized and emphasized the need for political engagement required for legal reform[117] and embraced "higher political goals."[118] With respect to proposals for the legalization of consensual divorce, Savigny argued that these proposals had not properly engaged with all the moral dimensions of laws with regard to marriage, and that it is based on a "false presupposition that law has no other purpose but to ensure the highest individual freedom" and that there are no policy principles involved in a marital relationship.[119] With respect to legislative proposals relating to mortgages, Savigny argued that the proposals were "mechanical"[120] and that they were based on simplistic a priori assumptions that mortgage law can be built based on universal formal principles (such as publicity and specialty), which can easily be implemented in any country with no regard to the political context.[121] He unequivocally states: "this merely formal perspective on legislating I consider pernicious."[122]

Therefore Rückert's and Behrends' reading of Savigny's general theory as being grounded in a constant back and forth between the individual and the social, the technical and the sociological, and the abstract and the empirical, seems persuasive and very instructive for one's understanding of Savigny's PrIL theory. Behrends argues that this duality is most evident in Savigny's distinction between the legal relation and the legal institute.[123] The latter represents the "legal elements which grant legal structure" to the legal relation, while the former represents the empirical,

James Q. Whitman, *The Legacy of Roman Law in the German Romantic Era* (Princeton University Press 2014).

[113] Behrends, "Geschichte" (n. 7) 261, n. 6, 267, n. 17, 270, n. 26, 298–9 (referencing how the "Vertrauensprinzip" is fully integrated in Savigny's theory, but is explicitly excluded in Kant's).

[114] Ibid., 280. See Friedrich Karl von Savigny, *Vom Beruf unserer Zeit für Gesetzgebung und Rechtswissenschaft* (Mohr & Zimmer 1814) 31, 32 (hereafter Savigny, *Vom Beruf*) (pleading for the revival from the Roman Republic of the "lively, vivid political spirit").

[115] Ibid., 48. [116] Behrends, "Geschichte" (n. 7) 280.

[117] Savigny, *Vom Beruf* (n. 114) 16. [118] Ibid.

[119] Friedrich Karl von Savigny, 'Stimmen für und wider neue Gesetzbücher' (1817) 3 Zeitschrift für geschichtliche Rechtswissenschaft 11, 25.

[120] Ibid., 26. [121] Ibid., 28. [122] Ibid.

[123] Behrends, "Geschichte" (n. 7) 287ff.

sociological part of private law, reflective of life experience.[124] In other words, injecting politics—albeit a certain kind of politics—meant focusing on legal relations and underscoring what human needs, desires, and purposes they are meant to serve. The political dimension was precisely the underscoring of private law relationships' social goals.[125] Property, for example, is not determined by the formalistic and abstract notion of individual will,[126] but is derived from the observation that the individual secures the means of his existence "through the extension of his power over its natural borders."[127] Therefore, as Behrends notes, legal relations, including property, are for Savigny "not abstract forms, but rather purposeful rules which must not be interpreted schematically, but according to life experience."[128]

By focusing the analysis in PrIL on legal relations, rather than legal institutes, Savigny believed he can better underscore how the application of one law over another is anchored to and therefore impacts the way in which we think of particular legal relations. When he argued against "the mistaken notion that the adoption or rejection of universal succession is something absolute and independent from which a further inference can be drawn to the rights of succession, and the local law that governs it" he was quick to explain that "the two are identical and universal succession is only the juridical form and the technical expression for that view of rights of succession which places their seat universally at the domicile, without distinguishing between the different portions of the estate."[129] In other words, "from the standpoint of the countries and the writers that deal with succession with reference to the estate as a whole, the *lex domicilii* is decisive, even for immoveables: from any other standpoint it is not."[130] This means then, that there is a cross-reference between the application of a particular law and a particular characterization of the nature of a legal relation. If one thinks of succession by reference to a—possibly presumed—intention of the decedent to have the law of his domicile decide the fate of his entire estate and if a law recognizes this inference either by considering individual autonomy important or because of practical considerations attempting to avoid parallel litigation and possibly conflicting decisions as to various parts of the estate, or on both considerations simultaneously, that legal system considers the application of the law of the domicile appropriate. The respective characterization of the nature of the legal relation of succession informs the application of a particular law, which in turn reinforces that particular characterization. The fact that different legal systems might perceive of the nature of legal relations differently and might be inclined to apply different laws was, according to Savigny "not disputed in any quarter."[131] Therefore, contrary to the contemporary interpretation given to Savigny's theory in PrIL scholarship, Savigny's goal was not to turn a blind eye to the implications the application of one law would have for our understanding of transnational legal relations, but precisely to underscore those implications. Shifting from the analysis of legal institutes/norms—"the technical expression"—to the analysis of legal relations was precisely the tool to make these implications more obvious since a particular

[124] Ibid., 288, 291. [125] Ibid., 291. [126] Ibid., 285.
[127] Savigny, *System 1* (n. 82) 344. [128] Behrends, "Geschichte" (n. 7) 291.
[129] Savigny, *Private International Law* (n. 102) 278. [130] Ibid. [131] Ibid.

nature of a legal relation is a particular "view of rights" which gets transferred to the transnational realm.[132]

In the historical development of PrIL, the shift of focus from the legal norm to the legal relation as an analytical tool for solving choice of law matters, was either hardly perceived as significant or interpreted as exclusively liberal and individualistic. Jitta, on the other hand, celebrated Savigny's analytical shift to legal relations as "the dawn of the modern development of Private International Law."[133] He believed that this enabled one to shift back and forth from social reality to legal determinations.[134] Private law relations could be explained, analyzed, and possibly assigned a policy substratum (see Jitta's notion of the "jus gentium privatum" described in the next chapter) by reference to interpersonal social reality and social needs, while at the same time being more minutely specified and contextualized within different national laws responding to different sociopolitical contexts.[135] In two volumes, Jitta broke down the vast area of legal obligations in categories and subcategories[136] and went back and forth between general observations about the needs of "international social order" and a comparative analysis of various legal provisions. An excerpt of his analysis of the social nature of the agency relationship provides some insight into his theory. In an initial account of the agency relationship Jitta argues that:

> We can explain, by an inter-human social duty, the obligations arising from the management of another's business, without recourse to a quasi-agency. The person who, without being thus obliged conducts the business of another, could be held to continue such business for a reasonable time because by involving himself, he prevented the intervention of another, and the spontaneous interruption of the managing of affairs could cause damages to the one for whom he is managing the affairs. In turn the one whose affairs were usefully managed has a duty to reimburse the agent; this is more than a duty of recognition, the social order is interested that the agent does not sustain the damage in this case; that would discourage those who are willing to serve. In case of full success we could even say that the one for whom the affairs were managed is unjustly enriched at the expense of the agent, if he is able to save the expenses that are attached to the management of the affairs, however it is not the measure of the enrichment which serves to establish the rights of the agent. The reasonable social order also requires that we do not encourage too much an interference with someone's affairs, which could be indiscrete.[137]

However, this general examination of the various interests and social expectations involved in the agency relationship is then followed by a comparative analysis of various laws, which then brings to the surface "a great number of very serious

[132] Ibid.

[133] D. Josephus Jitta, *The Renovation of International Law on the Basis of a Juridical Community of Mankind, Systematically Developed* (M. Nijhoff 1919) 90.

[134] Ibid., 94–9.

[135] Jitta applies this dual comparative legal/sociological perspective in his analysis of the area of obligations. See Josephus Jitta, *La Substance des Obligations dans le Droit International Privé*, 2 vols. (Belifante Freres, 1906, 1907).

[136] Ibid.

[137] Josephus Jitta, *La Substance des Obligations dans le Droit International Privé*, vol. 1 (Belifante Freres 1906) (hereafter Jitta, *Substance des Obligations* 1) 39.

nuances."[138] Once the different interests and perspectives are extracted both from a quasi-sociological examination of what Jitta refers to repeatedly as "the reasonable order of social life" and a comparative analysis, it appears impossible to Jitta to presume that the complexity of transnational relations could be reduced to an a priori choice of a national law. Rather, Jitta argued that one must "resort to the circumstances."[139] This initial step in Jitta's search for a methodology of PrIL differentiates his theory from Savigny's in various respects. Like Savigny, Jitta agreed that focusing on a legal relation as opposed to a legal norm encourages a more empirical, more sociological analysis of transnational life. He also agreed that the application of a particular law is a reflection and reinforcement of a particular way of perceiving the nature of legal relations. But while Savigny remarked almost on the side that the nature of a legal relation could be perceived differently by different legal systems, this realization took center stage in Jitta's account. Jitta's theory not only incorporated Savigny's method of focusing on the nature of a legal relation; it also focused on highlighting the social and political background of private law norms in different states. For Jitta, the method of focusing on the nature of a legal relation is precisely what revealed its politics, the different ways in which different political processes and circumstances generated different understandings of a legal relation.

What enabled Jitta to acknowledge this much richer political background was the comparative analysis. In his study of obligations for example, Jitta starts from a broad, quasi-sociological analysis of a legal relation to establish, wherever possible, an international substratum. In a second stage he focuses on a detailed comparative analysis sometimes to question what initially appears as a modicum of universal understanding, and sometimes to qualify a particular international substratum and show the high level of contestation among legal systems with respect to different aspects of legal relations. For example, he argued that while one could identify at a certain level of generality a duty of restitution for unjust enrichment, the conditions, limitations, and variations of this principle are so many that it is hardly possible to identify a common nature of restitution and unjust enrichment, even among the legal systems following the Roman law tradition.[140] Similarly, he argues that just as one "should not elevate to the level of a general common principle" the statement "nobody should enrich himself on the expense of another," one should also avoid positing as a principle of international common law that "the spontaneous management of another's business gives rise to mutual obligations."[141] There are, in other words, too many variations in the laws, making it impossible to assign any universal nature to those legal relations and therefore impossible a priori to deduce the applicable law. Therefore, one would need to go back and forth between the various interests and circumstances of the case and the "local sphere of social life" with which they are most closely connected in light of the policies identified in the various laws.[142]

[138] Ibid., 207. [139] Ibid., 211. [140] Ibid., 412–42. [141] Ibid., 442.
[142] This is the methodology most thoroughly exemplified in his volumes on the law of obligations.

3. Private and public law

Precisely because relational internationalists placed private law relationships within a national context, the relationship between private and public law is somewhat muddled in their analysis. Relational internationalists certainly relied on the private/public law distinction in order to center the analysis on interpersonal relationships, rather than interstate relationships.[143] But the extent to which this initial public/private divide spills into a substantive private/public divide varies.

At a certain level of generality, relational internationalists, precisely because they place private law largely with a particular national socioeconomic context—rather than natural law—acknowledge that this context informs the way in which each law apportions rights and obligations among individuals. This is precisely why their analysis starts from an attempt to localize a particular relationship in a particular community—or several—rather than to refer to some body of natural law or to individual autonomy. This is also why, as explained in the previous section, relational internationalists take for granted that a certain image of the individual, of the value of property, of the benefits of interpersonal trust etc. informs a certain structuring of correlative rights and obligations in private law. Savigny, for example, while distinguishing between private and public law as two "equally important parts of the law,"[144] wrote that the state and public law are "the highest level of legal development"[145] and that they have "the most determined influence on the development of private law."[146] Both private and public law join forces to fulfill the "general purpose of law" and are anchored in "the Christian way of life."[147]

Savigny argues that there is no need to distinguish a "separate" principle of national economy under the name of "the public good" since "to the extent the aim is to enlarge our dominion over our external nature (resources), this can only enlarge and improve the means through which man achieves moral freedom according to his nature. But a separate goal is not therein present."[148]

Rückert is therefore right to point out that Savigny's distinction between private and public law should not be analogized "to the natural law-liberal distinction between private and public law."[149] Rückert also tellingly points out that the difference between the natural law-liberal distinction and Savigny's is connected to Savigny's constant integration of the individual and freedom into a larger whole.[150] In Rückert's words, "in reality Savigny did not ignore the fact that any exercise of freedom requires an examination of the larger point of view, the 'Christian way of

143 Savigny, *System 1* (n. 82) § 9,15,52; Daniel Josephus Jitta, *La Méthode du droit international privé* (Belinfante 1890) 68 (hereafter Jitta, *La Méthode*).

144 Savigny, *System 1* (n. 82) § 9, 15, 52; Rückert, *Idealismus* (n. 5) 359.

145 Rückert, *Idealismus* (n. 5) 359.

146 Savigny, *System 1* (n. 82) 24.

147 Savigny, *System 1* (n. 82) 53–4:

> This general scope of all law is based on the Christian way of life; since Christianity is not only recognized by us as the rule of life, but it also transformed the world, so that all our thoughts as foreign and hostile as they might seem to it, are nevertheless disciplined and permeated by it.

See also Rückert, *Idealismus* (n. 5) 359.

148 Savigny, *System 1* (n. 82) 54.

149 Rückert, *Idealismus* (n. 5) 359.

150 Ibid.

life' in which law has its 'ultimate truth.' In this un-discharged voltage of his private law formulas, any abuse of freedom activates the 'general' element."[151] By emphasizing the cross-reference between private law norms and a particular national context relational internationalists did not mean to suggest that it was impossible to ever apply foreign law. Depending on the various contacts between a particular relationship and a jurisdiction, as well as the background assumptions and policies of the laws in conflict, it is, in principle, possible to consider a foreign law more suitably applied to a particular interpersonal relationship, even if one understands that each private law is placed within a national socioeconomic and political context.

At some point in their analysis however, relational internationalists concede a certain overwhelming of private law by public law values. As explained in the last chapter and the previous sections of this chapter, for Savigny public law values may overwhelm private law norms in a great number of cases, whenever the state wishes to protect a certain class of individuals and whenever the state pursues economic and social goals through private law norms. Two examples from his conflict of laws writing provide some insight into Savigny's distinction between private and public law within the realm of PrIL. After designating the law of the decedent's domicile as applicable for intestate succession matters irrespective of the nature of the property, he examines certain kinds of laws, which seem to disprove his general choice of law rule for succession:

> If a law attempts to promote the preservation of a well-to-do order of peasantry by so fixing the order to succession in peasant properties, but without any limitation of property, and in particular of the right to alienate, that the oldest (or even the youngest) son shall always succeed as sole heir, such a law is of the following nature. It excludes testamentary succession, the partition of the property, the succession of daughters so long as sons exist. It is thus, indeed, a law of succession; but it has a political purpose that lies beyond the domain of pure law, and it is therefore a statute of a coercitive and strictly positive character. Such a law is a real statute, and embraces all the peasant properties in the country ... It does not, therefore, like ordinary laws of succession, propose to assign to the estate of deceased inhabitants the most appropriate destiny; but it seeks to advance certain political ends by the way in which it disposes of a certain kind of immoveables ... All the cases here adduced, however different they may be in themselves, agree in this, that the laws as to the order to succession do not aim at devolving the estate of a deceased person in an appropriate direction, but are rather intended to regulate the destiny of certain special immoveables, or classes of immoveables.[152]

The "domain of pure law" therefore aims to "assign to the estate of deceased inhabitants the most appropriate destiny."[153] This is in turn informed by a variety of considerations, namely the probable intentions of the deceased, as well as a quasi-sociological examination of the hardship imposed on the decedent and the heirs depending on whether or not the estate is governed by the state of domicile or the various laws in different jurisdictions where the property is situated. As mentioned in the previous section, Savigny admits that different states might have different views on "the most appropriate destiny" of the estate but does not attribute these

[151] Ibid., 360. [152] Savigny, "Private International Law" (n. 102) 279–80.
[153] Ibid.

differences immediately to "political purposes." The differences could arise from a different understanding of the value of property for individuals, from a different understanding of the probable intentions of the decedent, from different safeguards put in place elsewhere in the law to minimize confusion about the fate of certain goods, which are part of the estate and so on. For Savigny this entire background context in which private law relationships are set still belongs to private law itself, unless it becomes clear that the state wishes to protect particular classes of property, of individuals, or effectuate a certain distribution of goods through the rules of succession.

Another example further explains the distinction and shows how far reaching the overwhelming of private by public law can be in Savigny's framework. Savigny not only agrees, as American legal realists emphasized repeatedly, that laws limiting the possibility of suretyship for women, those limiting the possibility of donations among spouses, or laws limiting the ability of minors or lunatics to enter into certain contracts pursue a political purpose of protecting a certain class of individuals. His explanation of guardianship is also illuminating:

> There is an essential distinction between guardianship and the legal institutions hitherto discussed. Only in the most ancient Roman law could it be regarded as an institution of purely private law. It has since gradually assumed the character which it presents in the modern common law of Germany, as well as in other legislations. Guardianship in the present day is the exercise of the protection, which the state is entitled and bound to give to the most numerous and most important class of those who need such care, pupils and minors. So viewed, guardianship belongs essentially to the public law, and only some special consequences fall within the province of private law. In conformity with this view, however, guardianship is not only subject to different rules in different countries, but even in one and the same country is susceptible of a less rigid treatment, on the part of the public authorities, than legal relations belonging to the strictly private law. These differences appear not merely in the rules of law themselves, but even in the selection of the local law by which these rules are fixed.[154]

Savigny distinguished between law in its "pure and direct" form and the instantiations of the legal element in an "indirect and mixed form."[155] The pure and direct form refers to the rules that clearly specify the conditions of individuals' rights and entitlements, whereas the "mixed" elements of law represent principles, policies, and values that need pragmatic balancing and weighing in individual cases.[156] This duality is found in Savigny's PrIL as well.[157] The more public policies and interests we identify in private law, the more balancing and openness is needed not only in

[154] Ibid., 303. [155] Ibid., 55ff.

[156] Ibid., 55 (including under this category: 1. Moral goals (boni mores) including in the new law religious goals; 2. Observance of state interests; 3. Fatherly provisions, as well as "promotion of exchanges," protection of various classes of people, such as women and children, against particular dangers). For a discussion of the social law vision that emerges from Savigny's duality between individualistic premises and other-considering duties, see Behrends, "Das Sozialrecht" (n. 82) 91 (noting that "Savigny's historical legal school which recognized the pertinent motives of the French revolution but also wished to maintain the republican freedoms, came in this search for the 'true,' meaning the correct social model.").

[157] In his eight volumes, Savigny cited his discussion on the various types of laws from his first volume. See Savigny, *Private International Law* (n. 102) 77ff.

the national norms which are in conflict but in our analysis on the applicable law in the transnational context. Savigny did not include in his PrIL analysis an argument discouraging or delegitimizing the inclusion of strong political, public values in private law. His method simply relies on an analysis of the extent to which these values can be identified in the laws and what their nature might be.

Behrends notes that in this back and forth between various values and policies, Savigny "allowed for room for any social policy, including protection for the working class."[158] By elucidating the context of the Roman sources that Savigny relied on, Behrends argues that "Savigny's system was obviously open for social law, in principle in the same way as the current social Rechtsstaat incorporating fundamental rights."[159]

But this social law is not based on a complete integration of private law into public law, because this would allow for the state's "full disposition over education, the work force and the distribution of goods."[160] Rather, it is based on a perpetual consideration and balancing of different policies and different images of the individual within a social community. Behrends explains that in this "historically grounded balance [. . .] the value of the individual and personal freedom of the adult capable of independence is placed at the forefront and the requirements of solidarity and serving others are implemented in both areas [of freedom and solidarity] to the protection of the first."[161] Behrends shows that the achievement of economic independence and therefore self-reliance rests at the core of the image of the individual in the social state and in Savigny's system, and has its historical roots in the Roman society of small families aspiring to economic self-reliance:

> If one recognizes in this way the adult individual capable of self-reliance as the model of the law it becomes clear that social law takes account of an image according to which the individual within the citizenry to which he belongs or amongst which he lives requires attention and solidarity and, to employ the *jeu de mot* by mister Eberhard Echenhofer, wants to be and must be *solidaire*, not *solitaire*. It is an aspect, which belongs to the human condition. Everyone is at some point young, constantly aging and in need of help, many temporarily or long term incapable of working or unemployed; and everyone is, from the beginning until the end, in need of information.[162]

Much of the same reasoning found in Savigny's writing can also be found in Jitta's PrIL scholarship, but with some important nuances. Like Savigny, Jitta also seemed to distinguish between an open acknowledgment that private law is set within a national socioeconomic and political context and situations in which public law values almost overwhelm private law per se. The distinction also follows similar lines as in Savigny's theory. A general socioeconomic and political context provides for a different view on the individual subject of law, different views of the value of property, different views on interpersonal solidarity etc. In turn this creates a different structuring of correlative rights and obligations. But all this, for Jitta as for Savigny, still operates within the realm of private law. While Savigny also acknowledges that

[158] Behrends, "Das Sozialrecht" (n. 82) 19, n. 46. [159] Ibid., 20. [160] Ibid., 24.
[161] Ibid., 24. [162] Ibid., 24.

private law norms are placed in a sociopolitical context and rejected a natural law perspective, he did not anticipate much deviation in the general private law proper. By contrast, Jitta thought even this general social/political background of private law can create significant differences in private law and will generate all sorts of thorny questions of conflict of laws. His comparative law analysis showed that even within a general grounding in Roman law in the major European legal systems, there is significant deviation in private law. So whereas Savigny thought only the direct and explicit incorporation of political goals in private law created significant divergence, Jitta saw important differences among different national private laws even just because private laws are set within a particular sociopolitical national context.

Both agreed that matters take a very different turn when it is obvious that the state pursues very strong public policy interests through private law. For example, when looking at labor contracts, Jitta argued that there is a strong, consequential and political debate occurring at the time of his writing about how to provide for increased freedom of labor while curbing various kinds of abuses. Jitta acknowledges that it is ultimately this political debate, which gives shape to a particular apportionment of rights and liabilities between the employee and the employer.[163]

Furthermore, it would be fair to say that these laws "impose certain obligations on the employer where the true creditor is the entire state, such that these obligations penetrate to a smaller or greater extent into public law."[164] Jitta, like Savigny, does not argue that this is wrong, or an affront to individual autonomy, or reprehensible. The only conclusion to be drawn from this acknowledgment that in some instances states function almost as creditors and rely on private law as an instrument to pursue broader public interests is that one can deduce "almost a definitive localization from this type of regulation. They are made, for each nation, for the local sphere of social life. In this sphere of social life, they apply exclusively."[165]

Jitta's analysis of contracts for rail transport also provides helpful insights into his consideration of the possibility of public law values entirely taking over private law relations and issues. Jitta notes that in the context of the rising importance of rail transportation:

> Even private law was not enough. Administrative law came to its aid. Public security, the interest of the post in the security of the mail, territorial security and so many other interests generated an ever-increasing involvement of the state in the exploitation of rail transportation, to the extent that the state itself engaged in the exploitation. The private law relating to rail transportation entered such a boiling phase under the influence of such burning questions of social philosophy that its character of private law almost evaporated. This is true with respect to the contract between the respective business and its personnel and this is also true with respect to the contract for transport of goods. Once the law imposes an obligation to the entrepreneur to provide transportation, establishes the extent of limiting liability, sets the price and all other conditions of transportation and defends any individual value, the contract of transportation acquires a very rigid character, not common of private law

[163] Jitta, *Substance of Obligation* 1 (n. 137) 183, 184. [164] Ibid., 183.

[165] Ibid., 173–8. See also 190–1 for a more detailed analysis of the way in which public law goals are included in various areas of contract law.

contracts. . . . The influence of administrative law on private law in the area of rail transportation and the rigidity this influence caused for private law makes a comparison of the laws almost useless for private international law. The laws are made for the national sphere of social life, the only one that administrative law can cover. By contrast, it is particularly interesting to compare the laws from the point of view of the politics involved in each state's exploitation of its railroad.[166]

Like Savigny, Jitta recognizes that political goals can define a particular area of private law and like Savigny he argues that in such cases states will always be inclined to apply their own laws to fulfill the political purposes underlying them. Interestingly, while Savigny thought the incorporation of public values in private law made the analysis less rigid, Jitta thought the opposite. This is because while Savigny understands private law as a domain fixing quite stringently the rights and obligations of individuals amongst themselves, Jitta imagines private law in looser social, relational terms.

4. Freedom and responsibility

Once one understands that relational internationalists were not rejecting or even discouraging the inclusion of public values in private law it is easier to understand that they were open to both broadening the scope of the public policy exception in PrIL and determining the applicable law based on an interpretation of the legislative policy at stake.

But relational internationalists also argued for a certain substratum of interpersonal morality within private law. Principles of "boni mores," "bona fides," and interpersonal trust ("Vertrauensprinzip") provide further relational context and social limits within which individual freedom can be exercised *within* private law.[167]

Okko Behrends shows persuasively how, in Savigny's case this was the result of the influence of two different schools of Roman law. Behrends argued that:

on the one hand Savigny's Christian-Enlightenment anthropology is related to the skeptical-academic individualistic tradition. On the other hand, his legal theory, which grounds the historical truth of legal principles, reflects the general assumptions of the natural law stoic school of thought and establishes therefore a true methodological parallel between Savigny's and the Stoic legal theory.[168]

This enabled Savigny to create "an equilibrium between the formal rules of individual freedom and material principles that ground other-considering duties."[169]

166 Ibid., 270–1.

167 Behrends, "Geschichte" (n. 7) 293, 294. See also Okko Behrends, 'Die *bona fides* in *mandatum.* Die vorklassischen Grundlagen des klassischen Konsensualvertrags Auftrag' in Okko Behrends, *Institut und Prinzip. Siedlungsgeschichtliche Grundlagen, philosophische Einflüsse und das Fortwirken der beiden republikanischen Konzeptionen in den kaiserzeitlichen Rechtsshulen. Ausgewählte Aufsätze,* vol. 1 (Wallsteig 2004) 806 (hereafter Behrends, "Bona fides").

168 Behrends, "Geschichte" (n. 7) 297.

169 Ibid.

This equilibrium is partly reflected in Savigny's "Vertrauensprinzip" and bona fides. The general Roman law context for this principle, on which Savigny drew heavily, is well explained by Behrends:

> The self-serving ius civile, the ius civile in the narrow sense, is the area of self-responsibility and freedom of citizens and therefore of the self-centering. This separates people. The area of ius naturale or ius gentium is the area of *aequum et bonum* or *bona fides* and is dominated by principles of others-considering duties. It unites people regardless of the ius civile and aims at trustworthy cooperation and solidarity.[170]

Savigny tried to create a duality and mutual reference between two dichotomies: on the one hand individual freedom/social responsibility and on the other hand the structure/value or rule/principle dynamics of the law.[171] Behrends thought the linking element between the two extremes within each set of dichotomies is the "trust principle" (Vertrauensprinzip) of "loyalty and faith" (Treu und Glaube).[172]

On the one hand this principle was meant to counterbalance individual freedom and social responsibility and was thought of as a vehicle enabling the weighing of values and goals.[173] Savigny recognized openly that the balance might tilt in different directions depending on the case, as well as the socioeconomic conditions of each period[174] and already noted "the extended importance of *bona fides*."[175]

On the other hand, the principle was "partly extra-legal social and partly juridified."[176] This enabled him to go back and forth between "life constructed socially with no legal coercion"[177] and "life viewed from one angle only, namely the legal."[178] Extracting principles of bona fides from social custom and general reasonable expectations meant openness to referring to social life and life experiences, as well as to acknowledging the "social application of private law."[179] Undoubtedly this reference to social custom and general reasonable expectations is often bound to replicate patterns of discrimination and injustice. This is for example reflected in the

170 Behrends, "Bona fides" (n. 167) 827.

171 Okko Behrends, 'Struktur und Wert. Zum institutionellen und prinzipiellen Denken im geltenden Recht' in Okko Behrends, *Institut und Prinzip. Siedlungsgeschichtliche Grundlagen, philosophische Einflüsse und das Fortwirken der beiden republikanischen Konzeptionen in den kaiserzeitlichen Rechtsshulen. Ausgewählte Aufsätze*, vol. 1 (Wallsteig 2004) 51, 58–9 (hereafter Behrends, "Struktur und Wert").

172 Behrends, "Geschichte" (n. 7) 294 citing, among others, Friedrich Karl von Savigny, *System des heutigen römischen Rechts*, vol. 5 (Bei Veit & Comp. 1841) 108.

173 Savigny, *System 1* (n. 82) 5.

174 Behrends, "Struktur und Wert" (n. 171) 59:

> Savigny's model is in conformity with ancient precepts also in that the form-value dichotomy belongs to the nature of law, but the particular resulting counterbalancing is a task that occurs in each era and which is not always best attained in each era. It is therefore no accident that Savigny rediscovered the duality between form—pure legal element—and value—mixed legal element, but was aided in this discovery also by the Christian-secular view that the individual needs to attain moral freedom, a space of formal legal freedom. For Jhering this concept is then overwhelmed by a strong cultural optimism, which considers legal structures and values the product of human culture.

175 Savigny, *System 1* (n. 82) 5. 176 Behrends, "Geschichte" (n. 7) 293.

177 Ibid., 294. 178 Savigny, *Vom Beruf* (n. 114) 30.

179 Behrends, "Strucktur und Wert" (n. 174) 60.

fact that Savigny's focus on interpersonal morality did not contest the application of the law of the husband's domicile in family law matters, but merely argued that the husband cannot unilaterally change his domicile and thereby violate the wife's rights and reasonable expectations, where reasonable expectations are thought to be aligned with the notion of dependent domicile.

However, it is precisely in this albeit limited gradation and constant cross-reference between individual liberty and social responsibility that Behrends saw yet another striking difference between Savigny and Kant. While Kant rejected the Roman "bona fides" as a principle determining in any way individual responsibility,[180] Savigny tried to "incorporate social reality under the political life principle of law"[181] precisely through the Roman law principle of bona fides translated into "loyalty and faith."

The same principle of social responsibility is found repeatedly in Jitta's theory under another, but very similar terminology. Much of the analysis of transnational private law relations is based for him on a principle of interpersonal, social "trust." As in Savigny's theory, the principle is partly extra-legal and socially constructed, "based on the demands of universal social life" and partly juridical.[182] This means that either the applicable national law or the rights and obligations of individuals directly can be derived from the various elements of the interpersonal relationship and its transnational context.[183]

According to Jitta, one should be attuned to the reasonable expectations that individuals create in each other and in the third parties whom their actions involve or affect.[184] One should also examine, based on this principle of "social trust" into which "sphere of social life" individual actions have penetrated and which individual and community interests they have affected.[185]

However, Jitta's theory seems to use the principle of social trust differently from the way it is referenced in Savigny's theory. First, for Savigny the bona fides was used as a medium to counter individualism and inject social obligations. For Jitta, the distinction between liberty and social responsibility is less clear and it is less clear overall whether there is a duality between liberty and social responsibility or whether the principle of social trust becomes the main vehicle of analysis—not alongside but sometimes instead of the concept of individual freedom. His adage "if private law is social, PrIL is doubly social" is meant, I believe, to emphasize precisely the significance of what he constantly referred to as "the social duty of person to person" underlying both private law and PrIL.[186]

Second, for Savigny it seemed important to recognize individual freedom and social responsibility as counterweights to one another precisely in order to provide some stability, predictability, and structure to legal reasoning, whereas Jitta might be criticized for falling in the trap of the "free law judge." He seems to have been much less concerned with judicial discretion than Savigny and even Story might have been. From that point of view, "the mixed legal element" of bona fides, which

[180] Behrends, "Geschichte" (n. 7) 298. [181] Ibid., 300.
[182] See for example Jitta, *Substance des Obligations* 1 (n. 137) 220. [183] Ibid., 218.
[184] Ibid. [185] Ibid. [186] Ibid., 213.

embraces and references open ended appreciations of social interactions, takes up much more analytical space in Jitta's work than in Savigny's. In part, this is explained by the particular intellectual context in which they employ the terms. Savigny took them from Roman law and its particular legal and social context. Jitta was interested in a sociological analysis and interpretation of law. This also explains why Jitta might have felt quite comfortable in taking relationality to another level of analysis. While for Savigny the individual is both a self-responsible self-referential being and a *solidaire*, Jitta seemed to think of the individual as always socially bound.

Therefore, while Jitta openly admitted that the principle of reasonable expectation, social trust, and interpersonal duty is itself controversial and subject to different interpretations and gradations in various legal systems,[187] he argued that this regrettable lack of uniformity in the interpretation or the substance of the principle of interpersonal morality should not lead PrIL back into the formalism of choosing between laws, because this would take the field away from what Muir Watt calls "the sensitivity to life experience."[188] In this way, Jitta seems to have been captured by what Behrends calls "the false alternatives" of either "formal law or free judge law," while in Behrends' view Savigny tried to navigate between them.[189] Jitta therefore argued that until a common conviction existed between national laws the judge should be able to express his reasoned "conviction" as to the reasonable way of solving the PrIL matter based on the principle of "inter-personal trust" as determined by the "demands of the international social life."[190]

Although it is hard to pin down what relevance and implications for our legal assessments of rights and duties in cross-border interpersonal relations the principle of interpersonal trust might have, it is possible to underscore a few of its instantiations. First, the principle of interpersonal trust functions, for Jitta, as a way of anchoring the principle of localization in a social environment. In this way, localizing an interpersonal relationship in a particular community must account for the expectations of third parties and international society at large. In Jitta's account it is a heuristic principle, which attempts to focus the analysis of the applicable law on the interests of a wider pool of interested individuals and communities.

A general principle of interpersonal morality also features strongly in Savigny's analysis of the way in which individuals could shop for a forum and/or a law to the detriment of the other party of the legal relation. This is a consideration to which Savigny gives quite a lot of thought such that in virtually every area of law the test of interpersonal trust/morality is applied to probe the soundness of any determination on the applicable law. For example, after arguing that the law of domicile should govern claims to marital property, he considers whether the domicile at the time of marriage or at the time of the action should be operative:

[187] Ibid., 221.

[188] Horatia Muir Watt, 'Future Directions?' in Horatia Muir Watt and Diego P. Fernández Arroyo (eds.), *Private International Law and Global Governance* (OUP 2015) 343, 375.

[189] For a very interesting discussion of Savigny's model versus the newer strands of judicial discretion or interest jurisprudence, see Behrends, "Struktur und Wert" (n. 171) esp. 60–2.

[190] Jitta, *Substance des Obligations* 1 (n. 137) 220.

If, at a place where the law establishes as the rule universal communion of goods of the most extensive description, a marriage is contracted by a rich man with a poor woman, the estate becomes common by the completion of the marriage. If the man afterwards changes the domicile to a place where the dotal regime prevails, the wife must, according to the second opinion, lose in a moment, and against her will, the share of the estate to which she had already acquired right.[191]

In other words determining the law of domicile at the time of marriage as applicable ensures that the reasonable expectations of both parties are taken into consideration and prevents abuses of freedom in interpersonal relations. From the point of view of interpersonal morality the matter seems to be settled:

When the marriage was about to be contracted, it was entirely in the wife's option, either to abstain from it altogether, or to add certain conditions touching patrimonial rights. She has made no such contract, but has accepted the conjugal rights as fixed by the law of the domicile, and naturally has reckoned on its perpetual continuance. The husband now changes the domicile by his own mere will, as he is undoubtedly entitled to do, and quite a different distribution of the conjugal estate is thus introduced for this marriage.... Precisely in order to exclude this unjustifiable one-sided power of the husband over the rights of the wife, was the existence of a tacit contract presumed by the defenders of the first opinion.[192]

This is not the end of the matter, however. A strong public policy at the place of new domicile could bring other considerations, such that the principle of interpersonal morality, while a serious consideration, is merely one among others:

The second opinion must indeed be adopted, if a law as to conjugal property of a strictly positive nature should exist at the new domicile. This would be presumed if a law were there enacted prohibiting any marriage whatever to be contracted, or if instituted elsewhere, to be continued, otherwise than under the dotal regime, or otherwise than with the communion of goods.[193]

The same kind of principle trying to balance various kinds of freedoms in interpersonal relations features in his discussion of cases in which a debtor enters into an obligation at his personal domicile:

If that debtor capriciously changed his domicile, or if he dies, his previous *forum domicilii* has, as such entirely ceased. But in the quality here established, as the special forum of the obligation, it still continues: it follows the emigrant in his new domicile; it binds the heir in case of death, although he should have a different domicile. The reason of this peculiar rule is, that the debtor, by undertaking the obligation here, creates an *expectation* that he will also submit to its consequences at the same place. This expectation must not be disappointed; neither ought the debtor to be prevented from changing his domicile at pleasure.[194]

Similarly, Savigny argues that prescription should fall under the law of the contract, rather than the law of the forum, because:

Thus the plaintiff cannot select for his action just that one of several concurring jurisdictions under which there is the longest term of prescription. In the like manner, the

[191] Savigny, *Private International Law* (n. 102) 296–7. [192] Ibid., 294.
[193] Ibid., 296–7. [194] Ibid., 205.

defendant cannot, by changing his domicile to a place where there is a shorter term of prescription, obtain an advantage to himself, seeing that both the local law and the special forum of the obligation are immutably fixed or the debt contracted by him at the former domicile.[195]

Thereby:

This doctrine is not only correct in principle, but it is also recommended by a certain equity, since every capricious exercise of free will by one party to the detriment of the opponent is excluded by the clear settlement of the period of prescription that results from it.[196]

Establishing a certain level of equality among the parties to the private law relationship was very important to Savigny. And unlike state-centered internationalists or those taking a political legitimacy perspective, for Savigny the determination of the applicable law had to maintain a sober perspective on how individuals may structure relationships differently in order to undermine other individuals' expectations and opportunities.

5. Social legitimacy

In contrast to Brilmayer's political legitimacy theory centered on the individual-state relationship, the individual-centered theory that I have attempted to recover and reconstruct in the previous sections creates what can be seen as a form of "social legitimacy." This theory embraces Singer's proposition to "shift our focus from viewing individuals as abstract citizens whose relationships to each other are governed by rights enforced by the state to viewing them as active participants in shaping their relations in daily life."[197] But in so doing, it provides for various layers of analysis of the legitimacy of applying one particular law over another. There are three different layers embedded in the theories of the relational internationalist authors discussed here, although they inevitably bleed into each other and reference one another's analytical nuances.

First, relational internationalists cite individuals' reasonable expectations as to the applicable law and/or as to the substantive outcome of the dispute as an important consideration. This is, for example the case when Jitta argued that it seems reasonable for individuals to assume that the authority of their state of citizenship does not follow them so as to prevent them from obtaining a divorce even after they have established domicile elsewhere and therefore moved their legal relation to the social context of another state.[198] It also features, for example, in Savigny's examination of the scope of restriction of donations among spouses:

[195] Ibid., 250. [196] Ibid., 250.

[197] See Singer, "Nihilism and Legal Theory" (n. 4).

[198] Josephus Jitta, *The Renovation of International Law on the Basis of a Juridical Community of Mankind* (Martinus Nijhoff 1919) 120:

The State, according to my opinion, exceeds the reasonable limits of its sovereignty, by enacting a rule which forbids divorce to its subjects in such a manner, that the prohibition

It cannot be maintained that the marriage entered into at a place under the Roman law [which disallows donations among spouses], and afterwards transferred to another place, was constituted under the tacit contract that an effectual donation between the spouses could never take place at any time. The prohibition of gifts is rather a mere restriction of freedom to which the spouses must accommodate themselves, not a legal institution imported into the marriage by voluntary submission. On the other hand, it cannot be admitted that such laws should be applied to immoveable property lying within their territory, even when the marriage subsists in a country that knows no such restriction of freedom. For the purpose of these laws is not to ward off a danger from the things, as if they could suffer injury from gifts *inter conjuges*, but, rather, as already stated, the preservation of purity of morals in the marriage. The legislator addresses himself, therefore, to married persons living within the territory, without respect to the situation of their estate.[199]

Second, relational internationalists cite private law values, including the concepts of social trust and *bona fides* as informing a certain substratum of interpersonal morality to which individuals can be held accountable in their transnational dealings. In the case of *La Jeune Eugenie*, Story felt comfortable subjecting property rights to universal values and morals, and tried to excavate the variety of values underlying private law categories in his determination of jurisdiction and the applicable law.[200] Jitta considered a particular law applicable to legal matters relating to letters of exchange based on the confidence such letters inspired in the particular communities where they were circulated. Savigny argued that the husband cannot change his wife's entitlements to maintenance through a simple change of domicile because this would constitute a complete disregard for her agency.[201]

Third, relational internationalists hold individuals accountable, as Jitta made explicit, to the degree of their penetration in these social communities. While their methods of localization of a legal relation differ, as I have explained in the previous chapter, none imagined private law relationships as immune from legal authority, but instead as accountable to the laws of different communities as determined by the particular link between a transnational private law relationship and one or various communities. Certainly one could now question Savigny's possibly essentialized analysis of the nature of private law relationships, as Jitta did. And, of course, one could disagree with Savigny's view of the nature of any one private law relationship and could downplay the element of individual liberty in relation to the element of social responsibility. But all of this would be in line with the relational internationalist perspective. Since, in my reading, these authors did not operate with nor wish to construct false alternatives between the individual and the state, individual liberty, and social responsibility, rearranging any of these values would not appear as an abrupt change. It is only when one argues either that the litigating parties disappear

is absolutely indestructible. Husband and wife, especially the wife, must be at liberty to establish their home, *cum animo perpetuitatis,* in the realm of another sovereign, and to obtain a divorce there, the effect of which must be recognized everywhere. The regulation of the jurisdiction, of course, must be in accordance with the general rule.

199 Savigny, *Private International Law* (n. 102) 297.

200 See Chapter 8.

201 Savigny, *Private International Law* (n. 102) 294.

for a while in the PrIL division of authority among states, or that an individual can impose side constraints on state authority that the recalibration between the individual and the social, which Savigny, Jitta, and Story left open, seems a drastic move in either direction.

To highlight the way in which relational internationalists constructed a theory of legitimate authority which integrated both reasonable expectations, interpersonal justice, and public policy analysis, it is useful to look at the way in which their reasoning intersects with that of the American realist scholar, David Cavers, whose views on PrIL were discussed in Chapter 5.

The American realist school of thought in PrIL was in large part constructed by reference to laws, which deny the capacity of certain classes of individuals (in particular, at the time, married women without obtaining the prior consent of their husbands) to enter into particular contracts. In Currie's methodology, focused on state interests, a state would presumably always apply its own law if it protected or granted a benefit to its domiciliaries. A domiciliary could therefore plead want of capacity in relationship to a non-domiciliary. By contrast, Lea Brilmayer argued that it was unfair for a state to impose a restriction or a burden on a non-domiciliary, thus reversing in this case Currie's analysis. While Currie thought it was legitimate to apply a law that benefits a domiciliary, Brilmayer thought it was an illegitimate imposition of authority on a non-domiciliary.

By contrast, David Cavers took a different and much more nuanced perspective on legitimate authority, which relational internationalists embraced as well. Cavers certainly agreed with his follow realists that one must underscore the policies of the laws in conflict and acknowledge that the purpose (or a possible purpose) of some laws is to protect a particular class of individuals from being induced into particular transactions. But in determining whether it was legitimate to impose this particular policy one had to take into account a variety of differentiating facts. Thus, in the case of a contract between a merchant and a married woman "[t]he fact that the publisher's agent went to the defendant's home would be material," as well as whether she "first clipped the coupon," or "whether the sale was part of a sales campaign waged in that state and not an isolated transaction," or whether "the bargain was struck by mail," or whether "the transaction comprises a sale of books ... or shares of stock ... or, on the other hand, some article, a vacuum cleaner perhaps, which barely lay beyond the concept of the 'necessary'."[202]

Arguably all of these factors have an impact on the parties' reasonable expectations in relation to one another. All these factors would need to be considered under the analysis of principles of interpersonal trust. According to Cavers, "the degree to which sustaining this bargain would impair the protection which state A insists is due its infant matrons must be measured against the degree to which its avoidance will frustrate the reasonable expectations of business men from without the state."[203]

[202] David Cavers, 'A Critique of the Choice-of-Law Problem' (1933) 47 Harv L Rev 173, 180–9.
[203] Ibid.

In Cavers's framework the question of which law could legitimately apply to a particular relationship is a balancing act between underscoring and giving the broadest possible application to the policy of the laws, while at the same time policing the actions of individuals in relationship to each other to prevent abuses. This is why, in his correspondence with Brainerd Currie, Cavers conceded that while who "clipped the coupon" might be a marginal "differentiating fact" there are other elements in the conduct of the parties that might be important in a decision whether to deny or grant the protection each party claims: planning a transaction to by-pass a known law, for example.[204]

Although hardly ever discussed in accounts of Savigny's PrIL theory, the same kind of cases discussed by American realists feature prominently in Savigny's own writing. And much of the same reasoning is employed. With respect to restrictions on capacity to enter into particular contracts Savigny, like Currie, would apply the law of domicile of the person receiving the benefit, since this seems to be the purpose of the law.[205] However, like Cavers, Savigny ponders on the kind of inequity that this might create for the other party. Much like in Cavers's framework, Savigny also envisions a certain kind of tradeoff between the protection due to a particular class of individuals and the legitimate expectations of the other party to the contract. For example, as to bills of exchange he argues that as a general matter it would not be unfair to the merchant to apply the law of the person whose capacity is limited by virtue of her law of domicile. This is because one could reasonably assume that the merchant would be cognizant of the different laws in the different areas of his trade:

> The difficulty, however, is less in reality than it may at first sight appear. The cautious purchaser of a drawn bill, although it has travelled through various parts of the world, and is covered with numerous signatures, will generally look only to a few subscriptions, which he knows from his own experience to be safe; and all besides these may be immaterial to him.[206]

Based on this rationale therefore, it seems wise to keep the protection of the laws denying capacity in place. A different analysis might be warranted however, when the law recognizes capacity to issue bills of exchange only to particular classes of individuals, which are hard to ascertain:

> The ascertainment of that quality was especially difficult in consequence of the statutory rule, that where guilds of merchants existed, only their members should have the privileges of merchants, and consequently the capacity necessary for bills. This very peculiar restriction originated, doubtless, in a paternal care for those who might be disposed rashly to contract debts. On account of the strict execution connected with them, bills were considered particularly dangerous; and the use of these dangerous instruments for the enhancement of credit was denied to all to whom it was not indispensable on account of their special mercantile relations.[207]

[204] Ibid.
[205] Savigny, *Private International Law* (n. 102) 159.
[206] Ibid.
[207] Ibid., 161.

In these circumstances, one might be inclined to uphold the validity of the bills on the following considerations:

> If a Berliner in Paris draws a bill on a Frenchman, it would certainly be extremely unfair to require of the Frenchman, in order to satisfy himself as to the future right of action on the bill at Berlin, not only to know the Prussian laws (which perhaps might be practicable), but also discover whether the drawer is a member of the Berlin corporation of merchants, or the possessor of manorial lands (Rittergutsbesitzer), or tenant of demesne lands—qualities which are certainly not easily ascertainable. Such an injustice would, however, immediately meet with retribution, inasmuch as the credit of Prussians who happened to be abroad would be undermined, in respect at least to bills.[208]

Jitta adopted a very similar kind of balanced reasoning on the question of which law could legitimately apply. However, he also incorporated more of Currie's skepticism regarding states' unwillingness to give up on a particular policy in their law in order to apply a foreign law. As to laws limiting capacity for donations for example, Jitta argues that a state would likely want to have its limitations on capacity enforced for its domiciliaries abroad, while preventing the application of these limitations for out of state domiciliaries when they affect property in the territory in order to protect "the security of national land credit."[209]

Similarly, when asking what law would apply to the formal validity of a donation made by a French person in Germany in conformity with German rules, Jitta argues that while the donation would be valid from the point of view of the German judge, the French judge could find "in the spirit of its law" various reasons for denying validity.[210]

Certainly Jitta did not agree with Currie that a state would always apply its own law. However, Jitta thought that there is such a wide range of policies that can be identified in a law, such that the balancing of regulatory policies and legitimate expectations of foreigners is always contentious and complex.

E. Conclusions

The state-centered internationalist perspective created a framework of interstate legitimacy whereby the application of a particular law is justified relative to a foreign sovereign, based primarily on a uniform neutral division of state authority. The same principles of neutrality, coupled with individual freedom generated theories of legitimacy based on consent, either conceived of as a free choice of law, or based on the political relationships of domicile or citizenship.

In contrast, the relational internationalist perspective took neither extreme position. Instead, the question of legitimacy was answered in a more fluid context in which the individual is neither separated from his or her private law relationships or from the state nor subsumed under them. Various layers of analysis were used

[208] Ibid., 162. [209] Ibid., 172–4. [210] Ibid., 177.

without the sense that a particular choice between them is inevitable or that any one choice is suited for all private law relationships. Individuals' reasonable expectations, the extra-legal social context, as well as the legal and political context, all played a different role depending on the private law relationships and to a different degree in the writings of each author. The possibility for the recalibration and the rethinking of the values underlying private law relationships and their projection in the transnational context was, in my reading, always left open.

8

Universalism Versus Uniformity

A. Introduction

In 1953 the German scholar Gerhard Kegel wrote a highly influential article that sought to push PrIL from "legalistic jurisprudence" (Begriffsjurisprudenz) toward "interests jurisprudence" or to achieve a proper balance between the two.[1] Unlike the American realist school, Kegel's theory was not meant to create a paradigmatic shift in PrIL.

Rather, it claimed to provide the best theoretical justification for PrIL's underlying justice dimensions.[2] On the one hand, Kegel wanted to clarify that previous terms of art in PrIL, such as the center of gravity, the nature of the legal relation, Natur de Sache and so on, should only be understood as short forms for the existence and analysis of various underlying interests.[3] On the other hand, he introduced a much debated, much contested, and some argue much misunderstood distinction between material justice and conflicts justice, suggesting that there are particular interests to which PrIL, as opposed to substantive law, caters.[4] Lastly, he used his theory of conflicts justice to argue that PrIL deals primarily with individual and private law interests, and thereby to contest the highly political, state-centered focus of Currie's theory.[5]

[1] Gerhard Kegel, 'Begriffs—und Interessenjurisprudenz im internationalen Privatrecht' in Hans Lewald et al. (eds.), *Festschrift Hans Lewald: bei Vollendung des 40. Amtsjahres als ordentlicher Professor im Oktober 1953 überreicht von seinen Freunden und Kollegen mit Unterstützung der Basler Juristischen Fakultät* (Helbing & Lichtenhahn 1953) (hereafter Kegel, "Interessenjurisprudenz").

[2] Klaus Schurig, 'Interessenjurisprudenz contra Interessenjurisprudenz im IPR: Anmerkungen zu Flessners Thesen' (1995) 59 RabelsZ 229, 235 ("Currie wanted even a limited change of paradigm. Such a thing either works or not. In contrast, interest jurisprudence aims to set the current PrIL on a rational foundation and to make judicial decision processes more transparent and therefore easier to contest, to understand and to replicate.").

[3] See Kegel, "Interessenjurisprudenz" (n. 1) 270ff.

[4] Gerhard Kegel, 'The Crisis of Conflict of Laws' (1964) 112 Recueil des Cours 91 (hereafter Kegel, "The Crisis"). For a list of publications by Gerhard Kegel, see Alexander Lüderitz and Jochen Schröder (eds.), *Internationales Privatrecht und Rechtsvergleichung im Ausgang des 20. Jahrhunderts. Bewahrung oder Wende? Festschrift für Gerhard Kegel* (Alfred Metzner 1977) 479 (hereafter Lüderitz and Schröder, *Festschrift Kegel*).

[5] See Kegel, "Interessenjurisprudenz" (n. 1) 287; Klaus Schurig, 'Das Fundament trägt noch' in Heinz-Peter Mansel, *Internationales Privatrecht im 20. Jahrhundert: Der Einfluss von Gerhard Kegel und Alexander Lüderitz auf das Kollisionsrecht* (Mohr Siebeck 2014) (hereafter Schurig, "Das Fundament").

Nineteenth-Century Perspectives on Private International Law. Roxana Banu. © Roxana Banu 2018. Published 2018 by Oxford University Press.

These different analytical moves and Kegel's general interest theory have all had a profound influence on the development of PrIL in Germany, even though Alex Flessner argues that the impact of Kegel's theory was not equivalent to that of Currie's theory in the United States.[6] But according to Kegel's collaborator, Klaus Schurig, Kegel's theory represents, after Savigny's and Franz Kahn's theories, a third stepping stone in the "fundamentals" of contemporary PrIL in Germany and possibly other European states.[7]

Kegel's initial articulations of interest jurisprudence in PrIL have generated intense debates and critique and have created a school of thought in its own right, at least in Germany.[8] Within this school of thought, many aspects of significance regarding the state-centered/individual-centered analytical duality in PrIL have been discussed. Scholars debated on how individual interests should be defined or discovered; what the relationship between individual and broader public interests might be; whether individual interests can only be referenced in geographical or also substantive terms; how the interests of order and uniformity are to be evaluated from an individual-centered perspective, and what the relevance of the transnational context of individual interests might be.

All of these questions bring to light important and often underappreciated nuances regarding the articulation of individual-centered perspectives in PrIL, and this chapter therefore begins by providing a broad overview of the main insights of interest jurisprudence on these questions. However, my interest is not only to recover these German interest jurisprudence debates as an important variation of individual-centered perspectives developed in the second half of the twentieth century. My goal is also to use these debates as an entry point to outline the way in which nineteenth-century relational internationalists reflected on some of the same issues regarding the articulation and relevance of individual interests in the transnational realm. This chapter in particular focuses on the way in which relational internationalists referenced the transnational context of individual interests and how the pursuit of order and uniformity fits within the relational internationalist perspective.

This reference back to history from the twentieth-century articulation of interest jurisprudence to nineteenth-century relational internationalists is not only a useful entry point to reveal yet other layers of the relational internationalist perspective. Interest jurisprudence theorists themselves engaged in a conversation with the past when articulating their views. For example, Gerhard Kegel considered the way in which his conflicts/material justice distinction differs from Jitta's and Cavers's theories,[9] while Alexander Lüderitz reflected on the way in which interest jurisprudence

[6] Alex Flessner, *Interessenjurisprudenz im internationalen Privatrecht* (J.C.B. Mohr 1990) (hereafter Flessner, *Interessenjurisprudenz*).

[7] Schurig, "Das Fundament" (n. 5) 9 (arguing that after Savigny "further architects were needed to create the fundamentals of modern PrIL") and 11 (arguing that both Savigny and Kahn brought important developments to PrIL, but that the theories remained "rather intuitive and unstructured" until interest jurisprudence was developed).

[8] For a discussion of the various criticisms, which were brought against interest jurisprudence along the years, see Schurig, "Das Fundament" (n. 5).

[9] See Kegel, "Interresenjurisprudenz" (n. 1) 271, 272.

links to but also departs from Savigny's theory.[10] And as recently as 2014, an edited volume published in Germany inquired into the way in which twenty-first century PrIL might still be influenced by Kegel's and Lüderitz's twentieth-century PrIL writings and how those, in turn, might be influenced by nineteenth-century classical (presumably Savignian) theories.[11]

In introducing the main tenets of interest jurisprudence in the first section of the chapter, I am therefore particularly attuned to the way in which its proponents position themselves in relationship to nineteenth-century individual-centered theories. I then offer my own account of how the two constellations of theories relate and depart from each other.

B. Gerhard Kegel

In the 1950s the German PrIL scholar Gerhard Kegel began to publish a series of writings focusing on the question of justice in PrIL.[12] Kegel perceived himself as reacting to two different themes referenced in PrIL theory up until that time.

On the one hand, Kegel believed the "classical" thinkers had failed to provide a true theory of justice for PrIL. He perceived Savigny's "theory of the seat," or von Bar's term "the nature of the situation" or Gierke's theory of "center of gravity" as mere "images" or metaphors that cannot explain the particularities of PrIL's justice dimensions.[13] Rather, he argued that one must identify the interests particular to PrIL matters. In other words, as later German interest theorists (and often quite different from Kegel) would argue, PrIL can only legitimate itself as a distinct field if it caters to distinct interests.[14]

On the other hand, Kegel argued that theories, which explicitly or implicitly identify state interests as the particular stakes of PrIL had to be wrong. He was thereby attacking Currie's governmental interest approach as well as the formalist state-centered European theories. Whereas the latter were allegedly wrong to assume that PrIL was governing relationships between states,[15] the former was allegedly wrong both for mixing governmental with private interests and private with public law, and for mixing questions of substantive justice with conflicts justice.[16]

According to Kegel:

the justice we are seeking in private international law demands an evaluation of interests, just as any other legal decision does. However, here we are concerned not with governmental

[10] Alexander Lüderitz, 'Anknüpfung im Parteiinteresse' in Alexander Lüderitz and Jochen Schröder (eds.), *Internationales Privatrecht und Rechtsvergleichung im Ausgang des 20. Jahrhunderts. Bewahrung oder Wende? Festschrift für Gerhard Kegel* (Alfred Metzner 1977) (hereafter Lüderitz, "Parteiinteresse").

[11] Heinz-Peter Mansel, *Internationales Privatrecht im 20. Jahrhundert: Der Einfluss von Gerhard Kegel und Alexander Lüderitz auf das Kollisionsrecht* (Mohr Siebeck 2014).

[12] See Kegel, "Interessenjurisprudenz" (n. 1).

[13] See Henri Batiffol, "Les intérêts de droit international privé" in Lüderitz and Schröder, *Festschrift Kegel*, (n. 4) 14 (hereafter Batiffol, "Les intérêts").

[14] Lüderitz, "Parteiinteresse" (n. 10) 53.

[15] Batiffol, "Les intérêts" (n. 13) 12.

[16] See Kegel, "The Crisis" (n. 4), Chapter XII.

interests, but with the interests of private persons, be it interests of individual parties or interests of undetermined persons, which might be called the interests of commerce [...] For the sake of order and uniformity, this cannot be ascertained in individual cases according to fluctuating and unstable criteria. It must rather be determined with reference to the broadest possible means.[17]

Furthermore:

[J]ustice, together with the interests that it regulates, cannot be divided into disconnected parts, that is, into justice and interests in the area of substantive law and justice and interests in conflicts law. The interests of conflicts law predominate as a rule, but in exceptional cases the interests of substantive law prevail. Accordingly, justice in the field of conflicts law regularly takes precedence over that of substantive law, and the rules of conflicts law govern; but as an exception, in cases where the application of foreign substantive law would violate the public policy of the forum, justice in the field of substantive law is given priority over that of conflicts law and the foreign substantive law is not applied.[18]

It was this division between conflicts justice and substantive justice that provoked the most criticism of Kegel's theory. Recently, Klaus Schurig, Kegel's collaborator, argued that Kegel was misunderstood as pleading for the *independence,* as opposed to the *separation,* of conflicts interests from substantive interests.[19] Instead, "changes in the substantive norms and the corresponding appreciation of substantive interests spill into PrIL, since they imply different conflicts interests."[20]

This ambivalence is reflected in Kegel's attempt to position himself relative to Cavers' theory. Since for Kegel, "it is in principle wrong to make the choice of a law dependent on what is perceived as the better substantive result,"[21] Cavers, "who made the most progress in this direction" seems an appropriate intellectual opponent.[22] But Kegel was also unsure about how to read Cavers in light of the conflicts justice/substantive justice division:

Since he [Cavers] does not touch upon the difference between substantive and conflicts justice, it is possible that what he aimed at was a refinement of conflicts justice. In that case, his contribution would lie only in proving and refining the conventional PrIL rules in light of conflicts justice. His "fresh approach" would be less provocative, but more significant.[23]

In addition to dividing substantive and conflicts justice, Kegel distinguished sharply between private and public law. Allegedly, in private law "the state gives its benevolent sanction to a *de facto* system of private law, rather than bringing this system into existence by legislative fiat."[24] And while he admits "this is no doubt an exaggeration [it is] a necessary one if we are to underline the essential difference between public and private law."[25] Political interests cannot in general guide the choice of law question, since they are "foreign elements to *Private* International Law," even though their relevance is recognized on a case by case basis under public policy.[26] While Kegel remarked that private law deals with "the correct and proper ordering

[17] Ibid., 186. [18] Ibid., 189. [19] Schurig, "Das Fundament" (n. 5) 12.
[20] Ibid. [21] Kegel, "Interessenjurisprudenz" (n. 1) 270. [22] Ibid., 271.
[23] Ibid. [24] Kegel, "The Crisis" (n. 4) 183. [25] Ibid.
[26] Kegel, "Interessenjurisprudenz" (n. 1) 269.

of relationships among private parties" this translates into the proposition that one should acknowledge the fact that "the state does not decide its own affairs, but those affairs of others."[27] The "affairs of others" stand for the affairs of "individual parties" or "of undetermined persons, which might be called interests of commerce."[28]

These interests are, in turn, defined in abstract terms based on general a priori assumptions. The following passage provides much insight into the possible arrangement of interests that Kegel anticipated, as well as the normative grounding for these interests:

> The interests of the party himself are best served by the application of the law of the state of which he is a *citizen*. For in most cases it will be this state that is also the state where he grew up, learned to acquire respect, consciously or unconsciously, for his social obligations and whose law, in the last analysis, he has come to accept and trust. In most cases the law of *domicile* stands in less intimate relationship with the individual. To choose the *lex domicilii* means to give consideration to the interests of others with whom the party is living, that is, to the interests of the local society in which the foreigner has established his domicile, in other words, the interests of commerce. These interests of *commerce* are also protected, apart from the domicile factor so suitable for personal, family and inheritance rights, by the *lex loci contractus* for the form of the contract, by the *lex rei sitae* for things (since most people come into contact with a movable or immovable thing in the place where it is located) and by the *lex loci delicti* for torts (since tortfeasor, victim and helping third party are able to follow this law with the most ease and certainty).[29]

In a rather diffuse way, the interests of individuals and/or of the repeatedly personified "commerce" lead to the pursuit of "order" playing "a vital role for the determination of [PrIL] rules."[30] It is no wonder then that interests of commerce are equated with interests in the "facilitation" and "ease" of commerce.[31] Kegel referred repeatedly to the need for structure, order, and uniformity of results. He seemed to link the pursuit of order directly with private interests or the interests of commerce. For example, he cited passages in which Currie referred to the "rights of the litigants" and "justice to the parties" as rare instances where Currie allegedly must have acknowledged the "interests of order" in PrIL.[32]

Overall, according to Kegel, "the interests of *order* play a vital role in the determination of legal rules. In conflict of laws, moreover, there are special interests of legal order."[33]

> There is a definite interest here in avoiding solutions containing gaps, overlaps and contradictions, i.e. there is an interest in *substantive uniformity* (homogeneity) of *result*.[34] Another

[27] Kegel, "The Crisis" (n. 4) 182.

[28] Ibid., 186. It is possible that these remarks can be explained less by a desire to push for a natural law, apolitical version of PrIL but by a different understanding of the private/public divide in the European context, as opposed to the American one. For a useful perspective on the differences, see Nils Jansen and Ralf Michaels, 'Private Law and the State: Comparative Perceptions and Historical Observations' (2007) 71 RabelsZ 345.

[29] Kegel, "The Crisis" (n. 4) 187.

[30] Ibid.

[31] Kegel, "Interessenjurisprudenz" (n. 1) 274.

[32] Kegel, "The Crisis" (n. 4) 179.

[33] Ibid., 187.

[34] Here Kegel was making the important point that PrIL should be interested in avoiding the creation of so-called "limping" relationships, which are valid in one jurisdiction, but not in another.

essential interest of order is the interest in *international* (or interstate) *uniformity of result.* However, since every state has to ensure the achievement of justice on its own, these interests are, despite widespread opinion to the contrary, rather sharply delimited. No state will give in to another on important points in the absence of a comprehensive and satisfactory international or interstate agreement. Here, even if for other reasons, namely for considerations of justice rather than governmental interests, I share Currie's restraint.[35]

C. Individual-Centered Intuitions

In Kegel's theory individual interests become the main justification for interests of order. Yet it is not exactly clear how one should perceive the association between these two types of interests. Since Kegel's interest jurisprudence is framed around geographical, rather than substantive, factors, it is not exactly clear whether individuals are presumed to have an interest in intransigent choice of law rules, whatever the outcome of their application might be, or whether Kegel presumed individuals to have an interest in the avoidance of contradictory decisions in substantive terms. Furthermore, Kegel's initial articulation of interest jurisprudence in PrIL leaves somewhat unsettled what the universalistic dimensions of PrIL might be. On the one hand, it remains unclear how the transnational social context determines particular individual interests. On the other hand, it remains unclear how PrIL, by reference to individual interests, appears to generate a heightened interest in order.

Fellow German scholars, Alexander Lüderitz and Alex Flessner, have further pondered on these questions. The former scholar sought to concretize and refine the notion of "parties' interest." In so doing he made two points discussed below. On the one hand he argued that the interest of order is a public interest from which deviation is not only possible but necessary when individuals have chosen a particular law. Anything else, allegedly, would amount to a "state's attitude of superiority." [36] On the other hand, he argued that the systematic nature of PrIL must be maintained such that one should limit as much as possible the application of exceptions, including public policy.[37] Like Kegel, Lüderitz argued that one should reason on any PrIL matter, even when attempting to deviate from a choice of law rule, through PrIL's methodological arsenal rather than by reference to substantive values or equity.[38] Alex Flessner agreed with Lüderitz that interests of order represent broader, public, interests. If one adopts an individual-centered perspective, argued Flessner, the interest of the parties in a particular *outcome*—most clearly evidenced by parties' choice of law—should always have precedence.[39] In the scholarship of modern German PrIL scholars, the conceptualization of the relationship between order and private interests has taken an interesting turn. Whereas Kegel initially intimated that order is a private interest—presumably in the facilitation of

[35] Kegel, "The Crisis" (n. 4).

[36] Karsten Otte, 'Betrachtungen zur Interessenlehre' in Heinz-Peter Mansel, *Internationales Privatrecht im 20. Jahrhundert: Der Einfluss von Gerhard Kegel und Alexander Lüderitz auf das Kollisionsrecht* (Mohr Siebeck 2014) 27, 32 (hereafter Otte, "Betrachtungen").

[37] Ibid., 34–5. [38] Ibid., 29. [39] Ibid., 36.

commerce—Lüderitz and Flessner argued that the principle of order could stand in the way of private interests.

Before focusing on the responses to Kegel's theory by fellow German PrIL scholars Alexander Lüderitz and Alex Flessner, the chapter takes a detour to outline the way in which Kegel's theory was received by Henri Batiffol in France. In Chapter 4 I argued that Henri Batiffol's theory of systems coordination did not provide a framework, which would radically transform the liberal thinking in PrIL in the mid twentieth century. I explained that English scholars reviving the vested rights theory and focusing on individual liberty found great support in Batiffol's general philosophy of PrIL. While Batiffol described himself as a critic of individualistic theories in PrIL, increasingly liberal theories in England were thought of as entirely compatible with Batiffol's theory on the continent. Here I want to suggest that Batiffol's review of Kegel's theory reflects a similar ambivalence. While Batiffol expresses skepticism about Kegel's initial individual-centered starting point, he confesses being struck by the similarities between his and Kegel's theory. Where the two theories are most in accord is the focus on systematicity and on the coordination of norms through PrIL's methodological arsenal.

Ultimately then in the mid twentieth-century new versions of vested rights theories, Batiffol's systems coordination theory, and Kegel's interest jurisprudence connected through their strong liberal dimensions. They all shared a fundamental interest in PrIL techniques and methodology and attempted to secure the coherence of PrIL as a legal field by minimizing the use of exceptions in the name of equity or transnational substantive values. English theories of justice in PrIL further connected with German conflicts justice theories through their focus on individual liberty, increased freedom of choice of law by the parties, and their distrust in public policy analysis.

In this theoretical trio, the universalism of PrIL appears to be constructed mostly by reference to securing if not increasing commercial activity and interpersonal relationships across borders. By contrast, this chapter shows that because relational internationalists did not construct such sharp divides between private and public law and justice and private and public interests, their universalistic ideology attempts to simultaneously reference a broad range of interests in the transnational realm.

1. Henri Batiffol

The French PrIL scholar Henri Batiffol (1905–1989) shared with Kegel the disapproval of the European state-centered theories of Zitelmann and Pillet. Batiffol admitted that when his PrIL scholarship began "in the inter-war period, the constructions of Pillet or Zitelmann who looked within PublIL for principles and solutions to conflict of laws issues, understood as reciprocal obligations among states, seemed from another era and quite sterile."[40] But Batiffol also saw himself as an opponent of individualistic theorists, among whom he included Savigny, who, we

[40] Batiffol, "Les intérêts" (n. 13) 12.

are reminded, wrote in line with liberalism "which professes that the final scope of all juridical construction is the protection of the individual, and primarily her liberty."[41]

Since Batiffol found neither the PublIL argument nor individualistic liberalism were acceptable, he applauded the German so-called "third-school"[42] for shifting the focus in a direction he personally favored. Allegedly this school "considers national systems as positive law, against an abstract and unreal universalism, but works towards their reconciliation through comparative law."[43]

Batiffol became famous for putting a name to this revised universalistic theory of PrIL in the twentieth century. He argued that PrIL deals with the coordination of legal systems, pled for a revival of the renvoi doctrine, and generally argued that PrIL ensures the coexistence of different legal systems.[44]

From a philosophical point of view, in a book titled *The Philosophical Foundations of PrIL* Batiffol argued quite thoroughly for focusing PrIL theory on the private law relationship, even though he did not give much credit to Savigny for having already made this move.[45] He also pled for a more substantive focus in PrIL drawn from an analysis of private law norms and ideals, as well as for emphasizing state and interstate interests.[46] However, it remained unclear how his theory of coordination was any different from Pillet's and Zitelmann's. Although his philosophical work in PrIL had implicitly uncovered potential areas of reform, he did not seem able to transform those philosophical ideas into his own theory of coordination, which remained quite vague. Chapter 4 showed how Graveson looked to the theory of coordination to emphasize individual liberty, and how French courts, in fact, used Batiffol's theory as a platform for liberal jurisprudence. Furthermore, Phocion Franceskakis and recently Andreas Bucher criticized the theory of systems coordination for being overly technical and for failing to illuminate whose interests are served through various forms of intersystem coordination.[47] This ambivalence between his disavowing of extreme liberalism, while incorporating liberal and formalist principles in his own theory may be a result of the fact that Batiffol tried to reconcile state-centered and individual-centered perspectives by bringing them all together, yet without articulating the links between them. PrIL would deal with individual liberty, but also with private law relations and private law values, with public law principles, and with state, as well as interstate interests.

Given this lack of clarity about the relationship between individual- and state-centered perspectives, it is therefore not surprising that Batiffol considers his theory of coordination quite similar to Kegel's theory of conflicts justice and confessed to being "struck by the fundamental convergences."[48] He found an ambivalence

[41] Ibid., 15. [42] Ibid. [43] Ibid.

[44] Henri Batiffol, 'Réflexions sur la coordinations des systèmes nationaux' (1967) 120 Recueil des Cours 165; Henri Batiffol, *Traité élémentaire de droit international privé* (3rd edn., Pichon & Durand-Auzias 1959). See also Chapter 4.

[45] Henri Batiffol, *Aspects philosophiques du droit international privé* (Dalloz 1956) 222.

[46] Ibid., 15–16 and 222–7.

[47] For Franceskakis's critique of Batiffol's theory, see Chapter 4. See also Andreas Bucher, 'La dimension sociale du droit international privé: cours general' (2009) 330 Recueil des Cours 1, 92–4.

[48] Batiffol, "Les intérêts" (n. 13) 20–1.

in Kegel's reference to private interests. To the extent Kegel referred to interests of individuals in relational terms, Batiffol welcomes the emphasis because this would be different from an individualistic approach. But since Kegel referred to the interests of an "average individual," Batiffol was unsure whether Kegel maintained or departed from an individualistic premise with the reference to parties' interests.[49] Similarly, he was unsure whether Kegel referred to the interests of commerce as "interests of third parties" or to more abstract sets of interests. The former would temper the liberalist tendencies Batiffol saw himself reacting against, so to the extent Kegel had those interests in mind, Batiffol was happy to subscribe.[50] Lastly, Batiffol was in agreement with focusing on the interests of order and uniformity of solutions, depending on what that might mean. If they were used as proxy for interstate interests and "international order," he could subscribe to them too, so long as they did not lead to "undue compromises" in the name of decisional harmony.[51]

With these comments Batiffol indirectly highlighted two important aspects regarding Kegel's theory. He showed that the categories of interests identified by Kegel needed a corresponding theory of the individual's relationship to the state, a theory of law and a theory of autonomy. But at the same time, Batiffol showed that one could freely fill in these blanks. Both Batiffol's and Kegel's theories were broad and indeterminate enough to converge on the moderate account that Batiffol aimed to construct in his review, without making any specific ideological commitments.

2. Alexander Lüderitz

It was precisely the vagueness of Kegel's first account of interest jurisprudence[52] that another German interest jurisprude, Alexander Lüderitz, sought to overcome. In an article in a festschrift dedicated to his mentor Gerhard Kegel, Lüderitz argued that the element in need of most refinement was the category of "private interests." Better articulating this main category would clarify the rest of the theory as well.[53]

Lüderitz opened his review with a critique of the perpetually state-centered development of PrIL. He argues that in an initial step, Zitelmann and other European state-centered theorists had structured PrIL around PublIL, thereby failing to account for any interests and expectations of the actual individuals involved in the PrIL matters.[54]

Writing in 1977, Lüderitz thought not much had happened to temper those initial state-centered theories. He believed that "PrIL had barely found its model as private law, that it was already challenged in light of an alleged shift in the function of private law generally."[55] PrIL, in other words, had never had a chance to articulate

[49] Ibid., 15–16. [50] Ibid., 17. [51] Ibid., 18.

[52] Klaus Schurig explains that Kegel meant the initial essay to open a conversation on the possible category of interests that might factor into the PrIL decision. See Schurig, "Das Fundament" (n. 5) 12.

[53] Lüderitz, "Parteiinteresse" (n. 10) 35. For an analysis of Lüderitz's theory, see also Karsten Otte, 'Betrachtungen zur Interessenlehre' in Heinz-Peter Mansel, *Internationales Privatrecht im 20. Jahrhundert: Der Einfluss von Gerhard Kegel und Alexander Lüderitz auf das Kollisionsrecht* (Mohr Siebeck 2014) 27.

[54] Lüderitz, "Parteiinteresse" (n. 10) 33. [55] Ibid., 34–5.

and construct its private law dimensions, which for Lüderitz are of profound humanistic value.[56]

Lüderitz believed that the critique of Savigny contributed to maintaining the field's state-centrism. But in his view, as in Schurig's view, this critique was the result of a misunderstanding of Savigny's premises.[57] Schurig recently argued that no theory, including the conflicts justice theory, should be thought of as Savignyan, but rather, if at all, as a refinement, a challenge, or a reconceptualization of Savignyan traces.[58] That said, insofar as even the slightest association between classical PrIL and German interest jurisprudence was regarded cautiously because Savigny's theory is commonly perceived as formalistic or overly liberal, Schurig thought that this misunderstood Savigny.[59] Schurig showed how Savigny reacted to the formalism of previous theories and in fact anticipated a much larger scope for political and public policy considerations than we now recognize in his writing.[60] Savigny, remarks Schurig, "never had the blindfold he was attributed."[61]

Thus, rather than prompting a return to a problematic theory, Kegel was simply one more architect in a series—together with Savigny and Kahn—to have set the fundamentals of PrIL, in Schurig's view.[62] For Schurig, then, interest jurisprudence was a stepping-stone in a series of developments from Savigny. Lüderitz, however, thought that in some respects, we had not made enough use of Savigny's intuitions.

Lüderitz's general insight is that over time, scholars unduly narrowed Savigny's theory, and augmented its formalism and universal implications.[63] Lüderitz argued that Savigny's theory consisted of two steps. The first one could be translated as the thesis of equality between nationals and foreigners. It was this step that motivated Savigny to argue that, in principle, the place of litigation (determined by the plaintiff's unilateral choice) should not determine the outcome of the case. Thus, preventing forum shopping and striving for uniformity of decisions should be among the goals of PrIL because, and to the extent that, a certain kind of equality between the parties is a goal as well.[64] Lüderitz argued, as I have done in previous chapters, that we have tended to raise this initial rather formal principle of equality, to the level of formalizing the entirety of PrIL. In other words, Savigny's principle of formal equality between nationals and foreigners was increased to a point where "the entire justice substratum collapses into brute order [. . .] PrIL becomes technical law and for many a senseless game."[65]

Lüderitz argued that while PrIL scholars focused on and enlarged the scope of the principle of formal equality, they lost sight of the second step of Savigny's analysis, namely the principle of "free submission."[66] As I have shown in previous chapters, Lüderitz argued that this principle is sometimes concretized through various empirical elements of freedom (choice of domicile, purchase of foreign land) and sometimes through a fluid determination of reasonable expectations that individuals raise in one another in their transnational dealings.[67] Lüderitz pointed out that

[56] Ibid. [57] Ibid., 31–2. [58] Schurig, "Das Fundament" (n. 5) 5–6 and 11.
[59] Ibid., 8. [60] Ibid. [61] Ibid., 9. [62] Ibid.
[63] Lüderitz, "Parteiinteresse" (n. 10) 32–3. [64] Ibid., 31–2. [65] Ibid., 32.
[66] Ibid. [67] Ibid.

these expectations could either refer directly to the application of a law or to the substantive center point of a legal relation, which in turn informs the application of a particular law.[68]

Lüderitz seemed to believe, as I have argued as well, that we have lost sight of Savigny's fluid analysis of the various elements of what Lüderitz calls the interpersonal "interaction field"[69] and have started to focus on the pursuit of order and uniformity at all cost. Lüderitz showed for example how Savigny's focus on domicile was uncritically replaced with a focus on citizenship, by ignoring the important implications for autonomy and self-determination.[70] Similarly, he argued that Zitelmann's scholarship further formalized and increased Savigny's more moderate universalistic thesis.[71]

By contrast, Lüderitz thought that the decision to apply a particular law must be made by reference to the predominant interests of individuals in large sets of interpersonal relationships. Lüderitz referred to the interest in being able to ascertain the law that is to govern one's rights and liabilities,[72] an interest in integration in a particular community,[73] the interest in the continuation in the enjoyment of certain emancipatory rights and privileges, as well as the recognition of relationships already entered into.[74]

In light of these interests, Lüderitz argued, for example, that allowing name changes according to the law of the domicile of immigrant couples enables them to integrate faster into the new country.[75] In particular, it allows a smoother integration for the children of such families into local schools.[76] At the same time, it might construct a more difficult relationship with the enlarged family left behind in the state of citizenship.[77]

Similarly, norms that apply to questions relating to the parents' rights to and methods of the education of their children have widespread implications for a variety of relationships. Applying German law as the law of domicile might provide more protection to the children of migrant workers and would offer equal rights to both parents in the education of their child.[78] At the same time, it might create conflicts between the children who would become more integrated into the German culture and ways of thinking and the parents who might still be attached to the culture and customs of their homeland.[79]

Furthermore, Lüderitz argued that one could not make broad personal assumptions about the nature of these various relational interests. He perceived Kegel's appreciation of the "normality" of one's attachment to one's state of citizenship as highly problematic for people's autonomy and self-determination.[80] Instead, he argued that one would need to resort to empirical data and studies of family sociology, historical accounts of patterns of immigration, and so on[81] before constructing a PrIL rule that has important implications for all those interpersonal relations. This

[68] Ibid., 32–3. [69] Ibid., 37. [70] Ibid., 33. [71] Ibid. [72] Ibid., 36.
[73] Ibid., 36–7.
[74] Ibid., 38–40. Recent debates on recognition, discussed at greater length in Chapter 6, could find a useful anchor point in Lüderitz's interest jurisprudence in PrIL.
[75] Ibid., 37. [76] Ibid. [77] Ibid. [78] Ibid., 38. [79] Ibid.
[80] Ibid., 38. [81] Ibid., 39.

also means that choice of law rules might differ between temporary guest workers and long-term immigrants, or between temporary guest workers in one county over another.

Alexander Lüderitz introduced an important distinction and relationship between interests, on the one hand, and purposes and goals, on the other. As Karten Otte remarked in his account of Lüderitz's underlying philosophy of PrIL:

> ... purpose is not the same as interest: interests are the needs of those under the authority of the law, which can be discovered empirically or presumed. Purposes specify whose interests to prioritize. Interests must be appraised and weighed and thereupon prioritized in the decision on the applicable law. The goals referenced in this evaluation are the elements of justice.[82]

Lüderitz maintained the conflicts/substantive justice divide.[83] A principle of substantive justice, according to Lüderitz, will always imply a *lex fori* bias, which might simply be covered up through broader appeals to equity.[84] Unlike relational internationalists, Lüderitz did not envision any universalistic methodology appealing to substantive values or a combination of substantive and geographical factors that could break the *lex fori* bias. Furthermore, Lüderitz considered a comparative law analysis in PrIL, much like Jitta envisioned it, simply too demanding.[85] For normative, as well as pragmatic reasons, the conflicts/substantive justice divide was to be maintained.

When it came to referencing the impact of the conflicts/material justice divide on a certain substratum of interpersonal justice however, Lüderitz's reasoning was more nuanced. Lüderitz thought that an express choice of law should be honored as a direct indication of parties' interests. Disregarding it would qualify as states' attitude of superiority.[86] Parties' choice of law would settle the question of conflicts justice as being the most accurate indication of private interests. On the other hand, Lüderitz clarified that the principle of free choice holds only when there is equal bargaining power. When such equality is in doubt, for example in consumer contracts, it seems that no interest in the application of the law as such (conflicts justice) could trump the interest of the party with the weaker bargaining power in the application of protective norms (material justice).[87] Here, the conflicts/material justice divide should not function to disregard or eliminate substantive considerations, but to highlight them. Lüderitz argued for example that by separating the two considerations it becomes clear that neither the consumer, nor the businessperson appeals to the application of a particular law because it is familiar to any one of them (via citizenship or domicile), but rather because of the particular protection it grants. In this way, the decision-maker in PrIL is forced to make a direct—substantive—determination as to which party it aims to protect in order to restore equality within the private law relationship.[88]

Finally, Lüderitz shifted the normative justification for order, as well as the degree of order that Kegel had postulated for PrIL. What was needed, according to Lüderitz,

[82] Otte, "Betrachtungen" (n. 36) 31. [83] Ibid., 31–2. [84] Ibid., 32.
[85] Ibid. [86] Lüderitz, "Parteiinteresse" (n. 10) 48–9. [87] Ibid., 49, 53–4.
[88] Ibid., 49–50.

was not order or decisional harmony per se. This postulate could in fact clash with parties' interests, especially when parties choose a different law than the one that would otherwise apply. What was needed was to construct categories of interests based on particular repeating circumstances and empirical data. "Complete justice in individual cases cannot be obtained in this way. Where wood is chopped, splinters must fall."[89] The typifying of interest constellations was instead a rule of law consideration. Case by case determinations "would be incompatible with current notions of law, would overwhelm the courts, would completely undermine certainty (and thereby 'trust') and would mean de lege ferenda to absolve the legislator of any responsibility."[90] Lüderitz aimed to position his theory somewhere in between the case by case analysis and the pursuit of order and structure at all cost. Unlike in Cavers's theory of the principles of preference, Lüderitz arguably thought that deviating from the rules set out through a determination of predominant interests in particular sets of cases still needed to be made through PrIL's methodological arsenal and technical reasoning, rather than through vague appeals to material justice or an overall better substantive result.

3. Alex Flessner

Lüderitz tried to pave a middle road between a case by case evaluation of private interests and the pursuit of order and structure even to the detriment of private interests.

Alex Fressner thought the moderate position was untenable. In 1988, Flessner argued:

> It is extraordinary that in the area of private law, the individual is subsumed under a state legal order, in which he is placed long term (in family or inheritance law) or from case to case (in the area of obligations and property law) through the operation of the choice of law norm. This repeated attempt of Private International Law to subordinate people (under a state, a nation, and its law) misses the conditions that made Private International Law necessary in the first place, namely the fact that all these nations, states, and legal systems, which raise the plea for application, coexist internationally, constantly compete with each other.[91]

In this constant insecurity and relative chaos, the individual, argued Flessner, "does not operate within a legal system but in between legal systems—and some sensible solutions need to be drawn from this for individuals."[92]

These humanistic underpinnings cause Flessner to raise the same critique to Kegel's theory as Lüderitz did: one must identify the real interests of real individuals, rather than the presumptive interests of average individuals.[93] Similarly, Flessner also believed the pursuit of order and uniformity is, on its own, a dubious interest

[89] Ibid., 40. [90] Ibid.

[91] See "Das 'Private' und das 'Internationale' des internationalen Privatrechts. Diskussionsbeiträge von Alex Flessner und Rainer Pitschas" in Erik Jayme and Heinz-Peter Mansel (eds.), *Nation und Staat im internationalen Privatrecht. Zum kollisionsrechtlichen Staatsangehörigkeitsprinzip in verfassungsrechtlicher und internationalprivatrechtlicher Sicht* (C.F. Müller 1988) 340, 341.

[92] Ibid., 343. [93] Flessner, *Interessenjurisprudenz* (n. 6) 57.

within an individual-centered interest-based theory.[94] Individuals do not have an interest in the pursuit of uniformity and order, but rather an interest in having their interests acknowledged, discussed, and weighed. Yet for Flessner, contrary to Lüderitz, this realization should translate in an evaluation of private interests in each case and a general low regard for internal structure, order, and consistency of PrIL rules and determinations.

Flessner gave the example of a PrIL matter in the 1970s generated by a Spanish couple's divorce case brought in Germany. The couple were Spanish citizens; Spanish law did not allow divorce due to the Catholic underpinnings of its marriage laws at the time. German law, by contrast, recognized the right to divorce.[95] Flessner argued that it was unhelpful to suggest that the right to divorce should be denied because the law of citizenship applies and then to justify the application of that law on the abstract assumption that individuals are connected to their state of citizenship.[96] Furthermore, it would be unhelpful to argue, as Kegel did, that the matter is actually "procedural" versus "substantive" or "an incidental question,"[97] since this allows one to hide a policy choice behind a dogmatic insistence on "internal structure."[98] Flessner argued that this mode of argument simply obscured the question whether the substantive interest that the couple claims—in divorce—should be recognized based on an analysis of the relevant individuals/communities affected and on a balancing of the respective interests.[99] Not only was this abstract justification of conflicts justice not addressing the particular "substantive" interest of the parties to a divorce. It also did not capture the relevance, if any, of the Spanish state's interest in preventing its citizens from divorcing when they no longer live in Spain. Flessner argued that it is unhelpful to suggest, as Kegel did, that the right to divorce is denied because of the interest in preserving order, structure, and consistency within PrIL by the unvarying application of the nationality principle. Flessner repeatedly and rhetorically wondered who the addressee of uniformity was in such a context and why their interests weighed more than those of the spouses.[100]

The proposition that considerations of order and uniformity might interest the broader national or international community was always perceived with skepticism by Flessner even more so than by Lüderitz. But occasionally this appeared as a corollary to a broader skepticism regarding broader public or community interests in the area of private law generally. Here Flessner joined conflicts justice theorists in

[94] Ibid., 45, 66. [95] Ibid., 26ff; BVerfGE 31, 58 in (1972) 36 RabelsZ 145.

[96] Flessner, *Interessenjurisprudenz* (n. 6) 28. [97] Ibid., 29.

[98] Ibid., 28:

> There remains a conflict between the interest of avoiding limping marriages and the interest of the couple in entering into a marriage or, in other words, between paternalism and respect for a legal institution, and self-determination and consensus of the spouses. For the settlement of policy conflict one would need to develop a relevant criterion from the will of the historical legislator as well as the entire value structure of the present legal order.

[99] It is interesting to note the similarity between the case that generated much of the methodological and theoretical debate in Germany in the 1970s and the case with which this book opened, namely that of the same-sex couple seeking divorce in Canada.

[100] Flessner, *Interessenjurisprudenz* (n. 6) 28.

injecting a skepticism, if not agnosticism, to referring to any public interests alongside private interests. While Flessner, like Lüderitz, occasionally seemed to assume that a properly formulated interest jurisprudence will clearly account for all kinds of interests and interest bearers,[101] he, like Lüderitz,[102] was skeptical that any interests other than those of the parties are implicated in the majority of private law disputes.[103] Ultimately Flessner too argued that PrIL should grant large scope to party autonomy and free choice of law.

D. Interest Jurisprudence and Relational Internationalism

The ambivalence that Batiffol noticed in Kegel's initial account of interest jurisprudence, between an individualistic and a relational perspective, is carried through in Flessner's as well as Lüderitz's theory. While interest jurisprudence initially appears to plead for the identification of all interests and interest bearers, the separation between private and public, and between the individual and the state often translate into an assumption that private interests predominate in all or most private law matters. Often the initial proposition that one should *distinguish* between private and public interests, and between material and conflicts justice turns into a preference for the private and/or conflicts justice.

I suggest that much of this is explained by the analytical starting point of interest jurisprudence. Kegel, Lüderitz, and Flessner started with a humanistic concern that the interests of people and their views about justice, freedom, and security are easily marginalized within state-centered theories, if not deliberately ignored. This is a fundamental concern that they share with nineteenth-century relational internationalists. The latter, however, shifted from a focus on the state to a focus on the private law relationship. The initial unit of analysis is the private law relationship, rather than isolated individuals. Story structured his treaties on different kinds of private law relationships, as did Savigny. Savigny explicitly rejected a focus on individuals in isolation. Jitta adopted the analysis of legal relations as the dawn of modern PrIL theories and broke large private law categories into different types of legal relations. Because they focused on the nature of legal relations, they could extract policy elements from both the extra-legal social context and legal norms and principles.

Interest jurisprudence, however, asks us to take a step back from an analysis of the nature of the legal relation. Kegel's remark that the terms of "nature of a legal relation" or "most connected law" are signposts for an analysis of the interests at

[101] Ibid., 62–3.

[102] Lüderitz, "Parteiinteresse" (n. 10) 50: "One should not deny that in the vast number of relationships one balances and offsets primarily private interests; how one does it impact the community, but generally not in such a way that it has an interest in decisions in PrIL following its substantive values."

[103] Flessner, *Interessenjurisprudenz* (n. 6) 62. See also at 86–7: Flessner argues that he did not question "the value prescription of the political school, but rather its veracity." In other words, Flessner argued not that political interests should not be considered when they can be ascertained, but that they should not be presupposed in all private law scenarios, when they are not ascertained. Flessner further argued that interest jurisprudence is guided by "the legitimate expectations of the litigating parties or the general community" and pointed out that this is already noticeable in Savigny's theory, at 86–7, n. 261.

stake in the dispute is an important one, although not particularly novel. As shown in previous chapters, many authors had already argued that Savigny's notion of the nature of a legal relation was a fluid, rather than a dogmatic concept. But interest jurisprudence distanced itself from the nature of a legal relation analysis also because this analysis might "disproportionately favor substantive considerations."[104]

Moving away from a focus on the private law relationship therefore meant moving further away from a substantive analysis both of the way in which individuals understood their relationship and of the values that are embodied in the various national laws relating to the particular relationship. In keeping with interest jurisprudence, this allowed a refocusing on conflicts justice considerations, that is, on the application of a law without regard to its substantive content.

It is at this junction that the two kinds of individual-centered theories diverge. Relational internationalists took the relationship as the first element of analysis, referenced a set of values particular to the relationship, as well as the laws regulating it, and then proceeded to analyze the embeddedness of the legal relation in ever larger social circles.

By distancing itself from an analysis of private law relationships, interest jurisprudence disconnected itself from an otherwise rich substantive analysis. Yet from a different angle, interest jurisprudence, especially in Alexander Lüderitz's account, brought to light a particular set of relational considerations, which while often implicit in the nineteenth-century theories, was not as explicitly developed.

Alexander Lüderitz's account implied an argument that individuals have an interest in the application of a particular law because they wish to establish certain terms of fair interaction with other individuals and communities. For example, he argued that at least certain categories of migrant workers have an interest in being integrated in the host country community;[105] children have an interest in having the maintenance obligations of parents being adapted to the living conditions and costs of the community in which they live, in order to fully take part in the social life of that community;[106] the parent whose parental relationship to the child is in dispute has an interest in having the law of his/her domicile applied, for example, in order to comply with formal requirements that are common in her social environment, and so on. [107] Once it is clear that individuals' access to, participation, and integration into particular national communities are linked to the application of particular laws, it becomes clear that the parties to the legal relation might have different such interests. Lüderitz was clear that ultimately PrIL represents a value judgment about whose interests should prevail in which cases. Here substantive considerations could provide a factor of interpretation and of choice between the relevant interests.[108]

[104] Otte, "Betrachtungen" (n. 36) 32 and n. 27.

[105] Lüderitz, "Parteiinteresse" (n. 10) 41. [106] Ibid., 43. [107] Ibid.

[108] Ibid., 37,40. See also Otte, "Betrachtungen" (n. 36) 31 noting that Lüderitz, unlike Kegel, made a distinction between interests and aims:

> For the decision of conflicts of interests Lüderitz offered premises. More important than the interests themselves are the aims of a particular conflicts decision. The aim is not the same as the interest: Interests are the empirically determined or presumed needs of the ones under law's purview. The aim establishes whose interest one should give priority to. Interests must

What could result from Lüderitz's analysis is a kind of sociology of the transnational realm. Human mobility in the transnational realm is taken at face value and analyzed in social, legal, and even political terms. And because of the complexity of social life understood in this way, Lüderitz pleaded for "recognizing color" rather than making black and white appreciations.[109] Order and uniformity are important human interests and rest at the foundation of legality, but they should not be used as a slogan that prevents the recognition and weighing of human interests.[110]

Because the conflicts justice theory sought to divide, at least methodologically, private from public interests and states from individuals, the universalistic dimension of their theory rested primarily on uncovering a set of possibly universal interests of fairness that should be given consideration in devising conflict of laws norms. Since, other than in Flessner's theory, individual interests were not generally premised on particular substantive outcomes and particular legislative policies, conflicts justice theories did not have to ponder much on how different policies underlying different laws would have to be balanced and how individuals' expectations with respect to the application of particular substantive policies had to be correlated to broader public purposes, national or international. Yet because relational internationalists premised their analysis on the nature of a private law relationship they inevitably struggled to correlate individual reasonable expectations and autonomy with broader public purposes, national sovereignty with international cooperation and solidarity, and national legislative policies with natural law principles.

The next section seeks to reveal the precise way in which the relational internationalist perspective can be thought of as internationalist, yet not committed to a formalist pursuit of order and uniformity at all cost. It starts by considering the much discussed blend between particularistic aspects—reflected in the focus on territoriality—and universalistic aspects—reflected in the focus on comity, in Story's writings. By reference to Story's reasoning in the case *La Jeune Eugenie*, the chapter further discusses how Story attempted to correlate private interests and reasonable expectations with governmental interests and regulatory policies.

Before outlining the universalistic contours of Savigny's and Jitta's PrIL theories, I briefly consider the contours of their general universalistic ideology. I show how Savigny's universalistic ideology can be explained by the various elements of the romanticist and historicist perspectives to which he was drawn. The chapter then elaborates on how those same general views on reconciling universalism with particularism, and national self-determination with natural law were picked up and elaborated by Jitta.

be evaluated by weighing them against one another and therefore establishing priorities in every decision on which law to apply; the aims which are invoked in this evaluation of interests are building blocks of justice. One is therefore in search for the purposeful evaluations of all elements of a dispute.

[109] Lüderitz, "Parteiinteresse" (n. 10) 38. [110] Ibid., 32.

1. Joseph Story

Much like Savigny's and Jitta's theories, Joseph Story's PrIL theory has received different interpretations depending on which element of his theory—the focus on territoriality or on comity—has been highlighted in the interpretations. Joel R. Paul writing in PrIL for example, has suggested, by reference to Story's decision in *La Jeune Eugenie*, that Story's references to comity and international justice enabled him to reconnect private with public international law.[111] Phillip Marshall Brown on the other hand, writing in PublIL, argued that Story's theory is remarkably particularistic and a step back from PublIL, by focusing so strongly on territoriality.[112] Historians have similarly pondered on how to best understand Story's internationalist premises. While some have read Story's writing as strongly relying on natural law and reason,[113] recently it has been argued that in *La Jeune Eugenie*[114] Joseph Story attempted to blend particularistic, territoriality-based arguments with universalistic, natural law arguments because of particular political circumstances, rather than theoretical convictions.[115]

Yet Story's theory is best understood as a blend between universalistic and particularistic premises, which in turn is a reflection of his theoretical and normative convictions, most thoroughly exemplified in his writing in PrIL. *La Jeune Eugenie* can then be understood neither as an attempt to discard any private law elements and focus on PublIL, nor as a departure from theoretical and normative convictions in light of particular political circumstances, but rather as an example of his overall framing of PrIL issues.

As will become apparent from the discussions of Savigny's and Jitta's theories, the blend of particularistic and universalistic premises is common to all relational internationalist theorists discussed in this book and a reflection of their attempt to position states both as distinct normative units and as members of a larger community in search for cooperation and solidarity.

Chapter 2 already illustrated that Story's PrIL theory is framed around the notion of comity, which simultaneously presupposes that states are independent sovereigns as well as parts of a larger community longing for cooperation and reciprocity. In the area of PrIL, Story intimated that the main reason for cooperation is the need to secure the rights and reasonable expectations of individuals in their transnational relationships. This is why Story references repeatedly the need to avoid pernicious consequences, which would result for individuals from an unprincipled application of the forum's law in all cases. As Chapter 2 showed, in Story's theory comity serves primarily as a notion, which explains why states might apply foreign law although they are not obliged to do so. This notion had a similar function to Savigny's notion

[111] Joel R. Paul, 'The Isolation of Private International Law' (1988) 7 Wis Int'l L J 149, 164–8.

[112] Phillip Marshall Brown, *Foreigners in Turkey* (Princeton University Press 1914) 104.

[113] Note, 'International Norms and Politics in the Marshalls Court's Slave Trade Cases' (2015) 128 Harv L Rev 1184 references in note 9 (hereafter "International Norms and Politics").

[114] *United States v. The La Jeune Eugenie*, 26 F. Cas. 832 (C.C.D. Mass. 1822). (hereafter, *La Jeune Eugenie*).

[115] "International Norms and Politics" (n. 113).

of the community of laws, as will be shown in the next section. And like Savigny, Story attempted to illustrate at different points in his PrIL writings, what the limits of comity might be. It is in his illustrations of the limits of comity that the particularistic/universalistic pendulum of his PrIL is best highlighted.

In the area of contract law for example, Story explains that "generally speaking, the validity of a contract is to be decided by the law of the place, where it is made. If valid there, it is by the general law of nations, *jure gentium*, held valid everywhere, by tacit or implied consent."[116] This rule is founded, according to Story "not merely in convenience, but in the necessities of nations" and is ultimately reflected "in universal consent of courts and jurists, foreign and domestic."[117] An initial universalistic starting point is therefore found in *coordinating* the application of domestic laws to enable "commercial intercourse" and prevent utter isolation.[118] Precisely because the initial basis for the application of foreign law is based on mutual interest and convenience, it can be reinterpreted and reassessed continuously and subjected to various exceptions. The most important exception, argues Story, is that:

> No nation is bound to recognize or enforce any contracts, which are injurious to their own interests, or to those of their own subjects. This exception results from the consideration, that the authority of the acts and contracts done in other states, as well as the laws, by which they are regulated, are not, *proprio vigore*, of any efficacy beyond the territories of that state; and whatever is attributed to them elsewhere, is from comity, and not of strict right. And every independent community will, and ought to judge for itself, how far that comity ought to extend. The reasonable limitation is, that it shall not suffer prejudice by its comity.[119]

Because the application of foreign law results from mutual beneficial *coordination* the benefit of this coordination might not outweigh the danger to national interests, policies and domiciliaries. Story certainly did not argue, like Currie, that this would always be the case if domiciliaries do not receive the benefit of the law of the forum, but he certainly drew a cautionary remark about overly sacrificing domestic policies and interests too easily in the name of international comity qua coordination of laws.

> Mr. Justice Best has with great force said, that in cases turning upon the comity of nations (*comitas inter communitates*), it is a maxim that the comity cannot prevail in cases, where it violates the law of our own country, the law of nature, or the law of God. Contracts, therefore, which are in evasion or fraud of the laws of a country, or the rights or duties of its subjects, contracts against good morals, or religion, or public rights, and contracts opposed to the national policy or institutions, are deemed nullities in every country, affected by such considerations; although they may be valid by the laws of the place, where they are made.[120]

Yet in Story's theory comity does not only have a *coordination* function, but also one of international *cooperation* on substantive matters. When states ponder on the

[116] Joseph Story, *Commentaries on the Conflict of Laws, Foreign and Domestic, in Regard to Contracts, Rights and Remedies and Especially in Regard to Marriages, Wills, Successions, and Judgments* (Hilliard, Gray 1834) 201 (hereafter Story, *Commentaries*).

[117] Ibid., 202. [118] Ibid. [119] Ibid., 203. [120] Ibid., 204.

scope and limits of the application of foreign law they also ponder on how they could maximize each other's policies, again out of comity. Therefore, Story argues that:

> A broader principle might be adopted; and it is to be regretted, that it has not been universally adopted by all nations in respect to foreign contracts, as it has been in respect to domestic contracts, that no man ought to be heard in a court of justice to enforce a contract founded in, or arising out of, moral or political turpitude. [. . .] Unfortunately, from a very questionable subservience to mere commercial gains, it has become an established formulary of the jurisprudence of the common law, that no nation will regard or enforce the revenue laws of any other country; and that the contracts of its own subjects, to evade or defraud the just rights of other nations, will be enforced in its own tribunals.[121] Sound morals would seem to point to a very different conclusion.[122]

Grounded in this dual function of comity, the PrIL analysis was sequenced between universalism and particularism. Comity as coordination would start the analysis from the premise of the application of either *lex fori* or a foreign law. Since this was based on the need to avoid pernicious consequences for individuals in their transnational dealings, their expectations would be weighed in. Comity as cooperation would then function as a check to the proper balance of national vs. foreign state and individual interests. A case decided at the time in Louisiana illustrates this sequenced reasoning, which Story judged as having "great force."[123]

The case concerned a man running away with a thirteen-year-old girl, without the consent of her parents, married her in Mississippi and then returned with her to Louisiana. After the girl's death, the mother demanded her property, which she would have been entitled to according to the law of Louisiana, but not according to the law of Mississippi. Much like in Story's theory, the court relied on comity in various ways. It first postulated that because of comity qua "the law of nations" courts will apply foreign law in contract, provided first, that the parties "really intended to be governed by those laws" and that by applying the foreign law "this government would not injure its own rights, or the rights of its citizens."[124]

Since the limits of comity understood as coordination in the application of law are constructed by reference to both individual and larger communal interests, the court went to great length to establish the intentions of the parties, as well as the policy of Louisiana of "watch[ing] with particular care" over minor women who might be "seduced into an escape from her mother's dwelling, and removed in haste out of her reach."[125] The court concluded that Louisiana law should apply to the

[121] Citing *Boucher v. Lawson*, Cas. Temp. Hard. 85,89,194. See *Boucher v. Lawson*, in T. Cunningham, *Reports of Cases Argued and Adjudged in the Court of King's Bench, in the Seventh, Eighth, Ninth and Tenth Years of King George the Second, During Which Time the Right Honorable The Earl of Hardwicke was Lord Chief Justice of the Court* (3rd edn., Stevens & Haynes 1871) 247:

> But if it should be laid down as a principle, that because the goods are prohibited to be exported by the laws of any foreign country from where they are brought, therefore the parties would have no remedy or action, it would cut off all benefit of such trade from this kingdom, which would be of very bad consequence for the principal and most beneficial branches of our trade, nor does it seem to have been ever admitted.

[122] Story, *Commentaries* (n. 116) 204–5. [123] Ibid., 155. [124] Ibid., 156.

[125] Ibid., 158–9.

case to protect the women domiciled in the state since otherwise "it would be unnecessary for us to legislate. In vain should we endeavor to secure the persons and the property of our citizens. Nothing would be more easy, than to render our precautions useless, and our laws a dead letter."[126] The court concludes by invoking the law of nations once again, this time as a principle of cooperation and solidarity among states in fostering each other's policies as much as possible. The court argues that "we cannot, here, hesitate to believe, that the Courts of our neighboring Territory, far from lending their assistance to this infraction of our laws, would have enforced them with becoming severity."[127] This principle of cooperation is again referenced as a "general principle of natural justice, by which nations have tacitly agreed to govern themselves."[128]

Story believed the reasoning of the Louisiana court would "form the basis of the American jurisprudence on this subject. They have much to commend them in their intrinsic convenience and certainty, as well as in their equity; and they seem best to harmonize with the known principles of the common law in other cases."[129]

Story employs much the same reasoning navigating in between individual and state interests, particularistic and universalistic concerns, in *La Jeune Eugenie.*[130] This was a libel case against the schooner La Jeune Eugenie for being engaged in the slave trade off the coast of Africa. Under the authority of acts prohibiting United States' citizens to engage in the slave trade Captain Stockton captured La Jeune Eugenie on a suspicion of slave trade even though it was sailing under the French flag, having French papers. The allegations asserted an offense against United States' law and against the general law of nations. Three elements of Story's reasoning in the case highlight his PrIL theory and methodology along the state-centered/individual-centered and particularistic/universalistic spectrum.

First, Story fully acknowledged the contentious political circumstances of the case[131] since it had "become the subject of diplomatic intercourse between our government and that of France."[132] However, Story asserts a duty "to my own country, to France, and to the world" to decide the matter and contends that he "cannot seek shelter under the wings of executive authority."[133] Story therefore dismisses the suggestion of the United States government to remit the case to French courts because of his duty to the private individuals involved in the case:

> If it had seemed fit to all the parties, whose interests are before the court, to agree to the course held out by this suggestion, it would have relieved my mind from a weighty responsibility, which has been most heavily pressed upon it. But the French claimants resist this course, and require, that the property should be delivered over to their personal possession, and not to the possession of their sovereign. Under such circumstances this court must follow the duty prescribed to it by law, independently of any wishes of our own government or of France.[134]

[126] Ibid., 158. [127] Ibid., 159. [128] Ibid., 159. [129] Ibid., 160.

[130] *La Jeune Eugenie* (n. 114).

[131] For a very helpful analysis of these political circumstances, see "International Norms and Politics" (n. 113).

[132] *La Jeune Eugenie* (n. 114), 840. [133] Ibid. [134] Ibid., 851.

Second, Story recognizes the tension in the case. On the one hand, he had to agree that "no one has a right to sit in judgment generally upon the actions of another... It would be inconsistent with the equality and sovereignty of nations, which admit no common superior."[135] On the other hand, slave trade appeared to Story as unequivocally "abhorrent to the great principles of Christian morality, mercy, and humanity."[136] Story tries to reconcile this tension both in relationship to the parties and to the foreign state.[137] As a matter of private law he constructs the case as a capture and seizure,[138] which is either deemed "rightful and bona fide" or tortious because it infringed upon legally recognized rights of the ship owners.[139] In this way, this seemed like a regular tort case, rather than a matter of foreign relations or general public international law. From this point of view, Story sees himself obliged to judge on the rightfulness of the capture in relationship to the ship owners, rather than portray it as an infringement of sovereignty rights held by the French state. Since Story judges the slave trade to be against the law of nations, which he bases, like all relational internationalists discussed in this book, both on natural law and reason, and on custom and state practice,[140] he shifts the burden to the defendant to prove that his country tolerates the slave trade.[141] This is Story's way of simultaneously considering the interests of the parties and of the states concerned, as well as of reconciling universal principles of justice with national sovereignty.

Lastly, Story references comity throughout the decision precisely in the dual coordination/cooperation function assigned to comity in his PrIL theory. By grounding any deference the court might give to the French government in comity, rather than absolute right, Story claims to be deciding the case by the "dictates" of his "deliberate judgment."[142] And if one thought that comity as coordination imposed any strong obligations to defer to state sovereignty, either of the forum, or of a foreign state, Story clarified that his judgment cannot be "bound by considerations of mere convenience or comity, or a blind obedience to the wishes of any sovereign."[143]

In this first invocation of comity, Story clarifies that the determination of the case is not constrained, but rather loosened because of comity:

> I think, I have a right to say, that the American courts of judicature are not hungry after jurisdiction in foreign causes, or desirous to plunge into the endless perplexities of foreign jurisprudence ... But it is to be remembered, that while the court is not rashly to engage in asserting jurisdiction over foreign causes from the odium ... it also has a public duty to perform, from which it dare not shrink, to pronounce its own judgment of the law [...].[144]

[135] Ibid., 847. [136] Ibid., 840.

[137] Ibid., 845. Interestingly, Story ponders on the unusualness of hearing a claim based on "the law of nations" in a civil court and concludes:

> In the cause of The Diana, 1 Dod. 95–100, Sir Wm. Scott, in commenting on an analogous proceeding for the condemnation of a slave ship, did not deny the competency of a court of civil jurisdiction to adjudicate upon a question of this sort, upon proper allegations to direct its inquiries. If there be any right to be asserted by the libellants, I am not aware, that the mode, which is here adopted, is in substance, however it may be in form, exceptionable.

[138] Ibid., 843, 848. [139] Ibid., 848. [140] Ibid., 834–6, 845.

[141] Ibid., 834, 849. [142] Ibid., 849. [143] Ibid., 840. [144] Ibid., 851.

But Story also references comity as cooperation. The argument had been raised on behalf of the French party that even if French law also prohibited slavery, this policy could not be applied or relied upon by an American court. Here too, Story considered that this argument sounded too much in international relations, rather than in tort. Whereas national sovereignty prohibited a state from enforcing another state's penalties, in civil proceedings it seemed entirely natural to apply a foreign policy, whether private or public, to decide on the rights and obligations of individuals in relationship to each other. Not only could the argument against the application of foreign public law be refuted by challenging that considerations of sovereignty are implicated in private law proceedings to a large extent. Comity itself dictated that states should cooperate with each other in enforcing each other's policies when adjudicating transnational private law matters:

> It is said, that the cognizance of penalties and forfeitures for breaches of municipal regulations exclusively belongs to the tribunals of the nation, by whom they are enacted. And this, in a general sense, with reference to the right to originate proceedings for the sole purpose of enforcing such penalties and forfeitures, may be true. But that any court may take notice of the laws of a foreign country, whether civil or penal, which come incidentally before it in the exercise of its general jurisdiction over persons or property, can admit of as little dispute.[145]

In other words, in his judgment in *La Jeune Eugenie*, just like in Story's analysis of choice of law in contract, Story's reliance on comity as *cooperation* signifies, indeed mandates, a step back from the public law taboo.[146] But Story is aware of a possible contradiction: the public law taboo itself could be seen as a principle of interstate and judicial restraint of authority and ultimately justified by comity. Story therefore needs to clarify that comity as *coordination* merely postulates the possibility of applying either forum or foreign law but does not dictate when one should apply the one or the other. Comity as *coordination* is therefore not a choice of law rule, but merely an anchor point that explains why a court would ever apply foreign law to begin with. Comity as *cooperation* indicates a clear case when foreign law should apply, at a minimum, when the foreign policy—private or public—is shared by the forum or is a rule of customary international law. Comity as coordination, explains Story, is not an *essential* element of the law of nations, but comity as cooperation is, since it constructs a larger community of shared goals and policies:

> It is often said, that no country takes notice of the revenue laws of a foreign country, or holds itself bound to repudiate commercial transactions, which violate them. But this is a rule adopted from a motive of policy or comity: and is not an essential ingredient in any system of the law of nations. If any nation were disposed to discountenance any smuggling in violation of the laws of a foreign country, and in cases coming regularly before its own courts were to refuse to recognize any rights of property founded on such violation, I am not able to perceive, what just ground of complaint the offended nation could have against such conduct. It seems to me, that it might with more justice complain of the refusal to enforce such laws, and

145 Ibid., 849–50.

146 For a description and analysis of the so called "public law taboo" in PrIL, see William Dodge, 'Breaking the Public Law Taboo' (2002) 43 Harv Int'l L J 161.

to discountenance such violations. But where a title to property originates in what a nation deems in its own subjects a public crime, more specially if it be an aggravated crime founded on fraud and rapine; and it finds, that another nation deems it a crime of a like nature, and prohibits it as such, and confiscates the property of its subjects engaged in the commission of it, I do not perceive, why such property, so polluted by crimes, should, if it falls into the custody of a court of the former nation, be so sacred from judicial touch, that it must be restored to the wrongdoer. And I would ask, where is the authority, that requires such a court to act in this manner, when the public policy of its own, as well as of the foreign, government is avowedly engaged in endeavoring to suppress that crime? If in a case before this court, acting in rem, a title to property, founded on theft or other municipal crime, or on a fraud committed in a foreign country, were set up, until my judicial conscience is better instructed, I should have extreme difficulty in recognizing such a title, if the property was once legally in the custody of the court.[147]

In other words, comity as cooperation reverses what at first sight appears as an overreach of jurisdiction:

It enforces the policy, common to both nations, of repressing an odious traffic, which is denounced by both. It makes our own country, not a principal, but an auxiliary, in enforcing the interdict of France, and subserves the great interest of universal justice. I am not aware of any obstacle in the constitution of a court of admiralty, proceeding in rem, to the adoption of such a practice; and I am greatly mistaken, if it does not carry in its bosom the seeds of peace and reconciliation, instead of animosity and recrimination.[148]

2. Friedrich Karl von Savigny

Much like Story's theory, Savigny's theory has also been differently read, depending on whether one focuses on his natural law premises, or his discussion of national sociolegal particularities, on his references to individual liberty or the communal underpinnings of the *Volk*. Similarly to the discussion of Joseph Story's theory, this section shows that the defining element of Savigny's PrIL theory is precisely his attempt to reconcile natural with positive law, and particularistic with universalistic elements.

There are various paths to understanding Savigny. The one adopted by Okko Behrends was to trace Savigny's thinking to the Roman law sources that he cited and seemed more favorable toward.[149] Another path, adopted by Joachim Rückert, was to trace Savigny's thinking to the German romanticist tradition and subscribe to him an "objective idealist" philosophy, which although unique to Savigny, nevertheless finds its roots in early German romanticism.[150] Finally, another path, proposed by Frederick Beiser, is to follow the various steps that contributed to Savigny's thinking, from "the young romantic," to his strong critique of natural law and Kant, and to his "mature work" in the System.[151] Interestingly, all these ways of capturing

[147] Ibid., 850. [148] Ibid., 851.

[149] For Okko Behrends's understanding of Savigny's theory, see Chapter 6.

[150] For Joachim Rückert's understanding of Savigny's theory, see Chapter 6.

[151] Frederick C. Beiser, *The German Historicist Tradition* (OUP 2011) (hereafter Beiser, *German Historicist*).

Savigny's thinking converge on one aspect, which is of particular interest for this chapter, namely the blend between natural law and positivism, between universalism and relativism.

Okko Behrends argues that Savigny incorporated universal principles of ethics and social cooperation from the stoic-natural law philosophy, while preserving a belief in particular national laws that purport to define and structure those general principles "in a particular way."[152] Within the eight volumes of the System, PrIL was merely an example of Savigny trying to simultaneously reference the individual and the social, the particular and the universal.[153]

Rückert too identifies in Savigny a "Hoheitsdrang" (an aspiration to the higher and the universal), while maintaining his faith in national self-determination and a strong cultivation of the individuality of each "Volk."[154] Finally, Beiser tries to capture Savigny's universalistic/particularistic and natural law/positive law duality by situating Savigny in the context of three different influences: the romanticist school, the rejection of Kantian precepts, and the historical school. Beiser's analysis is particularly helpful in explaining Savigny's mix of universalistic and relativistic elements and ultimately his universalistic/particularistic ideology within PrIL. This section therefore starts with a brief account of Beiser's explanation for the ideological duality in Savigny, before showing how this duality might be captured in Savigny's PrIL writings.

a) Savigny's triad: romanticism, anti-Kantianism, and historicism

In 2011 the leading scholar of German Idealism, Fredrick Beiser, wrote a compelling account of the ideology of the various protagonists of the German historicist tradition, including, most important for this chapter, the philosopher Johann Gottfried Herder (1744–1803) and Savigny.[155] In the chapter dedicated to Savigny, Beiser traces Savigny's thinking, from his "most formative years" in Marburg under the influence of the romantic tradition, to his decisive critique of natural law and Kant, to his historicist views, and finally to his mature work in the System and the puzzling return of several "natural law-like" precepts.[156]

Beiser shows in a first step that as a "young romantic"[157] Savigny started with a strong inclination to natural law and aspired to show "how law originates from the necessary laws of our own consciousness."[158] But under the influence of the powerful intellectual movement known as the "Frühromantik," sometime between 1800 and 1802 Savigny completely lost faith in the natural law tradition,

[152] Okko Behrends, 'Geschichte, Politik und Jurisprudenz in Savignys System des heutigen römischen Rechts' in Okko Behrends, Wulf Eckart Voss, and Malte Diesselhorst (eds.), *Römisches Recht in der Europäischen Tradition: Symposion aus Anlass des 75. Geburtstages von Franz Wieacker* (R. Gremer 1985) 257, 269 (hereafter Behrends, "Geschichte").

[153] Ibid., 271.

[154] Joachim Rückert, *Idealismus, Jurisprudenz und Politik bei Friedrich Carl von Savigny* (R. Gremer 1984) 238, 358.

[155] Beiser, *German Historicist* (n. 151) Chapter 3 (Herder) and Chapter 5 (Savigny).

[156] Ibid., Chapter 5. [157] Ibid., 218–19. [158] Ibid., 221.

and through his critique of Kant's moral philosophy, he lost confidence "in the power of reason to provide substantive practical principles."[159] Furthermore, Beiser notes that:

> Savigny began to recognize that legal doctrines cannot be given a transcendental foundation independent of a particular society and state. He now realized that traditional natural law doctrines, which assumed that human beings have a fixed identity and nature prior to their entrance into society and the state, began with a false abstraction. Human beings are social and political animals, whose very identity is determined by the specific society and state in which they live. Thus, a natural law for all human beings seemed as plausible as the ideal of a single universal language.[160]

Fully engaged with the early historical and romantic tradition, Savigny wrote in this period about "the spirit of humanity" identified with Christianity not found in any particular church but whose basic value is "the education of the human race."[161] He argued for a reintegration of the passions of love and friendship in philosophical ethics, a focus on the concrete human being, rather than the abstract entity endowed with reason, and for an ethic of "self-realization and individuality."[162] In line with the *Frühromantik* tradition, he looked back with nostalgia at the Holy Roman Empire, which had many independent sources of authority serving "as sources of local autonomy and belonging."[163]

Savigny subsequently engaged in a strong and repeated critique of Kant and natural law, which paved the way for his historicism and his theory of the *Volksgeist*.[164] He was critical of Kant's disregard of what Savigny viewed as the moral virtues of love and friendship,[165] and wrote against Kant's theory of punishment[166] and Kant's categorical imperative and pure reason.[167] Savigny therefore purported to establish a new theory of jurisprudence, neither Kantian, nor grounded in natural law, but rather in history. He argued that the genesis of law must be linked to the social and political context,[168] against any a priori method of finding the law and generally against formalist jurisprudence.[169] He now argued that law is not the product of reason, but that it reflects the beliefs and ways of life of an individual people. As Beiser notes, Savigny believed that:

> civil law is as characteristic of a nation as its language, customs and constitution; and to separate it from the culture of a nation is an artificial abstraction. The law therefore grows with a people, and it dies with them when a nation declines. The proper seat of the law lies in the common consciousness of the nation.[170]

The way in which Savigny thought of his historical jurisprudence, in contrast to the philosophical school, was aptly summarized by Beiser:

159 Ibid. 160 Ibid., 222. 161 Ibid., 222–3. 162 Ibid., 223.

163 Ibid., 223. ("For the early romantics, the chief evil of modern politics was centralization, the amassing of all power in a single executive and bureaucracy, which would crush all diversity and local liberty. They found such centralization not only in the absolutist regimes of the eighteenth century, but also in the revolutionary government in France.")

164 Ibid., 225. 165 Ibid. 166 Ibid., 226. 167 Ibid., 227.

168 Ibid., 230. 169 Ibid., 233. 170 Ibid., 238.

The problem with the philosophical school, he argues, is that it makes an artificial and arbitrary separation of the part from the whole. This part can be the individual citizen, who is separated from his family, country and state; or it can be the present generation, which is separated from history [. . .] It is clear from Savigny's argument that the historical school represents a methodological holism. This school claims that each individual has to be understood from his place in a whole, whether the part/whole relationship is synchronic or diachronic, whether it is that of a citizen to the state or that of a generation to history. Hence the basic fallacy of the philosophical school is hypostasis: it separates the part from the whole and gives it a self-sufficient identity, when in reality the part is intelligible only within the whole.[171]

These initial articulations of his historical theory of jurisprudence are further developed in the System. There, Savigny argued that every right:

is part of a larger network of rights (legal relation), and that its meaning and extent depends upon this network [. . .]. Savigny insisted that "the spiritual element of jurisprudential practice" consists in constantly keeping in mind these two organic factors; in other words, in treating any individual case, we have to consider the relationship of all the parts and how they changed or developed.[172]

Furthermore, law exists "in the common consciousness of the people," so "positive right is also national right."[173] The historical theory is now definitively separated from the social contract theory and Beiser explains Savigny's charge toward the latter in these terms:

He makes two basic objections against it. First, it assumes that each individual could exist apart from his society and state, that he could just as well have chosen to live in some other society and state from that in which he happens to live. But this does not agree with the fact that wherever we find human beings they exist in a community and live according to laws. Second, the theory is circular, because it assumes the powers to deliberate and make laws that people could have only through society and the state. Though a collection of distinct individuals need the law, they still do not have the power to create it.[174]

These themes were merely a continuation of Savigny's life-long focus on three elements: (i) the rejection of the theory of pure reason and philosophical a priori deductions; (ii) his insistence on the particularities, traditions and values of each people, and (iii) the relational and organic embeddedness of the individual and individual rights within a larger whole. In all these respects Savigny was well grounded in the *Frühromantik* and the Historical School. But Beiser also notes "one of the most striking passages of Savigny's System" in which natural law seems to make a comeback for Savigny who now argued that the context of law can be "individual, the characteristic of a particular people; or it can be universal, i.e. that common to human nature."[175] Beiser describes Savigny's new take on natural law:

[171] Ibid., 244.

[172] Ibid., 246–7. ("Further, the institution of right should be understood organically, i.e., in its living interconnections and its progressive development, so that it is seen as part of a whole, the wider web of legal relations and higher laws, which also have an organic nature.")

[173] Ibid., 274. [174] Ibid., 251. [175] Ibid.

Savigny sees these as two necessary aspects of all right, and he complains that they have become separated in contemporary jurisprudence. There are those who stress the individual aspect of right, as if general principles play no role, and there are those who emphasize the universal aspect of rights, as if general principles had their meaning independent of particular cases. Normally, Savigny criticizes the second party, the formalists who had developed the universal side of the law; but here, as if to admit that they too have their point, he insists that we should not neglect "the sense for the whole, and therefore the higher meaning of the institutes of right." The universal content of Volksrecht appears as "the moral nature of right" and it involves such concepts as "the moral worth and freedom of man." The task of the legislator, Savigny insists, is to keep in mind both these aspects of law and to fuse them into a unity, so that the universal principles take on a concrete meaning and particular cases have a general significance. [...] Hence, in the second book of the System, Savigny discusses the universal concept of right, which he defines as the sphere in which a person can act freely without the influence of others. The need and existence of right is the result of our human condition, Savigny says, and it does not depend on contingent historical circumstances alone.[176]

Savigny concluded that the universal ideal is the development of "ethically/morally responsible freedom"[177] and the "ethical development of human nature" even though "it is the historical task of each Volk to develop it in its own way."[178] This was Savigny's way of avoiding both abstract formalism and absolute positivism, and to reconcile relativism with universalism.[179] This also makes it possible for Savigny to distinguish *jus gentium* from natural law. According to Savigny, *jus gentium* is "first extracted from experience, empirically" and then based on its "grounding element," "namely the consciousness of human nature."[180] This, he argued, made it possible for the Romans to think of *jus gentium* as "jus civile, as a positive law which arose and developed historically."[181] This meant that one must exercise "extreme caution" when moving from the universal to the particular in order to not destroy the national spirit of the laws of the people, while still having in sight "the equal ethical worth and freedom of individuals."[182]

Certainly one way of understanding this recurrence of universal principles in Savigny's System is to adopt Behrends' proposition that Savigny always incorporated human rights, ethical dimensions of social life from the stoic tradition. But another useful way of understanding Savigny's incorporation of universal elements is made possible when Savigny is placed within the historical tradition in which he was writing, and in particular when his nineteenth-century historical tradition is placed in relationship with the earlier historical tradition of the eighteenth century, in particular that of Johann Gottfried Herder. My concern here is not with the debate on whether or not Savigny read Herder extensively[183] or whether or not Herder

176 Ibid., 251. 177 Ibid. 178 Ibid.

179 Behrends, "Geschichte" (n. 152) 269.

180 See Friedrich Karl von Savigny, *System des heutigen Römischen Rechts*, vol. 1 (Bei Deit & Comp. 1840) 113.

181 Ibid. 182 Ibid., 56.

183 See Christoph Mährlein, *Volksgeist und Recht, Hegels Philosophie der Einheit und ihre Bedeutung in der Rechtswissenschaft* (Königshausen & Neumann 2000) 127 (discussing the way in which Herder's influence on Savigny has been discussed in PrIL scholarship and contesting the assumption that Savigny read much of Herder's historical philosophy).

is actually the main "gateway through which to understand Savigny."[184] Rather, the usefulness lies in understanding how the relationship between the relative analytical dimensions of the *Volk* and the universal elements of natural law featured in the earlier historical tradition of the eighteenth century, which helps explain, I argue, the way in which they featured in Savigny's writing.

In their analysis of the German historical tradition and in particular the relationship between the earlier eighteenth-century and the later nineteenth-century school, both F.M. Barnard and Beiser find it striking that while in the eighteenth century Herder kept traces of universalistic, natural law inspired elements, the later nineteenth-century generation to which Savigny belonged, "self-consciously and explicitly rejected the natural law tradition."[185] Adepts of the eighteenth century historical school of thought, including Herder, were extremely critical of natural law for "illegitimately universalizing the values of 18th century Europe as if they held for all epochs and cultures."[186] But if Herder and Humboldt "still clung to the concept of natural law" it was because they were "very reluctant to surrender it for fear of relativism."[187]

To be sure, Herder was concerned with the imperialist connotations of natural law and its individualistic underpinnings, since he, like Savigny, conceived of the individual as a social being, who cannot be understood apart from her social context.[188] But Herder was equally concerned with the potential of relativism, which would allow the state, especially the centralized bureaucratic states of the modern world, a free hand for despotism.[189]

Therefore, natural law was to be maintained, even though it needed to be stripped of the individualistic connotations.[190] According to Herder, the universal element is not the isolated individual, but "humanity," which symbolizes interhuman cooperation, rather than the mere accumulation of isolated individuals.[191] Common to all states was therefore the pursuit of happiness[192] and ethical self-realization and perfection[193] even though each state achieves it differently in different times.[194]

As for Savigny,.Christianity, though not associated with any particular church, would ground humanity generally because "religion, as Herder viewed it, is

[184] See Franz Wieacker, *Privatrechtsgeschichte der Neuzeit unter besonderer Berücksichtigung der deutschen Entwicklung* (2nd edn., Vandenhoeck & Rupert 1996) 393.

[185] Beiser, *German Historicist* (n. 151) 13; F.M. Barnard, *Herder's Social and Political Thought, From Enlightenment to Nationalism* (Clarendon Press 1965) 153–67 (hereafter Barnard, *Herder's Social and Political Thought*). See Johann Gottfried V. Herder, *Outlines of a Philosophy of the History of Man* (T. Churchil, tr., Bergman Publishers 1800).

[186] Beiser, *German Historicist* (n. 151) 13.

[187] Ibid., 217. ("In Savigny there is no such reluctance [to abandon natural law], there is no such fear. He was indeed heartless and relentless in banishing the concept from his writing and the lecture hall. Only later in his career would he discover that the concept is not so easily abandoned.")

[188] Ibid., 156 ("Against Hobbes and Rousseau, he argues that man is naturally social, and that he cannot survive, let alone prosper, without the aid of others.")

[189] Ibid. [190] Ibid.

[191] Ibid., 155, 157. Barnard, *Herder's Social and Political Thought* (n. 185) 77. ("By humanization Herder chiefly meant the provision of education and social welfare under conditions of political freedom. This, Herder insisted, presupposed as the most basic requirement the absence of political censorship and the abolition of absolutist rule.")

[192] Beiser, *German Historicist* (n. 151) 134. [193] Ibid., 156. [194] Ibid., 158.

essentially man's consciousness of his social obligations. Christianity, in its purest form, is the expression of this consciousness in social conduct and in man's attitude to his fellow-man."[195] Furthermore, for Herder, and similarly for Savigny, the law of nature demands the realization of individuality, whether the individual is a particular person, culture or state.[196] Under humanity Herder included "everything having to do with what I said about man's noble education toward the use of reason and freedom, toward finer senses and drives, toward the finest and strongest health, toward the fulfillment and domination of the earth."[197]

Although it might seem as surprising as Savigny's universalistic postulates in the System appeared, Herder too argued ultimately that "the basic norms by which we should govern our life are those that ensure, as their minimal precondition, that we can live autonomously and rationally. Hence, for Herder, the two fundamental characteristics of humanity are the use of reason and freedom."[198] Yet these are formal characteristics only, so that the content of what should count as rational and what one should choose as a free being will depend according to circumstances.[199]

Herder believed that all these elements, Christianity, education toward use of reason and freedom, as well as the common social nature of mankind, would lead to more "humanity" which he associated with "Billigkeit," which in turn translates into reasonable, fair, just, and equitable interpersonal relations.[200]

> Increasing trade in particular would, Herder felt, create a community of interest transcending national boundaries. Though he agreed that trade did not spring from the noblest of human motives, he nevertheless regarded it as one of the most powerful "organic" forces in that it combined two fundamental human drives, the instinct of self-preservation and the sensus humanitatis. When he was advancing, therefore, the principle of partnership as a basis of international relations, he presumably thought in terms of a fusion between the economic and ethical springs of human behavior, leading to an ethical code of commercial relations, which could give birth to a sense of partnership between nations.[201]

The relativist view of different peoples with different climates, social, political, cultural, and ethnical backgrounds combined together with a search for universal humanity as well as the pursuit of fair and equitable interpersonal relations—ultimately with individual ethical self-realization and perfection. "Such was Herder's ultimate solution to the problem of the one-in-many in history, of how there could be a single rational standard amid incommensurable national ones."[202]

I do not mean to settle whether Savigny's reference to Christianity, to the universal pursuit of ethically responsible freedom, or to the self-realization and perfection of the individual, be it one people or one individual in a social context, mirror similar concepts in Herder. What I meant to suggest by creating a parallel between

[195] Ibid., 139, 158, 156; Barnard, *Herder's Social and Political Thought* (n. 185) 9.
[196] Beiser, *German Historicist* (n. 151) 159. [197] Ibid., 156. [198] Ibid., 162.
[199] Ibid. [200] Barnard, *Herder's Social and Political Thought* (n. 185) 98.
[201] Ibid., 105.
[202] Beiser, *German Historicist* (n. 151) 162. ("Freedom prescribes only that we choose effective means to ends, whatever those ends might be; and reason prescribes only that we find sufficient evidence for our beliefs, whatever these beliefs might be. The formality of these requirements, Herder assumes, makes the standpoint of humanity compatible with historical change and cultural diversity.")

Herder's and Savigny's historical ideology is that in the historical tradition the blend of natural law alongside the relativist concept of the individual *Volk* was a way of ensuring national autonomy and self-determination, while also creating an ethical basis for law and interhuman cooperation as well as individual self-determination. For example, Barnard argued that the German political romanticists who followed Herder and made use of his concepts (among whom he counts Savigny as well) had in fact brought those concepts to the nationalist front, ignoring Herder's more universalistic and humanistic views, such as "middle-class leadership, reform from below, cooperation, rather than subordination, and popular participation in government."[203] Barnard argues that because Romanticists over-emphasized the significance of the state and could not conceive of human existence outside the state, they increased the potential for human subordination and extreme nationalism, which were out of tune with Herder's ideology of empowering people to self-realization and perfection through ethical social cooperation.[204] He therefore found it unsurprising that romanticists denied any virtue for natural law and includes Savigny in this camp.[205] He argues that contrary to the later Romanticists, Herder "upheld the notions of both Volk and Humanität as equally relevant value considerations."[206]

Viewed from this angle, then, Savigny's attempt in the System to reemphasize both the national and the universal could be understood as precisely the kind of ideological tempering and human empowering beyond and within the state that Barnard saw in Herder, but not in the Romanticists. Savigny's life-long attack on natural law and a priori value judgments was now to be tempered by an appeal to human freedom and self-realization where the development of ethically responsible freedom and Christian social values were perceived as universal values beyond the state.

b) Back to PrIL

To the extent this interpretation or reconstruction is plausible, it allows for a different appreciation of the way in which both universalistic and nationalist, both private and public elements are combined in Savigny's PrIL, confirming Behrends' own intuition that Savigny's PrIL theory could be read as simultaneously combining these elements.[207] On the one hand, Savigny's choice for domicile as the connecting factor over nationality can be understood precisely as a means of allowing individuals the personal freedom outside and beyond the state that Barnard thought nineteenth-century historicists lost through their attack on natural law. Savigny's repeated references on the way in which individuals inevitably extend into various jurisdictions because they enter into a variety of relationships vital to their development allude precisely to the idea of the ethic of self-realization and freedom within and outside the state, which Herder thought would be inevitable for human flourishing and development.[208]

[203] Barnard, *Herder's Social and Political Thought* (n. 185) 154. [204] Ibid., 156.
[205] Ibid., 159. [206] Ibid., 166. [207] See Chapter 6.
[208] Beiser, *German Historicist* (n. 151) 155.

Furthermore, the previous chapter showed that this freedom would be "ethically responsible"[209] both within the private law relationship and in relationship to the communities in which it is embedded.[210] The broad public policy and the relational perspective would temper individual liberty. Christianity and the appeal for an international juridical community would encourage universalism, but a legal relation would still be localized in a community. Elements of the private law relationship and elements of legal policy would factor into the localization of a legal relation, but to a different extent and depending on the particular relationships.

This chapter aims to highlight a different dimension of Savigny's pendulum between universalism and particularism, namely Savigny's attempt to simultaneously anchor PrIL in a community of laws, while trying to establish its limits. Savigny anchors PrIL in "an international community of nations having intercourse with one another; and this view has in the course of time always obtained wider recognition, under the influence of a common Christian morality, and of the real advantages which result from it to all concerned."[211] In prescribing this level of internationalism, as well as replacing citizenship with domicile as the most significant connecting factor in a broad range of PrIL matters,[212] Savigny makes a significant departure from Roman law,[213] which he defends as entirely in line with his overall historical method.[214]

[209] Ibid., 251.

[210] It is notable that Ludwig von Bar criticized Savigny for having included too broad a public policy exception, making it unlikely that foreign law would apply in many circumstances. See Ludwig von Bar, *Das internationale Privat- und Strafrecht* (Hahn'sche Hofbuchhandlung 1862) 109–110. ("Most laws which are not logical consequences of general principles may be referred to reasons of this description (of politics, police, or political economy), and there would be really little room for the application of foreign law.")

[211] Friedrich Karl von Savigny, *Private International Law. A Treatise on the Conflict of Laws: And the Limits of Their Operation in Respect of Place and Time*, vol. 8 (William Guthrie tr., 2nd edn., T. & T. Clark 1880) 70 (hereafter Savigny, *Private International Law*).

[212] Ibid., 134:

> The great influence of this voluntary submission to the territorial law has always been very generally recognized. It might have been doubted in Roman law, according to which personal dependence on a particular local law was chiefly determined by municipal citizenship, which everyone normally obtained, not by his own free will, but by birth. But every possible doubt disappears in modern law, in which personal subjection to particular law is determined by domicile; for as domicile itself is fixed by perfectly free choice, so in regard to particular legal relations the normal faculty of subjecting oneself at will to any territorial law admits of no doubt.

[213] Ibid., 71–2:

> This standpoint of the community of law among independent states, from which has arisen an approximate uniformity in the treatment of conflicts among different positive laws, was unknown to the Romans. The intercourse of nations had to receive the enormous impulse which we observe in modern times, before the felt want of such principles could bring them to recognition and development.

[214] Ibid., 13–14:

> The author cannot be charged with having changed his mind in this respect (that some of Roman law can be refuted as presently irrelevant), as he has publicly expounded most of the views referred to for a period of from thirty to forty years—a fact which proves the utter baselessness of the charge which has been made against the historical school in general, and against myself in particular.

It is in Savigny's postulate of the community of laws that critics of PrIL read Savigny's alleged naiveté and extreme liberalism. By positing a community of laws Savigny is believed to have either failed to appreciate or deliberately downplayed national interests and public policies. But Savigny writes his universalistic theory of PrIL in constant conversation with scholars, like Carl Georg von Wächter, who had suggested a presumptive application of the law of the forum in PrIL matters.

Savigny does not disregard particularists' concern with public policy, but rather the methodological implications and reasoning. Thus, the presumption of the application of forum law is refuted precisely because it is a *presumption*. It simply states, without probing, whether "the prevailing view of modern legislation were the jealous maintenance of its own authority."[215] Furthermore, it ignores the fact that since there are multiple grounds of jurisdiction, if each state applied its own law the plaintiff would be able to determine the fate of the defendant's rights and reasonable expectations.[216] This is, according to Savigny, "a special reason which makes the application of this principle very dangerous."[217] More importantly, Savigny ridicules the *lex fori* presumption for being merely a postulate, not a theory:

> A modern writer gives to this view the following very appropriate expression: We will admit that every judge has to administer the laws of his own country; but then he must apply them only to the persons and the cases for which they are made. *Whether*, then, the legislator has intended his law to apply to cases (legal relations) in themselves doubtful, and in which there is a collision of territorial laws: *this*, says that writer, is the *only* difficult point.[218]

By contrast to the *lex fori* theory, anchoring PrIL in a community of laws meant for Savigny that one could make a universal methodological proposition, namely that every judge should apply the law to which the legal relation belongs, according to its nature, regardless of whether this is its own, or a foreign law.[219] More importantly, it meant that Savigny could presuppose or prescribe a certain degree of reciprocity:

> We might suppose the interest of our own fellow-subjects to be imperiled, if in some cases a landed estate in our country were to fall by inheritance, according to the rules of a foreign country, to a foreigner, instead of a native. But the opposite result might as probably occur, in the particular case, in applying the foreign rules of law; and besides, every such danger, if people will use that word, is completely removed by the reciprocity we have assumed to exist. Or it might be supposed that the dignity and independence of our country would be endangered, if foreign rules of law were applied to the succession of the estate on its soil. But this objection also is refuted by the supposed reciprocity, which, more generally viewed,

[215] Ibid., 144.

[216] Ibid., 145: "But a principle which leads to such results cannot possibly be regarded as correct. The hardships and arbitrariness to which the principle may lead is very striking, if we imagine it applied to the countries in which the *Landsassiat* has full sway." The translator explains in n. 2 that "The Landsassiat is a rule peculiar to certain German states, by which the acquisition of certain kinds of property, or of rights in such property, involves complete personal subjection to the law of the country, and the necessity of taking an oath of allegiance."

[217] Ibid., 145.

[218] Ibid., 145 citing Heinrich Thöl, *Das Handelsrecht. Als algemeines in Deutschland geltendes Privatrecht mit Berücksichtigung des ausserdeutchen Handelsrechts*, vol. 1 (Fues 1841) 28.

[219] Savigny, *Private International Law* (n. 211) 76.

resolves itself into an international community of law, as the foundation and highest aim of our whole doctrine.[220]

Savigny argues that it cannot be *assumed* that the application of foreign law always causes an injury to the forum. Furthermore, the principle of a community of laws, if universally adopted as the anchor point of PrIL, would serve as an informal basis for reciprocity. Therefore, one should not start from a *preference* for the application of the *lex fori*. However, Savigny notes that:

> [T]he true elements of the principle here contested [of the a priori application of the *lex fori*] must be noted, and that rather because the admission of them may perhaps facilitate the reconciliation of conflicting opinions.[221]

Therefore, Savigny argues not only that "if the judge finds a domestic law on the question of conflict, he must follow it unreservedly, even if it should not coincide with his own theoretical view" and that the judge must always apply its own procedural law[222] but also that:

> The judge must never apply a foreign territorial law, if its application is excluded by the limits above fixed for the legal community of independent states ... Thereby it will become apparent that the practical difference between this theory and the view which I maintain is, in fact, not so great as it first appears.[223]

Savigny argued that there are "many kinds of law, whose peculiar nature does not admit of so free an application of the community of laws"[224] including laws resting on moral grounds, or "on reasons of *public interest (publica utilitas)*, whether these relate to politics, police, or political economy."[225] Understanding the parameters of this class of laws that are beyond the scope of the community of laws is, in Savigny's words "perhaps the most difficult part of this subject."[226]

Savigny therefore did not reject the insight of focusing on public policy and statutory intent that the *lex fori* school of thought was offering. Rather, he rejected the simplicity of the method, which ultimately ignored precisely the analysis of the various policies and their reach. Furthermore, he rejected the presumption that states should be perceived as isolated units, rather than in need and search for cooperation and reciprocity. Just as individuals should not be perceived as isolated units, states too should be perceived in relational terms. Therefore, in Savigny's view the proposition that the judge should always apply his own law "disturbs and hinders the desirable and gradually approaching accord in deciding cases of conflict in different states."[227]

Savigny not only placed states within a community searching progressively for uniform choice of law rules. In his analysis of the nature of legal relations, Savigny also seems to imply a certain homogeneity of substantive law among states, based on the Roman law tradition. Here too one might assume that Savigny's reference to Roman law obscured significant differences in substantive laws and public policies among states of very different legal culture. The previous chapter showed that

[220] Ibid., 138. [221] Ibid., 146. [222] Ibid. [223] Ibid., 146.
[224] Ibid., 76. [225] Ibid., 78. [226] Ibid., 76. [227] Ibid., 145.

Savigny does not ponder much on significant differences among laws following different legal traditions. Virtually all western PrIL scholars of the nineteenth century reference and compare primarily western laws and legislative policies. However, methodologically, Savigny did not confine his analysis to Roman law. Rather, his initial reference to Roman law in the analysis of the nature of a legal relation is often followed by an analysis of national legislation at the time of his writing.[228] Furthermore, Roman law sources are presented as guiding, rather than determining, the nature of the legal relation analysis:

> If in this inquiry we closely follow the statements of the Roman law, the correctness and consistency of which, from the standpoint of the common law, cannot be questioned, we must not forget of what character these statements are. They do not contain rules of positive law, but leading points of view from which the probable and natural thought of the parties is to be discovered, and along with which, therefore, the special circumstances of each case are to be attended to. Where, therefore, the circumstances might lead to another decision, we act entirely in the spirit of these texts of the Roman jurists, if we do not practically apply them.[229]

By referencing the community of laws among states, as well as determining a large category of exceptions, Savigny tries to reconcile universalism with particularism. Similarly, by using Roman law sources as guiding points in the analysis, Savigny tries to reconcile both common law/*jus gentium* with national legislative particularities, and to navigate somewhere between the rules/approach divide in PrIL methodology.

3. Josephus Jitta

Many of Savigny's initial articulations on the universalistic/particularistic pendulum were further developed by Jitta. Like Savigny, Jitta also argued for focusing on the autonomy and self-determination of a nation, as well as natural law and universal principles of justice. Much like Savigny, he tried to distinguish natural law from *jus gentium*, while at the same time reconciling natural law and *jus gentium* with positive law. Also in line with Savigny's intuition, Jitta argued that the blend between the national and the universal should be understood as a corollary to human existence. The focus on humanity as well as the state is merely an attempt at capturing both the national and the international existence of individuals.

Jitta perceived his own theory as navigating somewhere between universalism and particularism as a corollary to what he described as the general pendulum of individuals between "the cosmopolitan spirit and the national sentiment."[230] In other

[228] Ibid., 325:

> Hitherto the special rule of law as to the form of legal acts has been considered from the standpoint of a universal customary law, which has sprung from an acknowledged want, and has been further developed by jurists. The question is still to be answered: What position does positive legislation occupy towards that rule? First, that which is the foundation of the common law (Roman and canon law), and then some modern legislation.

[229] Ibid., 203.

[230] Josephus Jitta, *La methode du droit international privé* (Belifante Fréres 1890) 27 (hereafter Jitta, *La Methode*).

words, individuals' identity is constructed through their existence both within and outside a state of citizenship, domicile, residence or other affiliation. PrIL theory must follow this very fragile balance between the cosmopolitan and the nationalist spirit, rather than exaggerate on either front.[231] It should also develop more toward one or the other side of the spectrum by constantly readapting to individuals' own relationship to their social context—more toward the national sentiment or toward the cosmopolitan spirit.[232]

In PrIL Jitta believed that an appreciation of both universalism and particularism could be achieved by focusing on a comparative analysis of the regulation of particular interpersonal relationships in different legal systems.[233] Comparative law would enable one to understand the actual complexity of the field. This is because in the transnational context "the facets of the various legal relations are much more complex than in purely national circumstances, and human individuality is significantly modified by the various relationships with various juridical groups which exist within humanity."[234]

Acknowledging the complexity of legal relations and the transnational context in which they take place made Jitta skeptical of Savigny's method of localizing a legal relation in a single jurisdiction in every case. In Jitta's view a legal relation could only be localized if it was absolutely clear that such relationship has a preponderant element defining its nature and this element caused the legal relation to penetrate in a local sphere of social life.[235] When this was not the case, Jitta believed the localization of a legal relation in a single jurisdiction disregarded the complex transnational social context and the policies of the laws involved.[236] Rather, he believed that one should try to construct the "reasonable principles of international social life" following a thorough comparative analysis.[237]

Jitta believed that an appropriate comparative analysis might at times reveal "international-common rules of law."[238] Like Savigny, Jitta goes to great length to

[231] Ibid., 27–31. [232] Ibid.

[233] Josephus Jitta, 'Le Droit Commun International comme Source du Droit International Privé' (1908) 4 Revue critique de droit international privé 36, 36:

> As I became convinced that a larger view of Private International Law, as the private law of legal community larger than a nation, should replace the narrow view, which perceives of this science as an ensemble of formulas meant to settle conflicts, I was led to a more and more detailed comparative analysis of laws and judicial decisions, before approaching any question of private international law.

(hereafter, Jitta, "Droit Commun 1").

[234] Jitta, *La Methode* (n. 230) 218.

[235] D. Josephus Jitta, *La substance des obligations dans le droit international privé*, vol. 2 (Belinfante Frères 1907) 495, 498 (hereafter Jitta, *Obligations*, vol. 2).

[236] Ibid.

[237] Jitta repeatedly pleads for the alignment of law and life, a departure from abstraction and formalism and much more nuanced and sociological analysis of relationships in this international context. See D. Josephus Jitta, *The Renovation of International Law on the Basis of a Juridical Community of Mankind, Systematically Developed* (M. Nijhoff 1919) 3 ("the reasonable principles are not to be found by philosophical abstraction, but by observation of life's phenomena"). D Josephus Jitta, *La substance des obligations dans le droit international privé*, vol. 1 (Belinfante Frères 1906) 4–45 (hereafter Jitta, *Obligations*, vol. 1).

[238] Jitta, *The Renovation* (n. 237) 91.

explain how these common rules of law might be distinguished from natural law, ideal law, and public international law.

Jitta's understanding of natural law in the private law realm was explained in the following terms:

Private law must ensure the equality of all individuals before the law, but it does not mean the identity of law for all individuals. This identity would be in contradiction with the conditions of life, which give each person *a distinct individuality,* both because of differences in morals, sex, age, education and level of culture and of social differences, which are so many that we can say that there are no two people that have identical conditions of existence. Among those conditions, which result from today's reality, we must include the intimate connection that exists between an individual and one or more states, because of race, language, place of domicile, birth or even residence. Private law must take account of all those conditions, it is not enough to ensure all individuals the same level of liberty, one must grant each person, *taking account of her individuality and the individuality of others,* the greatest level of freedom compatible with the accomplishment of the same condition for other individuals, and with the maintenance of the social order. It is in this sense that I speak of a natural private law, which is the pillar of the just and unjust.[239]

Jitta clarified that this principle of natural private law not only refutes the formalist principle of freedom, which is usually associated with natural private law, but also rejects the notion that natural law "is either unchangeable or constructed for an ideal humanity."[240]

No doubt its principle is true everywhere, but since its principle takes account of human individuality generated by a large variety of conditions, law based on human individuality will vary as well. Because of this it is impossible to detach [private] law from reality, which reflects the current conditions of human individuality. [. . .] In this way, natural and positive law can coordinate with each other; the abstract notion of just and unjust does not have a strength of its own in disregard of human consciousness, and human consciousness does not deserve the force it may exercise if it does not take account of the just and unjust. [. . .] It is therefore the duty of our legal field to coordinate the positive private law of humanity with the natural demands of social life.[241]

Jitta clarifies that in his theory the "international common law" does not stand for "philosophical law, founded solely on natural reason."[242]

I do not make of philosophical law the source of a duty that a judge must sanction in the name of society [. . .] Common international law is different and composed of principles of law recognized by all nations, as the emanation of natural reason [. . .] Philosophical law and the common international law have a common element: natural reason. But for philosophy natural reason is an ideal, whereas for the international common law it has penetrated the juridical consciousness of all nations. It is for this reason that I consider the latter positive law.[243]

[239] Jitta, *La Methode* (n. 230) 60. [240] Ibid. [241] Ibid., 60–1.

[242] Jitta, *Obligations*, vol. 2 (n. 235) 498.

[243] Ibid., 499. It is precisely the fact that Jitta does not predetermine a universally valid law, but tries to discern it from comparative analysis which made Beale, Baty, Lorenzen, and Pound appreciate Jitta's version of "jus gentium." See Chapters 3 and 4 for an outline of how Jitta's theory was perceived by the United States legal realist school.

International common law, discovered through comparative law, is, argues Jitta, "positive law, not a philosophical abstraction."[244] Jitta was rehearsing here Savigny's proposition that *jus gentium* is to be recovered empirically and that it is the widespread use and adherence to its norms that qualifies it as "rational ." Jitta, for example, seeks to discern how the natural law/positive law blend might operate by asking whether promissory obligations can be understood as natural and universal. He argued that neither autonomy in the realm of private law, nor promising as such, should be viewed as principles of natural law.[245] The level of autonomy granted to individuals within a particular legal relation inevitably depends on the law that regulates such relationship.[246] Similarly, a promise cannot be understood by reference to autonomy and cannot create a universal obligation. Instead, much like current philosophical accounts of promissory obligations suggest,[247] Jitta believed that the underlying rationale for giving any weight to a promise is the degree of confidence that one individual generates in another by virtue of her promising.[248] "The field of application of the principle of autonomy can thus obtain the scope it deserves by reference to the principle of confidence raised in others."[249]

Since international common law is to be extracted from comparative law and therefore from "customary law," meaning the practice of states as embedded in their legislation and national judicial decisions, Jitta clarifies that it should be distinguished from "ideal law."[250] Slavery, remarks Jitta, was once considered *jus gentium* although entirely repugnant to natural reason.[251] This is why Jitta is cautious in tracing any direct genealogical line from old notions of *jus gentium* to his notion of the international common law.[252]

Furthermore, given Jitta's life-long attack on the public international law school of thought in PrIL, he is careful to distinguish his notion of international common law from public international law. Here again, Jitta thought that slippage in the notion of *jus gentium* could lead one to equate the two:

> While paying tribute to the old *jus gentium* I do not wish to gather the support of modern public international law, although international custom also plays a significant role there as well. International common law, as a source of private international law, belongs to private law and not public law. It concerns itself with inter-personal relationships. Consensus among national laws and uniformity in national jurisprudence are facts from which we may deduce the constant legal conviction of the universal social body.[253]

The distinction between international common law and public international law is a distinction along the state-centered/individual-centered spectrum. It is not a private/public distinction in a substantive sense, nor a national/international distinction in the jurisdictional sense. International common law is different from public international law because the former refers to interpersonal relationships. But this

[244] Jitta, "Droit Commun 1" (n. 233) 554. [245] Jitta, *Obligations*, vol. 2 (n. 235) 500.
[246] Ibid., 505.
[247] See Ronald Dworkin, *Justice for Hedgehogs* (Harvard University Press 2011) 302–3.
[248] Jitta, *Obligations*, vol. 2 (n. 235) 500. [249] Ibid., 502.
[250] Jitta, "Droit Commun 1" (n. 233) 554. [251] Ibid. [252] Ibid., 555.
[253] Ibid., 555.

does not mean that whatever states agree to in international treaties, even in the realm of public law, cannot have an impact on private law cases. Jitta clarifies that international treaties of any kind can bind not only states, but also national judges and individuals.[254]

Furthermore, international common law is international also in the sense that the collective enterprise, the common conviction of nations expressed through customs, matters. Therefore, whereas a national judge could disregard the customary law of another state, it would have to take a fundamentally different perspective on *international* customary law, "which rests on the legal community of the universal social body, manifested by facts":[255]

> Its authority is independent of national legal rules, with respect to whether or not customary law is a source of law in national law. The call to international customary law is not a call to the *lex fori* or to *jus fori*. Without a doubt it is impossible for a norm of international customary law, properly established, to be contrary to the principles of the *lex fori* in a civilized state, but, in applying the international customary norms, the judge recognized its authority as such. It does not blindly apply the law of its own state.[256]

International common law is to be placed, in Jitta's view, in between "international codified law" and a more general "ideal law" referred to as ""the nature of things," "general principles of law," "natural equity."[257] International common law is therefore "less precise" than codified law, "less vague" than ideal law, but certainly "not a myth."[258]

Overall, Jitta believed that "the common international law, when it exists, is a subsidiary source for the international legal relations that do not penetrate through a predominant element into a local sphere of social life."[259] Jitta recognized that in his theory, the role of the judge is extremely important in conducting a thorough analysis of the legal relation, determining into which local spheres of social it penetrates and why, and what the common international rules might be.[260] But at this stage of the analysis, when the judge finds that the relationship cannot be localized in a single sphere of social life and searches for international common law, Jitta maintains that the conscience of the judge is not "free." This is because "as sources of positive private law, aside from the law, the treatise, and customary law" Jitta includes "neither the nature of things, nor general principles of law, nor general equity."[261] International common law must make reference to actual state practice, conviction, and reasoning. Only when no international common law can be asserted, in a final analytical step, the judge must decide according to his juridical conscience:

> The general principles of ideal law and the opinion of its interpreters will clarify his conscience, but will not bind it. It is free. The *lex fori* and the general system to which they serve as a basis should not act as gap fillers for the lack of international positive law. If the judge finds inspiration in international law, despite its silence on the question of international law, which

[254] Ibid., 559. [255] Ibid. [256] Ibid., 559. [257] Ibid., 553–4.
[258] Ibid., 554. [259] Jitta, *Obligations*, vol. 2 (n. 235) 500. [260] Ibid., 502.
[261] Jitta, "Droit Commun 1" (n. 233) 560–1.

he is asked to resolve, it is by virtue of a free magistrate, and not by virtue of the obedience he must give to his national sovereign.[262]

Jitta thought of the "juridical conscience" as an important element of law's power of justification, reflection, and debate.[263] While Jitta reassured his reader that "he has not abused this resource [the conscience of the judge],"[264] he was also very critical of doctrinal perspectives in PrIL that "ensure the mechanical certainty of the rule of law only by putting the juridical conscience to sleep."[265]

Jitta openly admitted that his approach might lead to different appreciations of "the reasonable principles of international social life" as between different national courts and legislators. Yet to Jitta, this disagreement, when following an actual analysis of the requirements of international social life seemed preferable to abstract uniformity.[266] However, Jitta was remarkably realistic about the divergence in legal interpretation depending on the judge asked to decide the matter:

> The outcome is that a law might be completely differently interpreted by a timorous judge or by a bold judge. This is the case even when the law is identical, as it is the case when different states have laws of common origin. I just want to state the difficulty.[267]

Therefore, Jitta admits:

> I must confess frankly that the international-common rules and the reasonable principles, the latter being considered as a subsidiary positive law, do not give the world great certainty as to the applicable rule, but the way out is by no means the establishment of mechanical rules for the solution of the so-called conflicts of laws, *it is the involvement of unions of States and, in the last resort, of the collectivity of the States*. The State, acting in isolation, cannot give the world the uniformity of the juridical rules, whilst the collectivity is in possession of the full power of mankind on the human species.[268]

Overall, Jitta's view of the universalistic dimensions of PrIL is remarkably nuanced. The methodology of PrIL he embraces is sequenced, moving from the attempt to localize a legal relation in a local sphere of social life according to its social scope, placing the legal relation in a transnational social context potentially governed by universal customary law and finally allowing the judge to make a reasoned legal determination of the case based on his juridical conscience. This determination is, in turn, influenced by national law and socioeconomic circumstances, as well as by transnational legal and factual elements.[269]

262 Ibid., 560.
263 Jitta, *Obligations*, vol. 2 (n. 235) 502.
264 Ibid.
265 Ibid., 503.
266 Jitta, *Obligations*, vol. 2 (n. 235) 502.
267 Jitta, "Droit Commun 1" (n. 233) 561.
268 Jitta, *The Renovation* (n. 237) 91. See also Jitta, *Obligations*, vol. 2 (n. 235) 503:

> Particularly for international legal relations, which can neither be localized, nor regulated by international common principles of law, there is a strong difference between my analysis and those systems which pretend to achieve the application of one particular law through all combinations possible. If those systems achieve mechanically the certainty of the applicable law, they only achieve this result by putting the consciousness of the judge to sleep.

269 Jitta, "Droit Commun 1" (n. 233) 570.

The value of Jitta's analysis of international common law does not rest in the findings, but in the methodology. Jitta is clear that his findings of commonality are meager[270] and admits openly that acknowledging the absence of uniformity of law following a comparative analysis is as important as finding commonality.[271]

The value of Jitta's study is therefore primarily in the method. Whereas state-centered internationalists as well as modern individual-centered scholars argue that in the presence of general diversity of national legal rules PrIL is meant to provide order and uniformity, Jitta took a different course. In Kegel's framework PrIL's universalism is not of a substantive, but of a structural nature. In the scholarship of nineteenth-century relational internationalists, especially in Jitta's scholarship, PrIL's universalism is more layered. A private law relationship's embeddedness in an ever wider social circle (a state—several states—humanity) implicated a different set of norms and principles. A private law relationship's embeddedness in a national sphere of social life makes the application of that nation's law legitimate and only "international public policy" may trump it.[272] By contrast, when a legal relation is embedded in a number of national communities or appears to be embedded in international social life generally, the appeal to norms may, in a staggered fashion, reference national law, international customary law, judicial conscience and responsibility. The relational insight travels through Jitta's entire analytical framework: an individual is embedded in a private law relationship which in turn is embedded in one or various national communities; the judge borrows from his national legal, economic, and political culture, but is also embedded in a sort of universal community of decision makers dealing with international private law relationships; states present an individuality, but are simultaneously embedded in a community of common legal judgment reflected in state practice.

E. Conclusions

The pursuit of order and uniformity has always been an important principle of PrIL theory and methodology. Yet its normative justification, as well as its relationship to other PrIL principles is not always clear. Previous chapters showed that the principle rests very much at the core of the state-centered internationalist perspective, which tried to create an analogy between PrIL and PublIL.

The principle of order and uniformity, however, is generally associated with Savigny. Furthermore, the intransigent pursuit of order and uniformity is generally associated with a liberal ideology, a clear separation between private and public law, and a disregard for national politics and national self-determination.

[270] Ibid., 567, 568, 570 (also noting that absent consensus on a particular legal issue, the judge will be influenced by national debates on a particular controversial issue of private law); See also Josephus Jitta, "Le droit commun international comme source du droit international privé" (1909) 5 Revue critique de droit international privé 485, 488, 493.

[271] Jitta, "Droit Commun 1" (n. 233) 558.

[272] Ibid., 561.

This chapter argued that this understanding of the PrIL canon might have been enshrined in PrIL when Gerhard Kegel put forward a theory of conflicts justice, in which he outlined an association between private interests and the principle of order and uniformity, alongside the private/public and conflicts justice/material justice dichotomies. Yet following the intuitions of Kegel's fellow interest jurisprudes, I argued that this normative justification for the pursuit of order and uniformity is certainly not inevitable and does not map onto the relational internationalist perspective.

Instead, this chapter aimed to show that the universalistic ideology of the authors referenced throughout this book is, in fact, considerably more fluid and more restrained than the intransigent pursuit of order, uniformity, or the appeal to the internal structure and logic of PrIL. Both Savigny and Jitta were particularly keen on achieving a fragile balance between national autonomy and self-determination, as well as universal principles and values, including individual self-determination and social cooperation. Their reconstruction of *jus gentium* and natural law was placed alongside their insistence on the particularity of each people and the articulation of individual self-determination was placed alongside a relational perspective. In their theory, expectations regarding the application of a particular law in geographical terms informed or supplemented expectations regarding a particular substantive outcome for various legal relations.

All of these various dimensions were then to be systematized (possibly over-systematized in Savigny's theory) into various principles of international reasonable social order and/or choice of law rules. But those were meant to be the result of an analysis, that sought to integrate, not separate, the national/universalistic, geographical/substantive and private/public dimensions. This universalistic "method" of the relational internationalists is different in many respects from the way in which we have come to insist on the pursuit of order, structure, and uniformity by adopting the broadest and possibly most abstract element of analysis (for example state sovereignty, individual choice, broad appreciations of average individuals' attachments to various countries).

Savigny himself argued that "we must never forget that rules of law are made for the parties, whose real interests it is to further their purpose impartially and that the interests of the parties are not to be made subservient to the uniformity or consistency of the rules of law."[273]

[273] Savigny, *Private International Law* (n. 211) 138.

9
Conclusions

In 1949 André Bonnichon remarked: "modern scholars of PrIL commonly state that conflict of laws boils down to a conflict of sovereignties."[1] This conventional wisdom was perplexing to Bonnichon because:

> While Public International Law scholars freely recognize that sovereignty is one of the most complex notions and some even deny its existence as such as an attribute of state power, those who write in the field of Private International Law pretend to be employing a clear concept and to derive rigorous consequences from it. Allegedly, the object and nature of Private International Law, its characteristic place among different branches of law, the solution of general problems such as renvoi and characterization, are all to be solved by reference to state sovereignty.[2]

A year later, Bonnichon argued that it was necessary to discern the fundamental influence of this conflict of sovereignties theory on PrIL, as well as its inevitable limitations. His own conclusions about the idea of conflict of laws as conflict of sovereignties were as follows:

> A notion born relatively late in the development of a science. [...] It appeared capable of becoming the core of a new thesis. [...] Then this clear notion proves to be complex. We can discern the ambiguities, which make the reasoning easy and the conclusions fragile. It proves an insufficient instrument and we go back to ancient concepts, although we disguise them under the new vocabulary. [...] As so many like it, it must be put in the category of ideas that served, can still serve, but cannot play the central role that we once attributed to it. This I believe, must be the destiny of the idea of conflict of sovereignties in PrIL. The science of conflicts that existed before the end of the 19th century was long content with the aspects that I called functional or essential, namely with principles of justice and the nature of the relationships. The new theories of public law internal and international, the Napoleonic codification, the need for synthesis and the rejection of the notion of comity constituted favorable circumstances for the rise of the idea that conflict of laws is nothing but conflict of sovereignty. But the mere notion of sovereignty is unclear.[3]

It is hard to determine how much has changed since Bonnichon's account. PrIL scholars have continued to be fascinated by the idea of PrIL as conflicts of sovereignty,

[1] André Bonnichon, 'La notion de conflit de souverainetes dans la science des conflits des lois' (1949) 39 Rev crit dr int privé 615, 615 (hereafter Bonnichon, "La notion, 1949").

[2] Ibid., 615.

[3] André Bonnichon, 'La notion de conflit de souverainetes dans la science des conflits des lois' (1950) 40 Rev crit dr int privé 11, 31–2 (hereafter Bonnichon, "La notion, 1950").

Nineteenth-Century Perspectives on Private International Law. Roxana Banu. © Roxana Banu 2018. Published 2018 by Oxford University Press.

and with the prospects of using this metaphor as a way of reconnecting PrIL with PublIL.[4] And just as at the time of Bonnichon's writing, the discussions about and the perspectives on sovereignty are very much internal to PrIL. PublIL scholars are still contesting conventional notions of state sovereignty and the abuses and injustices brought by the state-centered dimensions of PublIL.[5] Just as Bonnichon described in mid-twentieth century, little of the PublIL critique of statism is translated into PrIL state-centered theories. This lack of critical engagement with state-centered premises in PrIL is exacerbated by a sense that there is no alternative on which to construct an international theory that takes account of social justice and global justice generally. Even more so than in Bonnichon's time, it is hard to remember that any fruitful theories were forged in the nineteenth century before the association between PrIL and PublIL. And to the extent those theories that Bonnichon calls "functional or essentialist, focusing on principles of justice and the nature of legal relations" still form part of the intellectual memory of PrIL, they are attributed to a theory of PrIL dismissed as overly liberal or libertarian.

This book has argued that both of these premises are wrong. In the first place, the nineteenth-century PrIL-PublIL association and its focus on state sovereignty did not represent the enlightened quest for the global good that it is thought to have been. PrIL and PublIL traditionally connected at a structural rather than normative level. Both at the end of the nineteenth century and as late as the 1970s when F.A. Mann recovered the state-centered internationalist theory in England no argument was made that substantive norms of PublIL should guide the analysis in PrIL and even less so that private actors have obligations deriving from such norms. Understanding the history of the PrIL-PublIL association should make us more skeptical of general appeals to reconnect PrIL with PublIL. However, it is not the goal of the book to pre-empt projects pleading for the application of PublIL norms in PrIL or to pre-judge the value of any theory trying to reconnect the two fields. There is a remarkable tendency to re-create the nineteenth-century structural connection between PrIL and PublIL even in contemporary projects.[6] Understanding the limitations of this association in the history of PrIL would prevent us from romanticizing just any kind

[4] See more recently Alex Mills, *The Confluence of Public and Private International Law: Justice, Pluralism and Subsidiarity in the International Constitutional Ordering of Private Law* (CUP 2009) (hereafter Mills, *Public and Private International Law*).

[5] For a range of perspectives, see James Der Derian et al., 'How Should Sovereignty Be Defended?' in Christopher J. Bickerton, Philip Cunliffe, and Alexander Gourevitch (eds.), *Politics Without Sovereignty: A Critique of Contemporary International Relations* (UCL Press 2007) 187. See also 'The Transformation of Sovereignty' (1994) 88 Am Soc Int'l L Proc 1. For an interesting critique from a feminist perspective, see Karen Knop, 'Borders of the Imagination: The state in Feminist International Law' (1994) 88 Am Soc Int'l L Proc 14; Karen Knop, 'Re/Statements: Feminism and State Sovereignty in International Law' (1993) 3 Transnat'l L & Contemp Probs 293. See also Eyal Benvenisti, 'Sovereigns as Trustees for Humanity: On the Accountability of States to Foreign Stakeholders' (2013) 107 Am J Int'l L 295 (trying to maintain, yet reconstruct the notion of state sovereignty, as trusteeship for humanity).

[6] See Mills, *Private and Public International Law* (n. 4). Roxana Banu, 'Assuming Regulatory Authority for Transnational Torts: An Interstate Affair? A Historical Perspective on the Canadian Private International Law Tort Rules' (2013) 31 Windsor YB Access Just 197 (arguing that the Canadian Supreme Court's attempt in the 1990s to "adapt Private International Law to modern realities" can, in fact, be best understood as recasting the nineteenth-century PrIL-PublIL association).

of appeal to connecting the two fields. But the nineteenth-century variation of this connection is by no means inevitable. Those who believe there is much to be learned from PublIL should continue to insist on it, but the task is twofold. Contemporary iterations relying on the PrIL-PublIL association for social justice reform should engage with historical variations of the PrIL-PublIL relationship to understand its potential limitations and perils. At the same time, recognizing the limitations of the nineteenth-century state-centered theory means that contemporary scholars wishing to pursue a reconnection between PrIL and PublIL may have to construct it anew, rather than pointing to the historical alignment between the two fields.

Acknowledging and revealing the limitations of the state-centered internationalist perspective in PrIL, the book then pondered on the value of individual-centered theories in PrIL. Just as it has argued that state-centered internationalist theories should not be over-romanticized, it argued that individual-centered internationalist theories should not be overly demonized. Private law-focused theories of the nineteenth century did not all plead for an overarching principle of individual liberty or adopt an individualistic, libertarian perspective on private law. To the contrary, in many respects they were much more nuanced and flexible than state-centered theories. Indeed, several authors of the nineteenth century portrayed a more relational, socially constituted image of the individual. They relied on the association between PrIL and private law both to counter state-centered premises and increase the agency of individuals in the transnational realm, and to point to various dimensions of responsibility and respect individuals owe to one another and the communities in which they operate. Analogizing PrIL to private law led them to various premises: that one should focus on a relationship, instead of an isolated individual; that one should draw from both extra-legal social expectations and the law; that one must justify the application of a law or another to the individuals; that the framework of justification should reference the level of embeddedness of a private law relationship into a community; that the level of embeddedness of a private law relationship should be based on an analysis of both geographical connecting factors and the policies of the laws regulating the respective private law relationships; that there is a floor of inter-personal equality that private law, like PrIL, must respect and so on.

These conclusions summarize the relational internationalist perspective as a theory that places individuals at the center of a range of concentric circles representing different dimensions of relationality. Relational internationalists placed the individual in relationship to the other party(ies) of the private law relationship, emphasized the relationships that individuals have with various communities and groups apart from their private law relationships, embedded private law relationships within various national communities, and finally integrated all these relationships into a broader notion of humanity.

In all of these respects, I have argued, the relational internationalist perspective is worth recovering and revisiting, but not necessarily transplanting with an unaltered content, into the twenty-first century. Just as I have argued that nineteenth-century individual-centered theories should not be read from the prism of contemporary libertarian private law theories, so they should not be read through the lens of contemporary relational theory in feminist jurisprudence, private law, or moral theory generally. Nor should they be read as a moment in a long line of progress to any particular theory of international law, private or public, or of domestic private law, or of relationality.

One should be open to engage with these theories much in the same way as David Kennedy invited us to engage with the scholarship of what he calls "primitive legal scholars" such as Francisco Victoria and Francisco Suárez.[7] Kennedy argues that:

> The distinctive style and method of primitive texts suggest a more uniform faith in universal principles than does the methodological argument of traditional work. But the patters of primitive authority seem incoherent and diffuse, while those of most traditional scholars seem unified and internally coherent ... This confusion arises only from the perspective of modern scholarship which accepts the validity of uniform principles only when methodologically defensible but at the same time is skeptical of all methodological defenses.[8]

To a modern reader the attempt to separate and then reunite the individual with the community, the state with a community of states, the private and the public, might seem incoherent, yet these moves seem entirely unproblematic to the relational internationalists presented in this book. To some extent this is because they too, like Kennedy's "primitive scholars," conceive of the part—the individual, the state, law—as deriving from a larger whole, be that Christianity, natural law, or reason. This is why their description of similarities and differences between *jus gentium,* natural law, and positive law mirror to some extent those of the primitive scholars. While relational internationalists don't as unequivocally subscribe everything to a universal legal/moral order as the primitive scholars did and while they still make some of the classical distinctions between a state and an international community of states, the individual and the community, the private and the public, they nevertheless feel quite comfortable reverting back and forth in between the particular and the universal and ultimately reuniting every part in a larger whole. For Jitta this is based on his proposition that the authority of a single state is derived from the universal juridical community of mankind. Similarly, Joachim Rückert showed persuasively that Savigny created "distinctions" without "separation"[9] and ultimately reconnected everything in a larger whole,[10] be that Christianity[11] or equal moral worth and freedom.[12] Furthermore, Rückert showed that Savigny does not provide any proof for his constructions of separating and then reuniting individual peoples with humanity, individual citizens with the past and present of their nations, the origin of law in the spirit of the people or of humanity with its ultimate contingency.[13] The plausibility of such constructions is simply presupposed.[14]

This means that the theories of the relational international scholars presented in this book could be as perplexing for a modern reader as Kennedy suggested the

[7] David Kennedy, 'Primitive Legal Scholarship' (1986) 27 Harv Int'l L J 1 (hereafter Kennedy, "Primitive Legal Scholarship").

[8] Ibid., 6–7.

[9] Joachim Rückert, *Idealismus, Jurisprudenz und Politik bei Friedrich Carl von Savigny* (R. Gremer 1984) 314.

[10] Ibid., 310. [11] Ibid., 367. [12] Ibid., 366. [13] Ibid., 314–15.

[14] Ibid., 315.

scholarship of primitive scholars in public international law might be. Furthermore, Lüderitz's cautionary remark about situating Savigny's scholarship in any one philosophical school (Kantian, Hegelian etc.) holds for the scholarship of all relational internationalists:

> The task [of situating Savigny's theory in one philosophical school] is . . . understated, because it cannot be too easy to correlate merely implicit and unsystematic references to philosophical precepts with systematic philosophers.[15]

This means then that the nineteenth-century relational internationalist perspective recovered here should not be equated with any particular contemporary relational theory. Relationality in the theories presented in this book is an insight that creates and justifies various conclusions for the theory and methodology of PrIL, but it is not a theory in itself. By contrast, contemporary scholars in various domains attempt to create a coherent theory of second-personal morality,[16] relational autonomy,[17] or relational justice in private law.[18] Their ambit and ambition move beyond the contours of the relational insight in the theories presented here. The relational internationalist perspective cannot be read as an early articulation of contemporary relational theories.

Yet just as Bonnichon thought PrIL should have been mindful of debates around the notion of sovereignty outside of the field, relational internationalism could be brought in conversation with, and possibly partly traded off for, newer insights on relationality within other legal fields and policy debates. This project, commenced elsewhere,[19] is beyond the scope of these concluding remarks.[20] Nevertheless, in the last section of these conclusions I wish to propose, but by no means exhaustively set, the boundaries of a conversation that might fruitfully be had between nineteenth-century relational internationalism and contemporary relational perspectives and other academic debates that resonate with some of the elements that I have identified as defining the relational internationalist perspective. This section builds on the recovery of a complex and nuanced theoretical perspective within PrIL's intellectual history in this book and suggests how this perspective can be an important bridge

[15] Ibid., 287.

[16] Stephen Darwall, *The Second-Person Standpoint: Morality, Respect and Accountability* (Harvard University Press 2009).

[17] Jennifer Nedelsky, *Law's Relations: A Relational Theory of Self, Autonomy and Law* (OUP 2011) (hereafter Nedelsky, *Law's Relations*).

[18] Hanoch Dagan and Avihay Dorfman, 'Just Relationships' (2016) 116 Columbia L Rev 1395 (hereafter Dagan and Dorfman, "Just Relationships").

[19] Roxana Banu, 'A Relational Feminist Approach to Conflict of Laws' (2017) 27 Mich J Gender & L 1 (hereafter Banu, "A Relational Feminist Approach") (showing how relational feminism could inform the analysis in PrIL). An earlier version of this article, awarded the ASIL Prize for Best Text in Private International Law in 2016, places relational feminism in conversation with the nineteenth-century relational internationalist perspective (unpublished manuscript, on file with author).

[20] Some of the relational theories, which might be relevant in the transnational context, were developed concomitantly with or after the drafting of this book. See Hanoch Dagan and Avihay Dorfman, 'Interpersonal Human Rights' (unpublished manuscript, available at <https://papers.ssrn.com/sol3/papers.cfm?abstract_id=3038380>, accessed on December 10, 2017; Jean Thomas, *Public Rights, Private Relations* (OUP 2015). Bringing these theories in conversation with the relational internationalist perspective in PrIL is the subject of an ongoing project.

between PrIL and a broad range of academic debates, including: private law theory and feminist perspectives on relational justice, global justice debates, as well as debates about the role of intellectual history studies generally.

A. Concentric Circles of Relationality

The relational internationalist perspective described throughout this book is premised on a strong humanistic concern. PrIL, Jitta wrote at the end of the nineteenth century, "has become a species of supreme law, a law of laws, placed to such extent above the individuals, that it can disregard them."[21] The main concern of authors like Jitta was that the state-centered paradigm would subsume individuals under broader categories of states and nations, and would eliminate their voice and self-determination. They feared that the conceptualization of conflict of laws as conflict of states or state sovereignty would create the illusion that PrIL did not have the burden of justifying its methods, its principles, and its norms to individuals directly. The main target, especially for Jitta, who had witnessed the height of the state-centered perspective, was the implicit contention, which Pillet made explicit, that in this interstate distribution of sovereignty the "litigating parties disappear for a while."[22]

Once the humanistic premises of the relational internationalist perspective are fully captured, the relational underpinnings of the theory also become clearer. The goal of relational internationalists was not to separate the individuals from each other or from the state, or to create a strict separation between private and public, or the market from politics. Their main goal was to bring back the voice, the interests, and the concerns of individuals as they navigated the transnational realm. It would have appeared impossible for these authors to disconnect individuals from the large framework of relationships in which they are embedded because they were interested primarily in accounting for the individual *as* a transnational agent. The relationships and connections that transformed an individual from a citizen of a state to a transnational agent were precisely the elements that rested at the core of relational internationalism.

The analysis of the relational internationalists starts from the realization that PrIL regulates relationships between individuals in the transnational realm. All relational internationalists are keen to show that PrIL must account for the interests and expectations of all parties to the dispute. Story spoke about conflicts between creditors and purchasers, Savigny explicitly denied any attempt to derive the applicable law from the geographical affiliations, interests and expectations of one party only, and Jitta adopted the focus on relationships as the dawn of the modern theory of PrIL.

[21] Josephus Jitta, *La methode du droit international privé* (Belifante Fréres 1890) 5 (hereafter Jitta, *La Methode*).

[22] Antoine Pillet, 'Droit international privé consideré dans ses rapports avec le droit international public', Annales de l'enseignement superior de Grenoble (F. Allier Père & Fils 1892) 309, 335 (hereafter Pillet, "Rapports").

They insisted repeatedly that PrIL must remain attuned to the fact that it is dealing with correlative rights, obligations, and expectations, and that PrIL rules should prevent any party from a unilateral determination of such correlative interests.

Because the private law relationship is the primary unit of analysis from which their theory starts, they focused less on describing the image of the individual coming into the private law relationship. Accounts of individuals' pre-existing affiliations to different communities and groups, and the corresponding socio-economic makeup of individual identity prior to entering into a private law relationship are occasionally found in Story's theory, but not so much in Savigny's theory. I have argued in Chapter 8 that twentieth-century German interest jurisprudence includes, in the writings of Alexander Lüderitz, more sophisticated accounts of this level of relationality. But in the writing of Josephus Jitta, the last protagonist in my account of relational internationalism, the multi-faceted human identity that is brought into the private law relationship is clearly underscored. Jitta wrote that private law and PrIL must take account of each person's "*distinct individuality*, both because of differences in morals, sex, age, education and level of culture and because of social differences, which are so numerous that we can say that there are no two people who have identical conditions of existence."[23] These diverse conditions of existence "include the intimate connection that exists between an individual and one or more states because of race, language, place of domicile, birth or even residence."[24] For Jitta this picture of the diverse conditions of social life translates into the argument that both private law and PrIL must account for substantive, rather than formal autonomy and liberty:

> Private law must take account of all those conditions, it is not enough to ensure all individuals the same level of liberty, one must grant each person, *taking account of her individuality and the individuality of others,* the greatest level of freedom that is compatible with the accomplishment of the same conditions for other individuals, and with the maintenance of the social order.[25]

This complex context upon which relational internationalists reflect manages to situate not just individuals, but also their inter-personal relationships in a pendulum between "the cosmopolitan spirit and the national sentiment."[26] Therefore, every private law relationship is embedded in a social community and/or a state. All relational internationalists try to find links that place private law relationships in the realm of a community and/or a state. And by the time Jitta articulated this "localization" principle, it becomes clear that this too has a social dimension. Since "every relationship has a social purpose," every jural relation is embedded in a social reality.[27] To localize a private law relationship in a particular community, then, means to underscore "the link that may exist, in a social sense, between the fact and a local sphere of social life."[28]

[23] Jitta, *La Methode* (n. 21) 60. [24] Ibid. [25] Ibid. [26] Ibid., 27.
[27] Josephus Jitta, *The Renovation of International Law on the Basis of a Juridical Community of Mankind* (Martinus Nijhoff 1919) 99 (hereafter Jitta, *The Renovation*).
[28] Ibid., 97.

Once the embeddedness of a private law relationship is explained in social terms, it becomes obvious that a private law relationship could be simultaneously embedded in various communities and ultimately within humanity at large. For relational internationalists, this translates into many different analytical dimensions. On the one hand, they all reference several universal principles of interpersonal morality, interpersonal trust and solidarity. On the other hand, they all reference a certain substratum of universal law and *jus gentium*. Yet they are careful to situate this concept at the border between positive and natural law, in order to ensure enough room for national self-determination and legal particularities, while at the same time committing law to higher, universal standards.

Furthermore, the embeddedness of individuals and their relationships within humanity means that a private law relationship can have such a wide systemic social impact that "it may belong to international social life" in a much broader sense.[29] The social sphere for which one must account is much wider when one understands that a private law relationship can simultaneously impact and become embedded in so many local spheres of social life.

Emphasizing all these levels of relationality made Jitta at the end of the nineteenth century "beg to remind the reader that international social life is knotty, and that it is better to untie the knot patiently than to cut it through with a sharp knife."[30]

B. A Conversation Between the Past and the Present

The various ways in which the relational sensibility seeks to situate the individual within various spheres of social life point to the value of recovering the relational sensibility, which PrIL has lost from its historical memory. Recasting this nineteenth-century relational internationalist perspective challenges the common assumption that PrIL has no internal resources to rethink its regulatory function in an increasingly inter-connected world. Instead, this perspective resonates with strikingly contemporary and critical insights. Theoretically and methodologically, this perspective encourages a much needed contextual analysis, fosters inter-personal responsibility, mutual trust, and respect in transnational dealings and brings a much needed awareness of the wide range of elements that constitute individual identity in a transnational context.

But to make up for what would have been more than a century of development and refinement, one also needs to rethink, reconstruct, and partly trade off some of the insights of the nineteenth-century relational perspective in light of contemporary debates within feminist scholarship and private law theory, as well as to ponder on the role of further intellectual historical accounts for the current development of PrIL.

[29] Ibid., 136–7. [30] Ibid.

While I certainly cannot hope to treat these topics exhaustively here, I wish to sketch what a conversation between the past and the present might look like along the lines of these contemporary topics.

1. Private law and feminist theories of relationality

Relational internationalists constructed much of their theory by reference to private law, and their relational insights in many ways started from, though did not remain at the analytical level of the private law relationship. Interestingly, various contemporary private law theories focus on emphasizing various layers of inter-personal solidarity and a substantive notion of equality and self-determination underlying private law relationality, in contrast to the conventional neo-Kantian notion of correlativity.[31] Furthermore, feminist theories have long criticized the classical notion of correlativity in private law, as well as the formal equality principle, and have in many ways pioneered much of the work on relationality.[32] In order to make use of a reconstruction of the nineteenth-century relational internationalist perspective for the development of PrIL, the field should tap into and engage the rich debates occurring within these areas of law and policy, in particular along five areas of inquiry.

a) Contextual analysis, medium-level relationality versus ideal relationships

Both within private law and feminist writings, there is a lively debate about whether a focus on relationships is merely a proxy for engaging in a contextual analysis, or if it represents a normative argument in favor of a particular kind of relationship and community between people.[33] Furthermore, in both private law and feminist

[31] See, e.g., Hanoch Dagan and Avihay Dorfman, 'Justice in Private: Beyond the Rawlsian Framework' (forthcoming in Law & Philosophy, 2017) (hereafter Dagan and Dorfman, "Justice in Private"); Dagan and Dorfman, "Just Relationships" (n. 18); Joseph William Singer, *Entitlement: The Paradoxes of Property* (Yale University Press 2000); Eduardo M. Peñalver, 'Property as Entrance' (2005) 91 Va L Rev 1889; Joseph William Singer, 'Democratic Estates: Property Law in a Free and Democratic Society' (2009) 94 Cornell L Rev 1009; Gregory Alexander, 'The Social Obligation Norm in American Property Law' (2009) 94 Cornell L Rev 745 (hereafter Alexander, "The Social Obligation Norm"); Anthony Townsend Kronman, 'Contract Law and Distributive Justice' (1980) 89 Yale LJ 472 (hereafter Kronman, "Contract Law").

[32] See generally Nedelsky, *Law's Relations* (n. 17). Catriona Mackenzie and Natalie Stoljar (eds.), *Relational Autonomy: Feminist Perspectives on Autonomy, Agency, and the Social Self* (OUP 2000); Martha Minow and Mary Lyndon Shanley, 'Relational Rights and Responsibilities: Revisioning the Family in Liberal Political Theory and Law' (1996) 1 Hypatia 11; Martha Minow, 'Paradoxes of Rights' in Austin Rata and Thomas R. Kearns (eds.), *Identities, Politics, and Rights* (University of Michigan Press 1995); Samantha Brennan, 'The Liberal Rights of Feminist Liberalism' in Amy R. Baehr (ed.), *Varieties of Feminist Liberalism* (Rowman & Littlefield 2004).

[33] John Christman, 'Relational Autonomy, Liberal Individualism, and the Social Constitution of Selves' (2004) 117 Philosophical Studies 143, 158:

> It is one thing to claim that social conditions that enable us to develop and maintain the powers of authentic choice and which protect the ongoing interpersonal and social relationships that define ourselves are all part of the background requirements for the development of autonomy [. . .] It is another thing, however—and a more dangerous and ultimately problematic move, I have argued—to claim that being autonomous *means* standing in proper social relations to surrounding others and within social practices and institutions.

writings the endorsement of particular substantive relationships ranges from a medium level relationality, according to which the individual participates in relationships and community, while relying on a potential right of exist, to a thick notion of community, according to which the individual is thought of as always constituted by and socially responsible to others within a particular relationship/community.[34]

Framing the individual as an inherently social being, aiming to establish relationships with other people in the transnational realm enabled relational internationalists to construct a much more contextual and nuanced analysis than state-centered theories. While Robert Leckey argued that the value of relationality to push for contextual analysis is less important in areas that are already prone to contextual analysis,[35] I hope that it will have become apparent that in the case of PrIL it was precisely relationality that provided an impetus for more contextual analysis.

But while the nineteenth-century relational internationalist perspective relies on the insight of the individual's inherent social nature to push for a more contextual and nuanced analysis of PrIL matters, it is not always clear whether it also pleads for a particular level of social embeddedness emerging from transnational interhuman relationships. This rests on the fact that while all relational internationalists pleaded for the integration of elements of good faith, inter-personal trust, and solidarity as analytical elements for choice of law matters, they did not provide much insight into the level of solidarity that these analytical elements push for or encourage.

As the contemporary debate between legal theorists Hanoch Dagan and Gregory Alexander suggests, our conceptualization of the level of integration within a private law relationship will dictate a different level of social responsibility. And, in turn, the level of interdependency one envisions within private law relationships will dictate what individuals and communities can demand of each other.[36] These insights are extremely important for PrIL in elucidating the kind and level of responsibility and care individuals owe to each other and to the communities that their transnational relationships inevitably affect.

b) *Inherent versus constitutive relationality*

Part of the debate around the level of inter-connectedness that should inform private law norms relates to a debate about the value of community and relationships for individuals. Feminist scholars have long argued that liberal private law is only able, if at all, to account for "inherent relationality" as an attribute of human nature.[37] Feminist relational insights highlight the fact that autonomy and human flourishing are constituted, and therefore perpetually impacted by relationships with others.[38]

[34] See Robert Leckey, *Contextual Subjects, Family, State, and Relational Theory* (University of Toronto Press 2008) 3–31 (discussing the various layers of relationality within the feminist scholarship).

[35] Ibid.

[36] Gregory Alexander, 'The Social Obligation Norm in American Property Law' (2009) 94 Cornell L Rev 745; Hanoch Dagan, *Property: Values and Institutions* (OUP 2011) Chapters 2 and 3.

[37] Jennifer Nedelsky, 'Reconceiving Autonomy: Sources, Thoughts and Possibilities' (1989) 1 Yale JL & Feminism 1, 9, n. 4.

[38] Ibid.

Similarly, conceptualizing the embeddedness of an individual as an expression of a common concern for everybody's "human flourishing" as Gregory Alexander does, or as a necessary condition for individual autonomy as Hanoch Dagan does, will generate different levels of social cohesion and self-sacrifice for others, within and beyond the private law relationship.[39]

The nineteenth-century relational internationalist perspective fluctuates between a concern for inherent or constitutive relationality, and is often less attuned to the potential tensions. In Jitta's theory, the relationships with various communities and the socio-economic context are clearly constitutive of each person's distinct individuality. But when Story and Savigny in particular plead for the recognition of individuals' expectations, they presume that this would enable and foster more equitable and smoother transnational inter-individual relationships. And while they are mindful of the correlative dimensions of expectations, they may be less attentive to the inequitable relationships and conventions that construct those initial expectations, and what consequences their recognition would have in terms of structuring these and similar transnational relations. Feminist insights would help further illuminate the way in which various layers of relationships shape one's expectations and capabilities, and how those are further projected into transnational legal relations.

c) Formal versus substantive autonomy

A corollary to the distinction between inherent and constitutive relationality is the debate over formal versus substantive autonomy. Feminist writers generally, and Jennifer Nedelsky in particular, are keen to emphasize a thick notion of relational autonomy, according to which autonomy is shaped by factors such as race, class, gender, as well as citizenship and others. This insight has translated into private law theories. Anthony Kronman already showed that the libertarian notion of autonomy underestimates the impact of market power, poverty, social status and others on individual autonomy, and that it fails to account for and reverse disparities caused by those factors, through private law norms.[40] Hanoch Dagan and Avihay Dorfman have recently argued that individuals, and not just states, private law, and not just public law, must respect and accommodate individual particularities and "ground projects" such as disabilities, religion, class, gender, or ethnicity.[41] Jean Thomas recently argued that one could extrapolate private rights and duties from public law rights, by illuminating the "relational dimension" typical of private interactions[42]

[39] Gregory Alexander, 'The Social Obligation Norm in American Property Law' (2009) Cornell L Rev 745; Hanoch Dagan, *Property: Values and Institutions* (OUP 2011) Chapter 3.

[40] See Kronman, "Contract Law" (n. 31).

[41] See Dagan and Dorfman, "Just Relationships" (n. 18).

[42] Jean Thomas, *Public Rights, Private Relations* (OUP 2015) 157: "The formal relationality of a right is already suggestive that a right is also *responsive*, normatively, to facts or judgments concerning relational structures between purported right-holder and associated duty-bearer, just as it has to be responsive to value in the form of individual interests."

and the extent and level of dependency that individuals experience in their interactions with others.[43]

Nineteenth-century relational internationalist PrIL scholars were aware of the fact that private law relationships impact and construct parties' autonomy. Jitta clearly disavowed a formalist notion of equality and autonomy when arguing that it is not enough for private law and PrIL to ensure all individuals the same level of liberty, but that "one must grant each person, *taking account of her individuality and the individuality of others*, the greatest level of freedom which is compatible with the accomplishment of the same conditions for other individuals, and with the maintenance of the social order."[44] Yet it is not always clear to what extent and for what factors individuals are supposed to accommodate each other in their transnational private law dealings. Sharpening the implications of incorporating a thick, substantive notion of autonomy would be extremely valuable for PrIL. For example, it would make much less plausible the common proposition that the law of the tort applies to all transnational torts because this is the jurisdiction to which all parties are most connected or which they implicitly agreed to. While the rule might pose fewer problems in the case of a minor car accident, it has wide-ranging implications in the case of mining operations of transnational corporations in developing countries. Injecting a strong awareness for disparities in market power, level of income, cultural and ethnical background, among other factors, would often challenge or at least refine the implied consent argument which rests at the foundation of many choice of law norms.

d) *Conflicts of rights and interests versus resulting patterns of relationships*

Once autonomy is reconceptualized as constituted by and dependent on relationships with other individuals and communities, it becomes clear that one of the most important roles of law is to structure healthy relationships that support and enable autonomy. Feminist writers have made an important contribution by analyzing rights, including private rights, as relational.[45] Rights are viewed not as reified and immutable entitlements, but instruments through which to construct particular types of relationships. Consequently, feminist writers challenge legal determinations cast in terms of conflicts of individual rights or interests. Rather, they argue for a critical analysis of the patterns of relationships that result from the institutionalization of particular rights over others.[46]

Nineteenth-century relational internationalists similarly disavow a reification of rights and the vested rights doctrine, including because those concepts rely on the atomistic, rather than a relational image of the individual. They attempt both to

[43] Ibid., 188: "In most cases that dependency is mutual: normal relations of friendship and commerce can be reasonably described as ones of *inter*dependence. But there is also a subset of private relations in which the degree of dependency is sufficiently substantial as to merit the same special normative scrutiny that we apply to the relation of individual and state."

[44] Jitta, *La Methode* (n. 21) 60.

[45] See, e.g., Jennifer Nedelsky, 'Reconceiving Rights as Relationships' (1993) 1 Rev Const Stud 1.

[46] Ibid.

maintain the empowering element connotative of rights, and to deny their immutability by referring to conflicts of reasonable expectations or interests. While this is already a major improvement over the vested rights theory, it is not clear that nineteenth-century authors are particularly attuned to the overall patterns of relationships that emerge through various PrIL norms. By contrast, feminist perspectives raise a deep concern for the potential violence of and subordination within the various types of private law relationships, including familial and personal ones. Incorporating those insights within PrIL would allow one to maintain the relational sensibility that comes with private law theories, while preventing us from idealizing existing relational structures within private law and PrIL.

Incorporating insights from the feminist debates on relational rights would make PrIL sensible to the patterns of relationships it structures through its norms and decisions. For example, determinations on the applicable law for the rights of foreign parents to the education of their children born in a country different from that of the parents' citizenship would become sensitive to the way in which these norms structure the relationship of migrant workers with their host and home country respectively. It would also make the choice of law analysis attuned to whether applying one national law over another would generate conflict between children whose rights are informed by host country standards, and the parents, whose cultural practices are informed by their home state. Similarly, PrIL would become sensitive to the kind of patterns of relationships it creates when it enables corporations to take advantage of lower standards of care, and quantum damages in developing countries when they engage in tortious activity in those countries.

e) Relational justice versus distributive justice

An implicit assumption in the feminist writing might be that desirable patterns of relationships imply and foster distributive justice. But feminist perspectives have also been criticized for focusing on a particularized ethic of care, which posits care and responsibility exclusively within a relationship. Similarly, if the relational lens is meant merely to create a certain kind of relational justice, this might inhibit reflection on distributive implications.[47] Interestingly, the same debate is now cast not only within legal and political philosophy,[48] but also within private law theories. Hanoch Dagan and Avihay Dorfman explicitly argue that relational justice is separate from, though not antithetical to distributive justice.[49] Gregory Alexander also argues that focusing on human capabilities to be fostered within relationships and communities does not have to translate into welfare maximization.[50] All these debates might simply outline a preference for ultimate values. But considering the

[47] See Robert E. Goodin, 'Structures of Political Order: The Relational Feminist Alternative' in Ian Shapiro and Russel Hardin (eds.), *Political Order. Nomos 38* (New York University Press 1996).

[48] See Samuel Scheffler, 'The Practice of Equality' in Carina Fourie, Fabian Shuppert and Ivo Wallimann-Helmer (eds.), *Social Equality: On What it Means to Be Equal* (OUP 2015).

[49] See Dagan and Dorfman, "Justice in Private" (n. 31).

[50] See Alexander, "The Social Obligation Norm" (n. 31).

extent to which deontological arguments, which might define relational justice, would inhibit awareness of values outside the relationship or the community seems important.

Nineteenth-century PrIL authors embracing the relational internationalist perspective were particularly attuned to the relevant dimensions of justice within a private law relationship. The relational sensibility would often allow them to extend this analysis to third parties and to the various communities that are affected by the particular private law relationships. But they were less attuned to the relationship and potential conflict between relational and distributive justice in a transnational context. Incorporating the insights of the current debates within private law and feminist writings into PrIL will help illuminate and sharpen those connections.

Overall, connecting PrIL with feminist scholarship and private law theories on relationality via the nineteenth-century relational internationalist perspective is likely to bring contributions going in both directions.[51] Feminist perspectives are virtually nonexistent in PrIL[52] and among private law theories only the neo-Kantian version has been applied to the field.[53] At the same time the transnational arena of interhuman interaction poses more complicated and diverse challenges than the national context for which most of those theories were written. Applying them to PrIL will reveal the potential, as well as the limitations of incorporating relational insights in the transnational context.

2. Global justice debates

Recovering and adapting private law theories from PrIL's intellectual history might at first sight appear counter-intuitive, since it is precisely the private law heritage that is presumed to hold PrIL in isolation from global justice considerations. The perception of PrIL as an impoverished field of law, both intellectually and politically, has made many critics of PrIL lose hope that PrIL might have any vocabulary and doctrinal tools of its own to align the field with global justice considerations.

[51] Karen Knop and Annelise Riles, 'Space, Time, and Historical Injustice: A Feminist Conflict of Laws Approach to the Comfort Women Agreement' (2017) 102 Cornell L Rev 853 (bringing conflict of laws to bear on feminist issues under the purview of public international law). Conversely, Banu, "A Relational Feminist Approach" (n. 19), bringing feminist perspectives to bear on conflict of laws methodology.

[52] Notable exceptions are Annalise Acorn, 'Gender Discrimination in the Common Law of Domicile and the Application of the Canadian Charter of Rights and Freedoms' (1991) 29:3 Osgoode Hall LJ 419 (on dependent domicile); Ivana Isailović, 'Political Recognition and Transnational Law. Gender Equality and Cultural Diversification in French Courts' in Horatia Muir Watt and Diego P Fernández Arroyo (eds.), *Private International Law and Global Governance* (OUP 2015) 318; Horatia Muir Watt, 'Future Directions?' in Horatia Muir Watt and Diego P Fernández Arroyo (eds.), *Private International Law and Global Governance* (OUP 2015) 343 (recovering a framework of recognition inspired, among others, by feminist writings); Karen Knop, 'Relational Nationality: On Gender and Nationality in International Law' in T.A. Aleinikoff and D. Klusmeyer (eds.), *Citizenship Today: Global Perspectives and Practices* (Carnegie Endowment for International Peace 2001) 89; Karen Knop, Christine Chinkin, 'Remembering Chrystal MacMillan: Women's Equality and Nationality in International Law' (2001) 22 Mich J Int'l L 523 (on dependent nationality).

[53] See Sagi Peari, 'Savigny's Theory of Choice of Law as a Principle of Voluntary Submission' (2014) 64 UTLJ 106.

Therefore, a call for reform in PrIL now generally translates into a broad proposal to connect the field with global justice debates occurring elsewhere: in legal and political philosophy, public international law, human rights, environmental law, law and development, etc.[54] Some suggest that we should stop thinking of PrIL as an independent legal discipline altogether.[55] While these reformers rightfully seek to re-invigorate normative debates about PrIL's global justice dimensions by importing insights from the global justice scholarship, it is often unclear what precisely PrIL can learn from these insights and how it can change in light of them. Indeed, it is not even clear what analytical and conceptual elements of the global justice debates connect to PrIL.

But a fruitful strategy of reform might be to connect particular perspectives in the global justice literature with normative approaches excavated from PrIL's own arsenal. And here again, though possibly counter-intuitive, past private law theories map onto global justice perspectives much more than state-centered theories. In this section I want to underscore four points of interesting connections between current global justice theories and the relational internationalist perspective.

First, contemporary debates in the global justice literature suggest that states' duties of solidarity toward non-citizens should be viewed as a corollary to the various forms of duties individuals have in the "lifelong of inter-subjective relations."[56] Fair principles of inter-subjective interaction in which individuals meet either as "citizens of their respective nations" or as "citizens of the world" translate into a responsibility of states to consider and weigh the interests of all parties to these interactions.[57]

This way of constructing a framework of global solidarity, which connects to various levels and degrees of interhuman solidarity in different social contexts is very useful for PrIL which operates at the micro-level of interhuman interaction by examining cross-border private law relations. Making the legitimacy of a PrIL determination dependent on the extent to which the court hearing the PrIL matter has examined the level of consideration, respect, dignity and care individuals owe each other in their cross-border private law relations would create an important layer of global justice in PrIL. Relational internationalists have similarly argued that moral principles of inter-personal interaction should translate into the responsibilities of states toward foreign constituents who are involved in and affected by various private law relationships in a transnational context.

Second, global justice authors, such as Eyal Benvenisti, try to shift the perception of national courts, from viewing themselves only as the trustees of their

[54] See the introduction for a discussion of this perspective.

[55] Horatia Muir Watt, 'Future Directions?' in Horatia Muir Watt and Diego P. Fernández Arroyo (eds.), *Private International Law and Global Governance* (OUP 2015) (hereafter Muir Watt, "Future Directions?").

[56] Sergio Dellavalle, 'On Sovereignty, Legitimacy, and Solidarity, Or: How Can a Solidaristic Idea of Legitimate Sovereignty Be Justified?' (2015) 16 Theor Inq L 367.

[57] Ibid. See also Sergio Dellavalle, 'Opening the Forum to the Others: Is There an Obligation to Take Non-National-Interests Into Account Within National Political and Juridical Decision-Making Processes?' (2014) 6 Göttingen Journal of International Law 217 (2014).

executives, to increasingly acknowledging their fiduciary duties toward litigating parties, whether national or foreign.[58] Several state-centered theories encouraged courts to perceive their determinations as informed by their duties toward their executives or the legislative branch, rather than foreign nationals and foreign interests. Yet relational internationalists similarly suggested that courts in PrIL should realize or almost "pretend" that PrIL litigation is not embedded in the much more politically contentious interstate matters of PublIL.[59] They argued that this should enable courts in PrIL to construct "a public duty" toward humanity and toward the litigating parties, obliging them to an equitable weighing of the interests of domestic and foreign parties alike.[60]

Third, global justice scholars increasingly plead for a departure from a statist view of the world,[61] emphasizing the way in which groups, investors, corporations, government officials, and discrete minorities disenfranchised by globalization look to various decision fora in order to regain the democratic voice that they might have lost in their respective jurisdictions.[62] The appeal to disaggregate state interests in order to allow for the voice of various individuals and groups rested at the core of relational internationalists who wrote precisely against the dominant school of thought, which tried to conceptualize interhuman relationships in the international realm as interstate relationships.

Finally, global justice theorists argue that both the use and distribution of sovereign authority should be linked to human rights.[63] In other words both questions of who gets to regulate a legal matter and how the legal matter is to be regulated must be linked to norms and principles of human rights.[64] Furthermore, human rights would need to be theorized, "inter alia, [as] claims for inclusion in a political society that operates on the terrain of global politics."[65] Determinations about who gets to

[58] Eyal Benvenisti, 'Reclaiming Democracy: The Strategic Uses of Foreign and International Law by National Courts' (2008) 102 AJIL 241; Eyal Benvenisti, 'National Courts, Domestic Democracy, and the Evolution of International Law' (2009) 20 EJIL 59; Eyal Benvenisti and George W. Downs, 'The Democratizing Effects of Transjudicial Coordination' (2012) 8 Utrecht L Rev 158; Eyal Benvenisti, 'Sovereigns as Trustees for Humanity' (2013) 107 AJIL 295.

[59] See the "as if" analogy underlying PrIL methodology in Karen Knop, Ralf Michaels, and Annelise Riles, 'From Multiculturalism to Technique, Feminism, Culture, and the Conflict of Laws Style' (2012) 64 Stan L Rev 589. For the proposition that PrIL should dissociate itself from the contentious nature of PublIL, see Robert Wai, 'In the Name of the International: The Supreme Court of Canada and the Internationalist Transformation of Canadian Private International Law' (2001) 39 Can YB Int'l L 117; Robert Wai, 'The Interlegality of Transnational Private Law' (2008) 71 L & Contemp Probs 107.

[60] See, e.g., Story's reasoning in La Jeune Eugenie, discussed in Chapter 8.

[61] Joseph Singer, 'The Player and the Cards: Nihilism and Legal Theory' (1984) 94 Yale LJ 1; Joseph Stiglitz, *Making Globalisation Work* (W.W. Norton 2007); Thomas Pogge, *Realizing Rawls* (Cornell University Press 1989); Charles Beitz, *Political Theory and International Relations* (Princeton University Press 1979); Martha Nussbaum, 'Beyond the Social Contract: Toward Global Justice' in Grethe B. Peterson (ed.), *The Tanner Lectures on Human Values*, vol. 24 (University of Utah Press 2004) 413.

[62] Eyal Benvenisti, 'Exit and Voice in the Age of Globalization' (1999) 98 Mich L Rev 167.

[63] Patrick Macklem, 'What is International Human Rights? Three Applications of a Distributive Account' (2007) 52 McGill L J 575 (hereafter Macklem, "Three Applications"); Evan J. Criddle, Evan Fox-Decent, 'A Fiduciary Theory of Jus Cogens' (2009) 34 Yale J Int'l L 331.

[64] Macklem, "Three Applications" (n. 63).

[65] Joshua Cohen and Charles Sabel, 'Extra Republicam Nulla Justitia?' (2006) 34 Philosophy & Public Affairs 147.

decide upon the rights and liabilities of individuals in a transnational context are the bread and butter of PrIL. Yet connections between these determinations and human rights are rarely under the purview of PrIL norms.[66] Relational internationalists however not only incorporated a layer of horizontal human rights norms under the term "jus gentium," but were also aware that individuals pursue particular claims in particular courts as part of their quest for recognition and integration in various communities.[67]

Just as in the case of the parallel between the relational internationalist perspective and feminist relational perspectives, the parallel with global justice debates can bring contributions going in both directions. Overall, connecting global justice insights with the intellectual history of PrIL is likely to illuminate the current unjust dimensions of the field, but also the value of the reconstruction of PrIL's own intellectual history. It also quite clearly brings PrIL in conversation with global justice theories and identifies its own inner potential to contribute to global justice. But the relational internationalist perspective also has much to offer to global justice debates. First, it deliberately includes the private and economic dimensions of transnational life within the purview of global justice debates. Second, it situates those dimensions neither in the domain of the unfettered individual autonomy, nor in the exclusively statist framework. Thirdly and relatedly, it combines appeals to humanity with references to the virtue and autonomy of national communities; positive law and lucid comparative law analysis with references to universal inter-personal morality and ethics, and *jus gentium*; and navigates back and forth between inter-personal relationships and the relationships of individuals to broader communities and groups.[68] In the case of PrIL, this translates into a fluid, but structured and more technical analysis and methodology, which in turn might provide more structure and anchorage to legal and ethical analysis around cosmopolitanism.[69]

[66] See Muir Watt, "Future Directions?" (n. 55). [67] See esp. Chapter 8.

[68] This maps onto the analysis provided by Robert Wai regarding the value of bringing perspectives from transnational law in conversation with debates around cosmopolitanism. See Robert Wai, 'The Cosmopolitanism of Transnational Economic Law' in Cecilia M. Baillet and Katja Franko Aas (eds.), *Cosmopolitan Justice and its Discontents* (Routledge 2011) 153. See also 156:

> A cosmopolitan perspective on the global economy must recognize that while the nation-state is clearly one venue for norm-generation, the forms of community are multiple and so likewise are sources of relevant norms of conduct. Normative communities are complicated and dynamic, and exist at many levels, from the local—including private or exclusive worlds like the family—through to the world public affairs of states. Consequently, a consideration of transnational economic law may in some respects offer a better model for the simultaneous consideration of both state and non-state normative orders, and their interrelationship. If the particular contribution of law comes from its synthesis of practical relevance and normative promise, then it is all the more important to consider the full range of normative practice in the global society.

[69] For a wonderful exposition of the possibilities and advantages of PrIL's techniques, see Karen Knop, Ralf Michaels, and Annelise Riles, 'From Multiculturalism to Technique, Feminism, Culture, and the Conflict of Laws Style' (2012) 64 Stan L Rev 589.

3. The value of intellectual historical analysis for PrIL

There are potential cross-references at all the different points of conversation between the present and the past outlined above. This book focused on recovering a relational sensibility that is part of PrIL's own intellectual history. This particular perspective illuminates quite explicit dimensions of global justice and restores *jus gentium* as a moral point of reference for law, distilled, in part, from states' own practice.[70] It replaces a framework of recognition focused on isolated individuals with a framework of recognition of relationships and various facets of inter-personal interaction. All these themes are found in current debates on law and policy outside of PrIL, to which PrIL could and should connect. In turn, these debates would have much to contribute to sharpening and possibly correcting some of the insights of relational internationalism.

This book started by noting the contrast between an increasing interest in rethinking the theoretical foundations of PrIL and a decreasing interest in the intellectual history of the field. I suggested that the lack of interest in the intellectual history of the field has much to do with the conventional understanding of nineteenth-century PrIL on which the call for jurisprudential rethinking is premised. I hope by the time the reader has arrived at these conclusions, she will be persuaded that the conventional understanding is in many ways flawed and that PrIL's intellectual history holds much valuable material to be recovered and rethought.

But in these concluding paragraphs I want to consider more broadly how studies of intellectual history can help in the process of rethinking PrIL's theoretical foundations.

An immediate and rather straightforward value of intellectual history in PrIL is to separate what many of the "canonical" writers of PrIL meant to say from the way in which their theories were read and altered. In a 2005 volume dedicated to Pierre Lagarde (Henri Batiffol's collaborator), Pierre Gothot argued compellingly about the need to separate Savigny from "Savignyism."[71] Gothot argues that at least in Europe, Savigny is "no longer an interesting and inventive scholar, he is above all a reference 'like no other,' often decisive, an 'authority' in the sense closest

[70] For a contemporary jurisprudential recast of *jus gentium* and the blend of natural and positive law that it incorporates, see Jeremy Waldron, *'Partly Laws Common to All Mankind': Foreign Law in American Courts* (Yale University Press 2012). See also Rafael Domingo, *The New Global Law* (CUP 2011); Neil Walker, *Intimations of Global Law* (CUP 2014) 198–9 (noting how certain intimations of global law under which current recasts of *jus gentium* could be included are premised less on natural law and universal reason, but rather "upon the idea of law as a joint construction, as a collective accomplishment"). In PrIL Horatia Muir Watt also drew attention to the loss of *jus gentium* as a normative dimension of PrIL and argued that "the conceptual divide between international politics and global market led to the immunity of cross-border private economic expansion from the moral and legal constraints previously carried by the *ius gentium*." See Horatia Muir Watt, 'Private International Law Beyond the Schism' (2011) 2 Transnatl Leg Theory 347, 359.

[71] Pierre Gothot, 'Simples réflexions à propos de la saga du conflit des lois' in *Le droit international privé: esprit et methodes, Mélanges en l'honneur de Paul Lagarde* (Dalloz 2007) 343.

to the etymology of the word."[72] But those references are mostly to Savigny's disciples, "very different from each other, who did not retain much from Savigny other that the community of law metaphor and the analytical method."[73] This is how, in Gothot's view "Savignyism arose, and with it we lost the interest in Savignyan thought."[74] Much the same can be said of the other "canonical" figures of the nineteenth century. Intellectual history can help restore the "canonical" thinking both on its own terms, and revise the canon altogether.

On the one hand, further intellectual historical work can reveal the common perceptions about the theoretical foundations of PrIL. For example, revealing the conventional association between PrIL and PublIL shows that it is not enough to reclaim the association today as a way of increasing PrIL's social justice dimensions. Instead, acknowledging the formalist underpinnings of the nineteenth-century association makes it possible to reveal and criticize its contemporary reinvention, rather than idealizing any attempt to reconnect the fields.

On the other hand, intellectual history can reveal paths not taken in the development of the field. Re-engaging with Savignian thought generally and in PrIL in particular, might reveal insights and perspectives which were lost in the "prejudices and misunderstanding"[75] or "misleading simplifications"[76] about Savigny's theories. As Joachim Rückert remarked, especially in a field much influenced by Savignian thought, such as PrIL, revisiting Savigny might allow us to "not only learn history but learn from history."[77] Similarly, acknowledging an alternative to both the formalist and the state-centered late nineteenth-century perspectives in the writings of Josephus Jitta, means breaking the spell of inevitability that very much marks PrIL as a field. It shows that different imaginaries were constructed in the intellectual history of PrIL, some of which were marginalized, misunderstood or even failed to register as possible alternatives. Bringing them back for the purpose of analysis and critique can contribute much to the jurisprudential rethinking of PrIL. As Annabel Brett notes:

> In this sense, to do intellectual history just *is* to do philosophy. If philosophy has a further task, it is not to gain a better insight into reality, but analogously to poetry, to stretch our imagination and our language and thus to help create a new world for living in. We might add that doing intellectual history can itself be understood as poetic in that sense, for intellectual history does not merely unravel the structure of what we have inherited but can also unearth what we have lost.[78]

[72] Ibid., 350. [73] Ibid. [74] Ibid., 354.

[75] Joachim Rückert, 'Friedrich Carl von Savigny, the Legal Method, and the Modernity of Law' (2006) 11 Juridica International 55, 57, referring to three main "prejudices and misunderstandings" about Savigny: "(1) the Left Hegelian and Marxist point of view, that Savigny was just a juridical reactionary; (2) the opinion that he only wanted to preserve conservatively what has become obsolete already; (3) and, especially, the view that his theory of legal method had become obsolete and useless."

[76] Ibid., 67. [77] Ibid.

[78] Annabel Brett, 'What is Intellectual History Now?' in D. Cannadiene, *What is History Now?* (Palgrave Macmillan 2002) 113, 127.

Intellectual history, therefore, should not be opposed to, but rather form part of rethinking the theoretical foundations of PrIL in a world of increasing inter-dependence and human mobility. It is my hope that this book might help to open the door for further engagement with PrIL's intellectual history on its own, and as a path to rethinking the premises and aspirations of PrIL for the future.

Bibliography

Abdelal, R. and Ruggie, J., 'Principles of Embedded Liberalism: Social Legitimacy and Global Capitalism' in David Moss and John Cistermino (eds.), *New Perspectives on Regulation* (Tobin Project 2009) 151.

Acorn, A., 'Gender Discrimination in the Common Law of Domicile and the Application of the Canadian Charter of Rights and Freedoms' (1991) 29 Osgoode Hall LJ 419.

Alexander, G., 'The Social Obligation Norm in American Property Law' (2009) 94 Cornell L Rev 745.

Arminjon, P. (ed.), *Mélanges Antoine Pillet: reproduction de diverses études et notes de jurisprudence écrites par Antoine Pillet* (Sirey 1929).

Arminjon, P., 'La notion de droit acquis en droit international privé' (1933) 44 Recueil des Cours 1.

Armitage, D., *Foundations of Modern International Thought* (CUP 2013).

Azoulai, L., 'The European Individual as Part of Collective Entities' in Loïc Azoulai, Ségolène Barbou des Places, and Etienne Pataut (eds.), *Constructing the Person in EU Law: Rights, Roles, Identities* (Hart 2016) 203.

Azoulai, L., Barbou des Places, S., and Pataut, E. (eds.), *Constructing the Person in EU Law: Rights, Roles, Identities* (Hart 2016).

Bachellier, M.N. et al. (eds.), *Le droit international privé: esprit et methodes, Mélanges en l'honneur de Paul Lagarde* (Dalloz 2007).

Baehr, A.R. (ed.), *Varieties of Feminist Liberalism* (Rowman & Littlefield 2004).

Bähr, O., *Der Rechtsstaat: eine publizistische Skizze* (Scientia 1961).

Baillet, C.M. and Franko Aas, K. (eds.), *Cosmopolitan Justice and its Discontents* (Routledge 2011).

Baker, B., 'Interstate Choice of Law and Early-American Constitutional Nationalism. An Essay on Joseph Story and the Comity of Errors: A Case Study in Conflict of Laws' (1993) 35 McGill L J 454.

Banu, R., 'A Relational Feminist Approach to Conflict of Laws' (2017) 27 Mich J Gender & L 1.

Barnard, F.M., *Herder's Social and Political Thought, From Enlightenment to Nationalism* (Clarendon 1965).

Bartin, E., *Études de droit international privé* (A. Chevalier-Marescq 1899).

Bartin, E., 'La doctrine des qualifications et ses rapports avec le caractere national du conflit des lois' (1930) 31 Recueil des Cours 561.

Bartin, E., *Principes de droit international privé: selon la loi et la jurisprudence françaises* (Domat-Montchrestien 1930).

Basedow, J. et al. (eds.), *European Encyclopedia of Private International Law* (Elgar 2017)

Batiffol, H., 'Les tendences doctrinales actuelles en droit international privé' (1948) 72 Recueil des Cours 1.

Batiffol, H., *Traité élémentaire de droit international privé* (2nd edn., Librairie Générale de Droit et de Jurisprudence 1955).

Batiffol, H., *Aspects philosophiques du droit international privé* (Dalloz 1956).

Batiffol, H., *Traité élémentaire de droit international privé* (3rd edn., Pichon & Durand-Auzias 1959).

Batiffol, H., 'Principes de Droit International Privé' (1959) 97 Recueil des Cours 431.

Batiffol, H., *Droit international privé* (4th edn., Librairie générale de droit et de jurisprudence 1967).

Batiffol, H., 'Réflexions sur la coordination des systèmes nationaux' (1967) 120 Recueil des Cours 165.

Batiffol, H., 'Pluralisme des méthodes en droit international privé' (1973) 139 Recueil des Cours 79.

Batiffol, Henri., 'Droit et nature de choses dans la philosophie française du droit' in *Choix d'articles. Rassemblés par ses amis* (Librairie generale de droit et de la jurisprudence 1976) 387.

Batiffol, H., 'Les intérêts du droit international privé' in Alexander Lüderitz and Jochen Schröder (eds.), *Internationales Privatrecht und Rechtsvergleichung im Ausgang des 20. Jahrhunderts. Bewahrung oder Wende?* (Alfred Metzner 1977) 11.

Batiffol, H., 'Reflections on the Co-ordination of National Systems' (1985) 15 Seton Hall L Rev 793.

Baty, T., 'A Modern Jus Gentium' (1909) 20 Jurid Rev 109.

Beale, J.H., 'Dicey's Conflict of Laws' (1896) 10 Harv L Rev 168.

Beale, J.H., *A Treatise on the Conflict of Laws: Or, Private International Law*, vol. 1, part 1 (Harvard University Press 1916).

Beatson, J. and Zimmermann, R. (eds.), *Jurists Uprooted: German Speaking Emigré Lawyers in Twentieth-century Britain* (OUP 2004).

Behrends, O., Eckart Voss, W., and Diesselhorst, M. (eds), *Römisches Recht in der europäischen Tradition: Symposion aus Anlass des 75. Geburtstages von Franz Wieacker* (R. Gremer 1985).

Behrends, O., 'Geschichte, Politik und Jurisprudenz in Savignys System des heutigen römischen Rechts' in Okko Behrends, Wulf Eckart Voss, and Malte Diesselhorst (eds.), *Römisches Recht in der Europäischen Tradition: Symposion aus Anlass des 75. Geburtstages von Franz Wieacker* (R. Gremer 1985).

Behrends, O., 'Die *bona fides* in *mandatum*. Die vorklassischen Grundlagen des klassischen Konsensualvertrags Auftrag' in Okko Behrends, *Institut und Prinzip. Siedlungsgeschichtliche Grundlagen, philosophische Einflüsse und das Fortwirken der beiden republikanischen Konzeptionen in den kaiserzeitlichen Rechtsshulen. Ausgewählte Aufsätze*, vol. 1 (Wallsteig 2004).

Behrends, O., *Institut und Prinzip: siedlungsgeschichtliche Grundlagen, philosophische Einflüsse und das Fortwirken der beiden republikanischen Konzeptionen in den kaiserzeitlichen Rechtsschulen; ausgewählte Aufsätze*, 2 vols. (Wallstein 2004).

Behrends, O., 'Das Sozialrecht. Sein Wert und seine Funktion in historischer Perspektive' in Behrends, Okko and Eva Schumann, *Gesetzgebung, Menschenbild und Sozialmodell im Familien- und Sozialrecht*, Neue Abhandlungen der Akademie der Wissenschaft zu Gottingen, vol. 3 (De Gruyter 2008).

Behrends, O. and Schumann, E., *Gesetzgebung, Menschenbild und Sozialmodell im Familien- und Sozialrecht*. Neue Abhandlungen der Akademie der Wissenschaft zu Göttingen, vol. 3 (De Gruyter 2008).

Beiser, F.C., *The German Historicist Tradition* (OUP 2011).

Beitz, C., *Political Theory and International Relations* (Princeton University Press 1979).

Benvenisti, E., 'Exit and Voice in the Age of Globalization' (1999) 98 Mich L Rev 167.

Benvenisti, E., 'Reclaiming Democracy: The Strategic Uses of Foreign and International Law by National Courts' (2008) 102 AJIL 241.

Benvenisti, E., 'National Courts, Domestic Democracy, and the Evolution of International Law' (2009) 20 EJIL 59.

Benvenisti, E. and Downs, G.W., 'The Democratizing Effects of Transjudicial Coordination' (2012) 8 Utrecht L Rev 158.

Benvenisti, E., 'Sovereigns as Trustees for Humanity: On the Accountability of States to Foreign Stakeholders' (2013) 107 Am J Int'l L 295.

Bernard, M., 'Review of Antoine Pillet, Principes de Droit International Privé' (1904) 31 Journal de droit international privé et de la jurisprudence comparée 769.

Bollée, S., 'L'extension du domaine de la methode de la reconnaisance unilatérale' (2007) 96 Rev crit dr int privé 307.

Bomhoff, J., 'The Constitution of the Conflict of Laws' in Horatia Muir Watt and Diego P. Fernández Arroyo (eds.) *Private International Law and Global Governance* (OUP 2015) 262.

Bonnichon, A., 'La notion de conflit de souverainetes dans la science des conflits de lois' (1949) 39 Rev crit dr int privé 615.

Bonnichon, A., 'La notion de conflit de souverainetes dans la science des conflits de lois' (1950) 40 Rev crit dr int privé 11.

Boullenois, L., *Traité de la personalité et de la réalité des lois, coutumes, ou statuts, par forme d'observations* (Guillaume Desprez 1762).

Brennan, S., 'The Liberal Rights of Feminist Liberalism' in Amy R. Baehr (ed.), *Varieties of Feminist Liberalism* (Rowman & Littlefield 2004).

Brett, A., 'What is Intellectual History Now?' in D. Cannadiene, *What is History Now?* (Palgrave Macmillan 2002) 113.

Brilmayer, L., 'Rights, Fairness, and Choice of Law' (1989) 98 Yale LJ 1277.

Brilmayer, L., 'The Problem of Provenance: The Proper Place of Ethical Reasoning in the Selection of Applicable Law' in Donald Earl Childress (ed.), *The Role of Ethics in International Law* (CUP 2012).

Bucher, A., *Grundfragen der Anknüpfungsgerechtigkeit im internationalen Privatrecht (aus kontinentaleuropäischer Sicht)* (Helbing & Lichtenhahn 1975).

Bucher, A., 'La dimension sociale du droit international privé: cours general' (2009) 330 Recueil des Cours 1.

Butler, M. and Kirkby, C. 'Same-Sex Marriage, Divorce and Families: Selected Recent Developments' (2013), online: Library of Parliament Research Publications http://www.lop.parl.gc.ca/content/lop/ResearchPublications/2013-74-e.htm.

Cannadiene, D., *What is History Now?* (Palgrave Macmillan 2002).

Cavers, D., 'A Critique of the Choice-of-Law Problem' (1933) 47 Harv L Rev 173.

Cavers, D., *The Choice-of-Law Process* (University of Michigan Press 1966).

Cavers, D., 'Cipolla and Conflicts Justice' (1970) 9 Duq L Rev 360.

Cavers, D., 'Contemporary Conflicts Law in American Perspective' (1970) 131 Recueil des Cours 85.

Cavers, D., 'A Correspondence with Brainerd Currie 1957–1958' (1982) 34 Mercer L Rev 471.

Cavers, D., *Selected Essays 1933–1983* (Duke Univ Press 1985).

Cheatam, E., 'Review of The Logical and Legal Bases of the Conflict of Laws' (1944) 93 U Pa L Rev 112.

Cheatham, E. and Reese, W.L.M., 'Choice of the Applicable Law' (1952) 52 Colum L Rev 959.

Childress III, D.E., 'Comity as Conflict: Resituating International Comity as Conflict of Laws' (2010) 44 UC Davis L Rev 11.

Childress III, D.E., *The Role of Ethics in International Law* (CUP 2012).

Christman, J., 'Relational Autonomy, Liberal Individualism, and the Social Constitution of Selves' (2004) 117 Philosophical Studies 143.

Schmitthoff, C.M., *The English Conflict of Laws* (3rd edn., Stevens 1954).

Cohen, J. and Sabel, C., 'Extra Republicam Nulla Justitia?' (2006) 34 Philosphy & Public Affairs 147.

Collins, L., 'F.A. Mann (1907–1991)' in Jack Beatson and Reinhard Zimmermann (eds.), *Jurists Uprooted: German Speaking Emigré Lawyers in Twentieth-century Britain* (OUP 2004) 381.

Cook, W.W., 'The Logical and Legal Bases of the Conflict of Laws' (1924) 33 Yale LJ 457.

Cook, W.W., 'The Scientific Method and the Law' (1927) 13 ABA J 30.

Cook, W.W., 'The Jurisdiction of Sovereign States and the Conflict of Laws' (1931) 31 Colum L Rev 368.

Cook, W.W., *Selected Essays on the Conflict of Laws, Reprinted from the Harvard Law Review* (Harvard Law Review Association 1940).

Cosack, K., *Lehrbuch des deutschen bürgerlichen Rechts* (1st edn., Gustav Fischer 1910).

Criddle, E.J. and Fox-Decent, E., 'A Fiduciary Theory of Jus Cogens' (2009) 34 Yale J Int'l L 331.

Crome, C., *System des deutschen bürgerlichen Rechts* (J.C.B. Mohr 1900).

Cunningham, T., *Reports of Cases Argued and Adjudged in the Court of King's Bench, in the Seventh, Eighth, Ninth and Tenth Years of King George the Second, During Which Time the Right Honorable The Earl of Hardwicke was Lord Chief Justice of the Court* (3rd edn., Stevens & Haynes 1871).

Currie, B., 'Married Women's Contracts: A Study in Conflict-of-Laws Method' (1958) 25 U Chicago L Rev 227.

Currie, B., *Selected Essays on the Conflict of Laws* (Duke University Press 1963).

Decker, T., *Das kollisionsrechtliche Werk Ernst Zittelmanns (1852–1923)* (doctorate in law, Osnabrück University, 2004) (unpublished).

De Chassat, M., *Traité de statuts (lois personelles, lois réelles), d'après le droit ancienes et le droit modern, ou du Droit International Privé* (A. Durand 1845).

D'Oliveira, H.U.J., 'Die Freiheit des Niederländischen Richters bei der Entwicklung des internationalen Privatrechts: Zur antizipierenden Anwendung des Benelux-Einheitsgesetzes über das Internationale Privatrecht–ein Requiem' (1975) 39 RabelZ 224.

D'Oliveira, H.U.J., 'La Pollution du Rhin et le droit international privé' in *Rhine Pollution: Legal, Economic and Technical Aspects* (Tjeenk Willink 1978).

Dagan, H., *Property: Values and Institutions* (OUP 2011).

Dagan, H. and Dorfman, A., 'Just Relationships' (2016) 116 Columbia L Rev 1395.

Dagan, H. and Dorfman, A., 'Justice in Private: Beyond the Rawlsian Framework' (2018) 37 Law and Philos 171.

Dane, P., 'Vested Rights, "Vestedness," and Choice of Law' (1987) 96 Yale LJ 1191.

Darwall, S., *The Second-Person Standpoint: Morality, Respect and Accountability* (Harvard University Press 2009).

De Nova, R., 'The First American Book on Conflict of Laws' (1964) 8:2 Am J Legal Hist 136.

De Nova, R., 'Historical and Comparative Introduction to the Conflict of Laws' (1966) 116 Recueil des Cours 437.

De Szászy, S., 'Choice of Law by the Parties to a Contract with Principal Reference to the English and American Law' (1934) 20 Transactions of the Grotius Society 156.

Dellavalle, S., 'Opening the Forum to the Others: Is There an Obligation to Take Non-National-Interests Into Account Within National Political and Juridical Decision-Making Processes?' (2014) 6 Göttingen Journal of International Law 217.

Dellavalle, S., 'On Sovereignty, Legitimacy, and Solidarity, Or: How Can a Solidaristic Idea of Legitimate Sovereignty Be Justified?' (2015) 16 Theor Inq L 367.

Der Derian, J. et al., 'How Should Sovereignty Be Defended?' in Christopher J. Bickerton, Philip Cunliffe, and Alexander Gourevitch (eds.), *Politics Without Sovereignty: A Critique of Contemporary International Relations* (UCL Press 2007).

Dicey, A.V., *A Digest of the Law of England with Reference to the Conflict of Laws* (Stevens and Sons 1908).

Dodge, W., 'Breaking the Public Law Taboo' (2002) 43 Harv Int'l L J 161.

Domingo, R., *The New Global Law* (CUP 2011).

Dworkin, R., *Justice for Hedgehogs* (Harvard University Press 2011).

Ehrenzweig, A., 'A Counter-Revolution in Conflicts Law? From Beale to Cavers' (1966) 80 Harv L Rev 377.

Ehrlich, E., 'Les tendances actuelles du droit international privé' (1908) 4 Rev dr int privé 902.

Eichhorn, K.F., *Einleitung in das deutsche Privatrecht: Mit Einschluss des Lehenrechts* (Vandenhoeck & Ruprecht 1836).

Ely, J.H., 'Choice of Law and the State's Interest in Protecting its Own' (1981) 23 Wm & Mary L Rev 173.

Endemann, F., *Lehrbuch des bürgerlichen Rechts. Einführung in das Studium des Bürgerlichen Gesetzbuchs* (9th edn., C. Heymann 1903).

Flessner, A., *Interessenjurisprudenz im internationalen Privatrecht* (J.C.B. Mohr 1990).

Fourie, C., Fabian, S., and Wallimann-Helmer, I. (eds.), *Social Equality: On What it Means to Be Equal* (OUP 2015).

Franceskakis, P., 'Review of Gerhard Kegel, Begriffs- und Interessenjurisprudenz im internationalen Privatrecht' (1954) 43 Rev crit dr int privé 238.

Franceskakis, P., 'Perspectives du Droit international privé actuel a propos de la deuxième édition du Traité de M. Henri Batiffol' review of Henri Batiffol, *Traité élémentaire de droit international privé*, 2nd edn., (1955) 7 RIDC 349.

Franceskakis, P., 'De conflictu legum, Mélanges offerts à R.D. Kollewijn et J. Offerhaus à l'occasion de leur soixante-dixième anniversaire' review of M. von Overbeck, 'Les règles de droit international privé materiel' (1963) 53 Rev crit dr int privé 866.

Franceskakis, P., 'Review of Jessurun D'Oliveira, La Pollution du Rhin et le droit international privé' (1979) 59 Rev crit dr int privé 266.

Francescakis, P., *La pensée des autres en droit international privé: comptes rendus bibliographiques (1946–1984) réunis en hommage à leur auteur* (Université Aristote de Thessalonique, Faculté de droit 1985).

Franceskakis, P., 'De coflictu legum, Melanges offerts a R.D. Kollewijn et J. Offerhaus a l'occasion de leur soixante-dixieme anniversaire,' review of M. Blagojeviç, 'Théorie des statuts à la lumière générale de l'évolution de la société' in Phocion Francescakis, *La pensée des autres en droit international privé: comptes rendus bibliographiques (1946–1984) réunis en hommage à leur auteur* (Université Aristote de Thessalonique, Faculté de droit, 1985) 211.

Freund, O.K., *The Growth of Internationalism in English Private International Law* (Magnus Press 1960).

Gaudemet, E., 'La thèorie des conflits des lois dans l'ouvre d'Antoine Pillet et de la doctrine de Savigny' in Pierre Arminjon (ed.), *Mélanges Antoine Pillet: reproduction de diverses études et notes de jurisprudence écrites par Antoine Pillet* (Sirey 1929).

Gidel, G., 'Droits et devoirs des nations, théorie classique des droit fondamentaux des États' (1925) 10 Recueil des Cours 537.

Glenn, H.P., 'The Ethic of International Law' in Donald Earl Childress (ed.), *The Role of Ethics in International Law* (CUP 2012).

Goodin, R.E., 'Structures of Political Order: The Relational Feminist Alternative' in Ian Shapiro and Russel Hardin (eds.), *Political Order. Nomos 38* (New York University Press 1996).

Gothot, P., 'Le renouveau de la tendance unilatéraliste en droit international privé' (1971) 60 Rev crit dr int privé 1, 209 and 417.

Gothot, P., 'Simples réflexions à propos de la saga du conflit des lois' in *Le droit international privé: esprit et methodes, Mélanges en l'honneur de Paul Lagarde* (Dalloz 2007).

Graveson, R.H., 'The Doctrine of Evasion of the Law in England and America' (1937) 19 Journal of Comparative Legislation and International Law 21.

Graveson, R.H., 'The Comparative Evolution of Principles of the Conflict of Laws in England and the United States' (1960) 99 Recueil des Cours 21.

Graveson, R.H., 'Aspects Philosophiques du Droit International Privé Anglais' (1962) 51 Rev crit dr int privé 397.

Graveson, R.H., 'Comparative Aspects of the General Principles of Private International Law' (1963) 109 Recueil des Cours 1.

Graveson, R.H., *Conflict of Laws* (7th edn., Sweet & Maxwell 1974).

Graveson, R.H., *Comparative Conflict of Laws. Selected Essays*, vol. 1 (North Holland 1977).

Green, M., 'Legal Realism, Lex Fori, and the Choice-of-Law Revolution' (1995) 104 Yale LJ 968.

Gutzwiller, M.C., *Der Einfluss Savignys auf die Entwicklung des Internationalprivatrechts* (Gschwend, Tschopp & Co. 1923).

Gutzwiller, M., 'Zitlemann's völkerrechtliche Theorie des Internationalprivatrechts' (1923) 16 Archiv für Rechts- und Wirtschaftsphilosophie 468.

Gutzwiller, M., 'Le développement Historique du Droit International Privé' (1929) 29 Recueil des Cours 237.

Harrison, F. and Lefroy, A.H.F., *On Jurisprudence and the Conflict of Laws* (Clarendon 1919).

Hatzimihail, N., 'Pages of History: Friedrich Juenger and the Historical Consciousness of Modern Private International Law' in Leonel Pereznieto Castro, Tullio Treves, and Francesco Seatzu (eds.), *Tradition and Innovation of Private International Law at the Beginning of the Third Millenium—Liber in Memoriam of Professor Friedrich K. Juenger* (Juris Publishing 2006) 81.

Herder, J.G., *Outlines of a Philosophy of the History of Man* (T. Churchill, tr., Bergman 1800).

Hofer, S., *Freiheit Ohne Grenzen? Privatrechtstheoretische Diskussionen im 19. Jahrhundert* (Mohr Siebeck 2001).

Holland, T.E., *The Elements of Jurisprudence* (Clarendon 1880).

Huber, U., *Praelectionum Iuris civilis tomi tres* (Expensis Iosephi et Ioannis Roland fratrum, 1788).

Hueting, R., *Rhine Pollution: Legal, Economic and Technical Aspects* (Tjeenk Willink 1978).

Isailović, I., 'Political Recognition and Transnational Law. Gender Equality and Cultural Diversification in French Courts' in Horatia Muir Watt and Diego P. Fernández Arroyo (eds.), *Private International Law and Global Governance* (OUP 2015) 318.

Jansen, N. and Michaels, R., 'Private Law and the State: Comparative Perceptions and Historical Observations' (2007) 71 RabelsZ 345.

Jayme, E. and Mansel, H.P. (ed.), *Nation und Staat im internationalen Privatrecht. Zum kollisionsrechtlichen Staatsangehörigkeitsprinzip in verfassungsrechtlicher und internationalprivatrechtlicher Sicht* (C.F. Müller 1988).

Jayme, E., 'Die kulturelle Dimension des Rechts—ihre Beudeutung für das internationale Privatrecht und die Rechtsvergleichung' (2003) 67 RabelsZ 211.

Jayme, E., *Internationales Privatrecht und Völkerrecht* (C.F. Müller 2003).

Jayme, E., 'Menschenrechte und Theorie des internationalen Privatrechts' in Erik Jayme (ed.), *Internationales Privatrecht und Völkerrecht* (C.F. Müller 2003).

Jayme, E., 'Völkerrecht und internationales Privatrecht—eine entwicklungsgeschichtliche Betrachtung' in Leibe, S. and Ruffert, M. (eds.), *Völkerrecht und IPR* (Jenaer Wissenschaftliche Verlagsgesellschaft 2006).

Jayme, E., *Internationales Privatrecht: Ideengeschichte von Mancini und Ehrenzweig zum Europäischen Kollisionsrecht* (C.F. Müller 2009).

Jitta, J., *La Méthode du droit international privé* (Belinfante 1890).

Jitta, J., 'Das Wesen des internationalen Privatrechts' (1899) 14 AOR 301.

Jitta, J., 'Alte und neue Methoden des internationalen Privatrechts' (1900) 15 AOR 564.

Jitta, J., *La substance des obligations dans le droit international privé*, 2 vols. (Belinfante Frères 1906 & 1907).

Jitta, J., 'Le droit commun international comme source du droit international privé' (1908) 4 Revue de Droit International Privé et de Droit Pénal International 553.

Jitta, J., 'Le droit commun international comme source du droit international privé' (1909) 5 Revue de Droit International Privé et de Droit Pénal International 485.

Jitta, J., *The Renovation of International Law on the Basis of a Juridical Community of Mankind, Systematically Developed* (M. Nijhoff 1919).

Jitta, J., 'The Development of Private International Law through Conventions' (1920) 29 Yale LJ 497.

Joerges, C., *Zum Funktionswandel des Kollisionsrechts: Die Governmental Interest Analysis und die Krise des internationalen Privatrechts* (Mohr Siebeck 1971).

Jouannet, E.T., *'Qu'est-ce qu'une société international juste? Le droit international entre développement et reconnaissance?'* (Pédone 2012).

Jouannet, E.T., 'The International Law of Recognition' (2013) 24 EJIL 667.

Juenger, F., 'A Page of History' (1984) 35 Mercer L Rev 419.

Juenger, F., *Choice of Law and Multistate Justice* (M. Nijhoff 1993).

Juenger, F., 'The Lex Mercatoria and Private International Law' (2000) 60 La L Rev 1134.

Kaeckenbeeck, G., 'The Protection of Vested Rights in International Law' (1936) 17 Brit YB Int'l L 1.

Kahn, F., 'Gesetzeskollisionen, Ein Beitrag zur Lehre des Internationalen Privatrechts' (1898) 39 Jherings Jahrbücher für die Dogmatik des Bürgerlichen Rechts 1.

Kahn, F., 'Gesetzeskollisionen, Ein Beitrag zur Lehre des Internationalen Privatrechts' (1899) 40 Jherings Jahrbücher für die Dogmatik des Bürgerlichen Rechts 1.

Kahn, F., 'Gesetzeskollisionen, Ein Beitrag zur Lehre des Internationalen Privatrechts' (1890) 30 Jherings Jahrbücher für die Dogmatik des Bürgerlichen Rechts 1.

Kahn, F., *Über Inhalt, Natur und Methode des internationalen Privatrechts* (G. Fischer 1899).

Kahn Freund, O., 'Reflections on Public Policy in the English Conflict of Laws' (1953) 39 Transactions of the Grotius Society 39.

Kalenský, P., *Trends of Private International Law* (Czechoslovak Academy of Sciences 1971).

Kegel, G., 'Begriffs- und Interessenjurisprudenz im internationalen Privatrecht' in Hans Lewald et al. (eds.), *Festschrift Hans Lewald: bei Vollendung des 40.Amtsjahres als ordentlicher Professor im Oktober 1953 überreicht von seinen Freunden und Kollegen mit Unterstützung der Basler Juristischen Fakultät* (Helbing & Lichtenhahn 1953).

Kegel, G., 'The Crisis of Conflict of Laws' (1964) 112 Recueil des Cours 91.

Kegel, G., 'Paternal Home and Dream Home: Traditional Conflict of Laws and the American Reformers' (1979) 27 Am J Comp L 615.

Kegel, G., 'Story and Savigny' (1989) 37 Am J Comp L 39.

Kennedy, D., 'International Law and the Nineteenth Century: History of an Illusion' (1998) 17 Quinnipiac L Rev 99.

Kennedy, D., 'Law and the Political Economy of the World' (2013) 26 Leiden J Int'l L 7.

Knop, K., 'Citizenship Private and Public' (2008) 71 Law and Contemp Probs 309.

Knop, K., 'Lorimer's Private Citizens of the World' (2016) 27 Eur J Internat L 447.

Knop, K., 'Relational Nationality: On Gender and Nationality in International Law' in T.A. Aleinikoff and D. Klusmeyer (eds.), *Citizenship Today: Global Perspectives and Practices* (Carnegie Endowment for International Peace 2001) 89.

Knop, K., 'Re/Statements: Feminism and State Sovereignty in International Law' (1993) 3 Transnat'l L & Contemp Probs 293.

Knop, K. and Chinkin, C., 'Remembering Chrystal MacMillan: Women's Equality and Nationality in International Law' (2001) 22 Mich J Int'l L 523.

Knop, K., Michaels, R., and Riles, A., 'From Multiculturalism to Technique, Feminism, Culture, and the Conflict of Laws Style' (2012) 64 Stan L Rev 589.

Knop, K. and Riles, A., 'Space, Time, and Historical Injustice: A Feminist Conflict of Laws Approach to the Comfort Women Agreement' (2017) 102 Cornell L Rev 853.

Kochenov, D., 'European Citizenship and the Difficult Relationship Between Status and Rights' (2009) 15 Colum J Eur L 169.

Kogan, T.S., 'Toward a Jurisprudence of Choice of Law: The Priority of Fairness over Comity' (1987) 62 NYUL Rev 651.

Kollewijn, R.D., 'Conflicts of Western and Non-Western Law' (1951) 4 International Law Quarterly 307.

Kollewijn, R.D., 'Quelques considerations a propos de la doctrine de Savigny' (1968) 15 Neth Int'l L Rev 237.

Korn, H., 'The Choice-of-Law Revolution: A Critique' (1983) 83 Colum L Rev 772.

Koskenniemi, M., *The Gentle Civilizer of Nations: The Rise and Fall of International Law 1870–1960* (CUP 2004).

Kramer, R., 'Interests and Policy Clashes in Conflict of Laws' (1959) 13 Rutgers L Rev 523.

Kraus, H.C., 'Begriff und Verständnis des 'Bürgers' bei Savigny' (1993) 110 Zeitschrift der Savigny Stiftung für Rechtsgeschichte Romanistische Abteilung 552.

Kronman, A.T, 'Contract Law and Distributive Justice' (1980) 89 Yale LJ 472.

Lacapra, D., 'Rethinking Intellectual History and Reading Texts' (1980) 19 History and Theory 245.

Lassalle, F., *Das System der erworbenen Rechte, Eine Versöhnung des positiven Rechts und der Rechtsphilosophie* (Brochhaus 1880).

Lassalle, F. and Bernstein, E., *Ferdinard Lassalle's Reden und Schriften* (Vorwärts 1891).

Leckey, R., *Contextual Subjects, Family, State, and Relational Theory* (University of Toronto Press 2008).

Lehning, P.B., 'European Citizenship: Towards a European Identity' (2001) 20 L & Philosophy 239.

Lewald, H., *Règles générales des conflits de lois; contributions à la technique du droit international privé* (Helbing & Lichtenhahn 1941).

Lewald, H., *Festschrift Hans Lewald bei Vollendung d. 40. Amtsjahres als Ordentl. Prof. im Oktober 1953* (Helbing & Lichtenhahn 1953).

Logemann, J.H.A., 'Biography of Roeland Duco Kollewijn' (1962) 9 Neth Int'l L Rev 17.

Lorenz, E., *Zur Struktur des internationalen Privatrechts. Ein Beitrag zur Reformdiskussion* (Dunkler & Humblot 1977).

Lorenzen, E., 'Huber's de Conflictu Legum' (1919) 13 Ill L Rev 375.

Lorenzen, E., 'Review of The Renovation of International Law by D. Josephus Jitta' (1920) 29 Yale LJ 700.

Lorenzen, E., 'Territoriality, Public Policy and the Conflict of Laws' (1924) 33 Yale LJ 736.

Lorenzen, E., 'Story's Commentaries of the Conflict of Laws—One Hundred Years After' (1934) 48 Harv L Rev 15.

Lorenzen, E. and Heilman, R., 'The Restatement of the Conflict of Laws' (1935) 83 U Pa L Rev 555.

Lüderitz, A. and Schröder, J. (eds.), *Internationales Privatrecht und Rechtsvergleichung im Ausgang des 20. Jahrhunderts. Bewahrung oder Wende? Festschrift für Gerhard Kegel* (Alfred Metzner 1977).

Mackenzie, C. and Stoljar, N., *Relational Autonomy: Feminist Perspectives on Autonomy, Agency, and the Social Self* (OUP 2000).

Macklem, P., 'What is International Human Rights Law? Three Applications of a Distributive Account' (2007) 52 McGill L J 575.

Mährlein, C., *Volksgeist und Recht. Hegels Philosophie der Einheit und ihre Bedeutung in der Rechtswissenschaft* (Königshausen & Neumann 2000).

Mancini, P.S., 'De l'utilité de rendre obligatoires pour tous les Etats, sous la forme d'un ou de plusieurs traités internationaux, un certain nombre de régles generales du droit international privé pour assurer la decision uniforme des conflits entre les différentes legislations civiles et criminelles' (1874) 1 Journal de droit international privé et de la jurisprudence comparée 221 and 286.

Mancini, P.S., *Diriti Internazionale, Prelezioni* 1 (Giuseppe Marghieri 1873).

Mancini, P.S., *Della nazionalitá come fondamento del diritto delle genti* (Instituto Suor Orsola Benincasa 1988, originally published Torino: Tip. Eredi Botta 1851).

Mann, F.A. et al., 'Prerogative Rights of Foreign States and the Conflict of Laws' (1954) 40 Transactions of the Grotius Society 25.

Mann F.A., 'The Doctrine of Jurisdiction in International Law' (1964) 111 Recueil des Cours 1.

Mann F.A., 'Conflict of Laws and Public Law' (1971) 132 Recueil des Cours 107.

Mansel, H.P., *Internationales Privatrecht im 20. Jahrhundert: Der Einfluss von Gerhard Kegel und Alexander Lüderitz auf das Kollisionsrecht* (Mohr Siebeck 2014).

Marshall Brown, P., *Foreigners in Turkey* (Princeton University Press 1914).

Mayer, P., 'Les methods de la reconnaissance en droit international privé' in Pierre Mayer, Marie-Noëlle Jobard-Bachellier (eds.), *Droit international privé, esprit et methods: mélanges en l'honneur de Paul Lagarde* (Dalloz 2005) 547.

Mayer, P., and Jobard-Bachellier, M.N. (eds.), *Droit international privé, esprit et methods: mélanges en l'honneur de Paul Lagarde* (Dalloz 2005).

Meijers, M., 'L'histoire des principes fondamentaux du droit international privé a partir du moyen age, spécialment dans l'Europe occidentale' (1934) 49 Recueil des Cours 547.

Michaels, R., 'Globalizing Savigny? The State in Savigny's Private International Law and the Challenge of Europeanization and Globalization' in Adrienne Windhoff-Héritier, Michael Stolleis, and Fritz Wilhelm Scharpf (eds.), *European and International Regulation After the Nation State: Different Scopes and Multiple Levels* (Nomos 2004).

Michaels, R., 'Economics of Law as Choice of Law' (2008) 71 Law & Contemp Probs 73.

Michaels, R., 'Public and Private International Law: German Views on Global Issues' (2008) 4 J P Int'l L 121.

Michaels, R., 'Party Autonomy in Private International Law—A New Paradigm Without a Foundation?' (2013) 15 Japanese Yearbook of International Law 282.

Michaels, R., 'Story, Joseph' in J. Basedow et al. (eds.), *European Encyclopedia of Private International Law* (Elgar 2017).

Michaels, R., 'Waechter, Carl Georg' in J. Basedow et al. (eds.), *European Encyclopedia of Private International Law* (Elgar 2017).

Mills, A., *The confluence of Public and Private International Law: Justice, Pluralism and Subsidiarity in the International Constitutional Ordering of Private Law* (CUP 2009).

Minow, M., 'Paradoxes of Rights' in Austin Rata and Thomas R. Kearns (eds.), *Identities, Politics, and Rights* (University of Michigan Press 1995).

Minow, M. and Shanley, M.L., 'Relational Rights and Responsibilities: Revisioning the Family in Liberal Political Theory and Law' (1996) 1 Hypatia 11.

Morris, J.H.C., *Cases in Private international law* (2nd edn., Claredon 1951).

Moss, D. and Cisternino, J. (eds.), *New Perspectives on Regulation* (Tobin Project 2009).

Moyn, S. and Sartori, A. (eds.), *Global Intellectual History* (Columbia University Press 2013).

Moyn, S., 'The Nonglobalization of Ideas' in Samuel Moyn and Andrew Sartori (eds.), *Global Intellectual History* (Columbia University Press 2013) 193.

Muir Watt, H., 'European Federalism and the New Unilateralism' (2008) 82 Tulane L Rev 1983.

Muir Watt, H., 'Private International Law Beyond the Schism' (2011) 2 Transnatl Leg Theory 347.

Muir Watt, H. and Fernández Arroyo, D.P., *Private International Law and Global Governance* (OUP 2015).

Muir Watt, H., 'Future Directions' in Muir Watt, Horatia and Diego P. Fernández Arroyo, *Private International Law and Global Governance* (OUP 2015).

Muir Watt, H., 'Party Autonomy in International Contracts' in Horatia Muir Watt (ed.), *Private International Law and Public Law*, vol. 2 (Elgar Press 2015).

Muir Watt, H. (ed.), *Private International Law and Public Law*, vol. 2 (Elgar Press 2015).

Muir Watt, H., 'Batiffol, Henri' in Jürgen Basedow et al. (eds.), *Encyclopedia of Private International Law*, vol. 1 (Edward Elgar 2017) 64.

Müller, H., *Der Gundsatz des wohlerworbenen Rechts im internationalen Privatrecht* (Friederichsen, de Gruyter 1935).

Nadelmann, K., 'Wächter's Essay on the Collision of Private Laws of Different States' (1964) 13 Am J Comp L 414.

Nadelmann, K., 'Bicentennial Observations on the Second Edition of Joseph Story's Commentaries on the Conflict of Laws' (1980) 28 Am J Comp L 67.

Nedelsky, J., 'Reconceiving Autonomy: Sources, Thoughts and Possibilities' (1989) 1 Yale JL & Feminism 1.

Nedelsky, J., 'Reconceiving Rights as Relationships' (1993) 1 Rev Const Stud 1.

Nedelsky, J., *Law's Relations. A Relational Theory of Self, Autonomy and Law* (2011).

Neuhaus, P.H., 'Savigny und die Rechtsfindung aus der Natur der Sache' (1949) 15 RabelsZ 364.

Niboyet, J.P., *Traité de droit international privé français* (Sirey 1938).

Niboyet, J.P., *Cours de droit international privé: à l'usage des étudiants de licence et de doctorat* (Sirey 1946).

Niemeyer, T., *Zur Methodik des internationalen Privatrechtes* (Duncker & Humblot 1894).

Niemeyer, T., *Vorschläge und Materialien zur Kodifikation des internationalen Privatrechts* (Duncker & Humblot 1895).

Nussbaum, A., 'Rise and Decline of the Law-of-Nations Doctrine in the Conflict of Laws' (1942) 42 Colum L Rev 189.

Nussbaum, A., *Principles of Private International Law* (OUP 1943).

Nussbaum, M., 'Beyond the Social Contract: Toward Global Justice' in Grethe B. Peterson (ed.), *The Tanner Lectures on Human Values*, vol. 24 (University of Utah Press 2004).

Offerhaus, C.J., 'L'Université d'Amsterdam et le Droit international privé' in *Ius et Lex—Festgabe zum 70. Geburtstag Max Gutzwiller* (Helbing & Lichtenhahn 1959).

Oppenheim, L., *The Collected Papers of John Westlake on Public International Law* (CUP 1914).

Paul, J.R., 'The Isolation of Private International Law' (1988) 7 Wis Int'l L J 149.

Peari, S., 'Savigny's Theory of Choice-of-Law as a Principle of "Voluntary Submission"' (2014) 64 UTLJ 106.

Peñalver, E.M., 'Property as Entrance' (2005) 91 Va L Rev 1889.

Pereznieto, C., Tullio Treves, L., and Seatzu, F. (eds.), *Tradition and Innovation of Private International Law at the Beginning of the Third Millenium—Liber in Memoriam of Professor Friedrich K. Juenger* (Juris 2006).

Pillet, A., 'Droit international privé consideré dans ses rapports avec le droit international public' in Annales de l'enseignement superior de Grenoble (F. Allier Père & Fils 1892) 309.

Pillet, A., 'Essai d'un système general de solution des conflicts de lois' (1894) 21 Journal de droit international privé et de la jurisprudence comparée 417.

Pillet, A., 'Le droit international public, ses elements constitutifs, son domaine, son objet' (1894) 1 RGDIP 1.

Pillet, A., *Recherches sur les droits fondamentaux des États dans l'ordre des rapports internationaux et sur la solution des conflits qu'ils font naître* (Pedone 1899).

Pillet, A., *Principes de droit international prive* (Allier Frères 1903).

Pogge, T., *Realizing Rawls* (Cornell University Press 1989).

Pound, R., 'Uniformity of Commercial Law on the American Continent' (1909) 8 Michigan L Rev 91.

Puchta, G.F., *Pandekten* (10th edn., Johann Ambrosius Barth 1866).

Reppy, A., *Law, a Century of Progress, 1835–1935: Contributions in Celebration of the 100th Anniversary of the Founding of the School of Law of New York University* (New York University Press 1937).

Rückert, J., *Idealismus, Jurisprudenz und Politik bei Friedrich Carl von Savigny* (R. Gremer 1984).

Rückert, J., 'Friedrich Carl von Savigny, the Legal Method, and the Modernity of Law' (2006) 11 Juridica International 56.

Sack, A.N., 'Conflicts of Laws in the History of the English Law' in A. Reppy (ed.), *Law, a Century of Progress, 1835–1935: Contributions in Celebration of the 100th Anniversary of the Founding of the School of Law of New York University* (New York University Press 1937).

Salcedo, J.A.C., Le Renouveau du Particularisme en Droit International Privé (1978) 160 Recueil des Cours 181.

Scanlon, T.M., *What We Owe Each Other* (Harvard University Press 2000).

Schäffner, W., *Entwicklung des internationalen Privatrechts* (JD Sauerländer 1841).

Scheffler, S., 'Immigration and the Significance of Culture' (2007) 35 Phil and Public Affairs 92.

Scheffler, S., 'The Practice of Equality' in Carina Fourie, Fabian Shuppert, and Ivo Wallimann-Helmer (eds.), *Social Equality: On What it Means to Be Equal* (OUP 2015).

Schurig, K., 'Interessenjurisprudenz contra Interessenjurisprudenz im IPR: Anmerkungen zu Flessners Thesen' (1995) 59 RabelsZ 229.

Schurig, K., 'Das Fundament trägt noch' in Heinz-Peter Mansel (ed.), *Internationales Privatrecht im 20. Jahrhundert, Der Einfluss von Gerhard Kegel und Alexander Lüderitz auf das Kollisionsrecht* (Mohr Siebeck 2014) 9.

Shapira, A., 'Protection of Private Interests in the Choice of Law Process: The Principle of Rational Connection Between Parties and Laws' (1970) 24 Sw L J 574.

Singer, J., 'The Player and the Cards: Nihilism and Legal Theory' (1984) 94 Yale LJ 1.

Singer, J., 'Real Conflicts' (1989) 69 BUL Rev 3.

Singer, J., 'A Pragmatic Guide to Conflicts' (1990) 70 BUL Rev 731.

Singer, J., *Entitlement: The Paradoxes of Property* (Yale University Press 2000).

Singer, J., 'Democratic Estates: Property Law in a Free and Democratic Society' (2009) 94 Cornell L Rev 1009.

Skinner, Q., 'Meaning and Understanding in the History of Ideas' (1969) 8 History and Theory 3.

Sommières, M., 'La synthese du droit international privé' (1900) 27 J dr int privé 5, 158.

Steenhoff, G.J., 'Daniël Josephus Jitta' (1854–1925) in *The Moulding of International Law: Ten Dutch Proponents* (T.M.C Asser Instituut 1995) 237.

Steenhoff, G.J., 'Roeland Duco Kollewijn—1892–1972' in *The Moulding of International Law: Ten Dutch Proponents* (T.M.C Asser Instituut 1995) 382.

Story, J., *Commentaries on the Conflict of Laws: Foreign and Domestic, in Regard to Contracts, Rights, and Remedies, and Especially in Regard to Marriages, Divorces, Wills, Successions, and Judgments* (1st edn., Hilliard, Gray 1834).

Story, J., *Commentaries on the Conflict of Laws, Foreign and Domestic in Regard to Contracts, Rights, and Remedies, and Especially in Regard to Marriages, Divorces, Successions, and Judgments* (3rd edn., Charles C. Little & James Brown 1846).

Story, W.W. (ed.), *Life and Letters of Joseph Story*, vol. 2 (John Chapman 1851).

Symeonides, S., 'The American Choice-of-Law Revolution in the Courts: Today and Tomorrow' (2002) 298 Recueil des Cours 1.

Symeonides, S., *American Private International Law* (Wolters Kluwer 2008).

Symeonides, S., *Codifying Choice of Law Around the World* (OUP 2014)

'The Transformation of Sovereignty' 88 Am Soc Int'l L Proc v (1994).

Thomas, J., *Public Rights, Private Relations* (OUP 2015)

Tittmann, F.W., *De competentia legum externarum et domesticarum in defiendis potissimum iuribus coniugum* (Gebauer 1822).

T.M.C. Asser Instituut. *The Moulding of International Law: Ten Dutch Proponents* (The Hague: T.M.C Asser Instituut 1995).

Treggiari, F., 'Nationales Recht und Recht der Nationalität—Mancini' in Erik Jayme and Heinz-Peter Mansel (eds.), *Nation und Staat im internationalen Privatrecht. Zum kollisionsrechtlichen Staatsangehörigkeitsprinzip in verfassungsrechtlicher und internationalprivatrechtlicher Sicht* (C.F. Müller 1988).

Vareilles-Sommières, G., *La synthèse du droit international privé* (Pichon 1897).

Von Bar, L., *Das internationale Privat- und Strafrecht* (Hahn'sche Hofbuchhandlung 1862).

Von Bar, L., *The Theory and Practice of Private International Law* (G.R. Gillespie, tr, W. Green & Sons 1892).

Von Bar, L., 'Neue Prinzipien und Methoden des internationalen Privatrechts' (1899) 14 AOR 1.

Von Mehren, A.T. and Trautman, D.T., *The Law of Multistate Problems; Cases and Materials on Conflict of Laws* (Little, Brown 1965).

Von Mehren, A.T., 'Recent Trends in Choice-of-Law Methodology' (1974) 60 Cornell L Rev 927.

Von Mehren, A.T., 'Special Substantive Rules for Multistate Problems: Their Role and Significance in Contemporary Choice of Law Methodology' (1974) 88 Harv L Rev 347.

Von Mehren, A.T., 'Choice of Law and the Problem of Justice' (1977) 41 Law & Contemp Probs 27.

Von Savigny, F.K., *Vom Beruf unserer Zeit für Gesetzgebung und Rechtswissenschaft* (Mohr & Zimmer 1814).

Von Savigny, F.K., 'Über den Zweck dieser Zeitschrift' (1815) 1 Zeitschrift für geschichtliche Rechtswissenschaft 1.

Von Savigny, F.K., 'Stimmen für und wider neue Gesetzbücher' (1817) 3 Zeitschrift für geschichtliche Rechtswissenschaft 11.

Von Savigny, F.K., *The History of the Roman Law During the Middle Ages* (E. Cathcart, tr., Adam Black 1829).

Von Savigny, F.K., *System des heutigen Römischen Rechts*, vol. 1 (Veit and Comp. 1840).

Von Savigny, F.K., *System des heutigen römischen Rechts*, vol. 5 (Veit and Comp. 1841).

Von Savigny, F.K., *Private International Law. A Treatise on the Conflict of Laws: And the Limits of Their Operation in Respect of Place and Time* (William Guthrie, tr., T. & T. Clark 1869).

Voskuil, C.C.A., 'A Survey of Dutch Scholarly Practice Concerning Private International Law From 1938 till Present' (1970) 17 Nethl Int'l L Rev 11.

Vrellis, S., 'Conflit ou coordination de valeurs en droit international privé a la recherché de la justice' (2007) 328 Recueil des Cours 189.

Wächter, KG, 'Über die Collision der Privatrechtsgesetze verschiedener Staaten' (1841) 241 AcP 230 and (1842) 251 AcP 1, 161, and 361.

Wagner, A., *Briefe von Ferdinand Lassalle an Carl Rodbertus* (Puttkammer & Muehlbrecht 1878).

Wai, R., 'In the Name of the International: The Supreme Court of Canada and the Internationalist Transformation of Canadian Private International Law' (2001) 39 Can YB Int'l L 117.

Wai, R., 'The Interlegality of Transnational Private Law' (2008) 71 L and Contemp Probs 107.

Wai, R., 'The Cosmopolitanism of Transnational Economic Law' in Cecilia M. Baillet and Katja Franko Aas (eds.), *Cosmopolitan Justice and its Discontents* (Routledge 2011).

Wai, R., 'Private v. Private: Transnational Private Law and Contestation in Global Economic Governance' in Horatia Muir Watt and Diego P. Fernández Arroyo (eds.), *Private International Law and Global Governance* (OUP 2015).

Waldron, J., *"Partly Laws Common to All Mankind": Foreign Law in American Courts* (Yale University Press 2012).

Walker, N., *Intimations of Global Law* (CUP 2014).

Watson, A., *Joseph Story and the Comity of Errors: A Case Study in Conflict of Laws* (University of Georgia Press 1992).

Wieacker, F., *Privatrechtsgeschichte des Neuzeit unter besonderer Berücksichtigung der deutschen Entwicklung* (2nd edn., Vandenhoeck and Rupert 1996).

Windhoff-Héritier, A., Stolleis, M., and Wilhelm Scharpf, F., *European and International Regulation After the Nation State: Different Scopes and Multiple Levels* (Nomos 2004).

Wortley, B.A., 'Expropriation in International Law' (1947) 33 Transactions of the Grotius Society 25.

Wortley, B.A., 'The Concept of Man in English Private International Law' (1947) 33 Trans Grotius Soc 147.

Wortley, B.A., 'The General Principles of Private International Law from the English Standpoint' (1947) 71 Recueil des Cours 1.

Wotley, B.A., 'The Interaction of Private and Public International Law Today' (1954) 85 Recueil des Cours 239.

Wortley, B.A., 'Observations on the Public and Private International Law Relating to Expropriation' (1956) 5 Am J Comp L 577.
Wortley, B.A., 'The General Principles of Private International Law' (1958) 94 Recueil des Cours 85.
Wortley, B.A., 'The Protection of Property Situated Abroad' (1961) 35 Tul L Rev 739.
Wortley, B.A., *Jurisprudence* (Oceana 1967).
Zitelmann, E., *Internationales Privatrecht* (Duncker & Humblot 1897).
Zitelmann, E., *Die Unvollkommenheit des Völkerrechts* (Duncker & Humblot 1919).

Author Index

Subject Index